EROTIC VAGRANCY

Erotic Vagrancy

Everything About Richard Burton and Elizabeth Taylor

by Roger Lewis

riverrun

First published in Great Britain in 2023 by

riverrun

An imprint of

Quercus Editions Ltd
Carmelite House
50 Victoria Embankment
London EC4Y 0DZ

An Hachette UK company

A CIP catalogue record for this book is available
from the British Library

HB ISBN 978 0 85738 172 9
TPB ISBN 978 0 85738 173 6
EBOOK ISBN 978 0 85738 277 1

10 9 8 7 6 5 4 3 2 1

Typeset by Jouve (UK), Milton Keynes

Printed and bound in Great Britain by Clays Ltd, Elcograf S.p.A.

Papers used by riverrun are from well-managed forests and other responsible sources.

To the memory of
Beatrice Lilian Lewis
and
Martha Evelyn George

– my Welsh grandmothers

'. . . the damp, dark prison of eternal love' – *Quentin Crisp*

CONTENTS

Author's Note

Everything about Richard Burton and Elizabeth Taylor? Hardly. That's like expecting the whole history of Ireland to be contained in the novels of James Joyce, even if Joyce kept maps of Dublin about him wherever he was in his exiles, as a nostalgic reminder. There will always be sins of omission, errors of fact and interpretation. For a long time, I wanted my subtitle to be 'Studies for a Biography of Richard Burton and Elizabeth Taylor', using the word in the same way Francis Bacon called his paintings 'Three Studies for Figures at the Base of a Crucifixion' or 'Three Studies for a Self-Portrait', and so forth, the idea being nothing can ever quite be finished.

I may as usual be making a fatal commercial miscalculation (there are people – not on the face of it mental defectives – who have never heard of Federico Fellini or Orson Welles), but I am assuming general readers will be familiar already with the names Elizabeth Taylor and Richard Burton, with their glare and noise; and that what none now wants is another fat, conventional or 'authorised' biography, if by biography we mean a chronicle of events, where it can be made to matter what is supposed to *happen next*.

As with Marilyn Monroe, or for that matter Ernest Hemingway, or Napoleon, there are already plenty such works on Taylor, more appear all the time, mapping her out, plenty on Burton, and plenty on Taylor and Burton as a partnership. All excellent, my personal favourites being Maddox and Amburn (on her), Bragg and Rubython (on him) and Kashner and Schoenberger (on them). There are glossy albums, gushing commentaries, feminist tracts by lady academics, rubbishy academic tracts by frightening feminists, plus of course the usual *leper's death puke* by the late Alexander Walker and the late Sheridan Morley.

Two key texts, central to any understanding of my subject, are *Richard Burton: My Brother* by Graham Jenkins, but actually written, in 1988, by Barry Turner, and *The Richard Burton Diaries*, edited, in 2012, by Chris Williams for Yale University Press. The latter is not only one of the great show business books: as a human document it stands comparison with the Goncourts' *Journals*. Burton is better, in my view, less self-conscious, when hastily jotting things down ('You stupid cow! Just show your big tits!') than when he tried to sound like what he thought authors should sound like ('I love you more than anything on the sad face of this raped earth'), i.e. when he came across as a broken-down Dylan Thomas. I am grateful to Swansea University, which holds the copyright, and to Yale University Press, the publisher, for kind permission to make comprehensive quotation.

Despite the welter, the profusion, nobody, it seems to me, in any of the biographies and associated studies, has, with any exactness, paid attention to, has perceived, Burton and Taylor's art, their cinematic legacy: the minute realities, contours, intercellular spaces, oscillating corpuscles – to borrow phrases from natural science. After examining a jellyfish, Louis Agassiz described its anatomy as 'little more than organised water'. That's the sort of comparison I'd yearn to make – for I love watching Burton and Taylor's films, and can, I think, discern patterns of growth and form, images within images.

What I have produced – and I have spent many years gathering my material and boiling it down, reducing it like a lobster sauce – is more in the way of a novel of manners, the style and form evolving naturally from those previous publications on the histrionic or music hall personality – my books ('studies') about Peter Sellers, Laurence Olivier, Charles Hawtrey and Anthony Burgess.

Actually, my ideal readers, should they exist outside the mind of

God, will be those who have perhaps never heard of Taylor and Burton. Taylor and Burton will be beings come across in these pages for the first time; beings who have no external links and whom I have entirely imagined, as a by-product of insomnia, anxiety, lowered oxygen and benign prostatic hyperplasia, at least I hope it is only that.

For isn't that what Taylor and Burton were all along – sheer *fantasy figures*? To invoke Joyce again, they grew to have 'greater reality for me than reality'.

R.L.

Normandy, 2010–2023

Prologue

What Antony and Cleopatra most feared wasn't death or subjugation by an alien power but that they'd be ripe for ridicule: 'the quick comedians / Extemporally will stage us ... Antony shall be brought drunken forth ... I shall see / Some squeaking Cleopatra ...' It could be said Richard Burton and Elizabeth Taylor were precisely these as advertised fools of fortune, when Twentieth Century Fox took over Rome in the early Sixties – he was certainly drunken and she always did a lot of squeaking – and in their own turn, Burton and Taylor were to be caricatured, e.g. by Steve Coogan and Rob Brydon in *The Trip* (2011), where they compare and vie with their Burton voices over the dinner table, or in *Scrooged* (1988), where a trio of tramps at Karen Allen's soup kitchen mistake a frantic, bad-tempered Bill Murray for Burton, companionably call him 'Dick' and invite him to come out for their benefit with famous lines from his films ('Give us something from *The Sandpiper!*') – Murray does a strange rendition of haughty, unintelligible cod-Shakespearean muffling, and you think: is this what Burton has been reduced to, only four years after his death? Six years before his death saw Alan Bennett's *Me! I'm Afraid of Virginia Woolf*, with Leeds replacing New England, though the provincial squalor is intact – a canteen with sauce-encrusted bottle-tops, fuggy interiors, pleasureless evenings. The Burton/George character is now called Hopkins, an uneasy, uncertain, bookish, harmless, high-strung polytechnic lecturer – to his mother's dismay. He teaches English but she thinks he's in charge of woodwork. Julie Walters, in an orange wig, is an apparition of Taylor/Martha, who announces,

'They've sent my sputum to Newcastle.' The bonny and frizzy-haired yoga instructress (Carol MacReady) is another manifestation of Taylor as unscrupulous flirt. 'Those ski-pants haven't seen Zermatt,' says Thora Hird, with her trademark scorn. Then there's Benny Hill, who in a sketch called 'Who's Afraid of Virgin Wool?' is Rich Burt. It's a remarkable impersonation, actually – the bloated boozy face and the carefully-arranged dark hair. Benny was also always funny as grotesques like Fanny Cradock or Jimmy Savile. Is that Bob Todd as Taylor? (No, it's Benny again – he's brilliant in drag.) In Mike Leigh's *Career Girls* (1997), another one of his films about abortion, alcoholism, unemployment, obesity and dead-end lives, Mark Benton's character, with his twitches, stuttering and skin allergies, is called Richard ('Ricky') Burton: 'I don't look like him or anything. My mother was a fan.' Leigh's feral folk in high-rise flats, flailing and getting on each other's nerves, would seem to be a far cry from the real Burton, the real Taylor. Or maybe not.

Taylor's fate was to be impersonated by Roseanne Barr and John Candy, also Dawn French. 'I laughed the loudest,' said Taylor, 'but it hurt inside.' No wonder, as they all turned her into a giant panda. Most cruel was Joan Rivers, especially on her (1983) album *What Becomes a Semi-Legend Most?* 'I went pretty far with Elizabeth Taylor,' the comedian conceded, though she assured Roddy McDowall, 'I only make jokes about people who make forty million dollars a year.' Examples: 'If Liz Taylor filmed *Cleopatra* today, they'd have to widen the Nile'; 'Liz isn't fat? Her blood type is Ragu'; 'This woman could moon Europe.' According to Melissa Rivers in *Joan Rivers Confidential* (with its snappy subtitle: 'The Unseen Scrapbooks, Joke Cards, Personal Files and Photos of a Very Funny Woman Who Kept Everything'), a book assembled after Joan's death, Joan's archives contained 847 similar boffs, meticulously typed, cross-referenced and indexed. They met once – as co-hostesses, in 1985, for a dinner at Spago, Beverly Hills, to benefit 'battered children'. Joan was thrilled. 'I knew people would pay a thousand dollars a plate to see Joan Rivers and Elizabeth Taylor walk in together.' Taylor was splendidly unimpressed: 'Joan who? Who's that? Is she that awful blonde?'

Taylor became a lampoon of herself quite early on, much to the dismay of Rex Reed, who having seen *Secret Ceremony*, in 1969, commented, 'The disintegration of Elizabeth Taylor has been a very sad thing to stand by helplessly and watch. Something ghastly has happened over the course of her last four or five films. She has become a hideous parody of herself, a fat, sloppy, yelling, screeching banshee.' What's wrong with being any of those things? And I personally love *Secret Ceremony* and its predecessors, which by Reed's calculation will have to include, going backwards, *Boom!*, *The Comedians*, *Reflections in a Golden Eye*, *Doctor Faustus* and *The Taming of the Shrew*. The 'something ghastly' that had 'happened', of course, was her marriage to Burton, with its luxurious trappings and bad taste, a time, for both of them, of inelegance and sparkling filigree.

Burton, it has to be said, hadn't done himself any favours, finally rejecting, in 1978, *King Lear* on Broadway, in favour of another provincial tour of *Camelot*, much to the exasperation of John Dexter, who directed him in *Equus*, hoped to direct him as Lear, and who in exasperation called the star 'a lazy drunken fool', whose performances as Dysart for twelve weeks in the Shaffer play were 'absolutely bloody dreadful', Burton's style redolent 'too much of the pulpit and the pub.' No doubt – but when Burton had said, 'Lear is a Welshman,' perhaps one of the reasons for his avoiding being in any actual stage production was a belief he'd already had his fill of the character. 'Fuck you, I *am* Lear,' he'd been heard to say; and if he fully, if melodramatically, identified with the angry monarch ('I am, after all, the kind of authentic dark voice of my tortured part of the world, Wales'), it's because as a star Burton had been hedged about with a retinue – he and Taylor (Queen Lear: not a role Shakespeare got around to conceiving, unless she was Lady Macbeth who'd somehow survived, moved south and remarried, as Taylor always survived and remarried) would turn up, expecting hospitality, expecting to be received. 'I drove Richard . . . to the North Gower Country Club, introduced him to the delighted landlord and some of the staff,' remembered David Jenkins, his brother, of a return journey of the prodigal. One envisages Lear's knights, with jangling bridles. On another occasion they are in Cecil Road, Gowerton, where 'it was still quite an event ... having Elizabeth Taylor to tea.' Her knee-length suede boots matched the colour of the sitting-room carpet. When she stood up, it was as if half of her had disappeared. And if it is about nothing else, *King Lear* explores issues of family commitment, family secrets – in Burton's case, the horror of his daughter Jessica's concealment in a mental home and then the puzzle of his brother Ivor's death, and whether he, Burton, was culpable. (I think he was.)

Lear, the man, is thoroughly forthright, wanting his needs and comfort met without question. If Burton and Taylor took a commercial flight, they purchased all the first-class seats, so as to have the cabin to themselves – a very money-no-object, imperial thing to do, which I can imagine Lear doing, or any similar dictator. If he suspects he has been crossed, or mildly discountenanced, Lear quickly recourses to bombastic language ('Come not between the dragon and his wrath'), whether in the court or on the heath, where the storms and thunder crashes are a mixture of inner and external rages. 'Lear,' said Burton, 'when he lets off steam, when he really lets go, is utterly Welsh' – and he himself could bang about in a similar fashion. The actor surprised and surpassed even himself on occasion – for instance in July 1969, as Henry VIII, shooting a scene for *Anne of the Thousand Days*: 'I went over the top ... I had to say to an actor called Marne Maitland, "Get out! Limp back to Rome and tell His Holiness the Pope that I will have the marriage annulled. Get out. Get out. Get out." The last "get out" was delivered with such murderous virulence and at the top of my voice that Mr Maitland's feet left the ground and he tripped and fell down.' As in art, so in life. Taylor said her influence on him was only marginal: 'He's not less volatile. He just chooses when and where to be volatile with more

8

discrimination,' as if that were feasible. In his diary, Burton was more liable to recognise a less discriminating Lear-like crack-up: 'There are times when I think I am slightly out of my mind' (May 1969), and drinking aided the process easily enough. 'I am drinking too much,' he recorded that same month, 'and though I like to drink I have a fear that eventually it might affect my brain. Already, I've noticed, it has affected my memory. Or maybe I am getting old.' He was forty-three. That summer, in Puerto Vallarta, drinking 'tequila after tequila' only led to marital bickering and 'venomous malice'. Four years earlier, in May 1965, Burton had reflected, 'I am drinking too steadily – lunchtime and dinnertime . . . Am still a bundle of nerves.'

Burton was like a broken-down king without a kingdom, fumbling with a chalice, adrift in hotel suites, private yachts, executive jets – and in the end I think I agree with him. He never did Lear – so what? He *was* Lear. But everyone was tantalised for decades. 'One hopes, one thinks, he must play Lear,' said Warren Mitchell, who served with Burton in the RAF. 'The prize he was pursuing was King Lear,' wrote Keith Baxter in his memoirs. Baxter met a disconsolate Burton in the Italian Alps, where Taylor, in 1973, was starring in *Ash Wednesday*, and Burton was at a loose end. In an interview transcribed in *Acting in the Sixties* (1970), Burton told Kenneth Tynan the only role he 'longed to appear in on the stage' was Lear. 'I have to go back and face that live audience. With a bit of luck, maybe in five years.' (In five years he instead was in an uncompleted and lost film called *Jackpot*, with Charlotte Rampling.) In October 1969, Burton had mentioned a thoroughly implausible scheme, whereby 'I shall play *King Lear* in East Germany with the Berliner Ensemble in German.' He was going to 'learn it phonetically'. A year earlier he'd come up with another impossible dream: 'What I'd like to do now . . . is *King Lear* and then just disappear from view.' Ten years later, when 'I have to play Lear as a kind of obligation,' he said he 'knew the play by heart,' and having, as John Dexter complained, 'already wasted so much of my time,' another director's name came up – Elia Kazan. Burton backed out of that commitment as he didn't want to do matinees. Another excuse was the money was inadequate. When Liza Todd brought her future husband Hap Tivey to meet the family in Gstaad – they were married in 1984 and divorced in 2003 – Burton, noticing a copy of *King Lear* on the shelf in their bedroom, started reciting quite extensively from the play. 'What the fuck is going on here?' wondered Tivey, who was a conceptual artist specialising in light installations.

The other role he eluded was Prospero, though he did play Ferdinand (at Stratford in 1951 – Michael Redgrave the magus) and Caliban (at The Old Vic in 1953 – Michael Hordern the magus). Ideas for a film went nowhere. Sir John Gielgud, the putative director, found an ideal location for *The Tempest* in Tobago, another in Japan, and tried to seduce Burton with a landscape that was, he said in 1967, 'sometimes sand ... sometimes rocks, with strange tracts of deserted scrub ... shadowy woods and jungles, changing to marshes and dangerous pools – strange animals and insects.' Nevill Coghill, collaborator on *Doctor Faustus*, mentioned Garnish Island, or Ilnacullin, in Bantry Bay, off the coast of Eire: 'Marvellous lights and cloud effects, due to Atlantic weather conditions ... a paradise of flowers ... every sort of rhododendron ... Believe it or not, there is also a rustic Italianate palace, which is just what I imagine Prospero would have conjured up for himself.' In the telegram Burton sent in response, you can see him slithering away: '*Tempest* could not possibly begin for at least a year and a half or two years because of other commitments,' which for the record were *Boom!*, *Where Eagles Dare*, *Candy* and *Staircase*. In the autumn of 1982, Anthony Quayle, Falstaff to Burton's Hal at the Shakespeare Memorial Theatre, Stratford, thirty years earlier, had rather hopelessly begun wanting to interest and enlist Burton in his new Compass Company – with Burton meant to play Prospero in Leicester and Manchester, before arriving at The Old Vic. Quayle visited Burton at Céligny early in 1983. He turned up again in New York, during the run of *Private Lives*. Burton did nothing but prevaricate: 'Let's talk about it tomorrow.'

Lear-like, Prospero-esque: Burton had absorbed the lines and words, and something about his refusal to play these roles officially ('Of course,' he said, two months before he died, 'people are always trying to shove me back into doublet and hose') reveals him totally. They'd entered his imagination, extending into all areas of his life and existence, and to put on a costume and move around on a stage or film studio, surrounded by a cast, a crew, an audience, doing things and declaiming for effect, striking attitudes and poses – he'd be like an animal in captivity, and all this was compromising, standardising. Shakespeare ('There was hardly a line there I didn't immediately know but seeing the miraculous words in print again doomed me to a long trance of nostalgia, a stupor of melancholy,' he wrote in 1970) was Burton's way of looking at the world, its shadows and reflections. He was as Lear or Prospero in his sense of loss and his exiles, the torment of multiple separations – from his mother and Pontrhydyfen; from his elder sister and Taibach, when he was scooped up by Philip Burton; from the Welsh language, when his education was in English; from the working class to Oxford's and the RAF's officer class; from the West End to Hollywood stardom; from Sybil Williams, the first wife, to Taylor; and with Taylor from everything else to world fame.

His later partners, Suzy Hunt and Sally Hay (his widow) were Cordelia figures, or Mirandas, nursing an old devil prematurely decrepit with sciatica pains, limps, arm and shoulder stiffness, gout. 'When I met her,' he said of Suzy, whom he married in August 1976, 'I was on the edge of self-destruction and Suzy changed my life.' She got rid of Burton's sycophantic staff, redecorated Céligny, installed bookshelves. Nevertheless, people thought she was 'insane concerning the subject of Elizabeth Taylor', and a photograph of Taylor with Burton had to be cut out by hand by the usherettes from ninety thousand *Camelot* programmes. She played the piano and Burton read ten hours a day. Unable to cope with his alcoholism, Suzy eventually delivered him to his sister Cecilia's house in Hadley Wood, and left him there. As for Sally, 'I couldn't believe life could be so good to me,' said Burton, when he married her in Las Vegas, in July 1983. 'She can do everything,' he announced, 'cook, type, do shorthand' – none of these on the face of it Taylor's accomplishments.

Burton was good at playing soldiers, military philosophers of action and purpose (*The Desert Rats*, *Alexander the Great*, *Bitter Victory*, *The Longest Day*, etc.); and when young he'd excelled as Henry V, Coriolanus, Hamlet, Othello, Philip the Bastard in *King John*, authoritarian sorts who can do what they want (and who are dead at the finish) – but doing what you want can involve anarchy, and the realisation dawns, like for Lear, or Prospero on his island, that society, order, decency, reliability, the system of values and conventions one has lived by, are lies, fictions; are sham, easily disposed of – by 'oak-cleaving thunderbolts' (Lear), 'the sharp wind of the north' (Prospero); and in Burton's case, by the appearance of Taylor in his life, when she split him like an atom. 'He loved Elizabeth; he also loved Sybil,' said Robert Hardy. 'He would have loved to have been married to both of them,' said Burton's brother, Graham. But love mystified him, as it mystified Taylor, too. For them it was something obsessive, psychotic, maimed, disturbed, haunted. 'I wish I didn't love people,' Burton said in December 1968. 'And I wish I didn't shout at people.' Burton and Taylor's apparent entwinement actually involved disagreement and discord. 'I was mad with guilt – or just plain mad,' was Burton's summary of their courtship, during *Cleopatra*, when he was torn between conflicting emotions, filled with disunities and divisions and dissatisfactions, tempted by fantasies of possession (the jewels, the antique steam yachts), whilst at the same time (as a Welsh puritan) finding hateful that which impaired his integrity. This is why, in the end, Burton strikes me as a lonely person; and the nature of the loneliness makes me continue wondering about him, because it all seems connected to his curious reluctance, or ambivalence, about being an actor, as if what he disliked was the dissimulation and display, and what he most required was a means of avoiding exposure – exactly the dilemma of Alec Leamas, in *The Spy Who Came in from the Cold*, one of Burton's finest characterisations, who to operate as a double agent and assume an identity to fool Moscow Centre has to identify with what he has invented: 'the restless uncertainty, the protective arrogance concealing shame were not approximations, but extensions of qualities he actually possessed ... When alone, he remained faithful to these habits ... Only very rarely ... did he allow himself the dangerous luxury of admitting the great lie that he lived,' to quote John le Carré's novel.

Burton was one of those, who as Iago might say, 'keeps yet his heart attending on himself'. He preferred to be silent, reposeful, as if the films, the acting, was something he did, and received applause (and money) for, but was against his will. 'This is my sixtieth film,' he told John Boorman, director of *The Heretic*. 'I've never seen any of them except the first two. I was shocked. I was looking at my father's face. Unbearable.' It's interesting, I think, that his favourite theatre was an empty one. In 1979, when appearing as Hamlet at The Old Vic, Derek Jacobi said Burton materialised in his dressing room after the show, intending to invite him out to dinner – they'd got to know each other when Jacobi had a small role in *The Medusa Touch*, made the previous year. 'He waited while I changed, and as we were leaving he said, "Do you mind if we go up on stage? I haven't stood on a stage for twenty-odd years." It was a very moving experience for him, and tears filled his eyes.' Dick Cavett had a similar encounter in New York, the following year. Burton, wearily playing King Arthur in *Camelot*, wiped off the make-up, made his way with his guest out of the darkened playhouse, stopped near a work-light, and, 'his coat draped over one shoulder, gazed out at the empty house, tilted his head back, and with the famous, full-chiming resonance, began, "O, for a muse of fire, that would ascend / The brightest heaven of invention."' *Henry V*'s Prologue, moreover, more than a set piece, is about the importance of the mind's eye; nothing exists unless thinking makes it so – 'Think, when we talk of horses, that you see them . . . 'tis your thoughts now must deck our kings.' What we picture (or listen to) will be superior to anything we watch – especially with Burton, as the tradition he was exposed to, raised to be in, the Victorian classical English theatre, was conscious of itself as premeditated art, constricted and formal (Irving to Olivier the line of descent). Christopher Isherwood saw *Henry V* at The Old Vic in February 1956 and couldn't believe what a museum piece it was: 'When the Chorus swirled his cloak, a cloud of dust flew out of it.' But Burton was a revelation, 'often very moving.' Isherwood and Don Bachardy would have walked out, 'but ended by being glad we'd stayed, because of Burton. I am amazed to find him so good.'

It was Taylor who showed him another way, her Pop Art gaudiness and smeared pigment contrasting with his Pre-Raphaelite fancy methods where, as it were, one weighed one's words. If annoyed with him, Taylor could always cry sarcastically, 'I'm always fascinated to know what a wonderful stage actor you were,' her use of the past tense or pluperfect a blow, as well as the implication being classical theatre avoids carelessness, avoids awkwardness, is unlikely to persuade us into any kind of intimacy – and it's true Burton (as Alec Leamas in *The Spy Who Came in from the Cold*, Paul Andros in *The V.I.P.s*, as Thomas à Becket, and Dysart in *Equus*) will always cut us off (Burton had a secretive quality), and in 1977 he was heard to say he'd like to be invisible really, observing and recording, 'to be able to do that in absolute anonymity would be very desirable.' Remove the human element from *King Lear* and *The Tempest* and what remains? Look at the language, as Burton did. About people's misfortunes there's nothing to be done. What lasts is the sound of the sea, larks ascending on treeless mountain-tops, weeds flourishing in the green corn, burdocks, hemlocks, nettles, cuckoo-flowers.

* * *

From roles he never played on stage or film to a person he never was (unless it's Caliban looking at himself in the mirror): Rachel Roberts, who in his diaries Burton calls 'Maniacal . . . totally demented . . . stupendously drunk . . . totally uncontrollable . . . a mad case of alcoholism.' On one occasion, Roberts stripped naked, flashed her pubes at sailors ('I can take any three of you') and molested a basset hound. 'Outrage in Rachel's case has now become normal,' wrote Burton in 1968, when he additionally noted her 'very cheap-looking dyed blonde hair.' Roberts, an oratorical actress, as Burton was an oratorical actor, and both of them self-lacerating, was Ceres when he'd been Ferdinand in *The Tempest*, at Stratford, in 1951, and she doubled the roles of Mistress Quickly (the mother-figure) and Alice (one of the spoils of war) in Burton's *Henry V*, at The Old Vic, in 1955 and 1956, with Isherwood in the Dress Circle. During that season, Roberts was also Bianca, when Burton and John Neville alternated the playing of Othello and Iago – on at least one occasion 'after celebrating too well one lunchtime', both turning up on stage blacked-up. 'The audience noticed nothing unusual,' believed William Donaldson, 'nor did Burton and Neville.' Rachel Roberts is Burton's careworn wife in the television play, *A Subject of Scandal and Concern*, broadcast in November 1960.

Roberts was born in Llanelli, in 1927, two years after Burton's birth in Pontrhydyfen, twenty-three miles to the east. Roberts was the daughter of a Baptist minister, the Reverend Richard Rhys Roberts, and though she yearned, as a child, for a more exotic and dramatic world than was on offer in South Wales – she fancied dressing up; she wanted to be noticed – Roberts was always tormented by a puritan conscience, which made her ill at ease in Hollywood, mistrustful of success and happiness; the puritan conscience that dictates 'everything I did was wrong'. As she wrote in her own diary, 'Yes, I have a sweetness and a warmth and intelligence and talent, but I have also a devastating psychological flaw that is finally crippling me.' The roles for which she is best known – Albert Finney's mistress

Brenda in *Saturday Night and Sunday Morning* (1960) and Richard Harris' mistress Mrs Hammond in *This Sporting Life* (1963) – capture Roberts' turmoil. She's the headmistress whose pupils vanish in *Picnic at Hanging Rock* (1977) and Wendy Hiller's Teutonic companion in *Murder on the Orient Express* (1975), where Finney is Poirot.

Roberts could portray women whose brief pleasure had to be followed by endless bleak punishment. As Richard Gere, who played another of her younger lovers, in *Yanks* (1979), was to comment, 'I always sensed something fragile about her, tensed up, ready to snap.' Fully aware that, temperamentally, she was 'personally adrift and promiscuous and unstable', in 1955, after graduating from RADA, and with stints in Rep in Swansea and at Stratford, Roberts married the character actor Alan Dobie, in the hope he'd bring her a steadying domestic calm. Unfortunately, not only does life not operate like that, 'Alan's dourness was beginning to depress me,' and in her search for colour and raciness she latched on to Rex Harrison.

They met during a production of Chekhov's *Platonov* at the Royal Court in Sloane Square, in October 1960 – 'Rex cut such a dash … There was something Edwardian about him, something silky and ruffled' – and Roberts' love for him had an intensity which oscillated with hatred: 'Days of deep shock, rage, anger, terror, relief and hope.' Was she too domineering for him? Was there too much berserk energy? Their wedding was in Genoa in 1962, when Harrison was in Italy making *Cleopatra*, but a chill soon descended – Roberts hit him with a shoe and had assignations with the chauffeur. 'My large personality needed Rex's existence,' she said, but his exalted status and stardom only served to rub in Roberts' feelings of inadequacy. Harrison didn't like to mix with audiences or the ordinary public. He was driven in a Rolls to Warner Brothers. He had prestige and power – and Roberts fed off this, and loathed herself for doing so: walking through the mimosas in the South of France, travelling first class on the Golden Arrow and the Rome Express, swishing into The

Dorchester lobby in furs: 'I basked in the sun.' Crammed with contradictions, Roberts, who in Llanelli had known only an outside lavatory, lapped up the luxury and celebrity, whilst also saying she despised it – fame cut a person off from warmth and honesty and was 'pathetic and paltry'. She also yearned to be a leading lady and then disliked the vanity of such an ambition. She had strong features, which though never beautiful, were not improved by plastic surgery. There was a noisy scene after the premiere of *A Flea in Her Ear*, in 1968, in which Roberts had appeared with Rex. When the press photographers preferred to focus their cameras instead on the Burtons, Roberts screamed after them, as who could blame her, 'I'm the star of this fucking show not that fucking Elizabeth Taylor.'

Harrison eventually tired of the antics, which had exposed him to public humiliation – Roberts crawling around on all fours barking like a dog and biting Robert Mitchum; Roberts demanding an uncooked egg in a posh restaurant; Roberts singing Welsh rugby songs and wearing tarty clothes, such as transparent tops, suede miniskirts, hot-pants and thigh-length boots. The last straw was her misbehaviour at the royal screening of *Staircase*: 'Princess Margaret had no time for Rex Harrison's sloppy-looking, drunken, noisy wife,' said Roberts, putting herself in the third person. They separated in December 1969, were divorced two years later, and Roberts went off her rocker. She started to swallow overdoses and was regularly having her stomach pumped. 'I want to fucking kill him,' she said of Harrison to a doctor at the Cedars of Lebanon Hospital. When her lawyer Aaron Frosch sent a basket of cheese, she threw it out of the window, saying the gift was 'vulgar and pretentious'. Roberts went on Russell Harty's chat show, called the host 'a silly cunt' and said of her cats, 'all they want to do is screw.' Harty's other guests, Sir Peter Hall, Elton John and Barbara Cartland, fell into an embarrassed silence.

What are we to make of all this? First, Roberts was right to be indignant that were she a man, her bad behaviour would have won applause, even admiration. It irked her she should be chastised as a nuisance and for not 'obeying the rules of civilised behaviour. Yet Rex often doesn't. Robert Shaw didn't. Burton didn't. O'Toole didn't.' Very true. Throughout his diaries, Burton catalogues Roberts' pissed and maudlin capers with disapproval, without reflecting on his own behaviour – and yet the similarities are troubling: the way the Welsh actor and the Welsh actress always felt harassed, had nothing to cling to, propelling themselves about, alcoholism a symptom of deeper disturbance. In fact, Burton did on one occasion see a parallel, or anyway Taylor told him that 'last night I behaved just like Rachel Roberts. Probably I did . . .' And throughout her own journals, which were left in the conservatory of the Los Angeles house, 2620 Hutton Drive, where she was found dead, Roberts sees nothing except resemblances ('Poor Richard Jenkins – snap!'): South Welsh people swept away into marriages with big international stars, and for whom paradise was lost. Roberts' addiction to Harrison was like Burton's for Taylor – an addiction identical to her addiction for the bottle. Roberts' family, back in Llanelli, said of Burton, and by implication of Roberts, 'He had everything, but he drank.'

Secondly, therefore, Roberts is a warning about what can happen if you become over-dependent: 'I didn't make a life of my own . . . I lived entirely through him,' she said of Harrison, under his spell as if he'd literally had her conjured. A decade after the divorce, she was still dreaming of a reconciliation: 'I still love my special, dynamic, silly, crusty, unbearable Rex.' Her connection with the past, by some quirk of fate, was Sybil Burton, whom she'd known since Stratford, in 1951, when Roberts was in *Henry IV, Part II* and Burton was Hal. Twenty years on, everyone's marriages having sprung apart, and Sybil and Roberts now neighbours in California, Roberts attempted to reminisce: 'Come on, Syb, don't tell me you don't grieve for those days?' 'Absolutely not!' said Sybil, refusing to be drawn. Another one who wanted to bring up the past was Kenneth Williams. 'We sat there,' he said in May 1964, 'with fags and glasses of sherry, grimacing and giggling for hours, gossiping about the divorce and Taylor and Richard ... [Sybil] never loses that sense of perspective, or her ability to send everything up, including herself. So nothing is tragic.' Nor was anything comic, in the sense of light-hearted. Sybil's cheerful and stoical front was regularly mistaken for resignation, almost relief. I don't think this was ever so. What Sybil did recall was that Harrison had lent Taylor and Burton his Portofino villa, when they were conducting their affair during *Cleopatra*. Roberts, likewise, was upset about this, that her ex-husband had given use of the place to 'that man and his woman,' and it preyed on her mind – she didn't want Sybil thinking she'd been complicit. It's 1978, fifteen years later, and she keeps apologising to Sybil – it's all a means, obviously, of keeping being able to work Harrison into the conversation. Roberts thought Sybil organised and confident, and she envied her this – Sybil held down an ordinary job to fill the working week (a manuscript reader at International Creative Management), she'd raised a family: 'She knows nothing of genuine loneliness. I know she's suffered great pain, too ... Talk to her about Rex, I suppose that reminds her of Burton.'

Finally, there is Roberts' Welshness – the chippy Celtic strain uneasy (as Lindsay Anderson neatly saw it) with Anglo-Saxon cool. (Anderson scattered Roberts' ashes upon the Thames – mingling them with the ashes of Jill Bennett.) Comparing her fate with that of Burton, Roberts said they'd become 'croppers in the eyes of the world', because though they'd wanted to impress, actually they were 'insecure, cursed with feelings of inadequacy'. Despite manifest gifts and public recognition (Roberts won BAFTAs and was nominated for Oscars), 'underneath, the uncertainties and the instabilities bubbled away.' There were other resemblances between Roberts and Burton, too. Dissipation, frayed nerves, adrift from one's origins, an inability to settle. The Welsh are supreme at being actors and actresses because flamboyance is suppressed; it is the guilty secret, which bursts out now and again in lunatic ways, quick and fierce. There's a sense of flight, dispersal, a splitting up of mental states. Yet what is the alternative? To be respectful and dry? The Philip Burton or Reverend Richard Rhys Roberts approach is to remain formal, poetry and drama treated as something elevated – whereas (as Burton discovered – as Isherwood noticed when he saw him perform) if any good, art is brutal and wild, as well as being clean and definite. Interestingly, Roberts and Burton each had pedagogic hankerings, as if what they had accomplished could nevertheless be transmitted or imparted – Burton wanting to be an Oxford don so he could recite Gerard Manley Hopkins and Roberts trying to lecture on *King Lear* at the Yale School of Drama, New Haven. Unfortunately, used by now to grand hotels, she didn't like the shabby accommodation on offer – she was reminded of theatrical digs – and was soon slung out of academe: 'My behaviour had been mad and terribly out of control,' like a female Lear on the heath. Roberts killed herself in November 1980, at the age of fifty-three. The most horrible death imaginable – Nembutal, Mogadon, washed down with weedkiller. In her agony she crashed through a glass door.

She had strong feelings, was capable of real concentration. As she had said, 'I still have emotional power, but it is locked up inside me, devastatingly, eating me alive.' Born in Glamorganshire, in 1960, I'm not dissimilar.

* * *

Though it was almost comical, the way Taylor's body played up – illness after illness: throat and bladder infections; 'incipient ulcer, colitis and 'flu'; impaired circulation because of the tight costumes (thrombophlebitis) during *Giant*; 'a congenital anomaly of the spine'; 'severe lower back strain and possibly a ruptured intervertebral disc' (I am quoting from Warner Brothers' doctors' insurance claim reports); appendicitis (how many times did she have one of those out?); ovarian cysts; adhesions from her Caesareans; a twisted lower intestine, causing retching and vomiting; tracheobronchitis;

staphylococcal and/or fulminant pneumonia (which shut down *Cleopatra*), when she had a tracheotomy and was put on a Barnet Ventilator; hundreds of hospitalisations plus stints in the Betty Ford Center, at the Eisenhower Medical Center, Rancho Mirage (Betty Ford in person was Taylor's sponsor), etc. – nevertheless, Taylor would never have caved in, as Roberts did. With Taylor, illness was part of her strength, a sign of vitality. 'I get ill because I live too hard,' she said. 'I give too much, out of a lust for life. I never back away.' She had pulmonary viruses, sinus infections, thrush and weight 'issues'. There was extensive dental implant surgery. On 8 December 1956, Taylor underwent an operation at the Harkness Pavilion, New York, to replace three spinal discs with bone taken from her pelvis and hip. She said her leg was so numb, 'it started to atrophy.' Numerous reasons were given for the original injury: a fall on Beaverbrook's yacht in heavy seas, when she hurt her coccyx; being bent over backwards and kissed too strenuously by Robert Taylor during *Ivanhoe*; or an accident during riding lessons for *National Velvet*. The chief consequence for Taylor, however, was the opportunity for a gruesome self-dramatising anecdote: 'They cut away all the dead bone right down to the nerve centre.' In February 1997, she had a brain tumour removed, which had been preceded, she said, by 'seventeen falls, breaking my ribs and ankles,' when she lost her balance. Taylor received 42,000 get well cards. On 18 August 1999, she endured 'a compressive fracture of the twelfth thoracic vertebra'.

It was always as if she was about to die, but never did. Burton, meanwhile, when he was alive, would be on pins: 'I worried a lot about Elizabeth this morning ... and how awful it would be to lose her. I worked myself up to a rare state of misery' (3 November 1966); 'E. was in agony to the point of tears ... went for X-ray of ribs. No cracks but two spots on lung ... The most agonising hour of my life ended at approx. 1 p.m. ... I had [been] in the most terrible fear for Elizabeth's and my life. Sleep was no palliative ... I love her mindlessly and hopelessly' (4 October 1975). The lung cancer fear was immediately discounted by the specialists, who presumably found a smudge on the radiography lens, and she always bounced back. When she had phlebitis in her right leg she reminisced, 'The experience I had was painful, but beautiful, too.' She was never so prostrate she couldn't apply lip gloss in the ambulance. Only occasionally would Burton suspect her of hypochondria. Taylor was 'in such pain that I fancy she's going to end up in a wheelchair,' he wrote on 14 December 1968. She was drinking, taking too many tablets, 'ill only when she chose to be' – and the moment *The Only Game in Town* was completed, and she got to Gstaad for Christmas, she was leaping about, throwing snowballs. Then Burton says she was only 'semi-articulate' come the evenings, because of the drugs she'd been prescribed – in 1985, a year after Burton's death, Taylor was declared long addicted to Percodan (oxycodone hydrochloride), Hycodan (hydrocodone bitartrate), Demerol (meperidine hydrochloride), Dilaudid (hydromorphone hydrochloride), Morphine Sulfate (an opioid) and Halcion (a benzodiazepine derivate). In 1982, two years before Burton's demise, Taylor swallowed six hundred pills during an average sixteen-day period.

She was meant to be a goddess, after all, and goddesses can't die – Taylor was affronted by the idea of genuine death, consigning such an event to her film roles. For example, the sickly girl in *Cynthia* (1947), whose pampering parents intensify her ailments – 'a modern teenage Camille,' according to the studio synopsis; all the way to Cleopatra's stage-managing of her own death, the terminally ill Sissy Goforth in *Boom!* and the woman seeking someone to kill her in *The Driver's Seat*, which is sometimes known as *Identikit*. In contrast to the plethora of deathbed scenes, Taylor's own strength and indestructability ('I've been through it all, baby. I'm Mother Courage. I'll be dragging my sable coat behind me in old age') could almost work against her. Though now and again desperate and miserable, she rather luxuriated in her own anguish – and I never feel I pity her. There's too much savagery and pride. For Taylor's own life was so unlike the life the rest of us lead, or are told we should lead – all her illnesses, all her marriages, all her crown jewels (Laurence Harvey said, 'Her health was her favourite subject after diamonds') – yet there's nothing genuinely camp about her, either, despite her flamboyance and the association with homosexuals, to whom she was attentive: Montgomery Clift, Rock Hudson, Roddy McDowall, Franco Zeffirelli, Frankie Howerd – Taylor to Frankie: 'Did anyone ever tell you that you are the funniest man in the world?' Frankie to the assembled company: 'What a nice lady, and so intelligent.'

With everything done on an operatic scale, did Zeffirelli find her similar to Callas, when he put her in *Young Toscanini*? Self-destructive, but only seemingly: Taylor always survived. Furthermore, her vulgarity was not contrived. Taylor had a naturalness that's the antithesis of camp. (I don't think Burton would have tolerated camp, either.) With Taylor, there's more of a fairy-tale element, as if she's a creature who has only borrowed human shape and form – there's something about her that's elemental, from the forest floor. In 1945, her mother had been telling the *Los Angeles Times* that her daughter 'whinnies like a horse, and she also chirps like a squirrel and makes bird noises,' rather than display human speech. As Cleopatra she is surrounded by cat, ibis and serpent imagery. In *BUtterfield 8* she sniffs perfume bottles and picks over discarded clothes, as if silently examining a fox's earth. *Secret Ceremony* sees Taylor go through a wardrobe filled with furs. She puts on different coloured wigs, her face reproduced in mirrors and glass cabinets, silver-backed hairbrushes and the blade of a knife. She's an animal in her den, selecting clothes, dressing and undressing, checking her reflection, like a deer in a pool, or when she is Martha in *Who's Afraid of Virginia Woolf?*, poking about in the fridge, chewing the leftovers, Taylor is openly feral. I can't think of any other actress whose lengthy scenes are quite so inconsequential, devoid of the dramatic – and Taylor does seem oblivious, like a creature unaware of when it is being observed, snuffling and going about its business in its natural habitat, where there is no need for speech, only little grunts and snores. *X, Y & Zee* is similar: costumes and plumage. Orange fringes, yellow ponchos, purple capes with triangular tassels, lime-green bodices and beads abound. In the film, the sadomasochistic erotic games with Michael Caine, the emotional choreography, is that of birds of paradise going through a mating ritual, probing and rejecting, with Taylor emptying and filling suitcases, in constant jiggling, jouncing motion, literally and figuratively flighty. 'You love the uncertainty,' she tells her partner. 'You don't know what I'm going to do today, and neither do I.' We also see Taylor out in the street, kicking dustbins over – a hell-cat.

Taylor had an affinity with animals, more than with men – Burton delighted, incidentally, during their erotic vagrancies, in watching her 'become the animal that all men seek in their women', and when, in his diaries, and elsewhere, he goes into rhapsodies about 'your smell and your paps . . . and your round belly and the exquisite softness of the inside of your thighs,' I not only visualise a smirking, heaving Gloucestershire Old Spot sow, I also realise, once I've got over what Kingsley Amis called, in reference to intercourse, 'the horror or nastiness of it all', that when it comes to explicit sexual description, a little goes a long way. But my point here is not any of that – it's to affirm Taylor's identification with hostile and beautiful creatures, which crouch unblinking in the steaming woods and jungles: her pet monkeys, parrots and bush babies. In her early phase, her pets included a springer spaniel, a cocker spaniel, a golden retriever, a pair of poodles (one black, one white), two cats, a squirrel, two horses and a chipmunk, Nibbles, who was her swain. 'He is happy with me,' she said, 'He keeps showing me that he is. Can you wonder that I love him so much?' I *do* wonder, in fact, and, indeed, much needing to be known about Taylor's psychology can be found in or inferred from *Nibbles and Me*, a short book she wrote out studiously in pencil and illustrated, and which in 1946 was published by Duell, Sloan & Pearce Inc. Taylor renewed the copyright in 1974. There was a second edition, with an Introduction and 'additional illustrations', in October 2002. The project clearly meant a lot. Taylor had composed it originally, she explained, as 'a thirteen-year-old girl . . . leaving childhood behind.' Whether she ever did leave childhood behind is a big question, and in 1946 she was fourteen, not thirteen, yet nevertheless, *Nibbles and Me* is like something the friendless person in *The Secret Garden* would produce, or the girl in *The Nutcracker*, and Taylor, aged seventy when the book was reprinted, evidently felt it was important to remind everyone, 'Over the years, animals have remained my sweetest and most cherished friends.'

Nibbles is a North American rodent with a striped pelt, and you long to squash him with a boot or knock the little fucker sharply on the head with a stick; but he also could be an allegory or premonition of any of Taylor's husbands, the way she coos over his antics, weeps over accidents and disasters. Nibbles, 'venturesome and curious', falls down the lavatory, hops in a bubble bath ('Poor Nibbles, wet and shivering'), investigates a snake's nest, gets stuck in drains and pipes and explores under the floorboards. Throughout there is this unrestrained emotionalism – uninhibited and sincere, and not a little mad. When Nibbles reappears, after his numerous scrapes, 'We were speechless. We just sat there on the floor with our hearts brimming with thankfulness.' Referring to herself with the plural pronoun, Taylor might be making a regal proclamation. She is convinced she can talk to animals, commune with them – rabbits, turtles, snakes, baby lambs, guinea pigs and kittens. And when she remembers her earliest childhood, there's a J.M. Barrie preciousness: 'It was like going to bed in fairyland with the windows all wide open and the firelight flickering on the ceilings and walls.' Sounds dangerous and combustible to me – cold draughts, naked flames.

Nibbles came Taylor's way when she was making *Courage of Lassie*, at Lake Chelan, and befriended the wrangler. 'I'll never forget how thrilled I was when he put that soft furry little thing in my hand.' Fancy. Taylor constructed a cage of logs and turf, 'with berries, nuts, seeds, apples, grapes and brown bread' for Nibbles to eat – a green and gold affair, with an exercise wheel, a sort of Oliver Messel Suite for chipmunks. Unfortunately, Nibbles is crushed by a door: 'My heart was broken.' Taylor cried her eyes out, 'and then I knew that in reality there is no death,' not because she'd been vouchsafed a meta-physical vision to rival anything in the gospels, but because it was plain Nibbles could easily be replaced – chipmunks are pretty much identical. She captured at least seven Nibbles duplicates, in the same way Taylor went through eight wedding ceremonies, two of them with Burton. 'He will never grow up and never grow old,' Taylor said of her Peter Pan-ish succession of rodents, whom she kept in her pocket, took on the train, and kept on 'a lovely long gold chain ... with a dear little gold ring on one end for my finger and a collar for Nibs on the other with a nameplate on it.' Is that how Nicky, Mike Wilding, Mike Todd, Eddie, Burton, Senator Warner and Larry Fortensky ('a blue-collar boy of Polish extraction,' in the description of Nobel Laureate Joseph Brodsky) reckoned they were treated? Alternately pushed around and pampered, at least until the time came to put them in the wrong?

Taylor put down sunflower seeds and pine nuts for Nibbles, saw him fight off other chipmunks – his nose and leg were nearly chewed off – and when he goes missing, 'My head and my heart were bursting with agony ... Can you imagine how I felt? I wanted to go off and cry and cry. I felt shaky all over.' The only comparable moments I can discern (what follows is only a selection) are when Todd was killed in the plane crash – 'She's screaming like a maniac,' said her butler, Dick Hanley; 'She's lost the will to live,' said her doctor, Rex Kennamer; 'Mike, Mike! You can't leave me here alone!' said Taylor herself, falling on top of the coffin, at the Waldheim Cemetery in Chicago. Or then there was the death of James Dean, her co-star in *Giant*, who crashed his Porsche 550 Spyder near Cholame in San Luis Obispo County – Taylor was immediately indisposed and suffered from 'extreme nervous tension' and 'extreme mental duress' as a consequence, according to a studio physician's memo, copied to the insurance adjustors, Toplis & Harding. A surgical procedure on her ovaries in 1957, preventing further pregnancies, a tubal ligation, was 'the worst shock of my life. Like being killed.' The courtship with Burton was 'terrible heartache ... There was terrible pain ... What ballooned the unbelievably insane quality of everything was the insanity going on at the *Cleopatra* set every day. They would actually misplace fifteen hundred spears.' Everything about her involved hyperbole. 'I love Richard Burton with every fibre of my soul,' she told the press in 1974, announcing not union and harmony but their first divorce. That's how she was. The terminal pancreatic cancer of Laurence Harvey, the male lead in *BUtterfield 8* and *Night Watch*, set her off, which irritated Harvey's oncologist ('She struck me as very, very shallow, interested only in her own feelings and not anyone else's') as well as Harvey himself, the dying man finding the way Taylor went on about 'life and death' in his wretched presence thoroughly egocentric. She even tried to climb into bed with him, despite the tubes and drips. 'He was one of those people I really loved in this world,' Taylor told reporters, when Harvey joined the Choir Invisible, in November 1973, aged forty-five. 'He was part of the sun.' Taylor organised an Episcopal Memorial Service, even though Harvey was a Lithuanian Jew. 'I can't believe I'll never see him again. I just can't believe it.'

Death, love, loss – it all came back to Nibbles. When she decided to release Nibbles back into the wild, she asked her brother, Howard, 'to help me be strong and not mind about the heartache ... The world at that moment seemed so black and empty.' Taylor went to her mother, 'and the tears rolled down both our cheeks ... I couldn't stop crying. I knew I would cry for days but that didn't matter,' because she enjoyed it really, never felt better in her life. Taylor enjoyed disaster, illness, drunkenness, drugs, violence, lechery, insults and acrimony. Taylor's mother, by the way, Sara, spent her last years in a Rancho Mirage condo, playing cards with Zsa Zsa Gabor's mother. Sara died on 11 September 1994, aged ninety-nine.

It had been Taylor's dream to advance from a chipmunk to an elephant. Travelling to the Far East with Victor Luna, one of her post-Burton partners, she saw an elephant and wanted Luna to buy it. 'No, Elizabeth. You can't take an elephant home,' he said. Luna wasn't to last. In 1991, Taylor gave a five-ton elephant, named Gypsy, to Michael Jackson, for the private zoo at the Neverland ranch. The sinister compound, with its funfair and floral clock, and with the interior walls painted the colour of Taylor's eyes ('The painters never stopped mixing colours, but they never got it exactly right' – how hard is lavender to achieve?), was abandoned in 2005, in the wake of Jackson's trials and tribulations. The zoo dispersed, Tippi Hedren taking the tigers. Nobody knows what happened to Gypsy.

* * *

What do famous people become in the end? A series of shocking and for preference discreditable feature articles in a tabloid-shaped newspaper? A re-heated obituary page? A policeman's unadorned reconstruction of actions and whereabouts, as if used in evidence at the magistrates' court? The autopsy report, with statistics about the state of livers and kidneys? Public appearances as raw material for novelists and playwrights, who turn history into a narrative plot, with a bit of clever psychological analysis shoved in? Signed photographs, lost in a drawer? How fast household names require explanatory footnotes. I recently saw a reference to 'the comedian Terry-Thomas', to distinguish him, I imagine, from the professional wrestler Terry-Thomas or the chemical engineer from Hove Terry-Thomas. Of the narrators hired to be alongside Taylor for *That's Entertainment*, in 1974, the feature-length compilation of highlights from the MGM archives, who remembers Bing Crosby, Donald O'Connor, James Stewart or Mickey Rooney, at least in any detail – except for the likes of me? Such was the force of Taylor's personality, however, in a film where she had only a silent cameo, as Lola Comante, the President's procuress, in *Winter Kills*, she still somehow takes over, permeates. In this silly story by Richard Condon about the Kennedy assassination (corrupt cops, mobsters, spy networks – everybody bumping everyone else off), Taylor descends a staircase and surveys the guests at a party; watches a helicopter land; is in an office having her offers of financial assistance rebuffed – and we note those lips, those eyes, plus her white hats made from orchid stamens. She's like something from a botanical garden. Uncredited in the title sequence, Taylor, by 1979, was so famous, she didn't require any announcement – she briefly materialises and dematerialises, like a night bloom. The cinematographer, Vilmos Zsigmond, invented a special lens to slim her down.

Burton, too, made visitations. In a blood-red outfit he's a man in a bar in the zany *What's New Pussycat?* to whom Peter O'Toole bemusedly says, 'Give my love to what's-her-name.' He's also 'himself' in an episode of *The Fall Guy*, 'Reluctant Travelling Companion', broadcast on 24 November 1982. Lee Majors' Colt, a part-time bounty hunter and part-time stuntman, who to pursue (or escape) baddies in Seventies suits has regularly to dangle off helicopters, which are thankfully never far off the ground, and leap upon lorries speeding at a snail's pace, is taking a woman criminal to face justice, three thousand miles by train from Philadelphia to Los Angeles. Burton is the man in the next compartment, trying to study a script. 'You're Richard Burton!' says Colt. 'Lower your voice. I'm incognito,' says Burton, his own voice so deep and growly, the bass notes resonate more than the big steel wheels gripping the polished tracks. The woman criminal is herself a banshee. She screams and bites, won't shut up. Burton assumes rape and kidnap are under way, or a kinky sex game – he sees Colt has been using handcuffs. Burton must be disturbed by the racket half-a-dozen times, keeps coming in and out to make a complaint, his courtesy getting increasingly sarcastic. Finally, he is knocked unconscious by the woman criminal, played by one Mary-Margaret Humes, who mistakes Burton for someone else, though we are not told whom. When he comes round, the black steward brings him an ice-pack and a bottle of Scotch.

The programme is clumsy, cheap-looking, plastic, and in his 'Special Appearance' as himself, Burton is stiff and awkward, looking at best bashful in a white blouse, blue slacks and red cravat. It is the case, I think, that when they are 'themselves', celebrities become strangers to themselves, silly and self-conscious. Never more so than when Burton and Taylor played Burton and Taylor in *Here's Lucy*, aired on 14 September 1970. Lucille Ball is hard to take on any day of the week, her frog-voiced yelps and contrived slapstick, her (in Burton's brilliant phrase) 'false ecstasy of amusement'. The idea, in 'Lucy Meets the Burtons', is that to escape his hordes of fans, Burton, fed up of being stuck in a hotel room, has to disguise himself as a plumber. Lucy thinks he's a real plumber and insists he immediately comes into her office to mend her 'faucet', or what I'd think of as her tap. Hilarious misunderstandings ensue, as Lucy is the only person in the world in 1970 not to recognise who this man really is – her 'partner' Gale Gordon, expostulating in a Peter Glaze manner, is dumbfounded when he finds Burton hunched over the washbasin with a plunger: 'It's *you!*' he says, and starts quoting cod Shakespeare. Burton, in turn, quotes (badly – though the studio audience applauds respectfully) from *Richard II* ('Let us sit upon the ground and tell sad stories of the death of kings'), and Lucy remains unconvinced: 'You'd better stick to your plumbing,' she says, pulling a face. It's time for the actor to unmask himself: 'I'm Richard Burton,' he announces. 'Oh, and *I'm* Elizabeth Taylor!' replies Lucy. 'Believe me, you're not,' says Burton, which gets a mild laugh. The next thing we know, Lucy has got the Krupp Diamond stuck on her finger, 'and now my knuckle is all swollen.' She squawks a lot, pulls many more faces; Gale expostulates even more, like Peter Glaze with toothpaste in his eye, and Burton expects a fearful bollocking from his spouse, as 'I'd promised Elizabeth I'd get her ring fixed.' Agreeing, finally, that Burton is who he says he is, Lucy knocks over a typewriter and chokes on her chewing gum – thoroughly pathetic stage business.

30

After plenty of time for more of the same, she comes out with the killer line, 'How's the missus?'

Following the commercial break, Taylor comes on, to considerable clapping, wearing a psychedelic trouser-suit and matching headband. According to the credits, her hair was mussed by Sydney Guilaroff, who must have been specially brought out of MGM retirement, or even back from beyond the grave. Lucy tells Taylor that Burton, when impersonating a plumber, had 'fixed' her 'leaky pipes'. The camera cuts very quickly away from Taylor's reaction, in case there was a risk of innuendo. The ring immoveable on Lucy's finger, at a subsequent party scene, Lucy has to hide behind a curtain and shove her arm in the sleeve of Taylor's gown, pretending her hand is Taylor's hand – the false arm gags are like *Dr. Strangelove* or Harry Corbett doing Sooty. We end there, thank Christ – and basically it has been thirty minutes of caterwauling. What a combination of voices, shrill, piercing, wrenching, grinding, like a munitions factory on nights. Lucy and Taylor are so loud – and actually quite similar. They have a confrontational style. They weren't refined in their appearance, but coarse. They had resilience, and this is what curbed, or allowed them to survive (or surmount), their recklessness. They didn't much care what others thought of them, of their opinions and judgement. They were capable of courage, and temper. Taylor and Lucy had defiance – and the camera captured this. Nothing about them was relaxing.

Lucille Ball's one joke was that she was very big and television is very small. For decades she dominated the medium, playing a housewife unsuccessfully seeking domestic calm, a showgirl trapped in a world of cookers, washing machines, pastry-making and (as Burton discovers) sinks. Taylor, too, was very big as a star – and *Here's Lucy* diminishes her, as Burton, too, is diminished, his skin over-suntanned, burnt, his accent slipping back impatiently from grandiosity to South Welsh-Port 'Tarlbot'. What is confirmed, also, in this example of televisual shoddiness, is how Burton did not possess a comic spirit.

He had no humour, other than irony. When he laughed, e.g. in *The Spy Who Came in from the Cold* or as Petruchio, it is a derisive, scornful, cruel sort of snickering. His laughter is a lashing out. He cannot trifle. On the receiving end of a joke or if somebody is being obviously funny, he looks startled, bemused. He steps aside, as it were. Disengages himself. I myself, in the past, have always written about, dwelt on, comic genius – but Burton had a tragic sense of things. His element was despair, almost despondency.

* * *

Burton's sidekick, the prince's dog, Brook Williams, is in *Here's Lucy* as a hotel manager. He's dithering, effete. No wonder he rose no higher in the scheme of things than carrying Burton's bags, opening bottles. Nevertheless, Taylor, Burton, and Brook (his character is called 'Mr Williams'): they become Lucy's puppets. They are turned into cartoons. The process is extended or intensified in biopics, when other people appear on screen mimicking Taylor and Burton, ostensibly as in themselves they were usually meant to have been like – but the question actually arising is: when we look at far-off periods and places, and at people moving about in those contexts, do they become more real to us, or more fictional? For when I think of them as the one, they turn into the other. When I watched *Liz: The Elizabeth Taylor Story* (1995), for example, I realised the Taylor and Burton story could be told with fidelity in a variety of ways, as comedy or farce or tragedy. Here, with Sherilyn Fenn as Taylor, Angus Macfadyen as Burton, and Nigel Havers as Michael Wilding, however, they opt for soap opera, with big hair and over-lit plush interiors. (It looks like a cheap hotel where business conventions take place.) People address each other by their full names, so we know who they are: 'Spyros P. Skouras, meet Joseph L. Mankiewicz.' And it is comical or absurd, the way Taylor goes from man to man, each time always claiming to have found the love of her life at last – but she has no idea what this means or entails. Fenn's Taylor craves stimulation, excitement, even brute force, yet has no real feelings for others. What she mostly demonstrates is sentimentality, and a need for lots of pets – she's often clutching a dog to her bosom. Macfadyen's Burton is so atrocious, I thought Jerry Lewis' nutty professor had wandered into shot. The Welshman is portrayed as a selfish bighead, awash with beer. Cast as Taylor, Fenn gives a passable impersonation of Joan Collins.

In *Liz and Dick* (2012), Grant Bowler's Burton is a man determined to make a conquest – not only of Taylor, but of his accent. Bowler is Australian, I believe, possibly even a New Zealander, and his idea of being Welsh is to go in for a lot of brooding and glowering, singing hymns about Taylor's breasts or busty substances. He pronounces Ivor as 'Igor', as if Burton's brother was Frankenstein's hunchback assistant. Everyone is in Rome, for *Cleopatra*, with Taylor personally bringing an end to the Golden Age of Hollywood by bankrupting Twentieth Century Fox. Burton is married with children and yet, totally arrogant, he is also proud of himself for betraying family 'values', for shirking tedious domestic responsibilities and for making a fool of Sybil. It is much more exciting, squiring Taylor about the place, with press photographers' flashbulbs going off. 'Igor' keeps reminding him of their shared Welsh chapel background, wants Burton at least to seem torn and acknowledge a sense of duty. When 'Igor' is later paralysed in an accident, Burton howls, 'I killed my brother!' and it's as if the path of a Greek drama has been followed, hubris never doing anyone any favours.

Taylor, meanwhile, played by Lindsay Lohan, is interested only in cigarettes, booze, swimming pools, jewels, jets and fame. All she requires from life is one lavish treat after another. In this (interesting – plausible) interpretation, Taylor doesn't know how to play with her children, Michael, Christopher and Liza, because she's never been a child – only a child actress. There's also an erotic dimension to her habitual chaos, as Lohan's Taylor is aroused by mess, bad behaviour, the upending of conventional rules. Only when matters are extreme can she feel anything – hence her illnesses and suicide attempts ('How many did you take?'); hence perhaps the sheer number of her weddings. Sara Taylor [Theresa Russell]: 'Not that I'm counting, you just ended, what, your fourth marriage?' – Taylor: 'Oh, who's counting?' To distract us from the dialogue, the clothing of the Sixties and Seventies is shoved into our gaze, the fabrics, feathers, shoes. Lohan had one hundred and seventeen costume changes.

Caricatures though the performances are, the general thesis of the biopic is one I'd concur with for this biography – that it's not so much that Burton and Taylor's films and performances paralleled their lives, or extended or explained their lives, but that their works replaced their lives, e.g. when Burton and Taylor were George and Martha in *Who's Afraid of Virginia Woolf?* or when Burton was Bluebeard. There is an interfusion of public and private selves, also something that grew to be ugly about their relationship. Burton lost his self-worth when robbed of the Academy Award seven times. He was bad, it would seem, as was Taylor, at being out of favour – a lot of boredom, a lot of booze. In a way, or in this way among others, Burton and Taylor balanced each other out – but it was a wobbly sort of balance or pivot, vibrating, trembling. 'Life is so made that opposites sway about a trembling centre of balance,' wrote D.H. Lawrence, no doubt having himself and Frieda in mind (good parts for the Burtons), and that's how it was for many of these celebrity couples, from Lucille Ball and Desi to the Duke and Duchess of Windsor. We hardly need *Liz and Dick* to show us how love can be an addiction, as bad as nicotine or narcotics: loving someone is not enough, they have to be loved in the right way. What's good about love, what's bad: this is the Burton and Taylor romance, containing tragic fire.

There's not much tragic fire in *Burton and Taylor* (2013), where Dominic West and Helena Bonham Carter portrayed the megastars as playful, loopy and drunk, when in 1983 they were reunited for a final time, playing sixty-three performances of *Private Lives*. The trouble is,

Bonham Carter and West are not drunk enough, not chaotic enough. Old Etonian West is not in the least like Burton – he's better at being Prince Charles. He's too courtly and sober, wholly lacking in danger. Bonham Carter relies on blowsiness. As if to prove they'd run out of imagination, the production contains lots of shots of the cast lining up and bowing before the audience, at the Lunt-Fontanne Theatre. I suppose the ingenious point to make is Burton and Taylor may have been in *Private Lives*, but they had no private life. Indeed, Taylor said as much, to Warhol's *Interview Magazine* in November 1976: '*Private? What makes you think my life is private?*' Public opinion was the pond in which they swam. Apparently, the entire Noël Coward production was a ruse by Taylor to get Burton back, which only emboldened him to fly to Las Vegas one weekend during rehearsals and marry Sally Hay, the continuity girl from *Wagner*. Taylor's illnesses and indispositions were further stratagems.

Bonham Carter's Taylor is controlling, rattle-brained, inconstant – all the things Taylor genuinely was when she wanted to get her way. But when watching this television drama, the Burton who kept coming to mind was Tim Burton, Bonham Carter's partner – and Bonham Carter's portrayal of Taylor belongs with the characterisations she gives in *Planet of the Apes*, *Sweeney Todd*, *Alice in Wonderland* and *Dark Shadows*: her odd pout and look of admonishment and surprise; her look of sudden disappointment; the way she affects to be stunned and dazed, but is actually appraising, running her big eyes over someone and summing them up. These mannerisms adapt quite straightforwardly to her idea of Taylor, who in this broadcast is a comic strip drawing of someone old and fat and rheumatic, on the brink of cracking up. Bonham Carter has also been Enid Blyton, Princess Margaret and Noele Gordon – she likes witches and monsters – and it is the easiest thing in the world to exaggerate Taylor's hairstyles, fag-haggery and the rest. But despite the capacity for self-satire, there was an air of detachment and stewardship with the real Taylor, and this met a similar unsettling quality in

(Richard) Burton. They liked giving things a shove – and this made them dangerous and frightening, in ways no biopic can capture, unless we could go back to the days of German Expressionism. Dissolves, cuts, bizarre edits.

* * *

The Motive and the Cue, which ran at the National Theatre between May and July 2023, and was based on Burton's appearance on Broadway as Hamlet, in 1964, when he starred in a production directed by John Gielgud, was convoluted and contrived, frowsty. As a play about the rehearsing of a play, it was like an episode of *Gogglebox*, the programme where we watch other people watching television. We, the actual audience, are at such a remove, it was hard to become engaged, especially as here were actors playing other actors playing Shakespearean roles – David Tarkenter as Alfred Drake as Claudius, Janie Dee as Eileen Herlie as Gertrude. Two of the original company, William Redfield and Richard Sterne, had published behind-the-scenes books, which are what gave Jack Thorne his source material.

For it to make sense, you also needed an A Level or Open University familiarity with *Hamlet*, its plot and characters, from Rosencrantz and Guildenstern to Barnardo and Osric. *The Motive and the Cue* (the title a quotation: 'What's Hecuba to him, or he to Hecuba, / That he should weep for her? What would he do, / Had he the motive and the cue for passion / That I have ?' Act 2, Scene 2) stopped dead periodically so everyone can listen to a recital of the famous soliloquies – and I thought, why doesn't the National Theatre, having employed Sir Sam Mendes, simply put on *Hamlet*, scrap the extraneous stuff? It also helped for patrons to know who Hume Cronyn (Allan Corduner–Polonius) was, and that he was married to Jessica Tandy – so it also helped to know who Jessica Tandy was, likewise. ('You do mention her a lot. I think it's sweet,' Taylor tells him in the play, slightly acidly.) I felt like Larkin, visiting a deserted church; that I was 'one of the crew

/ That tap and jot and know what rood-lofts were,' seeing and spotting esoterica. Most ticket holders at the National will, without prompting, probably have worked out that 'Larry' was Laurence Olivier.

The Taylor character for the most part was at a loose end in her magenta hotel suite. The role seemed shoved in, despite a spirited impersonation by Tuppence Middleton. For example, she has breakfast with Gielgud to tell him things he'd actually already have long known all about: 'A man called Philip Burton, his teacher and the man whose name Richard took, must have been the one who brought him to see you,' she says, before going on to mention Port Talbot. Gielgud, for the record, and I'm a pedantic old shag pointing this out, had directed and appeared on stage with Burton in *The Lady's Not for Burning* (1949) and *The Boy with a Cart* (1950) – so he knew Burton rather better than Taylor did, even though the impression given in *The Motive and the Cue* is that Burton (Johnny Flynn) and Gielgud (Mark Gatiss) are encountering each other professionally for the very first time. In April 1964, Burton was thirty-eight and Gielgud sixty.

And this is built up into a clash of styles (Gielgud's Victorian manner, linked to the Terrys and the Trees; Burton's proletarian Welsh roughness), a clash of personality (Gielgud's reticent homosexuality; Burton's swaggering heterosexuality). I'm not sure there were ever quite such divisions, quite such an incompatibility. Nevertheless, this did give Jack Thorne's play its own dramatic impetus – Burton's drunken tantrums, Gielgud's old-fashioned gentility – Burton wrathful and Gielgud so soft and hesitant he couldn't yield even to the blandishments of a rent boy: 'You should probably go. Use my time on the clock ... to grab some of that fabulous pizza you people like so much.' Indeed, we were meant to feel Gielgud was incapable of connection in any field; that as an actor he went in for mood music, mellifluousness, in contrast to Burton, who sought emotional truth. But I don't believe that either – Burton was never naturalistic, never modernistic. If, in his work, and diaries, he left us in no doubt he possessed a painfully tortured soul, he did this through a sort of sorrowful oratory. He knew or was taught how to declaim – and his voice, his firmness and distinctness, the product of elocution, he took care of what he was saying and how he said things.

Gatiss, who in the Noele Gordon biopic played Larry Grayson as a lonely, faded old trouper, brought this sad, defeated quality to Gielgud. (Though in fairness he did get a lot of laughs.) Surely the real Gielgud was tougher – the Gielgud who said to Charlton Heston, who kept fluffing his lines on the set of *Julius Caesar*, in 1970, 'Oh Chuck, why don't you fuck off back to *The Planet of the Apes*.' He never evinced the melancholia of camp, at which Gatiss excels. So, there was never, in actuality, this sense of lachrymose failure and rejection, which is where *The Motive and the Cue* leaves him, even if Tuppence's Taylor is suddenly granted prophetic powers, as if seeing in the far distance Gielgud's Academy Award-winning butler in *Arthur*: 'You are going to be fine you know. And I really do believe it. There'll be a moment when the world adjusts, and then you'll be treasured again, just like you should be.' Gielgud would also work with Burton again, as a courtier, Pfistermeister, in *Wagner*. Immediately after directing *Hamlet* there was hardly unemployment – there was *Chimes at Midnight* with Orson Welles, then the Peter Brook *Oedipus* and, in the West End, Alan Bennett's *Forty Years On*.

One regret, another thing existing only in my imagination – Gielgud and Burton would have been well matched as the cryptic antagonists, Hirst and Spooner, in *No Man's Land*, the Pinter play in which Gielgud (Spooner) triumphed with Ralph Richardson (Hirst) at the National Theatre in 1975. There is something faintly echoing that battle of wills, that psychological entanglement, in *The Motive and the Cue* – the one character wheedling, a supplicant, the other abrupt and lordly: 'Do I detect,' says Spooner, 'a touch of the hostile? Do I detect, with respect, a touch of too many glasses of ale followed by the great malt which wounds?'

* * *

And if biopics are distortions – egregious and artificial – where does that leave biography? Or what I choose to call the biographical fallacy? Apart from there being, obviously, a tombstone at the far end, a summing-up in the papers should you be notable, despite what biographies allege, a life has no predictable shape or stability. Unless narcissism is extreme, when, to quote Norman Mailer, 'the eye of one's consciousness is forever looking at one's own action,' nothing is done by a person with any awareness of narrative sequence. Life is contingent, zig-zaggy, made up of discordant moments; and though the history and fortunes of Burton and Taylor seemed to come along or accumulate like a Dickens novel in weekly instalments, even with them, living their lives as they pleased, much of existence simply passed by, or was soon forgotten – appetite, scraps, events, sub-plots, which slowed down, speeded up, sank in, or failed to register. 'Bought cigs, books, sandals,' said Burton in June 1965 – nothing out of the ordinary there. 'Now for the long bore of Christmas,' he sighed in December 1968. Like for everyone else, there were plenty of days when 'the weather [is] not dramatically bad, no winds, no tempests, no howling blizzards, but simply a low grey cloud that squeezed the spirit . . .' Sometimes, time itself seemed to drag to a halt. 'Read nothing yesterday,' Burton jotted in September 1970, 'simply stared about in a generally stunned way.' A lot of us feel like that.

What precisely were they exposed to, therefore – the phenomena, the turbulence, filling their hours and days? What was absorbed? What impressions were formed, as the life or lives of Burton and Taylor went on much as before? ('We were invited to have lunch with the King and Queen of Greece anytime we like this week'; 'Last night as I lay reading in bed . . . I asked [Elizabeth] what are you doing? She said like a little girl and quite seriously, "Playing with my jewels."') Whether we are rich and privileged or sitting on the bones of our arse, how little of what we do is ever under conscious control. Nothing is where it belongs, in the human comedy. As Joan Didion says in *The Year of Magical Thinking*, 'Life changes in an instant.

You sit down to dinner and life as you know it ends,' e.g. when a loved one has a sudden coronary or a child is hospitalised. 'The clear blue sky from which the plane fell, the routine errand that ended on the shoulder with the car in flames.' There are turning points, disjunctions.

Yet they might not be the ones you expect, which is why biographies work one of two ways for me. First, with Keats, for instance, and Romantic poetry, which is deliberately numinous, I'm keen to know what drugs these people were on or knew of, the diseases and chronic illnesses they suffered from; I want the facts about Keats' medical training. It makes him less adolescent, knowing such. On the other hand, I loved Philip Larkin's poem, 'We Met at the End of the Party', which contains the beautiful lines, 'We walked through the last of summer, / When shadows reached long and blue,' and all this was spoiled somehow when I discovered, or was told, the precise autobiographical details it had recorded – who his partner was, what the occasion was. It lost its impact because for me Larkin's poetry works when it has a vagueness or ambiguity: 'The Building', for instance, which could be a cathedral as much as a hospital; nothing is specified ('in the hall / As well as creepers hangs a frightening smell'); maybe it's a hotel none can leave. Biographers, of course, want to provide a photograph of the Hull Royal Infirmary, opened by the Queen in 1967. The uncertainties, the diffuseness, the elements of indeterminacy, associated in Larkin's imagery and consciousness with the grey, pale skies of the north-east, are obliterated. Similarly, by linking the love poetry and everything else to the Monicas and the Maeves and the Bettys, and to the politics (sexual politics) of the Brynmor Jones Library: biography reduces Larkin's achievement, when all is found and marked on the map, when every deed is spelled out. Sometimes I really don't appreciate *information*. Like being told Bulmer's cider factory in Hereford contains the world's largest vat, with a capacity to hold 1.63 million gallons, or in 1979 Emma 'Baby Spice' Bunton was born in Hastings.

Conventional or traditional biographies are about corpses, reclining figures on tombs. Samuel Pepys recorded in his diary coming across an excavation in Westminster Abbey, when the skull of Jane Seymour was discovered. Pepys 'kissed the skull on the place where once the lips had been,' and that's what biographers are doing, in a sense. 'Everything can be explained in nine-hundred pages,' said Paul Theroux, reviewing Zachary Leader's authorised *Life* of Kingsley Amis. It cannot – and that bloated effort is a particular deadweight, every illicit embrace in Swansea, for example, traced directly to spots of adultery described in the novels. Why should that interest anybody? None of it is illuminating. Biographers, it seems to me, affecting a universal authority, see or notice only one thing at a time, remain on the surface, where they make themselves busy handling circumstances, tidying them up. A place for everything and everything in its place, as my maiden aunts used to say in South Wales. The process is bogus, the whole boiling is overly settled – too much carried away by and credence given to balance and fairness. There's no understanding that reserve and secrecy are a part of life, possibly more than (verifiable) events are, than action is. I fully agree with Taylor's contempt, or alarm, when another biography or biographical film came along and she said, 'There is no possible way they could know what was going on unless they were under my carpet or under my bed' – or inside her head. Biography is historical fiction, seldom provable, full of fishiness and titillation, and, despite its heaps of minutiae, insufficient. Since 2015, The Elizabeth Taylor Foundation has been putting together the Elizabeth Taylor Archive, which contains everything her mother, Sara, had salvaged – childhood drawings, Christmas cards, school reports, plus Taylor's business records, financial and legal documents and press material. Like urns in a row, there are a thousand linear feet of identical cartons, kept in climate-controlled conditions. 'Drawn shades protect [the archive's] treasures and inside it hums with the energy of an extraordinary life,' promises the website. It is like Cleopatra's mausoleum – or the Thatcher Memorial Library in *Citizen Kane*, a hushed sepulchre, over-reverent. Apparently, there are 20,000 digitised items. One day some poor wee bastard will start sifting through it all – Kate Andersen Brower reports there are 7,358 letters, notes and clippings and 10,271 photographs. My contention is this – that Taylor's actual meaning and presence are not going to be found there, just as any answer to the 'Rosebud' riddle is not amongst the papers examined by the reporter in Welles' film.

The illusion of biography is that real people are not perishable and that they can be restored. But people are perishable. They come to an end, go out of fashion, require exegesis. But matter, to use the word in the sense of physical properties, doesn't, or doesn't quite. It is infinite and limitless, like light. The nearer you think you get to the subject(s)-in-hand, the more distant they now appear. Writing, or biographical writing, for me anyway, is like what Francis Bacon said to David Sylvester about portrait painting: 'The longer you work, the more the mystery deepens of what appearance is, or how can what is called appearance be made in another medium. It needs a sort of moment of magic to coagulate colour and form, so that it gets the equivalent of appearance . . . In a second you may blink your eyes or turn your head slightly, and you look again and the appearance has changed . . . Appearance is . . . continuously floating.' Everything is still to be done.

* * *

If my own study, or studies, of Taylor and Burton has taken well over a decade, one reason is the first versions I destroyed, as too conventionally structured, too obvious. Nothing bloomed. It came too easily and I was not getting across what I had been seeing, what I'd deduced about impulses and motives, when I watched the films. In the end I went back to the beginning, to the spontaneity of my notebooks, where a scrawled rapture was to be found. In any event, I've always had an affinity with shuffled stories, follies, ghosts glimpsed in mirrors. As Leonard Woolf put it, 'If one is to try to record one's life truthfully, one must aim at getting into the record of it something of the disorderly discontinuity which makes it so absurd, unpredictable, bearable.' By extension – if trying to record anybody's life, not only one's own life. So, I've been scraping off the paint or rubbing at charcoal marks, to get rid of excrescences, whilst no doubt adding to others. The fragments remaining, though seemingly distracted, conflicting, compressed, had, I felt, vitality, movement – the movement of rocks in an avalanche.

For if I may be permitted to be anecdotal, or more to the point reminiscential, I fell ill on Boxing Day 2011: fevers and chills, swellings, lassitude, pervasive aches and night sweats. As usual, I think I'm dying, my consciousness disintegrating. In bed for five weeks, and in a High Dependency ward for three weeks – plus the trips to the clinic for blood tests, X-rays and abdominal scans – I found myself when recuperating watching all those overblown films Burton and Taylor made. *Boom!*, for example, or *Hammersmith Is Out*, *The Comedians* and *The Sandpiper*. Dismissed at the time, they now have a weird attraction, a distinct pleasurableness, or at least they do for me. Whilst I was languishing with a high temperature, rheumatic pains, pancreatitis, and which-what, these gaudily-coloured Sixties movies – *Cleopatra*, *The V.I.P.s*, *The Taming of the Shrew* – as often as not fruitily scored by Nino Rota, suited my mood. I gave in to them without a struggle, and I am perhaps less interested in Burton and Taylor historically and biographically, than in isolating them culturally, as carnal and fantasy figures who floated about in a world of child stars, faded grandeur, alcoholism, promiscuity and Lassie. If they remain significant, desirable, it is because what I watch and absorb in the end isn't a performance but a personality, a presence. Taylor is supple and soft, with her perfumes and furs – yet there is also something demonic and lethal about her. Burton, in his turn, with his ravaged, handsome face, looks as if he is lit by silver moonlight, when perhaps he'd turn into a wolf. His films have the atmosphere of intense dreams – dreams filmed with guilt and morbidity.

What I have been working on for many years now is a book about these two creatures – and it is also about the clash of worlds: the coal filth and industrial decay of South Wales and the grandeur and elegance of Old Hollywood (where Taylor had been a public baby at MGM – *National Velvet, Courage of Lassie*, etc.) – Michael Sheen once asked Taylor, 'How sweet is the air between the Welsh Valleys and the slopes of Olympus?'; a book about love and hatred and obsession; men and women and their incongruities; the issues of manhood and narcissism; the nature of ravishment and conquest and of suffering and ultimate risk; the fantasies we have about film stars and the fantasies the Burtons had about each other. What did they hope and desire for themselves? Why did they seem incapable of calm or satisfaction?

Everywhere is discrepancy. 'Our way of life,' said Burton, 'was a first-class recipe for organised suicide.' For her own verdict, Taylor echoed Othello's remark to Lodovico – his moment of self-discovery – that he was the one who'd loved not wisely, but too well. 'Maybe we love each other too much,' Taylor stated. The Burtons were a Sixties supercharged couple, in an era of supercharged couples: Mick and Bianca, Frank and Ava, Peter and Britt, John and Yoko, Margaret and Tony, many of them destined to become brand-image Warhol screen-prints. But to describe their cool world now, in the twenty-first century, is to describe a lost civilisation, with people in their sharp black clothes drinking and smoking, spending time in two-bedroom suites at fading grand hotels, the Sacher in Vienna and the Alfonso XIII in Seville, shooting their movies at Cinecittà, Rome, and buying villas in Puerto Vallarta, Mexico, in tax-efficient Switzerland and Papa Doc's Haiti: 'All those places in Hampstead, Mexico and Beverly Hills were with Richard. They're all just sitting there empty now,' said Taylor in 1975.

It is another planet – and it always was. In *The Last Picture Show* (1971), Peter Bogdanovich's portrait of a decrepit Texas town, set in 1951, where nobody is capable of happy relationships, and sex is furtive and joyless, and kitchens are piled with unwashed crockery – where life is a mean trap – what the populace watch at the cinema is Spencer Tracy and Elizabeth Taylor in *Father of the Bride*: the characters' rich and privileged home in that, their clothes, the decor, the salubriousness, are quite impossible to replicate in reality. The contrast with reality couldn't be more complete (it is almost a reproach) – and this is the world the Burtons came to embody, or Rex Harrison, Julius Caesar to Taylor and Burton's Cleo and Antony, came to embody. On a hill above Portofino, amongst the mimosa and lemon trees in Italy's coastal province of Liguria, Harrison built the Villa Genesio. A flag would be raised when the master was in residence. Here the Burtons became frequent guests – though because Rex's mad fourth wife, Rachel Roberts, as described earlier, was a friend of Burton's first wife, Sybil, there were fireworks. Indeed, explosions and eruptions were everywhere in that summer of 1962. During the making of Twentieth Century Fox's $31 million laborious Roman epic, the Burtons' 'much-publicised love affair often made work pretty tiring for me,' said Harrison. 'For at the height of it, Elizabeth and Richard kept hitting each other and giving each other black eyes.'

Their erotic relationship – their need to be transported by irresistible powers, which disturb and arouse – had an intensity and force, excitement and fervour. Burton and Taylor were spellbound by each other, enchanted, as were Antony and Cleopatra; and like Cleopatra, Taylor was her own singular and flamboyant creation, whose own needs were paramount. One thinks of bellicose Ethel Merman singing: 'Some people may be content / Playing bingo and paying the rent / But some people *ain't me*.' Interestingly, as an actress, Taylor adapted herself to her numerous husbands, at least she did so initially: the bright-eyed virginal toy bride for Nicky Hilton, the Fifties little woman for Michael Wilding, the broad for Mike Todd, the Jewess for Eddie Fisher, each other's idea of fun for Burton, the politician's consort for John Warner, the fellow redneck drug-addict wearing white fringed cowboy boots for Larry Fortensky – but she'd never compromise for long, by which time it was all their fault, the misunderstandings, the dissatisfactions. By these means Taylor was never defined by her relation to a man, despite appearances – and she stood up to Burton, who was not used to this. Indeed, he may well in the long run have come to agree with a formulation of Kingsley Amis' in *Stanley and the Women*: 'If you want to fuck a woman she can fuck you up. And if you don't want to she fucks you up anyway for not wanting to.' Interesting.

Quite forgotten now (it must be rediscovered) is a film Burton and Rex Harrison made together in Paris, in 1969, called *Staircase*, for which Dudley Moore composed the score, and in which the former Antony and Caesar played homosexual hairdressers: 'I didn't see it as a story of homosexuals but about two neurotic individuals who needed each other desperately for consolation,' said Burton. It is nevertheless a decided oddity, almost sinister in intensity. 'Most actors are homosexuals,' Burton alleged. 'We cover it up with drink.' Now to what degree did he really mean this? Nobody to my know-ledge, by the way, has quite got to the bottom of Burton's relationship with his teacher and mentor at Port Talbot Secondary School, con-genital bachelor Philip Burton, notable for his refined manners – who in 1943 had adopted as his legal ward the youth born as Richard Jenkins. 'Phil, if it hadn't been for you,' said Taylor, 'I probably would never have met Richard – I thank you with all my life for that.' This was sweet of her, considering that when Philip found out about their affair, he didn't speak to his 'son' for a full two years. He was so heart-broken about what he admitted was 'the fear of losing Richard', he fell ill. His tongue came up in boils. He never stopped longing to be with him, and the business seems straight out of Jean Genet to me. To cele-brate or mark the original guardianship, Burton gave Phil a copy of A.E. Housman's *A Shropshire Lad*. To think this was all being allowed *in Wales*. Phil later settled in Key West, Florida. 'It was extraordinary to find how many friends I had in my new home town.' A far cry from

Port Talbot, in anybody's estimation. Another sinister debonair sort prowling around in the early days was Emlyn Williams. He gave Burton his first professional cinematic engagement, in *The Last Days of Dolwyn*, in 1949, and presided at Burton's Memorial Service, on 30 August 1984. John Gielgud, as shown in *The Motive and the Cue*, was another admirer, who directed Burton on stage and told Edith Sitwell (in 1953): 'Richard Burton ... Stocky, Welsh, tough, yet beautiful in repose ... He is the new rage, full of potentialities.' When Burton was in *The Seagull* in Swansea, in 1950, his understudy was Kenneth Williams, who quickly became his beggar-maid, his bitch. 'Richard Burton is really charming,' Williams wrote in his (usually caustic and critical) diaries. 'A personal triumph for Richard Burton,' added Williams after the opening night, on 28 August. 'Colossal applause ... He deserved every bit of it. I got his drinks for him between acts. Privileged.' I was recently sent a copy of the programme: 'The Arts Council of Great Britain / presents / The Swansea Theatre Company / in / *The Seagull* / Monday August 28 / For Two Weeks'. On crinkled ochre paper and in faded crimson print, the advertisements have a period flavour: high-class fruiterers and florists; general drapery, hosiery and garment repair specialists; electrical accessories and 'Gifts for Every Occasion'; tasty snacks ('Good Service and Civility') at the Cosy Corner Café; 'For Quality and Personal Service try Vernon Toomey & Sons, Nelson Street'. In amongst instructions about the soft drinks 'obtainable in the bar' and the request, 'Ladies are respectfully requested to remove their hats', what gave me pause was that, according to the cast list, Medvedenko, the schoolmaster, was played by Wilfrid Brambell, Old Man Steptoe himself. I'd give a lot to have seen Wilfrid Brambell, Kenneth Williams and Richard Burton sharing the same stage. In the pit, two pianists, Edward Marks and Leonard Dyson, strummed Tchaikovsky.

In this book I try to evoke the age of Sixties excess – the freaks and groupies, the private jets and jewels and the steam yachts sailing in an azure sea; the mess and splendour of material goods; the magnificent bad taste and greed and money smelling like jasmine. 'I have a lust for diamonds,' said Taylor, 'that's almost like a disease.' With multimillion-dollar fees and a percentage of gross receipts, whims could be indulged. ('If I'm pounced on wearing white fur it's because I like white fur. I do what I damned well please.') Taylor would order hamburgers to be specially flown to London or Rome by Pan-Am or TWA from Chasen's in West Hollywood, and from New York, steaks from Gallagher's and cheesecake from Lindy's. When she flew to Leningrad to make *The Blue Bird* in 1975, she took 2,800 lbs of excess luggage. Economising was as abhorrent to these spoilt and beautiful beasts as it would have been to – well – Antony and Cleopatra. 'I thought you ordered Lafitte-Rothschild, Richard. What's this junk? Are you trying to save money again?' barked Taylor, the conspicuous consumer.

When they were at The Dorchester, the Burtons kept a boat anchored on the Thames for their dogs and cats, which couldn't come ashore because of quarantine restrictions. Taylor, as I've mentioned, and will keep mentioning, had every disease known to man – rabies might well have been next on the list, or foot and mouth. She also retained a suite at The Beverly Hills Hotel on a year-round basis, for some of her XXL frocks and stretch-kaftans. Chauffeured limos were kept on a twenty-four-hour call. Publicity photographers were incessant – what the Burtons gained was life-as-spectacle; three bottles of vodka a day made them into bladders of booze ('I go raving mad on gin,' said Burton. 'Uncontrollable. Vodka's the thing. Or whisky. Or tequila when I'm in Mexico'); week-long parties at the Intercontinental Hotel in Budapest; 33.19-carat Krupp diamond rings (a prop for Lucille Ball) ... Yet for all their notorious carousing, there is nevertheless much melancholy in Burton's story. It was as if he was contemptuous of his talent – his acting is suffused with guilt, with a sense of loss, with the water of life flowing by. Why might this be – because I personally think it must have been wonderful to be so irresponsible? The answer is that, though meant to have been a young Welshman, fearing nothing, the ghost of Richard Jenkins, the person he was before, was always there, or often there, his shadow, haunting him.

Yet had Burton stayed in Wales, he'd have wasted away (he sensed this when labouring at the Co-op) – but paradoxically, becoming an international star made him fretful, filling him with inhibitions and uncertainties. Social climbing and mixing with Jackie O and Aristotle Onassis, Wallis and David, and sundry Rothschilds, was both glamorous and a source of dissatisfaction and emptiness – magnificent and ridiculous. Being photographed with Taylor alongside Marshal Tito and his stout First Lady during an official visit to Yugoslavia, during location shooting for *The Battle of Sutjeska*, hardly demonstrated or consolidated what Philip called 'Richard's abiding identification with the working class'. As the unreality of Hollywood only made him aware of his agitation and hollowness, he was drawn back sentimentally to his birthplace, or to the idea of his birthplace, and he drank himself to death when he saw only wasted opportunities: 'I loved my silly image as the besotted Welsh genius, dying in his own vomit in the gutter,' he said unconvincingly.

* * *

What's fascinating about Burton is that we have this self-conscious elaborate cultured Shakespearean Englishness (or Anglo-Welshness), which is accountable for the veneer, the shine, the cold detachment of his performances – he always had clarity and he was intensely theatrical (in the style of Laurence Olivier: 'One day I'll take on Larry!' he told Tynan); and then there's the fact that he found worldwide fame in the movies, a form which ought to require a naturalism, an avoidance, indeed, of the theatrical and the application of a theatrical effect – so in Burton they clash, they collide, the two schools, the two traditions, and he's always brooding or ill at ease, I think, because of this – as if he knew something wasn't right, wasn't harmonious.

Yet out of this did come greatness: *The Spy Who Came in from the Cold, Becket, Look Back in Anger, Equus.* Burton's hedonism coexisted with his puritanism, and his improprieties were also penitential – he was always working through his guilt, taking pleasure in it. Words when he spoke them had a lyric potency and plangency, the sounds coiling and lingering, like a stream among pebbles.

Of Marlowe's *Doctor Faustus*, in which he appeared in 1966 at the Oxford Playhouse, a production later put on film in Rome, with Taylor as Helen of Troy, her face as glossy-white as leprosy, Burton, anguished, unsatisfied, was to say, 'It was the one play I didn't have to do any work on. I *am* Faustus.' Mind you, he also said the same of Winston Churchill, whom he portrayed in *The Gathering Storm*, also known as *Walk with Destiny*, in 1974. 'After weeks of study and research I'm beginning to feel as though I am Churchill.' What Burton actually was, was a disappointed romantic, and as he registered his own downfall, his life became intolerable to him. With Burton, the concept and traps of damnation were alive and well, as was what D.H. Lawrence called 'the art of self-hate and self-murder'. He was therefore in his grave at Céligny, in Switzerland, at the age of fifty-eight. Taylor died in California in 2011, having reached her eightieth year, a Dame of the British Empire, who in spite of her illnesses was always grasping life, an honorary drag queen whose energies were channelled into Aids charities. She was happier, probably, with Rock and Roddy and Monty than with anyone else. She was Maid of Honour when Michael Jackson married his chimp, Bubbles.

Apart from Mike Nichols' *Who's Afraid of Virginia Woolf?*, the films Burton and Taylor made together were critical and commercial disasters, but none of that matters at this distance, for when watching *The V.I.P.s, Doctor Faustus, Under Milk Wood, The Comedians, The Taming of the Shrew*, and so on and so forth, and not forgetting the emblematic *Cleopatra* – which is not about Ancient Rome but Rome in 1962 – I am intent on seeing and discussing how they were when on screen together, how they affected each other, how they transformed each other. What's the true strength of their feelings? That their creative work was misbegotten is why I personally find it deeply appealing, for there is an element of poignancy, too, underneath the luxury and sleaze and rattle of gold. I find it almost unbearable, seeing the England and the Europe on view in the Burtons' location scenes: fewer people on the streets or vehicles on the roads; the architecture (since demolished) and the clothes (back in fashion); and the courtly manners of supporting players (Michael Hordern, Cyril Cusack, Dennis Price) – immaculate, urbane – that are now lost, spirited away. Dinocittà, the De Laurentiis Studios, fifteen miles south of Rome, where many of Burton and Taylor's films were made, which had been built in 1962 at a cost of $30 million, went bust and closed, the site abandoned. (In 2014 it was redeveloped as a 'theme park' with an ice rink, paddling pools, camel rides and a 'zombie walk'.)

Like some of my favourite bedside books – Roland Barthes on Japan or the fashion industry, Stefan Zweig on Mary Queen of Scots or Susan Sontag on photography and illness as metaphor (except *Erotic Vagrancy* has more of an irresistible tidal pull of comedy and satire than they'd manage in a thousand years) – I make no apology for this being a visionary book, a fierce book, a prose version of a portrait in pinks and lilacs and orange and yellow; a book about more than it seems at first to be about, in which the fame of great stars is to be contrasted with our own unimportance and silliness. For the point of great stars and their living fire is that they displace us, make most of us seem like nothing in particular – and with Burton and Taylor, illusion and reality became the same thing. It is an infernal story; an alcoholic story; a Pop Art story; an occult story. Their art, their catalogue of films, is determined by eroticism, or at least by amorous fantasy. Burton and Taylor were Bacchus and Venus, icons of indulgence, animal spirits. They were libertines. Everything had an erotic charge – jewels, limousines, cigarettes, drinks. Everything was an emblem of physical fulfilment. Yet though we may think that here we have the permissiveness of the Sixties and Seventies in action, in fact when we examine the entanglements, the conflicts, the divisions and the scheming (and the legal and financial consequences): sex was not any kind of liberation. The Burtons were under a net, shackled by desire; absorbed by each other, yes, by the fantasy and potency and anticipation of each other – but there was also a social and moral trespass, Holy dread, as Taylor knew well enough, when she wrote in her memoirs, of her initial meeting with Burton, and its aftermath, 'I think it was a little like damnation to everybody.' Hence, the public rebuke in *L'Osservatore della Domenica*, the Vatican newspaper: 'You will finish in an erotic vagrancy, without end or without a safe port.'

PART ONE
WET DREAMS

The principal Elizabeth Taylor section – decay and disaster and death (e.g. the immolation of Mike Todd); her urgent sexual needs and desire (e.g. the marriage to Eddie Fisher). Her hundreds of hospitalisations and the (demonic) mysterious relationship between her physical disorders and her mind, as if she was moving in poisoned air. 'Symptoms of disease are nothing but a disguised manifestation of the power of love; all disease is only love transformed,' says Thomas Mann in The Magic Mountain.

The time, the place: *Ivanhoe* is set in twelfth-century England, in the era of the Crusades; 1194, to be exact. Exciting places like Sheffield, Leicester and York are mentioned. King Richard is held hostage in Austria. Prince John fulminates in Ashby-de-la-Zouch. Sir Walter Scott's novel was published in 1819, the year of Queen Victoria's birth – so what we have is nineteenth-century Medievalism with plenty of fancy dress, costume armour and chivalric romance unfurling against a picturesque backdrop of stained glass and ecclesiastical architecture, with buttresses doing plenty of flying. We are additionally in the summer of 1951 at the MGM-British Studios, Borehamwood, where a tournament scene required twelve trumpeters, thirty Norman and Saxon squires, twenty-five 'special' foresters and a hundred and thirty-five 'ordinary' foresters (i.e. Robin Hood's merry men – one of whom was Frank Williams, in later life the vicar in *Dad's Army*), one hundred and sixty 'rough' Saxons for the crowd, one hundred and twenty Normans for the pavilions, sixty horses and six cows. Mountains of mutton, fish and venison were ordered for the feasts. What I mostly remember from this bustle is Finlay Currie wiping his greasy hands on his dog.

Elizabeth Taylor, who'd left Hollywood for England to make the film (and replace Deborah Kerr) on 15 June, was therefore travelling in hyperreality, a place of fanfares and jousts, chain mail and distressed damsels – and she's not the only one of the latter: Joan Fontaine, in yellow chiffon, is also after the hero and like Taylor's Rebecca is harried by George Sanders, a black knight who goes around saying, in reference to Sir Wilfrid of Ivanhoe, 'I carry his death warrant here against my breast,' which is surely as good a place as any. But I want to begin with this film because Taylor is quite beautiful, slender and drooping, like a snowdrop. She slinks and shimmers into view, glimpsed behind bead curtains, framed in gothic doorways or the tent flap. In pastel colours she poses in a mirror, is seen through glass. Her Rebecca, apparently a sorceress, such are her medical skills ('Swear to me his wound will mend,' Joan's Rowena demands, when Ivanhoe takes a bashing), is allowed little dialogue – but when her movements are accompanied by Miklós Rózsa's viola arpeggios, Taylor reminds me of my belief that she's the last of the great silent movie actresses. She has a mournful complexity here, Rózsa's Central European sounds (Hungary and Vienna were always in his orchestrations) starting up whenever Rebecca appears – emphasising a sadness, which was often Taylor's best quality: the sorrow that underlies joy, which Taylor, her eyes like purple oil, conveyed in everything from the *Lassie* series, when she is separated from her collie, to the eleven films she made with Richard Burton, where their shared ecstasy is in danger of tipping over into dissipation, to her duplication in the smudges and smears of Andy Warhol's screen-printed portraits. After all her fairy tales and adventure stories, Taylor's final dispersal was to be as a perfume. Parenthetically, let's all pause for a moment and think about

Jeanne Moreau's summary exposition: 'Love is like a fragrance. It doesn't last.'

By hyperreality, Umberto Eco, who coined the word – as *iperrealismo* – meant 'an artificial environment that seems actual'; it's a terrain where 'the boundaries between game and illusion are blurred', where we'd find (or place) holograms, automata, wax statues, moon rock, freak shows, wildlife parks, 'Sensurround' in cinemas, and 'collections of inconsequential wonders', like garish posters or period movie magazines – Taylor appeared on the cover of *Life* fourteen times by the way. Biography, in my understanding of the genre – or my deconstruction of it – involves a similar fossicking. As with *Ivanhoe*, with its overlapping of the Middle Ages, Victoriana and the Fifties, the centuries or decades merge or collapse. We assume we know the emotions of the past (though *which* or *whose* past?), are able to discriminate amongst the references and influences – except of course we can't. What we are looking at is a Technicolor garden, a newly constructed cardboard castle with moonlight flooding through the backlot casements. As Eco said, disapprovingly, when he visited Hearst's San Simeon, with its plundered antiques, its mad jungle of building styles, the net result can be 'psychedelic', having a 'barbarian grandeur' and a 'sensual perversity', which is thoroughly fake, like the chapels and groves of Forest Lawn, which though a cemetery avoids all mention of death and loss, insisting instead, said Eco, on fantasies of immortality and preservation and serenity. Personally, I relish the contradictions, salute the bad taste, especially as Taylor's remains were placed in the Great Mausoleum, next to the Last Supper diorama, in Forest Lawn Memorial Park, Glendale, on 24 March 2011.

Give me anachronisms, mixed-up appearances, collisions of popular culture and high art. That Taylor first saw *The Wizard of Oz* in a screening-room at San Simeon, for example, is a fact containing numberless ramifications. (Richard Thorpe, the director of *Ivanhoe*, was one of the many directors associated with the Judy Garland

classic) – the nine-year-old child actress, already busily auditioning
for Universal and MGM, a guest at Kane's Xanadu; her contentment
with the towering artifice, the mad majesty: Taylor was at home with
the place, could easily measure up to it. Taylor, moreover, was insistent she'd never be crushed by the moguls, as Judy Garland was – Judy
who, said Taylor, 'never talked back. She followed the studio's orders.
They pumped pills into that poor girl to keep her awake, to put her to
sleep, and to keep her slim.' Judy felt herself watched, organised, got
at, shut in. Taylor was not to be controlled, but she did have, I think,
a sense of continuous panic – particularly as, all her life, she was
looking (as Judy was) for love, which is to say, for her idealised version of love, which perhaps she never distinguished from romance,
and was as full of fancifulness as *The Blue Bird*. She gave herself over
to it a million times – Nicky Hilton, Michael Wilding, Mike Todd,
Eddie Fisher, Burton, John Warner, Larry Fortensky – but she gave
herself as an actress gives of herself, with a paradoxical combination
of self-delusion and scrupulous detachment, as if somehow it's happening to someone else, perhaps an identical twin. Her description,
in 1965, of watching Burton coming towards her, and the thrill going
through her body, is telling: 'I sort of detached myself, as though I
were floating upward and looking down with great clarity on the two
of us, like in a Chagall painting.' It is distance, intangibility, which is
depicted or described here: the unbearable lightness of being. It is
Chagall who created the frescoes on the ceiling of the Paris Opera
House, or Palais Garnier, winged creatures holding bouquets and
playing flutes, horses, cockerels, baskets of fruit – mighty swirls of
blues and greens, vaguely modernistic in the opulent neo-classical
theatre's acres of red plush and gold leaf. The work was unveiled on 23
September 1964 – was Taylor aware of this? *The Taming of the Shrew*,
as *La Mégère Apprivoisée*, the Zeffirelli romp, received a gala premiere
at the Palais Garnier on 28 September 1967. On her head Taylor wore
a two-inch-high jewelled rose, the petals fashioned from nine-carat
diamonds by Van Cleef and Arpels. The entire confection, designed

by Alexandre de Paris, the hair stylist, was valued at $1,200,000. It was Taylor, on this occasion, who looked like she'd fallen from Chagall's canvasses – Burton, in the Pathé newsreels, is bloated and perspiring, his eyes unfocussed. Pissed, no doubt.

* * *

Biography is bricolage, as is *Ivanhoe*, which anticipates *Cleopatra* and Fox's Rome and Egypt, a decade hence. Eddie Fisher, hardly a friendly witness, was not wrong to say of his (then) wife and Burton, who would turn into Antony and Cleopatra for real, or hyperreal, 'they were two powerful forces crazed by passion, fuelled by alcohol, fighting the world. Who could resist that?' None did. What I like about Taylor's Rebecca, therefore, is the demureness, the solemnity. Everything is being banked up, awaiting future use. She has to spend a lot of the film looking after Felix Aylmer – *Ivanhoe* contains Felix Aylmer *and* Finlay Currie – who is as doddering as ever and whitters away about how, 'My heart broke long ago, but it serves me still,' surely a cardiological miracle. He's Isaac of York, a Jew who pledges money for King Richard's ransom. Everyone seems very against this scheme, especially Prince John and his henchman, De Bois Guilbert – George Sanders, who struts about in a suit of chain mail. Guilbert's political machinations, however, never overcome his amorous machinations, and he is after the womenfolk every chance he gets. Joan Fontaine is locked in a turret, as is Taylor. 'I shall possess you, Rebecca, if I die for it,' he tells her, though what good would that do him? Not one to give up, he comes to her room, or turret, to rub in his intentions: 'Rebecca, you mistake the nature of our bargain. I want you alive, not dead' – Taylor had started to heave herself over the parapet. 'When next I come to you, meet me with desire on your lips and fire in your breast, or no man's life is saved this day!' Is that how Sanders spoke to Zsa Zsa Gabor and Benita Hume, to name two of his wives? A demand for desire on their lips and fire in their breast? Any male person in his

59

prime might make the same request, but Guilbert, though evidently a blackguard, in Sanders' hands acquires a surprising conscience. Seemingly a rapist and a pillager, with Sanders playing him, his love for Rebecca is real – and Ivanhoe's, in Robert Taylor's incarnation, is non-existent. Sanders wants to be able to save Taylor's character from torture and death, to find a way to be merciful. And I do savour Sanders' world-weariness, his doom-laden voice. Whether in Hitchcock's *Rebecca* – and when he speaks to Rebecca here, his enunciation of her name is identical – or (my favourite) *Journey to Italy*, it's always like he'd wandered back from the dead. It was no surprise when, in 1972, he committed suicide, at a hotel ten miles south of Barcelona, the Rey Don Jaime, in Castelldefels. ('Dear World, I am leaving you because I am bored. I feel I have lived long enough. I am leaving you with your worries in this sweet cesspool. Good luck.') In his scenes with Taylor, it's as if he knows her tantalising beauty is something he'll never possess, so he channels self-hatred into the film's many scenes of armed combat – broad swords, maces, lances. A fan of the film, incidentally, was Picasso, who made a linocut, 'The Knight and the Page', where a horse, an engine of war, is covered with armoured plates, flags, pennants and spikes, as if off to a bullfight. Is that Taylor looking on, the damsel in the watchtower? Pageantry predominates. Taylor's staunch curves will have appealed to the old Spaniard. *Ivanhoe* also appealed to Bob Dylan, the old songster. He once told Taylor he'd been watching it on the telly: 'In every movie you're a queen. In real life too.'

It's interesting to jump ahead to 1962, and compare Taylor and Sanders with Taylor and Rex Harrison, another quick-tempered and selfish man, but one who didn't have Sanders' dry cynicism, which was thoroughly metaphysical, belonging with cemetery railings and tombs. Harrison's moods, by contrast, were caused by nothing more significant than the chauffeur being late with the car or a producer omitting to organise his dry-cleaning. Harrison was mercurial; Sanders' stale and acrid manner suggested actual pain and desolation – and

I'd like to have seen Sanders as Caesar. Though filled utterly with pessimism, he had a sense of the absurd, which militated against any meanness, any twistedness. Taylor, though of course there's no telling what the ensuing ten or twelve years would do to her, is sucked up by Sanders, here in *Ivanhoe*, as if she's nectar – she's not belittled or quelled; and she becomes part, somehow, of his melancholia; of his idea that life is a condemned playground. With Harrison, Taylor bickers, she answers back – they could be Lucy and Desi.

Apart from Joan Fontaine and Taylor, who are anyway there solely for the men to abuse, *Ivanhoe* is a masculine film – personnel with beards from Olivier's Shakespeare pictures sternly issue edicts and crouch at incredibly solid-looking wooden trestles – Basil Sydney, Olivier's Claudius, Norman Wooland, Olivier's Horatio; the production designer is Roger Furse, who'd made the scenery for *Henry V*, *Hamlet* and *Richard III*. They sit down and stand up in alarm, shaking fists. Taylor was correct in her memoirs, *Elizabeth Taylor* by Elizabeth Taylor, to call *Ivanhoe* 'a big medieval western', for so it is – rowdy bands having a go at each other, lots of horses, outlaws, in-laws, sheriffs, taverns, warring tribes. It is a story about challenges – literally, gauntlets are flung down. There are lots of battles, with arrows pinging off stone walls. Emlyn Williams is the oddly named Wamba, a cackling jester, who dies with a grisly scream in the castle fire – he also dies with a grisly scream in *The Last Days of Dolwyn*, Burton's first film. 'I'll squash you like a plum,' says the exasperated Finlay Currie, and I'm with Finlay. The interesting point here is Williams therefore worked with Taylor long before Burton did – knew her, had doings with her – which gives additional animus to the fact, when Burton abandoned Sybil for Taylor, he, Williams, flew to Rome to issue a personal reprimand. That other fusspot, Philip Burton, was keeping watch: 'Emlyn Williams ... had gone to Rome to make a direct appeal to Richard on behalf of Sybil and the children ... I myself admired Emlyn for his initiative, and was very grateful to him for his concern.' A little later: 'Emlyn Williams came to New York in

July [1962] – he had to replace Paul Scofield in *A Man for All Seasons* – and I had some good and reassuring meetings with him. He hadn't given up hope of a reconciliation between Richard and Sybil.' But come the following month, 'Emlyn Williams advised me not to be too optimistic; he did not think Elizabeth Taylor was out of the picture.' Nor was she – nor was she ever to be. The impression given is Williams and Philip thought her a witch, who cast an evil spell upon their protégé – and in fairness that is how Burton often saw things, though more delightedly: 'Bewitched. Bewitched by her cunt and her cunning,' he memorably jotted in his diary, a quotation recurring more times than I can count. Though not the language of Sir Walter Scott, it's a sentiment crossing the face of De Bois Guilbert as Sanders plays him, when Taylor's Rebecca is in the vicinity.

The centrepiece of *Ivanhoe*, for me, isn't the tournament, or anything to do with the Crusades, dungeons, towers or moats, it's the trial scene, where Taylor stands accused of witchcraft, the menfolk, Sanders to the fore (though his feelings are mixed) wanting to drag her to the stake. Rebecca, says Megs Jenkins, an unreliable witness, is capable of turning into a black swan. She's the sort of person who knows about poisonous flowers, toads, vials and jars of bubbling juices and smoky liquids – and I suspect Taylor did also. Look how many witches she did in fact play – Susanna Drake, in *Raintree County*, Maggie the Cat, Catherine Holly, in *Suddenly, Last Summer*, Gloria Wandrous, in *BUtterfield 8*, Cleopatra, Albee's Martha, a midnight hag, dozens more: Taylor had the power to turn the milk, foul the sugar, raise storms, spoil crops, dance with the devil and send furniture splitting and flying about a room. She rode horses bareback by night (*National Velvet*, *Reflections in a Golden Eye*). She talks with animals and birds (*Lassie*, *The Sandpiper*). She is imbued with mysticism, or magic realism. She is capable of setting loose demons from a boiling sea (Coward's Witch of Capri and Burton's angel of death, in *Boom!*). In *X, Y & Zee* there's a half-joking reference to her broomstick. In *The Blue Bird*, Taylor is an actual witch, with hooked nose, claws, the works.

What I'm actually saying, by cataloguing the psychomancy, is Taylor had unique intensity, its sources other-worldly. She was thoroughly intuitive, having little need to rehearse or mug up – what she did came unaffectedly. That her healing arts (or science) cured Ivanhoe is the prosecution's apogee – a misogynistic one, too. Taylor's Rebecca has interfered with nature. Throughout it all, Taylor simply halts there, in the dock, in a dress of white silk with small gold stars. She has a faint yellowish glow, isn't required to say very much – she poses, and her beauty dominates the scene. Taylor exists to be gazed upon, standing alone in the well of the court. She was nineteen here, and had already been married twice.

* * *

If I belabour discussion of *Ivanhoe* – I suppose I could equally well have chosen another costume piece, *Beau Brummell* (released on 6 October 1954), after the making of which Taylor's co-star Stewart Granger said, and it surely takes one to know one, 'She knew that I knew that she was a cunt' – it is because I'm interested in how everything was filtering into it, how everyone who came into the studio (and who went to the cinema) was surrounded on all sides by the post-war customs and conventions, which is why in the Fifties there were these entertainments about chivalry, domestic decorum, behaving properly; the themes explored are suitability, respectability. So, too, Burton on Broadway, in 1960, in *Camelot*: more pseudo-medievalism, Celtic sagas, accusations of witchcraft (this time Guinevere is sentenced to death by fire), Round Tables, Grail quests and swords in stones – paraphernalia representing Eisenhower's America and the search for peace and good order, the Fifties utopia, with villains routed, and everyone in full acceptance of their moral, civic, cultural duty. And this was the ideology Taylor and Burton, on the set of *Cleopatra*, were breaking down, when they were branded as decadent and diabolical – though what they chiefly revealed, when masks of virtue were removed, was love as something that brings unhappiness. The other aspect of *Ivanhoe* to be mentioned here is that, regarding Taylor, we can see what the world is going to do to her. When people later on mocked the actress for her obesity, it's because they remembered her earlier perfection: 'Elizabeth Taylor used to be the one woman in America every other woman wanted to look like,' joked Joan Rivers, 'and now we all do.' Permit me, therefore, to contrast everything I've been describing thus far by looking at *X, Y & Zee*, sometimes called *Zee and Co*, released on 24 February 1972. Here Taylor is loud and kitsch and aggressive – and gives merit and authority to these usually pejorative connotations. As Iris Murdoch observed in *The Bell*, and I agree, 'When something's fantastic enough and marvellous enough, it can't be in bad taste.'

The time, the place: London in September 1970 (the date on Edna O'Brien's screenplay) – which from my twenty-first-century perspective is already as historical an epoch, as fantasticated, as Walter Scott's Waverley. We are also, I surmise, as far as O'Brien's inspiration went, in Rome several crucial years earlier, for *X, Y & Zee* is an examination of Burton and Taylor's marital and courtship shenanigans, as amply covered in the press at the time, even if we don't have Burton but Michael Caine in his Harry Palmer spectacles. Perhaps Burton felt he'd traversed this territory sufficiently in *Who's Afraid of Virginia Woolf?* and *The Taming of the Shrew*, and in place of his Lear-like rages and Welsh sonic boom, Caine, with sticky hair and a furtive, startled expression on his face, does seem, well, more ordinary. He shouts and rants (as Taylor does), but the result is peevish ('Get out of here, you slut!'). He sulks and walks out of a restaurant. He walks with lots of little short steps – where what Burton did was swagger. 'They all rely on you, the female sex,' O'Brien's script calls upon Caine to say, and though I'd believe this of Burton, I can't of Caine, who is the chipper Alfie, unreliability his watchword, with numerous dolly birds on the go – his character, Robert Blakeley, visits his tearful secretary in her seedy flat. Burton is or was too lordly for all of that; he's always Bluebeard, courteous towards the wenches in his castle. Caine is more Elephant and Castle than castle, more Old Kent Road than Lear's vassal, Kent. No disrespect is meant here – for Caine has reality, modernity. He's good at showing the aggravations of a man aware he's running out of steam, no longer youthful, his jawline losing definition – a man starting to become stale. Nevertheless, when Taylor's Zee Blakeley says of Caine's character, hurling a home truth, 'Men from poor backgrounds never get over it, do they?' it is a remark directly applicable to Burton. Robert is 'conditioned to constant battling,' as Burton grew to be. 'You like the tussle. You like the uncertainty,' Zee tells him. The blonde calm of Stella, played by Susannah York, seems like a welcome relief – but Zee is quick to point out how Robert will miss her own spirit and gumption. 'I'll fight her a duel any day, and win,' Zee says – and how like Sybil, Burton's wife, Stella sounds, especially when she acknowledges she's not 'a bitch the way some women are'. Zee is thoroughly Taylor – the Taylor whom Taylor had become: her seeming conviviality, her appetite (there are many scenes at table, lots of talk about food – Zee grabs snacks from the fridge, follows recipes from the colour supplements), and her conviction, 'real men don't like skinny women'. Initially she thinks Susannah York is no threat because she's 'a bag of bones'. As during the famous off-screen dramas when making *Cleopatra*, there are suicide attempts: Zee, like Taylor, when bandaged and in hospital, is enacting another ploy to get her way. She eggs Robert on to drive dangerously, too, as Taylor did Burton in Italy: 'That's right, kill us. Let's die together as all true lovers do . . . Let's die together.'

The title is a clue – O'Brien wanting to assign algebraic configurations to people swept up by emotion and gonads, as if by strong chemicals. This person, X, breaking away from that person, Y, binding with another person, Z: allegiance, alliance, new compounds formed – as if the narrative feelings of adult life can be expressed as formulae in chalk on a blackboard. 'Have you ever thought,' Taylor's character says, 'that you get your happiness at the expense of someone else, me of you, you of me, and so on and so forth.' We proceed less by addition and multiplication than by division, subtraction – all this predictable loss, mess, confusion: 'all this wrangling, all this hell.' *X, Y & Zee* begins with a ping-pong match, and everything else is a sexual game, including bondage, lesbianism and role play. There's a lot of dressing up. 'I love you in bright colours,' are Zee's first words to Robert, when the couple is getting ready for Gladys' party. Gladys, ghoulish and gurgling in a fright wig, and as over-the-top as Mrs Slocombe from Grace Brothers, is Margaret Leighton, by now married to Michael Wilding – another ramification. 'They're all darling people,' she says of her guests, but they are not. The group scenes are a jungle, lots of jostling and wariness, though I like the appurtenances, as fixed in their period as items displayed by the National Trust: brown and orange retro crockery, revolving Long Playing vinyl records taken gingerly from their sleeve, dark glasses with chrome-effect frames, hotel foyers of brass and gold, wind chimes. Taylor is always looking through her vast wardrobe, is often changing her outfits, clobber as it's begging to be called, and gazes in a mirror. Stella runs a boutique, where Zee makes a sudden appearance in a purple witch's cloak. She tries on lots of brightly-coloured frocks, ponchos, hot-pants (*X, Y & Zee* is as pink and orange as *Who's Afraid of Virginia Woolf?* is black and white) – the shop is a riot of shawls, masks, hats, beads, curiosities, boas. Pretty Gavin with his bolts of violet cloth is the future Right Honourable Baron Cashman of Limehouse in the London Borough of Tower Hamlets CBE. The decor, however, can't distract from the fact a duel has indeed begun – Zee has come to see her rival, who is cool, doesn't rise to the challenges. When Stella says that a red hat Zee wants is not for sale, and Zee replies, 'Mustn't take what isn't ours, must we,' Taylor may indeed be thoroughly Taylor, but she's also like dragon queens Bette Davis or Joan Crawford, more or less emitting puffs of furious green smoke. At one point, when thwarted, she rampages up and down the street.

As it concerns a man and two women, *X, Y & Zee* is about Taylor and Burton and the melodramas behind *Cleopatra* in reverse, with Taylor in the Sybil part, the wife who is to be strung along and dumped – except Taylor is not somebody who can be left. She can't be ditched. 'I'll always be your baby,' she says to Caine's Robert, 'no matter whose lover you are or whose husband.' When Zee yells '*Robert!*' it is like Taylor screeching '*Richard!*' Burton's dilemmas, too, are here, when, in 1962, he couldn't keep things trivial and was torn by guilt – will he go off with his new mistress or stay with his wife? 'The more he wants to get out, the more he has to protest to you that he wants to get in. It's always like that with a cunt.' I quote from the screenplay. In the finished film that last sentence is deleted. 'I've made up my mind,' says Robert. 'I'm going to leave her,' yet he cannot and spends the entirety of the film going back and forth between the women's houses, exactly as Burton did, when he was prowling around Rome, driving around Italy, flying to Paris and London. Zee is convinced Robert will never leave her, that the novelty of Stella will wear off ('Everyone's a good listener at first') – and had Sybil been in Stella's position, these are exactly the things Sybil would say: 'You're [i.e. Robert is] everything I ever despised and I'm everything I vowed not to be. That's where our love has got us to.' Her remarks to Robert about Zee would exactly sum up Sybil's for Taylor: 'I do love your company and all that, but I didn't reckon for her and she's too much, she's everywhere.' Similarly, Zee's remarks to her husband about Stella are Taylor's sneering sentiments about Sybil, who was tranquillising and soulful, and 'sees beauty in everything, especially in shit'.

Taylor was too much. Taylor was everywhere. Her raucous laughter (which is not joyous) fills the soundtrack, along with plinky-plonky music. Her face when she succeeds in riling Caine's Robert is an expression of victory. Were we in *Ivanhoe* still, Taylor would now be

George Sanders. Susannah York is Rebecca or Joan Fontaine's Rowena, mouthing platitudes: 'Somehow I don't ever see us as perfectly happy'; 'People never want to admit they were in love once it's over.' Taylor's Zee is good at strategy and intrigue. She's rampageous, can never be shaken off. At one level, *X, Y & Zee* is an erotic frolic. Edna O'Brien was annoyed the producers didn't have the courage to include her climax: 'The last we see are their three bodies – arms, heads, torso, all meeting for a consummation,' is what she writes in the script published by Weidenfeld in 1971. Instead, on screen, Susannah York is crying in bed, Taylor stares meaningfully (or meaninglessly) from the doorway, and Caine is at a complete loss. There are then, as the credits roll, freeze-frame close-ups of everybody's eyes, which is simply confusing. The last thing that seems likely is an orgy. But there has been enough secrecy and deception, lies and cover-ups, to show how the games (as in *Sleuth*, where Caine duels with Laurence Olivier, under the direction of *Cleopatra*'s Joseph Mankiewicz) are about power. Zee is spiteful, tormenting, but also terrified by the threat of rejection, the prospect of loneliness – of being a woman abandoned: she cannot yield to that. Burton in his diaries several times expressed his admiration for *X, Y & Zee*, with its theme of a woman clinging on to her man. Perhaps, as Zee flings Robert's luggage out of a window, he recognised the truth in her comment, 'He likes women to be a mess. That's why he's still with me.'

* * *

When was Taylor at her absolute loveliest? For me her glamour is truly apparent in *A Place in the Sun* (1951), when she makes an entrance, as Angela Vickers, 'a rich girl with nothing to do', down a long polished hallway, and she's covered in white fur. The film is noticeable for the blackness of the black, the whiteness of the white – Taylor's costumes, her motor car, the harsh neon of the city scenes, are like ink and milk. The contrast is decisive and ravishing, like

Othello and Desdemona. Despite the title, the sun is in eclipse, reaching the earth only in small flecks – the atmosphere is of cold shadows, a night garden, a lake at evening, a hushed late afternoon, with the forest floor covered in dusty pine cones. You know at once that the prolonged and hungry kiss between Taylor and Montgomery Clift's George Eastman ('Tell mama, tell mama all') sets the seal on a love that is fatal, doomed. Nothing good will come of it – and out of the night come talons, beating wings, in the character and shape of Shelley Winters' Alice Tripp ('I'm in trouble, real trouble'), the factory girl whom George has impregnated.

Having encountered Angela, 'a pretty girl you read about in the papers', George now feels only a clammy hatred and resentment – and fear – when faced with Alice, who threatens to pull him back into poverty and an existence of dull duty. Clift is so appealing and earnest as the striving young man, who 'wants to work and get ahead, that's all', as he says at his job interview; he is so nervous, flighty and friendless – when I watch the film I quite side with him and identify with him. Who'd not behave as he does, given the circumstances? Of course Shelley Winters has to be murdered ('Are you crazy, coming up here?' he says to her). Clift's character has been trapped – trapped into having to become a killer. He was, in any event, Clift, a furtive actor – or am I letting his lupine looks sway me? I think of Clift as slinking away into the birch trees, his quarry in his jaws. He was frequently sideways-looking, with a glistening grin, which never quite turned into a confident or easy smile. I'm not sure he managed to be handsome, either. He burns without heat. A cloud was always crossing his sun. There is a sombreness, an awkwardness. He was anxious and stammering – in *A Place in the Sun*, as in *The Heiress*, made a year previously, he covets a life he can't legitimately possess. He has to kill Shelley Winters – she is in the way – and we feel the pressures on him of this whining scold. He's the one, also, as Morris Townsend, who'd seduced Olivia de Havilland's Catherine Sloper, solely to get at her money – and who abandons her at midnight when it looks like she'll not turn out to be as substantial an heiress as had been forecast. (Taylor accompanied Clift to the premiere of *The Heiress*, though whether this was the New York one, on 6 October 1949, or the Los Angeles one, on 20 October 1949, or the London one, a year later, I have not ascertained.)

Clift was good at portraying shabby self-interest – he's always risking exposure and humiliation, putting himself in positions where his different background and origins only emphasise his unsuitability. Does it help (or hinder) that we can't but be aware of his guilty homosexuality and drug abuse? Truman Capote had a story of a deranged Clift taking cashmere sweaters from a shop and kicking them along the pavement, putting a lot of effort into soiling them. 'He can't go on like that,' said Taylor, when she heard, 'it will kill him,' which it duly did, in 1966, when Clift was forty-six. He was himself the sort of soiled American male Arthur Miller wrote about, who gradually realises nothing is happening as it ought. It's interesting that John Huston cast Clift as the Viennese wizard in *Freud*, and in *Suddenly, Last Summer*, he's a psychiatrist: a student of the murky mind. It's a realm the actor seldom strayed far from – for as he once said, 'When you throw yourself into an emotional scene, your body doesn't know you're kidding, when you become angry, tearful or violent for a part.' It's all, as it were, true.

A Place in the Sun is a film about desperation, and aspiration. George toils at the textile factory, folding and boxing up blouses on the production line; and his loneliness coincides with Alice's – she's dowdy, careworn – and they hold hands. The fundamentals of sexual need and sad solitude are very unromantic. Their scenes are filled with rain, which drips on parked cars. The boarding-house rooms are dismal, though the set decorators placed a clue on the wall – a print of Millais' drowning Ophelia. Indeed, the film is full of premonitions – owls screeching, dogs snarling and barking, electric bells, sirens, clocks chiming, and mockingly jolly Hawaiian holiday music on the radio. The omnipresent radios also broadcast news bulletins and weather reports, predicting high temperatures.

Winters was always good at being oppressive, either by chirping, chuckling, warbling or else howling in pain and wretchedness – Charlotte Haze in *Lolita* (where she is run over – and how perfect that the future mother of Dolores Haze should be Taylor's mirror opposite in *A Place in the Sun*); the mother whose throat is slit by Robert Mitchum in *Night of the Hunter* (we see her corpse sitting up in a submerged car, her hair streaming like weed, her mouth set for ever in a sullen pout); and in *The Poseidon Adventure*, she expires after a heroic underwater swim. Here, washed out and abandoned by George, she gets to be increasingly mean and demanding. She threatens to phone the newspapers, to turn up and embarrass George in front of his new friends – because by this time he has discovered Elizabeth Taylor, the boss' daughter, 'popular leader of society's younger set', having been invited by the boss to drop in on him at home, a home that is a palace of chandeliers and white plaster pillars. When Angela appears, in an evening gown designed by Edith Head, which is embroidered with thousands of tiny glass flowers and stars, it's as if George has been wafted to another world – one in which he'll only ever fit in fitfully ('What are we going to do about him socially?' asks Angela's mother prudently, if snobbishly.)

Anne Revere, as Clift's gloomy mother, who runs a religious mission, makes off-screen telephone calls, heavy with dramatic irony: 'Promise to be a good boy, not to waste your time on girls.' But the warning comes too late. The dour girlfriend is pregnant, wants an abortion, but the doctor won't help; the beautiful girlfriend is a vision of Venus, water-skiing and splashing about in the big pond by the vacation cabin – a pond Clift shortly takes Winters out to explore in a rowing boat, as darkness is fast falling. (As the director, George Stevens, said of his extensive hunt for the location – Cascade Lake, Idaho, Lake Tahoe and Echo Lake, in Sierra Nevada – 'I was trying to find a good lake to drown a pregnant girl in.') Alice tipped into the drink, the remainder of the film is about pursuit. Screaming sirens close in, the orchestral strings reach a discordant climax, and when Taylor's character hears what has happened, she collapses dramatically, sinking in an overhead shot on a circular rug.

A Place in the Sun concludes with Clift's character going to the electric chair. Taylor's Angela is seen back at school, with a school choir warbling on the soundtrack, as the teacher drones on – a scene to show how young she is, how she's not an adult. But the question remains, what would you have done? Obligingly marry Winters' Alice, with her nagging and whining, or try and keep the dream alive with Elizabeth Taylor, and remain for as long as possible in her world – a world you didn't expect to penetrate, which in any event is going to be lost to you, as how can anything like that conceivably last?

There's a montage sequence capturing the themes and dilemmas: as Clift dances with Taylor, and moves towards a midnight terrace with tropical foliage, slow lap dissolves disclose both Anne Revere, gazing imploringly at her unringing telephone, and Shelley Winters, waiting and being stood-up. Even before he is pursued by the law, George Eastman is pursued (and trapped – hemmed in) by responsibilities. Taylor, slender and immaculate, represents a test of independence, a challenge. She is a sorceress, with a sensuous immediacy, who'll make men lurch, and fall, beyond rectitude. Stevens cast her because 'there's been a smouldering spirit of revolt in Elizabeth for a long time', and, murder aside, her effect on Clift's character, her sexual allure and power, was exactly the same as her effect on men generally – not excluding Richard Burton, who was bedevilled by her instantaneous affections.

Like George Eastman, Burton was the working-class person tempted by one touch of Venus, and who inhabited two worlds, South Wales, with its dark river water, and Hollywood; and who suffered moods, said Taylor, 'like a whirlpool of black molasses, carrying him down, down, down.' Yet Taylor never minded his agony. It added to the ecstasy. When I look at her films, and Burton's films, and the films the pair of them made together, what I notice is the intensity and force, excitement and fervour. Their art was determined by eroticism, by their fantasy and anticipation of each other. And this is the additional, or incidental, importance of *A Place in the Sun*, as far as I am concerned – it is like a prophecy, an illumination. Burton, when he met Taylor, like the Clift character when he meets Taylor, suddenly found himself beyond limitation. All was permitted, and he felt elation. In magazine photographs, posters and advertisements, there they are, emblems of comfort and success, emblems of physical fulfilment, oblivious of everyone but themselves. Everything had an erotic charge – minks, limousines, cigarettes, drinks and cologne. On the grain or silver chips of the celluloid we have their sunburnt skin, a Mediterranean glow. On recordings, there's Burton's voice, like seawater washing over a scallop shell. His spoken words always had a lyrical potency ('You couldn't converse with him. You could only listen,' said a witness), and as he made language coil and spurt, it was an acoustic version of Taylor's wearing a Burmese ruby necklace, bracelet and drop earrings in a swimming pool at Cap Ferrat: 'Since there was no mirror,' she remembered, 'I had to look into the water. The jewellery was so glorious, rippling red and blue.'

Flash objects associated with the Burtons, the saloon of the steam yachts decorated with Impressionists, the Vuitton luggage, the Cartier baubles and the snowbound villas and grand hotels, imply sensuality (or greed) – thirsting, melting, hungering, swallowing. As Taylor's Cleopatra says to Burton's Antony, in dialogue that turned Shakespeare into a novelette, 'To have waited so long, to know so suddenly. Without you, this is not a world I want to live in' – and Antony replies, 'Everything that I want to hold or love or have or be is here with me now.' They lived in fairyland, or a pantomime transformation scene, where white mice are ponies and the pumpkin becomes a coach – in they'd get and drive away to their high fortune.

* * *

Taylor was a filthy beast, nevertheless. A slattern. Until she became a patient at the Betty Ford Center for drug and alcohol rehabilitation, in December 1983, Taylor had never coped without servants – her housemaids, daily women, gardeners, gardeners' boys and milkmen; she had never cooked or cleaned, done the laundry, or gone shopping for groceries. She knew nothing of ordinary life ('I can't remember a day when I wasn't famous'), and if her pets fouled the carpets, well, somebody else would deal with the messes. Indeed, she was a nightmare guest or visitor. When she came out of a bathroom, it was 'as if a cyclone had hit a Bloomingdale's cosmetics counter,' said a clerk at the Beverly Hills Hotel. When she borrowed Calvin Klein's house on Fire Island, 'he was horrified, as were the maids'. Mattresses and rugs were always having to be replaced at The Dorchester. After she'd rented a property in Natchez, Mississippi, during the making of *Raintree County*, a writ was issued by the owner, who'd returned to find 'liquor spills all over the house. The walls were full of grease. Her make-up covers the bedspreads; imprints of her hands appear on shower curtains; ditto on window sills.' Taylor grudgingly paid $400 in compensation.

Michael Wilding found that his marriage to Taylor was in immediate trouble when, the newly-weds having taken up residence in 1375 Beverly Estate Drive, he was relegated to a position slightly below that of the animals. His wife, he complained, spent 'as much time with the dogs and cats as she does with me. One of our Siamese cats even spends nights in our bed.' The dogs, cats and ducks roamed freely, crapping at will. When, after staying at the Plaza, in New York, Taylor was presented with a $2,500 surcharge, she summoned Roddy McDowall and Montgomery Clift and the three of them ransacked – or re-ransacked – the suite, chopping up the curtains and bedsheets and shoving pillows in the lavatory. Her treatment of the Park Lane Hotel, also in New York, was worse, because in addition to addle-pated Eddie Fisher, Taylor's room contained Matilda, a monkey which chewed the furniture. (Matilda was left with Roddy McDowall at Central Park West – and never retrieved.) Sandra Lee Stuart, in her history of the Beverly Hills Hotel, says Taylor managed to deposit lipstick smears on the ceilings, which baffled science as the actress, even in high heels, was never taller than five-foot-three. Dominick Dunne, bidden to the Grand Hotel in Rome, in 1973, for champagne and caviar, entered to find Burton 'on the floor in a green velvet dinner jacket picking up with a Kleenex dog shit left by their unhousebroken Shih Tzu, on which Elizabeth doted. Her dogs were never house-trained.'

Couple this habitual slovenliness with her eating habits – Taylor went in for ketchup and mashed spuds with gravy; spinach with ice cream ('Aren't you fat enough already?' Burton used to ask incredulously) – and it is fair to say, despite her poise on screen (Cleopatra in golden robes; Frances Andros in *The V.I.P.s* in fur muffs; Sissy Goforth in *Boom!* on a crystal throne), the actress did not suggest purity and refinement – only voluptuousness. This was apparent from the beginning. Orson Welles, Rochester in *Jane Eyre*, in 1943, said he understood the impetus of *Lolita* 'because of my contact with Elizabeth Taylor as a child. I have never encountered anyone like her.' Fred Zinnemann, who directed her screen-test for *National Velvet*, in 1944, glanced at the burgeoning bust under the white blouse and commented, 'The camera loved Elizabeth Taylor.' James Agee, who in his script for Laughton's *Night of the Hunter* showed an eerie interest in the massacre of innocents, in the December of 1944 watched the completed *National Velvet*, and those budding breasts rendered him insensible: 'I have been choked with the peculiar sort of adoration I might have felt if we were both in primary school,' he said, as if confiding his crush to the actress personally. Agee further remarked on Taylor's 'natural grace' and 'natural-born female's sleep-walking sort of guile'. He appreciated her 'semi-hysterical emotion', her 'frightened nobility', her 'odd sort of pre-specific erotic sentience'.

We get the picture. Taylor's sexuality – her appetites – is (are) what we see and share, after a fashion, in all her performances, from the

days of the child star right up to, say, *Secret Ceremony* or *X, Y & Zee.*
She was always emotionally charged, fondling and savouring, and in
National Velvet the object of the nymphet's affections, of course, is a
horse. And I use the word nymphet advisedly – in the Nabokov sense.
Nymphet has implications not expressed by child; there is a sort of
knowingness, a self-conscious indulgence of a trope, when it comes to
the character of Dolores Haze, heroine of *Lolita*: 'Light of my life, fire
of my loins. My sin, my soul. Lo-lee-ta,' says Humbert Humbert,
James Mason in the Kubrick film. There is what my friend Steve Jacobi
calls a 'kind of blushing irony' built into the idea of the nymphet,
which is Nabokov's point. Thus, in *National Velvet*, and in *Life with
Father* and *Little Women* particularly, Taylor, beribboned, gives performances which are full of gestures that are too old for her – there's
an unwelcome, abundant sexuality, an animality. It's as if she knew
instinctively – or did her mother urge this, train her for this? – that
when it came to men she had a duty to flirt, connive, be imperious and
arbitrary; to engage in what Anita Brookner, in one of her novels,
called 'heartless and pointless stratagems, to laugh, pretend, tease, have
moods, enslave and discard'. As a youngster, and as a crone, there's an
air of calculation to Taylor's sulks, jealous rages and desires. Sometimes,
though, I have to confess, I do prefer Taylor as a child actress than as a
grown-up actress. She's brighter – the lissom star is not connected
with the coarse old broad of *Who's Afraid of Virginia Woolf?*, and the
rest of the show-pieces. There is also something charming about
Hollywood's reconstruction of the England into which she was placed:
Sussex re-imagined in California, in *National Velvet*. Everything is
green and mossy, with stone bridges, brooks, ponds. We hear bagpipes. Scotland, Ireland, the Yorkshire Moors – topography is jammed
together. Poor people sit down to supper at tables groaning with hams
and pickles, crusty loaves, wheels of cheese. Mickey Rooney, who
always struck me as being a hobgoblin, is a former thief and tramp,
now working for Donald Crisp as a butcher's boy, with access to cleav-
ers and knives. In *National Velvet*, he shears Taylor's hair so that,

wearing the yellow and pink silk riding colours, she can ride in the Grand National – her Rosalind moment in disguise. As Velvet Brown passes the finishing post, she faints – it's as if she's swooning with an orgasm, like St Teresa. Though she's disqualified when unmasked as 'an adolescent female', Velvet doesn't seem to mind. Consummation has occurred. 'What does it feel like to be in love with a horse?' she had been asked, earlier in the film, and when she lies in bed dreaming of The Pie (the name of the nag) – 'Come on, faster, faster!' – we scarcely need Dr Freud to offer an exegesis. 'The Grand National. Large dream for a little girl,' says Anne Revere – this time she's Taylor's mother, where seven years later, in *A Place in the Sun*, she'll be Clift's.

Velvet's dream (or nightmare) is about control, about power. In a painfully desiccated fashion, the themes recur in the film (and stage play) Burton would be making in 1977 – *Equus*, where as the psychiatrist, Martin Dysart, he regrets how academic timidity has prevented him from experiencing true passion and free expression; from ever feeling, as his patient, Alan Strang, explicitly has felt, the eroticism of the horse's conjunction with a man, in the shape of a centaur: the animal's strength and the hot sweat of its flanks; the twisting of the neck; the bridles, harnesses and whips. (Equine imagery is everywhere in the film: Harry Andrews, as the stable owner, paces the room like an angry horse. He snorts. He shies.) Jenny Agutter, who in fact could be Taylor at the stables, in jodhpurs and blouse, teaching Peter Firth how to groom a stallion, and make the creature 'fresh and glossy', gives the boy a brush and tells him, 'the harder you do it, the more the horse loves it.' The idea is that Strang, stripping off and caressing the horse in the moonlight, mounting, panting and ejaculating ('with my body I thee worship'), is sensing the presence of dark gods, to which Dysart is blind. They are the same gods, I think, with which Taylor was instinctively in tune. In *Lassie Come Home* in 1943, and *Courage of Lassie*, three years later, it's dogs.

Again, the postcard colours, the fluffy trees, the Scottish castles painted on glass, and Donald Crisp as a taciturn yeoman, who sells Lassie to Nigel Bruce – 'Finest collie I've ever set eyes on,' blusters the actor best known (only known) for impersonating Dr Watson. Taylor, as Bruce's granddaughter, Priscilla, objects to the way the dog is shut up in the kennels. The dog must agree, for it burrows out under the mesh and returns to Roddy McDowall, time and again. Bruce, who plays a duke, moves north to his shooting lodge for the grouse season – Lassie still makes repeated dashes for it, going back to Yorkshire by way of the Canadian Rockies, a river in Colorado, Dame May Whitty's house, everglades, a peddler's caravan, etc., and Priscilla hears about these adventures approvingly. In her blue coat and bonnet, Taylor is dressed like Princess Elizabeth or Princess Margaret Rose, except Roddy McDowall's comment on his co-star, years later, that she was 'a tiny adult walking up with this exquisite face,' must put us on our guard. For Taylor is unmistakably a dark little doll, an Edward Gorey puppet, not quite human, whose soul is projected, voodoo-fashion, into the indefatigable pooch – and I'm always somewhat concerned by the treatment of Lassie, who gets into vicious fights, sustains injuries and limps, its paws damaged by rocks and thorny tracks. Lassie staggers about, and no dog can act any of this, in the sense of faking it.

Come the sequel, Taylor is now a tomboy shepherdess, sitting high in a tree that's laden with red apples. We have at least half an hour of wildlife documentary, including a wolf swept downstream to its death; owls, ravens, bears, eagles, foxes, squirrels and deer. It's like Janácek, the way Lassie (and Taylor) gets on well with the different species. It is paradise, and when Taylor, in the role of Kathie Merrick, finally appears, she's Lolita, sunbathing and lolling on a log, flicking through a magazine, the camera concentrating on her tanned limbs. Lassie, as forward as Humbert Humbert, snatches her jeans. 'Don't run away! I won't hurt you!' Taylor cries.

In *Courage of Lassie*, we see Taylor in a sylvan or elemental habitat, as if she's present at the beginning of the world. Alone and absorbed, seemingly unaware that she's on a film set, she already possesses the concentration, and obliviousness, of her mature performances, e.g. in *BUtterfield 8*, where she wanders around a boudoir, putting on and removing a pair of stockings, like Eve making the discovery of clothes. We then switch to hell, with the arrival of men. Lassie is shot by hunters, and Taylor's Kathie, with a quiver in her voice, and her eyes filling with big tears, suggests that the dog, instead of being destroyed, could do the state some service by enrolling at the Army War Dog Training Center. The battle scenes are a real inferno. Lassie scurries across No Man's Land, dodging bullets and sinking into the mud. He has a nervous breakdown and keeps snarling. He leaps from a troop train, runs through the woods, hides in a cave, and bites Elizabeth Taylor. 'I know you didn't mean it,' she says. I think he bloody well did. The picture fades out on a plea for 'patience, love and understanding' for the returning wounded veterans.

After pets, and before husbands, it was fathers: *Father of the Bride, Father's Little Dividend, Life with Father.* I like the latter, made in 1947, as William Powell gives a considerable comic performance, as the domestic tyrant who loses every argument, who is always outwitted. Once more, Taylor is inhabiting artificial landscapes, the colours like seed packets. We are in Warner Brothers' idea of 1883, with horse-drawn trams and city mansions on canvas back-drops. Taylor, in powder-pink bows, twirling a pink and white parasol, is a confection of pink sugar. You can see her breathing in and out in her tight dress, a costume that is designed to display her figure, her noticeable chest. 'There are things about women that I think you ought to know,' says Powell to a prospective son-in-law, and his quibbling facial expression does hint at a wealth of dark, exasperated knowledge.

Taylor gives essentially the same performance in *Little Women*, two years later. It is gorgeous to look at, the gazebos with potted palms and ferns, the velvet curtains and etched glass. The March family appears to live in a music box, surrounded by tinkles and bells. 'We are better off than a lot of people,' say the sisters – and indeed who else has the orange leaves of autumn and the Christmas tree candles arranged for them by MGM? Taylor is Amy, the one who tries to be ladylike, the 'affected young goose' in a vast array of auburn ringlets, mauve frocks and pink petticoats, whose justification is, 'a princess always knows she's a princess.' Quite.

I like the way the characters are grouped in these Holman Hunt parlours. They wear pinafores and huge hooped skirts, which scorch before the coal fires. The sisters sacrifice their pocket money to help the poor, smuggle food into the slums – and Taylor's Amy is the only one who is not annoyingly earnest; she isn't irritatingly sweet and weeping fat glycerine tears. 'You can tell a lady by her gloves,' she says, putting on airs and fibbing that she's off to attend a millionaire's ball. Except that was precisely what lay in Taylor's own future, even though 'Marmie' (Mary Astor), with a prophetic skill that is uncanny, warns that she doesn't want any of her little women ever to be 'queens on thrones without peace or self-respect'.

I much prefer Taylor's Amy March to the ostensible centre of the story, Jo, who claims, 'I'll never get over my disappointment at not being born a boy.' (Parenthetically, in the twenty-first century, it's interesting how these old films have modern relevance and resonance, have things to teach us, regarding 'identity' politics.) Jo (June Allyson) is a rude and rompy crosspatch lesbian, a militant Velvet Brown, who cuts off her hair and sells it, as 'I don't think I'll ever marry.' The film concludes, nevertheless, with a wedding – Janet Leigh's – in what must be one of the bonniest tableaux in American art, a domestic interior to frame Elizabeth Taylor: there she is in a bronze coat and plaid bonnet, an amber dress trimmed with russet-coloured taffeta patches. We have an intimation of Cleopatra here, as if the actress is already covered with gold leaf.

No wonder Louis B. Mayer was alarmed. 'She looks like a little tart,' he said. 'Can't something be done to rectify her attire?' Taylor was still a schoolgirl. Found doodling in class, Amy is made to hold up a slate inscribed, 'I am ashamed of myself.' Taylor in real life was never once that. She refused to be meek, or to apologise for her desires. 'Just be quiet, *Daddy*,' she once sarcastically snapped at Michael Wilding, who in fairness was a full twenty years his wife's senior. To Senator John Warner, whom she married in 1976, and who was a scant five years older, she was heard to growl in public, 'Don't tell *me* what to do, *buster*.' Such language could make her harsh and grotesque ('You know what, I hate your guts,' she said to Burton – but their erotic play was complex), and it certainly made Taylor unpopular with other women. Anne Revere said, 'She reminded me of a mechanical midget with buck teeth.' Irene Dunne found her 'extremely agitated', and Mary Astor's recollection was that there was a look in those violet eyes 'that was somewhat calculating'. Calculating and precocious is what Taylor was in the two films with Spencer Tracy, and you can see what Bette Davis meant when she said with her trademark disdain that Taylor 'brought the little lost princess image invented for her at MGM,' variously distilled and sweetened, or else filled with remorse and misery, to all she did.

Father of the Bride, released in 1950, on the face of it is a comedy about profligacy, the ruinous cost of putting on a wedding. Far from being 'a joyous occasion', the day quickly turns into 'a business convention', as the list of invitees lengthens and the bills mount up. Spencer Tracy, as Stanley Banks, glowers and expostulates to an extent that reminded me of Oliver Hardy. He has that heavy-set integrity of the firm-but-fair patriarch, who of course will be won over. But note Tracy's thin, straight little mouth, his coal-black eyes. He was Rouben Mamoulian's Mr Hyde, as well as Dr Jekyll. In *Bad Day at Black Rock*, handicapped with one arm, he can still knock out every man in the bar. He was capable of violence, menace, and these feelings are implicit when Kay, i.e. Taylor, his only child, brings home her fiancé, Buckley Dunstan: 'He walks in here and we hand him Kay!' he says with disgust and outrage to his wife, Ellie Banks, played by Joan Bennett.

From being a jovial film about the extravagance of florists, caterers, photographers, and so forth, *Father of the Bride* gets to be tribal, almost anthropological – it is about possession, ownership, handing over the virgin at the altar, the innocent girl going from one alpha-male to the next, as a new alliance is formed. Taylor, with a slight quaver in her voice, is the idealising daughter, looking up to the strong man. She has a teasing self-possession, nevertheless, and has been used to boys sniffing around her and paying her attention since she was, we are told, fifteen. Meanwhile, Tracy has a hard time relinquishing his Freudian (or Nabokovian) urges. 'You have a little girl,' he bleats. 'She looks up to you.' And suddenly there is a rival, the father / child bond (or enslavement) is broken. There is an interpolated nightmare sequence (designed by Salvador Dalí), where a nauseous Tracy tries to make his way up the undulating aisle of the church – the ground has turned into rubber. The spell is broken by Taylor emitting a horror movie scream.

As I mentioned in the Prologue, in *The Last Picture Show*, Peter Bogdanovich's celebrated black-and-white Texan anthem, *Father of the Bride* is what's on at the fleapit, and the idea is to underscore how, in this more adult tale of affairs and annulments, Cybill Shepherd's Jacy Farrow, 'the richest and prettiest girl in town', is a sort of sister to Taylor's Kay, a girl about to be lost to the social claustrophobia in Fifties Americana – just as the likes of Cloris Leachman, Eileen Brennan, and the rest of Bogdanovich's provincial characters, are as washed-out as Anne Revere. And in *Father of the Bride* itself, the matrimonial liturgy is a kind of curse, an ending rather than a beginning: 'Who giveth this woman to be married to this man?' Taylor is indeed no longer a child, and throughout the film she tries to remind her parents of this fact. 'I'm twenty and Buckley is twenty-six and we're grown people,' she is compelled to assert. Actually, Taylor was seventeen. As everyone approaches the big day, misgivings intensify. 'The wedding's off!' Kay announces, with firmness. She is indeed the 'spoilt brat' Buckley accuses her of being – as her chief objection is that the groom's idea of a happy honeymoon is fishing in Nova Scotia, like Prince Charles wanting to take Diana to meet the midges of Balmoral.

82

One way and another there's a reconciliation and we end with Tracy opening the front door and Taylor, in her bridal finery, is reflected over and over in a series of big mirrors. 'Pops, you've been just wonderful,' she reassures him. 'I love you. I love you very much.' He calls her 'kitten', and also 'a princess in a fairy tale' – and how horrible really to have to be that, to be those things, stuck in a castle, a victim of unrealistic expectations, the prey of talking-beasts (as Angela Carter called a certain sort of man) and demon-kings. Is that what Tracy is, in fact, in Kay's life? In *Father's Little Dividend*, of 1951, we are back where we started, with Stanley Banks referring proprietorially to 'My Kay, the darling of my heart', and when he bends over to tie up his shoe laces, he gives the camera his Mr Hyde face as he lets us know he hates the idea of his son-in-law's crimes: 'First he steals my daughter, now he makes a grandpa out of me.' (The child's name has already been put down for Harvard, Class of '73.) But what about Taylor becoming a mother? She gets the vapours, feels ganged up on, gives Buckley a hard time. 'I don't know if you know it,' he tells Tracy, 'but your daughter has got a terrible temper.' The menfolk are in agreement at last, and if Kay's moods are meant to be, well, plain (female) moodiness, Taylor in real life, and in the performance she gives here, is slightly more dangerous than this – there's almost a madness to her, with shadows and hints of irresistible powers, which disturb and arouse. She's always leaving Buckley, as she'd leave her own many husbands, disappearing, wanting to end it, the minute a relationship stopped being wonderful. The tensions and apprehensions Taylor conveys on screen are serious and real, though the jaunty soundtrack music tries to pretend otherwise. Though this film, and its predecessor, are inevitably sentimental, Taylor herself doesn't have soppy scenes – these are left to Joan Bennett. Taylor is troubled, and flighty: the nervous horse, the fleeing dog.

* * *

Or the chattering monkey. Indeed, Elizabeth Taylor was born fully hairy, like a monkey. 'Her hair was long and black. Her ears were covered with thick black fuzz,' as were her shoulders and arms, and everywhere else, according to her mother, speaking to a journalist in 1953. Sara Viola Warmbrodt (1896–1994) was a minor actress, the daughter of a German who ran a laundry in Oklahoma, who as Sara Sothern had appeared on stage with Edward Everett Horton and Bela Lugosi. Taylor's condition, Sara explained, and it makes Taylor sound like an experiment in Lugosi's lab, was called hypertrichosis. Taylor's cheeks had a peachy down. She always had to pluck her eyebrows, or else they'd grow together, like Frida Kahlo's. In May 1950, when she went on honeymoon with Conrad Nicholson Hilton, an indiscreet steward on the *Queen Mary* caught a glimpse of Taylor and, 'I couldn't believe my eyes. She had black hair all over her arms and was as hairy as a little ape.' When Burton first saw her, he exclaimed, 'Dark, dark, dark, dark. She probably shaves.' Is this why *Cleopatra* was such a notable success in India, where they were still queuing up to see it in 1975? 'She would have made a perfect maharani. Beautiful, plump, jewel-studded – and very hairy,' said Burton with Welsh gallantry. His nickname for her was 'Monkey Nipples'.

This may begin to explain why she spent hours in the bathroom, depilating. Though, when describing one of her near-fatal illnesses – or her return to consciousness, molecule by molecule – Taylor, seldom commonplace, would leap into the fantastic and have us believe she was so entirely self-created, she'd managed to give birth to herself ('When I came to, it was like being given sight, hearing, touch, [and a] sense of colour. Like I had just come out of my own womb'), a more probable scenario, anyway, is Taylor was sprung from Sara's loins, if not Lugosi's bell jar, as Elizabeth Rosemond Taylor, on 27 February 1932, at 'Heathwood', 8 Wildwood Road, Hampstead (Golders Green, actually), which meant that she'd always be at least as American as Bob Hope (Eltham) and Cary Grant (Bristol), and her accent, with its parakeet modulations, would equally be as manufactured as theirs. Her father, Francis Lenn Taylor (1896–1968), was from Illinois, a homosexual and drinker who'd therefore drifted into the art business. Taylor's parents had met whilst pupils at Arkansas City High School, had married in 1925, and under the tutelage of an affluent uncle, Howard Young, Francis had been sent to London to manage a gallery situated in 35 Bond Street, which specialised in Gainsborough copies and sketches discarded by Augustus John. On 23 September 1939, for instance, John wrote to Maud Cazalet to tell her, 'Francis Taylor is selling all my beloved drawings, many of which I tore up … in a fit of madness, but he has pieced them together again.' Pieced them together rather expertly, too – forty-four of them, ripped up into confetti and reassembled, were offered for sale by Christopher Wilding, Taylor's son, at Chiswick Auctions on 25 August 2010. Most were fragments in pen and ink of John's wife Ida Nettleship in the nude.

Francis also dealt in the odd canvas sold in a hurry by Jewish refugees. Burton in his diaries divulged as much. The Vuillards, Vlamincks and Utrillos once belonged to people who were 'apparently all knocked off by the Nazis during the Occupation. They were Jews.' It is no mitigation that know-all Andrew Sinclair, who saw the stock in 1970, when it was stored at Squire's Mount, Burton's compound in Hampstead, said all the pictures were copies. The boastful Sinclair ('I had been a Cambridge don'; he needed to tell everyone he met about 'my Nash terrace house in Regents Park') also spotted a fake Rouault and a counterfeit Modigliani. Burton, who'd not have appreciated the upmanship, especially as Sinclair was there to talk about their film of *Under Milk Wood*, reacted by saying his and Taylor's more important collection was in any event kept aboard the *Kalizma*. 'Oh I see,' said Sinclair, who perhaps deemed himself a wit, 'Your travelling pictures …' Sinclair wore a leather coat because 'I wished to unsettle any stranger who might approach me,' though if they did it would only have been to scoff at his bushy comb-over.

Less absurd altogether was the controversy in 2004 over the rightful ownership of Van Gogh's 'Vue de l'asile et de la Chapelle de Saint-Rémy', which Taylor (and Burton) had acquired at Sotheby's on 14 April 1963. If Francis Taylor had taken advantage of Jewish refugees, buying their hoards cheaply, there's something even more distinctly unpleasant about the later saga – Elizabeth Taylor's rapaciousness, selfish naked greed, exposing the shallowness, phoniness, of her own claims to be a Jewess, as she ground opponents down with legal threats and counter-threats. It was Francis, in fact, who did the bidding at the auction. Taylor and Burton's involvement was kept secret. The price paid was $257,000, or £92,000 at the time, and the oil painting was displayed in the salon of the *Kalizma*. Forty years later, the descendants of Margarete Mauthner (1863–1947), a Jewish collector who'd been forced to flee Berlin in 1939 for South Africa, wanted it back – and a Californian court was asked to decide whether the Van Gogh, by then worth at least £10 million, was 'among Jewish-owned works of art that disappeared during the Nazi period'. If so, would Taylor make restitution? Would she arseholes. All that was required, legally, was for the claimants, Mauthner's four great-grandchildren, to prove the picture was once owned by the family and 'that it was lost as a direct consequence of the Nazis' official policy of persecuting Jews and dispossessing them of their finances and assets'. Taylor refused to believe the Van Gogh had had to be sold to finance the journey to Johannesburg; she did not believe it was disposed of because of Hitler. The claimants 'have provided not a shred of evidence that the painting ever fell into Nazi hands or any information concerning how or when Mauthner "lost possession" of it,' even though the Van Gogh catalogue raisonné confirms 'La Chapelle de Saint-Rémy' as still being owned by Mauthner in 1939, shortly before she had to leave Germany or face the concentration camps. 'The reason she didn't have it thereafter,' said her family, 'was the direct result of Nazi policies towards the Jews.' Mauthner, incidentally, had been the translator of Van Gogh's letters and was instrumental in making his works well known.

Taylor's lawyers, who on her express instructions 'chose the path of aggressive litigation', countered by saying too much time had elapsed – there was a statute of limitations pertaining to the Holocaust Victims Redress Act. Amazingly, the Supreme Court agreed. 'The descendants waited too long to bring their claims demanding that Taylor return the artwork,' it was stipulated in 2007. Another technicality was that the Holocaust Victims Redress Act was intended to act at governmental level and 'does not give individuals the right to sue private art owners'. What's galling is that the Mauthners got nowhere alleging Taylor 'must have known when she bought the Van Gogh that it had been stolen by the Nazis', particularly as the Sotheby's catalogue had clearly stated its history and had specifically mentioned it had once belonged to one Margarete Mauthner – but then Taylor's father had form in all these areas. So, here's a weird thing. In 1956, Francis had visited Augustus John at Fryern Court, Hampshire, and sat for his portrait. The rendering in black, brown and white chalk is like one of those virulent caricatures of large-nosed, Jewish businessmen, glistening with drool, as used to appear in *Der Stürmer* throughout the Twenties and Thirties. What had John possibly detected or decided to put there?

The Van Gogh picture was sold at Christie's in London in February 2012 for £10,121,250.

* * *

Taylor was never educated. She went to Vacani's Dance Academy, which was visited one afternoon by Princess Elizabeth and Princess Margaret Rose, and if I may make a note here – horses, dogs, diamonds, flashes of silver and gold: if we shift forwards a century more or less, Elizabeth Taylor and Elizabeth II would come to have the same degree of grandeur. They were women set apart from what the rest of us think of as reality (bills, queues, pension plans, practical inconveniences, manila envelopes) for the entirety of their lives; they were aware of all that was to be expected of them; and every public moment, every entrance, every exit, was captured by cameras and newsreels. And yet nobody knows what they are or were really like – not even themselves.

This will have occurred to the late Roger Michell, too, as throughout his documentary about the Queen, made for the Platinum Jubilee in 2022, *Elizabeth: A Portrait in Part(s)*, interspersed, almost subliminally, amongst the clips of Her Majesty are clips of Taylor – Taylor arriving at premieres, wrapped in furs, and the Queen and Prince Philip, in their finery, being received at the Palladium or Covent Garden; Cleopatra on her barge side-by-side with the Royal Yacht *Britannia*; the burning of Windsor Castle and shots of the set of *Cleopatra* being demolished at Pinewood, the pillars and temples crashing down. Juxtaposed in these ways, the question is raised, which was the less artificial, a monarch or an actress? They are both equally forms of intricate celebrity, is the answer, national and international property, surviving on celluloid, in archives of newsprint. Not that Princess Margaret, Countess of Snowdon, would have thanked anyone for making comparisons. 'She's a common little thing, isn't she?' Her Royal Highness said to Emlyn Williams about Taylor, stating a fact, not venturing an opinion.

Sara generally kept Taylor away from her father – 'My dear wife won't let me near her,' Francis lamented. 'She wanted the child all to herself. She dotes on her night and day.' There was a distinct element of emotional smothering. Taylor had no friends – and weekends were spent at the estate in Shipbourne, Kent, 'Fairlawne', of Francis' intimate friend, Victor Cazalet, the son of Augustus John's friend Maud and the member of parliament for East Islington. Cazalet bought the infant Elizabeth a pony, generally behaved as her champion. An association with the family, and tangentially with royalty, was retained. On 15 June 1968, the Queen Mother and Princess Margaret, with Taylor, Burton and Noël Coward, attended the wedding of Sheran Cazalet, daughter of Victor's brother, royal racehorse trainer, Captain

Peter Cazalet, to Simon Hornby, at St Giles' Church, Shipbourne, Kent. The reception was at 'Fairlawne'. Taylor, Burton and Coward, arriving early in a Rolls, had entered the saloon bar of an adjacent pub, The Chaser, and ordered three large vodkas and tonic. These were possibly not the first drinks of the day. 'I was resplendent in my morning coat and grey topper,' said Coward in his diary, on 23 June. Not so actually. He looked like a crumpled and sozzled sea turtle. He was overheard to say to Taylor, 'What are you nervous about? It's not your wedding.' 'That's why I'm nervous,' Taylor replied.

During the war Victor commanded the 83rd Anti-Aircraft Battery at Sevenoaks, where the Officers' Mess was stocked with provisions sent down from The Dorchester. One of his men, so to speak, was Dennis Price, who when he was offered a film role was told, 'Of course, old boy, off you go. No need to bother about parades for a couple of days,' and this is the degree of discipline that in due course would appeal to Taylor. When Alec Guinness paid a visit to the Sevenoaks depot – the Duke d'Ascoyne, as it were, checking up on Louis Mazzini – he was so shocked to see some sergeants knitting, he immediately joined the Royal Navy Volunteer Reserve instead, eventually seeing action in Sicily. Cazalet himself was killed in July 1943, in the plane crash off Gibraltar with General Sikorski. But he'd still had plenty of time to confirm an eccentric status. He held a fondness for Mussolini, was a supporter of Franco, and had said of the concentration camps that they were 'quite well run'. The Taylor family was eager for his social connections, nevertheless (Ascot, Royal Garden Parties, First Nights), and it was Cazalet who, seeing war looming, had advised them to return to the States, where they would be safer. Francis set up his art gallery in an arcade at the Beverly Hills Hotel, his daughter enrolled at a dance studio in Pacific Palisades, and Sara began an affair with Michael Curtiz, who'd direct *Life with Father*. Visitors to the home at 703 North Elm Drive recalled a creature being trained to be another Shirley Temple. 'Sing, darling, sing!' Sara commanded. Taylor's mother would then ask the company in a theatrical, rhetorical way, 'Have you ever seen a more beautiful face, more beautiful hair, more beautiful teeth?' Outside of the champion's ring at Cruft's, no.

Taylor said of her childhood that 'the child in me was suppressed. It worked, it was paid, it was on the screen, but it was not me.' Does this mean she didn't recognise herself in the performances she gave? That her authentic self was elsewhere, otherwise engaged? How peculiar to objectify yourself, alienate yourself, push everything away decisively to the third person. It was a frequent ploy – Taylor's means of absolving herself from responsibility for her actions, so that other people could assume the burdens, cope with the consequences. 'I'm absolutely sick of being Elizabeth Taylor,' she said in 1976, when she abandoned acting to be a politician's wife. Yet she didn't like not being Elizabeth Taylor, either, and before long, the marriage to John Warner in jeopardy, she was saying, 'I lost confidence in Elizabeth Taylor as a person.' As a person? Or as a star? Or as a brand? What? What you realise is that nothing was solid, everything is unstable, and this is something that dawned on her before her brain tumour operation in 1997: 'Even if I survived, would I still be me?' It's the kind of question about identity and consciousness that philosophers have been asking since the days of Plato. The additional problem with being a child actress, like Taylor, is that she became an adult too soon – which paradoxically meant she never grew up, and is why in 1941 a beflummoxed casting director could report, 'Her eyes are too old. She doesn't have the face of a child.' To interviewers Taylor would say, 'I was born a baby.' To Firooz Zahedi she said, 'I was born as a child.' You'd not think this was unique – but to Taylor it evidently was. Taylor experienced none of the adolescent psychological jostling, the experimentation and hesitation of any intermediate stage. It's as if she'd said to herself, we waste too much time with preliminaries. Why take things gradually? She had an innocence, but no conscience – hence her blithe willingness to damage other people (Debbie Reynolds, Sybil Burton), when defending her own needs.

'Mike's dead and I'm alive!' she famously announced when, newly widowed, she was fucking Eddie Fisher before Todd's ashes had cooled – outraging the public, who deluged her with hate mail and voodoo dolls stuck with pins. Taylor had boldness, and she suggested a definite link to darker forces that Burton, in particular, couldn't resist ('If you're my girl, come over here and stick your tongue down my throat'); but because she had no capacity for self-analysis, nor was there any limit to bad behaviour. Her life was built on force, exploitation, getting beyond constraint, with the result that her hair-stylist, Alexandre de Paris, could say with authority: 'She plays a brilliant Elizabeth Taylor, on stage and off. It's her single greatest role' – and Evelyn Keyes, one of Mike Todd's mistresses (and John Huston's wives) concluded: 'Elizabeth Taylor is the love of Elizabeth Taylor's life,' because even when desolate and hurt, the emotions existed for her as things to flaunt, to exhibit; as instances of a further movement of her will.

The studios had insisted on a toy existence. MGM, in Culver City, contained a zoo, gardens, lakes, and thirty sound stages. 'Everyone looked so happy and seemed to be enjoying themselves,' recalled Taylor of this slightly chilling domain. Such education as Taylor ever received was provided in the 'Little Red Schoolhouse', next to the Thalberg Building. The studio booked flights, reserved hotels, provided chauffeurs, and when you threw a party, they hired the band and organised the catering. It is when set against this royal background, or upbringing, we can see how Taylor, flying to Paris to finish *The Sandpiper* in 1965, was going to require twenty-one suites at the Lancaster; or why when filming *Who's Afraid of Virginia Woolf?* at Smith College, Northampton, Massachusetts in 1966, she insisted on Warner Brothers finding a plane that would bring her and Burton straight to Bradley Field, in Connecticut, without the bother of needing to refuel in Chicago. She then insisted on swapping houses with Mike Nichols, because his was nicer – fourteen rooms and nine fireplaces. The Burtons were guarded by the police as if they were the President and the First

Lady in the care of the Secret Service. Bodyguards were ordered not to speak to the stars, 'unless they initiate the conversation, and then make it brief. Do not ask them any questions'. As Ernest Lehman, the script-writer, put it, somewhat sceptically, Taylor and Burton 'had it the easiest of any of us ... All they had to do was show up.'

Yet what more is required of a star? A star is irresistible – and Humphrey Bogart early on had assured Taylor, 'You're one of the major stars in this town.' A star can be parodied, impersonated (John Belushi in drag portrayed Taylor choking on a chicken bone), but not replaced. Stardom is not the same thing as celebrity. Celebrity is available to anyone. To be celebrated is a human achievement. Star-dom is extra-terrestrial – and so when Sara said to Hedda Hopper, 'Make my daughter a star!' the injunction was already not necessary. Oscar De Mejo, a painter married to Alida Valli, visited 703 North Elm Drive and remembered Taylor's being there, when 'she wore a light blue cotton dress that clung and crept about her legs. She emit-ted an air of ageless, inculpable eroticism.' The inculpability is inter-esting, and key. Taylor's sensitivity as an actress (like Monroe, a lot of what she accomplished was not visible until directors screened the rushes) was related, I think, to her insensitivity and callousness. For nothing was premeditated, in the same way that a fox's stark treat-ment of a rabbit or a chicken is simply (and helplessly) natural. By this light, Taylor was not capable of dissimulation. There was no dis-tinction between preparation, and rehearsals, and actual execution, which was always intuitive and always unlimited.

Men were wanting to possess her for this reason. In October 1948, the portrait photographer Philippe Halsman, known for his Elizabeth Arden lipstick advertisements and for the famous shot of the jump-ing Duke and Duchess of Windsor, peering through his lens, told Taylor, who was sixteen, 'You have bosoms, so stick them out!' Yes, she was a lesson in human anatomy, and her breasts had ripened like fruit; she had a throbbing heart; and then there was the sound of her panting and breathing. But a million barmaids and waitresses and nannies share those attributes, and there's more to Taylor than this – there were always unseen forces, currents of sexual tension, which culminated in her relationship with Burton. I adore the Burtons for going too far with the drinking and smoking and fucking; for taking risks – maximum intensity: extreme bliss, ravishment, ecstasy, which you can find in pornography, if we are honest. (Kevin McClory, one of her lovers, said Taylor was 'totally pornographic'.) It needn't involve emotional (or spiritual) intimacy, as a matter of fact. This is sexuality as a necessary animal, biological urge, which is instinctual – and once again here we are with Taylor as an instinctive, hormonal artist, in tune with lunar rhythms and cycles. (She always took days off contractually for menstruating: it was a weekly occurrence, and joke, for the crew at Cinecittà, during *Cleopatra*, to receive the phone call from her shrill factotum Dick Hanley, 'Elizabeth's got the rag on.') Her directness is what's appealing. I am reminded of Francis Bacon's saying what most interested him about human behaviour was when it operated on or at the level of instinct: 'I mean, pleasure is such a strange thing, really . . . And so is pain. We experience them the whole time, but it's impossible to say clearly what they are.'

* * *

I'd agree; though it's not *completely* impossible – as we can be sure violation, domination and submission are a large part of it; an annihilation, a surrender, even if these are chiefly abstract considerations. (It's what Bacon painted, Mapplethorpe photographed.) Taylor's own views on sex were very clear, indeed explicit: pleasure and pain were the same thing; fucking was inseparable from danger and suspense: 'A woman will try and dominate a man,' she explained. 'She will try and get away with it. But really, inside herself, she wants to be dominated. She wants the man to take her.' It's like an incitement to rape, the way she sketched it. If the male is docile and compliant, refuses to be abusive, if nothing lurid happens, the female, according to Taylor, 'becomes bitter. There is no more dialogue, they have no rapport.' Antony and Cleopatra are like this; as were George and Martha; or the couple in *The V.I.P.s*; or Petruchio and Katherina; and also the disintegrating pair played by the Burtons in *Divorce His, Divorce Hers*, set in Seventies Rome rather than Ancient Rome: 'It's no fun behaving badly if you're not going to punish me,' says Taylor's character. 'Beat me black and blue, but please don't leave me.' She and Burton, in everything they did together, were Venus and Bacchus, embodiments of indulgence and animal spirits. We may think, how wonderful to be irresponsible, that here was the permissiveness of the Age of Aquarius in action; but when Burton wanted to replace Sybil with Taylor, when you examine the entanglements, the conflicts, the disloyalties and division – the scheming – sex quite quickly was not any kind of liberation. Taylor and Burton were under a net, to use Iris Murdoch's image: the shackles of desire, and the issues of social and moral trespass, let alone the legal and financial consequences ('I gave away everything I had,' said Burton of his divorce settlement, 'I wanted to start again from scratch'), were to prove a suffocation.

Another consequence was the loss of privacy – all those newspapermen and cameras; the court they surrounded themselves with. It was only when visiting Burton's freshly dug grave, at dawn in August 1984, that Taylor was able to reflect, 'I couldn't help thinking it was one of those few occasions ever that Richard and I were alone.' What they'd gained was life as a spectacle – or to be more precise, Burton gained it ('How else am I going to become a Hollywood star?' he'd reasoned, when embarking on his seduction); Taylor never knew anything other than champagne parties and sunny blue pools, ruby-encrusted coffee spoons and buffets beneath palm trees, with celery and olives in silver dishes served by valets wearing white gloves, and the glasses and bottles in sparkling rows. As Shelley Winters said, she was 'a Hollywood baby who never had the experience of living on her own. She was afraid of the real world and longed for it at the same time.' Was Burton the real world? Were all men, with their sexual possibility? It's as if, knowing from puberty that she could arouse male curiosity, Taylor exploited her supposition that, as Freud could have told her, or Schnitzler, Wedekind and Alban Berg, that eroticism is the basis of human motivation. If she gloried in her own distress and torment, regarding her love life, this was a way of not feeling artificial. Henry Wynberg, a lover she knew in the Seventies, put it interestingly: 'Sex was one of Elizabeth's great discoveries. She had indulged in it relentlessly.' This makes her sound like a pioneer, like Tesla and his coils of alternating current. It made her not false, at the same time as it made her heightened, with an unselfconscious strength and focus.

She was first engaged to be married at the age of eighteen, and was first divorced two months before she was twenty. Before even this episode Taylor had public liaisons with Glenn Davis, a Korean War veteran, Howard Hughes, who wished to purchase her from her parents for $1 million, and William Pawley Jr., a radio station owner, whose father was American ambassador to Brazil. In 1949, she sent sixty love-letters to Pawley, which were sold at auction in Amherst, Massachusetts, in 2011. She'd tell him things like, 'I've never known this kind of love before – it's so perfect and complete – and mature.' (Mature?) Pawley gave Taylor a $16,000 engagement ring, which when it was all over, she kept. The official fiancé, however, was Conrad Nicholson Hilton Jr., the hotel chain heir, who was already addicted to heroin, alcohol and gambling. His sixty-four-room Bel Air mansion, Casa Encantada, 10644 Bellagio Road, had gold silk walls and golden carpets. There were twenty-six lavatories with gold taps. There were five kitchens – multi-course meals were served on gold plates by liveried waiters. (It sounds like a flagship Hilton hotel.) Sara was dazzled. 'You are never going to do any better than Nicky Hilton.' Her daughter concurred. 'He's my darling,' said Taylor. 'I'll love no other man until my dying day.' She was the sacrificial virgin.

95

'Nicky' Hilton, cruel, silly, and bored, found her receptivity alluring, and repulsive. On their honeymoon, without warning or preamble, he punched his wife in the belly: 'That'll teach you.' He had the dark force of a killer – but what is it he punished her for? He hoped to teach her what? I think he wanted to remove her from the movie star trance, which was a provocation. For almost as perverse as Hilton himself were MGM's arrangements for the wedding, held at five p.m. on Saturday 6 May 1950 at the Church of the Good Shepherd in Beverly Hills, and attended by the Hollywood aristocracy. Taylor was working on *Father of the Bride* at the time (it was released on 6 June), and the nuptials were a continuation of (and publicity for) the film, even to the extent of Taylor's white satin dress embroidered with beads and pearls being a replica (made by costume designer Helen Rose) of the one worn by Kay, her brittle character. Guilaroff did her hair. Two hundred policemen held back the fans. Taylor's limo had six motorcycle escorts. She ripped her veil on the car door. In the church, which Hilton hotel officials and MGM set designers had filled with carnations and lilies tied with silk bows, the organ broke down. There was a glut of wedding gifts, selected by Sara from Marshall Field in Chicago – fine china, crystal, silverware, lace-trimmed linen. Taylor received shares in the Hilton Hotel Corporation, which she retained, and by 1994 her portfolio was valued at $21.7 million. This stock was about the only element in the marriage that was not the product of artifice, of nothingness. Louis B. Mayer's paying for the bridal gown; the wedding breakfast at the Bel-Air Country Club, enjoyed by (presumably the Marx Brothers were detained) Gene Kelly, Bing Crosby and Fred and Ginger, Esther Williams, Mickey Rooney, and from *Father of the Bride*, Spencer Tracy and Joan Bennett; the blue silk going-away frock with mink stole and trousseau created by Edith Head; the seventeen steamer trunks piped aboard the *Queen Mary*, where Taylor and Hilton shared the decks with the Windsors: it was a dream that would swallow any ordinary person down, do away with them. Everything was a lie: fake love, fake joy, fake bonhomie. It is almost possible to feel sympathy for Hilton, when he said, 'I didn't marry a girl. I married an institution.' All Taylor did, said Elsa Maxwell, who saw the honeymooners in Paris, was 'flash her diamonds and show off her cleavage.' The only aspects that were real, if primitive and gross, were Hilton's kinks. 'I really had no idea what was coming,' said Taylor later.

Hilton, who died in 1969, aged forty-two, at least had a big penis. His other partners, including his own stepmother, Zsa Zsa Gabor, and Joan Collins, were never in any doubt about his endowments. 'He had absolutely the largest penis, wider than a beer can and much longer, I have ever seen,' said a starlet named Terry Moore, still alive in her nineties. 'To make love to him was akin to fornicating with a horse.' Tastes form. Taylor would always be appreciative of meaty cocks. Eddie Fisher's stamina was attributed to his amphetamine addiction. No matter. 'He would reach climax and immediately he would have another erection,' said Angela Sweeney, his voice coach, clinically. Taylor would say of John Warner that 'he's the best lover I ever had,' and she ostentatiously went shopping for his extra-large underpants on Rodeo Drive. Even Burton was heard to boast, 'If I'm called upon, I can sometimes summon up a good eleven-and-a-half inches. But of course, I'm only joking.' The amount of vodka he consumed, I'm sure the promise of pleasure was often followed by emptiness and boredom – a sick joke, beyond question.

With her first marriage, too, Taylor was being shown pain and humiliation were a possible response to sexual arousal. On their honeymoon in Europe, Hilton drank, gambled, and beat his wife up. Perhaps it wasn't all buffetings. In June, they attended Royal Ascot – though even there, tumult, impetuousness, continued to be discharged: Churchill was late because his car had collided with his protection officer. In Rome, Taylor went to see Guilaroff, who was working on *Quo Vadis*, and told him her marriage was a cruel farce, 'nothing like the romantic parts she had played on screen.' She was wearing long sleeves to conceal her bruises. It was more like the narrative of De Sade's *Justine*, culminating in Taylor's announcement, 'I had terrible pains . . . I left him after having a baby kicked out of my stomach . . . I saw the baby in the toilet.' They were married in the spring, separated officially on 14 December, and the divorce decree was obtained on 26, 29 or 30 January 1951 (sources differ), so that was a quick gestation. Taylor immediately went into hospital, Cedars Sinai, with what was discreetly called 'recurring ulcerative colitis', but her psychological legacy was longer lasting. For it's as if, having been taught by Hilton that sex and violence were connected, that desire can also mean a desire to hurt, and that the senses, literally and figuratively, were there to be assaulted, torment was something she found she sought – and sought to inflict. For what's fascinating about Taylor is that, ever afterwards, she'd challenge masculinity with the way she'd now fight back, playing false with the servile position, and becoming, in her turn, something of a despot ('Nobody tells me who to love or not to love, who to be seen with and not to be seen with,' she told the Twentieth Century Fox lawyers, when they threatened to bring suit on the basis of the morals clause in her *Cleopatra* contract); and yet though she effaced grace and softness, because they signified weakness, she'd still tell Montgomery Clift, 'I yearn for a big strong guy to look after me, to buy me lots of jewellery and to pay the bills,' so as a feminist Taylor was something of an anti-feminist, coquettish as much as she was aggressive, wanting to be free and kept. 'I love you! I love you! I can't live without you, my dear, dear, darling Monty,' she also gushed – and it is part of her generous sexuality that she always embraced, or could incorporate, homosexuality, was never revolted by it, and in her final years was a champion for Aids research. Perhaps the way physical possession could never be carried through, sealed, so to speak, with Clift (and Rock Hudson – and Michael Jackson) was tantalising – unattainability was erotic, despite the courtship, the flirtation – and if Taylor, like Judy Garland, and the rest of the divas, had that distinct element of drag queen – of sleaze and exhaustion never far off, behind the effort going into appearances (the hair, the make-up, the wardrobe); then it is the paradox of men who don't like women, or who are incapable of fucking women, that they always like this kind of woman. Taylor, alternately slender or bloated, dazzling or aged (made to look old for *Who's Afraid of Virginia Woolf?*; made to look young in *Ash Wednesday* – which Burton called 'a fucking lousy nothing bloody film'), is always a fantasy figure. 'That sure is a beautiful animal,' says Rock Hudson in *Giant*, when he first sees Taylor riding side-saddle on her stallion. 'Too spirited for anyone else to ride,' replies her father, taking Rock literally, thinking he meant the horse – but maybe Rock didn't only mean Taylor, who in this great film is called Leslie, an ambiguous or androgynous male or female name, like Nicky.

* * *

Released in 1956, *Giant*, at 201 minutes, and in which Taylor had forty-one changes of costume, is about gigantism. The huge brown dusty flat planes of Texas, which generate vast wealth; the vast cattle herds; the vast fields of oil wells, the derricks, like iron reptiles, pecking at the soil; Jett Rink's vast hotel and the massive banquet; and not forgetting Rock Hudson's sheer size, as if he's been put together from hams and tenderloin, brisket and rump steaks. Then there's this gloomy gothic mansion, as magnificent as the Ambersons', constructed as if from gingerbread, with gables and weather-vanes, in the middle of a yellow nowhere. Reata Ranch's stately home is redecorated over the years, in accordance with changes in fashion and developments in the plot. At first it is masculine and mahogany, with black leather furniture; by the end it is white and suburban – and it is the setting for over-scaled emotions, heated family arguments, chiefly to do with Leslie's progressive views about wifely duties (she refuses to be demure) and her treatment of the Mexican servants (she isn't a racist). *Giant* is a return to *Elephant Walk* in those respects: a big safari lodge, with blood-red walls, and women excluded from men's talk, and Taylor's fury at the chauvinism.

Yet though it is an American epic – the railroads, the distances – it is the small personal details that register: Leslie's asking Jordan 'Bick' Benedict when she first meets him, and she hears about his half-a-million acres, 'Why aren't you married, Bick?' – a question repeated when she gets to know the local oddball, played by James Dean: 'When are you going to get married, Jett?' There is a profound homosexual theme in this story, which has nothing to do with effeminacy – everything to do with loneliness. (Mercedes McCambridge as Luz, Bick's sister, is gruff and mannish.) Dean, indeed, is a miracle of awkwardness and nervous fidgeting, as he tries out various poses, experiments with how to drape a shotgun across his shoulders. In his jeans and, in profile, his big cowboy hat tilted over his face, he is an icon of androgynous male beauty. His semi-articulated affinity with Taylor's character – his awareness that he is drawn to her (and towards something she represents), and that he can never act upon this, is emotionally true, in ways Rock's behaviour never is. (With Bick, everything is a threat to his masculinity: it's as fundamental and unvarying as that.) Dean comes across, in this film he never saw, because he'd been killed in the car crash long prior to its release, as a sad romantic, whose insolence sees off self-pity. Was Taylor ever in a more affecting scene than the one where Leslie goes to visit the friendless Jett in his scruffy hut, with its pots of geraniums on the windowsill: so he has planted and tended them, has he? They drink tea, Jett surreptitiously taking a swig of Scotch to give himself courage; the politeness is strained to breaking point – but the point is, it doesn't break. Dean mumbles in a sing-song way. He stares into space, leaves odd pauses and gaps in his delivery of the dialogue. It is as mannered as Restoration Drama, and Dean is wonderful. Ivan Moffat, who co-wrote the screenplay, was quite wrong to complain Dean 'did nothing to help the girl', i.e. Taylor, as his awkward infatuation and lack of connection is what creates intense emotion. He's neither natural nor unnatural – perhaps he is supernatural? The mud around his compound is blackish and filthy – filthy with oil. 'My well came in big,' he says, as he capers about, drenched in the sticky liquid. With no one to spend his new riches on – with no one in his life – alcoholism grips him, and in the later scenes, in grey hair and dark glasses, shuffling like a living ghost around the Vegas-style hotel he has had built – and how lonely does a person have to be to inhabit his own empty hotel? – Dean is impersonating Howard Hughes, juddering with neurosis. (You realise Mark Rylance and Leonardo di Caprio studied this performance at an impressionable age, as did the Day-Lewis of *There Will be Blood*.) Michael Wilding said Dean told him his ambitions were to play Hamlet and Faust.

As with Clift in *A Place in the Sun* (and *Giant* was also directed by George Stevens), Taylor is at her best reaching out to characters, personalities, who can't be reached. And isn't this what would draw her to Burton? She sensed his emphatic loneliness. He had acquaintances, employees, the dozens of relatives in South Wales, drinking buddies, with whom he could appear hearty, but Taylor could see at once he was not sure of himself – and this helplessness, and his regretful smile, was an enticement, and a warmth poured from her – as it does in *Cat on a Hot Tin Roof* (1958), which is almost a film about lingerie, as Taylor gazes in the mirror and peels her silk stockings off, examines herself in satin straps and ribbons, slips in and out of cashmere robes. The film is also an inadvertent comedy about a man (Paul Newman as Brick Pollitt, a name that chimes with Rock's Bick Benedict) refusing to take the hint – he can't see his wife's sexual frustration, in this humid southern setting. Taylor wants to fuck, he pushes her away with the comment, 'I've seen that look before.' She caresses herself absent-mindedly, clutches the phallic posts and struts of shiny brass bedsteads, with their plant-like knobbly decorative tendrils; she poses in doorways in her petticoats, and in silhouette behind muslin curtains. She looks first class in her skirt and blouse and an orange belt. Yet Newman – he is so pretty, with those blue ice-chip eyes, loafing about and drinking – is disgusted by her ripeness. With his injured leg, he is symbolically crippled, like a stammer or club foot in a Maugham story. The agony of homosexuality is represented the better for being encoded – 'You can't stand drinking out of the same glass, can you?' Taylor, as Maggie the Cat, says to him with genuine puzzlement. 'I get so lonely,' she sighs with regret.

What a grotesque family they are (Tennessee Williams' imagination is not dissimilar to Charles Addams'), yammering, scratching, sneaking and spying on each other, trying to win the affection and approval of Burl Ives' Big Daddy, who is 'irritable from too much devotion'. Only Taylor's Maggie refuses, like Cordelia, to spout about her gratitude, and Big Daddy respects her for this. He confides in her about his terminal cancer – 'I'm going to live, Maggie! I'm going to live!' he says, meaning the opposite, as they lean on a fence and gaze at cantering horses. But willpower won't defeat terminal cancer, nor will bravery. Big Daddy refuses morphine injections, as 'When you've got pain at least you know you're alive.'

Ives, imposing and thunderous, is what Rock's Bick may have become – a giant patriarch in a mansion with porticoes and verandas (that ensure no privacy), an American Lear, not skilled at delegating or relinquishing power, to whom people suck up because he has the money. He flirts with Taylor ('I can tell he likes me. He's still got an eye for young girls,' she tries to joke), and he grabs her wrist at the picnic. 'Will you put some honey on this?' he asks her, at the meal-table. A sensation of warped, misdirected, sexuality is in the air. The lie of Big Daddy's cancer (Big Mama, Judith Anderson, refers to his ailment as a spastic colon), is one amongst many other malignancies, and mendacities, and to the atmosphere of illness and disease, infection and pollution, in the film, Taylor's Maggie is immune. Ghastly children run amok ('no-neck monsters', 'those five screaming monkeys'), and she refuses to coo sentimentally. Big Mama keeps pretending Big Daddy is being humorous and ironical ('You don't know nothing and you never did!' he snarls), and Maggie can see how her in-laws talk around things, leaving things unsaid and unspoken. Chiefly, there's Brick's 'occupation of drinking' – and Big Mama blames Maggie for his unhappiness – exactly as, in *Suddenly, Last Summer*, again written by Tennessee Williams, Taylor plays a person who is told they are at fault for causing queerness, or as it is framed for her, childlessness and impotence; similar accusations fly back and forth in *Who's Afraid of Virginia Woolf?*. The drinking and the marital arguments ('In all these years, you never believed I loved you,' says Big Mama – what a shame Taylor never played the role later on in her career); the family feuding and the family feeling; everyone speaking and being frantic; everyone full of hate and hardness – Taylor's character rises above the ensemble in always wanting individual attention. She panics if not at the centre of it. The screaming and weeping, in the bedroom with Newman, turns into a contest between their eyes: her purple peepers are aflame as she says, 'I'm alive! Maggie the cat is alive!' Having been called, contemptuously, 'a cat in the heat', she grasps the sobriquet, instead of recoiling at the insult. Taylor blooms in the southern temperatures, with its ceiling fans, sticky heat, and rain and swamps full of death. 'I'm not living with you,' she says to Brick – or maybe he says it to her: it makes no material difference. 'We occupy the same cage, that's all.'

In *Suddenly, Last Summer* (1959), adapted for the screen from Tennessee Williams' play by Gore Vidal – and note how Williams and Vidal rather relish presenting their proclivities as filth, as perversion; they wallow in self-disgust – liberation, the key to the cage, to freedom, is offered by a transorbital lobotomy. 'You are going to witness an operation never performed before in this State,' the student doctors are promised, as if they are gathering to enjoy a circus trick. Montgomery Clift's bushy eyebrows appear above the cool sharp knives, the clamps and surgical saws. He's Dr Cukrowicz, and 'more than twelve hundred mental cases' await his scalpel. I had the shock of my life when I spotted Rita Webb, the comedy crone, cackling in a creaking rocking chair in the background at the County Asylum, but then the studios used by Columbia were in England, at Shepperton.

Gary Raymond, also in the credit roll, is Burton's room-mate, Cliff, in *Look Back in Anger*. Malcolm Arnold, responsible for the jaunty St Trinian's school song, composed the score. Oliver Messel, who designed filigree suites at The Dorchester, created the scenery. Jack Hildyard, who photographed *The Millionairess* and *Casino Royale* with Peter Sellers, focussed the cameras. What we have, therefore, is Southern Gothic as imagined in Surrey. Everything is slightly *off*. Perhaps this is why the star of the film – it is a character in its own right – is the horror garden, a dense tangle of dripping trees, lizards and foul air. Horticulture is symbolic of psychology, which is itself symbolic of the curse of memory. *Suddenly, Last Summer* is like a Hammer zombie film, with a top-notch cast, chief amongst whom is Katharine Hepburn, who as Violet Venable, a rich and merciless widow lurking in (another) baroque mansion, appears and disappears in an ornate lift, like a rising and falling throne. Violet is a human Venus flytrap, a 'devouring organism', who goes on and on about her dead son, Sebastian, whom she idolises to an unsavoury degree. She is appalled that Sebastian's cousin, Catherine, who was with him when he died, has divulged secrets 'of an unspeakable character'. Catherine, Taylor at her most dazed, is surely having crazy visions, as she has been babbling like 'a wild animal . . . the things she says, terrible, obscene things.'

It is a film about erotomania. Sebastian's abandoned room is an altar of homosexual taste, the pictures of martyred saints, nude neo-classical statues, white silk clothes made in Rome. In her slightly younger days it was Violet who procured the boys – 'Violet and Sebastian', a quasi-incestuous couple, egotistical and superior, in Venice and Madrid, the mother pimping for her son. That Catherine, Violet's niece, is expected to assume these duties, attracting the men by lolling in the surf – and here Taylor is physically splendid, kneeling in the sand, the phosphorescent sea running through her thighs – is intensely disturbing. 'Hungry young people' do indeed gravitate towards this apparition (it could be by Botticelli), and yet there is a sort of confusion, a skirmish, as Sebastian (whom we never see clearly) interposes himself and is then pursued, away from the beach and up into the hills. We are meant to believe he is there eaten alive by 'savage, devouring birds'. A cannibalistic orgy is implied. No wonder Taylor's character needs to be placed in 'a custodial home for the insane', as anyone would flip after experiencing what she went through: 'suddenly, last summer, Cathy knew she was being used for evil.'

The paradox is that Taylor's character is the only sane one in the film. Hepburn, with her downturned mouth and white mask-like shrivelled features, is like someone who is already dead, Ernest Thesiger, say, or Peter Cushing. She wears white robes and starched gowns with high collars and veils – she is a construction. All she wants, to protect the family name, is that Catherine is lobotomised: 'This operation of yours,' she asks Clift, 'does it really work? The sharp knife in the mind to kill the devil in the soul.' She promises to donate a few million to the hospital, if this order is carried out – and the venal medical authorities are keen to put ethics aside and accept the loot. Catherine's mother – Mercedes McCambridge, wandering in from Reata – is also happy to consent to her daughter's enforced psycho-surgery, if this will ensure a bigger eventual legacy for her other child, Gary Raymond. It gets to be quite a thriller. Who can Taylor trust? Who will save her? What is the extent of Cukrowicz's guilty conscience? 'You're very like him, Doctor,' says Violet, imagining Sebastian's reaction, trying to flatter, though the impression is more that it is Hepburn herself who is the one dangerously detecting the homosexual strain in Clift. 'He would have been charmed by you,' she adds meaningfully.

Taylor's Catherine is watched, and wrongly accused. There's a nightmare sequence where she is pursued through the asylum, groped by the inmates – another day's pay for Rita Webb. Under sedation, groggy on the bed, rolling her sleeve up for the injections without having to be asked, Taylor is convincingly gripped by hysteria and fear: 'I lose all track of time, with all these shots.' Catherine isn't mad – she is maddened. By the end, Violet is directly blaming her for Sebastian's murder, like Big Mama blaming Maggie for failing to arouse Brick: 'Sebastian was famished for blondes. Fed up with the dark ones.' Will Taylor have to go on Dr Cukrowicz's operating slab because of the colour of her hair? How did anyone ever believe lobotomies were humane, beneficial procedures? It fits perfectly, however, and Taylor fits perfectly, into this boiling-over atmosphere of sexual frenzy that Tennessee Williams always cooked up, which is stronger for remaining elliptical, not fully spelt out, represented only by that sinister jungle garden, the giant leaves, haunted houses, tropical claustrophobia – which Burton will endure in *The Night of the Iguana*, which Burton and Taylor combined will explore in *Boom!* (I have heard that Burton was considered for the role of Dr Cukrowicz: interesting if true.) Taylor clearly made much use of Williams' work, was drawn to it, and so what was it that appealed? That his women are actually men? That the vampishness, madness and disease are metaphors for delinquency? Hepburn, too, grasped this about the playwright's work, praising it for being 'brilliant and full of poetry', but she also wanted Mankiewicz, the director, to tone down the script, to keep it from being 'cheap and sensational' – though, to my mind, these are the very qualities that Taylor, through some alchemical means, always makes rich and absorbing. Taylor, I think, was like Maria Callas. She played over-wrought characters, but it's a mistake to say she was tarnished by camp. There's an underlying seriousness, not frivolity. I therefore disagree with Hepburn, when she said of Taylor, in *Suddenly, Last Summer*, that she was 'posing unnecessarily. It was simply vulgar.' Taylor always took lust, desire, betrayal and jealousy as her ruling principles – and they are destructive principles. You can't really live with them on a regular daily basis. They belong only in opera (or soap opera). It is pulverising – and Hepburn's criticism, despite her repeated qualifications ('I think she is a brilliant actress, truly brilliant. Especially with the Williams stuff. Look at her . . . as Maggie the Cat') reveals a lot about the difference between them as artists. They were both big stars, forthright and

ferocious women, very sure of themselves. There are plenty of superficial similarities – men in common (Louis B. Mayer, Howard Hughes,
George Cukor, John Huston, Spencer Tracy); attitudes towards the
manly men they needed and respected ('Did he leave because he was
bored or did he leave because he couldn't bear to say goodbye? The
eternal question' – Hepburn on Tracy, but it could be Taylor on
Burton); they each played Katherina in *The Taming of the Shrew*; they
were Cleopatra; they were in *Little Women*, though not the same version. But where Hepburn was thin, clipped, nipped, darting and
acidulous, and as serpentine as a swan's neck, Taylor was fleshly, over-
flowing, sloppy. Hepburn suggested an austere sexuality, a puritanical
East Coast frugality. You can't picture her splashing out. (When Sidney
Poitier comes to dinner it will be a spare repast.) Her clenched voice
reaches us as if through a cloud, a brittle far-off warble. Her laughter is
never carefree – a puzzled frown is never distant. She has pink-rimmed
eyes, glass-lidded eyes. Her face was like a lighted candle, a taper. How
raucous and open Taylor is by contrast, how wild – a conflagration of a
person, a forest fire. (We realise why the gangs were provoked by
Taylor's Catherine in ways they weren't by Hepburn's Violet.) They
were regal and assertive, confident, in different ways. Yet they were
equally as tremendously aware of themselves, of the dash they were
cutting. They were women familiar with being photographed, and possessed overwhelming vanity. What they chiefly had in common is
determination: nothing will stop them. A remark Hepburn made,
whilst making *The African Queen*, could equally have been Taylor's
motto: 'Live dangerously. There's a lot to be said for sinning ... If you
obey all the rules you miss all the fun.'

* * *

It's strange, all these films where Taylor is rejected by men, yet her
reputation, as an actress now in her prime, was, as Jack Warner said,
'She can play herself and that's about it. She's at her best when the

plot revolves around sex.' If we ignore the dismissiveness of the tone, in fact Warner was correct. The point I'd emphasise is, though she was quick to sulk and smart – the day after Dean's death she went into hospital with stomach cramps, called Stevens 'a callous bastard!', and had herself assigned a wheelchair, crying when she tried to walk: nevertheless, she could still skip after Rock Hudson ('Hey, wait for me!') – and despite always being hours late at the studio, blaming her tardiness on nervous exhaustion and racing heartbeats: by playing herself, the child actress succeeded by the young woman, the mature lady, the scold and eventually the old trout, Taylor (it is possible to witness her growing up), had limitless material to hand, and what the camera records are her states of consciousness, her inner world. Burton knew this. In his diary for 30 January 1972, he said he'd been watching *X, Y & Zee*, yet again, and, 'I was still fascinated . . . There are always little subtleties in E's performance to be discovered anew.' I once spent many years writing about Peter Sellers, who was an impressionable blankness. I studied Laurence Olivier, a monster of egotism, who despite the opulence of his acting was similarly hollow, and like Sellers a master of mistaken identities, giddy deceptions, camouflage. Or then there was Charles Hawtrey, who seemed to come from a fantastic realm, of unicorns and the phoenix. And Anthony Burgess, who wrote millions of words to conceal the fact he was not any good as a writer (he was a carnivalesque showman, a role being assumed by Manchester schoolteacher, John Wilson). None of these was warm, enveloping. They had no sense of any real textured self to fall back on. They were cold personalities. Taylor, by contrast, was never a cold actress. I think of her as a stream of sparks, a scatter of ash, a hearth glowing with coals – as Tolstoy says of Anna Karenina (which would have been a good part for her): 'Her face shone with a vivid glow, but not a joyous glow – it resembled the terrible glow of a conflagration on a dark night.'

And, of course, she made any plot revolve around sex – what else can risk, delay, complication and rapture, which shrivels away into disappointment, bringing pain, loss and grief, i.e. the rudiments of any narrative, possibly have to do with? If the smell of soap and scent, as it were, in Taylor's earliest films, culminated in her being pummelled by Nicky Hilton, her response, when making *Ivanhoe* in England, in 1952, was to get quickly married to a chivalrous Englishman, who could have stepped from the pages of Walter Scott. Her engagement to Michael Wilding was announced on 14 February 1952 and the civil ceremony was conducted at Caxton Hall, seven days later. 'It must be those huge breasts of hers,' said Marlene Dietrich. 'Mike likes them to dangle in his face.' Wilding, said Taylor, 'represented tranquillity, security, maturity,' and these qualities soon irritated her enormously. 'She sought me out for comfort,' said Guilaroff, to divulge to him how Wilding was a flop. Indeed, Wilding is not only Taylor's forgotten husband, he is forgotten as an actor. Within a few years, Taylor had even forgotten about him herself. 'It's very difficult for me to remember,' she said in 1964, 'what it was like to be married to Michael Wilding.' She thought of him as 'an island, an oasis', particularly after the volatility of Nicky – yet all that affability scarcely registered. His calmness ('he restored all sanity') came to feel like indolence – an English complacency (and which is decidedly not a Welsh, or Celtic, trait, either: we are busy, irritable, fly), which can come across, did to Taylor, as a person pretending to be helpless. Wilding was the sort of chap who wore a yachting cap, particularly inland.

It is always held that the husband of Taylor's whom Burton most resembled was Mike Todd, who was thoroughly thuggish and thrustingly masculine and pugnacious. I disagree, Burton was like Wilding, for whom acting was a means of infiltrating high society. Not that Wilding, born in Leigh-on-Sea in 1912 into a family of bishops and ambassadors, was exactly ever in proximity to the South Welsh coalfields – but there is the same sense of the performing arts as a way of escape. Wilding was urbane and spruce. In his films, *Piccadilly Incident* (1946), *The Courtneys of Curzon Street* (1947), *Spring in Park*

Lane (1948), amongst them, he is always going in and out of Mayfair front doors with Anna Neagle. Smiling, dashing, charming – if somewhat floaty (John Le Mesurier is a later example of the type) – jollity must always supplant torment. In Wilding's films, which are about romances during bombing raids, how to manage during the blitz, how to cope with class divisions and how to behave with servants, and so forth, though there's nothing to suggest deep, churning emotion, there's nevertheless the air, if not of comedy, then of irony, even whimsy. English virtues, to be sure – was Taylor too American by now to appreciate these? The valet's slight shrug, the poetic properties of a suitor's restraint . . .

Wilding wanted to be a painter, and didn't have much to say for theatricality. 'I hate acting and I hate actresses,' he'd said to Taylor when they met – music to her ears, as she was already threatening to pack it in. ('Husband, home and children are purpose enough in any woman's life,' she told the press. 'If she does them well' – and did she believe she did them well, I wonder?) Wilding was an art student in Bruges, 'a city full of beautiful girls who seemed to have no difficulty understanding me in any language,' whey-hey, and having been rejected as unfit by the military (owing to his epilepsy), instead of war service he was recruited by Michael Balcon and Herbert Wilcox to work at Ealing, and they encouraged him to be an actor, in all those romantic thrillers. Wilding was the typical English gentleman, shy and distant in manner – David Niven made an international success of the formula, though Scottish and though he had more glint. The actor who 'has haunted me like a spectre down the years' was Rex Harrison. Wilding would have been good as Professor Higgins; he'd have been good in *The Ghost and Mrs Muir*, which is about the spectre who haunts Gene Tierney down the years.

Wilding met Taylor when he was making *Trent's Last Case*, which was released on 29 October 1952. Orson Welles, who had a cameo as Sigsbee Manderson, another of his megalomaniacs with a putty nose, also had another encounter with a sexually provocative Taylor when, as during *Jane Eyre*, she treated the studio canteen as a catwalk, walking the length of the room to find the salt cellar, 'wiggling her hips,' remembered Wilding. 'Then she'd wiggle her way back.' Technically too old to be Lolita now, nevertheless, 'That girl didn't ought to do that,' grumbled Welles. 'Upsets the digestion.' Continuing with the theme of food, with dyspepsia, and with Taylor wanting to persist in being tempting, teasing, Wilding suddenly heard her say, 'Why don't you invite me out to dinner tonight?' He found her 'a seething mass of feminine wiles', which is everything a man wants in many ways, but it is not everything a man needs. Wilding escorted Taylor to the plane back to New York, after the completion of her scenes in *Ivanhoe*, on 7 October 1951. She was also required in America to publicise *A Place in the Sun*, released two months previously. Taylor attempted to use the separation to her advantage, angling for a proposal of marriage, accusing Wilding of shilly-shallying when he demurred. In a way, as Stewart Granger said, Wilding was aware (as Burton would be likewise) of careerist advantages. 'Michael thought Elizabeth's stardom would rub off on him somehow.' Finally, he might be able to compete with Niven and Rex. On the other hand, though she was *Elizabeth Taylor*, she was twenty years his junior, and there's something slightly paedo about the way Wilding described the way 'I kissed her very thoroughly' on their initial date. 'Am I doing the right thing, Herbert?' he asked Wilcox, when the engagement was settled – 1952 was a Leap Year. Taylor had popped the question. 'Am I doing the right thing?' Wilcox thought not. This marriage, he confided to Anna Neagle, was 'sad, unnecessary, tragic,' though that didn't stop three thousand fans gathering outside Caxton Hall to watch. 'This wedding was supposed to be entirely private,' said a MGM spokesperson disingenuously. Helen Rose once more designed the bridal outfit, in grey wool ('My job was to keep Elizabeth Taylor looking like Elizabeth Taylor'). Anna Neagle was the bridesmaid. 'This is, for me, the beginning of a happy end,' said Taylor, still only a few days shy of twenty.

Wilding found himself presenting his wife with thirty necklaces, bracelets and earrings, set with diamonds, sapphires and emeralds. 'We're broke, but we don't care,' said Taylor with bravado – yet though she also said, 'Michael, I know you are all I need in the world,' she was soon to find him in private (and public) the last thing she wanted in the world, i.e. a person who expected her to be domesticated, grateful, knuckling under. A wiser course all along would have been for Wilding to have treated Taylor as an escort, somebody who'd expect to be bought drinks, have her cigarettes lit. Instead, Wilding had to buy her a whole house. Their first abode was a two-bedroom apartment, downstairs from Janet Leigh and Tony Curtis, at 1060 Wilshire Boulevard, Westwood – though this was seemingly not grand enough, even if the newly-weds never had as much money as they wanted or expected. 'I don't think Hollywood will understand you,' Wilcox had warned Wilding – and sure enough, the studios, believing Wilding might be the next Rudolph Valentino, mistaking the English reserve for Latin languor, could only think to put him into ridiculous costumes, e.g. Wilding is the Pharoah Akhnaton in *The Egyptian* (1954) and the Prince in Ruritanian garb in *The Glass Slipper* (1955), a Cinderella musical with Leslie Caron. Nevertheless, he took an advance on his MGM three-year contract to buy the marital home, 1771 Summitridge [sic] Drive, Beverly Hills, where he and Taylor, plus two poodles, three cats and a duck, lived from the summer of 1952 until July 1954. The cost was $75,000 and Taylor needed a further $40,000 for remodelling. There were six cars and a staff of five. The address is now (2022) a Substance Rehabilitation Facility, belonging to a charity called Southern California Recovery. Whilst here, Taylor gave birth, on 6 January 1953, to Michael Howard Wilding Junior. The studio put her on suspension during the pregnancy, and one rather wants to shake her by the hand for her calling them 'those shit-assed motherfucking faggot cocksuckers'.

Though the couple was, as Wilding said, 'always existing on borrowed money', they left the baby behind with its grandparents so they could gallivant to Rome, Copenhagen and Madrid. Home life was less halcyon. 'I just want to be with Michael and be his wife,' Taylor reiterated. 'He enjoys sitting at home, smoking his pipe, reading, painting . . .' Her real feelings were more in line with what she later said to Art Cohn, one of the victims in the Mike Todd plane crash: 'I was dead. Old at twenty-four.' The idea she'd be the little woman and have to keep house was anathema – and Wilding was astounded at her incompetence, which amounted to rebellion. 'Elizabeth has very little of the housewife in her,' he said incredulously. 'Forgets to order dinner.' She never got used to the habit of picking up grocery staples or having a look in the fridge. 'Elizabeth couldn't even fry eggs,' Wilding went on, aghast. 'She can't cook and shows no sign of trying to learn. She is untidy to the point of disaster. She makes a room look as if a tornado has hit it. It's a kind of disease with her.' Taylor also had no sense of time. 'Unpunctuality is a sort of disease with Liz.' All these infirmities, epidemics, infections. How like a testy Fifties husband Wilding sounds – Lucy and Desi would make their fortunes dramatising domestic mishaps and kitchen calamities, as would, in England, Terry Scott and June Whitfield, or sitcoms with Wendy Craig. But with Taylor it's not that she was falling short, failing to warm the slippers, heat the plates, put the laundry on or show herself disinclined to be a drudge. It's more she was shaping up as a destructive force, what Kingsley Amis would call a wrapped-up-in-herself female – and such was her capriciousness and her wilfulness, I wonder if, after all, there might not be something in the pre-feminist belief that your females, traditionally going in for superstition, religious mania, folklore, horoscopy and witchcraft, are generally less rational, more instinctive and immediate, than your males. Wilding certainly sensed this – that Taylor possessed superhuman powers of endurance and was a shrew never to be tamed: 'She is incapable of worry. To me, I think, the most important thing about Elizabeth is that she is very brave. Brave about actual physical things, afraid of no person and no animal, nor of any illness that may affect her as a person. And apart from physical dangers, illnesses and such, she is undismayed by life.' This is a perceptive tribute – though by being undismayed by life, Taylor, by being always tough, by not wanting to be shown any opposition, by being uninhibited, could be heartless – the other side of the way she could be charming.

'Very simple, very quiet,' Taylor said of the marriage. 'Two babies were born. We didn't do much.' Well, they must have done something – the second son, Christopher Edward Wilding, was delivered by Caesarean section on 27 February 1955. The family had moved the previous summer to 1375 Beverly Estates Drive, high in the Hollywood Hills, north of Beverly Hills, overlooking Laurel and Benedict Canyons. 'My crow's nest house,' Taylor called it, a Fifties gem constructed on a two-acre lot in 1953 by the architect George MacLean, who was appointed Christopher's godfather. There were intercoms, automated doors and curtains, and light-dimmers. There was an indoor waterfall and a mossy rock pool 'with trees growing out of it', as Taylor remembered it. The house, made of stone and glass, consisted of low-level sections connected by roofed walkways – one section contained three guest bedrooms; another was for the kitchen and servants' areas; lastly there were two main bedrooms and a carpeted living-room dominated by the fireplace. Through picture-windows were views of the Santa Monica mountains and the ocean. The decor was 'all the colours I loved, off-white, white, natural woods, stone, beigy marble'. Ferns and orchids abounded in a central courtyard. All very Fred and Wilma Flintstone, actually – and Taylor's final film, in which she is appropriately cartoonish and bulbous, was to be *The Flintstones* (1994), based on the Hanna-Barbera animated series. As Pearl Slaghoople, Fred's mother-in-law, Taylor says to Wilma, 'You could have married Eliot Firestone, the man who invented the wheel.' The yabba-dabba-doo home, which cost the Wildings $150,000, in 2022 was on the market and valued at $8,854,900. From the 'realtor's' particulars, it looks minimalist today, featureless, with palm trees and a crappy fountain or birdbath in the garden.

The poodles, spaniels, a golden retriever and (by now) four cats were in residence full-time (I find no more mentions of the duck – possibly eaten, as in *Peter and the Wolf*), but Wilding was often absent, drinking during the day in seedy bars. He'd discovered the Los Angeles specially reserved for Englishmen, as wonderfully described by Christopher Isherwood as a place possessing 'a kind of psychological dankness which smells of anxiety, overdrafts, uneasy lust, whisky, divorce and lies ... California is a tragic country, like every Promised Land.' Wilding's boon companions were Errol Flynn and John Garfield. 'You'd better watch out,' these old soaks warned him, 'or you'll be known as Mr Elizabeth Taylor.' He didn't really rise even to that level of attainment. Wilding sat there, 'watching my career turn to ashes'. Which it certainly did. Though there'd be brief appearances in *Waterloo* (1970) as Major-General Sir William Ponsonby, killed in slow-motion by French lancers, *Lady Caroline Lamb* (1972) as Lord Holland, and *Frankenstein: The True Story* (1973) as Sir Richard Fanshawe, in his later years, and after a stint as the 'front man' for Hugh French's agency, Chartwell Artists, 'meeting the [clients] and listening to their problems about their work and private lives', and after another failed marriage, Wilding was to be found working as the maître d' at a restaurant in Brighton called The Three Little Wilding Rooms. 'The whole ghastly thing embarrassed me ... I was profoundly grateful when eventually the place closed.' Meanwhile Taylor, who'd said once upon a time, 'When I'm married to Mike, I don't care if I stop acting,' was in constant demand: replacing Vivien Leigh in *Elephant Walk*, *Beau Brummell*, *The Last Time I Saw Paris*, *Giant*; the couple separated during the protracted shooting of *Raintree County*. 'The happiest years of our marriage,' Wilding told Taylor, 'were when you were dependent on me.' But how could he conceivably expect to keep her subservient, fettered? As Taylor understandably shot back, 'Oh Mike, I'm not your daughter. I'm your wife' – the end of the Lolita complex, and the start of the actress' reliance on railing and abuse. 'Our rows were one-sided,' wrote Wilding in his memoirs. 'Liz had a quick temper, but I am basically placid.' She hated to see him absorbed in *The Times* cross-word, snatched the paper and flung it on the fire. 'Of course we fight,' Taylor told the press. 'It would be garbage to say we didn't.'

Taylor treated Wilding shabbily – 'Liz cut off his balls' said Stewart Granger – and she was enraged when he refused to participate in her sado-masochistic games. 'Go on, hit me! Hit me, why don't you?' she demanded, according to Wilding's own aghast account. 'I've never gone in for hitting hysterical females,' he said, attempting to keep some dignity. 'If only you would,' she taunted. 'At least that would prove you are flesh and blood instead of a stuffed dummy.' His mild-ness, or restraint, earned her contempt. 'Why don't you give me a spanking, Michael? That's what my father would do.'

Was she remembering Francis? Or is it a generic older man's chas-tisement she's imagining? Thus far on screen she'd been taking orders from Nigel Bruce, Donald Crisp, Frank Morgan, William Powell, Spencer Tracy and Robert Taylor, plus Louis B. Mayer. I think Taylor was chiefly alluding to a taste for torment she'd experienced with Hilton, which formed the basis of what she feared and required, and which she could indulge fully when she met Mike Todd, whom she first saw in June 1956, during a cruise to Santa Barbara. Taylor and Wilding were also guests at a dinner Todd threw for Ed Murrow, and Todd immediately presented Taylor with jewels, roses, Impressionist paintings (borrowed from her father), and a Rolls-Royce Silver Cloud. He flew her to Chicago and Atlantic City for dirty weekends. 'They're two of a kind,' said Wilding resignedly. The Wild-ings separated in July 1956 ('We are in complete accord in making this amicable decision'); Taylor filed for divorce in Santa Monica on 14 November, citing 'extreme mental cruelty'. Taylor married Todd in Acapulco the following February. 'That terrible woman again,' said Marlene Dietrich, who saw Taylor as her rival as sexual empress. 'She ruined Michael Wilding's life and now she's going after Todd.'

* * *

Wilding remained pacific. 'I'm always available if she needs help in expediting any legalities.' He didn't account for Todd, who was hot-headed and thrived (said S.J. Perelman, who wrote the script for *Around the World in Eighty Days*) 'on turbulence'. Todd was fanatical, impatient, cocky, growling, snarling, snapping, prowling: he was like something coming after Sir Henry Baskerville on Grimpen Mire. His relationship with Taylor lasted 414 days, brief enough not for dis-illusion to set in. 'Mike was the greatest love I shall ever know,' Taylor said at the time. 'I shall never love anyone so much again.' I simply find him morbid. I imagine him baring his teeth and breathing heav-ily, his glistening pink tongue hanging out of a gaping black mouth. Todd's telephone calls were incessant. He inspected Taylor's sched-ules, expected to be granted final approval of her wardrobe, her shoes and hats – when she had difficulty choosing amongst a batch of fifty hats, Todd said, 'Oh, wrap up the whole fifty of them and send them to her hotel.' Taylor always fell for gestures like that. When *Raintree County* resumed, after Clift's car accident and plastic surgery, and Taylor departed for the location, in Danville, Kentucky, the phone was ringing the moment she set foot in her rented house. 'I didn't want you there one second before you talked to me,' said Todd down the line. Every day, when Taylor returned from work, there he'd be again: 'Shut-eye time for you! You've got a seven-a.m. call tomorrow morning . . . I know what time you break for lunch and I'll call you then, and I'll know when you wrap up the day's work, and I'll call you then.'

What would seem to any sensible outsider like control freakery – general and thorough interference (Taylor was presently twenty-four, Todd forty-seven) – Taylor interpreted as adoration. She was thrilled by this boldness. She yielded. Todd made her feel coquettish. He'd be doing his deals in Paris, London or New York, and the telephone never stopped jangling. 'Over those five weeks,' said Taylor, referring to her absence in the Blue Grass State, 'Mike Todd and I came really to know one another. I had never in all my life talked as I did with him.

There was nothing we did not discuss – ourselves, Broadway, Hollywood, food, people, travel, sex, everything ... I knew I had never met anyone with such integrity, honesty, and feeling.' Wasn't all this rather anonymous, though? The perfect being, at the end of a telephone – like a relationship conducted by correspondence, or someone in our own era conversing on the internet with a Thai bride. How could Taylor find the disembodied chatter appealing? Though she'd toy with the idea – all these toys: the toy wedding to Nicky Hilton; her toy aspirations – she'd not have wanted to be subsumed for long; for there to be somebody else deciding what's best for her; somebody else thinking they must stand up for her. 'I dress the way Mike wants. I wear my hair this way for Mike,' she said in a childlike way, as if describing a new game. She went on, 'I can't stop talking about marriage. It's because I understand it now. I know what it means.' You have to wonder. When did Taylor genuinely submit to anyone? When was she ever once utterly at a loss?

I always found Todd empty – hence his need for coarse bluster and pomposity. Look at *Around the World in Eighty Days*, his sole achievement, which won the Academy Award for Best Picture in 1956 (beating *Giant*): it is episodic, a flicker of famous faces, with nothing lasting long. (Todd was lucky in Niven; Cantinflas is a bore.) It is an Attention Deficit Hyperactivity Disorder movie. There's Sinatra at the piano, Dietrich singing in a saloon, Shirley MacLaine in brownface as Princess Aouda, Buster Keaton clipping tickets on a train. Richard Wattis and Patrick Cargill are unbilled. If it hadn't been the mid-twentieth century and cinema a profitable racket, Todd would have been prospecting for gold or drilling for oil, like James Dean's Jett Rink. He 'definitely belonged,' said Joe E. Lewis, the nightclub singer, 'on a runaway horse.' He was frantic, materialistic, an every-man-for-himself sort of person, and his marital plans with Taylor were a typical manic confusion. In January 1957, Todd had 'a battery of lawyers' working on Taylor's divorce from Wilding – in Mexico City, where the petition was denied. 'The public is against quick divorces and [re-]marriage,' said an official, whom Todd then called 'a fucking hillbilly son of a bitch' and wanted killed. Perhaps it was the altitude, as Mexico City is 7,200 feet above sea level. Another attempt was made in Acapulco, which succeeded – so the civil ceremony was held the very next day, 2 February, in Puerto Marques, at a villa belonging to Fernando Hernandez, a friend of the president, Miguel Aleman Valdes. The mayor of Acapulco officiated, and everything was conducted in Spanish, with bride and groom, guarded by troops from the Mexican army, having to say '*Sí!*' Cantinflas and Eddie Fisher were joint Best Men. Debbie Reynolds was the bridesmaid. It was all vulgar in the extreme – lorry after lorry bringing 15,000 white gladioli and bushels of orchids; crabs, lobsters, caviar; smoked ham and turkey; coconut halves filled with twenty-five cases of champagne. A firework display cost $100,000. I wonder how much it all cost to pull all the strings, shell out for the back-handers? The urgency? Taylor was three months pregnant with Elizabeth Frances, known as Liza – it was a pretence that the baby was born 'prematurely' on 6 August.

'I am the happiest, luckiest girl in the world,' Taylor averred. But what of poor old Wilding? Biographers have maintained he was very placable, flying down to Mexico 'on the Monday preceding the wedding,' to assist with legal formalities. 'My presence will simplify matters; I came here for one reason only, to sign my divorce papers. It's my divorce too, you know.' A slight peevish note there, I think. It is therefore mighty odd that in his own memoirs, Wilding mentions none of this – his narrative is quite different, anomalously different. Mexico and an Acapulco jaunt don't come into it. Instead, it came as a surprise to Wilding when, three days after 'a decree nisi was awarded to Liz by the Los Angeles County Court', he read in a newspaper that 'Liz and Mike Todd were married ... at the City Hall'. Wilding gasped to Joseph Cotten, 'I just don't believe it.' What has the ring of truth is his unwillingness to go and visit and pick up Michael Jr. and Christopher from wherever it was Taylor and Todd were living. 'I did not feel up to meeting face to face the man who had replaced me as Liz's husband.' Wilding was also correct to see the failure of his career and the failure of his marriage to Taylor as connected, were in fact the same thing.

* * *

'They're all just me,' Sid James said of his characters, 'just with different hats on.' The same might be argued of Taylor in performance, her temperament and achievement closely aligned and reflected back and forth in the cracked looking-glass, though she'd not have thanked you for making the observation. When Joseph Losey tried to get her to see the funny side of *Boom!* – 'This is a funny scene! It's the story of your life, so you ought to understand it,' i.e. 'it was a story about this woman who had eight husbands and so on,' Taylor's response was to take exception: 'I don't happen to think the story of my life is very funny!' Not from her own perspective perhaps ('My earliest memory is of pain' – as a toddler she'd grasped an electric fire, and everything went on from there) – but it is from mine. Taylor (and Burton) was a magnified being, a grotesque being, and everything had comic impetus – the dishevelment, the multitudinousness. To give a small example, on Sunday 14 February 1982 there was *The Night of a Hundred Stars* at Radio City Music Hall, held in aid of the Actors' Fund of America, which was building a retirement home in Englewood, New Jersey. Gina Lollobrigida said she was swamped by the crowds. 'What really happened,' said Peter Cook, 'is that she tripped over her own dress . . . Hardly anyone recognised her.' Larry Hagman was popular backstage because he'd brought a bottle of vodka along. James Cagney, who appeared on stage in a wheelchair, missed the cast party and 'supper ball' at the Hilton on Sixth Avenue because he'd been abandoned in a lift – a search party discovered him in the basement at four a.m. Taylor was in floods of tears. 'The worst thing that has ever happened to me in my life has just happened' – 'Elizabeth,' said Cook, 'knowing your life, that must be pretty bad.' Jane Russell had thrown an ashtray at her, 'for no apparent reason.' She, Russell, had to be sedated and taken to hospital. As the ashtray had ricocheted off Taylor's left breast, it's a miracle there weren't further mass casualties, a state of emergency declared.

The making of *Cleopatra* was farce – people bursting through lots of doors; *Who's Afraid of Virginia Woolf?* is Laurel and Hardy or Tom and Jerry; *The Taming of the Shrew* is humorous fisticuffs – though it is also fair to say high spirits were mostly used up in the long lunch breaks. It is a hungover film, the spilled drinks more or less on show. You can see this in the still photographs printed in the publicity booklet: the sheen of boozy sweat, the bad air, the screwed-up eyes, the panting and hesitation. Nor did Burton suit those costumes, the brocade codpieces and pheasant feathers insisted upon by Zeffirelli. He's like a man wearing fancy dress. He's not at ease in them – whereas with a bodice and arms akimbo, spitting straw from her mouth, Taylor romps happily, swinging those big hips. Despite the title, and the presence of jocose Peter Ustinov, *The Comedians*, paradoxically, is more thoroughly mournful – it's about Graham Greene's sense of sin – and Taylor's appearance as Helen of Troy, gliding through *Doctor Faustus*, whilst representing a pinnacle of the erotic ideal, manages to mock pride, covetousness, lust, anger, gluttony, envy and sloth by turning sins into nothing more than a deceptive dream. With each pose, Taylor seems to be saying, of her own majesty, 'Oh, come off it!'

In addition to Taylor's obvious absurdity and frivolity, running beneath the surface was always something bracing, a nature operating without pretension, because innocent of hypocrisy. Her marriages, spending sprees, travel, houses, hotel suites, fluffy clothes: it all seems improvised, in a rush, for the benefit of the public, her follies never hidden from us but almost insisted upon, like a parody of the glamour of Old Hollywood, where a star appeared only under klieg lights and glowed brightly, as for instance at the start of *A Star is Born* – the ferocious, sulphurous hissing and whooshing. As Taylor was to reminisce,

'Any carefree privacy had pretty much disappeared under the constant chaperoning, constant surveillance, constant work.' Spreads in *Photoplay* and *Movie Gems* were what counted, 'swimming-pool parties or let's-paint-your-fence parties', with everybody 'performing almost entirely for the camera'. Taylor was unique in deciding, 'Nobody was going to decide for me whom to date, what to wear, or put words in my mouth,' which is why, as a star, she's continuously present to us (there is latent humour) – from the little girl with trotting horses and panting dogs in the early films, all the way, say, to the hag in *Ash Wednesday*, in 1973, whom we watch undergoing a procedure at a plastic surgery clinic – the film begins with an elderly face, with pouches and wrinkles, which the surgeon slices and chops away at; the skin is given a chemical peel. Excess tissue is removed. The result of the operation is that the patient, hitherto cocooned, mummified, in bandages and cotton wool, is turned into Elizabeth Taylor, complete with furs and pearls, orange turbans and snoods, and a tomato-red trouser suit, designed by Edith Head. Alexandre de Paris does the hair. Taylor's companion at the hospital – a place so discreet, patients receive no flowers: no one is to know where you are – is Keith Baxter, who never did get to play Octavian in *Cleopatra*. He's a fashion photographer, an occupation popular in the period (Snowdon, Lichfield, Bailey), who says those who undergo nips and tucks have 'taken of the fountain of youth . . . We refuse to accept reality,' with its negativities, defeats, ailments. Taylor's excuse for undergoing the 'rest cure', with its stitches, bruising and injections, is that she wants to look as she did when she was first married – to Henry Fonda. His way of forgetting he's getting older is to demand a divorce and marry a girl younger than their daughter. Yet in this (neglected) film about being old and trying (forlornly) to be young, all I am reminded of is how Taylor's Barbara Sawyer is Taylor's Cleopatra – the thick pencil marks around the eyes, the imperious immobility, the way a rich person believes the ageing process can be arrested and reversed, withering overcome, or at least ignored, though the upshot of plastic surgery, of self-mutilation, is these people become freaks, who do not want to be seen in public with their grown-up children, as this is a giveaway about biological retrogression. 'You've got to be surgical,' says Baxter, extending the metaphor. 'Cut yourself off from the past.'

Did Taylor take this in? Disagree with it as a precept? Her character gazes at jewels in shop windows. She enjoys cream cakes. Some things cannot be altered. To what extent did Paramount expect audiences to recall the Ash Wednesday liturgy (Genesis 3: 19) when, at the beginning of Lent and a period of penance, the priest makes the sign of the cross with a smudge on the forehead and tells the congregation, 'Remember, that dust thou art, and unto dust shalt thou return'? That's to say, the title *Ash Wednesday* points to a satire on disgusting vanity. And of course, there's Eliot's poem of 1930, *Ash-Wednesday*, with its hyphen, which is about a spiritual search for something, I think faith, balance, harmony, one of those. Fonda anyway ignores his wife's rejuvenation, resenting Barbara's attentions, the gifts and drinks. 'We can't live on memories,' he says. But we can; we do. It's how we enter into another person's existence, living on our recollections of them, which are carried in the mind, come and go in the human consciousness, surfacing like treasures long hidden, pulled from a lake. For regarding Taylor's queens, damsels, daughters, tarts and matriarchs; her angels and demons; her resilient shrieking and palpitations; and all the *sheer stuff* printed by the newspapermen and the pictures taken by the cameramen who always accompanied her – where all of that welter (and outlandishness) has no diminution is as after-images in my memory, which is outside time, follows its own logic. 'To me,' said Picasso, 'there is no past and future in art. If a work of art cannot live always in the present it must not be considered at all.' Which is more or less true, and not unlike, I now see, the accumulation of impressions in those verses of T.S. Eliot: dry rocks, deserts, empty rose gardens, emblems of sterility, austerity, which are sent packing, superseded, by the poet's sudden acceptance of the fruit of the gourd, hawthorn blossom, figs, juniper trees, and other ideas (and ideals) of beauty and fertility, particularly all the symbols of water – flowing streams, bubbling springs, fountains, 'and the spirit of the river, spirit of the sea', which refresh the wasteland. In *Ash-Wednesday*, Eliot dramatises his own psychic struggles – and that's no more than Taylor, put here on this planet to be stared at, leered at, ever did, and particularly so in *The Girl Who Had Everything*, released on 27 March 1953, which is graphic about her need for different breeds of men.

It is hard to find. My disc is in Spanish, *La Chica Que Lo Tenía Todo*. In any language what you'll notice is the way Richard Thorpe, who'd directed Taylor in *Ivanhoe*, frequently immerses Taylor in water. Twenty-one years of age here, Taylor's Jean Latimer climbs in and out of swimming pools, emerges from the shiny water, shakes water from her hair. In lots of Helen Rose outfits, she's a water-creature, posing by ornamental ponds in scallop-shaped bras and bathing costumes, in frocks with elaborate lacy sleeves, like fins or fish scales. The smell of chlorine or wet grass – something saline – is suggested. It is black and white, but Taylor appears to scamper through purple leaves. The lawn and terrace are a greenish pewter. It is paradise, with dancing in expensive restaurants, sojourns in hotel suites with plenty of cut flowers in silver vases, though the setting is officially Kentucky. The house, where Jean lives with her widowed father, Steve, played by William Powell, a criminal defence attorney, has hewn rock walls and large reception spaces, decorated with statuettes of horses. (The house could be the Wildings' – I have seen a photograph of Wilding visiting the set, Taylor perched on his knee – husband and wife looking amused whilst Powell is launched on some story.)

Taylor's character has everything, as Taylor had everything. The conceit is that Jean is the spoilt and motherless only child ('It has been tough since Nancy died'), whose perfect life needs stirring up – so she exchanges her nice fiancé, Gig Young's Vance Court, for a Latin American hoodlum, Victor Raimondi, played with a Chico Marx accent by Fernando Lamas. Complicating matters, though simplifying them as regards getting a plot off the ground, is the fact Raimondi is Steve's client – and Steve knows what an ugly customer he is, ordering mob killings, bullying subordinates. The implication, nevertheless, is Taylor's Jean will now be receiving superior sex. At a horse auction, and when alone with Raimondi in the mansion he handily rents locally, Taylor is so aroused she throbs. There are a number of clinches, prompting a fast fade. Raimondi's badness is erotically compelling. The girl's deeper nature has been aroused – and what's notable is Jean is not misled by her new partner. She knows exactly what's on offer. When Raimondi suggests Jean drops by right now for a swim, Taylor gets a lot into the line, 'Now has always been my favourite time.' She's not a guileless blank, as regards the physical side of things.

Taylor is the only female to be seen in the entire film, perhaps in the entirety of Kentucky, with its racetrack fraternity, visiting racketeers, lawyers. (As with *Ivanhoe*, it's more laying siege: men determined to get what they want through brute force.) What a great comic actor Powell was, his delivery and bearing like Burt Lancaster, his posture and facial expressions reminiscent of Groucho Marx. He tilts himself backwards to look at people, to get them into focus, overdoing it occasionally as Steve is always fixing drinks at his well-stocked private bar, dropping ice cubes and olives into tumblers. In *Life with Father*, Taylor was, I think, Powell's niece, visiting from out-of-town. Here, though the daughter, she calls him not father but by his first name, Steve this, Steve that, and their familiarity, almost their equality, is both strikingly hip and modern and quaintly ancient: Powell and Taylor are Caesar and Cleopatra. Powell, in particular, has a wry knowledge-ability. He sees there's nothing to be gained from stopping Taylor's kittenish Jean insisting on her freedom, going to New York without his blessing to be with Raimondi. Even when she was a child, he was fully aware of 'the kind of girl she was getting to be' – and perhaps he's to be blamed for how forthright Jean has turned out, as he was seldom around: when she had (like Taylor in real life) 'that emergency operation on her ear', Steve was in Washington working on an important case. Whatever the reason, it's always been up to her – as it was for Taylor – to decide whether things are suitable or not suitable.

Powell, as in *My Man Godfrey* and *Life with Father*, imbues his character with assurance, with probity. He grasps at once that his daughter is wary of entrapment, that her experiment with desire with Raimondi, whom Steve is hired to defend before a congressional committee, is perhaps a necessity, when the alternative is the complacent, masculine, stifling little world of Gig Young's Vance. Powell can see that for Taylor – or Steve can see that for Jean, as Caesar saw for Cleopatra – abjection and delinquency are something she wants to experience, luxuriate in. It will do her good to taste forbidden things. Indeed, the Gig Young character – what he promises Jean is abhorrent, the uxorial cage, where he'll expect honour and obedience. Look at this exchange: it is as emotionally bruising as Raimondi's slappings. Vance says he'll always take care of her, and Taylor's character says, 'Will I marry you? I'm not ready to settle down.' Vance replies, 'Settling down could be a lot of fun,' over which Jean mutters, 'Let's face it, Vance, running a house, worrying about the meals and kids . . .' He then says, 'Be too dull and humdrum for you' – 'Could be' – 'But that's living, Jean. There's no substitute for it. No good one, anyway.' And Jean says, though it's Taylor's attitude too, 'Maybe, but if I let you pressure me into it, it would only be a big mistake.' Vance ends with a slight threat: 'But let's get one thing straight. I'm not going to stand by while you play the field.' He doesn't want to see how marriage can mean the loss of identity. It is a thoroughly adult scene, not in the least histrionic – one of Taylor's best. Dialogue is overlapped, the car radio is playing – music for *The Girl Who Had Everything*, incidentally, was provided by André Previn and it has the urgency and panic of the emotions: jazzy and clashing orchestral noises, with howling saxophones and trumpets; classical and decorous, and disruptive, yearning – the music pulling in two directions. As Taylor was pulled in two directions – for what is love meant to deliver? In this scene, her lovely face looks as if it is receiving blows, as what's on offer, the restrictions of conventional married life, are more horrible than life on the dangerous edge of things with a Bolivian mobster – and nor is it hard to see the crude autobiographical allegory: Vance is Michael Wilding, Raimondi is Michael Todd. 'Every time you look up, I'll be there,' says Raimondi to Jean, which is exactly the sort of extravagant promise Todd made to Taylor, phoning her incessantly, plying her with gifts and tributes. There's a scene in the film where Jean is given a chestnut colt by Raimondi – horses and stallions always having an erotic frisson where Taylor was concerned – and when Vance protests at the gall, the inexpedience, the vulgar inappropriateness, of such a grand gesture, Jean puts him down as Taylor did Wilding: 'What are you doing? *Comparing?*' Her contempt is mortifying.

In the film, Raimondi is conveniently shot dead by a rival gang at a traffic light – not quite a premonition of Todd's dramatic demise in the plane crash, but similarly as sudden. Jean 'comes to her senses' and reconciles with Vance, as Taylor never did with Wilding, who was soon past and gone, though perhaps Vance also prefigures Eddie Fisher. Vance, in any event, was 'right about Raimondi all along' – but Taylor's Jean was right about Raimondi all along: there was something arousing, vital, about his gambling, sporting pursuits, male drives, his 'illegal racing wire barbarism'. Fairness and niceness aren't life's chief essentials. That the arrogance echoed Todd's is no wild conjecture, as the screenplay for *The Girl Who Had Everything* was by Art Cohn, Todd's associate and biographer, who went down in flames with his master in *The Liz*, five years later, when love was turned into death. Gig Young met a sticky end too. He appeared with Wilding in *Torch Song* (1953), in which they vied for the affection of Joan Crawford. He lost his role in *Blazing Saddles* owing to alcoholism, and in 1978, in Apartment 1BB of The Osborne, Manhattan, he shot dead his (fifth) wife, Kim Schmidt, and then killed himself.

* * *

The relationship with Todd was savage. 'Out of my perversity,' said Taylor, 'I'd try to drive Mike mad. I'd be late, I'd love it when he would lose his temper and dominate me. I'd start to purr because he'd won' – yet didn't it mean she'd won? Taylor's mother had told *The Ladies' Home Journal* in 1954 that, as a child, Taylor had enjoyed boxing with her brother, Howard: 'She would light into him with all of her strength and would be furious if he didn't give her a good wallop back. "Harder, harder! Hit me harder, Howard!" Is it these pugilistic nursery games she was re-enacting? In public Todd and Taylor would be pushing, shoving, and slapping each other across the chops. Todd, a ghastly circus huckster, was continually pursued by lawsuits and criminal bankruptcy threats. He chewed twenty Cuban cigars a day. 'Made Especially For Mike Todd' was embossed on the band, which he neglected to remove. He was something of a nineteenth-century one-man Wild West extravaganza, switching on the charm. Keen to display charisma and drive, slamming doors, slamming into people, barking into five telephones simultaneously, he craved excitement and was never far from brutality. Was he a murderer, too? His first wife, Bertha Freshman Todd, died 'accidentally' in 1946, as a result of a 'self-inflicted stab wound', sustained when chasing Todd with a kitchen knife. Her jewels and furs went missing and were never recovered. Joan Blondell, wife number two, supported Todd at the inquest, where it was established Bertha had been 'slicing an orange', so he gambled away $3 million of her savings. When Joan complained, he dangled her by the ankles out of a sixteenth-floor window. Joan was left with a broken arm, a nervous breakdown, and nothing in the bank. Ever thus, 'Mike's courtship hit me like a tornado,' gasped Taylor. His proposal was novel: 'From now on, you'll fuck nobody but me.'

They recorded their grapples on a reel-to-reel tape recorder – the moaning and groaning; the bedspring sonatas – and Todd found it amusing to present a spool to Lord Beaverbrook, when they went aboard his yacht. Nonetheless, it was Taylor who fell over on deck and had to be flown to the Harkness Pavilion at Columbia-Presbyterian Hospital, New York, where her ruptured spinal discs were operated on. This didn't make the violence abate. Eddie Fisher, Todd's best friend, saw Todd knock Taylor to the floor at dinner. 'He really belted her. Elizabeth screamed, walloped him right back ... Mike dragged her by the hair, while she was kicking and scratching him.' Fisher concluded, 'She liked to be roughed up.' Debbie Reynolds, who also witnessed the ugliness, says Todd would be chewing on his food gorilla-fashion, and he'd look at Taylor and say, or threaten, 'I'd like to fuck you as soon as I finish this.'

This was not going to end well, though it did end. On 21 March 1958, with Taylor remaining in Los Angeles to shoot *Cat on a Hot Tin Roof*, Todd took off with Art Cohn in his private plane from Burbank for a Showman of the Year banquet at the Friars Club, New York. He crashed in New Mexico, the twin engines of the Lockheed Lodestar paralysed by what in the accident report was called 'surface ice accretion'. Todd was burned to a crisp, a cinder, identifiable only by his wedding ring. I have before me the Civil Aeronautics Board Aircraft Accident Report, File Number 2-0038, bearing the date 13 April 1959 and released to concerned parties on 17 April 1959. The document confirms the Lockheed Lodestar, model 18-56, serial number 2312, took off at 10.41 p.m. Pacific Time, on the Friday. The initial destination was Tulsa, Oklahoma. Rain was falling steadily. The pilot, William Stebbins Verner, forty-two, who'd spent 7,680 hours in the air, and the co-pilot, Thomas Barclay, thirty-six, who'd clocked up 4,500 hours, for some reason did not seek a briefing from the United States Weather Bureau forecasters 'the evening of March 21' and 'all evidence indicates that the flight would have encountered extensive cloudiness, numerous shower areas, and moderate icing in the clouds, and precipitation over 10,000 feet'. On the planned route, the freezing-level was 8,000 feet, with 'moderate-to-severe turbulence' expected at 5,000 feet and above.

Two hours after leaving Burbank, at 1.55 a.m. Mountain Time, to get above the storm front, Verner requested permission from Air Traffic Control at Winslow, Arizona, to ascend from the flight's assigned altitude of 11,000 feet to 13,000 feet. As the plane began to shake and vibrate, at 2.23 a.m. the pilot informed Air Traffic Control at Zuni, New Mexico, about the ice, which had seized up the instruments and air-speed indicators. The right engine rod and propellor failed. 'Complete loss of control followed and the aircraft struck the ground in a very steep angle of descent.' At 2.40 a.m., an Air Force B-36 reported seeing an intense explosion in a valley of the Cibola National Forest, twelve miles south-west of Grants, New Mexico, which lay at an elevation of 7,200 feet above sea level. The airway beacon at Grants, where 'it was raining when the flight passed overhead at 0230', had noted the considerable 'cloud bank to the west'.

It wasn't the weather, the ice, the clouds, however – the accident occurred because Todd had had two extra fuel tanks installed, housed in the baggage compartment and filled to capacity. The maximum certificated take-off weight for a Lockheed Lodestar was 18,605 lbs. Todd's plane was 20,757 lbs, i.e. at least 2,152 lbs in excess. 'The pilot ordered and supervised the full fuelling of the aircraft; it is inconceivable that he was not aware of the overloaded condition.' Not only that, 'no waiver of the certification weight limits was issued'. As, therefore, 'there is evidence of the aircraft being considerably over its maximum allowable weight at departure', when the plane, rendered even heavier by the residual ice accretion, tried to climb that additional 2,000 feet, it simply stalled: 'There is no doubt that control was lost as evidenced by impact markings on the ground.' If Todd had been reading, he'd have lost his place.

The four bodies, what was left of them, teeth and dentures mainly, were taken to Albuquerque. Taylor was hysterical, ran out into Schuyler Road screaming, and was comforted by Sidney Guilaroff, Irene Sharaff and Edith Head. How many other people would think to summon hairstylists and costume designers to be at their side in their hour of need? 'There was noise and confusion everywhere,' said Richard Brooks. Others who turned up to share the bad news: Debbie Reynolds, who looked after the children, Michael Wilding, Kurt Frings, even Greta Garbo, who said, 'Be brave!' Were the Marx Brothers still detained? Eva Marie Saint was there, to witness a Lucia di Lammermoor wraith. Taylor 'appeared halfway down the stairway but couldn't face any of us. She turned around and went back upstairs to her room. It was such a sad moment for all of us.' Paul Newman joined the queue on the landing, but because he'd complained about Taylor's unpunctuality on the set of *Cat on a Hot Tin Roof*, he was not to find favour: 'Get the fuck out of here!' snarled Taylor when she caught sight of him. 'I just put my tail between my legs and silently left in a state of disarray,' said Newman. Taylor wailed so much, her doctor, Rex Kennamer, said she should have her tonsils out. 'Nobody will ever know how much I loved him,' Taylor kept saying. The best account of the gaudy melodrama is found in a letter Marlene Dietrich wrote to Noël Coward on 24 March – which was clever, as Todd was not interred in the Waldheim Cemetery, Forest Park, Illinois, until 25 March:

Liz went to the funeral with a party of six. Her doctor, her dressmaker, hairdresser etc. The intimate 'family circle' the family wanted! And Mike would have been furious that I wasn't invited. So I sit here and read in the papers how hysterical she was and I think of the time Jimmy Dean died and she went hysterical and behaved like a bereaved wife right in front of our Michael [Wilding] – and then when Monty Clift had the accident leaving her house, again she went hysterical and behaved in the same way. Now it is real and I wonder if she can tell the difference?

Whilst I share Dietrich's scepticism about Taylor's histrionic strain, her abandoned woman pose, with her hair a shaggy mess, though her behaviour could be disproportionate, and inappropriate, it was not manufactured. As Stewart Granger, another person who couldn't stand her, sneered, Taylor was always 'searching for publicity, searching to be at the centre of everything', and if she was upset, she was upset on a titanic scale, like the mutinous winds that between the green sea and the azured vault set roaring war, as a magician once said. Despite what Granger, and Dietrich, maintained, however, there was something oddly impersonal, something earnest and absolute, about the states Taylor got herself into, because what counted was the immediate impression. Taylor did not have a reflective or mystical turn of mind. Nothing was planned. She couldn't arrange how she felt, control her distress or indignation. High anxiety and terror were as empirically true, as inhabited, as a high fever – a tingling of the blood cells, a pink flushing, as we can see on display in *Raintree County*, which was released in 1957. It was whilst making this film that Clift, leaving Taylor's house in a state of inebriation, crashed his car into a tree or lamp post, smashed his jaw (which had to be wired back together in three places), perforated his eardrum, fractured four ribs and lacerated his face acutely. Actually, the accident has been variously described – did it occur on 12 May, 13 May or 14 May 1956? Sources differ – some place Rock Hudson at the scene. Was the car, a Chevrolet Bel Air Sedan, about to plunge over a precipice into a ravine or wrapped around a telegraph pole? Numerous biographers, wishing to lend stage effects, swathe the crag with billowing fog. Taylor, scurrying to the scene, shoved her hand in Clift's mouth so he could breathe and fished out broken teeth from his windpipe, one of which she later had mounted on a ring. Or so I have heard. Had she used a pebble to smash the car window, or did she simply pull open the back door and climb right into the wreckage, 'cradling Monty's smashed face in her lap, wiping away the blood with the sleeve of her dress', in Wildings' words? In Taylor's words, Clift 'was bleeding from the head so much that it looked like his face had been halved ... There was a tooth hanging on his lip by a few shreds of flesh, and he asked me to pull it off because it was cutting his tongue.' No mention of incipient asphyxia or dental debris in the pharynx. Shooting was suspended on *Raintree County* for nine weeks.

* * *

It is *Giant*, in reverse. How parochial the big country actually is, when examined from the perspective of Raintree County, Indiana. The district is populated by citizens who believe themselves to be 'people with roots', and there aren't any cowboys anymore. These are men and women who instead want to be 'accomplished', i.e. suburban. Attire is elegant – ballgowns, trimmed hats, skirts with huge hoops, snowy white dresses and matching parasols. Furniture has been imported from France. There are lawns and carriages. Lee Marvin, as Flash Perkins, may say of himself 'I'm half-bull and half-alligator', and though he goes in for drinking bouts, he's not Oliver Reed. Eva Marie Saint is, as always, always sexy, always prim, the sweet blonde who is there to be hurt – in *The Sandpiper*, eight years later, Taylor will again poach Eva's man, the frustrated schoolmaster played by Burton. Her man on this occasion is Clift's John Wickliff Shawnessey, who perhaps because of that automobile accident is halting, self-conscious, furtive, and he totters about like Stan Laurel. We meet these young people as they graduate from college – their professor, Jerusalem Webster Stiles, is an affected, loquacious show-off played by Nigel Patrick. They have a picnic in a woodland – and America is a place of classical pastoral beauty; lakes, rivers, mossy stone walls. Clift, as the class valedictorian, even wears a cluster of oak leaves in his hair. He also walks in a field with a scythe, like a figure in a frieze.

When Taylor turns up, a visitor from New Orleans, paradise becomes a place she can ruin. Though filmed on location, as with those movies Taylor made as a child, these are not the colours of nature, of reality – bilious orange skies, caramel and straw-toned interiors. We first see Taylor's Susanna Drake when she is posing as a photographer's model. Clutching a bunch of white lilies, and wearing a billowing mauve satin frock, this 'charming ambassadress from the land of mint and magnolia', as the effete Stiles describes her, is soon romping in the foliage with Clift and she becomes instantaneously pregnant. This is soon enough revealed as a phantom pregnancy, a ruse, but by now Taylor and Clift are honeymooning on a paddle steamer and the sunset is as red and black as a furnace. Little bells tinkle on the soundtrack, and Taylor's Susanna leaves the audience in no doubt that she is insane – she rants about the 'seditious doctrine of abolition', claims her mother burned down the plantation mansion when her father's black mistress was revealed, and smashes her collection of porcelain dolls against a wall. She pounds at her reflection in a mirror, sleepwalks dangerously with an oil lamp, and squirms in her golden bed with nightmares. Then the Civil War breaks out, but that's as nothing compared with the 'war going on inside her' – for Taylor's Susanna has 'got a sickness and not all the loving care in this world can rid her of it'.

Taylor is the film's thing of darkness – increasingly agitated, a grown married woman clutching at her toys in the nursery. 'She's drained the very laughter out of you,' Clift is told, and he and Flash Perkins leave town, follow musket and fife, and fight in the Union cause. As in *Gone with the Wind*, however, the battles and military sequences are generally a distraction, a nuisance. I'd prefer to remain in Tara with Scarlett (and with Olivia de Havilland) – and parenthetically, though it is easy to accept Taylor as a mad presence (her tricks and selfishness; her hysterical fits), she's very different to Vivien Leigh, who had a clinical nervous splendour, a genuine manic illness, rather than, as with Taylor, a personality that only went over the edge when she wanted it to (not the same thing as saying she was putting it on: I don't think she did that). Clift and Marvin have scuffles with Confederate soldiers ('I come from Raintree County,' says Flash, fatally wounded, 'and I can lick anyone here!'), but again, I'd rather watch Taylor, by now confined to an asylum, sharing her ward with freaks and moaning creatures. 'She's normal enough to be wretched,' says a nurse, whose bedtime reading matter must be Samuel Beckett, and my chief image from this film, which I saw for the first time only the other day, is of Taylor swooping down the stairs and along corridors in a vast russet dress, which is decorated with cones and stripes, and the sleeves are as big as sails. Out she runs across the grass and she later sinks into a swamp, drowning so that Clift can be free to court Eva Marie Saint, which must have thrilled all concerned no end.

The film has the stately pace of grand opera, with a big symphonic soundtrack – the kind of opera Susan Alexandra Kane appears in, in *Citizen Kane*. *Raintree County* is a bloated parody of itself. The director, Edward Dmytryk, would direct Burton in *Bluebeard*, which is another essay in death and lunacy. The final shot, for example, is of the mysterious, mythical raintree, an orange burning bush, deep in the everglades, which no human eye in modern times has ever glimpsed, though Taylor expires under it. But despite the tawdriness, the fervour of the film is true to the actress' stronger feelings. When she and Clift visit the ruined pillared mansion, the scene of the fire, and Taylor swirls about remembering how it was 'all white when I was a little girl', and then grows panic-stricken as she reminisces about her mother, who 'went insane', there is a growing gothic atmosphere of hushed-up truth and lies, congruent with the tropical midnights, the eerie birds and forests in bloom, which Taylor's presence renders sinister, not idyllic; claustrophobic, not open and infinite. And in this she is revealing about her own experiences of attraction and recoil, the positive and negative emotional reversals and thrills – the horror and beauty of her concurrent life with Todd, and when he died, with Eddie Fisher. For nor did Taylor hang about: 'I thought I could keep Mike's memory alive,' she said. 'But I only have his ghost.' By 29 August 1958, she was dancing in nightclubs with Eddie, and Earl Wilson told readers of the *New York Post* that, 'having been Mike Todd's close friend', Eddie was now 'sort of an escort service for Liz'. She and Eddie went to the

Grossinger's Hotel in the Catskills, a kind of Jewish Butlin's, where the crooner had a residency. 'What do you expect me to do?' asked Taylor rhetorically. 'Sleep alone?'

* * *

The frenzy of *Raintree County* was apparent in her sinful and subversive life, and Todd left behind so many debts and legal muddles, his tax affairs were not settled until 1971. Taylor had sued the plane company for negligence, which meant, as Todd's widow, she sued herself – Michael Todd Company, Inc., and Ayer Lease Plan Inc., of Linden, New Jersey, were the joint-lessees. A settlement of $27,092.55 was reached in 1963, and the New York Federal Court directed the sum be paid to baby Liza.

Eddie's first job was to convert Taylor to Judaism. 'I feel as if I've been a Jew all my life,' she said on 26 March 1959 – and a lifetime later, in 1980, she received the Simon Wiesenthal Humanitarian Award 'for converting to Judaism, a courageous decision, for even in the best of times it has never been easy to live as a Jew.' His other job was to look after Taylor's sixty pieces of luggage. Eddie answered the telephones, walked the dogs, ordered the limos – an errand boy, who had to fuck the mistress. He said she liked to be fucked from behind, what is known as back-scuttling. She also liked to be pinned to the ground – 'Elizabeth loved to fight,' with sex as abrupt as rape. 'Eddie's favourite time to fuck is in the morning,' Taylor told the manager of the Waldorf-Astoria, ensuring no disturbance from maids until the afternoon. Eddie was also the nursemaid, because by now Taylor had become, as Eddie said, 'the world's greatest hypochondriac ... She enjoyed playing the invalid. It was a way of testing the devotion of those around her.' Racing yet again through the night in an ambulance, or wheeled away with double pneumonia, 'Get my lip gloss!' Taylor would command.

Insurance premiums for her illnesses cost $45,299 for *Raintree County*, $75,000 apiece for *Giant* and *Cat on a Hot Tin Roof*. With

Taylor, illness was real, as well as being a metaphor – a metaphor that expressed her character, her marvels and her mysteries; the ferments in her blood. We have a sense of this in *The Last Time I Saw Paris*, made just prior to *Giant*, where in a dandelion-coloured dress and a gash of red lipstick, Taylor is alluring as Scott Fitzgerald's death-haunted heroine, Helen Ellswirth, her joy and merriment somehow ominous, as what it mostly suggests is the despair that is on the other side of fun. Taylor is good at being in bed, wrapped in sheets and towels, padding to the bathroom, examining her bulges in the mirror ('I'll never be a Size 10 again'). She's living in Paris, with Van Johnson, a struggling novelist, who says patronisingly, 'I'm no good, Helen. Be a good girl and let me alone . . . I don't have what it takes.' Nor does he. Money suddenly comes in from an oil well, so Taylor has her hair cut, Van Johnson becomes a drunk ('When you've got enough money, no excuses are necessary'), but Taylor believes in him, as she believed in Lassie or The Pie. Then her patience runs out, as it did with Wilding. She's fed up with his lack of fun – 'You know me, always good for a couple of laughs,' Van says bitterly. 'He just sits there, in the dark, alone,' Taylor complains to Walter Pidgeon. Who should come to her rescue but Roger Moore, playing a tennis coach. 'I called the house. You weren't there' – 'That's because I'm here.' As punishment for such dialogue, Taylor walks around in the snow in an orange cocktail frock, ends up in an oxygen tent at the hospital, and expires upon a lame joke: 'I catch colds even from weather forecasts.'

Illness gave Taylor her power – she expected to be comforted. Making *National Velvet* she fell off the horse and complained about back pain for the rest of her life. The Pie trod on her foot and her boot had to be cut off, such was the swelling. In the *Lassie* films and *Little Women* she took sick leave for sinus trouble. During *Giant* she was absent with heat exhaustion, laryngitis, a bladder infection, intestinal obstruction (i.e. constipation) and migraines. She said she had thrombosis in her knees because her jodhpurs were too tight, and she insisted on hobbling about on crutches, saying it was sciatica.

Commonplace ailments always triggered exaggerated treatments. A teenage spot meant consultations with dermatologists. If she stumbled in high heels, or coughed, the emergency services were called. 'I heard the bone break!' she'd assure the ambulancemen. Her honeymoon with Nicky Hilton, on board the *Queen Mary*, was additionally notable for food poisoning. In Morocco with Michael Wilding, who was appearing in a film with Anita Ekberg, 'Everything was dirty,' said Taylor. 'I came home and went into hospital for a month.' She was hit by a swinging door, during *The Last Time I Saw Paris*, and because her character is locked out in the sleet and dies, in Japan it was entitled *Dies in Paris in the Rainy Morning*, which was something of a spoiler. When her daughter, Liza Todd, was delivered by Caesarean section on 6 August 1957, eight doctors were in attendance. When told afterwards that they'd taken the opportunity to give her a tubal ligation, Taylor said, 'It was the worst shock of my life, like being killed.' Her maternity wardrobe had cost $38,000, and the nanny was sent to buy toys with the instruction, 'Anything expensive will do.'

Out dancing, she trod on a matchbox, which ignited, setting fire to her front bottom. She fell off an exercise bike. She fell over a lot. She fell off John Warner's horse and broke a finger. A cat fell on her head when she was trying to rescue it from a tree, during the making of *The Taming of the Shrew*. She choked on a chicken bone ('She's lucky,' said the doctor. 'This could have lodged in her larynx and killed her'). She had a salivary gland infection, a facelift, piles and alopecia. 'Over the years,' said a hairstylist in New Orleans, 'with all the hairstyling and dyeing, it's very, very thin.' Taylor wore wigs, and her dressing room, for *Divorce His, Divorce Hers*, was filled with Alexandre de Paris hairstyle designs, 'coils and plaits, interwoven with jewels and flowers,' recalled Waris Hussein, the director. Burton had to deal with her piles: 'I heard her calling me and she was bleeding from her rectum,' he wrote in his diary for 10 April 1970. 'It turned out she had burst a pile ...' Kennamer was summoned, to whatever continent they were in, and, 'He mucked about and put a bandage around her arse.'

Illnesses were after all human symptoms, reminding the Hollywood goddess of biological origins, the limits of mortality, which she seemed to want to test, and she was thoroughly absorbed by her body's uproar and peculiarity. (Thoroughly absorbed, indeed, from the moment she first drew breath: 'My earliest memory is of pain.' Her opening line in the fantastical and disconcertingly weird *Boom!* is 'Pain! Injection!') In a group session at the Betty Ford Center she enthralled her audience by saying, 'I can feel the blood rush through my body, rushing like red water over the boulders in my pain-filled neck and shoulders.' When needing a blood transfusion, during *Cleopatra*, and plugged up to intravenous drips, a similar image had occurred to her – it was 'like boiling water flowing through my whole body.' Taylor saw herself as an emblem in Romantic poetry, a sea, a storm, rainy breeze. 'Even in the terrible darkness,' she continued, 'there remained within me that stubborn insistence on living.' The paradox with Taylor's ailments is that they gave her strength. If illness was to make the screen siren seem terrestrial, the plethora had the opposite effect. 'Throughout [my] many critical hours in the operating theatre, it was as if every nerve, every muscle, as if my whole physical being were being strained to the last ounce of my strength, to the last gasp of my breath,' she told the agog audience at a charity dinner for Cedars-Sinai. Illness was never a sign of surrender with Taylor, but a manifestation of her tyranny – when Eddie tried to appease her, soothe her fevered brow, etc., 'She would become even more ferocious,' he said. Disease was not debilitating. Her fragility was protected by a metallic survival instinct. Where, for the rest of us, disease means phlegm, mucus, sputum, with Taylor, her coughs and sinkings, and what she liked to broadcast as her death sentences, only reinforced the occult or supernatural components of her invalidism. Her body was not consumed or polluted by viruses and infections – it was augmented, an indication of her intense passion (she'd devise a perfume called 'Elizabeth Taylor's Passion') and sensuality, a symptom of going always to extremes. In this fashion, illness was an extension of eroticism, a manifestation of it, a place where her energy flowed, flooding every nerve. Injury and suffering and debility gave her a languor, a yearningness, and her mouth, with its crimson lipstick, opened in a roar of pain that would have satisfied Francis Bacon. (Or to quote a more graphic description by Richard Brooks, when he was directing *The Last Time I Saw Paris*, and he didn't like Taylor's make-up for the death scene: 'Your mouth looks like a bloody cunt.')

Yet then there were her addictions, for which we can blame Clift, who encouraged Taylor to take Benzedrine: 'You'll forget your worries.' She was already calming herself down with sedatives as a child actress, and by the time she was an elderly actress, in 1981, she was receiving literally hundreds of prescriptions for opiates, hypnotics, tranquillisers, antidepressants and stimulants, from Ativan to Xanax, with huge doses of Tylenol, Percodan, Hyocodan, Demerol, you name it, thrown in. Taylor had a habit of consulting lots of doctors concurrently, to add to her stash of Nembutal, Doriden, Luminal and Seconal, which she'd conceal in the many bathrooms of her hotel suites. The cross-effects of the elixirs caused a mix of hysteria, flu-like symptoms, and sprained ankles, from inflamed joints. Costiveness alternated with diarrhoea. Because she was Elizabeth Taylor, she never had the humble shits, only severe amoebic dysentery.

A lot of what was always going on with her, therefore, was an addiction to opioids, the powerful analgesic, morphine the best known, which slows the muscles controlling the gut – hence Taylor's constipation, as food stopped moving through the intestines. Absorbed into the blood stream from the gastrointestinal tract, the drug also suppresses coughs, there's a reduction in the breathing rate, and this leads to slow, shallow respiration. The pills or injections have sedative effects and interfere with brain function – and emotion. The body gets accustomed to it, and higher doses are required – addictive properties and withdrawal symptoms include anxiety, sweating, vomiting, heart arrhythmia, headaches and fainting, all Taylor's regular complaints. Furthermore, owing to an increased metabolic rate, high levels of carbon monoxide are produced – which are usually expelled by an increase in the rate and intensity of breathing, which will increase the amount of oxygen entering the lungs. Except morphine reduces the sensitivity of the respiratory mechanism in the brain – inhalation and exhalation – and breathing becomes slower, and may stop, as during *Cleopatra*. Sedation turns into coma.

Taylor was always collapsing like this, or else from barbiturates, like Seconal, which suppressed the central nervous system, causing drowsiness. The side-effects of overdoing it are anxiety, fevers, and breathing, again, can be depressed. Fluids build up in the muscles, lungs and brain, causing swelling (oedema) and pneumonia. As with opioids, the slower breathing rates lead to high levels of carbon monoxide remaining in the body, which isn't adequately expelled from the lungs. Oxygen deprivation leads to cyanosis: blue skin and nails. The cough reflex is suppressed, so it is difficult to clear fluid from the lungs. This explains a lot of what Burton was mentioning in his diary about Taylor: 'ill with tooth trouble and aching bones' (8 June 1965); 'internal bleeding' (29 March 1966); 'permanent nasal and bronchial irritation' (2 April 1966); 'she looked like death . . . Some filthy doctor had given her some shot to which she was allergic and therefore she was poisoned instead of helped' (20 April 1966); 'great discomfort with her left shoulder . . . nagging infuriating pain' (24 September 1966).

I am grateful to Eddie for a lot of the pharmacological information, for divulging that chronic medical problems and passing out mid-sentence were a consequence of Taylor's taking too many tablets, too many tumblers of Jack Daniel's. 'She being the movie star, naturally she won,' when she wanted a prescription repeated. Owing to legal settlements and threats, Eddie's recollections couldn't be published for years – and no wonder, for Taylor, in her fourth

husband's estimation, was a mad woman and a dope fiend. And he's
the one person I feel genuinely sorry for. Taylor was always nasty
about him, a reflection of her guilt and shame, possibly; and Burton
was contemptuous also – the mockery of the cuckolder. In his diary
entry for 16 November 1966, for example, he writes, 'Elizabeth is so
ashamed of herself for having married such an obvious fool. He really
is beneath contempt ... a gruesome little man.' Eddie's original
appeal was an intimacy with Mike Todd, who called him 'you little
Jew bastard', I'm sure affectionately. Indeed, it was Todd who got
Eddie to effect an introduction in the first place: 'Come over and talk
to her. Tell her how great I am.' If Todd ordered 144 pairs of custom-
made socks, Eddie, in Hong Kong, ordered 140 silk suits, 185
monogrammed silk shirts, 50 silk pyjamas and, to give to Taylor, a
40-carat diamond bracelet. It was Eddie, whom she married at the
Temple Beth Sholom, in Las Vegas, on 12 May 1959, who got to play
hospitals – indeed, the marriage unfolded in hospital rooms and
hotel rooms, with an oxygen cylinder in the corner. There was no
home, as such. When Eddie was singing at La Tropicana, Taylor had
a tonsillectomy. When he received his own recreational shots of
methamphetamine, barbiturates and phenobarbital, Taylor joined
him. BUtterfield 8 was made in a hallucinatory cloud, and Taylor's illnesses were openly connected to her embrace of disorder, impulse,
and to her fluctuation between pleasure and pain. 'Elizabeth Taylor
would not be in tomorrow,' ran a studio memo, dated 16 June 1960, a
fortnight after shooting had commenced. 'She had been crying for an
hour and is emotionally upset from nervous exhaustion.' Pandro
Berman, the MGM producer, was exasperated. 'She was constantly
sick and purposely late,' he stated. Yet her complete lack of discipline
was linked to the lack of restraint, which was pivotal to her character
in the film. Taylor always reckoned she disliked the film and its
themes and only participated out of contractual necessity, and then
very grudgingly. 'The leading lady is nearly a prostitute,' she said, as
if shocked. She won her first Oscar for the performance, which was

no accident (it is fully merited) – though in the film she is killed in a car accident, for the wages of sin can only be paid in a fatal currency. As Gloria Wandrous, John O'Hara's heroine, Taylor gives a heart-rending portrayal of a rich man's other woman – her loneliness and gumption. As with *Secret Ceremony* or *X, Y & Zee*, later in her career, where she moves and operates almost as a silent movie actress, what we get a sense of is Taylor's own spontaneous complexity – and proof of what Louise Brooks meant when she said sex is 'one of life's most powerful and defining aspects,' the key to a person's true character and deeds.

* * *

If Taylor's marriages broke up like meringues, it is because the chief difficulty she had with men is that they didn't seem to exist, in any pure sense. They were romantic projections, willed into existence on her terms. Her expectations were wholly far-fetched – 'I am now Mrs Hilton. You can take it from me that my romantic life is settled for-ever'; of Michael Wilding: 'He is so mature and that is what I need . . . I just want to be with Michael, to be his wife'; 'I have given Mike [Todd] my eternal love'; 'I love Eddie dearly . . . I have never been happier in my life,' she told the world. 'I love you and need you with my life for the rest of time,' she told Eddie personally, if a little inco-herently. 'I love you and need you with *me in* my life for the rest of time,' surely is what was meant? The sentiment was engraved on a pair of diamond-studded gold cufflinks – that's a lot of words to get on a pair of cufflinks. Taylor's syntax when communicating with Burton, in March 1974, during a rough patch, was a similar burble: 'I wish I could [tell] you of my love for you, of my fear, my delight, my pure animal pleasure of you (with you) – my jealousy, my pride, my anger at you, at times . . . Anyway I lust thee.' When they'd got mar-ried for the first time, in March 1964, she said, 'I'm so happy you can't believe it.' When they got married for the second time, in October

1975, she said, 'We are stuck like chicken feathers to tar, for lovely always.' A year later, Taylor was saying of John Warner, 'I want to spend the rest of my life with him and I want to be buried with him,' as if a wedding and a funeral were the same thing. I can't find anything Taylor said about Larry Fortensky, her eighth and final husband, whom she married on 6 October 1991, but he said of her she was 'a wild woman' in bed and he was smitten by her 'big breasts'.

The unreality of every relationship; of everything being artificial: the revolting Fortensky nuptials were certainly an extreme instance of that. By this stage in Taylor's life, the child actress had become a wicked, calamitous witch, who'd formed a mad alliance with Michael Jackson. In her view, Jackson was 'the brightest star in the universe. I loved him like a son,' and his Neverland Valley estate, with the carnival rides, swan-shaped boats, and air of Willy Wonka paedophilia, was the setting for the wedding ceremony, which cost $1.5 million. Fortensky, whom Taylor had met at the Betty Ford Center in 1988, was completely overwhelmed. 'Those cameras everywhere. Elizabeth was used to it. I never got used to it.' Michael Jackson's chimpanzee, Bubbles, was the bridesmaid. Fortensky would have been better off marrying the chimpanzee. Nancy Reagan, Gregory Peck, David Hockney and Franco Zeffirelli were guests. The Marx Brothers were no longer detained. They were dead. The tent was decorated with daisies. The bride wore a yellow dress by Valentino. Aside from fitting some wardrobes for Nancy Reagan, Fortensky did nothing. Bored and sloshed, he stayed at home and 'hardly got out of bed,' said Taylor crossly. She threw him out in 1996. He squandered his divorce settlement, was drunk on beer all the time, fell down the stairs and was in a coma. He then contracted melanoma and went into a coma. He was always comatose. Fortensky died on 7 July 2016, aged sixty-four.

Apart from Warner, who lived to be ninety-four, and who'd had an American nuclear submarine named after him, Taylor's beaux did not escape damnation. Nicky Hilton went mad and Rex Kennamer 'went away convinced that Nick should be locked up as soon as possible,' Burton recorded in his diary. He died on 5 February 1969. As for Wilding, Taylor 'paid no attention to him at all,' said Eddie, looking back and seeing premonitions of his own fate. 'He'd drink all day and he suffered from epilepsy,' for which he took medication, including Seconal. 'I was convinced that his love for Elizabeth had just about destroyed him.' Wilding died in July 1979, as a result of a head injury, sustained during an epileptic seizure. A spray of yellow roses appeared on the coffin at Chichester Crematorium: 'For dearest Michael. Love always, Liz.' He'd been living in the Sussex countryside with Margaret Leighton, at a place called Gauntlet Cottage. Some sources claim Taylor 'had flown seven thousand miles in order to be present at the twenty-minute service', though I have my doubts, as I have my doubts concerning Wilding's alleged presence at Mike Todd's funeral in Chicago. 'I am here in case I can help Liz,' Wilding was quoted as saying to the press. Perhaps he remained in the terminal at O'Hare. At the graveside Taylor was supported by Kennamer and Howard, her bearded brother. Wilding is not in the newsreel footage, nor was he in any of the rooms reserved at the Drake, nor aboard the TWA-DC-7 made available by Howard Hughes.

Todd's demise was the most dramatic, going up in a fireball like Cagney in *White Heat*. It is also fully in keeping that he didn't lie still and stay put, in Plot 66 of the Beth Aaron section of the cemetery, that he burst forth from his tomb. In June 1977, Todd's body was stolen. The 'rubber bag' containing his remains was found under a tree. According to police, 'toolmarks were found on the coffin lid and a glass top under the bronze lid had been shattered. Thieves had dug four-and-a-half feet to reach the coffin . . . There were no valuables on the body or in the grave.' By sheer force of will, which could in his day splinter oaks and gutter candles, Todd was surely staging an escape attempt. It must have outraged his ghost that his widow, after cavorting with erstwhile best friend Eddie, and everything that happened subsequently, was no longer answering the phone, as she had for ages following the plane crash, by saying, 'This is Mrs Michael Todd.'

For Burton to rise in Taylor's esteem, Eddie had to fall. 'I had lost her and she no longer needed me,' Eddie said during the *Cleopatra* debacle. 'I had a costume fitting with Irene Sharaff, then I had a drink with Richard,' Taylor taunted. You can't blame Eddie for obtaining a gun. 'Don't worry, Elizabeth. I'm not going to kill you. You're too beautiful.' When Eddie had had enough in Rome, Taylor, never the one at a loss, was the one to issue an ultimatum: 'If you leave me now, you'll never see me again.' I'm not sure she ever did, and her own views on their sacred union were distinctly morbid: 'Maybe with Eddie I was just trying to see if I was alive or dead.' She was drinking and taking tablets. Looking after her and scooping her up when she lost consciousness, 'It was like catching a dead person,' said Eddie, though he was the one who never quite sprang back. He took to vodka and Seconal, carried on getting married (Connie, Terry, Betty), was dropped by the RCA Victor label, recorded an Al Jolson tribute album, broke his hip and died, aged eighty-two, in 2010. Debbie Reynolds, who'd filed for divorce in 1958, and didn't see Eddie again until 1973, found he'd become prematurely 'an old, beaten man'. Eddie really should have heeded his own advice, when, in the Fifties, at a party in the Dakota, he'd first glimpsed Taylor, being loud and boisterous with Montgomery Clift: 'I fell in love with her that night, but she was out of my league.'

Though there's no doubting the strength of Taylor's feelings, those feelings could be diverted, switched, re-focussed on to other objects, so the effect was of impulsiveness, instability, ego. Whether she was addressing William Pawley in 1949 ('I've never loved anyone in my life before one third as much as I love you – and I never will') or Burton in 1974 ('O' Love, let us never take each other for granted again!'), it is the same as when she wrote to Cassius, her lost cat, also in 1974 ('You know always when I hurt and you made comfort for me, as I did once when you were a broken kitten . . . Please come back!').

She was obsessive and hysterical, her instantaneous decisions and elation (and dismissiveness) leading only to heartbreak and melodrama. Her need gradually eroded the spirit, my God it did. Burton, of course, was harder to expel, though even he threatened to commit suicide, telling Taylor, in 1973, 'You have enormous responsibility because if you leave me I shall have to kill myself.' Which he did, with the drink. Nor did Taylor encourage Burton to give up the drink, saying that when sober he was a bore, leading him to wonder, 'perhaps I should start drinking again,' as he'd noted in his diary two years previously, on 8 September 1971.

After two marriages and two divorces, they still ended up doing *Private Lives* together. 'How terrible a thing time is,' said Burton in his diary on 14 March 1983. 'Elizabeth gave me the terrors again. She is such a mess.' Taylor was avoiding rehearsals, claiming she had sickness and diarrhoea. Her teeth were falling out. She couldn't remember her lines. But she was more than an actress by then. With her dissimulations and plotting, making other people's lives a misery, undermining them, laughing and speaking with a spiteful intensity, Taylor in old age was the same as (or a magnification of) Taylor the child star, for whom (to adapt a sentence from Tolstoy's *Childhood*), besides herself, 'nobody and nothing existed in the universe, that objects were not objects at all, but images which appeared only when [she] paid attention to them.' Taylor had no ordinary life – indeed hers was its reverse. She believed nothing was unattainable. Hence, the belief in the concept of Eternal Love, which I am compelled to put in capital letters, if not ironic quotation marks. 'Eternal Love' can only usually be sustained when partners die young or youngish, in each other's arms. Suicide, murder, something nasty. It is irrational, destructive. Children and previous or concurrent (blameless) partners are discarded, without qualm. When Taylor had wanted Eddie to leave Debbie Reynolds and day after day the press called her a 'viper', 'harlot', 'thief', 'destroyer', 'cannibal' and 'barbarian', *so what?* She could ride any of that sort of thing out. With 'Eternal Love' nothing counts for anything, save divine inevitability, as in Wagnerian opera or some Richard Curtis shit. Taylor and Burton, for sure, didn't want to see beyond their love, or infatuation, which was absolute, despite the vexation and dismay everything they were doing was causing. It wasn't going to last for them, as it hadn't for Taylor with Nicky Hilton, Michael Wilding, Mike Todd, Eddie Fisher and, later on, with Senator Warner and jobbing carpenter Fortensky. Edna O'Brien realised as much or almost as much, when Taylor's character is told in *X, Y & Zee*: 'You always get them like that, quick, bang, before they know where they are, a punch in the face, a sniff of ammonia, but you don't keep them, you can't keep them, you cannot keep the love of a man.' Always excepting Nibbles and his replacements, Eternal Love hadn't worked out or ripened for anyone, and it never did.

* * *

As an actress, Taylor doesn't seem to act, as such. (Burton was always acting: he was never not conscious of his voice, of his bearing.) There's nothing between her and the audience, not even an awareness of the camera – except there was, of course: 'Once the camera begins to roll, she comes alive,' said Richard Brooks, when Paul Newman complained she wasn't doing anything during *A Cat on a Hot Tin Roof*. She doesn't withhold herself (though who knows what she was ever *thinking*? And what would her feelings in any event actually be *evidence of*?), and I am always mesmerised by those scenes where she is getting dressed, or undressed – these stripteases, where she gazes at her reflection, or rubs her ankle or her shoulder, like a bather in a Bonnard. The long first scene in *BUtterfield 8* (the title refers to the Upper East Side telephone exchange) is rivalled only by Janet Leigh's getting ready to take a shower in *Psycho* – and there's a similar sense of premonition. Gloria Wandrous has decay and disaster haunting her every hour, and what I admire about the film (unknown today) is that though it is about ordinary moments (waking up, cleaning one's teeth, making a phone call, gathering up one's clothes), these banalities are invested with immense stylisation, and the effect is unsettling. There is the surface life of shopping and going out, saying hello to the neighbours, generally filling the day, and then this operatic life underneath, seething with passion, hatred, a desire for death and extinction.

There is no dialogue for ages. Taylor is alone in this luxurious apartment on Fifth Avenue, a blue boudoir with a pink marble bathroom. The cold sun through the slats of the window blinds is harsh. The phone is off the cradle. Screwed-up cigarette packets litter the floor, along with discarded shoes. Taylor is like a forest creature gaining consciousness, or a child before it has learned to speak. She clears her throat, gargles. She takes a swig of whisky from a decanter. She sniffs the array of perfume bottles, examines the contents of the wardrobe, the gowns and furs. She then notices her own clothes are torn – has she been attacked by a werewolf? In a manner of speaking, exactly so. Her co-star is Laurence Harvey, born plain Larushka Mischa Skikne, in Joniškis, Lithuania. In October 1964, he would play Arthur in the Drury Lane transfer of *Camelot*, and 'unfortunately,' reported Noël Coward, 'does such an accurate vocal imitation of Richard Burton that if you close your eyes you might just as well be at *Becket*.' He always resembled a thinner Lugosi, and his screen (and stage) persona was as mean and cruel, and as foreign, as Dracula.

BUtterfield 8, like Bram Stoker's vampire novel, is about sex as a destructive force. Harvey, as the wealthy Weston Liggett, is an ascetic sensualist, shimmering amongst exclusive country clubs, rosewood executive suites, and manicured high society. He fully expects everything always to go his way – from the placing of a bowl of flowers on the breakfast tray to a substantial salary as a corporate lawyer. But then there's Taylor's Gloria: 'You bring out the wildness in me,' he says. We never see Harvey lose his composure, but we can sense it – and it is part of the demonic unreality of the film that Taylor, in the opening scene, must be bruised by the rough handling, her blood-stream full of drugs, and this is left to the audience's imagination likewise. Luckily, Eddie, cast as Gloria's pudgy well-intentioned best pal, spells things out for slower viewers: 'Sunday morning and the Scotch on your breath . . . You are boozed up, burned out and ugly.'

Taylor's resistance to *BUtterfield 8*, her off-hand behaviour and boredom, contributed to the playing of her role. Her numbness suggests Gloria is a Marilyn Monroe kind of characterisation – the call girl too dim to stop herself from being exploited, as in *The Prince and the Showgirl*, where Olivier, under lots of make-up, played a Lithuanian princeling. But Taylor's intelligence prevents Gloria from seeming dim, or pathetic. 'I'm not like anyone, I'm me,' is a line that she makes resonate with clarion assurance. (Monroe would have made it mournful, regretful.) What Taylor can convey is how sexual enjoyment will result in genuine bewilderment, if there isn't reciprocity – why has Liggett insulted Gloria with a cash payment, the $250 she eventually finds left for her in the apartment, and which provokes her to scrawl NO SALE in lipstick on the looking-glass? Sex is her form of being avid, even a man's equal, rather than the chance for a cheap betrayal. 'Put your assets away,' she jeers at Harvey. 'You haven't enough.' Monroe would never be in the driver's seat like that.

The scene in the hotel bar, where Liggett tries to win Gloria back, and she slowly and deliberately pierces his shin bone with her stiletto heel, is a pure sexual battle. Taylor is as inscrutable here as Cleopatra, in black velvet and white pearls. Gloria earns her living, we discover, and has a busy schedule, modelling clothes, a rented escort who is paid to patrol in the latest frocks around fashionable bistros and lounges. His leg surely needing A&E treatment, Harvey instead whisks Taylor away immediately to spend several days and nights in a cheap motel, an adventure that fills him with inevitable disgust. Returning to Manhattan, he contrives an argument and flings a mink coat in Taylor's face, saying anything she has touched is tainted. This remains the shrill moral – that sex outside the boundaries of marriage (and Liggett has a demure off-screen Wasp wife) is evil; that for a woman to enjoy sex is evil: so she must be branded as emotionally disturbed. Thus, for expressing herself erotically, over Gloria a long shadow of loneliness and fear has to be cast, and Taylor is given a big tearful speech ('all older men seemed like fathers to me'), about how she was abused at the age of thirteen: 'I loved it, every evil moment of it. I loved it . . . The deep shame of it didn't hit me until it was too late.' Until only the other day probably. Her punishment for the crime of being sexually confident is for her red Sunbeam Alpine to soar over a ditch and explode. 'Everything in her was struggling towards respectability,' says Harvey as an epitaph – piously and quite falsely, as nothing in Taylor's performance justifies the line. Whether Liggett himself will relinquish his own 'drinking, leching and lying', who knows? A man didn't need to in the Sixties.

It is Taylor who makes *BUtterfield 8* an intensely erotic film, where nothing explicit is shown. The New York on display, cool and autumnal, is her comfortable habitat. When the neon lights of the motels and diners pulsate, it is Taylor's animality that is not far off. Sex is implied in Taylor's movies with her clothes, with her petticoats, with the scene where Fisher's girlfriend mends her ripped dress with pins; with the way she is shampooing her hair. Unlike with Marilyn Monroe, there's never any lifelessness in her performances – and incidentally how different Harvey was from Burton. Harvey was a spiv, his suits too dapper. He is an on-the-make sort. When he and Taylor embrace on Fifth Avenue, it is an immaculate clinch – and Burton and Taylor were never like that, for all that Burton somehow embodied outmoded virtues like chivalry and honour, which is why he was so good at Shakespearean princes and as King Arthur in *Camelot*. (Harvey is more concerned about loss of face.) Taylor is bigger than *BUtterfield 8* – transcends it – because she intuitively understood the madness of sexual love, that it involved degrading each other, revulsion as much as desire, and a submission to radical instability, and to absolute fear.

* * *

BUtterfield 8 is a summary of Taylor's own sado-masochistic demands; her potency and her toying always – but toying only, before an innate stubbornness and sense of superiority reasserted itself – with the idea of relinquishing control. The sexual drive is not only at the centre of her life and doings – her life and her character's life – it was also a way of keeping a focus on her body and its cravings, even its cravings for illness and pain, which would be signified by the aches of her nervous system, her muscular spasms. She always knew as much. 'It was my subconscious that let me become so seriously ill,' she believed, of her many debilitations during *Cleopatra*. 'I just let the disease take me.' Being ill, you could say, was part of her feminine destiny. It connects Taylor with the heroines of nineteenth-century novels and operas, which are the forerunners of Hollywood: girls in nightgowns struggling through storms, adrift on ice floes, pursued by phantoms, vampires or bailiffs, gesticulating wildly about their helplessness and vulnerability as they desperately seek shelter. The squalid actual world – tuberculosis, abduction, rape, starvation, abuse – is transfigured, given a romantic fervour. Few have seen Taylor as Nadina Bulichoff in Zeffirelli's *Il Giovane Toscanini*, made in 1988, because it was hardly released, and never dubbed into English, but I always do think of Taylor as born out of her actual era, and fitting more into the era of the young Toscanini, and she is a woman who is like the image of Salome dancing before Herod in an oil painting by Gustave Moreau, hung in a heavily embossed frame on a dark wall. Here is a woman – Salome, Taylor – whose entire drama is playing out in public – the glitter and the beauty, the flashiness and bad taste. Taylor 'lacks taste', asserted Diana Vreeland, flinching at the lashings of eyeshadow; but that too, the actress' pomp and decoration, was a sign of her unashamed need for ecstasy, ferment. Her greed is linked here likewise. 'My taste buds get in an uproar and I get a lusty, sensual thing out of eating,' she crowed. 'Food is one of my major vices.' During the making of *The Taming of the Shrew*, directed, in 1967, by Zeffirelli, she scoffed, for example, platters of spaghetti, eggs, pancakes with lemon cream, and pots of caviar. Peter Cook said it was her glands behind it. He pictured them as independent, impish creatures, thinking nothing of force-feeding the star with two dozen chocolate eclairs and brandy chasers. Taylor's glands, indeed, scurried about the hotel suites like corgis or gremlins. 'No,' she'd scream, 'please, I beg you!' But her glands take no notice. You've never known glands like them, assured Cook. 'The trolley arrives and Elizabeth Taylor hides in the bathroom, but her glands take the eclairs, smash down the door and stuff them down her throat . . . Terrible glands.'

Her adult personality was a bundle of appetites; what counted with her was the supremacy of instinct, and she could spend hours absorbed in selecting a dress that would go with a necklace. 'Just a little $50,000 diamond would make everything wonderful for up to four days,' said Eddie, and he wasn't exaggerating. 'I mean, I love presents,' said Taylor, and she was always wheedling and demanding gifts and tributes from producers, like a monarch expecting bounty. She received a Cartier brooch worth $4,250 from the makers of *The Sandpiper*, after she'd asked rather rudely, 'What are you giving me?' In the Soviet Union to make *The Blue Bird*, in 1971, she saw a bejewelled bluebird in a cabinet in the lobby of her hotel. 'Oh, Henry,' she said to Henry Wynberg, 'buy it for me!' Wynberg wasn't so easily blandished. 'Ask George Cukor, let him buy it for you' – and Cukor did so, or else Twentieth Century Fox duly did so.

Taylor was a vessel of emotion and acquisitiveness on an imperial scale. She was her own singular and flamboyant creation – so no wonder Walter Wanger, who gave her an emerald that had belonged to Tsar Nicholas, offered her the earth to play *Cleopatra*. 'Elizabeth is the entire film,' he stated. One of the reasons she was disgruntled about *BUtterfield 8* was that it delayed her being able to play Cleopatra, who was a living deity to the Egyptians, and whose story involved the complexities of Roman political history and foreign policy, war and manoeuvres, usurpations, assassinations and fragile alliances. But mostly, with Cleopatra and Caesar, and Cleopatra and Antony, it is a story about sex and its proximity to hatred and destruction; suffering and physical horror; dreams and prophecy.

Though set in Ancient Rome (and Alexandria), *Cleopatra* is chiefly about Rome in the early Sixties, and London at the end of the Fifties. It is lavish, decadent, molten, with Taylor, in bold colours, as the full-mouthed vamp, a woman who will ruin men. The film was also shaped by illness, exacerbated by addiction, and it was not disclosed to the studio or to the insurance companies at the time that Taylor was by now, in the words of a memo only recently found in the (head of Twentieth Century Fox) Spyros P. Skouras archive, 'chronically dependent on sleeping pills and painkillers', which made her vulnerable to infections. Fisher would concur with this. His wife 'had become addicted to every pill on the market – pills to help her sleep, pills to keep her awake, pills to dull her pain, pills and more pills'. Shooting commenced at Pinewood on 28 September 1960, with Peter Finch as Caesar, Keith Baxter as Octavian, Stephen Boyd as Antony and Stanley Baker as Rufio, but there was no footage of Taylor as Cleopatra. She remained in The Dorchester with an abscessed tooth and a boil on the buttock, for which she was prescribed anti-inflammatory cream, and a course of pronestyl hydrochloride, because she complained of palpitations and shortage of breath. Then she decided she had meningitis, which she didn't. On 18 November she was declared 'unfit to work for the foreseeable future'.

The production was suspended, at a cost to Twentieth Century Fox of $121,428 a day. The director, Rouben Mamoulian, was replaced by Joseph Mankiewicz, who wanted to compose a new script, intending to deliver it and re-start the project on 3 April 1961. Fisher and Taylor went to Munich, where they stayed in the hotel where Mussolini had visited Hitler, and when Fisher didn't fancy going to a nightclub ('I was tired and needed some rest'), Taylor took an overdose of Seconal, a barbiturate. They returned to The Dorchester and, Taylor's tablet-taking exacerbated by heavy drinking, on 4 March 1961 she collapsed with breathing difficulties and underwent an emergency tracheotomy at The London Clinic, where to stimulate the lymphocyte responses in both T- and B-cells in her bloodstream, i.e. her immune system, her congested lungs were treated with staphylococcal bacteriophage lysate. 'I'm going to lose my girl,' cried Eddie for the press. 'If she dies, I die.' 'I died four times,' said Taylor. 'You feel yourself falling into a horrible black pit.'

Soon enough, she was drinking champagne in her room with Truman Capote. On 14 March she was eating custard and borrowing a commode, which her surgeon, Horace Evans – Lord Evans of Merthyr Tydfil, personal physician to the Queen Mother – claimed had been used by royalty on Commonwealth tours. Discharged on 27 March, Taylor returned to America and, a month later, assisted to the podium by Eddie and Rex Kennamer, she received the Best Actress Academy Award, from the hands of Yul Brynner, for *BUtterfield 8*. *Cleopatra* was to resume at Cinecittà, where the sets had been expensively reconstructed, on 25 September. The sets and costumes abandoned in Pinewood were later salvaged by Peter Rogers for *Carry On Cleo*. Kenneth Williams wore Peter Finch's toga. Charles Hawtrey, submerged in Taylor's sunken marble-effect bath, promised Joan Sims, 'I'll let you play with my rubber duck.' Taylor and her court, which included Rex Kennamer, plus five dogs, two cats, 300 dresses and 120 pairs of shoes, took up residence in the Villa Pappa, on the Via Appia Antica, or maybe the Via Appia Pignatelli or even the Via Appia Piatello (sources differ), where, each morning, all the pillows, flowers, candles and dinner napkins had to be changed and re-colour-co-ordinated. On 22 January 1962, Taylor met Burton for the first time in costume. 'You're much too fat. But you do have a pretty face,' were his opening words. There was nothing reticent or self-protective about either of them – they recognised each other at once as fellow creatures of sheer careless will, sharing a defiant belief in the illicit as representing liveliness; both of them also refused to suffer or sink under the weight of moral fearfulness and dogmatism. 'Don't leave me, Eddie. You must stay and help me exorcise this cancer,' said Taylor, realising she was in delightful danger. But you can't stop what's coming.

PART TWO
WILD JENK

The principal Richard Burton section ('Wild Jenk' or 'Jenks' was his nickname at school) – Burton's story being one of witchcraft and enchantment and damnation. It was as if he'd made a diabolical pact in exchange for sex, power, fame. 'He was always craving admiration,' said his first wife, Sybil. 'Perhaps that explains his need to go from woman to woman, seeking change and excitement like a frustrated unhappy child.' Claire Bloom, Mary Ure, Lana Turner and Susan Strasberg were amongst his conquests, but it was Elizabeth Taylor who dragged him down to Hell.

'Ma' lwc y diafol arnat ti,' he was told by his family over and over. 'You are touched by the luck of the Devil.' And so he was, like a character in an ancient fairy tale, who wasn't fully or thoroughly human; a change-ling or foundling, who wakes up as a prince, with easy access to wealth, success and beautiful girls, their golden hair tumbling in tresses. But was there an element of a curse, too? If Richard Burton, when he met Elizabeth Taylor, was like a man selling his soul to the devil for sex and fame and the rest of it – and if Taylor was the one to cast him into the flickering Inferno of Faustus or Don Giovanni – it is the case he'd always feared and expected damnation, which was a real and primitive punishment for moral transgression, for indulging the carnal senses, for commingling high spirits and evil spirits. 'Felt heavy weight of man's guilt at intervals,' he wrote in 1975, after a routine fuck. 'Thought about death too much . . . I look terrible and feel diabolical.'

How was he going to behave when the end was near, or at least fairly near – when the smell of sulphur was in his hair and clothes, and nothing to be done? When, in August 1984, the firework went off in his brain and a cerebral haemorrhage proved fatal, Burton was not as old as all that (fifty-eight), but death and decay and the red light of the furnace had shown on his face and in his bearing for years, giving him a passionate and perturbed hard-edged quality. Burton was unhealthily tanned, burnt, wreathed in cigarette smoke. Despite his beauty, which always remained, his eyes, his expression, held some combination of guilt, fear, misery. There was a grainy texture – illness and turmoil; a face filled with tension, and which was never glowing with pleasure. Burton's face didn't so much catch the light as sink into dagger-edged shadow.

Burton had a natural force – and a heartlessness ('What compassion I do have I find almost impossible to express'); 'he had a pagan simplicity about him' (Michael Powell) and everything about him ought to be inappropriate: the adulterous husband and feckless divorcee; he was licentious and uproarious. But Burton is steadfastly sympathetic. Why? Because of his charisma. Despite teenage acne, and the humps and pits of his complexion (which required cosmetics – applied daily by Ron Berkeley), 'He was the most beautiful-looking boy ... He seemed so calm and collected' (Gladys Henson); 'He is outstandingly handsome and robust, very masculine and with deep inward fire, and extremely reserved' (Nevill Coghill); 'He was a stunningly interestingly electric fascinating man personally' (Robert Hardy); 'He oozes such charm. If I were only a bit younger I'd definitely single him out romantically' (Margaret Rutherford). And with Burton, his schisms and conflicts were those of an exceptionally intelligent person seeking sensation, indulging the colours and rhythms of primeval energies; and if a capacity for damnation is a capacity for extreme behaviour – boldness, ambition, the willingness to be possessed, overwhelmed – there is nevertheless no need to go as far as Baudelaire ('My chief joy at the moment is in reading Baudelaire, in

French,' said Burton in 1971), who recommended such releases as 'rape, arson, poison or the knife'. But Burton did gravitate towards characters who went in for exactly this sort of deliverance, thoroughly identifying with Doctor Faustus, and with Marlowe's plot, which involves temptation, trial and seduction away from duty. 'I *am* Faustus,' Burton said to Nevill Coghill when, in February 1966, he and Taylor (playing Helen of Troy) spent three weeks in Oxford, rehearsing the play and giving six public performances. The production was later filmed in Rome, costing $800,000 of the Burtons' own money. Personnel from *Cleopatra* were involved, e.g. John DeCuir, the art director, who designed a gothic horror vault teeming with guttering candles, reliquaries, corridors lined with bones and coloured liquids in glass jars. There are trunks, cases, boxes, cabinets and puppet theatres; globes and astrological charts, coffins, cobwebs and pioneering telescopic instruments with distorting lenses. Illuminated manuscripts and dusty vellum books are piled high – and out of the purple fogs, the glut, comes Burton's own moral story ('the wages of sin is death'; 'this word damnation terrifies not him'); and here is a prince of devils, giving in to his own desires and secrets, giving in to luxury, vanity, cunning.

Burton's life before Taylor was 'such a dreary plain with only an occasional high peak of excitement,' as he wrote in his diary. In Céligny, where he'd settled as a tax exile in 1956, 'I had a superb convertible Cadillac, a large library, an insatiable thirst for knowledge and the means to satisfy it and every opportunity to play anything I wanted and I was terribly unhappy.' It was for Taylor he flung away everything, smitten, as Faustus is by Helen, by the anarchy she represented and embodied. Colour came into his life. Taylor was 'beautiful beyond the dreams of pornography. I'll love her till I die.' The decadence, splashiness – and in being released from worldly cares, a willingness to damage others: there was in Burton's behaviour something of what Rose Macaulay once described as 'letting things go to the devil and seeing what happens when they have gone there.'

As Mike Nichols remarked, 'I think Richard was in love with ruin . . . Nothing is more romantic than waste . . . He was enthralled by the idea of large, romantic self-destruction.' Burton was like floating fire or coals, everything burning and tormented, smoking and burning up, and when I think of him – as Alec Leamas, in *The Spy Who Came in from the Cold*, or as George, in *Who's Afraid of Virginia Woolf?*, though Burton is ash grey and the films in black-and-white, his face throws off the red flush of the flames.

Time after time, Burton played the devil – Chris Flanders in *Boom!*, McPhisto in *Candy*, Vic Dakin in *Villain*, Hammersmith in *Hammersmith is Out*, Morlar in *The Medusa Touch*, Colonel Kappler in *Massacre in Rome*, O'Brien in *Nineteen Eighty-Four*. Henry VIII, Bluebeard, Trotsky, even Jimmy Porter, are Satanic. These are all characters, as Burton plays them, for whom life was hell and everyone an enemy. They have made themselves alone. As Burton himself said, in March 1970, when staying at Puerto Vallarta, 'The sun is bright, the people around me are all engaging, but . . . I don't want to see any of them.' Burton's notable roles are wintry, sour-mouthed. These men smoke cigarettes in hungry drags, swallowing and gulping fire deep into the lungs, emitting from the nostrils currents of pale blue dragon breath – in the on-set photographs of *Anne of the Thousand Days*, Burton, in full Tudor garb, is never without a cigarette. Burton's eyes are always flecked with the red of poisonous berries – and if you observe him, even in those classical epics, where he wears a toga (*The Robe*) or steel armour (*Alexander the Great*), or those action films (*Where Eagles Dare*) where he brandishes guns, he was never supple, agile, physically at ease. His bones seem to be jarring, his movements clumsy, as if his blood is blighted. He rarely smiles. He looks too hot – the result of too much yelling and drinking. From the Sixties onwards, he had a face that should have been painted by Francis Bacon, who depicted (or unlocked) sensation, created images with his smears of pink, lilac, orange and yellow, which are at once tender and cruel, queasy and focussed, and always have grandeur, submerged in papal purple or cardinal red. Burton's George, in *Who's Afraid of Virginia Woolf?*, lit by a stark bare swinging light bulb in the garage, is a perfect Francis Bacon image.

Yet Burton never looked foolish, and was always faintly menacing, and his chief instrument of enchantment was his voice, its flavour and texture. 'I get an orgasm just listening to that voice of his,' said Taylor, happy to fall for its beauty, its direct appeal to the senses. With Burton, seduction was a product of eloquence, and his liquid way with words was like the booze, or tears, or drugs, or transfusion of blood; language as potions, spells, charms, which transform the normal world-weary consciousness. Burton's voice was certainly one of the twentieth century's great noises, roaring, swelling, delicate and bombastic by turns, the articulation and diction very precise – and it's what I hold most dear, what I find most engaging, about him, too, the inflections, nuances, elaborations and grain of his voice, the fire and the flint of things spoken. Everything one would want to know with Burton is present in the voice, which was rich and artificial, carrying a sense of fracture, of mournfulness. There were nightingales in it, in the keys and chords. He didn't, as Peter Sellers did, use his voice for mimicry or parody – he could be Winston Churchill or Marshal Tito and he was still Richard Burton. His voice was not a deceptive instrument. Nor did he rely on the College of Heralds fanfare of Sir John Gielgud or peevish rasp of Sir Michael Redgrave – with both of whom he worked on stage. Nonetheless, it is fair to say, it was the era of wonderful voices, of dynamic intonation – and in Burton's era, as they moved through rooms filled with cigarette smoke, everyone sounded like crimson: Miles Malleson, Roger Livesey, James Mason, Dennis Price, Robert Newton, Michael Redgrave, Harry Andrews, Emlyn Williams, dozens of them, ringing, piping, bubbling, swooping, swerving, spilling – and you could hear every word, there was always perfect control. And all this, and Burton as much as any, belongs to the nineteenth century. Burton was not a modern actor. He didn't go in for speed, overlapping dialogue, mumbling, fumbling. All is clarion, trumpet-toned, trumpet-tongued. The style he'd absorbed, to which he was receptive, was that of a tradition exemplified by Olivier, an acoustic scale made for battlefields, pulpits, the barn-sized theatres of the past, with red velvet and golden plaster cherubs, like The Old Vic.

The problem with oratory, however, is not that it is unnatural and declamatory – and even Taylor could tire of it when it came at her non-stop: 'He suffers from this intoxication with words. It's Welsh verbal diarrhoea . . . He is so full of shit,' she once vouchsafed. The problem is when a performance becomes a series of set pieces, and the actor is no longer present in those moments, which are too studied, which are literally an exercise in public speaking. Such a duty was required of him, nevertheless, when Burton narrated a twenty-six-part television documentary about Churchill, *The Valiant Years*, broadcast between November 1960 and June 1961 on ABC and in February 1961 on the BBC. 'Get that boy from The Old Vic,' Churchill had commanded, having grasped here was a person (like himself) who didn't speak, as such, he made incantations; who was very aware of how he sounded; who played to the gallery; who was conscious of his popularity – who was conscious, too, that his black moods were well-known and talked about. This old stager, aggrandising and 'weary and burnt-out', is the Burton whom John Boorman met in 1976, when he directed him in *Exorcist II: The Heretic*. 'He acted from the neck up, face and voice. His body was rigid, completely inexpressive . . . If I asked him to adjust his reading, he simply changed it without comment . . . He had no view of the character, and it was, I suspect, of no interest to him.' This is to underestimate the power of that face, that voice, which conveyed a sense of mist and vapour. For, in this sequel to *The Exorcist*, Burton, as Father Lamont, a priest sent by the Vatican to investigate the mysterious demise of Max von Sydow, still manages to suggest ineffable grandeur, even when saying, as he undergoes a metaphysical adventure with Linda Blair, 'Come, fly the teeth of the wind, share my wings!' Furthermore, there are always moments in any Burton film when close-ups of his eyes, the turn of his head, the pain expressed in speeches about death and repentance, when (as never with Olivier) we do seem to be on intimate terms with him, with his sense of damnation and degradation, his general uneasiness and moody gravity. As an actor he's not a wearer of masks – no false noses (Orson Welles) or funny walks (Alec Guinness, Peter Sellers). 'Richard couldn't wear a wig,' said Michael Hordern – yet he always has presence: a presence indicative of the smell or taste of sulphur on the tongue, minerals, black mud and black trees with scorched leaves.

As a man he was, his nature was, unpretending. Indeed, Burton was more dedicated than he pretended to be, when, for example, he liked to get us to collude with him, that theatre and cinema was fakery, effeminacy. 'All my life I think I have been secretly ashamed of being an actor and the older I get the more ashamed I get,' was a typical Burton remark. But there's a difference between the Burton who was mocking and the Burton who was acting; and when he said, in 1966, 'the mystery of the actor is the ultimate mystery, because no one even begins to know what it is,' what was it Burton was trying to realise in his work? There is a sense of detachment (even boredom – the bare minimum he's doing); yet what were his feelings? With what was he in contact – his responses, his perceptions? There's a lot of brooding (as he says in his diaries often enough, 'I turned into one of my mad moods last night'; 'acute unhappiness added to stupendous quantities of guilt, alcohol, laziness') – and he saw himself, I think, as a banished man, which helped sustain his melancholy. He was exiled, in his mind (because of choices made) from Wales and his childhood ('I lusted for London. I finally caught that train and never went back and never will') – after which everywhere was another galaxy; from England and the London and Stratford classical stage – to follow a career in Hollywood; from Britain and America – to be by a Swiss lake and avoid taxation; and from Sybil to be with Taylor and with Taylor's thoroughgoing egotism. It was an existence of transient accommodations – hotel suites, rented villas, boats, planes; the colour-supplement hedonism, the purchasing of expensive furniture, paintings, jewels. Darkness surrounded him, nevertheless. And believing himself, in his own estimation, cut off, wasting away, Burton could exult, after a fashion, in the idea of punishment sent from above – like all those bawling and defrocked priests he played, or Dysart in *Equus*, shouting at the Cosmos ('What's to become of me? What have you left me fit for?'); or Trotsky in Mexico awaiting the assassin's blow; or Leamas in and out of the figurative cold; or Antony in Alexandria, 'transform'd into a strumpet's fool,' as Shakespeare puts it – 'we see him sunk in luxurious enjoyments and nobly ashamed of his own aberrations,' as Augustus William Schlegel glosses it. Like his characters, Burton was always waiting for things to come – yet what was of value in the past? And before moving on (by going back) I'll just mention one of John Osborne's favourite stories: 'Someone suggested that Burton be invited to lead a National Welsh Theatre. A distinguished leader of the Principality asked what were Burton's qualifications. It was explained that he had played Henry V at Stratford and a Hamlet at The Old Vic applauded by Churchill. The reply, which evoked no surprise, was, 'Yes, I see that. But what has he done in *Wales*?'

* * *

'Oh, Wales!' said Diana Vreeland to Bruce Chatwin. 'I *do* know Wales. Little grey houses . . . covered in roses . . . in the rain.' Wales, where Burton was concerned, wasn't quite so quaint. It had more a mood and manner of the gothic literature of the eighteenth century – fast-flowing streams, icy mists, gloomy groves and mountains, where clouds drift and gather above the gorse and swallows winter at the bottom of ponds; fogs and valleys with giant ferns drenched by recent drizzle; the clang of hammer strokes and whoosh of gas flares, with red and gold sparks coming from the foundries and the steelworks. Wales was both a rural world, the hills shaggy with heather, and an industrial landscape, with smouldering fires and a hopeless pollution. The sounds of whistles and the rattle of iron wheels echoed along streets named after Crimean battles – Inkerman Row, Alma Terrace. There were lamplighters and women in headscarves and black dresses – though in the Sixties and Seventies they often weren't pinched and drab, for by then Taylor was in the habit of distributing her cast-offs amongst Burton's relatives. Bright orange belts, white-lace hot-pants embroidered with daisies, rhinestone and sequin-beaded organza jackets, velvet evening capes, couture outfits by Chanel, Givenchy and Valentino, and yellow kaftans made by Thea Porter and Vicky Tiel, would arrive from Hollywood in hampers. It must have been quite a sight, all these Glamorganshire ladies in cuboid outfits and psychedelic smocks, dusting the parlours crammed with antimacassars and horsehair sofas, going shopping in the Co-op. 'Elizabeth used to send trunks of clothes,' said Burton's sister Hilda, showing off an ermine cloak. 'That one cost a thousand pounds!' It was the star's habit to wear a garment once, then discard it. No alterations were needed at the Wales end, either. As Burton said, displaying a Celtic trait not to be awestruck, 'Elizabeth isn't particularly attractive physically. She has the shape of a Welsh village girl,' which tends to the dumpy and the hirsute. He was no doubt being affectionate when, singling out her double chin and short legs, he called her 'my old Fatty Taffy'.

A lot of Welsh words refer to smelting, forges, bridges, crossings, and to waterfalls and watermills, woods and rivers. The cemetery in Port Talbot is situated on the bank of the Ffrwdwyllt, or 'wild stream'. Burton's village, Pontrhydyfen, means 'place by the bridge over the ford'. The little fairy-tale house under the high viaduct where he was born, '2 Dan-y-Bont', means 'dwelling place under the bridge'. Burton's ancestors, according to research, were cattle dealers, drovers, joiners, smelters, millers, but by the turn of the century the workforce had all gone underground – and Burton always mythologised (and sentimentalised) the miners, saying the valleys were 'filled with song and poetry and beer', and 'the boys of the Rhondda Valley were nothing if not real men'. His father was a 'regal peasant' who'd hold up pit props with his bare hands, 'stole food so that his sons could grow into the strongest in the valley', who could sing five hundred Welsh songs without stopping and play the organ so well, the dead rose up again. They all might be giants, though in actuality, Richard Jenkins, or Dick, or Dic-Bach-y-Saer, or Daddy (or Dadi) Ni, born in 1876 at Efail-Fâch, was a midget, 'five-two only in his boots', who wagged his finger in the faces of normal-sized folk and said, 'Remember, boyo, the bigger you are, the harder you fall.' What an old tit he completely sounds. His other witticisms: 'See this glass of water? If God changes it into beer then I'll agree, He be'; 'You've got a face like a boot. Everyone wants to put his foot in it'; and his cure for hangovers was a spoonful of Vaseline before bed. 'He looked very much like me,' said Burton. 'A man of extraordinary eloquence, tremendous passion, great passion.' His philosophy was a resigned, 'Never mind, we're all dying.' He was so small, like a toddler he'd fall through the railings on the bridge. There's a famous photograph, taken in 1953, where Burton, who by now had received an Academy Award nomination for *My Cousin Rachel*, had appeared on Broadway in *The Lady's Not for Burning*, and had starred at Stratford as Henry V, is striding ahead on the bridge or viaduct in Pontrhydyfen. His diminutive father with a smirk on his face is in the background – Dick's expression denotes embarrassment, derision. He seems to be saying, who the hell do you think you are? He was impossible to impress, pretending to believe Hollywood 'was a small place on the other side of the Welsh mountains'. Burton is in pale flannels, and gives off a sort of subdued silver glow. He casts no shadow, yet he is on parade, marching off to conquer the world – and he often played soldiers, now I think of it, men in uniform in deserts; which is to say, men of power and risk. His father, Dick, holding back, is dressed in shabby black, at one with the cold dampness and distinct bare twigs and cloud wisps. Everything you see in the photograph is stone. The road, the parapet, the boxy seemingly windowless houses on the bleak hill. And Burton doesn't

look as if he could ever have been a part of this place. He was immediately famous, and this picture on the bridge is of a person who now
(who already) took himself for granted as a great man, and what he
had to do in his career was confront the limits of success, which as
Faustus says is to be 'in danger to be damned'. What I feel, seeing
Burton here, aged twenty-eight, is the majesty of his achievement
and the glamour of his rise and fall to come. What comes over is the
ever-present tumult and intensity; the wildness Burton expressed in
physical ways: smashing, rampaging, pulverising: 'You know, I used
to fight people all the time. Hit them, I mean. If anyone made fun of
my Welsh accent.' This rowdy energy is inherent in his stance, his
posture. He was always fighting with life.

* * *

Where Burton always described something elemental in his
birthplace – lakes, light, anvils, molten lava, clefts and caverns, like
the beginning of the world represented in Tony Palmer's *Wagner* –
Wales, during Burton's own early years wasn't a place of grand opera.
It was a place in the grip of the General Strike, with 84,000 miners
unemployed. There was tuberculosis and malnutrition, with people
digging for roots and standing in freezing water. It was Burton's habit,
as a youngster, to cook potatoes at night on open fires on the hill, as if
in a camp of devils. He collected dung, selling it to people for their
gardens. There was a newspaper round, a bottle harvest to get deposits
back. He was an enterprising imp, and had been born, as Richard
Walter Jenkins, into an extra-large family on 10 November 1925. Above
him already as mouths to feed were Thomas Henry, known as Tom or
Twm (1901–1980), Cecilia or Cis (1905–1993), Ivor or Ifor (1906–1972),
William (1911–1986), David (1914–1994), Verdun (1916–2002), Hilda
(1918–1995), Catherine or Cassie (1921–2011) and Edith (1922–1966). It
was an upbringing, an existence, 'crowded with affection', insisted
David, in his memoir, *Richard Burton: A Brother Remembered*. But with

the diminutive patriarch on the dole or in the pub – and even when given a job in the pit Dick only earned three pounds a week (£138 today) – circumstances were obviously straitened. Here was another aspect to romanticise. To New York reporters, Burton would say, 'I'm the son of a Welsh miner,' and they'd print stories about how 'he had to live in a shanty with no toilet facilities'. In Russia for *The Battle of Sutjeska*, which won the Best Anti-Fascist Award at the Eighth Moscow International Film Festival, he said, 'As the seventh son of a Welsh coal miner I know hardship at first hand,' which made him seem folkloristic and a man of the people. It was also a champion way of registering how far he'd come; a measure of the distance (psychological, financial) covered by his professional ascent. Newsreel footage exists of the Jenkins clan plus wives and husbands clambering aboard a train in Swansea or Cardiff and heading for Hungary – February 1972, this must be, and Taylor's fortieth birthday party in Budapest, where Burton was shooting *Bluebeard*. There they are, these squat cabbage-faced Welsh people in the railway carriage, ordering drinks from the steward, with the winter sky outside the rattling window. And it's impossible to see Burton has any connection with these merrily chattering characters. Physically, he's nothing like them; nor temperamentally, for he was suave, taciturn, distant – further evidence, if you like, he was a changeling or foundling: a creature from a fairy story about unicorns and hippogriffs, black and splintered and morbid. You can't reason it out.

* * *

Taylor was a spoilt and needy child, and so was Burton. The adored darling in a family of women, he was a clinging baby, crying and screaming, who possessed 'the spooky eyes of the devil' – Taylor, indeed, would later commend 'Richard's sexy Satan eyes', and Lauren Bacall, seeing the effect Burton was having in Hollywood, would remark, 'Wicked Richard is using those eyes again, making him

appear wickeder than ever.' But despite a plethora of sisters and aunt-
ies, the one female Burton never or barely saw was his mother. Edith
Maud Jenkins, née Thomas, born in 1883 in Llangyfelach, died of
septicaemia, or puerperal fever, on 31 October 1927 – Halloween.
She'd recently given birth to Burton's younger brother, Graham. The
only thing anyone could recall about her was she enjoyed wallpaper-
ing. Ten pounds had to be borrowed for the funeral, and Edith was
buried in the Jerusalem Chapel graveyard, Pontrhydyfen, a spot now
derelict. 'It was like a bad dream, the funeral and everything,' remembered Hilda. 'Graham in a cot and Mam in a coffin. It was a long time
before we got over it.' Burton never got over it. 'I watched my mother
die,' he said dramatically, in 1967, referring to a moment when he was
two years of age, when he'd have sensed drama and upset going on
around him, and was from the first compelled to make a series of
transformations or abrupt adjustments. Dick proved himself to be
absolutely useless. 'I certainly remember the shame and disgust his
drunkenness made me feel,' said David. 'Something akin to contempt for Father grew in us.' So, on 4 November, days after the death,
Burton was taken by Cecilia to live with her and her new husband,
Elfed, in Taibach, in the vicinity of Port Talbot – 73 Caradoc Street
was to be his home until 1943.

'He had no English and spoke all [in] Welsh to my sister,' said
Hilda. 'While her husband, Elfed, although he is a Welshman,
always spoke in English ... It was like going to a foreign country,' if
only a matter of four miles. Cis took Burton back to visit Pontrhydyfen
each weekend. 'He loved the atmosphere. He liked being with us ...
He grieved for the village,' discerning that, though cossetted (he
wore shoes not boots; he had a bicycle – Elfed had a white-collar
position in the Co-op), he was displaced, already fractured with self-
doubt, and beginning his search to be noble and unified. Though
surrounded by family, Burton was an orphan, or felt himself to be an
orphan: the child who will revolt against grown-ups; who would
want a free play of his passions; who never got over his experience

of loss. 'Completely wild was Richie when he lost his temper,' school-fellows recalled. 'Wild as a bloody hawk he was.' Burton's justification: 'It's different to be without a natural mother.' He was no delinquent, however. Nor was his father, when it came to books. 'If he had had a proper schooling, he could have been anything,' said Hilda of Dick, with surprising sympathy. 'Never without a book.' Burton received a proper (English language) schooling, and though 'I've always been in love with the Welsh language and missed hearing it in Port Talbot,' he, too, became a bibliophile, always changing his library books: 'I am reading on average about three books in two days,' he recorded in his diary in October 1940. The habit continued, and I doubt there's ever been in history a more literary, a more cultured international film star, who'd have known without needing to be told *Where Eagles Dare* comes from the line, 'The world is grown so bad that wrens make prey where eagles dare not perch,' as found in *Richard III*, Act 1, Scene 3.

Though he wasn't always reliably eloquent and elevated – 'Merry Christmas, Richard,' said Michael Caine, one Christmas. 'Why don't you go and fuck yourself,' replied Burton unseasonally – on the whole, 'He was a very serious and academic person,' said Warren Mitchell, and if his journals form an autobiography of alcoholism – as if Burton was a warrior in a mead hall drinking himself into a proud stupor: an abstemious day was a whisky and soda, a few glasses of wine, several brandies, and a few more whiskies and soda: 'Sometimes' (he jotted in 1969) 'I am so much my father's son I give myself [the] occasional creeps ... He had the same temporary violence ... We wave the same admonitory finger at innocence when we know bloody well when we are guilt-ridden' – the journals are also a record of wide and incessant reading. Taylor bought Burton the entire Everyman Library, bound under her direction in calf and green velvet, 'a sensuous delight just to hold and touch'. He was already familiar with the contents, knowing since his schooldays 'which sides of the pages my favourites lie on', the indexes lodged in his head. The treasured set was kept in Céligny, but has since been dispersed – in October 2022, for instance, nine books turned up in a shop in Cambridge, including Vasari's *The Lives of the Painters* in four volumes (£280), Macaulay's *Critical and Historical Essays* in two volumes (£140) and the *Poems and Plays* of Robert Browning in three volumes (£200). Each volume bore a label, 'From the Library of Richard Burton (1925–1984) bound as a gift from Elizabeth Taylor'. No markings or inscriptions to any of them, which is a shame. 'Text clean,' boasted the antiquarian bookseller, where what I'd have wanted were heaps of the actor's annotations, even scribbled laundry lists and suchlike marginalia.

Shakespeare Burton knew by heart; Dylan Thomas – his First Voice in the inaugural 1954 recording of *Under Milk Wood* is for the ages; yards of Gerard Manley Hopkins; Proust; Anthony Powell; Dickens; Joyce; Ngaio Marsh; Melville; Iris Murdoch – he was able to detect from her prose she was a cigar-smoking lesbian wearing 'disfiguring trousers and sweaters'. Burton competed with JFK, or was it Bobby, in spouting the Sonnets. He could do 'To be or not to be' in German and backwards. He played Scrabble with Sophia Loren, who beat him.

He called in to see Edna O'Brien in Putney, perhaps hoping for more than a literary discussion. According to Edna, 'Richard Burton rang the doorbell one Monday evening, late, and said he was in the neighbourhood,' which is an unlikely excuse, as what would Burton be doing in south-west London at any time, let alone by chance, unless on the prowl? The thick black bristles on the back of his neck twitching, his yellow eyes narrowing, he couldn't help smelling out witches – Edna let him in, and he 'mesmerised' and 'entranced' her by reciting Shakespeare and Dylan Thomas, 'torrents of it'. He told her he admired her short story, 'The Love Object', first published in 1968, in a volume entitled *The Love Object*. This was 'a favourite of his', and 'maybe because of it, he took me to be more [of a] libertine than I was. He could not understand why I did not want to go to the bed-chamber, wanting instead to sit and talk.' The *bed-chamber*?

What is this? Rapunzel's tower? (Edna wasn't so reticent when Robert Mitchum found himself in the neighbourhood, though Patrick Magee was a pest.)

'The Love Object' – the unnamed anti-hero could very well be Burton; I can see how he'd have wanted to recognise himself as the distinguished figure ('his eyes looked sad') who had (says the narrator) 'what I call a very religious smile. An inner smile that came on and off, governed . . . by his private joy in what he heard or saw.' He is fastidious, detached, uninvolved emotionally. 'Another thing he did that endeared him [to me] was to fold back the green silk bedspread, a thing I never do myself.' There's always a clothes brush in his luggage. It's a story about an affair – a map of love – and for the chap, sex is a purely technical business. He is already married – and, 'We just started to meet. Regularly. We stopped going to restaurants because of his being famous' – he's a media lawyer or some such; Edna is careful not to make him a film star or television personality. 'My jealousy [of his wife] was extreme, and of course grossly unfair.' For where the man has his job, his family, the woman, the mistress, gets to be ruined by the strength of her own feelings: 'I wanted to do everything and anything for him. As often happens with lovers, my ardour and inventiveness stimulated his' – until it all gets too much, and she's ditched.

The problems of intimacy are forensically examined. Everything is wonderful at first – the world's 'violence, sickness, catastrophes' are shut out, eclipsed. Life seems perfect. Then one day ('jocularly, just like that'), the man says, 'This can't go on, you know.' For the woman, who only once is given a name (Martha – there's a Martha played by Taylor in Who's Afraid of Virginia Woolf?; another in The Comedians), passion ends in deep depression: 'I have become infirm. I have lost the use of my limbs and this accounts for my listlessness . . . I am a cripple.' Where once the lovers had worshipped each other's little habits, now these same things are despicable – the non-poignancy of cigar ash, breakfast remnants. Sourness seeps in, chasms open up, degradation sets in. Martha spends hours waiting for phone calls that don't come – she is 'sitting on the edge of madness'. Emotionally she is stripped bare – 'nothing is a dreadful thing to hold on to'.

Burton would always reduce his women (Claire Bloom, Susan Strasberg) to these uncontrollable states – even Taylor, particularly in Rome, during *Cleopatra*, behaved like Edna O'Brien's heroine, with her suicide attempts; and the story demonstrates how the object of love is to create unhappiness: the disagreeableness of being taken over by another person; the sheer wreckage. And, to look at matters from the man's perspective, what a burden it can be, when someone is besotted with you – when in the tale Martha sees her paramour by chance at a Reception, 'He looked like someone I did not know.' He looked at her coldly, 'with aggression'. She has to be erased.

* * *

A lot of the erotic vagrancy in Burton's, and Taylor's, and Sybil's, existence is here in this story by Edna O'Brien – and if there's any lesson it is this: no one learns anything from what they read; no one ever applies literature's morals and truths. We continue fucking things up and fucking people up, even though Burton was to say his enduring, all-consuming affair was with language and literature, not women. He was happy to confess as much: 'The only thing in life is language – not love, not anything else.' It's why some of his performances (Jimmy Porter in *Look Back in Anger*, Becket in *Becket*, Chris Flanders in *Boom!*, Dysart in *Equus*, Wagner in *Wagner*, O'Brien in *Nineteen Eighty-Four*) have an element of recital, like Dietrich Fischer-Dieskau singing Schubert next to a grand piano. Osborne, Anouilh, Tennessee Williams, Shaffer, Orwell: their dialogue brought out Burton's formality, the Welsh intellectual puritanism; the Principality's starchy tendencies, the flinching from flamboyance, whilst courting it. And underneath, like the coal made from trees and leaves and hidden under the earth, the pressure of something aggressive, dark, strange, stormy, which characterised the flame of the man, his private sense of Hell. For if, in South Wales, Burton had learned to speak and read in English, in England, and a member of the Shakespeare Memorial Theatre's summer season, at Stratford in 1951, and everywhere after that, he exaggerated his Welshness: 'It made him feel different and apart from people,' said Anthony Quayle, Falstaff to Burton's Hal and, in 1969, Cardinal Wolsey to Burton's Henry VIII, in *Anne of the Thousand Days*. Quayle thought Burton's attitude consistently arrogant: 'Fuck you, I'll do it my way, and that's it,' more or less summed him up. When directed in *Hamlet* by John Gielgud, at the Lunt-Fontanne Theatre, New York, in April 1964, and Gielgud said, 'The Americans are the most dreadful snobs. They only appreciate Shakespeare when it is spoken in pure English,' and Burton had to remind him, 'John, you may have forgotten. I am Welsh.' Gielgud's equitable response was, 'Oh, very well, it is almost the same thing.'

It is and it isn't. The important point is, as Burton wrote in 1969, the South Welsh spoke English 'with a verve, a love and a vivacity unmatched anywhere'. This lesson had sunk in during his earliest schooldays, at Eastern Primary in Taibach, where he had been enrolled at the age of five, and at Eastern Boys', where he went three years later. At the latter Burton was prepared for the eleven-plus examination by a teacher called Meredith Jones, who later on became the Further Education Officer for Glamorganshire. As with everybody in Burton's past, Burton inflated the man, saying of Meredith, 'He was all electricity, sparking and flashing; his pyrotechnical arguments would occasionally short-circuit but they were never out of power.' I know the type. Often named Eifion or Teifion, Carwyn or Cadwaladr, they abound in Wales, or still did when I grew up there, masters of pomposity and bullshit, quick with the cane, bullies really, who mocked stutterers, the cross-eyed and the lame, drew attention to eczema. Burton was young enough to be impressed by the 'huge personality of the man', especially Meredith's 'dark-eyed insolence to take on an opponent in the opponent's special subject and destroy him with a fire of improbably and, to the specialist, infuriating irrelevancies.' One of his party pieces, as Burton explained in an article, 'The Magic of Meredith Jones', published in *The Sunday Times* on 17 June 1956, was to talk about the 'dichotomies between the Copernican and heliocentric cosmologies', which at least (or at most) made him seem almost a Glamorganshire Faustus, a philosopher sort, aware of the heavens and the firmament, ill at ease with his allotted and limited place in the scheme of things, i.e. a provincial primary school teacher, someone who was less really than a little water drop falling in the ocean, 'ne'er to be found' (Marlowe). In Meredith's case, a need to organise everybody and be important saw him take on the Warden's duties at the Taibach Youth Club, where Burton started in amateur dramatics. Meredith was Secretary of the Port Talbot Youth Committee, probably a notability in the W I. He was one of those Welshmen, as Burton put it himself – 'no short word for them if a longer one will do; men of brilliantly active vocabularies who love an audience.' Burton was one such himself, with mixed results. 'When Richard spoke, he was listening to himself and getting off on his own voice,' said Montgomery Clift with some disquiet. There is something in this: the hymns and arias; the bearing and manner of speech resounding and echoing as if from a vanished medieval idyll, with everyone in druidical robes. Burton would now and again come out with *amentaceous* (fern- or catkin-like), *sporiferous* (an agent of asexual reproduction) and *meldonium* (a drug to treat coronary disease and used by athletes to 'improve' performance). Taylor could only take so much of this. When Burton mentioned excrement, she finally said, 'Don't you think shit is a much better word?' Burton evidently added the Copernicus/heliotrope business to his own repertoire, except he didn't credit it to Meredith – he told Ava Gardner the idea was his father's, which is interesting.

In March 1937, Burton passed the scholarship exam for the Port Talbot Secondary, the first member of his family to be offered the chance of a grammar school education and, as he said in 1961, 'I was striving to acquire an education of almost any kind.' Though he'd always say Meredith 'taught me to love the English language ... He taught me to be a reader,' it was his next mentor who truly changed his life. Philip Burton was to be his Mephistopheles.

* * *

Philip Burton died, aged ninety, at the William Crane Gray Inn Nursing Home, Davenport, Haines City, Florida, on 28 January 1995. Biographers and commentators have always been very civil. Franco Zeffirelli called him 'a charming, well-informed gentleman', when Philip hung around the Dino De Laurentiis Studios, during the making of *The Taming of the Shrew*. He was the person, it is generally agreed, who instilled in the future actor a sense of craftsmanship – the player of Shakespeare and the classics, poring over textbooks; the hard-won artistry and decorum. But this, I think, could often result in a sort of false beauty – and one can grasp at once why Taylor, who was animated, ardent and spontaneous, who was 'soft, pulpy, slushy, oozy' (to use Keats' words when describing a nectarine), was going to be a powerful (necessary) counterbalance.

Philip was chiselled and precise; life (and art) was one long process of self-improvement. For him high culture was part of an urge for respectability, the concealment of early poverty and deprivation. Philip was born in 1904, in Mountain Ash, near Aberdare, in the Cynon Valley. His father died in a pit accident when he was fourteen. His mother scrimped to send him to the University College of Wales and Monmouthshire, later Cardiff University, and he graduated in 1925 with a joint honours' degree in history and mathematics. As a teacher, shortly the Senior Master, in Port Talbot, a grandee in his BA gown, he always had his favourites. Hubert Clements, Hubert Davies, Evan Morgan, Thomas Owen-Jones, who went to RADA and The Old Vic, Vivian Allen ... Richard Walter Jenkins was next in line, and Philip possessed what he preferred to call 'a Pygmalion

Complex. It's a very deep urge to fulfil myself as an actor or writer through another person. Perhaps I should be unkinder to myself and call it a Svengali Complex.' Is that how a paedophile attempts to explain it? Leslie Howard and Wendy Hiller, Rex Harrison and Audrey Hepburn, Moira Shearer and Anton Walbrook: there is always a sexual underpinning; the relationship isn't chaste and objectively professional – it is a destructive infatuation.

I have always found Philip drab and creepy, like a snail or whelk coiled inside its shell. One can imagine him robbed and beaten to death by sailors he'd taken home, which was the fate of George Rose, Burton's gravedigger in the Broadway *Hamlet*. Philip, fiercely repressed, well-spoken, was determined not to be effeminate, yet the scented talcum powder and a subdued tie offset with a signet ring or suede shoes only emphasised his genteel shabbiness – the pale face and carefully shaved cheeks, the spectacles with polished thick lenses. He smoked an occasional cigarette. His table manners were precise. Having been devoted to his mother, Philip lodged with motherly sorts – though as a 'paying guest': 'the word "lodger" was anathema.' He'd been with Mrs Elizabeth Smith, at 6 Connaught Street, since 1925. The crone attended to his needs, shopping, cooking, doing the laundry and dusting, crisply pressing his lumpy suit. I am reminded of Renée Houston in *Carry On At Your Convenience*, who says to Charles Hawtrey, 'I've put a new napkin in your ring.' Philip made himself useful in the locality as a church sidesman. He had a fine ear for music and played the piano for school assemblies. He knew about German songs. Pernickety, dainty, over-fastidious and cautious – cautious with money (the rented rooms – never a mortgage); cautious about his health (angina, diabetes, kidney ailments, always a worry: Burton would later pay his medical bills); a fusspot about medications and doctors' appointments – A.L. Rowse and Kenneth Williams were similar sorts, also Philip Larkin.

Philip was soon renowned, as the news got about he'd been to America, when most Welsh people hadn't been to Gloucester.

In April 1939 he received a travelling scholarship from the Guild of
Graduates of the University of Wales, and in New York had resided at
the Horace Mann School for Boys, doing what I don't know. In 1941,
he founded and commanded the Port Talbot (499) Squadron of the
RAF Training Corps, and as a Flight Lieutenant was awarded a military MBE. He directed plays at the Taibach Youth Club and the
YMCA. If he never had girlfriends or a wife, he could make this
appear by deliberate choice, as he had a devotion to a nobler calling,
sex and romance apparently disregarded, set aside, ferociously
sublimated. 'I'm quite happy on my own,' Philip said sniffily,
sounding exactly like Kenneth Williams when he added, 'and, you
know, a cultured person is never lonely.' When a female schoolteacher, a colleague, once visited Connaught Street, Philip refused
to escort her home: 'I didn't ask her to call,' he said to his landlady,
his proud misogyny barely containable. (She might have had
designs on him, see.)

There is a brand of South Welsh camp I adore – robust and witty,
and full of deliberate irony, outrage and frivolity. Ryan Davies was a
major specimen, as also my friend Molly Parkin, who in her own
words was 'given to excess, to put it politely,' and of whom (English)
people said, 'Well, she's Welsh like Dylan Thomas and Richard Burton,'
free-floating spirits known and admired for 'their hooliganism, their
verve and their vigour'. The colourfulness of valleys life; carnivals and
concerts, street floats and marching jazz bands. 'You know the Welsh,'
said Hilda. 'We're good at singing, we're good at parties, and we don't
feel shy.' Philip was never that, never any of these things, which from
his angle were working class diversions. He had an aversion to panto-
mimes and circuses. There was a sensation, with him, of darkness and
clamminess, of grotesquerie, which family and associates at the time,
and critics subsequently, have elected to ignore – though Stanley
Baker wasn't able to ignore it, when he described Philip as 'Richard's
adopted father who wanted to be much more.' And when, in her
Foreword to Philip's memoirs, published in 1992, Taylor said without

Philip the wider-world would never have seen Burton's 'cat-green eyes', the implication is how Philip's superior sensitivity would (literally) not have been blind to physicality – and as Burton himself once admitted, 'Never underestimate physical attraction. It opens doors.'

It was Philip who said, 'I was fascinated by him. I thought he had incredible potential and great need ... He had an obvious virility.' He also added, as paedophiles always do, 'He courted me.' What happened is that instead of sitting his School Certificate exams, to be set by the Central Welsh Board, in the summer of 1942, for which he was already expected to achieve 'matriculation standard', making him eligible for college or university entrance, Burton, distressingly, had been withdrawn from the classroom in April 1941 by Uncle Elfed, and compelled to earn a wage – one-pound-eight-shillings a week as a draper's assistant in the gents' outfitters' department of the Co-operative Wholesale Society, Taibach branch. 'I hate it! I hate it!' Burton said, and even years later, in 1971 to be exact, when making *The Battle of Sutjeska* in Yugoslavia, a film mostly involving explosions, commandos slithering down muddy hillsides and crossing roaring rivers on flimsy bridges, after mentioning, in his diary, about how Yugoslav soldiers singing around fires are 'a bit like my old Welsh lot', Burton's thoughts turned to domestic discomfort – damp, cold, dirt – and he writes with a shudder: 'I don't want to be reminded of Caradoc Street ... What a monster Elfed was.' Elfed was not his father and, for his part, Elfed, who thought Burton 'a devil of a lad', was acutely aware Burton was not his son. 'Rich and Elfed just didn't get on,' remembered Graham. 'When I stayed there, Elfed used to fall asleep on the sofa in the living room and Richard would look at him with contempt.' The quarrels with Cis' husband were something Philip could exploit.

Meredith, in particular, was outraged Burton had left or been made to leave school, as here was a pupil, never a slouch, who after handing in homework would diligently state, as in his pocket diary for 23 June 1940, 'I swotted very hard today and learned Chem[istry] practically off by heart.' Meredith, as Secretary of the Port Talbot Youth Committee, appealed to County Councillor Llewellyn Haycock, President of the Youth Centre, which had been inaugurated in 1941, as well as being a school governor, to get the prodigy reinstated – which Burton was, in September 1942, when he was nearly seventeen. As Burton said, here were people who 'swept me into the ambition to be something other than a thirty bob a week outfitters' apprentice,' where he was so truculent, he was known as Wild Jenk. He did learn to appreciate the cut of a jacket, however, and Burton always admired Rex Harrison's sartorial elegance, his way with clothes, which 'drape themselves around him, knowing they have come home at last.'

Burton considered becoming a Baptist minister; he wondered about joining the constabulary, and had visited the police station in Bridgend. But it was amateur dramatics he enjoyed. At the Youth Club he was cast in *The Bishop's Candlesticks*, a summary of *Les Misérables*. The producer was Leo Lloyd, who worked in the steelworks by day, and of whom Burton said, 'He channelled my discontent and made me want to be an actor.' One can see how the prolix role of Jean Valjean, escaped convict converted into magnanimous district plutocrat, would have appealed to Burton's romantic sense of himself: unfathomed nature! the forces of life! Acting made life endurable – or at least showing off before an audience did. In June 1942, Burton won second-prize in the Boys' Solo competition at the County Youth Eisteddfod in Pontypridd. He was also commended for English recitations, and it was Philip who was in charge of his elocution, 'breathing, delivery and movement ... The vowel sounds must be clearly distinguished and the consonantal sounds distinct.' The rain in Spain stays mainly in the plain. In Hertford, Hereford and Hampshire, hurricanes hardly ever happen. Come October, with Burton readmitted as a pupil at Port Talbot Secondary, Philip was directing him in the school play, *Pygmalion*. Burton was Professor Higgins. In real life he was Eliza Doolittle. 'I knew that he was potentially wild,' said Philip, and this was central to his, Burton's, appeal, now and always. In his deliberately misleading account of their relationship, Philip stressed how Burton jostled to get his attention, piping up in class, wanting to join the Air Training Corps to increase proximity. 'He saw to it that he did fire-watching duty on my nights.' Burton was soon a regular at Connaught Street, where Philip coached him in Hotspur's 'My liege, I did deny no prisoners' speech, from *Henry IV, Part One*, Act I, Scene 3, in which Harry Percy speaks of his impatient rage, after a battle, when he'd encountered a popinjay, and it had made him especially mad 'to see him shine so brisk and smell so sweet / And talk so like a waiting-gentlewoman / Of guns and drums and wounds.' I'd call this grooming, wouldn't you?

Mrs Elizabeth Smith remembered her gentleman lodger and his sixteen- or seventeen-year-old caller. 'Mr [Philip] Burton would be up with him at all hours, talking and studying.' Philip started buying little Richie his clothes, 'coached him, trained him, did everything'. But really, Mrs Smith added perceptively, 'he was the type of boy you couldn't alter. He had his own character,' which was under assault. Philip and Burton even ascended Margam Mountain. Philip didn't want shouting or 'the panting antics of ranting preachers. Let the voice speak clear and gentle and twitch the ears of that rabbit wrapped in one hundred yards of stillness.' Burton's ringing voice was a feature since he'd won a Scripture Reading competition at Eastern Infants. The inflections and formalities, the verbal melody and gorgeousness he'd owe to Philip; the charm was innate. It was a package that easily adapted itself to the decorous pseudo-medievalism of *Camelot*, which Philip worked on ('I was to receive no billing') in 1960. 'I'd never met a person before with such determination,' Philip was to say of his star pupil's early struggles – and it would have been Philip who first insisted no chance of life remained for him at home, in Caradoc Street; but everything could be altered: speech and voice, gesture, deportment. (There were to be lots of successive transformations.) It was also a question of class. 'It seemed to me,' Burton said in 1969, 'that coming where I came from, from the very depths of the working class, if I'm going anywhere, I must go as high as I possibly can,' where eventually you will disappear, separated, subtracted, from the rest of society, with its obligations and protocols. He was always reminded of how far he'd come, how far he'd risen – and if he revisited Pontrhydyfen in a Rolls-Royce Silver Cloud, driven by a black manservant called Bob Wilson, it was because, 'There's no point pretending I was still one of them.' What this meant was he belonged nowhere – a man coming to pieces, who wrote in his diary, again in 1969, 'There is no word quite as evocative in the English language as "home," especially if you don't have one' – a reflection also occurring to James Joyce, who had self-exiled Stephen Dedalus say 'home' was one of those words 'I cannot speak or write . . . without unrest of spirit.' Burton was residing on his steam-yacht the *Kalizma* at the time, which was moored on the Thames.

Elfed didn't appreciate the private Shakespeare tutorials, and there were angry scenes. Here is Philip's version: 'Rich' told him about 'the difficulties of his life at home', so Philip told him, 'There was a spare bedroom in Mrs Smith's house,' whereupon Elfed told Philip, 'You take 'im, Mr Burton. You take 'im.' Philip went to Taibach on a Sunday afternoon to press his case further: 'I promised that his [Richard's] further education would be no further burden to them, and that, after the war, I would see to it that he received a free college education.' This selfless philanthropy leaves out all the emotions which were by now involved: '[Richard] became my son, and very emotionally so' – and Philip on another occasion described Burton's arrival in Connaught Street as something less like a pupil wanting private coaching than Heathcliff at midnight coming to claim Wuthering Heights: 'I can't go home. I have no place to stay.' All agree, however, that it was 1 March 1943, St David's Day, when the teenager moved in for good. Burton would always celebrate the anniversary with a debauch. 'Drink up, or by this leek, I will most horribly revenge. On this St David's Day, I drink and drink, I swear,' he declaimed at Shepperton, for example, when Taylor was shooting *X, Y & Zee*, extemporising a speech of Fluellen's from *Henry V*. And as for Philip's fondness for quoting (as if in extenuation) Burton's comment, made in New York, during a press conference for *Hamlet* – 'He [Philip] didn't adopt me; I adopted him' – I find this positively queasy, like the abused expressing gratitude to his abuser. 'Phil virtually took me out of the gutter,' was another of his acknowledgements, made in 1968, and the image, with connotations of dark corners, filthy straw, suggests an angry latent bitterness.

Philip saw to it Burton became genteel, teaching him table manners, how to hold his cutlery. 'He used to like Shredded Wheat for breakfast. Mr [Philip] Burton was so spoiling him that he used to sprinkle the sugar on for him,' said Elizabeth Smith – he'd also be ensuring not too much sugar was being used up. There was more to it than speech therapy and lessons in the art of refinement, though. Where Philip fussed that 'it was distinctness, not volume, that mattered ... Make me hear you. Don't shout, but make me hear you,' Burton did the equivalent of Eliza flinging Higgins' slippers. There were quarrels and door-slamming. Philip would wait up until dawn for Burton to return. 'Where have you been?' – 'Sitting on my grandmother's grave all night meditating.' Are we to believe this? Pupils at Port Talbot Secondary sensed the tension between master and pupil. 'There were a number of occasions when it was perfectly obvious they hadn't come to school on the best of terms,' a classmate recalled. 'There'd been a row or something.' In lessons, Burton would ignore Philip, refuse to laugh at his jokes. 'It was rather sad in a way,' remembered Dennis Burgess. Burton started being cheeky to staff, intimidating people. 'What is it?' he'd ask sarcastically. 'Is it something we've got. Or is it something they lack?'

Though Philip said, 'He had very little free time because he was always most eager to work with me,' Burton returned to Caradoc Street to see Cis: 'He came straight from school to see me, for a long time. He wasn't happy there,' with Philip, who kept asserting, 'I was committed to him. He knew I was doing it out of love. I did feel very much his guardian and his father, and I was proud of him even in those days. It was a fine relationship.' Burton's response: 'It was Hell.' His skin erupted in cyclic acne, boils and carbuncles. He started to drink. 'You drink to overcome the shame.' Of what? Peter Glenville, on the set of *Becket*, a film and a story with a homosexual dynamic (as between Thomas à Becket and Henry II), asked the same question, and then answered it: 'There was something [Burton] did not want to face, and which drinking perhaps covered up.' Burton told Mary Ure that Philip 'made a pass', and what one of his schoolgirl mistresses, Rosemary Kingsland, who had to keep her uniform on during assignations, chiefly remembered is how furious Burton always was on the subject of Philip, 'very, very black and angry.' Burton confessed to her there'd been a sexual relationship going on – as he did to the press, though it was always assumed he was joking when he'd say, 'I drank because I was afraid of being a homosexual . . . Make-up isn't for men, but it is for actors.' He amplified this is 1975: 'Most actors are latent homosexuals and we cover it with drink. I was a homosexual once but not for long. But I tried it. It didn't work, so I gave it up.' Made his eyes water, no doubt. But he revealed it with drink. Douglas Wilmer, in Rome for *Cleopatra*, didn't like the way Burton became tactile towards the end of the evening, and in Hollywood, in 1959, 'Richard Burton got drunk and told Don [Bachardy] he was as beautiful as Vivien Leigh,' according to Christopher Isherwood. There'd remain on Burton's face expressions of ominousness; also, a brokenness – toughness and vulnerability. 'Oh, you poor baby!' were Taylor's first words to him, when, on the set of *Cleopatra*, in 1962, she came across Burton in a hungover condition. She thought him 'vulnerable and sweet . . . He was captivating. My heart went out to him.' Underneath, always, lay hopelessness and helplessness – a sense of what E.M. Forster, similarly sexually distressed, called 'panic and emptiness'.

Philip bought him a coat, which Burton promptly lost. He gave him the poetry books of Alexander Pope, Belloc and A.E. Housman (*of course*). Philip then had legal documents drawn up, an equivalent of the scrolls Faustus signs in blood, framed by Mephistopheles as a 'deed of gift'. He was to adopt the boy and in return his ward would 'absolutely renounce and abandon the use of the surname of the parent and shall bear and use the surname of the adopter and shall be held out to the world and in all respects treated as if he were in fact the child of the adopter Philip Burton who is childless and in good circumstances'. Dick Jenkins was deemed to be 'in poor circumstances', and money changed hands, fifty pounds was mentioned, for his signature, which all smacks rather of a Thomas Hardy short story, where offspring or brides are won or lost at the fair, with wrestling or weight-lifting exploits going on in the background. Philip also was to have 'uncontrolled custody and tuition' and was to pay for the adoptee (called 'the infant' in the paperwork) to be 'kept, clothed and educated'. Additionally, 'The infant shall reside in such places as the adopter think fit.' David Jenkins, who officially witnessed the guardianship agreement in Connaught Street, on 17 December 1943 – so Burton had already been there nine months – found Philip 'exceptionally courteous and charming'. Cis, like one of those innocent fans who doted on Liberace, said, 'Oh, I wish I had all that's in his head!' She'd not have wanted to know all that was in Philip's head. And yet how perfectly normal it was all made to seem, especially *in Wales*, and the Wales of those days, that two men should go off together on their own. Three weeks earlier, this was printed in the *London Gazette*:

NOTICE is hereby given that RICHARD WALTER JENKINS of Number 6 Connaught Street, Port Talbot, in the County of Glamorgan, Actor, a natural born British subject resident in the United Kingdom at the date of the coming into force of Regulation 20 of the Defence (General) Regulations,

1939, intends after the expiration of twenty-one days from the pub-
lication of this notice to assume the surname of Burton. Dated
22nd day of November 1943. R. IVOR REES, Alexandra Buildings, Port Talbot, Solicitor for the said Richard Walter Jenkins.

Burton found all this rather oppressing him. Behind the lawyer's dry
formula is a lot of yearning, Philip's for Wild Jenk, and Burton's to
escape from his background, which would, indeed, make him the
beneficiary of the older man's lust. Did Philip, therefore, or thereby,
damage Burton, or create him, or liberate him? As Elizabeth Smith,
the landlady, said, 'Richard has got to thank [Philip] for everything in
the world he's got' – like Mephistopheles making a bridge through the
moving air and revealing to Faustus images of sex and wealth. So,
when Burton said to Alan J. Lerner, 'I'm going to be the richest, the
most famous, and the best actor in the world,' what one realises is
Faustus' boasts, that he'll 'heap up gold' and 'live in all voluptuousness', did, as far as Burton was concerned, come absolutely true and
were absolutely real. Faustus' and Burton's magical powers were genuine. Burton did meet and marry Helen of Troy, the role Taylor played
on stage and screen, her face given a sheen by being buffed with
Johnson's Baby Powder. The pair of them appeared on over two thousand magazine covers between 1964 and 1974. The New York Botanical
Gardens had named a rose after Burton in April 1961, and after he won
a Tony for *Hamlet*, a fox at the zoo was given the appellation 'Richie'.
Faustus' soul is the actor's ego. And if, as Mike Nichols said, 'Richard
seemed to be prisoner of a fantasy of having sold his soul to the Devil,'
all his pacts and decisions – veering from duty or yielding to passion,
escaping poverty and his naked greed for money ('Larry [Olivier] has
a Rolls and a house in London and that's it. I decided I was not going
to do that. I was going to go for the money') – had to do with moral
scruple. 'Everyone is offered a choice,' Burton said. 'An obvious, easy
one, or a more difficult, rewarding one.' And it was Philip who was
the nagging conscience, a pedantic old priss he spent a lifetime

shaking off. Burton was, said Philip in old age, 'an integral part of my life,' and to Burton this was (the words he used in his diary in 1969) 'total agony.' But Philip's was a love that never failed. He followed Burton to Cardiff, when Burton was employed by Emlyn Williams ('We had a two-bedroom flat in the home of another delightful widow, Mrs Morris'), where they studied *Doctor Faustus* ('particularly the wonderful final soliloquy': 'The stars move still; time runs; the clock will strike; / The Devil will come, and Faustus must be damned'). When Burton married Sybil in 1949, 'I had a flat close to them,' in Hampstead. When Burton and Sybil appeared at Stratford together two years later (Burton was Hal, Sybil was Lady Mortimer), it's clear Burton was trying to keep a distance. 'A quiet day at home,' Philip wrote in his own diary, 'luxuriating in Rich's Stratford notices. This is bliss indeed.' He gave Burton 'notes' after a performance, missed his train, and had to wait over an hour on the platform in Leamington Spa.

* * *

In 1955, Philip trailed after Burton to New York, where he began to write bad plays and novels, which would be given titles like *A Forenoon Knell*; *You, My Brother*; *My Friend, the Enemy*; *They Call Me Gentleman Johnny* and *A Great Reckoning*. Burton's judgements: 'prissy, pious and pretentious', 'convoluted, pedantic and frequently opaque', 'perishingly dull', though this didn't stop him sending a copy of another one, amazingly called *A Sole Voice*, to A.L. Rowse. Philip wrote a play about Dante expressly for his ward ('I wanted to surprise him with a finished script'), which Burton set aside and never mentioned. 'One of the big disappointments of my life was that [Richard] never played it.' He wrote a movie script of *Coriolanus*, which was 'indefinitely postponed'. He wrote something about a German sailor, called *The Sea Devil*. Burton said it was 'not something for him'. He wrote a biopic about Simon Bolivar, 'a good vehicle for Richard', for which at least Philip received 'a token advance payment'. When James Mason asked him to polish a script, 'My weeks of work were unwanted and went unpaid,' Philip recorded. A screenplay of *The Beach of Falesa* was another failed project, which is surprising, as the Stevenson story, from 1892, had first been adapted by Dylan Thomas in 1948 and Burton had acquired the rights from Caitlin. The story of South Seas sorceries, involving a trader fooling the natives with demonic powers, which are actually conjuring tricks, luminous paint and sham harps, would have been a good one for Burton – and I don't know if any of Philip's material was retained, but in 1960, Hugh French, Burton's agent, offered the project to Christopher Isherwood. 'I think I can improve it,' said Isherwood, who saw a revision of Philip's draft by Jan Read, a Scottish author (d. 2015 in St Andrews, aged ninety-five) responsible for television's *Dr Finlay's Casebook*. 'It is a chance to air one of my favourite theories, that the truly evil man is the one who only pretends to believe in evil.'

When Philip, in an attempt to generate an independent career, mounted Off-Off-Off-Broadway a play called *Udomo*, about Kwame Nkrumah, the founder of the Republic of Ghana, where obviously 'the great majority of the cast . . . were black', the lead actor collapsed on stage and Philip had to bring down the curtain. The crew couldn't master the scene changes, the replacement lead actor never mastered his lines, and the producer disappeared 'without leaving money for the cast'. Philip's impressive-sounding American Musical and Dramatic Academy was always in the financial doldrums ('There was no money in our bank account'), and Aaron Frosch, Burton's lawyer, had to solve its tax problems, turning it into an official charitable organisation. Burton provided $27,000 towards initial running costs. At a fundraising reception, after a screening of *Who's Afraid of Virginia Woolf?*, the air conditioning broke down, as did the microphones, and the lights went out. In 1979, when Philip gave a 'lecture-recital' on *King Lear*, a man in the audience died of a heart attack ('an ambulance was called'); then the sound-system failed and no one heard a word.

Philip, as the President and Director of the American Musical and Dramatic Academy, was all set to direct a play for actual Broadway, but he was sacked in Washington, and the play (whatever it was) closed after two performances.

It is a sorry saga of disappointment and rejection. Here was 'the world to which I felt I belonged', and Philip was simply out of his depth. He had to sit in cinemas on his own, watching Burton 'with tearful pride'. He saw Burton's *Hamlet* from behind a pillar. 'We had a long and lovely session afterwards' – Philip was always usurping the director's role; this may be why Michael Benthall, artistic director of The Old Vic between 1953 and 1962, was not interested in casting Philip as Claudius opposite Burton, in allowing him near any professional production involving Burton, back in the Fifties. Eventually Philip realised, 'our shared dream of my directing [Richard] in Shakespeare in the London theatre was finally shattered . . . I wish I had worked with him on *Othello*,' a role Burton played at The Old Vic in 1955, when he was thirty. Even as late as 1982 there were pie-in-the-sky dreams. Burton was going to buy and run The Old Vic, rename it The Richard Burton Classic Theatre, with Philip as the consultant, selecting the repertoire. The productions were to be put on celluloid or videotape later. 'The whole thing came to nothing,' said Philip. 'I was relieved for Richard,' who was dying of the drink, 'but a bit sorry for myself.' There is a double sense of humiliation, when a person has been outgrown. You see only their littleness. Philip mentions Burton's 'uninterested brusqueness'. He was always waiting for 'a promised word from Richard – how often did I spend time doing that!' Burton 'broke appointments' and fitted Philip into his schedules 'with exasperating unreliability'.

What he received were scraps – Burton gave Philip the task of selecting a library for Puerto Vallarta: 'What a delightful assignment for a bibliophile like me!' Daphne Rye, of H.M. Tennent, to whom Burton was under contract, tried to get Philip walk-on roles in Blackpool and Bournemouth. Philip understudied Ernest Thesiger, who was never off. In New York, with Resident Alien status, he was a consultant in the script department of a film company run by Lester Cowan and Walter P. Chrysler Jr., he of the building. But the company was dissolved after six months, and Philip realised he was only there 'to get ready access to Richard'. He ended up escorting Chrysler's art collection in a van to Portland, Oregon, a journey taking two weeks. 'No good news awaited me professionally,' he bleated. He gave night classes to would-be actors. 'I had to bear all the initial expense of advertising and printing.' Philip also lectured at Barnard College 'as a temporary replacement for Mildred Dunnock', who though she may sound like a Marx Brothers character was an actress nominated for an Oscar as Willy Loman's wife Linda in *Death of a Salesman*, and who was in *BUtterfield 8* as Taylor's mother. Meanwhile, Burton was a tax exile in Switzerland.

* * *

Burton said of his two fathers, 'My real father gave me his love of beer. He was a man of extraordinary eloquence, tremendous passion, great violence. I was greatly in awe of him. He could pick you up with one hand by the seat of your pants. My adopted father is the exact opposite. A pedant, a scholar, meticulous in his speech, not given readily to passion. I'm still frightened of him. He still corrects my grammar.' Perhaps he was more like a mother? Dick Jenkins was a ne'er-do-well drunkard, inspiring in his son the off-screen antics and boorishness – all those dismal diary entries: 'Got sloshed' (14 June 1965); 'I was so fed up I had three glasses of wine and two large brandies in about half an hour' (12 April 1966); 'I drank steadily all day long' (5 May 1966); 'Became thoroughly drunk' (9 October 1966). Philip, however, though full of cant – he thought cinema 'a very inferior substitute' for Shakespeare on the stage – and ostentation ('Richard was the definitive Coriolanus, and Olivier agreed with me'), operated as Burton's more pervasive if turbid muse, contributing to the persona of sterility, deprivation, on view in (say) *Bitter Victory* (1958), which is about a commando operation behind enemy lines ('We need those documents from Benghazi!'), and Gavin Lambert's script brings out parched masculine values: honour, duty, strength, courage, the joy of destruction. Burton is a former archaeologist ('Besides, he's Welsh!') and gives a hushed and silent, whispered performance. How good he is at conveying intelligence – bleak, contained, his Captain Leith never in any doubt about what awaits him in life is death. His rival on the impossible mission – in and out of German barracks raiding a safe; the booby-trapped stairs and corridors (Burton will return to this kind of caper in *Where Eagles Dare*, but this one is dry, dark, unemphatic) – is Curt Jurgens' Major Brand. 'I'm a mirror of your own weakness,' Burton tells him, for it is Burton's character who shoots the wounded, stabs a sentry, and Jurgens who hesitates, and who is considered a coward for not being lethal. The theme is that of conflict revealing the real person – Hemingway's philosophy of grace under pressure. Lambert (or Nicholas Ray, the director) adds to the pressure by showing us Leith has been having an affair with Brand's wife. Early on there's an awkward nightclub scene; a sense of regret; parting – a lot of tension and sexual jealousy. But we hardly need to know the Jurgens role was intended for Alec Guinness to work out the queasy homosexual undercurrent, the sadomasochism of the soldiery – and that *Bitter Victory* is about deeply repressed emotions, hopeless fatalism, the things that matter being those which never can be expressed. Burton's severity never softens, never ameliorates – what he mostly is, is sardonic. Eventually, he is killed off. A scorpion crawls up his trousers and in due course, 'I'm afraid it's gangrene.' Dead and recumbent in the sand, Burton is very beautiful, like a Pharoah. Ray cuts back to the shot several times, as if to emphasise the perilous nature of human happiness and fulfilment, as everything is headed for destruction.

Jimmy Porter isn't in the Libyan desert, he's in an attic flat overlooking Derby. Except he isn't – as the locations captured by Oswald

Morris' camera for *Look Back in Anger* (1959) were in Harvist [sic] Road, Holloway, N7 (later demolished by Islington Council), Deptford, Romford and Dalston Junction. The graveyard, for the scene with Edith Evans, is St Mary's Roman Catholic Cemetery, Harrow Road, Kensal Green. Nevertheless, there is no foliage in the film – all is weedy pavements, scrub, dead grass, ash. The sky is ash white, the thick clouds like splotches on an X-ray plate. And though there are women in the film – the black-and-white photography gives Mary Ure a silver halo; Claire Bloom, narrowing her eyes and tilting her head, has the same demureness she had when confronting Olivier in *Richard III* (she brings out the monster, which she finds exciting) – there is psychological ambivalence here, as Jimmy's warmth, his rapport, extends only towards his Welsh flatmate, Cliff Lewis, played by Gary Raymond. It is Jimmy and Cliff who are more the married couple, fussing about breakfast eggs, the washing-up, the ironing. They enjoy music hall riffs and improvisations. They rugby tackle each other – puppies playfighting. If Jimmy, like Milton's Satan, is 'inflamed with rage', consumed with 'infinite wrath and infinite despair', it is because he feels crushed by conventional notions and expectations of marriage – women, with their caution and good sense, are a trap, blotting out the immediacy of experience, spoiling everyone's fun. Jimmy is not a man who wants to be properly handled, and Burton really is half-mad here, shouting and threatening, smashing crockery. His bachelor behaviour is menacing. He is the caged creature – a Francis Bacon figure suffocating in its surroundings – and when Ma Tanner (Dame Edith) asks, 'What do you really want, Jimmy?' his answer is, 'Everything. Nothing.' Later, she has a stroke, and her parting advice is, 'Don't let yourself down, son.' Burton emerges in the road and as if on The Old Vic stage belts out, 'Hell, hell, hell, hell!' and has a fight with his own overcoat. Though (we learn) Jimmy is a university graduate, he refuses to be urbane – and Burton's is a performance of brute force and cruelty, the misogyny, under Tony Richardson's direction, part of an attitude towards homosexuality, that it represents freedom (from domesticity, from ordinariness) – a bitter victory over illusions of prettiness, niceness. Women, in fact, with their alleged manoeuvring and rivalries, instil fear, so Jimmy has to keep saying they are wet; he taunts and resents them – and he sees it as his function to destroy the illusions Alison and Helena have about themselves. Was his degree perhaps in philosophy, as his vehemence makes him seemingly logical, but the arguments are abnormal, distorted. What Jimmy looks back at (not in anger; with nostalgia) is a lost pastoral world, an idyll; and it is the Fall of Man which enrages him, nothing less. Killing time in the flat, with Cliff and Alison, bored by the Sunday papers, the characters could be eating apples in a garden, Jimmy his own serpent. 'I'm for the first time ever looking forward to seeing a film in which I play,' Burton assured Philip. He was right to be impressed with himself.

The next one, *The Bramble Bush*, made at the Warner Brothers Studio, Burbank, in 1960 – the story is set in a small town in Massachusetts, the East Coast-looking backlot anticipating the college green of *Who's Afraid of Virginia Woolf?* – also contains biblical allusions: 'For every tree is known by his own fruit. For of thorns men do not gather figs, nor of a bramble bush gather they grapes' (Luke, 6: 44). Exclusivity, categories, precept, without which society is chaos. The bramble bush is that which brings forth evil and corruption – heavily symbolic here of spikes, prickles, entanglements, which are emotional, moral, sexual. Burton is the doctor, returning from Boston, to attend the deathbed of his best pal, who has cancer – a word the film doesn't utter, though we deduce Hodgkin's disease is meant. The patient is on increasing doses of morphine, and Burton gives him the booster shot to finish him off – a mercy killing. The law, however, insists a person should be kept alive, to suffer, for as long as possible. Killing is killing. Outside of all of that, Burton is pursued by Angie Dickinson, the nurse, and Barbara Rush, the best pal's wife, now widow. Plus, the small town's characters, the district attorney, newspaper editor, rector, drunks, and so forth – characters from a western – pile in. Jack Carson, as the burly political candidate, is in *Cat on a Hot Tin Roof,* in which he also incarnates the hearty bully. There are a lot of those in American cinema, men who are pushy, full of themselves, quick to bridle. Burton is low-key – one of his agonised performances (he's as agonised as the cancer victim); he's in church praying at one point. Then comes another Jimmy Porter session, and what he looks back in anger at is very specific: the memory of walking in on his mother in bed with her lover; his father, disgusted, leapt from the cliff onto the rocks. Burton has quite a monologue, divulging all of that, moving from a sofa to a chair, gazing at his mother's photograph, smashing it, smashing a table lamp, before running up the street in his shirtsleeves.

There's a soap opera pace, a soap opera locale (hospital corridors, the town square, where strangers and visitors stick out). But as one of the last people alive to have seen *The Bramble Bush*, I can tell you it's better than that. There's a Saul Bass title sequence, a cool jazz score, and Lucien Ballard's cinematography utilises a dilute biscuit palette, pale straw, sandiness, which infuses the screen with an atmosphere of sickness, jaundice. Fashions in attractiveness change (buxomness replaced the gamine), but Angie Dickinson is sexy still; she seems powerless to prevent terrible men from using her, as if she's not quite aware of how it happens. Her character, Fran, is always finding herself in motels or semi-amateur photographic studios. On the other hand, there's Barbara Rush, stiff and formal, seemingly ladylike, despite the way she pops coloured pills and drinks cocktails all day. Then there is Burton, with his expectancy and awareness, his restraint filling a room, his voice like bitter chocolate, gazing at everyone with horror and fascination – for here is a film that explores issues that are not mentioned or seen: abortion, adultery, pregnancy outside of Holy Wedlock, and the close friendship between Burton and Larry (Tom Drake) is a bond that's homoerotic. Love is expressed by bringing about death.

Liberty and social justice; tolerance and order; loss and error: choice is painful because it tests the limits of human reason. To quote Isaiah Berlin on the topic, 'Our natures are not fixed or finished; they are inherently incomplete, liable to self-transformation by the choices we make among the incommensurable goods and evils we confront unavoidably in our lives,' and confront every minute of every day. If Burton was good at making his characters' debates about conflicting values suggest his own inner conflicts and transgressions, it is because the subjects of his films were the dilemmas of his life – sexual freedom, erotic intrigues, physical existence; whether it is possible to become a different kind of a man, and to make an escape from what we are and move into a wholly new sphere. Hence, *Becket* (1964), about a libertine ('Nobody does it the way you do it, Thomas!') who is made Archbishop of Canterbury and becomes sanctimonious, who is given the Great Seal of England and becomes doctrinaire. The King simply cannot believe his friend has changed so fundamentally, has suddenly found all these new obligations – it's not what you'd expect, even from an ex-roisterer. *Becket* is also a double act between Burton and Peter O'Toole, who plays Henry II, the great-grandson of William the Conqueror. Burton is heavy-going, lugubrious, in comparison – serious. O'Toole was never serious. He has intensity – but it is a mad intensity. He was good at aristocratic lunatics, in the grip of mania: T.E. Lawrence of Arabia (O'Toole's Lawrence would not have translated Homer or been a Fellow of All Souls); *The Ruling Class, Lord Jim*, Tiberius in *Caligula*, any number of Anglo-Irish grandees. He had no spiritual dimension, as such, which Burton liked to show us he on the other hand possessed, but he, O'Toole, can be prone to hallucinations and dreams. As an actor he's a nervous stick insect, twitching, histrionic; and like Burton he's aware of a splendid (actorish) voice, given to fancy, quivering enunciation. As Henry, here and also in *The Lion in Winter*, he's syphilitic, ridden with rickets, cruel, in pain – the whole bundle can be camp at times, as O'Toole is never naturalistic, like ballet or opera are not naturalistic.

Showing how versatile he was, Olivier played both roles, Becket and the King, on stage in New York in 1960, alternating the parts with Anthony Quinn and Arthur Kennedy. Olivier is all over the film, too,

as O'Toole and Burton are intent on imitating him – the random
shouting, the declamatory style. The stateliness. The way they wander
around John Bryan's ecclesiastical sets and painted castles, very obviously *acting*. Lines are bellowed the full length of an empty cathedral
or throne room. (O'Toole and Burton are almost imitating Olivier
with a smirk.) O'Toole's monarch is bored, petulant; Burton is
reserved, solid – implying integrity. You believe in him as the courtier
and best friend, who discovers higher loyalties – yet this moral clash is
only the pretext for a deeper homosexual drama: the love between the
two men, who rub each other down with towels; the jealousies and
bitterness, as they try to elicit reactions, responses. The scenes in the
forest with the wenches, which actually look like rape; the laddish
leaping through the casements ('Quick, out through the window!');
the bits with Siân Phillips playing her lute and singing in Welsh – you
can't believe in their womanising. Pamela Brown (Eleanor) and
Martita Hunt (Matilda) as the queens have an arch quality. They could
be in Danny Kaye's *The Court Jester*. And the chief problem with the
film: despite back-projected horse rides there is no action, only lots of
dialogue or recitations in the cloisters, which gets to be tediously, fat-
uously 'literary' and no doubt everybody concerned (Hal Wallis,
Peter Glenville, Phyllis Dalton, Anne V. Coates) believed it was high
art. It's always a tonic, though, for me to see our character actors:
Donald Wolfit, in a purple velvet hood or helmet, making him resemble Marty Feldman, as a conniving bishop; Felix Aylmer as a doddery
prelate (when was he anything else?); Gielgud as the King of France,
enjoying the malice of diplomacy. 'Permit me to show you my aviary,'
he sniffs, though the budget didn't run to our being shown it. Yet it
doesn't expand, as an epic should. There's plenty of ceremony and the
ritual of the religious services – Burton in his episcopal attire. O'Toole
is seen howling and gnashing (he could be in the Arabian desert
again), and the conferences he presides over, as Henry II, where the
historical figures discuss the difference between the honour of the

throne and the honour of the Church: all this seems trumped up, our character actors, which now include Geoffrey Bayldon, Graham Stark and Victor Spinetti, frowning and looking solemn, as if they can't follow what any of it means. Burton, nevertheless, who played so many priests, here indulges his guilt – and I suddenly realise how good he'd have been as Inspector Maigret, who has a priestly gruff-ness and sensitivity. He is masculine, with his smoking and drinking, his spirits sagging, his face 'heavy, placid, and yet hard', in Simenon's words. It is *Murder in the Cathedral*, of course, the drama of Jean Anouilh's *Becket* – and Eliot's version of the same events is not only constructed like a detective story ('Who killed the Archbishop?'), it contains lines lifted from Sherlock Holmes. The difference with *Becket* is Becket's death is no puzzle. Henry has him stabbed out of petu-lance, out of the sadistic impulse to demonstrate 'a king must never weaken!' It is despotism, but it is also the showing off of a star actor – and it is on the brink of craziness, of blasphemy, as Henry is sexually jealous of – and his rival for Becket's affections is – Almighty God. Burton's Becket, you feel, would have been the wiser monarch, with a firmer idea of obedience and duty. In the end, it proves impossible to have O'Toole's king as a friend, because even friendship is something the king believes he can demand: 'I really am your friend, and you are wrong not to love me.' We end as we began – it's all taken place in flashback – with O'Toole stripped to the waist, flagellated by monks at Thomas' tomb, making penance, and it's very kinky, like Lawrence with José Ferrer and the Turks. Burton is present as a fibreglass effigy. 'His performance caused me to weep with pride,' said Philip, though he'd not have meant as the fibreglass effigy.

Plantagenet politics, in *Becket*, with all the personal taunts and recrimination it brings about, is a means of displaying two men's affection and hatred, the one aspiring to virtue, a higher life, the other ruthless and egocentric; and both of them luxuriant and neu-rotic and, in spite of themselves, romantic – which is to say, Thomas à Becket and King Henry II are aware, as Dorian Gray was, of 'how exquisite life had once been! How gorgeous!' Were theological debate replaced by camp bickering ('How's that for Holy Week'; 'Give us a kiss and I'll tell you who's peculiar!'), the relationship is the one in *Staircase*. 'It looks as though you've cornered the limp wrist market, duckie,' said O'Toole mockingly to Burton, though his co-star this time is Rex Harrison, who in his peerless Rex Harrison way pretended to get the wrong end of the tickling stick: '[It's] about two men living together, absolutely no servants, so they can't give dinner parties.' Whether or not he was calculatingly thoughtless by nature, none knew with Rex. It's another film I must be the first person in half a century to have watched – certainly I'm the first person to appreciate it, as the reviews, in August 1969, were stupid and hom-ophobic ('Shrill, flamboyant, sarcastic,' *Monthly Film Bulletin*; 'Harrison and Burton have dared risky roles', *Variety*), though the only thing off is it's set in the East End and doesn't look like London because it's filmed in Paris, so what we have is a French studio's idea of the architectural details and furnishings, the bricks and window frames, with the backstreet salon overlooking a cemetery. All this gives *Staircase* a necessary oddness, however, a bizarre quality. Harrison and Burton play a pair of ramshackle old queens ('male cosmetics, they're allowed, dear'), but not as any jape or joke. Burton, indeed, said later, 'I never got *Staircase* . . . out of my system,' and he was open (in his diaries) about 'my intense enjoyment playing a bald homosexual in *Staircase*.' The film is drab and sad and doleful – the filthy, stained, depressing brownish mauve flat, not painted or decor-ated exactly, more streaked and sickly. Cathleen Nesbitt is Burton's disabled mother, lying upstairs in pools of piss. She thinks her son is 'waiting for the right girl'. There's deliberately no garishness let alone elegance here – nothing of the musical, despite Stanley Donen's being the director. Burton (Harry) and Harrison (Charlie) are strangely unvain; they take the material seriously; they give perfor-mances. And it is about a marriage, one of their own marriages, perhaps: the screaming matches ('Oh, shut your mouth, keep the draught out!'), the inability to declare open affection, the rancour, self-hatred, loneliness and ego; the refusal to show each other they are needed; the hatred they prefer because love is sentimental. How much easier and safer simply to call your partner loudly 'an obscene flabby bag!' The drag artistes in the title-sequence, dressed in purple feathers and copper sequins, warbling about 'Help me climb life's staircase!' could be Taylor and Rachel Roberts.

There's a masculine strength in their voices, their roars. Burton and Harrison, in fact, only slightly exaggerate their usual manner, adding only more wistfulness, more polish. They are each, as always, contained, compact, masters of enunciation, Harrison with his wonderful scorn, Burton with his lyric baritone. Nevertheless, Burton has an unusual (for him) kindliness. He plays Harry as a babushka, his head bandaged to hide alopecia – he also looks as if he's had brain surgery, and the dead Burton in the Hôpital Universitaire de Genève (the cantonal hospital), Rue Micheli-du-Crest, cannot have been dissimilar. The film opens with Burton attending to Harrison's hair, deploying the curlers and pins, dabbing on the cologne, the shaving lotion, titivating the blue waves. As actors they are too proficient to do all this badly – and as Stanley Donen had directed Peter Cook and Dudley Moore in *Bedazzled*, a year earlier, it's no stretch to say the short dark Burton could be Moore (who provides the soundtrack) and the tall tapering Harrison could be Cook: Harry and Charlie are Pete and Dud roles, essentially, but they'd have played the relationship as comedy, whereas what we actually have is a tragedy. 'You must establish your credentials as a man pretty thoroughly before you can take the risk of playing a poof,' said Burton, joining in with the repellent way homosexuals are automatically there to be scoffed at. Yet then he added, 'I've been in training for this role for most of my life,' and the person he seems to be impersonating is the distressed Philip, with his complaining and nagging and grovelling, deflecting all those enquiries about why he'd never married. In *Staircase*, the

Harrison character, in particular, lives in fear of the police. He has received a magistrates' summons for breaches of the peace – for importuning. Stephen Lewis, later Blakey in *On the Buses*, in a blond thatch and a tan jacket, is his pick-up. Harrison pulls his boots off, helping him out of his 'damp clothes'. There's a lot of giggling behind a closed door. Lewis later shuffles off down the stairs, counting his money. With the trial coming up, Harrison, an aged falcon, is particularly fine and affected ('Can I help being artistic?'); he, too, is a version of Philip, for as a would-be big shot his biggest job, long in the past, was making an advertisement for duffel coats.

'Sometimes,' said Francis Bacon, 'a man's shadow is more in the room than he is,' and *Villain*, made on location in Notting Hill, Battersea, Kilburn, Bayswater, Hounslow, the Nine Elms Freight Yard, Wandsworth Gasworks and the Southern Industrial Estate, Bracknell, in 1971, sees Burton wanting to portray a homosexual as a killer. There was one of those Pop Art headlines (in the *Daily Mirror*), 'BURTON'S SECRET VISIT TO RONNIE KRAY', and Reggie and Ronnie Kray are no doubt the ostensible inspiration for Burton's Vic Dakin, a gangster who takes a razor to a croupier, beats up the clerk at the factory because the job involves 'silly little forms and pink carbon copies', and who trembles with rage at the sight of Colin Welland eating sandwiches. Dakin is revolted at the sight of a stripper ('Get out, slag!') and punches his reluctant lover (Ian McShane – 'He wants to see ya!') fiercely in the gut, before affecting to be considerate. McShane has recalled of his scenes in the film: 'After kissing me, he's going to beat the hell out of me and it's that kind of relationship. Rather hostile. It was very S&M.' Donald Sinden is a corrupt MP, Gerald Draycott, who gives false alibis, a role based on Robert Boothby. Joss Ackland swigs milk for his ulcer. Here is a late Sixties, well, early Seventies, London of Jags, Consuls, Rovers, Mini Coopers and Ford Zodiacs. There are signs for Double Diamond and Ind Coope. Victorian streets, railway arches and mansion blocks are being cleared for high-rise flats and hospitals surrounded by new motorways, inner-ring roads and service stations. Everything is going. At the funeral service for Vic's mother (Cathleen Nesbitt – Burton's mother again), this must be the last recorded use of the King James Bible: 'Thou knowest, Lord, the secrets of our hearts; shut not thy merciful ears unto our prayers.' Burton, his hair dyed red, is convincingly frightening as a man corrupt and megalomaniacal. (It's a pity the big crime we build up to is so paltry – a wage-snatch in a plastics factory.) There is a sexual frenzy to his attacks and outbursts. It excites him, laying into James Cossins, another person chomping sandwiches. It is a baroque role for him, power and evil making Burton shudder orgasmically. 'Sex is the overwhelming urge and driving force in all human beings,' Burton once said, perhaps paraphrasing Dylan Thomas' business about the force that drives the green fuse through the flower. As a homosexual psychopath, Burton's Vic Dakin presides over chaos and barrenness. Evil is something he can spread and inflict. It's like the destructiveness of alcohol – how it makes for evil, if you want to be in its grip, because it sets you apart from the world. And if you wonder what was Burton doing in the field of acting, it's that it set him apart from the world: 'I have achieved a sort of diabolical fame,' he said in 1963. 'I am the diabolically famous Richard Burton.'

* * *

1963: he ran off with Taylor; twenty years earlier he moved in with Philip. It amounted to the same thing, a fundamental separation from what had been going on before; an awareness that a sense of disruption was necessary – destruction almost had to be invited – if he was to have a big career; if he was to swoon before the fever of possibility and make it new. It was all part of a grand design, the exercise of violent or concentrated will. And along with all of that, there was sexual subordination and threat, which is why Burton could never be at peace. 'Oh, I know he *was* ...' he said, when taxed about

Philip's homosexuality. 'If one is sexually inclined in some way, there is a network of like-minded people they can trust and who will help.' Philip was 'part of this network', which included Gielgud (who said to Edith Sitwell: 'I should say Richard Burton is your man . . . *really* a good actor, intelligent, sensitive'), Nevill Coghill, Binkie Beaumont, Robert Helpmann (who sat through three consecutive performances of Burton's *Hamlet* at The Old Vic – and Philip was to say in his parasitic fashion, 'My only chance of ever playing Hamlet was through Richard'), Robert Hardy, Terence Rattigan, Kenneth Williams and Emlyn Williams. In August 1943, after Burton had achieved 'matriculation standard' in the School Certificate exams, an advertisement appeared in the *Western Mail*: 'Mr Emlyn Williams is looking for a Welsh boy actor' for his play *The Druid's Rest*, a farce about mistaken identities in the run-up to an Eisteddfod. Burton duly applied to the author / director, 'enclosing a recent photograph', writing to Williams at his London address, 15 Pelham Crescent. Williams was smitten: 'A boy of seventeen, of startling beauty and quiet intelligence . . . I was immediately struck with this very spectacularly handsome lad,' he said, after meeting him by appointment at the Sandringham Hotel, St Mary Street, Cardiff. It was Williams (Emlyn) who gave the Address at Burton's Service of Thanksgiving, held at noon in St Martin-in-the-Fields, Trafalgar Square, on 30 August 1984. 'Side by side with the light,' he said from the pulpit, 'the dark; behind exaltation, melancholy.' In between the harp solos and the hymns, Gielgud gave a reading from *Hamlet*.

I always found Williams, Wamba in *Ivanhoe*, don't forget, a poseur and a dandy, with a gardenia voice. Burton was unsure of what he thought about him, too. At a party Olivier threw in Hollywood on 19 March 1959, for example, to celebrate the tour of Williams' one-man Dylan Thomas show, *A Boy Growing Up*, Burton, according to Christopher Isherwood, started to recite Thomas' poetry and 'said Emlyn couldn't', which would have been a challenge and an insult, though none seemed to object. Come 17 May they'd all met up again,

'Olivier, Richard Burton and Emlyn very lively and drunk.' Nevertheless, Williams was a creepy character, who played creepy characters,
e.g. Caligula in the abandoned Laughton film. Like Robert Helpmann,
there's a genuinely perverse sense of evil, like a bat or a reptile or the
feline creatures in Saki. There's no redeeming warmth. His face is
like hard wax. He wrote books about Brady and Hindley. He imagined a diary for Crippen. His play *Night Must Fall* is about a charming
psychopath, who keeps a severed head in a hatbox. (Burton was in a
radio adaptation, broadcast in 1953.) There's never any touch of sympathy. I suppose Williams had charm and a dry wit, but he was chiefly
sulky, stamping, shrill, uncanny (like the other Williams, Kenneth).
He's like a thing sliding out of the tropics, rather than Flintshire.

Philip made sure he accompanied his ward to *The Druid's Rest*
audition, held across the road from the Sandringham at the Prince of
Wales Theatre, Cardiff. Burton wore his ATC uniform, and was
immediately picked out for the role of Glan Edwards, 'the small boy
whose starved imagination spins the web of misunderstandings', to
quote from the subsequent review in *The Times*. Daphne Rye, the
casting director for H.M. Tennent, was particularly impressed. It
was on this occasion Burton met Stanley Baker, also in the play,
which opened on 22 November, at the Royal Court Theatre,
Liverpool. *The Druid's Rest* then toured to Nottingham, Brighton,
Swansea and Cardiff, where the Jenkins clan was in attendance: 'Play
acting! That's not work!' The entertainment arrived at the St Martin's
Theatre, later home of *The Mousetrap*, West Street, London, on 26
January 1944.

Baker said Burton had been 'tense and highly insecure' at the audition, though soon enough there was plenty of rough-and-tumble in
the dressing room. 'You're uncontrollable kids!' said Williams. They
liked firing pea-shooters at girls, 'trying to hit their tits'. Baker remembered the antics fondly: 'We were like wild animals let loose to enjoy
the birds and the booze ... Two Welsh kids, totally disorientated,
absolutely free of any sort of control at all. We ran totally wild.'

Well, there was a war on. When the pair of them failed to turn up for rehearsals, Williams said, 'Where the hell are they? I shouldn't be surprised if they're behind the scenery having a wank.'

Baker is the only (Welsh) actor with whom Burton can readily be compared. They both had personalities like boiling water, plenty of masculine authority, and their backgrounds were broadly the same. Baker, raised in the terraces of the valleys, was 'eight or more likely nine when I got a milk round. I had to be at the milk depot by half-past five and finish it before school . . . My father was out of work. He only had one leg.' An ex-miner's son from Ferndale, Baker had an inspirational teacher, Glynne Morse, who taught him elocution, gave him books to read, got him into Ferndale Secondary School and brought out a strong natural intelligence – and a competitiveness, which in Baker manifested itself in the way he saw everything and everybody as a threat. 'I could make and break that cunt when I want,' he said savagely of a major HTV shareholder. He smoked and gambled and liked to boast about how he could afford to lose £1,600 a night at poker. 'Baker,' said Burton, 'didn't like people very much . . . and he hated to lose at anything and rarely did.' Baker, like Burton, felt compelled to leave the Principality behind ('To get the good things you had to get out of Wales'), and once he'd made a life for himself in the Mediterranean, where he settled at San Pedro de Alcántara, Spain, hell was to be pictured as 'sitting in that dreadful Chinese restaurant in Ferndale'. Baker's career (Burton's too to an extent) might be seen as revenge on poverty and ordinariness. He was hard, quick, angry, highly-strung, fast to take offence and bristle, slow at being polite. As Burton said when Baker died, in 1976, 'Unless you are Welsh, you couldn't possibly understand him.' He was a thin-lipped impatient driver, as if always behind the wheel of a getaway car. He made in performance an instantaneous impact, like Burton. There was a massiveness to him. He was conscious of the beauty of his dark voice, though never overdid the Shakespearean hollering – whilst it is Baker who played Richmond in Olivier's *Richard III*, filmed in Spain, in 1955, it was Burton who rode the horse Olivier had used in the Bosworth scenes, when *Alexander the Great* was filmed, in Spain, in 1956.

Baker's mother was unimpressed by Burton: 'Never, never mention that man's name in the same breath as my son,' she stipulated. In many obvious ways, Baker is better than Burton, especially in action scenes. Baker flings himself about in fights. There is real force behind the punches and karate chops, the crunch of an elbow in the neck or kidneys. He had more physical assurance than Burton. He also had a lanky grace. He looked good in those Sixties and Seventies suits and shirts, the yellow or orange matching ties. Baker had a pinched face, highish cheekbones, slightly slanted narrow brown eyes – vaguely oriental. (It's a facial aspect common in the valleys, and can be vulpine and handsome or rodent-like, sneaky. Michael Sheen is a bit of both: a flying squirrel.) Baker often had a bushy dark moustache, which gave his features body, symmetry. In his final decade, with lung cancer diagnosed, he did look ill, pasty. But there was never any stiffness about him (Burton could be halting) – and he had nobility, strength; and if there was a weariness, it's as if he was worn down finally by never wanting to trust anyone. All those criminals, policemen and intelligence officers he played, who were crossed and double-crossed, who were fully expecting treachery, represent this.

Baker is so similar to Burton – men who don't belong to anybody; whose heartiness never lasts long; they withheld themselves and would have us believe they are something other than only actors – yet in important respects they are not similar at all. They expected deference, preferential treatment, yet where Baker, for example, managed to remain real and efficiently natural, or enduringly proletarian, Burton ascends to a more poetic plane, suggested by his undertone of irony and lamentation, where he can look down on human beings, these blackened dots in frozen snow, and feel pity for them. Burton seems to serve a lost cause – he's romantic in that way – and brings with him a whisper of ghosts and stone memorials on deserted moors. With Baker, by contrast, there's nothing to suggest an obsession with heaven and hell. He's the pragmatic engineer in *Zulu* – Burton the disembodied voice at the end, his narration recorded in Paris. ('His ear was impeccable in all instances,' said Cy Endfield, despite the actor's three-bottles-of-white-wine-breakfast in the Hotel George V.) Baker is the Great Train Robber, in *Robbery*, implementing a detailed plan. When it comes to organising a team or gang, he is as scrupulous as any policeman or military figure, staring concentratedly at a stopwatch. The paradox with Baker, such is his rectitude, is he could portray crime as virtue – as in *The Criminal*, in fact, where Baker's character cold-bloodedly plots his revenge. In *Perfect Friday*, Baker is the office worker, again devising a complex criminal scheme, his eye on the clock.

As a businessman, with Oakhurst Productions, Greater Western Investments and Lion International (which owned British Lion Films, Shepperton Studios and Pearl & Dean the cinema advertisers), Baker had his eye on the balance sheet. In real life, he was quite the tycoon (e.g. as the executive producer of *The Italian Job*) – Burton would never have known or cared about 'collateral, audit techniques, inflation costing and world distribution'. Baker dealt with practicalities, logistics – and compared with all of this, with Burton, perhaps, by contrast, there was something about his performances that doesn't seem quite true: Burton played with vowels and cadences; the chapel oratory. He is exotic. He tends towards the mystical, rather than the expedient. There Burton is, in another dimension, with his priests and princes, his angels with horns, whilst Baker, with unappeasable resentment, remained in the mess, the prison cell, the hide-out, or Rorke's Drift, with the other men, the other-ranks, forced to be companionable, wary to the point of hostility. In *Accident*, surely a prime Burton role, Baker is an Oxford don, in the Senior Common Room, wearing a cardigan and whipping off and replacing a pair of heavy hornrims, and he's never less than slightly menacing. He's rugged and imposing, with a real presence in the Pinter duels, where every banal utterance is a threat: 'I've been to London to see the television people,' says Dirk Bogarde, 'And did you see them?' Baker eventually responds.

Though it was Baker who received the knighthood, shortly before his death from lung cancer at the age of only forty-eight, Burton kept a regal distance, as if always on a dais, like King Arthur in *Camelot*. They thought of each other as good friends, but wouldn't see each other for years. When Lady Ellen asked, 'When did you last see Richard, darling?' Baker refused to answer, pretended he hadn't heard. He never really forgave Burton for leaving Sybil, who also came from Ferndale, in the Rhondda. This was a breach of the puritanical code: marriage, duty, domestic felicity and responsibility, reputation, moral reassurance. If you want freedom from all of that, if you want to have things all your own way, and fulfil a dream of total independence, you'll disintegrate – as Baker thought Burton had disintegrated – because what frankly are the alternatives? Shamelessness and anarchy and lewdness. 'It's extraordinary that their marriage broke up,' said Baker at the time. 'It seemed to me they were a perfect match. Love? Elizabeth and Sybil are so diametrically opposed.' There you are. Taylor sabotaged Baker's thirty-fifth birthday party by phoning incessantly, alarmed Burton may have been in attendance with Sybil – so she, Taylor, gave everyone, Baker particularly, a taste of her hysteria. Baker had a small role in *Alexander the Great*. He was offered Rufio in *Cleopatra*, a role played in the Italian shoot by Martin Landau. Otherwise the actors did not associate, though as I have seen a photograph (dated 12 January 1964), where Baker is enjoying a drink and a smoke with Burton and Taylor in Puerto Vallarta, on the set of *The Night of the Iguana*, what is it that can be said with certainty about anybody else's friendships and enmities? Baker was not present, for example, when Burton recorded the *Zulu* narration – and though Burton requested no fee, when Baker had flown to New York to persuade him to do it, Burton kept him waiting for three days before meeting him, 'the shit'. It's an example of why I am growing sceptical of biography as a genre. It turns art (and artists) into mere formulaic exposition, a list of goings-on in daily life; statements; calculation; specification. There's a sense of finality, and biographies often have a very self-satisfied air, like one of Baker's audit techniques.

* * *

What can be written down (more or less) without question is that, in April 1944, Burton was accepted for the University Short Course BA degree, or semi-degree, maybe a diploma, even possibly only a summer school certificate, anyway, some wartime provision, taking place at Exeter College, Oxford, and which was on offer to servicemen – perhaps an equivalent of the conference Fred Kite remembered attending, in *I'm All Right, Jack,* when he commends to Ian Carmichael the 'preserves' he'd been served at tea in Balliol. This was a culmination of Philip's manoeuvring. 'The idea of a Welsh miner's son going to Oxford was ridiculous beyond the realm of possibility.' A Welsh schoolmaster's 'son', however, with ATC credentials, was a different thing. In 1969, shooting *Anne of the Thousand Days,* which is about Henry VIII's despotism, ripping up England, Burton, who was giving a performance full of threat, flinging goblets about, told his diary he'd only twice in his life known fear: 'Waiting for the letter from Oxford and the terror of not being accepted. I remember the torment of choosing between Kate [his daughter] and Elizabeth,' interestingly not Sybil and Elizabeth. Both times, which correspond in his mind, had had to do with uncertainty and disappointment; with whether it was going to be difficult to become someone else. Even so, Burton was not at Oxford long, six months maximum, though he'd exaggerate, lie, later about going up with 'an Exhibition in English, which I won'. When first in Hollywood, as he breezily states in his booklet *Meeting Mrs Jenkins,* he used to put it about that 'I was not long down from Oxford' – yet this was 1952. Burton hadn't set foot in the city for eight years.

As an Aircraftsman Second Class [AC2], Burton, number 3025224, in amongst Oxfordian studies, had to turn up for drill parades and lectures on navigation. By the autumn of the same calendar year, 1944, no longer a student, he was a navigator trainee, stationed at RAF Babbacombe, Torquay. This was the Aircrew Reception Centre, where Burton received his kit and inoculations. He proceeded to RAF Docking, at Bircham Newton, Norfolk, a base that gathered weather information and provided convoy escorts for North Sea operations. At RAF Staverton, outside Cheltenham, Burton attended the Observers Navigation School. RAF Wroughton, in Burderop Park, near Swindon, was a hospital for military patients. 'We all drank,' said Robert Hardy, who was at Magdalen and knew Burton at this juncture. Another companion-in-arms was Warren Mitchell: 'Richard spent his time reading, fucking and playing rugby,' no doubt possibly all at once. There was much barrack-room brawling, much daft bravado and boor-ishness. Standing on your head and holding your breath contests, tug-of-war contests, drinking bouts, punching windowpanes and avoiding being cut. 'I didn't get a single scratch!' said Burton. I suppose this was the closest he came to being Sebastian Flyte puking over Charles Ryder, or the hearties in *Decline and Fall*. With John Wain, later a Professor of Poetry, and a friend of mine, Burton played bar billiards and talked about the chapel preachers he had known.

The hooliganism, the laddish carousing, the all-male company, the beer and the fights, is the side of Burton I like least – the *Where Eagles Dare* machismo, on show also in *The Desert Rats* (1953), *The Longest Day* (1962), *Raid on Rommel* (1971) and *Breakthrough* (1978), probably others, and particularly found in *The Wild Geese*, which is a little evil-minded film I despise, devoid of any moral course or purpose. Burton, as if resurrecting his RAF days, is leading a group of slightly elderly mercenaries – machine-gunning Africans, throwing grenades at unarmed Africans. It is racist and fascist. The mercenaries even machine-gun each other – Burton lets Richard Harris have it, to save him from the Africans, who'd otherwise 'chop him up into small pieces' with their machetes. The premise is that men adore violence – the long prologue, before they go to Africa, consists of all these husbands bored by having to prune the roses, who have nothing to do save waste time in pubs. Ronald Fraser and Kenneth Griffith, eager for uniforms and camaraderie, announce they are in their forties – in their sixties if they are a day. The only woman in *The Wild Geese* is the one beaten up by the mafia in the nightclub. It is very Seventies, seeing a female covered with bruises. It is very nonsensical in any era, the plot relying on there being a helpful maverick missionary in the jungle with an airworthy Dakota. All this fuss and bother, and the African they are rescuing from other Africans dies anyway. Burton's entire performance is a snarl, his sunburnt face grimacing as he fires his gun. Released in 1978, it is the most nihilistic thing he did, even if Hayley Mills, Ernie Wise and Joanna Lumley attended the premiere at the Odeon Leicester Square, held in aid of the 'spastics' as they called them then. There was a meal afterwards at The Dorchester, where bread rolls and melon starters were laid out in advance. The Duchess of Kent went dressed as a milkmaid, if my eye is any judge.

* * *

Burton's chief achievement, nevertheless, at Oxford, brief though his stint there was, was to appear between 14 and 17 June 1944 in six performances as Angelo, in a Friends of the OUDS [Oxford University Dramatic Society] production of *Measure for Measure*, directed by Nevill Coghill in the cloisters of Christ Church. 'The boy is a genius and will be a great actor,' said Coghill. John Wain was Claudio. Perhaps because there was nothing on in London or they had nothing better in their diaries, and as a distraction from Normandy being invaded that week, in the audience at what was, after all, only a student show, were Gielgud, Rattigan and Binkie Beaumont. When Burton was demobilised on 16 December 1947, Binkie, remembering the evening, offered Burton a contract with Tennent's worth five hundred a year. Burton was never to worry where to go, what to do. This is why he never bothered to go back to Exeter College and attempt to become a genuine undergraduate, though he did hanker sometimes for an academic existence – *Doctor Faustus* (again with Coghill), which involved Burton and Taylor staying in Oxford for ten days of rehearsal and one week of performances, had the object of raising £8,000 for The Playhouse. Other five-, six-figure sums were bruited. Wolf Mankowitz, who adapted Marlowe's text for the subsequent film, gushed that this was 'the largest individual act of philanthropy made towards either the amateur or professional theatre in this country', and so it may have been, except by 1970, that is to say four years later, the theatre and the university hadn't received a penny. A lot of Taylor and Burton's activities at this period, *Villain* and the Andrew Sinclair *Under Milk Wood* amongst them, were tax diddles – deliberate 'losses' to offset against profits and launder their loot. A proposed Burton Taylor Theatre, where himself would essay Timon of Athens and Lear, obviously never came to pass. Other fiscal singularities included a five-hundred acre banana plantation in Tenerife and a horse stud in Ireland.

The impression I get is Burton liked the fancy talk, the grand gesture. In 1975, Michaelmas Term, as it might have been, wearing a BA gown to which he was unentitled, Burton managed to be a don for two days, as a Visiting Fellow (or something) at St Peter's. He and Taylor arrived by private jet at RAF Abingdon and stayed at The Bear, Woodstock. Burton had always hankered for such an appointment, believing himself, like Faustus, a man 'having attained to a great perfection in learning'. It was a slightly seedy, lubricious fantasy of his, too, that were he a professor, Taylor could 'give high tea to suitably selected undergraduates'. This is the world of *Who's Afraid of Virginia Woolf?*, when George Segal and Sandy Dennis are invited round to George and Martha's ('Drinks now, drinks for all!') to test the laws of hospitality. And as in the Albee / Mike Nichols film (which is like a prolonged Nichols and May sketch), Burton found the actuality of his forty-eight hours as a teacher very wanting. In the film, great care had been taken by the set decorator to create the filthy kitchen, the utensils and the peeling wallpaper. Burton found Seventies Oxford similar. 'Cheap. Everything very shabby,' he wrote in his diary. 'Clothes, cars . . . Students unattractive. Beer warm. Depressing.' Oxford didn't measure up – and it is exactly that feeling of dull stagnation that permeates *Measure for Measure*, where Burton's voice, said Robert Hardy, who saw the Coghill production, 'would sing like a violin' and also hold bass notes 'which could shake the floor'. John Wain never forgot 'the magnetic stillness of [Burton's] body as he spoke'.

Here's a play, indeed, and how significant it was Burton's earliest stage success, which is about physical needs and drives – the puritan intelligence, aware of human meanness and self-importance, and dogmatism, which asks what is it that controls our nature? Virtuous restraint? 'The tempter or the tempted, who sins most?' There can be no room, in such a programme, for ambiguities, ironies, insecurities. Angelo – and I can see how Burton was almost the person Shakespeare had had in mind when he developed the character – is the fallen angel, in a play where sex is 'abhorr'd pollution', 'a filthy vice', 'carnal stings', 'infected will'. Lust, death, illness: the subjects are mixed up. Everything is base, vile – nothing is ideal and noble; there are no happy endings – no heavenly grace or cosmic order. These are false consolations. Justice, spirituality, honour, and so forth, are abstractions – 'false seeming', in the words of the play. Fear, guilt, shame, suspicion: these are what have a reality – a reality to which Burton's Angelo, and Burton himself, was receptive. His encounter with Taylor, it could be said, was like Angelo with Isabella, his senses awakened by her beauty; beauty that has terror in it. And another, related, theme in *Measure for Measure* was already a theme in Burton's life long before he met Monkey Nipples, as he called Taylor. It is this: what does love consist of? Is love often more like ownership? Burton and Taylor were definitely two self-centred people, alert mostly to their own conflicting moods, so love, and the need to be seen to be loved, was for them a matter of pride, possessiveness, display – something that could be exclusive and glorified. It was something that would be presentable, hence the jewels, the toys, which were to be 'reckoned', as Antony says, added up, listed. Love was about prestige. Was it any different for Philip? Was Taylor so to speak an intensification of Philip? There were two great loves in Burton's life, both of which made him and unmade him, and Philip, as the first of them, was amongst the audience (of inflamed homosexuals) for *Measure for Measure*, of course he was. Burton had 'implored me to come up for the weekend'. Coghill 'arranged for me to stay at the college', where he intended to persist with his baleful policy of 'a close identification with the pupil', ex-pupil by now. Philip wanted to conduct a tutorial on the subject of Angelo – but Burton never turned up in Philip's guest room to celebrate the first night, or any of the other nights. He claimed he'd got stuck on a railing, climbing into the quad, or that he'd fallen asleep. (Exeter College has never had railings.) Sad, really.

* * *

According to the sources, when collated, Burton lost his virginity twice, each time in sordid circumstances. One account places him in Liverpool, where he thought he'd been plunged into Dante's Inferno. He was fucking on the hearthrug and scorched his feet on the fender: 'I dreamed I was in hell, suffering the torments of the damned . . . I'd had this strict chapel upbringing and had learned all about the wages of sin.' The second or other or alternative defloration was in Canada, during his RAF training. Writing about it in his diaries in 1971, Burton is filled with disgust. The woman in Winnipeg was 'horrifically filthy. Vile'. Revealed in the morning light, her face was as thick and raddled with face-powder as a Jacobean bawd, for instance, Mistress Overdone, from *Measure for Measure*. There was a baby in a cot behind a curtain. If this was (or these were) a formative experience, at least it accounts for Burton's misogyny, let alone his association of copulation with nastiness, bringing out everything involving what Tolstoy called 'cold animal hatred'. In 1973, during the making of *Massacre in Rome*, Burton said, 'I have treated women very badly and used them as an exercise for my contempt.' I'm put in mind of those Kingsley Amis anti-heroes who, whilst admiring from a technical point of view warm female flesh and tremendously prominent breasts, nevertheless prefer to find most women attention-grabbing howling bitches. Burton could have been a model for (or modelled himself on) Patrick Standish in *Take a Girl Like You*, except this novel didn't come out until 1960, and in the film, directed by Jonathan Miller, with a script by George Melly, they cast Oliver Reed.

Patrick Standish, we are told, is 'out for a good time, and [has] not much care for other people's feelings.' He sees marriage and monogamy as 'promising to work for another person for the rest of your life, in return for which you receive the privilege of promising not to go to bed with anyone else for the rest of your life. Oh, and the perks . . . like getting the food you've paid for cooked on the stove you've paid for in the saucepan you've paid for.' For Patrick, a woman-loathing womaniser, women are all too often 'so bloody keen on being a woman. Never [get] over finding out she was a woman', for whom being unpunctual is meant as charming, being lazy, hysterical and unreliable marks of distinction. 'But why aren't they ever interested in anything? I know they are interested in *people*, as if nobody else ever was . . . Look, what is this mental block they've all got about having their own bloody matches?' I laugh appreciatively at such rants, but Burton is there, in those mid-twentieth-century attitudes, and I'm not sure he even liked neck-nuzzling and kissing and the rest of the drill, as such. There was no tender emotion involved in his pursuit of erotic adventure, which, whilst as necessary as blowing one's nose, was only a stark struggle for power, conquest. Until Taylor came along, and sex was suddenly 'unimaginably delightful . . . I love its disgustingness and comicality,' it was more as if he was intent on destroying those girls (Claire Bloom and Susan Strasberg the most prominent – also Mary Ure: 'I love to be fucked, and Rich loved to fuck me'); or perhaps it's that he defeated in them, or awoke in them, a desire to face and be destroyed by carnal horrors. This yearning for destruction Taylor shared – which is another way of saying she was beyond embarrassment.

Burton said he had a 'primitive, atavistic fear' of being a homosexual, and it would be easy, facile, to attribute his womanising to a need to prove (over and over) heterosexual credentials. On the other hand, Helen Hayes said Burton's motivation was dermatological. 'How would you feel,' he asked her, 'if you had a pockmarked face like mine?' Hayes was 'too startled' to reply, but reflected later, 'He felt deficient because of his blemished skin. Conquering every woman who came within reach seemed to be his way of compensating for that liability.' Homosexuality, a damaged complexion: the sense of self-loathing, filthiness, it amounts to the same thing – marks of impurity, of corruption; and sin, or lewdness, is what he wanted the freedom to indulge. In his early days in Hollywood, for example, in 1955, when shooting *The Rains of Ranchipur*, the producer said, 'He is probably the most notable seducer of our times. He is sexually inexhaustible ... The girls come running.' Burton's co-star was Lana Turner, of whom Ava Gardner observed, 'That tramp fucked everyone. She fucked Frank when he was married to me. Of course, she fucked Burton.' Burton himself said, of his sexual appetite, 'I didn't want to control mine. I wanted to pursue it and satisfy it.' I like *The Rains of Ranchipur*, directed by Jean Negulesco, with its Far East vistas on painted glass, and the drawing rooms on Indian trains, and servants in white livery, and tiger hunts, and belly-dancers. I like these Fifties trashy melodramas because they are a dream world. Burton is in a silk turban as Dr Safti. 'I'm told you are a man of destiny,' Lana Turner says to him. 'You promised to show me the Mughal paintings.' There's no stopping her. As Edwina Esketh, she follows the social season – Antibes, Bermuda, Rome – accompanied by a bright-red set of matching luggage,

which is carried up the hotel steps in procession by uniformed por-
ters. The bags are the same shade of bright-red as Taylor's lipstick in
BUtterfield 8, when she inscribes 'NO SALE' on Laurence Harvey's
mirror. Michael Rennie is Lord Esketh, who is kept in his place. 'You
will do what I want,' Edwina tells him, on one of her many, typical,
disenchanted evenings. Blonde, bored, full (as it were) of an empty
hauteur, Lana Turner, in blue or pink dresses with matching parasols,
walking across the beautiful polished palace floors, is, we are told, or
rather it is her character who is, 'the most greedy, the most selfish, the
most decadent, the most corrupt ...' – who can resist? Not Fred
MacMurray, an ex-paramour, who for reasons I didn't take in is hanging around the ziggurat, and who says, 'I don't know what the word is
in Hindi, but in English she's a word of one syllable.' What? Bitch, slut,
cunt? Which?

Edwina is in India to purchase a stallion for her stables from the
Maharani, and the animal she selects is of course the doctor. Burton
is the child of Untouchables, raised in the palace when his parents
died of cholera. The Maharani, played by a Russian-sounding (and
indeed Russian) actress, Eugenie Leontovich, funded his medical
training. Safti is her special project, and when she says, 'I will have
nothing interfere with his career. For Ranchipur, I do what is necessary,' Edwina takes the hint. She starts smoking heavily. 'That's the
eighteenth cigarette in the last hour and a half,' says Safti, who can't
take his eyes off her, and in 1995, Lana Turner did die of throat cancer.
Cigarettes in silver cigarette-cases are further beautiful props, along
with the costumes and the make-up, Burton's red turban, Lana
Turner's red lips and red scarf, and the yellow and blue light, the lime
greens and peacock whites, casting shadows through the palace's
fretwork screens.

Essentially, it is Shaw's The Millionairess, with Sellers the Indian
doctor seduced by Loren's vampish Epifania, who learns humbleness
when shown the down-and-outs. Here, Burton is the innocent, the
mournful outsider, courted by a sophisticate. The theme now,

however, is temptation. 'Beauty provoketh thieves sooner than gold,' we are informed, so somebody in the script department at Twentieth Century Fox knew their *As You Like It*. The line comes when Rosalind and Celia are hiding in the Forest of Arden and fear rape, so disguise themselves as boys. In *The Rains of Ranchipur*, Dr Safti is the one in danger from Edwina; as in Arden there is a gender switch, the woman the one with the confidence, and they get into a clinch nonetheless when she squeals at a cobra. Burton's Safti thinks to run away with her, make himself a new person. His adoration changes Edwina, too, who as unlikely as this may seem plans to reform herself and stop being a manipulative nymphomaniac. Wise old Eugenie Leontovich is having none of it, sees the liaison as evil, and sends Lana Turner packing, literally packing, placing folded garments in her splendid luggage. 'If you send her away, I will go with her,' says the doctor, his innocence now looking like gullibility. But events and prospects are overtaken by bad weather, as ordained in the first reel, when either Nurse Gupta or Nurse Patel had said, 'We are all now praying for the rains to begin.' And begin they bloody well do. The raindrops get heavier. The sets collapse. Earthquakes, floods, a broken dam – are we meant to think lust (erotic vagrancy) has brought all this on? 'When there's something you can't stop, don't even try,' is the last line of the film, if you disregard, 'It's morning. Looks like the worst is over.' Edwina departs, reconciled with Michael Rennie, the doctor stays to look after the homeless, the cholera victims, etc. How boring and conventional of everyone – nothing disturbing and dissipated can be allowed to be prolonged. Yet here and there in the film the future, like the forthcoming deluge, is foretold: when Lana Turner gazes with longing at Burton, she is a Hollywood star who is in preparation for Taylor; when Burton's undesigning character exhibits a misery and a wish to be irresponsible, this is the Burton who will run amok in Rome. The basic tropes of desire and pursuit are present in *The Rains of Ranchipur*, as also in *Cleopatra*. We have here what Joseph Conrad called the shadow-line: when a person is on the brink of a tantalising and disquieting future, with its promises and designs, and its uncertainties.

* * *

Is that what Burton grew to despise about Sybil, and why he enjoyed the trouble he made – because of her clarity and calm, her common sense, good manners, fair play? If he found her and what she embodied excruciating, when Stanley Baker said, 'He felt ashamed. He knew he had treated her very badly over the years. I don't believe he ever forgave himself,' I hope the latter part of that was decidedly the case. Everything Burton said about Taylor was an insult to Sybil: 'Before Elizabeth I had no idea what total love was'; 'She is my everything, my breath, my blood, my mind, and my imagination. If anything happened to her, I would wither and die.' Everything Taylor represented was in opposition to Sybil, the star's inalienable strangeness, her lurid fire. Taylor was only ever aware of what was happening to Taylor. She was anxiously watchful, jealous, suspicious. When she said, very succinctly, to Graham Jenkins, on the set of *The V.I.P.s*, 'Sybil was yesterday,' this was true in so many respects. Sybil, in contrast to Taylor, not only came from Burton's past, she was a reminder of his earliest past. In his (derivative) Dylan Thomas-esque little book, *A Christmas Story*, published in 1964, the year of the Gielgud *Hamlet* on Broadway, *Becket* and *The Night of the Iguana*, Burton paid tribute to his sister, Cis, who'd raised him as if she'd been his mother: 'I loved my sister – sometimes with an unbearable passion . . . When my mother had died, she, my sister, had become my mother, and more mother to me than any mother could ever have been . . . I shone in the reflection of her green-eyed, black-haired, gypsy beauty.' Cis was 'naive to the point of saintliness, and wept a lot at the misery of others.' This is the paragon he'd found in Sybil. 'Sybil had Cissie's kindness, and her goodness, and her charm,' said Emlyn Williams, who had introduced them, steered Burton towards her, on the set of

The Last Days of Dolwyn, in 1948. This was Burton's first film, and the last one I managed to find and see. Sybil, aged eighteen, was an extra. She made no impression on me – I don't recall the most fleeting glimpse.

What I did think, however, is how often a Burton film involves catastrophe, the elements in a biblical frenzy – those rains in Ranchipur; the thunder, lightning and blizzards in *The Robe* (it took the construction workers 2,404 man hours to build Golgotha – the robe itself, woven by a Mrs Dorothea Hulse, a minister's daughter, was insured for $100,000); the snowstorm in Alaska in *Ice Palace* (a favourite Taylor insult: 'You were in *Ice Palace*!'); the snowstorms in Austria in *Where Eagles Dare*. Throughout *The Medusa Touch* there are floods, landslides, plus massacres, riots and a plane crash – the not very convincing Boeing 747 they used was a plastic model from a travel agent's window, constructed by Space Models of Feltham, if you must know. Burton's John Morlar, one of his devils, is responsible for the disasters, being a proponent of telekinesis. 'He has the most disconcerting eyes,' says Lee Remick. Indeed, he does. There are many close-ups of Burton's eyes – it's a film about his eyes – as the rest of him is bandaged up and immobile in a hospital bed. Jade green, they seem to be, with flecks of tiger-pelt yellow in the irises – sometimes there's a unique combination of lavender and orange, like a sodium flare. He has red-inflamed lids. In the final moments, Morlar brings down a cathedral on top of the Royal Family, whilst Harry Andrews, in police uniform, looks worried. Huge chunks of polystyrene pretending to be masonry cascade upon the congregation. Morlar then moves his attention on to a nuclear power plant.

Environmental destruction, therefore, if a frequent occurrence where Burton is concerned, must, first and last, have something to do with his energy, his demonic willpower, which was like Wordsworth's description of 'the roar of waters, torrents, streams innumerable', found in the vicinity of Snowdon's chasms and crags. And what happens in *The Last Days of Dolwyn* is that the Welsh town and estate of Dolwyn are inundated to create a reservoir. It's like a folk tale illustrated by Chagall – a magical reality suffuses this idyllic spot, the bakehouse, the grocery shop, the inn, with a wishing-well in the garden, the candle burning on the table. Hugh Griffith is the vicar, who preaches against the drowning of Dolwyn because it's the drowning of 'home', that emotive word. Edith Evans, with her poetic querulousness, is Burton's foster-mother, possibly auntie. She has a face that absorbs the light. Burton, with a note of attractive hesitancy, is a grocer's apprentice, who intercepts the lady of the manor on her walk through the woods. There he is, young and wary, as if he has all kinds of secrets. His guile, his pride: you can see what they all saw and desired in him, especially those golden eyes. Burton doesn't have the shapeliness of Cary Grant or the trim charm of David Niven – Burton is rather squat – yet there's carnality, eroticism, in a scene up at the hall when, during a dance, the string quartets fade out and are replaced by the Welsh villagers singing softly, and Burton hands over milady's lost elbow-length glove, pulling it from his pocket. The director (and author) Emyln Williams creates these shadows and sloping ceilings, worthy of Hitchcock – and Williams, who had worked with Hitchcock (*Jamaica Inn*), with great skill prepares us for the chaos about to be unleashed, with the sinister closing of the waters. The very sunshine is portentous, for soon clouds will take over. Williams gives himself a baroque and contorted role, too – that of a resentful local, Rob, who has made his fortune in Lancashire and returns, a fancy man, to buy up property, intending to destroy it. The Regency elegance of Dolwyn Hall will go, along with the bakehouse, the inn, the chapel and everything else. The populace is encouraged to move away quickly to Liverpool ('We're all going to be deported, to England'), a place Burton's character doesn't like the sound of, because 'The birds will not sing the same.' Liverpool is the sort of place where women wear false flowers in their hats and clanking trams screech towards you like mechanical dragons. Williams' Rob is a creature entirely from this realm – he's like the shape-changing owl with hidden claws in a ballet, never to be trusted. When he can't get his way, he sets fire to things. In the climatic episode, in the burning building, Rob and Burton's Gareth start to grapple. Rob is killed. Edith Evans, not at all like the imperious Lady Bracknell, and more a good witch from a fairy story, to cover up her foster-son's (or nephew's) possibly murderous deed – manslaughter anyway – unleashes the torrent, dynamites the dam. The film is an allegory of loss: the features of the landscape lost and altered by the deliberate tidal waves; Burton's character's life of breakdown and separation (Gareth's innocence lost); and in terms of Burton's own life, if only he could leave everything behind him, find an alternative, allow forces to wash over him, erase him.

* * *

Though, in January 1945, he appeared in a radio production, and on 9 September 1946, appeared on television, in adaptations of *The Corn is Green*, Emlyn Williams' parable of the Welsh boy ('He's got the devil in him!') encouraged to win an Oxford scholarship by his teacher, Miss Moffat – a role played in various revivals by Bette Davis, Katharine Hepburn, Sybil Thorndike and Ethel Barrymore: the female Philip Burton clearly appealed to vamps – Burton disappointed everyone, the Jenkinses in particular, by not returning to Exeter College, preferring, instead, after his demobilisation, to go to the London Film Studios, Isleworth, to make *The Last Days of Dolwyn*, and I wonder if his marriage to Sybil, born on 27 March 1929, the daughter of a colliery clerk, whom he said (or agreed) was 'a real sweet girl', was some sort of sop to his Welshness – a connection from whom he could be disconnected, detached, a mother-figure from whom he could expect unconditional forgiveness, even absolution, like the permanent indemnity he counted on from Cis, who said after the Taylor ructions, 'How could we be angry with him, he looked so sad.' The little boy lost act was one Sybil accepted. 'He was always craving admiration,' she said. 'Perhaps that explains his need to go from woman to woman, seeking change and excitement like a frustrated, unhappy child.' She'd also said, when they first met, 'I don't want him tamed.' Burton didn't seem to want her to be anything other than inconspicuous. 'I love her dearly and she assumes that I will marry her, so I suppose I shall,' he told Stanley Baker, without any sense of excitement. Fidelity was never on the cards. 'What the hell's the matter with your phone?' he'd lie. 'I tried again and again to get through to you. But nothing, bloody nothing.' Philip would've been used to these mendacious self-exculpations. The night before the wedding, which took place on 5 February 1949, in Kensington Registry Office, Burton, said Baker, was in 'dark despair. He really wasn't ready for marriage, so I asked him why he was marrying her.' 'She expects it. She expects the ring on her finger' – 'Don't do it, if it isn't what you want' – 'But I have to. Maybe it'll save me' – 'From what?' – 'Myself.' After the ceremony, Sybil had to get back to work. She was Stage Manager at the Prince of Wales Theatre, where there was a matinee of *Harvey* with Sid Field, the one about the alcoholic and the imaginary giant rabbit. Burton listened to a rugby commentary on the radio and went to bed with Daphne Rye's maid.

Presumably Sybil wasn't simple-minded. I am not prepared to believe she was only cosy and homely, with the implication of insipidity, tepidity. She had competence and vigour. Men as a rule go after the same kind of woman, and here with Burton we have women whose (feminine) weakness was their strength: Taylor with her illnesses ('take a tooth out and she's laid up for a fortnight. Graze her knee and it suppurates for a month'), Sybil with her quality of naturalness and unobtrusiveness. Yet there is still something that makes me uneasy. Sybil's attested saintliness and high spirits ('She was too good for him,' Lauren Bacall said of her; 'You have integrity,' Joan Crawford said to her; 'Sybil is a miraculous person,' wrote Kenneth Williams in 1956 – he never praised anybody); Burton's apparent adoration, which had a strong element of condescension ('I'll never hurt Syb. I'll never leave Syb') – but he betrayed her and humiliated her over and over; and as he made no attempt to conceal his philandering ('I was

confident and could never understand why any girl would resist me'),
and as Sybil remained perky, even coy, as he floated away, what was
important to her? It got to the point where she virtually facilitated his
womanising, condoned it – needed it, I wonder? She once returned
from the beach and said, 'There are two of them down there, Rich, both
your type. You'd better go before they leave.' How could she remain
humorous, teasing, unless it was part of some sado-masochistic sexual
game, that eventually got out of hand. As she'd reassured Eddie Fisher,
'Ever since Richard and I have been married, he's had these affairs.
But he always comes back to me.' Sybil's giving in to him always, letting him do as he liked, mobilised, I think, a combination of fear and
elation, a curious bubbling – a state of tension, moments of horror.
She knew she was a victim and wanted it (Sybil was briefly an actress,
don't forget, but wasn't really interested), and was able to look at
Burton from a distance – there was never, as with Burton and Taylor,
that clashing and merging of egos, that mystical love of theirs they
were so proud of, that was near to hatred.

Perhaps those other women, at least until the bigger adventure of
Taylor, weren't real to Sybil. She could be oblivious, whilst nevertheless
feeling or sensing her own repeated obliteration. Sybil's hair and col-
ouring prematurely grey and white like sleet contrasted with Burton's
glittering ferocity. Her response to his challenges (and predictable
antics) was to choose servitude, bondage. She kept in the background,
moving like a ghost: 'You do become an absolute nursemaid, because
your husband has to face the public every day. You worry about his
sleep and his health, the way you do with a child.' She also said, as if
keen to portray herself as a stock stoical figure, whom you'd find in a
Jane Austen novel sketching or taking up carpet-work, 'I performed
most of the household tasks, like cooking and cleaning.' Yet behind
the conventionalities of a dutiful, demure wife, Sybil had servants.
The children had nannies. Sybil's daily living was not typical of
South Wales – how many couples from the Rhondda in 1957 took
holidays in the Hotel Negresco, Nice? Perhaps Burton got tired of

her level-headed perfection; and did she subconsciously want to break away? When, after the divorce, Sybil married a rock star, Jordan Christopher, sixteen years her junior, and ran a disco in New York, admired by Andy Warhol for its 'dark brightness', and where Dudley Moore saw Sybil as a 'den-mother', was all that a preposterous change of direction, or actually in character? Looking back, it was virtually an arranged match, Burton and Sybil. 'I felt so responsible,' said Emlyn Williams, of the bust-ups in Rome. 'I had introduced the two of them. Sybil was a perfect wife. She was heartbroken.' Was Taylor an imperfect wife? Did she have a heart, capable of breaking? Her relationship with Burton was full of danger and disaster, also like something fated, a match arranged in the stars.

* * *

When Claire Bloom said, 'Oh Sybil, I'm so desperately in love with your husband, I don't know what I'm going to do,' Sybil was able to answer levelly, 'Darling, you must find something to do, because for me to hear this, well, it's not very pleasant.' Nor was it, but at least she was used to it. Bloom stretched across Burton's entire career. She was with him in Christopher Fry's *The Lady's Not for Burning* at the Globe Theatre, which had premiered in May 1948. The production then opened on Broadway, at the Royale Theatre, in the November of the following year, where it ran for five months. They were lastly in *Ellis Island*, the three-part CBS mini-series, broadcast in November 1984, three months after Burton had died. In the latter, Burton, with white streaks in his hair, looks splendid in his natty suitings – snow-white trousers, white collars, navy jackets. He is a senator of some kind, and doesn't have to do much, except look prosperous and solid. He's the Taibach Co-op tailor's dummy. Bloom pops up as the snooty mother of a ballerina. Between these poles, in 1953, Bloom was Burton's Ophelia. In The Old Vic season for 1954, she was Viola to his Toby Belch, Virgilia to his Coriolanus, and Miranda to his

Caliban. Bloom was in the films *Alexander the Great* (1956), *Look Back in Anger* (1959) and *The Spy Who Came in from the Cold* (1965). Enough to demonstrate she was Burton's most signal co-star, next to Taylor.

In his diaries he is sarcastic, calling her 'Clara Cluck'. In her own memoirs, Bloom describes Burton as the love of her life, though in fairness she had a terrible taste in men, with Rod Steiger and Philip Roth numbering amongst her husbands. Their sexual activities, hers and Burton's, 'sprang to a flame with an incandescence that astonished us both'. In this cross-eyed and dazed fashion, no doubt with the pair of them staggering about the room and falling over furniture, Bloom's capitulation was total: 'To feel so much pleasure from the body, mind, voice, mere presence of another, is a gift I am profoundly grateful to have received.' Ah, sweet mystery of life, at last I've found you. Sister Wendy Beckett used to be like this, standing in front of a Caravaggio. 'Many women,' Bloom generalised, 'go through life without ever knowing such happiness,' though take it from me, there are products on the market, the Rampant Rabbit and the Pocket Pleaser amongst them, which will give them a fair shot. Sybil was deliberately deceived, Bloom and Burton spending the night together: 'I came to dread the moment before dawn, when Richard had to go ... back to his wife.' They spent a dirty weekend in Norfolk as Mr and Mrs Boothby. 'Making love with Richard was something that had to happen,' Bloom said novelettishly.

She was smitten. She was enslaved. Everybody knew. Isherwood told his diary in September 1957, 'Claire is demure, but probably quite a bit of a bitch ... She is hopelessly in love with Richard Burton.' Bloom was not mousy exactly, and shrewish has the wrong connotations. Nor is she a mole or a slinking stoat. Yet she is like some perfectly formed dark stealthy creature rippling through leaves of pale blue grass, twisting and twitching, snapping its tiny teeth. A vole? She is a miniature and particular actress, burnished like ivory. Her autobiography aptly is called *Leaving a Doll's House*, and dolls have a hard, insidious quality. If Burton was disdainful in his journals and public comments – he tries to laugh her off and leafed through the Fergus Cashin biography hoping the author 'will make fun of Claire Bloom' – I think it is because he was embarrassed by the extent of her passion, and by her hurt, which was very real. He backed away from what he had sparked off in her – all that poltergeist-raising sex. Bloom was almost frantic, and if I think of her, on the screen, as a clipped silhouette, Taylor, by contrast, was always more undulating, always mobile, blurred, with a freely brimming erotic nature. Taylor, for example, could never have played (as Bloom did opposite Olivier) Lady Marchmain, who permits her by-the-book Catholicism to justify cruelty and monomaniacal coldness. Bloom's character in *The Spy Who Came in from the Cold*, indeed, Nan, could be the girl Lord Marchmain once fell for, as her, Nan's, Marxism is similarly doctrinaire, unyielding. She has simply soured over time, and as an actress Bloom is quite frightening, when playing malice and wateriness, as Doc Martin's loveless mother, for instance, or as those rich and poised matrons in Woody Allen films. Taylor would have no patience with such charming manners, with keeping up a pretence of being amiable. Bloom was refined, like sugar. Taylor is mayonnaise. Interestingly, in the Joan Hickson television version of Agatha Christie's *The Mirror Crack'd* (1992), the role Taylor had played in the film (1980), the has-been actress Marina Gregg, is played by Bloom, who is very narrow, focussed, dogmatic – a bitch, to use Isherwood's word. Taylor was never a bitch. Her Marina Gregg is dazed by her own stardom. On-screen or off-screen, it is all the same to her. She, Taylor, never lost her belief the world revolved around herself. Bloom was never in that league, and her Marina Gregg, poisoning the fan who'd once accidentally given her the rubella virus, is sharper and angrier, more febrile, spiteful, recognisably a citizen of St Mary Mead, not Hollywood.

* * *

It was whilst Burton was at Stratford, in the spring and summer of 1951, that he was encouraged to be off to California. Bogart and Bacall were on a cultural weekend, and Bogie told Burton, 'You're wasting your time on the stage. Come to the States.' This would have been the occasion when Burton's brother Ivor, or Ifor, though not Igor, picked Bogie up by the lapels, clean off the floor. 'A fantastic night, with Bogie's legs waving in the air.' Also backstage was Frankie Howerd: 'I can almost hear Shakespeare clapping his hands ... over his ears.' I'd give a lot to have seen Humphrey Bogart and Frankie Howerd encountering each other. Drink had no doubt been taken. Had drink been taken or was Burton stone cold sober, and what did he hope to accomplish, when he said to Sybil, according to Rachel Roberts, 'He hoped that one day someone would love her as she had loved him'? It should have been a lovely period, performing together as man and wife for seven months in the Shakespeare History Plays, everyone young and easy under the apple boughs, sharing a house at Oxhill in Warwickshire with Hugh Griffith and Osian Ellis, the harpist. 'It was one of the happiest times of [Burton's] life,' Robert Hardy, who played Scroop and Fluellen, insists. But it was the selfish happiness of Don Giovanni.

If Sybil loved Burton to distraction, it was so he could always be distracted. One of the saddest entries in Burton's diaries is found on the leaf for Monday 16 May 1960, when his lordship would have been making *The Bramble Bush*: 'Oh boy, I miss Syb already!!' – it is in pencil in a different hand: Sybil's. As Mike Nichols said, it was hard to believe Sybil never knew about all the girls, from Bloom to other young actresses, barmaids, cinema usherettes. Rosemary Kingsland, one of the paramours, was only fourteen, and says Burton rented a flat in John Adam Street, Covent Garden, for his trysts. 'Magnetism, instant magnetism ... Girls of fourteen are very sexual creatures. I was like a puppy on heat. I never felt that I was harmed.' So that's all right then. Rosemary had an abortion in 1955. Burton liked her to keep her school uniform on. Leafing through all the biographies and autobiographies,

Burton seemed to be having affairs with the following: during the making of *The Robe* with Jean Simmons, which meant cuckolding Stewart Granger, who threatened to kill him with a gun; Dawn Addams, also during *The Robe*; Maggie McNamara, on the set of *Prince of Players* (she killed herself in 1978); the cast of *Camelot*; Pat Tunder, who came back and forth to Rome; Mary Ure ('I have no idea if Claire knew Richard was fucking me. Poor Claire, she had no idea' – this was on the set of *Look Back in Anger*. She and Burton reconnected again during *Where Eagles Dare*); Lee Remick; Tammy Grimes; Sue Lyon (Lolita in *Lolita*); Ingrid Pitt; Geneviève Bujold (when Taylor was in hospital with piles); Nathalie Delon; Princess Elizabeth of Yugoslavia (when Taylor had her back in traction: 'I have a disintegrating vertebra. You can check the X-rays. Just ask my doctor'); a schoolgirl in Noto, Sicily, named Carmela Basile ('in the afternoon he came to see me at home'); Jean Bell, a *Playboy* 'Playmate of the Month' (October 1969 issue); Zsa Zsa Gabor; Miss Pepsi of Butte County (pop. 220,000); and Susan Strasberg, petite, dark, elfin, whom I place last because she wrote about Burton most, in her profoundly adolescent memoir *Bittersweet*, for which she received a $300,000 advance, published in 1980, where she recounts telling Burton in a P.S. to a letter: 'I'm going to make myself a peanut butter and jelly sandwich and go to sleep and dream of you.'

They'd met at the Morosco Theatre, New York, in the autumn of 1957. She was nineteen, he was thirty-two. The play was *Time Remembered* by Jean Anouilh. Burton was Prince Albert, who is mourning so much for a dead ballerina, his aunt, the Duchess of Pont-au-Bronc, played by the venerable Helen Hayes, hires a milliner, Amanda, to impersonate the lost girl, as if realistically that could have done anyone any good at all. Amanda was Susan, whose parents, Lee and Paula, Paula particularly, not content with fucking up Marilyn Monroe's life, berated their daughter in the dressing room after the first night, making sure everyone in earshot was aware they were unimpressed by her efforts: 'How could you? How could you do that to me? After all these years, all I've done for you, how could you be so terrible?'

They didn't mind Burton, who was illustrious enough to win approval. When the affair came to light, which it did immediately – Helen Hayes was annoyed at the racket they made when copulating: 'Even my radio turned up full blast couldn't drown them out' – 'instead of being annoyed or outraged, my mother was delighted,' said Susan. Apparently, Paula went in for the Philip approach to life: 'My mother lived vicariously through me.' With Lee, Burton discussed Shakespeare. With Susan, he was carnal – the grinning satyr. He bought Susan presents of diamonds and pearls: 'I was overwhelmed. He surpassed all my childhood fantasies when he laid his passion at my feet,' and not only there surely. 'His charisma and charm set him above the ordinary man, allowed him his own rules of life ... You could not judge someone like Richard. He was too alive to restrict.' With these admissions, with this discovery, on Susan's part, that love is less a lofty emotion than something more to do with subjugation ('I was torn between pain and ecstasy'), it is inevitable there's going to be trouble ahead. When Burton told her, 'I shall keep you in my pocket day and night. We will grow old together,' he was not proposing domesticity. He was declaring ownership. He'd rented an apartment for their assignations, but it was only a place to visit for the fucking, 'not the home I had envisioned,' says Susan. He bought her a white mink muff – she'd have preferred an apron. Susan soon found herself crying herself to sleep, crying on stage, smoking, taking tranquillisers. She was filled with apprehension and rage, waiting for the phone to ring, waiting for a cable. Messages, when they came, were so much mush: 'My beloved Susan. You may have gathered by now that I love a girl called Susan.' She had thrown herself into the relationship 'with total abandonment'.

So, what of Sybil? Sybil had been in Switzerland, where Katherine Burton, weighing six pounds and four ounces, was delivered by Professor Hubert de Watteville (1907–1984), Secretary-General of the

Conference of Gynaecologists and Obstetricians, on 10 September 1957. If named for Hepburn, as some have said, she'd have been Katharine – anyway, she's always been known as Kate, as in *The Taming of the Shrew*. On 11 September, Burton had left for Broadway, and evidently celebrated new fatherhood between matinees and evening performances, plus during the intermission, in a manner meaning Helen Hayes kept having to buy new batteries for her wireless. He was on his own with Susan for eight weeks, until the opening on 11 November, which Sybil came over to be present at. 'What are you doing here?' Burton snarled when he saw Sybil at the Morosco, babe-in-arms. Without waiting for an answer, he stormed off to his dressing room. 'Sybil looked stunned,' said Helen Hayes, who witnessed this scene – one which to me contains a sense of tangible evil.

The illicit relationship was completely openly flaunted – Burton organised Susan's twentieth birthday party, which was attended by Henry Fonda, Anthony Perkins, Olivier and Ustinov, hardly what you'd call publicity-shy persons. Sybil, when she arrived, played at being oblivious, despite press rumours. She was given a matching mink muff and concentrated on looking after the baby. 'I wondered if Sybil knew where [Burton] was and whether she knew about us. If she did, I thought she must be the most understanding wife in the world.' Again, it doesn't seem sufficient to say, as Robert Hardy did, '[Sybil] forgave him because she loved him profoundly and passionately.' Sybil's mind was not dreamy. She was entirely aware of the conditions of what life demanded of her – it's Susan who was on the edge of madness. 'I was frightened of the jealousy and anger I was feeling. In the worst moments, I contemplated suicide, to punish him' – Taylor was always getting her stomach pumped, likewise. 'The contrast of the intense pain and pleasure was too much,' and much desired, as in a tragic drama or opera; and is it because they are women they behave like this, needing a gesture, or because they are actresses? In an effort to be practical, Susan 'carried an alarm clock when I went to [Burton's] room, as I was afraid I would fall asleep in his arms.'

The run of *Time Remembered* completed, after 248 performances, the Burton family returned to Europe, and Susan was plaintive: 'You can't go, please don't leave me, you promised.' There was a long silence, Susan's letters went unanswered – she had to accept, 'He'll never leave Sybil, ever.' When she flew to London, where, in October and November 1958, Burton was shooting *Look Back in Anger*, Burton fobbed her off. 'It was incomprehensible; he was behaving like a stranger.' What he didn't want was for Susan to come across Bloom – and how alike the women were in appearance; at a glance, identical. Burton didn't want to be seen with Susan in the foyer of The Savoy, certainly not on the set of his film, but having decided not to hurl herself into the Thames, Susan looked closely at her paramour as if for the first time, and began to be repulsed: the nicotine stains, the fat fingers, and 'in his green eyes I saw the red veins of dissipation; on his sweet breath I smelled the alcohol; and in his poetic words I heard the lies.' Fair play, girl. Bloom had a similar epiphany, in Dublin, when filming *The Spy Who Came in from the Cold*: 'He was still drinking, still boasting, ... still reciting the same poems and telling the same stories ... I found him rather boring, as people are when they have got what they always wanted – a beautiful wife [Taylor by then], money ...' Even Taylor found herself disenchanted on occasion. Undergoing a hysterectomy, at the Fitzroy Nuffield Hospital, Bryanston Square, in 1968, she told Burton 'to fuck off' and that 'she couldn't stand the sight of my face', according to a diary item for 23 July. Burton assumed the anaesthetics were inducing hallucinations. Nevertheless, Burton could induce hallucinations all on his own, in that he had unhinged Bloom, and she gravitated to bastards afterwards, as did Susan Strasberg, who walked back into a dragon's den with Christopher Jones, who 'was beautiful, but a little too wild for my taste', so she married him.

Jones smacked her face. Jones' reasoning, if Susan smiled or talked to anyone else, was, 'You're so pure, I hate to see you cheapen yourself.' The world was a rival, as it was for Burton, where Taylor was concerned. Burton was jealous of Taylor's friendship with homosexuals, dogs, kittens, 'because her adoration ... is so paramount.' With Jones, Susan was topsy-turvily made to believe that, 'if I had loved him enough, he wouldn't have hit me.' Jones, who died in 2014, had a youthful demon-angel appeal, survived a prolonged nasty fight scene with Anthony Hopkins in *The Looking-Glass War*, and on stage, in 1961, was in *The Night of the Iguana*. He was altogether springier than Burton, lighter – there was less presence. He had a mumbling flat voice that was dubbed for *Ryan's Daughter* by Julian Holloway, Major Shorthouse in *Carry On Up the Khyber*. Susan and Jones had a daughter, Jennifer, who suffered from congenital heart defects. In April 1974, Jennifer was admitted to St John's Hospital, Santa Monica, for surgery. Elsewhere in the building, Burton was being treated for bronchial influenza and (the press were told) 'an injured left hand'. Actually, they were trying to dry him out, curb the three-bottles-of-vodka-a-day habit, which had imperilled the completion of *The Klansman*. Susan paid him a visit. He failed to recognise her. He had the shakes, dark circles beneath his eyes. He didn't much like hearing his 'Little Susan' was now a mother, that she'd grown up, as Wendy does in *Peter Pan*. 'My God, where have the years gone?' Burton said. The old devil was in decay. Susan, too, now has died, of cancer, in 1999, when she was sixty.

* * *

Whatever Burton was like on the stage, everything has disappeared. All that remains are Kenneth Tynan's remarks ('His Prince Hal is never a roaring boy ... The eyes constantly muse ... into a time when he must steady himself for the crown'); Emlyn Williams' remarks ('He drew attention by not claiming it. He played the part with perfect simplicity'); Burton's remarks to friends ('Playing Prince Hal was Hal becoming like me ... But I couldn't play Hal any differently, you see'); Michael Redgrave's remarks ('Richard Burton slipped into the part without even appearing to try . . . The atmosphere of a rugby final at Cardiff Arms Park was never far away'); Philip's remarks ('I feel proud, humble, and awed by God's mysterious ways'); the disobliging remarks of Meredith Jones, who'd have been storing up these alliterations for weeks ('You were a weak, pale, piping, pusillanimous imitation of Laurence Olivier' – just possibly a compliment coming from a Welshman, and Burton often used it as a joke against himself: 'I'm really called the poor man's Olivier'); and silly apocrypha, e.g. Burton's going into battle against Michael Redgrave over-refreshed and pissing in his armour.

What we do have to remember, nevertheless, and visualise, is Burton's career burgeoned when a war had flowed past. After six years, fighting had ended, church bells pealed, there were no more blackouts, no sirens sounded, but something had *happened*: there were craters in London from V-2 bombs, rusting coils of barbed wire, rationing, with queues at the bakery and the butchers' shops. Lanes remained without signposts. There were abandoned aerodromes, concrete pillboxes. Fields and hedges were shaggy with dog roses and honeysuckle, gardens overgrown, lawns lost under long grass. Ivy gripped and sucked the steps of collapsing, derequisitioned mansions, which if not demolished were converted to institutional use, as orphanages or coal board headquarters, with blocked-up windows. 'True it is we have seen better days,' to quote from *As You Like It* – and Burton, I think, captured the equivocal mood of post-war hope and optimism, under which lay a memory of death and sacrifice – the result being (you can see it in his face) a kind of accumulated tension. I say this having found three very early films, the title of the first of which is over-literary, scriptural: *Now Barabbas Was a Robber* (in some territories and upon re-release this was abbreviated to *Now Barabbas*); and it derives, as the chapel-going Burton would have known, from the Gospel According to John, Chapter 18, verse 40, in the King James Bible: the drama of Holy Week – accusations and counter-accusations;

arrest and betrayal; insurgency; Jesus in shackles up before Pilate and Caiaphas. Based on a stage play by William Douglas Home (brother of Sir Alec), which had been mounted at the Vaudeville Theatre in the spring of 1947, as a film it is a notable ensemble piece: Dandy Nichols pegging out the washing; Dora Bryan as a strapping floozie in a cinema; Sir Cedric Hardwicke as the prison governor; William Hartnell as an unsmiling screw, ultimately almost kindly when he gives a cigarette to Harry Fowler, whose mother has died. Others: Leslie Howard's brother Ronald as a thief, Martin Clunes' father Alec Clunes keeping watch over a condemned man, played by Richard Greene, famous for riding through the glen in 143 episodes of *The Adventures of Robin Hood*.

Now Barabbas begins with shots of bleak walls, spikes, armoured doors, window bars, razor wire. Bells toll. Gates slam. Men shout. We don't leave the prison precincts (save for short flashbacks) for the next eighty-seven minutes, as we meet various inmates: Leslie Dwyer as a bigamist; Kenneth More who confessed to having 'slipped again' and is serving six months for shoplifting ladies' gloves; and sundry smugglers, forgers and pilferers. Burton is Paddy O'Brien, his Irish accent not too terrible, but still terrible, his face wide and clouded, who has been given ten years' penal servitude for blowing up a railway line – an IRA saboteur. It's his ferocity which is instantly demonstrated. 'You shut your mouth!' is his opening line, and he never softens. Sir Cedric Hardwicke is almost impressed. 'I've always looked on you as one who walks alone,' he tells him – and indeed Burton is ill-fitted to joining in with the rest of the gang. He is quarrelsome, eager to pick fights. When Kenneth More tells tales about flying a plane down the Strand, Burton can't tolerate what he sees as lies and boasts, and pushes More about. He's particularly nasty to Medworth, a struck-off doctor (an abortionist, one suspects: a woman patient has died under the ether), played by Julian D'Albie. He hits out at the old man, knocks him to the ground. He accuses him of pomposity, of being too educated, too middle class. Medworth keeps saying he's old enough to be

his father, what's going on, where's his respect? It is more than bullying. The scenes jar. We don't know what motivates O'Brien's violent
rage; it is not quite possible to know the source of his anger – but we
know what was motivating Burton's disgust, which fuels the sequence.
Julian D'Albie could be Philip, hated for his air of fastidious superiority, and for his having known Burton at a time, still only a short five
years previously, when he was helpless and vulnerable.

Or such is my supposition. During the shooting of the film, he and
Sybil were married (5 February 1949); they bought their house in
Hampstead; Burton was appearing each evening at the Globe (now
the Gielgud) in *The Lady's Not for Burning*: all these significant steps,
taking him away from South Wales, away from Philip's formal, conventional, rigid idea of theatre, and moving him more towards a style
of acting (more real, more natural – more tasteless, when it came to
Taylor) that could cope with, encompass, Burton's degrees of hostility. You look at him here, at his male force, and think: everyone knew
how good he was going to be. In terms of *Now Barabbas*, the degradation of the other prisoners' existence, their resentment, is due to the
effects of the war. The mood of personal defeat, crushed existences,
waste – here are characters easily tempted into stealing stuff, lying,
pulling fast ones, lashing out (Richard Greene had killed a bloke
who'd mocked his girl, recognising her as an ex-prostitute), who have
been landed with bad luck. Yet in only the recent past they were soldiers, serving in Normandy, Germany and Greece, fighting men used
to rifles and drills. Now they are the war casualties, their existence
destabilised, distorted. How can anyone readjust to peacetime, to the
calm ordinary life? This is the message written on the face of
exhausted-looking Sir Cedric Hardwicke, on his forlorn pouchy features, his attitude of despair, as he imposes the rules and regulations
and opens the Home Office letter, confirming Richard Greene's
Tufnell is to be offered no reprieve from the gallows.

Secondly, *Waterfront*, released on 26 June 1950. Kenneth Williams
wrote to Burton about *Waterfront*: 'I thought yours was a lovely

performance, and the line, to the girl just before you went onboard ship at the end – "it will have to be a quick goodbye" – was incredibly moving. Somehow you got all the culminating emotions of the film into that one sentence.' It is Robert Newton's film, and in many ways a simplistic story. Newton – it was impossible for him never to over-act; he was always piratical, picking fights, lashing out – disappears into the Merchant Navy for fourteen years, then turns up again, expecting his tea to be on the table. Hard to believe as this is, *Waterfront* has the unadorned quality of a ballad, raw and stripped down to ele-mentals: men and women, parents and children; combat, murder, a hanging. Kathleen Harrison (one of my favourites – almost always startled and comic) is the mother, in her shawl; Kenneth Griffith (good at shits) is the boss' son, the seducer of one of the daughters, whisking her away in his motor car, dumping her later on easily enough. Whilst the film mostly concerns Newton's killing of the First Mate with a razor, it is Burton, low down on the bill, whom we watch. He's the fiancé of the other daughter, and is desperate to get a job as a ship's stoker. He wants to marry – but he wants to get away more. His combination of intensity and quiet is arresting. He is as sullen as the dark streets. The film looks like a lithograph, blocks of black ink – the Liverpool docks, the oil and steam, boilers, chains and spars. Burton merges in and out of this backdrop, is acclimatised to it, very suited to it. His coat, his hat brim – virtually Expressionist. Though he was heading towards being a notorious boozer like Newton – who is also in *Desert Rats* playing a nervous schoolmaster; who was like an actor sketched with a steel nib by Cruikshank; who was dead at fifty – Burton wasn't overblown like Newton. He was never Long John Silver all the time, even though he was aware, as Newton was, that acting was a showpiece, something aggrandising, the chance for a play of voices. 'I am much happier playing princes and kings,' Burton told Kenneth Tynan. 'I'm never really comfortable playing people from the working class.' And when he plays people from the working class, as here, they become princely, above and apart.

The same thing is going on in *Green Grow the Rushes*, released in November 1951, and shot on location in Romney Marsh, a place of rivers, ponds, the seashore: a watery realm. We are meant to be in an England that has miraculously managed to remain outside modern law and order – a favourite Ealing theme, where easy-going locals outwit the men from the Ministry (Colin Gordon is the bowler-hatted bureaucrat here); also a favourite Michael Powell and Emeric Pressburger theme, where the Englishness of English life is celebrated by a return to, a rediscovery of, medieval ways. The presence of Roger Livesey, he of the hooting, braying-bittern voice, Colonel Blimp himself, in *Green Grow the Rushes*, rather emphasises this for me. And in this film, we meet the sailors, publican, butcher and a newspaperman (Arnold Ridley), who could have been described by Chaucer. There is the squire, whose ancestors recovered land from the marsh, made the waves retreat, and we see the loveliness of the agriculture, the wheat meadows, verges of dried grass, woods, timber mills, beehives, oast houses and clapboard barns. The cinematographer, Harry Waxman, gives everything a haunted woodcut look, a deep and pure black-and-white, nothing grey, nothing misty, the black almost purple. Burton is a smuggler, his swift movements seen in silhouette, his face in profile in the caverns and castle ruins, where the contraband is stored. In the time-warp England of the film, a place to be found, perhaps, on the other side of the boundary of the known world – the real Kentish setting paradoxically adds to the artifice – Burton could easily be Elizabethan, like a figure in a William Morris tapestry; and this must be how he was on stage, at Stratford or The Old Vic, with an off-hand quality, an abruptness, before which Honor Blackman, who goes duck hunting in the reeds, or who shelters in a barn from a storm, immediately capitulates. Burton, or his character, Hammond, ensnares her by being cold.

It's interesting, the atmosphere the actor creates or casts about himself – an atmosphere of black smoke, everything irradiated, almost abstract. Burton has composure, is incapable of frivolousness.

He is half in darkness. There was always a touch of poetry about Burton, right to the end – I am a huge admirer of his *Wagner* for Tony Palmer, released as a ten-part miniseries in 1983. When I look at the early work, when I see how he was when he was young, instead of any of this leaving me feeling safe, secure, as if there's something eternal here, like the carved stone Norman church doorways Colin Gordon measures and examines, the emotions I experience, contemplating Burton, are the opposite, because latent (as in an X-ray – day-for-night) is oblivion, the pagan England Burton somehow embodies – and Harry Waxman shot *The Wicker Man* – and the town pageant with which *Green Grow the Rushes* concludes (everyone in historical costumes); this world of village louts, crooks and tarts, country dancing and writhing, people (or effigies) being burned at the stake: everything is sinking into hell.

The plot had concerned concealing brandy bottles from Customs and Excise. The easiest way of hiding it is to drink it, which everyone does. Ducks paddle in drunken circles on the duck pond. There's a runaway horse. There's a sort of frenzy. Robert Newton would not be out of place, with his scimitar and skull-and-crossbones. For the alcoholic, though, the drink, and the need to drink, goes deeper than tipsiness, carousing. Newton, Burton: they couldn't do without it, and the drink then becomes something to fill a person with fear, something incessant, evil. On screen, and by inference on stage, Burton had a lost, resentful quality, a sulky withdrawal, which women found enticing (which men found enticing) – they always believed they could save him from himself, that he was awaiting rescue. As with sex, as with drink: there was too much appetite – unlimited sensations, pleasure, followed by physical collapse and degradation. Like Faustus, Burton existed intensely. He had this strangeness, from the beginning, and his paradoxical genius could make saints and sinners the same thing, as no doubt he'd have managed to make cannibals and missionaries the same thing – and as George Jacob Holyoake, in *A Subject of Scandal and Concern*, set in 1842, a 'Sunday

Night Play' shown on the BBC in the winter of 1960, abstinence and asceticism are quite as destructive as libertinism, and Burton portrays an atheist who behaves like a priest, always bellyaching as if from the pulpit. Written by John Osborne, directed by Tony Richardson, it's ranting Jimmy Porter (or Luther, or Bill Maitland) all over again – a hero determined to show his defiance, make a meal of his conscience.

Burton, in round steel-frame glasses, mutton-chop whiskers ('bugger's grips'), and pouting his large lower lip (he has almost no upper lip – neither did Olivier, nor does Kenneth Branagh), stutters and stammers and tries to look academic or clerical. He gives himself a lot of impediments – Holyoake is flustered, introspective, perilously close to dull. He scratches, squirms. His home life is deliberately drab. Rachel Roberts, as his careworn wife, serves up soup, which is eaten with a wooden spoon. Her back to us at the hob, Roberts has the slow, deliberate movement of a dancer, and she's good at signalling her aloneness, her unhappiness and her alarm: 'You fly from brawling like a cat from water,' she tells her husband, who is 'not an easy man', though not as bad as Rex Harrison was going to be. For Holyoake has given a public lecture on behalf of the Social Missionary Society – and some of his remarks have been reported to the authorities as 'improper'. Holyoake, subsequently the defendant in a blasphemy trial, is accused of harbouring 'diabolical sentiments' about atheism, socialism and welfare reform. He has denied the existence of God – of some all-powerful, beneficent Deity – and (says Mr Justice Erskine – the Royal Court's George Devine) such a belief (or non-belief) if disseminated can only produce or engender public disorder and breaches of the peace, and Holyoake must surely be a 'wicked, evil, malicious, ill-disposed person'.

As with *Look Back in Anger*, Osborne's target is provincial peevishness – England in Victorian days (or modern days) is little better than in Tudor days, superstitious and dangerous. Having been arrested and locked in Gloucester Gaol, Holyoake is surrounded by characters from *Beyond the Fringe* – slimy and absurd Peter Cook lawyers, oiks reminiscent of Dudley Moore, smooth sorts based on Alan Bennett. The vicar is actually Andrew Keir. The one in the witness box with a false moustache is Nigel Davenport. Yet just as I was about to switch off and do something more interesting instead, Burton reappeared from the chalky, streaky vintage television images to deliver his big speech at the blasphemy trial – an Osborne aria about a man's right to hold honest opinions and make whatever metaphysical enquiries he pleases; a ten-minute (longer possibly) monologue setting out the essential requirements of intellectual freedom and condemning the constraints of religious orthodoxy and 'the will of bigots'. As Holyoake, making this speech in his own defence, Burton soars – a magnificent spectacle; here is proof of his greatness as an actor (in any medium); he is Shakespearean. I was in raptures. The stammering and stuttering fall away, as he convinces us we don't need any concept of God or empty worship as the foundation of good behaviour. Holyoake loathes passivity and blind obedience – people must work out their own moral code. Nevertheless, in his own nature or personality, he is as puritanical, principled, as any Jesuit – and as everything he says, in Burton's incarnation, is rousing and convincing, George Devine sentences him to six months.

One of the *Beyond the Fringe* people comes back on to say Holyoake was 'a pelican of the wilderness, an owl of the desert' (Psalm 102), and the human cost of his intransigence is marked out by Rachel Roberts. 'We did everything you instructed,' she says bitterly, giving her husband, who has fallen silent, a report of their baby daughter's funeral, a plain affair, with no procession, priest, ceremony or liturgy of any sort. 'It was just as you instructed ... I can't thank you for it.' It really doesn't do, the conclusion seems to be, for Holyoake, or Osborne, or Burton, or anybody, to keep asking why we are living as we are living.

* * *

'Burton is a huge success here,' Gielgud wrote to his mother, from Los Angeles, on 9 August 1952. 'He is making Daphne du Maurier's *My Cousin Rachel.*' So he was. Humphrey Bogart and Lauren Bacall, evidently still impressed after their Warwickshire weekend, had prevailed upon their friend Nunnally Johnson, the producer and screenwriter, to cast Burton in the picture, which had begun shooting on 21 July. George Cukor, having watched Burton on stage at the Lyric, Hammersmith, in April 1952, in a play by Lillian Hellman called *Montserrat*, also recommended the actor to Twentieth Century Fox, seeing in Burton 'the Victorian gentleman, Philip Ashley', du Maurier's hero. He, Cukor, had hoped to direct, but in the end, Johnson hired Henry Koster, who the following year also directed *The Robe*, and was considered reliable with period material.

Burton was already under contract to Alexander Korda, having been signed up for seven years (at a hundred quid a week), after the release of *Waterfront*. In his diaries, Burton says it was for five years, and in 1972, shooting *Bluebeard* in Budapest, he looked back and recalled a lunch at Korda's offices, in 146 Piccadilly – where the Hungarian mogul informed him, 'My friend and colleague Laurence Olivier told me that you are a natural aristocrat and now that I have seen you I know that he is right.' (Was the sentiment translated from Hungarian?) Burton never made a film for Korda – but that didn't matter. Korda loaned him out to other studios and with the fortune he received in fees for Burton's services he bought a Canaletto. For his own part, Burton went from £35 a week at the Shakespeare Memorial Theatre to $100,000 (and soon double that amount) per picture in Hollywood.

O, what a paradise it seemed – exactly as it had seemed for another Korda protégé and investment, Charles Laughton, a generation before. I'd venture to suggest the actor Burton most resembled, interestingly, is Laughton. Leaving aside aspects of physical beauty – though Laughton's repulsiveness, the undulation of his warty flesh, had a kind of paradoxical reptile-house beauty – here were two great

British actors, who abandoned the theatre for cinema, and who in the cinema were theatrical. All these stage effects – gesture and expression; their peculiar intensity. And both men had a sense of poetry. They were generally howled at by the press ('too many off-beat touches,' *Variety* said of Laughton; 'sceptics predisposed to give *Cleopatra* the needle,' the *New York Times* said of Burton), which was an intolerable distraction. There was the Welsh voice, the Yorkshire voice, with each actor capable of a dramatic rasp, a depth of vocabulary and style, which was always impassioned, though with a tendency, too, towards affectation, showing off. In the midst of playing a role they could seem, on occasion, as if they weren't quite willing thoroughly to subordinate themselves to the demands of the work they were actually in, and were giving, instead, a sort of running commentary on it – as if we needed to be reminded they were *Charles Laughton, Richard Burton*, rhetorical film stars, not (as it might be) Henry VIII (a monarch they each played). Bligh would have been a good one for Burton, Dysart in *Equus* for Laughton. Plus, offscreen, there was the pervasive guilt and sex, and lechery. All of which could be indulged in America.

'Last night,' said Gielgud, still writing to Mrs Gielgud, '[Burton] and his wife drove me [from the Beverly Hills Hotel, where they were all staying] to Malibu Beach to dine with the Selznicks. She is Jennifer Jones. Chaplin was there ... The parties are grand ... awful food, too much drink, rather noisy.' Gielgud mocked the garish clothes, the imitation Colonial, Tudor and Regency bungalows, the gardens, lawn sprinklers, pools, abundant palm trees, the hibiscus and the jasmine. His implication is it is all very vulgar, the colours, the plenitude; all too much for desiccated Sir John. Burton found Hollywood rich pickings; fertile. As James Mason's first wife Pamela remembered, 'Richard was quite noisy, riotous and full of fun. We all had the impression of an extremely lively and joyous person,' as usual at Sybil's expense. 'He is a philanderer,' said Pamela. 'He wants to be the centre of attention. He wants to be a personal hit.' Not so with Olivia de Havilland, Rachel

Ashley to his Philip Ashley, in the du Maurier film, he wasn't. 'Burton goes berserk when he is frustrated,' she said. 'He has these violent departures from control . . . He is a coarse-grained man with a coarse-grained charm.' Dame Olivia, whom I knew, my friend in Paris, where she was like an exiled grand duchess from the Imperial Russian Court, could see Burton's 'manliness was combined with a little boy quality', and unlike Taylor she didn't wish to be fooled. Her disapproval was something he was fully aware of. Interviewed on *Parkinson* a quarter of a century later, Burton recalled how, forgetting his lines ten times in a row, 'I finally went raving mad and started to kick the set and suddenly the whole thing started to fall in . . . Miss de Havilland didn't forgive me for a very long time.' Like until her dying day, for example, and she lived to be one hundred and four. Nonetheless, the antipathy works for *My Cousin Rachel*, because Olivia, as I finally got to call her, as a widow and the titular relative, spends the film going around poisoning people. Ashley's Uncle Ambrose, for example, goes to Italy for his health, meets Olivia's Rachel, marries her and drops dead. 'She has done for me at last,' is his melodramatic last utterance. Burton's character arrives on the scene in Florence and is distraught: 'Why was I not sent for at once?' When informed Ambrose croaked of a brain tumour, Ashley has his suspicions: 'May I ask what proof there is of that?' He returns to Plymouth, closely followed by Rachel, who must have embarked on the next packet, and who has designs – she knows so much about young Ashley, knows details about the house and its contents he has inherited, knows about the neighbourhood. Rachel's behaviour towards her cousin is motherly and gently flirtatious – organising everything, taking over. 'You mustn't make any alteration in your days because of me,' she says insidiously, presiding at tea, issuing invitations to strangers. Ashley gets interested in her sexually when her surreptitious evil becomes apparent; he is drawn in by her quiet calculation. (Philip must have been like this.) Rachel knows he is impressionable – she impels disaster.

Ashley gives Rachel a large allowance, and she still overdraws her account and runs through his fortune. There seems to be any number of shady former husbands and ex-partners of hers, who appear out of the rain to complain about 'unbridled extravagance and loose morals'. Heedless of any warning, Ashley gives Rachel all the jewels in the safe ('That's the most beautiful pearl necklace I've ever seen' – fancy), signs over the estate ('The completest folly,' says the incredulous solicitor) and like Antony with Cleopatra generally is obsessed. 'If I owned the world, it would be all yours, too,' he says, by way of a declaration. Rachel, now officially mistress of the house, doesn't want to marry him – she doesn't need to. She has everything. She makes tea with herbs ('an ancient art'), like a Borgia. Laburnum seeds are in the mix. Burton's Ashley starts having headaches and fevers. He staggers and limps. He tries to strangle Olivia de Havilland on the stairs. 'My blessed torment,' he calls her.

As with Hitchcock's *Rebecca*, a decade earlier, Cornwall has been recreated in California, the granite mansions and back-projected rocky coasts; the gibbets at the crossroads; the oak-panelled rooms and guttering candles. There is plenty of pewter plate. There is even more gothic mystery, danger and paranoia. Olivia is full of graciousness, which intensifies the obstinate sickly evil of her character, like someone out of Henry James. (One of her Academy Awards, on display in her Paris place, was for *The Heiress*, based on James' *Washington Square*.) Burton is saturnine, and has bounce. He plays Ashley as Heathcliff, full of obscure resentments. There is hidden, submerged erotic agitation in the material, emphasised by the surging Frank Waxman score, and when Dic Bach, Burton's father, saw *My Cousin Rachel* at the Odeon, Port Talbot, he was outraged. 'What the hell is all this kissing? What does Sybil say?' – 'But it's only acting, father' – 'Acting, be damned. It looks real enough to me.' The story is usually told jeeringly. The daft old bugger couldn't grasp it was made up. But as with the disingenuous Benjamin Partridge in *Tom Jones*, when he is taken to see Garrick's Hamlet, the painted backdrops and strangely dressed-up figures can automatically be ignored, overlooked, if the sentiment and delicacy of the main characters, the actual people there in front of you, convey honesty, instinctiveness, about human behaviour. The point isn't a glib one. It is profound, questioning the very meaning of let's pretend.

* * *

Burton, like Garrick, seemed too natural to be artful – his father perceived that – and with Fielding's Partridge might well have shouted out at the silver screen, 'Ay, go about your business!', reflecting similarly afterwards, 'I am sure if I had seen a ghost, I should have looked in the same manner, and done just as he did.' For this was not acting or seeming, but being – and being Burton, in this period, meant his relentless fucking, his need for indiscriminate erotic danger. Olivia de Havilland's chief objection was to his progress as rake, not his bashing up of the set or missed cues. As she said to me in 2015, and bearing in mind her idea of a gentleman was Edward Heath, 'I do remember Richard as a tempestuous young man, undoubtedly oversexed, his weekends studded with erotic encounters, which he felt impelled to recount to me on Mondays. I did not relish these confessions, as I, like everyone else, liked his wife, Sybil, and to learn of his infidelities was not a pleasant experience. That very nice woman, Sybil, was prematurely grey-haired at the age of twenty-six.' Meantime, Burton was writing letters to Bloom, pretending to be abstemious: 'I haven't looked at another woman. This has never happened to me before. You have changed me so radically, I have almost grown up.' The tragedy of Peter Pan is that he tries to grow up, but can't. Sybil functioned as Wendy, the sisterly mother, the motherly sister. 'Her sense of family,' said Mike Nichols, 'Richard's extended family of all his friends, provided the glue of his life . . . It was Sybil who called you back, Sybil who suggested a trip to New England. This was a very important part of any friendship with Richard.' A sister, a mother, a social secretary.

In Hollywood, he went to parties with the likes of Jack Buchanan, there making *The Band Wagon*, Stewart Granger and Deborah Kerr. When at a reception a foreign diplomat said, 'I had the benefit of an English governess,' Burton responded with not quite Oscar Wilde calibre wit, 'Oh yeah? Did you fuck her?' It was at one of these dos Burton danced with Jean Simmons, kissed her on the lips, and point-edly ignored Sybil, who gave him such a slap, 'It sounded like a bomb blast,' said Pamela Mason. I'm pleased to learn of this. I've never liked it that Sybil seemed to threaten nobody – where was her self-respect? Unless, to look at it differently, there was a masochistic playfulness, behind the mask of her stoical behaviour? Kenneth Tynan, a con-noisseur in these matters, said what gives pleasure to the masochist are threat, exposure, humiliation ('*these* are thrilling'), and what sat-isfies the sadist is the ability to say, as it were, 'Please forgive me for hurting you. Then I can go away and hurt you some more.' Did she and Burton still have sex? Or was that something they'd outgrown? Anyway, Sybil didn't go to parties again. She stayed at home and did the laundry, implicitly facilitating Burton's freedom to be involved with others.

There's an account of what typically happened in Penny Junor's biography, *Burton: The Man Behind the Myth* (1985), except there isn't. Jean Simmons' husband, Stewart Granger, sued, so the leaf bearing pages fifty-five and fifty-six was neatly removed, rewritten and replaced. Granger and Simmons are now 'a well-known screen couple', and Burton 'had climbed into their Hollywood mansion at night through the wood shed and made love to the woman on a big white rug in front of the fire while her husband slept peacefully in his suite elsewhere in the house.' What's killing is Stewart Granger's name remains in Penny's index, directing readers to pp. 55–6. Burton also first saw Taylor during this, 'my first time in California and my first visit to a swank house', as he put it in *Meeting Mrs Jenkins*, a little book published by William Morrow in 1966, and which had initially been an article, 'Burton Writes of Taylor', printed in *Vogue*, the previous year. It was one of those Sunday brunch jobs, with Bloody Marys beside the swimming pool, where Burton, in the company of Tony Curtis and Janet Leigh, Marlon Brando and Sammy Davis Jr., and seemingly (by his own testimony) a carefree bachelor, 'played for the others the part of a poor miner's son'. Taylor, the wife of Michael Wilding, was, said Burton, 'a combination of plenitude, frugality, abundance ... She was lavish. She was a dark unyielding largesse, and ... she was totally ignoring me.'

Even with Taylor, at least originally, it wasn't love but lust, and a component of their love was that they were each other's sexual tormentor; all that violent submission and domination, which by this time with Sybil had been overtaken for Burton by cosiness. What Burton liked was the novelty of face and figure and flesh; continual first-time excitement. He was possessive and sadistic with his women, getting them to recite a Welsh oath of loyalty: 'Who do you love?' – 'You' – 'Too faint,' he'd say, 'Not loud enough. Again' – 'I love you more than anyone else in the world,' they'd obediently respond. It was like a spell, a catechism. Susan Strasberg went through with it, learning the correct way to answer: *Mwy na neb arall yn y byd,* is anyway how she transliterated it; Method spelling. On Sunday 28 February 1982, Burton was reading from *Under Milk Wood*, at the Duke of York's Theatre, in the West End. The occasion: *Dylan Thomas: A Celebration*, a concert to raise funds for the installation of a plaque in Poets' Corner, Westminster Abbey. Taylor made an unannounced appearance on stage. *'Rwyn dy garu di mwy na un arall yn yr holl fyd,'* she intoned, 'in faultless Welsh,' said Burton's brother, Graham. 'Would you mind repeating that?' asked Burton. She did so, exiting to considerable applause. Burton had to be a woman's sole occupation – as he was for Bloom ('I waited only for the times when we could be alone together'); as he was for Susan ('Forever and a day, you belong to me,' Burton told her); as he was for Rosemary Kingsland ('She's mine now,' he asserted, having taken her virginity). Taylor, too, would often enough tell the reporters, 'I need strength in a man. I rely on him totally now . . . Richard is a very sexy man. He's got that sort of jungle essence,' like Tarzan, king of the apes, a man who could converse with leopards. Eddie Fisher, a biased witness, but still a witness, saw nothing worthy of commendation. Burton was 'an arrogant slob', 'a coarse, mean drunk', who was always angry. 'He was angry when he was sober, so his drinking just made that worse.' Eddie also overheard the 'Whom do you love?' – 'You' – 'Right answer. But it wasn't quick enough' routine, Burton the commanding Svengali, Taylor, still Eddie's wife, the hypnotised Trilby. In a letter to Susan, Burton said he expected her to follow him loyally 'into the house of dust, the worm's pasture, the grave', and it really was as if he'd kill them all in the end, as in *Bluebeard*, which is full of Count Dracula's trappings and familiars: hyenas, jackals, falcons, owls, a spitting cat, creatures contained in a Hungarian palace, the Wenckheim, an ornate neo-baroque fantasia, built in 1887. The building seems alive – creaking, tilting, wheezing walls and ceilings, with eyes and mouths appearing and disappearing in the abstract or Klimt-like pictures and photographs. Are we in the Emperor Franz Josef-Empress Sisi era of balls and Strauss, or the pre-Nazi era of jackboots and whips, or the Sixties?

The film is a lavish, gothic, campy edifice, photographed, as was *Doctor Faustus*, by Gábor Pogány. Everyone has strangely coloured hair and accents that are dubbed. The furniture is red and yellow. The backgrounds are ice-blue or ketchup-red. A deaf-mute hunchback servant-woman creeps along cobwebby secret passages, peeping through keyholes. We see her brush the locks of mummified corpses. Burton, as Baron Kurt von Sepper, plays at a *Phantom of the Opera*-sized pipe organ. The director, here in 1972, was Edward Dmytryk, who'd made the overheated *Raintree County* with Taylor, fifteen years previously. Burton must have had one of his alcoholic tantrums, because a letter of apology exists, where he says, 'Dear Eddie, please believe that the Richard you saw last night is not the real Richard Burton.' Apparently, the star had hopped into his Rolls with Nathalie

Delon, who was cast as one of Bluebeard's wives, and had vanished from the studio. (The other wives were Raquel Welch, Joey Heatherton, Virna Lisi, Marilù Tolo, and others – international early Seventies crumpet – a word deriving from the Welsh, *crempog*: something comforting and buttery, a naughty treat.) I own a poster, found in a Hastings junk shop, where in big letters inches high it announces 'BURTON is BLUEBEARD' and the bearded Burton, in the accompanying image, looks like Claudius, Hamlet's uncle, at prayer – when he says, 'My words fly up, my thoughts remain below: words without thoughts never to heaven go,' i.e. we are in an empty universe. And what's disconcerting about *Bluebeard*, despite the Hammer-style horror-movie special effects, the doors and windows blowing open and crashing, the concealed panels, stuffed rhino trophies and Expressionist Budapest alleys and cobbles, is that nothing is explained away as supernatural. All is sublunary. We are shown a realistic hunt, the boar, fox and deer fired at and killed, the bodies twisting and convulsing. Similarly, what is in the forbidden bloody chamber are von Sepper's wax-worky ex-wives, severed heads, dismembered limbs. It is daft, but it is psychopathic – a case study. 'They deserved to die,' says Bluebeard. 'They forced me to do it.' The film is a morgue. A singer is guillotined. Lesbians are impaled by antlers and horns. Raquel Welch, a nympho nun (whatever happened to those?) is shut alive in a coffin. Somebody else is strapped in an electric chair. A proto-feminist is beaten up, because she enjoys it ('Hit me again, please!'). All these birds, to use the noun of the period, models, are topless, posing on white fur rugs – borrowed, I wonder, from Jean Simmons and Stewart Granger's 'mansion'?

It is a lush and luxuriant film, cruel and mad. Von Sepper watches the girls through a grille (the Burton eyes in lascivious close-up), kills them and photographs them, as in Powell's *Peeping Tom* or Antonioni's *Blow-Up*, where the camera is an agent of misogyny, 'its shutter open, quite passive, recording not thinking' (*Goodbye to Berlin, Hello the Oxford Dictionary of Quotations*). 'They only begin to look human when they are dead,' says Burton's Bluebeard – and as Larkin likewise says in 'Lines on a Young Lady's Photograph Album', a girl in a snapshot is captured for all eternity ('We know *what was*'), and unlike Claudius with his empty phrases, an image 'holds you like a heaven', and you are affixed, you womenfolk, under the cosmic thumb, 'smaller and clearer as the years go by'. *Bluebeard* is decadent and neurotic, a cartoonish variation on the theme specifically expressed by Susan Strasberg of Burton: 'He absorbed, demanded, my complete attention ... I did not care about the consequences, Richard didn't seem to, either' – which makes the pair of them sound like Faustus blaspheming on the Bible, scorning God and his ministers, invoking the devil, beating the devil, finding tranquillity (his hope with Taylor) only in excess and luxury.

What this implies, this provocation and discord, is that, as with the characters he played, Burton had a puritan conscience, but a libertine's tastes. He wanted the freedom to turn things upside down, as George Holyoake does in *A Subject of Scandal and Concern*. He had the puritan urge for destruction, obliterating that which causes pleasure – in the seventeenth century this would have meant, for the Roundhead mentality, stained glass, carved woodwork, organs, alabaster saints, regalia and any liturgical ornamentation. The puritan has an awareness of folly and greed – yet also a belief in the power of the devil, which may well burst forth in theatre, opera, dance, sculpture; in music that wasn't only hymns, in literature that wasn't only sermons. In Burton's performances, in his depiction of suffering, in his irascibility, and his integrity, too, you feel the pressure of Old Testament savagery, of the threat of eternal punishment deriving from the chapel childhood. Off-screen, as well as on, he was like Dougal Douglas, in Muriel Spark's *The Ballad of Peckham Rye*, 'one of the wicked spirits that wander through the world for the ruin of souls', or at least to cause them horror, despair, perplexity.

I'm thinking of Sybil. If love and strength are the same thing, the greatest instance of strength Burton encountered was Sybil's – the way she finally withdrew from him, over Taylor, and never saw him again, didn't have anything to do with him again, which was the only way she had of hurting him. Her strength was endless. She was always the sanest person on view, her composure lost only once. This was when Philip complained to her – no doubt expecting sympathy or commiseration from her – after Burton had slipped him fifty quid, as a sort of (as Philip saw it) tip. Was Burton being thoughtless, spiteful, belittling? It does seem like a put-down, the master tossing a coin at the servant. Was it a mishandling? Yet Sybil's anger was at Philip, not with her husband. It's as if she wanted no glimpse, no information about, or reminder, of Burton's relationship with Philip, their intimacies or irritabilities. The mistresses were nothing, compared with that. 'Sybil,' said Rachel Roberts, 'was the good loving bride of Richard's, keeping house, making French fries, ignoring his infidelities,' but Philip was something other than an infidelity – he was someone who, though surrounding Burton with love and affection, had made demands on him, and there was still (would always be) a feeling of nightmare about Philip – and by mentioning the cash handout he imperilled Sybil's way of operating and continuing, where Burton was concerned, which was never to ask questions, because she didn't want to know the answers.

In September 1977, Burton and Susan Hunt, one of the later wives, spent five days with Philip at Key West, arriving by Lear jet. When they left, Philip found five hundred dollars in his study, left behind 'like an elaborate tip'. So, if it was a mishandling, it was one Burton repeated. If he was a person who felt a part of his life had been stolen, Philip was intimately connected with that, and it was a breach, for Philip to speak to Sybil as he did. It hinted at the moral rot, at something festering in Burton's soul, long before he'd become famous, long before he met Taylor, long before he met Sybil. And when he met Taylor, did his despair lessen? Exploitation, betrayal, greed: experience of these had made Burton the hopeless outsider whilst still in Port Talbot. He was metamorphic, not as an actor – he never changed on screen: a blue beard made no difference – but in (and throughout) his private life: all those disjunctions, absences, griefs, as he was separated from his mother, from his birthplace (with its traditions), from his talent as a classical actor; and from his own sense of himself, or his own easy relation with himself. I wonder, was he considered by Michelangelo Antonioni for *The Passenger* (1975)? Burton would have been ideal. It is about a man who wants to disappear. He switches his identity, sticks a different photograph in his passport, keeps the appointments in somebody else's diary and travels to London, Munich and Barcelona. He picks up a mysterious girl. 'I used to be somebody else,' he tells her, 'But I traded him in.' Jack Nicholson is on some weary unspecified personal quest – we keep watching because he interests us, grips us, as an actor. He is intent. Burton likewise has this capacity.

* * *

And then there is Jessica, I believe still alive, a patient these sixty years in the Devereux Hospital (or possibly 'Center'), Pennsylvania, which specialises in 'emotional and behavioural challenges' (as illnesses and disabilities these days are called), such as ADHD, anxiety disorders, bipolar 'issues', depression, and so on and so on. 'The shock to me of being told my child had the intelligence of a reasonably clever dog was considerable,' Burton said bitterly. His brothers, in their books, agree Jessica was the one subject never to be broached: 'Rich ... was not best suited to the needs of an autistic child' (Graham); 'He would clam up and look darkly at us if we talked of her. Eventually we all learnt to avoid mentioning her' (David). Jessica's doctors advised against visits. I often wonder what it must have been like for Burton, in the August of 1976, playing those prolonged scenes in *The Heretic* where his character, Father Lamont, visits a clinic for handicapped children and is surrounded by the withdrawn and weeping patients, the deaf, blind and malformed. Also on the ward is Linda Blair, demonically possessed. 'Wherever I look, I see only evil,' says Burton's priest, who in defiance of modern psychological methodology regards mental illness and epilepsy simply as evidence of an unclean spirit – maybe he's right: James Earl Jones puts in an appearance as a giant locust.

Jessica was born on 26 November 1959, a grizzly, fretful baby. It was Burton's sister, Cassie, a state-registered nurse, who was perturbed first. 'Was her crying normal? Was she happy? Was she healthy? What was the cause of her tantrums?' The word or diagnosis autism or autistic was not known or used in those days – instead, spastic and schizophrenia and retarded were unhelpfully bandied about, as if discussion and treatment of psychiatric complaints hadn't moved on much since eighteenth-century Bedlam. That would seem to be Burton's attitude, too. Mentions of Jessica in the diaries are fleeting and tinged with feelings of personal humiliation: 'It's hopeless ... Quite hopeless' (July 1969); when he sees Brook Williams' daughter: 'She has a mind and makes noises, unlike Jessica, poor bastard. I generally shut Jess out of my mind but sometimes she re-enters with staggering agony' (August 1969); and later that autumn, whilst finishing *Anne of the Thousand Days*, where the actual last shot is of the red-headed infant who'll grow up to be Gloriana toddling in a garden, Burton says of his own daughters: 'both of whom are alive and one of whom is dead.' Undead, therefore, and a sort of permanent reproach or incubus, a focus (or embodiment) of Burton's guilt and shame, like the woman with streaming hair, Antoinette Cosway, in Jean Rhys' *Wide Sargasso Sea*, a zombie, buried alive, hidden away in the attic, sanity slipping. Taylor once brilliantly said of Burton, 'If a prefrontal lobotomy was performed on his skull,' as in *Suddenly, Last Summer*, 'out would fly snakes, frogs, worms, tadpoles and bats.' I'm sure she was right. Burton was like the troubled man clutching at and slumped over a table, in the Goya aquatint, 'The Sleep of Reason Brings Forth Monsters,' from *Los Caprichos*, a suite made in 1797. It is an image of torment and foreboding, suggesting (a century before Freud) real truth is revealed only in nightmares and dreams.

Jessica, reported Graham, outwardly normal-looking, 'never smiled or showed pleasure in the silly games children enjoy.' The family was living in New York in the Bogarts' apartment, or what was now, as he'd died in 1957, his widow Betty Bacall's apartment, during the run of *Camelot*, which had opened at the Majestic Theatre on 3 December 1960. Jessica gazed in a blank way at the television screen, which 'incensed' her father, who'd have wanted her to be poring over books, solving puzzles. 'Why does she do that? It's not natural. Why the hell doesn't she do something, say something?' A severely autistic person is shut inside herself or himself, completely unable to connect with the exterior world, which is a source of terror and confusion. Roddy McDowall, Mordred in *Camelot*, says Jessica 'would scream and smash things. She became too strong to restrain', and Kate Burton told Paul Callan in the *Mirror*, twenty years ago, 'She became impossible to handle and obviously needed special care. There was a Welsh beauty about her. She is imprisoned in her own mind.'

As Burton felt himself to be. His diaries are full of succinct entries like 'temporary insanity', 'a state of nastiness', 'for some reason I suddenly turned from Jekyll into Hyde'. Jessica's cataclysmic will matched his – both had an otherness. The amount of alcohol Burton kept consuming induced what looked like – which partly were – epileptic seizures. (Susan Hunt kept a spatula in her bag, to release his tongue if he looked in danger of choking.) Somewhat against medical orthodoxy, Burton thought the uncontrollable shakes could be allayed by (rather than exacerbated by) booze in his bloodstream, that the booze was good for him, and he feared there was a genetic, or physiological, connection with Jessica's autism. 'She is lost through her own sad world of illness, which I may have led her into,' he told Roddy McDowall. And maybe he did – and maybe he was similarly in a lost world, as what he'd lost was ordinary life, natural life. Burton's brother David, a Chief Inspector of Police, as it happens, put it very soberly and devastatingly: 'We do know that Jessica had just begun to talk when Richard left; then, abruptly, all communication ceased. She became locked in her own mysterious world, where she has remained ever since.'

Jessica was the chief casualty of Burton's success with Taylor, and a living symbol and reminder of the malignancy within the relationship. Everyone was in Italy, being driven wild. Nothing mattered to Burton and Taylor other than possession, ecstasy. The world's press was avid for photographs, flashbulbs going off migraine-inducingly and incessantly, in faces, through windows and curtains, against glass. Jessica screamed in fear when reporters and cameramen invaded the rented villa. 'Jessica's illness,' said Chief Inspector Jenkins, making more than a surmise, and summing up the family's consensus, 'had been triggered by the emotional storm building up around her.' The serenity and the cool front Sybil presented, when Burton pursued his other women, and when he exploited her, broke down with Jessica, who was like a flame shooting up and engulfing a house. The first and very last coherent utterance she made was the name her father went by with his loved ones, which she turned into a baleful chant: '*Rich! Rich! Rich! Rich! Rich! Rich!*'

PART THREE
I.T.A.L.Y.

I Trust And Love You: Burton and Taylor meet making Cleopatra *at Cinecittà; it is the most expensive film in history. Their passion, obsession, and fidelity; and how they invented 'celebrity' and eradicated 'respectability'. Fast-forward half a century and the Burtons' existence is the one favoured by attention-seekers who want a 'profile' and totter along the red carpet in ludicrous hooker shoes. As Burton wrote in his diary, 'A lot of things happened to me – and us – in Rome.'*

'We seem to know a great deal on the basis of very little,' complained Iris Murdoch, in metaphysical rather than novelistic mode. What is the evidence? Where is the data? Can anything be said without falsehood? This is certainly true in the case of biography, when biographers assume the right to make a sweeping and authoritative summing up. 'She doesn't feel guilty,' said Brenda Maddox of Elizabeth Taylor. 'Through it all this woman refused to succumb,' concluded Kitty Kelley, implying a similar sentiment. 'Elizabeth did indeed know how to milk every gasp and every thrill,' gasped the thrilled William J. Mann. 'In the end, though,' said Paul Ferris of Richard Burton, 'it is he himself who has invited censure . . . by talking with such grandeur and pride . . . of the unachieved.' I sometimes wonder at the mentality and motivation of the biographer – as so very many biographies are disapproving. 'HBO even declined to tape *Private Lives*, on the grounds that Taylor's weight problem made it an unattractive television prospect,' jeered Sheridan Morley; and it is as if by being now in possession of all the *facts*; having ascertained and laid down the *chronology*; having decided what their subject had been *doing* and where they'd *been* – then this puts the biographer in a superior position, rubbed in by insisting on a cold degree of distance.

A morally superior position, too, impatient with frailties, and forgetful of just how difficult it can be *to get through a fucking day*, let alone live out a life, which at the time, and to the person concerned, will be unpredictable, full of decisions big and small. For myself, penetrating the consciousness of another person, an alien consciousness at that, coming to have an understanding of personal moments – let alone what T.S. Eliot called 'unattended moments' – and weighing up, and imagining, strengths and weaknesses: it is an affair of ghosts – listening to the resonant dead in Burton's voice ('I thought a lot about our lives and shades of mortality grew round me like a mist'); listening to Taylor justify herself ('I agree with Tennessee that I am an instinctive actress'). Because when it does come to hard facts and what anyone has been up to and where they might be found – conventional biographies, upon examination, are actually hilariously wanting.

In Tom Rubython's *And God Created Burton* (2011), Jessica Burton was born on 28 November 1959, and several hundred pages later, on 29 November 1959. (It was 26 November 1959.) The index to Chris Williams' edition of the *Diaries*, under the entry for Jessica, says Burton received a letter from her on 20 November 1968. But the note was from Burton's other daughter, Kate: 'It was sweet and repetitive of my letter to her . . . I wish I was her teacher. I'd teach her to avoid all the pitfalls of my half-baked education. As it is she is stuck with Syb's eighth-baked variety.' We are also told Jessica was in Switzerland with her father in June 1975 – but the 'JB' Burton mentions was Jean Bell, whom some books call Jeanne Bell. Her real name was (or is) Annie Lee Morgan. Burton had no further association with Jessica once she was placed with the Devereux doctors and nurses, when she was six. 'All I can do is make her rich, and she is rich,' Burton said, though she never had the means of enjoying the $10 million trust fund endowed in her favour.

As for the *Diaries* themselves, they are not to be trusted. On 'Tuesday 29 August 1975', Burton writes: 'Sunned. Had tea ... at D'Alleves.' That's Hôtel d'Allèves, Rue du Cendrier, Geneva. Yet 29 August was a Friday, and Burton, with Taylor, was in Jerusalem, causing a riot at the Wailing Wall. Or so says Yoram Ben-Ami, in *Guiding Royalty: My Adventure with Elizabeth Taylor and Richard Burton*. Except when he mentions the Israel trip in his journals, Burton has this event, preceded by a meeting with Ben-Ami in Switzerland, as taking place a month earlier, in the July.

So it goes on, biography a form of incomprehension. Melvyn Bragg says Burton's co-star in the NBC television version of *Wuthering Heights*, broadcast on 9 May 1958, was Yvonne Furneaux. Cathy was in the event played by Rosemary Harris, Burton and John Neville's Old Vic Desdemona. Michael Powell said, 'I had always hoped to work with Richard, ever since he joined the Stratford-Upon-Avon Shakespeare Memorial Theatre to play Hotspur and then Henry V, giving sensational performances of both for a young unknown Welsh actor.' Burton never played Hotspur on any stage anywhere in the world. At Stratford in 1951 the role was taken by Michael Redgrave. Sheilah Graham, in her profile of Taylor, refers to Burton's brother Ivor and his wife 'Gwyn' – it was Gwen. In *My Hollywood: A Celebration and a Lament*, Sheilah further says Taylor's Man Friday was Richard 'Manley', when it was Dick Hanley (1908–1971), who incidentally appeared on *What's My Line*, in March 1960, as 'Elizabeth Taylor's Secretary'. He couldn't have been more bursting with pride had he been Queen Elizabeth II's Lord Great Chamberlain. It was Hanley who broke the news to Taylor about Mike Todd's plane crash, and during the making of *Cleopatra* it was Hanley's rented Roman apartment which Taylor and Burton borrowed for afternoon trysts. Furthermore, when Sheilah says one of Burton's later girlfriends was Princess Elizabeth 'of Liechtenstein' she meant of Yugoslavia.

Penny Junor, in her Burton biography, calls Dylan Thomas' wife Caitlin 'Katlin'. Tyrone Steverson's *Richard Burton: A Bio-Bibliography* says *Boom!* was filmed in Corsica, when it was the Parco Naturale Regionale, Porto Conte, in Sardinia, forming the backdrop. Steverson also says Burton's third wife, Susan or Suzy Hunt, was previously married to 'world motor-racing champion, John Hunt'. Er, no. He's the one who went up Everest. The motor-racing champion was James Hunt. The Ritz-Carlton Hotel, Montreal, in the section of their website commemorating illustrious guests, asserts Taylor and Burton were married in the Royal Suite on Sunday 5 March 1964. The Reverend Leonard Mason, who officiated, remembered the date as 16 March. It was 15 March. One of John Osborne's biographers says *Divorce His, Divorce Hers* was shot in America, when the exteriors were done in Rome and the interiors in the Bavaria Studios, Geiselgasteig, south of Munich.

In the Endnotes to each of the three volumes of Christopher Isherwood's journals, the editor says Burton was in *California Suite*. It's a strange person who'd confuse Burton with Walter Matthau; nor was Peter Firth born in 1935, unless he was a very elderly teenager in *Equus*. Caroline Young, in *Roman Holiday: The Secret Life of Hollywood in Rome* (2018), says one of Burton's later wives was Sally Hunt, a neat conflation of Susan Hunt and Sally Hay, and a mistake Burton himself may have made. In 1965, he and Taylor could not have come to Europe, to film interiors for *The Sandpiper*, on board the QE2, 'booking all six first-class cabins', however, despite what Darwin Porter and Danforth Prince state in *Elizabeth Taylor: There Is Nothing Like a Dame*, as the ship wasn't launched until two years later. It's always sad to see people repeat the story that after *Cleopatra*, Mankiewicz never made another film and blamed the end of his career on Burton and Taylor, as if he was thoroughly washed up and bitter. In fact, in 1967, there was *The Honeypot*, with Rex Harrison and Maggie Smith, an interesting re-working of *Volpone*, and in 1972, *Sleuth*, with Olivier and Michael Caine – a battle of wills, replete with theatricality and dressing-up games, which was nominated for four Academy Awards, including Best Director.

Alan Bennett, who met Sybil in New York, in his diaries, *Writing Home*, calls her Sibyl. On the night of the day 'the divorce from Sibyl [sic] and the marriage to Liz was announced Sibyl [sic again] asked me to accompany her to the premiere of *The Criminal* with Stanley Baker ... I had been chosen because I was someone with whom no one could seriously imagine she had a romantic link.' Presumably Philip, Roddy McDowall and Dirk Bogarde were unavailable. Now, then – Sybil divorced Burton in Guadalajara on 5 December 1963, yet *The Criminal* had been first released in America on 24 May 1962, which is when everyone was still at Cinecittà, and on that particular day the Pope's dentist came in person to the set to treat Roddy McDowall, who'd broken a tooth. Maybe what Bennett went to see was *Zulu*? He tells the story again in his second collection of prose pieces, *Untold Stories*, and though he spells Sybil correctly, and mentions the day of the week and the year ('One Sunday in 1963'), otherwise Bennett now allows for a subjective vagueness, an element of mists-of-time doubt: 'in my memory the film was *The Criminal* with Stanley Baker ... afterwards I slipped away.' Perhaps they went to see a revival of *The Guns of Navarone*. The only point he really wants to get across in either version is his own sad desultoriness, to assert his unassertiveness.

I don't mind confusions and contradictions. In James Robert Parish's *Fiasco: A History of Hollywood's Iconic Flops*, Burton 'died in 1984 at age 54', which deprived him of four more years. Donald Spoto, in his biography of Taylor, confidently situates Salcombe in Norfolk and mixes up Hampstead and Hampshire. All this merely adds to the surrealism of the undertaking, the errors and ambiguities ensuring Taylor and Burton remain vivid and unusual, capable of being in two places at once, or nowhere in particular. That non-fiction is constructed on shifting sand, and biography, as a method, prone to defeat and collapse, is indicated by the way, when I examined heaps of them, to find out where the Burton family stayed during the endless months of the *Cleopatra* shoot, none was forthcoming. 'A handsome villa on the Appian Way,' says Rubython. Where? What was the actual address? I know Rex Harrison's digs – Via di Porta San Sebastiano, 13. (Though Taylor said Rex's house was 'on the Via Antiqua'.) The Burton 'contingent checked into a villa about two miles away from the Fishers,' says J. Randy Taraborrelli. Opacities reign. 'A villa one-and-a-half miles from the Taylor-Fisher residence,' says C. David Heymann, who reports Burton as complaining the rented property suffered smoke damage from a malfunctioning electric fire. Penny Junor, in her Burton book, *The Man Behind the Myth*, says the fire was caused by Burton's falling paralytic on the pillows with a burning cigarette in his hand. Sybil woke up to 'smouldering bedclothes', and a 'deeply asleep' Burton had to be carried into 'the safety of the garden'. Sybil then remembered Jessica, 'who was asleep on the top floor'. But we still don't know the whereabouts of this drama – a dramatic (and heroic) night for Sybil certainly – save it was 'in a villa on the Appian Way', and sometimes Roddy McDowall was moving in ('Burton arranged for Roddy McDowall, who was playing Octavian in the film, to vacate his hotel and come live at the house' – Rubython), and sometimes Roddy McDowall is moving out ('Roddy McDowall moved out of the Burton villa and into town' – Dick Sheppard, in his biography of Taylor).

Accommodation issues can be vexed. 'The Hampstead house where Francis and Sara lived had previously been owned by Augustus John, the Welsh painter,' assert Porter and Prince. 'When Augustus John moved out of his Hampstead house for other digs, he'd abandoned several of his paintings, leaving them still hanging on the walls,' these becoming part of Francis Taylor's purloined collection. Intrigued and sceptical, because this is a story widely repeated online, I wrote to Sir Michael Holroyd for some extra intelligence, as there is no mention of Francis Taylor let alone the infant Elizabeth Taylor in his 'definitive' biography, not even in the 1996 edition, which included new material. Sir Holroyd's office forwarded my letter to Rebecca John, who informed me, 'I am now the recognised authority on the work of my grandfather and can usually help to answer questions'. The upshot being – 'I have never heard or read anywhere that Augustus owned a house in Hampstead. His home from 1927 until his death in 1961 was at Fryern Court, Fordingbridge, Hampshire.' Miss John points out that the artist did rent 'the odd studio' in London in the Thirties and Forties – Pelham Crescent (where Emlyn Williams and Daphne Rye lived, incidentally), Tite Street and Mallord Street, SW3. I wonder if Donald Spoto's confusion of Hampstead and Hampshire set the ball rolling? Not that Taylor herself would have been any help. 'I was born in Hampstead,' she once told a journalist. 'Sorry, love, it was Hendon,' interjected Burton.

Nevertheless, Rebecca John does confirm her grandfather 'must have met Francis Taylor sometime in the Thirties, when Taylor was dealing from a gallery in Bond Street. They seem to have become friends – Francis visited Augustus at Fryern, and in 1956 sat for his portrait, which was reproduced in George Rainbird's *Fifty-Two Drawings*, published in 1957.' This was the chalk *Der Stürmer* sketch, which I described earlier on. 'When Francis Taylor left England in 1939, and having agreed with Augustus (I assume) to act as his dealer in California, he took with him a large stash of drawings and paintings straight from the artist's studio. He was indiscriminate, taking much work of inferior quality,' including the ripped-up pictures from the wastepaper basket.

Scraps and fragments – they can be as tantalising as follies, ruins, unfinished or abandoned castles, collapsed bandstands woven with myrtle leaves. I receive a similar frisson thinking about out-takes, deleted scenes, forgotten footage in a studio's vaults, such as the chunks of *Cleopatra* flung in the furnace: 'Zanuck destroyed an extremely good performance by Richard Burton that no one has ever seen,' Mankiewicz lamented to Tony Palmer. 'Literally, no one has ever seen'; or the sequences Burton shot for *Laughter in the Dark*

(1968) before he was replaced by Nicol Williamson; or the unfinished, lost *Jackpot* (1975), which prompted Terence Young, who'd been through this already, with *The Klansman*, the previous year, to remark, 'Burton had become really very irrational and unpredictable. I knew he wanted to quit [the booze] but he just couldn't. He didn't know what he was doing.' All this suggestiveness, the blurring and marring. And portraiture, which depends on suggestiveness, interpretation, expression, is not news photography or accurate reportage, just as biography isn't an anatomy lesson. As Augustus John depicted them, Dylan Thomas, Lawrence of Arabia or W.B. Yeats have faces that are peacock blue, pine green; poses are struck in spots and stripes of light and painted shadow. The works are fantasies of verisimilitude, like the dimensions, aspect, layout of Taylor's Roman lodgings, which cost Twentieth Century Fox $3,000 a month in rental charges. Unlike Burton's premises, at least the place had a name – Sheppard says it was 'the Villa Pappa [which] adjoined the Moroccan Embassy on the old Via Appia'. Lester David and Jhan Robbins, in *Richard and Elizabeth*, describe it as a 'fourteen-room garden-surrounded mansion with a swimming pool and a tennis court'. J. Randy Taraborrelli says it had fifteen rooms. John Cottrell and Fergus Cashin (whom parenthetically in his diaries Burton calls 'those two stupid failures ... Bloody clowns of hell'), in *Richard Burton: Very Close Up*, attenuate Villa Pappa to Villa Papa, and say the property contained seven bedrooms and six bathrooms, though Ruth Waterbury, in *Elizabeth Taylor: Her Life, Her Loves, Her Future*, says the Villa 'Papa' had 'seven bedrooms, almost no baths, [and] a staff of seventeen servants to run it.' Waterbury adds the Burtons had 'a smaller villa than Villa Papa but very near it.' Walter Wanger, the producer of *Cleopatra*, recalls the Villa 'Pappa' as having 'seven bedrooms, six bathrooms, a huge living room, another smaller salon'. Taylor loathed it, anyway, calling it, according to Kate Andersen Brower, the 'House of Pain'. Brower adds that it was a ten-thousand-square-foot property, later lived in by Franco Zeffirelli, and that the address was 448 Via Appia Pignatelli. In her memoirs

Taylor tells us the drains exploded one day and 'the whole kitchen was floating in sewage,' and whatever her numerous staff and courtiers were up to, they never expelled the vermin. 'Finally, I decided I'd better go to the pantry myself and duel with the rats,' she wrote. 'God, that was a filthy house.' Framed photographs of Mike Todd were dotted about.

Well, wherever it was, whatever it was called, however many lavatories there may or may not have been, Taylor soon filled it with her collection of ten dogs, four cats, rabbits, children and hangers-on, most of them, human and otherwise, incontinent and ill-disciplined: Michael Wilding Jr., Christopher Wilding, Liza Todd, Dr Rexford Kennamer, a governess, a handyman, a butler, cooks, a laundress, two chauffeurs. Kitty Kelley says the 'pink marble mansion' had two butlers and eight acres of pine trees. Taylor wanted the beds changed every day, the pattern of the sheets matching her collection of cigarette holders. She sounds like a Hanna-Barbera Princess Margaret. There was an office block at Cinecittà, specially converted and decorated in mauve and glazed chintz, to serve as Taylor's dressing room, with a retiring room, a storeroom for her costumes and wigs, a bathroom and shower, and a cubby hole for Eddie. I don't propose to catalogue inconsistencies in everyone's descriptions of it, though the mauve chintz is my own fanciful addition, and at least this time we have Taylor's own word for it that, 'Even my dressing room was five times normal.'

The point has been made, I think, in the foregoing, that as variants multiply, comically so, biography looks more like holography than anything else. The principal forms are there, Burton and Taylor, Taylor and Burton; they may even be three-dimensional, possessing perspective and being capable of movement. But they are zigzags of light, impossible to grasp. You can't describe them as objects. They are air, shadows, vibrations, illusions, utterly cut off, more strange than true.

What follows, therefore, my *Cleopatra* calendar, a distillation made or compiled from mountains of books, articles, newspaper clippings, archival rummaging generally, is meant to have the quality of farce – people running in and out of lots of doors, colliding, falling over, picking themselves up, falling over again. So, to begin at the beginning – easy enough for the poet to say, but with the making of *Cleopatra*, when did the beginning begin? I suggest:

13 *December* 1951

On this day, Walter Wanger, a producer who'd been in the business long enough to have worked with Garbo, and who was married to Joan Bennett, Taylor's mother, Ellie Banks, in *Father of the Bride* and *Father's Little Dividend*, shot Jennings Lang in the bollocks. 'That's the first hit Walter has had in ten years,' observed Walt Disney, a man not normally given to humour. Wanger believed Jennings, an agent with MCA, and who was later responsible for the series *Wagon Train*, had been having an affair with Joan, who denied everything. Wanger's defence was 'temporary insanity', and he spent four months in the bin. Whether the insanity was temporary or not, he was to be the producer of *Cleopatra*.

What's clear from his book, *My Life With Cleopatra*, co-written with Joe Hyams, is if Taylor's behaviour was often hateful and mad, Wanger was obsessionally dedicated to the project, to the point of ludicrousness. He knew his sources – his Plutarch, Shakespeare, Shaw and Théophile Gautier. Cleopatra, said Wanger, is 'the quintessence of youthful femininity, of womanliness and strength', and ever since first seeing *A Place in the Sun* ('I was overwhelmed') he knew Taylor was the only candidate for the role. Her subsequent performances, e.g. in *Cat on a Hot Tin Roof* and *Suddenly, Last Summer*, confirmed his hunch.

Wanger took his ideas to Twentieth Century Fox, where he was rebuffed by the Executive Vice President: 'Who needs Liz Taylor? Any hundred-dollar-a-week girl can play Cleopatra.' Indeed – any slinky Aphrodite on the half-shell. The name Joan Collins was mentioned. Incidentally, in *Sea Wife*, an oddity to be made on location in Jamaica in 1957, Joan plays a saucy-looking nun, cast adrift on a raft and marooned on a desert island with Burton, who quotes Keats and kills a pelican. Joan, with her dark hair, cheekbones, busty substances and an attractive overbite, looks a bit like Taylor – and she must have been the only nun in history to apply vermilion lipstick. On the desert island, the shellfish and coconut diet agrees with her, as she is never malnourished or diseased – indeed, Joan looks like she regularly shampoos her hair and her snow-white rags cling to her as becomingly as a shift by Balenciaga. Burton fortuitously finds a machete, builds a boat, and they set sail to safety. Despite the tropical heat, nothing happens – an inconsequential dead loss on the erotic front. Joan's nun does not yield to temptation, and she rather regretfully reflects, 'Nobody ever looks at the face of a nun.'

Matters simmered until:

November 1958
Wanger started mentioning Cleopatra to Taylor, telling her he envisaged a film about 'really a modern Cleopatra', which is to say, 'a woman of many moods, of many emotions, turning off and on her hate, her ambition, her love, her excitement, and her dreams' – which is a brilliant summation of everything Taylor had ever achieved (would ever achieve) on screen. Wanger repeated his words in a memo to Rouben Mamoulian on 27 June 1960.

December 1958
John DeCuir, the production designer of genius, started making preliminary sketches of the Forum and the Alexandria palaces, which were to be 'the last word in opulence, beauty and art'. Casting ideas at this stage: Olivier, Cary Grant, John Gielgud, Yul Brynner,

Curt Jurgens or Noël Coward for Caesar (*Noël Coward?*); Burton or Burt Lancaster for Antony. A script was commissioned from Nigel Balchin and Lawrence Durrell.

24 February 1959
Sophia Loren and Audrey Hepburn were asked if they were interested in playing Cleopatra. Carlo Ponti said, 'Italy is the only place to make it,' so Fox sent scouts to Pinewood. The initial budget forecast was $2,955,700, to cover sixty-four days' shooting.

July 1959
Bulldozers began excavating a site for the Alexandria set on the Fox lot in Hollywood.

1 September 1959
Spyros Skouras, the President of Twentieth Century Fox, and a man, according to Groucho Marx, who never made a horror picture intentionally, accurately predicts Taylor will 'be too much trouble'. His casting brainwave is Susan Hayward. Taylor 'started to cry' when she heard this. The budget is now $4,500,000. Rouben Mamoulian is assigned directorial duties, as he had 'an artistic reputation'. Wanger wanted Hitchcock as 'he would bring the right touch of suspense to the story'.

15 October 1959
Taylor signed a contract with Fox for $1 million. During negotiations, she'd said to Skouras, 'I don't need you!' and quick as a flash he retorted, 'Neither do we need you!' He was always falling asleep over his worry beads, fretful that Fox was starting to receive poison-pen letters, along the lines of: 'You are wasting money on Liz Taylor. Nobody wants to see her after the way she treated that sweet little Debbie Reynolds.'

2 December 1959
Wanger goes to Pinewood. 'It was rainy and cold, and Pinewood doesn't look like Egypt.' Nor does it, nor did it. Skouras wondered about shooting on location in Turkey and 'began negotiations with the Turkish government'. Fruitless scouting trips in Asia Minor were added to the budget.

7 December 1959
Taylor is in the Harkness Pavilion, 180 Fort Washington Avenue, New York, with double pneumonia. Everyone is fully aware Taylor 'is so susceptible to colds and bronchitis'.

8 March 1960
Taylor fell over on some ice in Philadelphia and was examined at the Nazareth Hospital, run by nuns and which, since 1940, had 'expanded the community's access to emergency hip fracture repair', with further X-rays at the Harkness.

9 April 1960
Burton travels from Lausanne to London by train, arriving the following day, to begin three weeks of rehearsal for John Osborne's television drama, directed by Tony Richardson, *A Subject of Scandal and Concern*, which is about 'a man who didn't believe in God . . . It is an interesting play,' wrote Burton in his diary on 2 April. He stays at The Savoy. His fee is £1,000. The production is recorded on 25 April and Burton returned to Switzerland on Wednesday 27 April.

3 May 1960
The external sets have been going up in England – temples, palaces, a four-acre lake, galleys, sphinxes fifty-two-feet high and sixty-five-feet wide – utilising 142 miles (is that the same as the 750,000 feet other sources quote?) of tubular steel, 20,000 (or 80,000 – again depending on the source) cubic-feet of timber, seven tons of nails, 300 gallons of

paint, and causing a shortage of skilled plasterers in the British build-ing trade. The scaffolding rental was costing $2,000 a week. The upper reaches of the Thames are diverted to flow through the set as a tributary of the Nile. Palm trees are shipped from Hollywood and fresh fronds flown in from Egypt and the Riviera.

British unions object to the employment of Sydney Guilaroff, as 'our using him is a reflection on the skill of the English hairdresser'. Guilaroff, who'd styled Taylor's wigs at MGM, was being paid $1,000 a week plus $600 in expenses.

19 *May* 1960
No wigs or costumes are ready and the workmen constructing Alexandria are already on overtime.

20 *June* 1960
Taylor and Eddie attend the heavyweight boxing bout, at the Polo Grounds, Upper Manhattan, between Floyd Patterson and Ingemar Johansson. The former knocked the latter out cold in the fifth round. Thinking the boos and hisses were directed at her, Taylor directed a variety of 'Fuck You!' gestures at the 50,000 capacity crowd.

25 *June* 1960
Skouras arrives in person at Claridge's. He is met at the airport with two bottles of Scotch and an envelope stuffed with English currency. 'England is the best place to make this picture,' he states. 'There's no sun,' says Wanger plaintively.

28 *July* 1960
Taylor re-negotiates her contract, stipulating 70 mm cameras have to deploy the wide-screen Todd-AO [American Optical] process, meant to be an improvement on Cinerama. Whether or not it was an improvement on Cinerama, the main benefit of the Todd-AO

system to Taylor personally is she'd receive royalties now that she owned it, having inherited it from Mike.

Another contractual obligation was that the schedule had to be adjusted to suit Taylor's menstrual cycle. As Kenneth Haigh was to confirm, 'We could only shoot Roman scenes in the Senate when Elizabeth was having her period.'

15 *August* 1960

Truman Capote writes to Cecil Beaton, somewhat bitchily passing on the news that Oliver Messel, Beaton's professional rival, is 'getting ten thousand pounds just to do Liz's clothes for Cleopatra'. Beaton will at least have been gratified when Messel was replaced later by Irene Sharaff.

In his letter to Beaton, Capote also mentions the weather: 'London, my God: rain, rain. I thought it was *winter*.'

31 *August* 1960

Taylor and Eddie arrive at the Port of Naples on the recently launched S S *Leonardo da Vinci* (scrapped in 1982). They attend the Opening Ceremony of the X V I I Olympiad in Rome. Taylor goes to see the water polo event and is pinched on the bottom by the judge.

She and Eddie make their way to London, where at The Dorchester they are installed in a 'large corner suite', i.e. the Oliver Messel Suite, comprising a bathroom, dressing room and living room, with an adjoining two double bedrooms, plus two further bathrooms and a sitting room. Plus, again, additional accommodation for the Wilding and Todd children and nannies. Taylor immediately has a sore throat.

14 *September* 1960

On Kennamer's express instructions, Taylor, 'who says she was unable to sleep and was having palpitations', is administered a quarter grain of morphine by a Dr Vernon.

21 *September* 1960

Dr Vernon injects Taylor with 2 cc of Paraldehyde, a central nervous system depressant, or sleeping tablet, which is what sent Evelyn Waugh around the twist and inspired *The Ordeal of Gilbert Pinfold* (1957). Kennamer is concerned for her ventricular arrhythmia.

23 *September* 1960

The patient is given Atarax or Hydroxyzine (used in the treatment of anxiety and nausea – with side-effects of headaches and drowsiness) and Phenergan (prescribed for short-term sleep problems, hay fever and allergies, cold and cough symptoms), obtained by Dr Vernon from John Bell & Croyden, a Wigmore Street pharmacy and Royal Warrant holder. Not for the first time, a Fox report says Taylor is 'hysterical'.

Dr Vernon, who gave Taylor pills at The Dorchester, was in love with the aunt of David Hare. Aged thirteen, the future playwright was thrilled to overhear all these stories about visiting show business royalty. The doctor was a devout Catholic, who alongside his private practice did good work for the NHS in Brixton.

26 *September* 1960

Taylor has costume fittings. Rushes of her camera tests (two-and-a-half hours' worth) are screened for her and Eddie at the Dominion Theatre.

28 *September* 1960

The first day of principal photography. The hairdressers go on strike, an unresolved union dispute because of Sydney Guilaroff, who'd created Taylor's tomboy cut for *National Velvet*. 'Well, Sydney, you're a star at last,' Taylor tells him pointedly and with exasperation. Oblivious to her irony, Guilaroff's view was, as he explained, 'Elizabeth remained adamant about working with me, insisting she was entitled to have a stylist who was familiar with her.'

When the production moved to Rome, in effect Guilaroff was sacked, as was Oliver Messel, who'd complained Guilaroff was being paid four times as much as he was. Messel, the costume designer, was found to have been duplicating the costumes he'd designed in 1945 for Vivien Leigh in *Caesar and Cleopatra* – and though Taylor and Leigh doubled for each other in long-shot in *Elephant Walk*, Leigh was rather slenderer than Taylor.

Not to be outdone, or left out, Guilaroff said he was the one who'd been asked to convey 'a copy of the script' of *Cleopatra* to Taylor, and had been asked personally by Walter Wanger 'to persuade Elizabeth to take the role'. He was then the one (usually it is Eddie) who called Wanger back and announced, 'Walter, she'll do it, for one million dollars.'

29 *September* 1960

Over at the O'Keefe Centre for the Performing Arts in Toronto, *Camelot* begins its pre-Broadway try-outs. Alan J. Lerner, producer and lyricist, keels over with a stomach ulcer and Moss Hart, the director, collapses with a heart attack and is either ill or dead. 'It was my dream that I might be asked in to help,' said Philip, and Burton, rather desperate, is able to facilitate this – though it is an unofficial arrangement.

Philip was like a convict worker, editing and directing, if covertly. 'I spent some six hours making notes on the script and last night's performance,' he noted in his diary for 7 October. He also privately coached Roddy McDowall as Mordred. 'I found him to be an unusually sensitive, intelligent actor.' Well, there we are.

'I was adequately paid,' says Philip, no doubt out of Burton's own pocket, but he was emphatically not credited in the programme or on the posters or anywhere – and his name has never been whispered by anyone who had anything to do with the show. Neither gratitude nor acknowledgement is extended in Lerner's (1978) autobiography, *The Street Where I Live*, for instance. Burton, however, did remain loyal – 'It was Philip who saved the show' – but this was hyperbole.

30 *September* 1960
The temperature at Pinewood is 7.2 degrees Centigrade, 45 degrees Fahrenheit, and there are two minutes and twenty seconds of sunshine.

1 *October* 1960
Taylor reported ill. Remains at The Dorchester. Eddie is being paid $150,000 by the studio to get her to the studio, ensure she gets early nights, watch her diet, walk her dogs, but he himself is addicted to methamphetamine. Taylor, we now know, was on an 'enormous amount of drugs', or so says Eddie, who added, 'She'd be popping pills and drinking most of the day.' Pills, cigarettes, alcohol – it wrecked Taylor's immune system. Truman Capote visits and finds 'the rooms were so crowded with shedding cats and unhousebroken dogs and a general atmosphere of disorderly paraphernalia that one could not easily espy the Messel touch.'

3 *October* 1960
There are two minutes and fifteen seconds of sunshine at Pinewood.

18 *October* 1960
Lord Evans, the doctor, says Taylor has 'a case of infection of doubtful origin'. The insurance companies want Taylor replaced – the production is already losing $121,428 a day – by of all people Marilyn Monroe. W.C. Fields once described Mae West as 'a plumber's idea of Cleopatra', which as a conception (not altogether a foolish one) is perhaps what the insurance people had in mind.

20 *October* 1960
Wanger reports he'd been with Eddie and Taylor to see *The Millionairess*, which starred Peter Sellers and Sophia Loren. In three

years' time, the director, Anthony Asquith, will direct *The V.I.P.s* and Wolf Mankowitz, who wrote the screenplay, will subsequently adapt *Doctor Faustus* and assist with the Yugoslavian project, *The Battle of Sutjeska*, in which Burton's Serbo-Croatian dialogue was put into English only for everything he said to be re-dubbed into Serbo-Croatian.

As regards *The Millionairess*, what would Taylor have made of that – the rich hypochondriac infiltrating a doctor's life and career, insisting on having her way, thinking she may have at last found love? Sellers playing an Indian ('Oh goodness gracious me!') would not be allowed today.

26 *October* 1960

Large cuts having been made and new scenes with different songs inserted, *Camelot* opens at the Shubert Theatre in Boston. It still lasted about five hours, which must have been like sitting through the Middle Ages in real-time.

29 *October* 1960

Taylor to The London Clinic, taken there, according to Guilaroff, by Guilaroff. 'I sat with her, stroking her hand . . . She was placed in an iron lung developed for polio patients.' Malta Fever was mentioned, which Eddie thought was an invented ailment. In fact, it is another term for brucellosis, which is caused by the ingestion of animal secretions – unpasteurised milk or undercooked meat, usually, but the slobbering of Taylor's innumerable and terrible pets, which shared her bed, may be to blame. Symptoms are joint and muscle pain, abdominal pain, nausea, vomiting, infections of the bone – and Taylor always had back problems, or spondylodiscitis.

6 *November* 1960

A Subject of Scandal and Concern is broadcast on BBC Television.

7 November 1960
Taylor discharged. The doctors say she had a 'boil on the buttocks' and 'an infected tooth'.

9 November 1960
Taylor re-admitted, having been taken to The London Clinic on a stretcher with 'a terrible headache'. Lord Evans and Dr Goldman in attendance.

13 November 1960
Lord Evans comes to see his patient, who seems to have returned to her Dorchester suite, and confirms Taylor has been poisoned by a tooth abscess. Eddie thinks she is faking symptoms to obtain drugs, particularly Demerol and Seconal, and that her acute fevers are brought on by binge drinking. 'She was eating Demerol like candy,' says her husband – Demerol being an addictive opioid, properly used only to treat severe pain. Overdosage results in stupor, respiratory depression (breathing issues), convulsions, all the symptoms Taylor manifested, though the entirety of the British medical profession, publicly at least, never put two-and-two together. Seconal, or Secobarbital, now discontinued, except in Holland, where it is administered intravenously for euthanasia, is a strong sleeping tablet.

18 November 1960
After another week in The London Clinic, the actress is still indisposed, the diagnosis they come up with this time being meningism – not meningitis (as some sources said), far from it, more of a migraine, characterised by neck stiffness, photophobia (flinching from bright light), general neuralgia. 'There is nothing more we can shoot without Liz. We must come to a stop,' says Wanger. Production officially halted, it is hoped only until 3 January. When the insurance people again urge re-casting, Skouras holds his nerve and is kindly: 'We cannot abandon [Taylor] just because she has been ill.'

The script is given another polish by Nunnally Johnson, for a $140,000 fee. Paddy Chayefsky is also consulted. Ambitions remained grandiose, as the film would be 'Covering for the first time in the theatre the contrasting lives of Caesar and Antony and the enmity of Octavian. All of this against the greatest panorama of world conquest.' Taylor insists on the elimination of any asses' milk bath scene and of a strip poker card game scene with Stephen Boyd.

21 *November* 1960
After her meningism and which-what, Taylor says, 'I've never been so glad to be alive. There were moments when I thought I would never see another day. It makes the world seem a doubly wonderful place.' Doubly? Trebly?

3 *December* 1960
Camelot opens at the Majestic Theater on Broadway. Burton is paid $4,000 a week plus eleven per cent of the gross.

9 *December* 1960
Taylor and Eddie leave for Paris and Palm Springs.

16 *December* 1960
Noël Coward records in his diary that with Marlene Dietrich he'd attended the opening of *Camelot*. They found it 'disappointing' and 'flat and vulgar' and 'music and lyrics uninspired and story uninteresting'. Burton, however, 'gave a superb performance and made the whole expensive evening worthwhile'. The 'vast' first night party was at Lüchow's. 'Enjoyable if you like vast parties,' which Coward did.

23 *December* 1960
Taylor and Eddie return to London.

28 December 1960
Taylor (and Eddie) actually 'showed up at the studio early this morning,' but as the sound stages weren't heated to her satisfaction, she returned to The Dorchester, where 'they live like royalty with children, dogs, cats, retainers and supplicants for favour all over the place'.

31 December 1960
Wanger invites Taylor and Eddie to a New Year dinner at The Caprice. A waiter, colliding into what Burton would one day call Taylor's 'apocalyptic' breasts, spills coffee everywhere, darkening her Dior.

3 January 1961
The new start date. Mamoulian manages six takes of the scene where, before an amused Caesar, Cleopatra rolls out of a carpet. No footage has subsequently been found. Was there film in the camera? A double in the rug? Mamoulian contemplates resignation.

6 January 1961
Michael Wilding Jr.'s eighth birthday. Eddie and Taylor take the family to Bertram Mills Circus.

14 January 1961
The Fox board, presented with a balance sheet showing the Pinewood shoot was losing $121,428 a day, accuse Wanger of 'letting Liz run the show'.

18 January 1961
Mamoulian, who had taken a ten-month lease on a flat in Eaton Square, resigns. 'Dreams have to be translated into flesh and blood,' he said, admitting he'd been defeated in this endeavour. 'Rain, mud, slush and fog. We didn't have one inch of film with Liz in it.' There really wasn't film in the camera.

25 *January* 1961

The new director is to be Joseph L. Mankiewicz, who'd been responsible for *Suddenly, Last Summer*. He saw Cleopatra as 'a genius in the art of attracting men'. He scrapped the ten and a half minutes of film shot by his predecessor – and there was now to be extensive recasting, replanning and rebuilding.

Taylor and Eddie go to Paris and thence by the Orient Express to Munich, to attend the pre-Lenten Festival or *Fasching*. If, as Eddie said, they stayed at the place where, on 18 June 1940, Hitler met Mussolini, then the Hotel Vier Jahreszeiten, on Maximilianstrasse, will have been used to raised voices.

Eddie said he was exhausted by the unremitting nursing duties, all the non-stop mollycoddling ('She was drinking and taking pills and passing out. She was constantly passing out') and for his sanity would have to leave in the morning. Taylor said, 'You're leaving in the morning? I'm leaving right now,' and swallowed a handful of Seconal.

Eddie felt he couldn't do right for doing wrong: 'I was the one who had tried to stop her from killing herself, and that had made her so angry she had tried to kill herself.' He decided to go into hospital to have his appendix taken out – for no reason except being in hospital gave him reprieve from Taylor for a few days. The ruse only irritated her. She didn't like having to get up in the morning to pay Eddie a visit.

Michael Jr and Christopher Wilding were in Munich with them – I have seen a photograph in the UPI [United Press International] Archive of the two children, Eddie and Taylor 'enjoying a carousel ride', as the caption has it. No one is enjoying themselves one little bit. Taylor's sons, in identical suits with matching ties and hankies, are alarmed, uneasy. Eddie looks frankly distressed, as if he wishes he was anywhere but there.

9 *February* 1961

Mankiewicz requires an additional $4,866,000 – taking the budget to $10 million. Forty different insurance companies and ninety syndicates of Lloyd's underwriters were going to be involved when on:

3 *March* 1961

Though the Foreign Press Association award Taylor a prize for *BUtterfield 8*, Dr Carl Heinz Goldman, Taylor's London physician, says she is 'quite ill'. *Quite* in the English sense of *very*. Goldman (1904–1992) had fled Nazi Germany in 1933, arriving in England with five pounds in his pocket. He was also Kay Kendall's doctor.

Breathing difficulties intensify. Taylor is comatose, with swollen ankles and a high temperature. Dr Middleton Price, who happens to be hanging about in The Dorchester, and with a portable pump, too, called a Barnet Ventilator, resuscitates Taylor by sticking a tube down her throat into the windpipe, to deliver high concentrations of oxygen directly into the lungs and drain the bronchial tubes. Back to The London Clinic everyone goes.

4 *March* 1961

She is attended by eleven doctors and the Queen's portable lavvy is wheeled in. X-rays show fully congested lungs. Taylor is given her famous tracheotomy – the scar visible ever after – by Professor Sir Terence Edward Cawthorne (1902–1970), an Ear, Nose and Throat Specialist, who held Chairs at King's College Hospital and the Hospital of Nervous Diseases, Queen's Square, and had published papers on vertigo. Double pneumonia diagnosed.

Dr Carl Goldman is now less ironic, starker: 'Miss Taylor was as near to death as she could be.' Skouras is distraught, venting his feelings like that other Greek, Zorba: 'Do anything, anything to make Liz happy. She is the only one who matters, the only one who counts, forget the picture.'

6 March 1961

Taylor takes to communicating by scribbling a plethora of notes, possibly on the bedsheets: 'Am I dying?', 'Can I die any more because I feel like I can?' She is drip-fed nutrients and antibiotics through a tube implanted in her ankle.

7 March 1961

The story goes that someone in America whose life had been saved by a drug called Staphylococcal Bacteriophage Lysate got in touch with Eddie, who got in touch with Dr Goldman, who authorised Eddie's agent, Milton Blackstone, to obtain twenty vials – which he did, in Philadelphia – and to send them top speed to Idlewild, thence London. Once administered, the patient 'vastly improved'.

Another scenario, involving less haring about, is Taylor was saved by Staphcillin (also called Methicillin), which is used against bacterial infections and had been developed in 1960 by the Beecham Laboratory, in Betchworth, Surrey. Possibly a combination of both drugs was involved, intravenously and as a nasal spray. But here's the thing – Staphylococcal Bacteriophage Lysate is normally only used by vets, on dogs.

8 March 1961

'I want my mother,' reads one of Taylor's notes.

9 March 1961

The Soviet Embassy offers Russian drugs and medical equipment. A gastro-nasal tube is inserted.

10 March 1961

Taylor has recovered sufficiently to entertain John Wayne, Tennessee Williams and Truman Capote at her bedside, though I don't know whether all at the same time. Tom Stoppard ought to imagine it in one of his little plays.

The doctors say, 'She put up a wonderful fight . . . Miss Taylor often struggled more than was good for her.' One pictures sharp judo shouts and throws, a boxer's clinch, fast sumo wrestling holds.

12 *March* 1961
Taylor fails to swallow a piece of orange, so is put on a diet of 'soups and broths', shoved in through the gastro-nasal tube.

13 *March* 1961
Tracheotomy tube removed.

15 *March* 1961
The decision is made by Fox to scrap the London production – it will take fifteen weeks to dismantle sets worth $600,000.

Michael and Christopher Wilding and Liza Todd visit their mother in hospital for the first time.

24 *March* 1961
'I didn't know there was so much love in the world,' Taylor says, looking at her get-well messages.

27 *March* 1961
Accompanied by Eddie, her parents and Kennamer, Taylor leaves The London Clinic in a green-leather wheelchair. Jostled by huge crowds, she falls out of it. She is taken to Heathrow in a Rolls, with her oxygen cylinder and breathing mask. Demolition of the sets commences. The props and costumes are also abandoned, as to crate them up and put them in storage would 'take about three months'. Seven million dollars had been utterly wasted on the Pinewood effort – though there doesn't seem to have been any salvaged Taylor footage, I have seen Peter Finch, Stephen Boyd and Keith 'Blodwyn of the Valleys' (copyright Joan Collins) Baxter footage. Baxter (as Octavian) had had four scarlet robes, beautifully

embroidered by the women who made Queen Elizabeth II's Coronation gown and train.

29 *March* 1961
After an overnight stay in New York, Taylor and Eddie return to Hollywood. Debbie Reynolds sends a get-well telegram.

4 *April* 1961
The date when once upon a time it was hoped Mankiewicz would resume shooting interiors with Taylor.

12 *April* 1961
The children (and nannies) follow from London.

18 *April* 1961
Skouras to Mankiewicz, expressing: 'the great confidence and respect I have in your showmanship ability and your integrity as an artist dedicated to the greatest medium of entertainment in the world.'

19 *April* 1961
Taylor receives her Best Actress Oscar at the Santa Monica Civic Auditorium for *BUtterfield 8*.

2 *May* 1961
'Liz is in excellent health,' reports Dr Rex Kennamer.

19 *May* 1961
Mankiewicz and Wanger finally convince Skouras 'that Burton is the right man to play Mark Antony'.
    Guilaroff again: 'I left *Cleopatra* to return to MGM, where I was needed,' but not before 'I advised Elizabeth to take a close look at the work of a Welsh actor named Richard Burton . . . [and

hence] I had unwittingly set in motion a chain of events that led to one of the most scandalous love affairs the movie world has ever seen.' On Sydney's say-so, Taylor apparently went to New York, saw *Camelot*, and said, 'You were right, Sydney. I'll telephone Fox immediately.' Taylor's seeing Burton in *Camelot* is backed up by no other source.

7 *June* 1961

Skouras authorises Wanger to offer Burton $250,000.

Taylor, meanwhile, is with Eddie, at The Sands for Dean Martin's forty-fourth birthday party. Also present is Marilyn Monroe, who kisses Eddie and says, 'It's important for me to be reminded of what turns Elizabeth on.'

8 *June* 1961

Wanger sees *Camelot* and dines afterwards with Burton (and his squeeze Patricia Tunder) at The 21 Club in West Fifty-Second Street. 'He exuded confidence, personality and sex appeal.' Burton tells Wanger, 'Don't worry. I want to do this. We will work out a deal.'

30 *June* 1961

Plans to shoot in Hollywood – and re-excavate the backlot – scrapped, as studio space presently utilised by George Stevens' *The Greatest Story Ever Told*. There was talk of Taylor playing Mary Magdalene, until the anonymous hate mail poured in: 'Surely you can find an actress of good moral character for the part?', 'A woman like Liz Taylor in a story about Christ – never, never, never', they ranted. I can't say I've heard of Joanna Dunham, who was eventually given the role. Presumably, when everyone set about the task, scouring the four winds like supplicants in a fairy story, 'an actress of good moral character' was in fact tricky to locate? Joanna, who came from Luton, and was educated at Bedales, the Slade and RADA, went on to appear as a customer in an episode of *Are You Being Served?*

Martin Landau (Caiaphas) and Roddy McDowall (St Matthew) would join the *Cleopatra* cast, nevertheless, along with the other 2,154 people soon to be on the Fox payroll, excluding laboratory technicians.

9 *July* 1961

At a fundraising dinner at the Beverly Hills Hilton for Cedars of Lebanon Hospital, attended by Bobby Kennedy, the Attorney General, Taylor, in her guise as 'a symbol of the miracle of modern medicine', gives her melodramatic speech about her illnesses, her loss and regaining of consciousness: 'The experience was both painful and beautiful, like childbirth.'

11 *July* 1961

During this lay-off period, Taylor and Eddie, having been to Las Vegas, went from New York to Russia with the ballet. They'd enjoyed a performance given in Los Angeles by the Igor Moiseyev State Academic Folk Dance Ensemble, which went in for synchronised leaping and hopping – typical USSR drilled acrobatics. As a consequence, they were now official delegates at the Moscow International Film Festival, staying at the Sovietsky (not Sovietskaya as some sources have it) Hotel, on Leningradsky Prospect.

Also on this day, Mankiewicz gives Skouras assurances that 'the greatness of the picture would be more effective if it were made in Italy', plus 'large sums of money could be saved if the production was made in Italy', owing to the dollar/lire exchange rate.

Up go sixty interior sets on seven sound stages at Cinecittà, plus thirty exterior sets. The Forum is twelve acres of brick and marble, costing $1.5 million and causing a shortage of scaffolding and steel throughout Italy. Tens of thousands of costumes and props, including ornamental horse saddles, are manufactured. 'We have brought a circus flavour to the lot and to Rome,' says Wanger.

Regarding the new plan to shoot in Europe, Eddie 'is worried about

Liz being so far away from her doctors', so Kennamer, on a retainer of $25,000, is to be on hand in Rome, 'until she was sufficiently advanced in the production'.

14 *July* 1961

At a Reception for dignitaries at the Kremlin, Taylor and Gina Lollobrigida turn up wearing identical white lace Dior frocks. Taylor says that hers was the original, Gina's a rip-off. In addition to Eddie, Taylor has been accompanied to Moscow by her agent, Kurt Frings, her hairdresser, Alexandre de Paris, and her American quack, Kennamer. At the film festival, which ran between the ninth and twenty-third, Peter Finch won the Silver Prize for *The Trials of Oscar Wilde*. The American entry was *Sunrise at Campobello*, about FDR's paralysis. It takes home nothing, though Hume Cronyn was in the cast.

27 *July* 1961

Mankiewicz arrives in Rome, installing himself at the Grand Hotel, where he is working on a wholly new script. He didn't like the existing script or any of its vestigial drafts. 'Cleopatra, as written, is a strange, frustrating mixture of an American soap-opera virgin and an hysterical Slavic vamp of the type Nazimova used to play' – though I think that sounds a fascinating characterisation, and what is it he thought he was going to end up with, with Taylor, who will have read and absorbed those earlier treatments?

25 *August* 1961

Taylor's quip, 'It will be fun to be the first Jewish queen of Egypt,' upsets Egyptians.

Pre-production work now underway at Cinecittà. Hermes Pan is rehearsing dancers, pole-vaulters, charioteers and archers. 'The horses won't work with the elephants in the big procession', however. A circus owner, Ennio Togni, sues, 'claiming we slandered

his pachyderms when we called them wild'. A Chipperfield elephant named Mary (b. 1947 in Ceylon) is shipped from England as
a replacement.

The location for the Alexandria scenes at Torre Astura is found to
be plugged with World War Two mines, which have to be cleared by
demolition experts, who kept finding dead soldiers.

$475,000 is being spent on 26,000 costumes – a bargain compared
with the $130,000 spent by Irene Sharaff on Taylor's sixty-five outfits.
Some sources say fifty-eight outfits.

1 *September* 1961
Taylor and Eddie arrive at the Aeroporto Internazionale di Roma-
Fiumicino.

11 *September* 1961
Rex Harrison's contract finally negotiated. The budget is now $14
million, though within two months will creep up to $15,214,348 and
21 cents. By November it is $20 million.

17 *September* 1961
Burton makes his final appearance in *Camelot*. 'He gave a superb
performance,' according to Philip. Lerner and Loewe are paid
$50,000 by Fox to release him from his contract. William Squire, an
Old Vic colleague, takes over the role of Arthur.

19 *September* 1961
Burton (who is on $250,000 as a basic fee plus expenses) and Hume
Cronyn (who is on $5,000 a week plus expenses) arrive from New
York, though don't work until the New Year, i.e. they are idle for
seventeen weeks. Roddy McDowall ($2,500 a week) is in Rome for
four months before he is required. Carroll O'Connor, as Casca, has a
fifteen-week contract, which was extended for ten months. He was
called on seventeen days. Robert Stephens anticipated six weeks'

work and got seven months' pay. John Hoyt (Cassius), expecting to be used for eleven weeks, stayed for seven months, and was required only for a fortnight.

Douglas Wilmer was there from beginning to end, as Decius, a conspiratorial Senator. His lines were reduced to two words, 'Goodnight, madam.' Elisabeth Welch, as a Nurse, had her scenes completely deleted. Ronald Allen, of *Crossroads* fame, is in there somewhere, God knows where. Likewise, Alan Browning, who married Pat Phoenix.

George Cole, as Flavius, a deaf-mute, turned up 'every morning at around five o'clock' to have a false beard fitted – for eighteen months, at his calculation, which suggests he was part of the original English shoot. Though Cole's every scene was eventually with Rex Harrison, Harrison never recognised him, always 'reacted as if he had never seen me before'. He referred to Cole as 'this little man with the beard and the tin tray'.

Time wasn't entirely squandered. Burton, along with Jessica Tandy (Mrs Hume Cronyn), Kenneth Haigh, Michael Hordern, Robert Stephens, Michael Gwynn, Douglas Wilmer and anyone else who was hanging around, e.g. Alan Browning and Martin Benson (and I'm sure my ear detects Finlay Currie), made a stereophonic three-disc boxed-set of *Coriolanus* for Caedmon Records / The Shakespeare Recording Society, under the direction of Howard Sackler, which was released in 1962. Robert Stephens' then-wife Tarn Bassett is Virgilia, wife to Coriolanus. I have heard it and it is *bloody good*.

25 September 1961
Mankiewicz's first day of principal photography. Everyone had high hopes for 'the most truly brilliant treatment of history in terms of people and not merely in terms of spectacle that the movies have ever attempted,' according to a Fox press release. Taylor, who describes herself as being 'healthy and radiantly happy', in Cleopatra's costume

of slate-blue veils and a silk tunic 'with a plunging neckline', makes offerings to Isis.

27 September 1961

According to Christopher Isherwood, who was staying in 11 Squire's Mount, N W3, one of the Burtons' Hampstead properties 'managed' by Burton's brother Ivor and his wife Gwen, 'Ivor and Gwen have had no direct news of Richard and Sybil in Rome.' Were silences and mystery beginning to build?

28 September 1961

Taylor and Eddie attend an awards ceremony at the Teatro Sistina, where, for *Suddenly, Last Summer,* or as it is called locally, *Improvvisamente, l'Estate Scorsa,* Taylor receives the Maschere d'Argento (Silver Mask), given by the Associazione Italiana Critici dello Spettacolo (Italian Association of Entertainment Critics) to 'prominent personalities in show business, fashion and sports'. Taylor's role is dubbed by Lydia Simoneschi, who had dubbed Joan Bennett in *Father of the Bride* and Shelley Winters in *A Place in the Sun.* In the future she will dub Mona Washbourne in *The Driver's Seat.* So, Simoneschi had a wide range when it came to shrieks and sobs. Huge crowds are partially held back by the police.

1 October 1961

Sybil, Kate and Jessica, plus Burton's brother, Ivor and his wife, Gwen, and Roddy McDowall, drive to Rome in two cars from Céligny.

14 October 1961

Taylor and Eddie throw a party at the Grand Hotel for Kirk Douglas, who is marking the first anniversary of the release of *Spartacus.* Guests present include Jack Lemmon, Cyd Charisse, Joan Collins and Gina Lollobrigida. Burton is seen topping up Taylor's glass.

With pointed irrelevance, *Il Giorno*, the national daily newspaper, comments: 'Miss Taylor must have her children and husband around her every free moment she has. She treats Eddie like a slave but acts madly in love with him.' Acts madly in love with him.

12 *November* 1961

To general hilarity, 'a vast and violent fire' breaks out in Beverly Hills and burns down Zsa Zsa Gabor's house and Walter Wanger's house, 'all of which goes to prove,' said Coward in his diary, 'that God's in his heaven and not just sitting there either. He's *doing* something.' Re-telling this story, John Osborne called Wanger Wagner, as in Rhine maidens and Valkyries and dwarves labouring inside mountains.

Wanger, feeling the pressure, undergoes blood tests, cholesterol level checks, swallows pills. Skouras announces he has bladder and prostate 'issues'. Choosing her moment, Taylor said to these executives, 'What do you care how much *Cleopatra* costs? Fox pictures have been lousy. At least this one will be great, though expensive.' Reassuring words, because by:

19 *November* 1961

Skouras calls a meeting at the Grand Hotel, attended by lawyers, heads of department, etc. He begs Wanger to 'show some real interest in the huge costs and many problems facing us'. Seven million dollars had been spent in recent weeks on life-size warships for the Egyptian and Roman fleets, operated by a genuine Italian admiral and six Italian Naval captains. Two of these, Cesare Girosi and Achille Zoli, had commanded Axis submarines during the war. (The Regia Marina had 116 submarines, 88 of which were lost in action.) Cleopatra's barge has golden oars. Unnecessary sets, which were of the wrong size anyway, were built on overtime for scenes that have been cut. Exterior sets which were required had to be repaired or reconstructed, as they disintegrated in the rain. In the minutes sent to the

Fox board, *Cleopatra* is described as having 'the worst planning and management in the world'.

28 *November* 1961

Philip arrives in Rome and stays with the Burtons at their 'wonderful house', though we are no nearer knowing the address. There was a party that evening attended by Rex Harrison, Rachel Roberts, Hume Cronyn and Jessica Tandy, also Ricardo Montalbán, who wasn't in the film. Burton and Philip drive to Naples and inspect the amphitheatre at Pompeii. 'We repeated our old Port Talbot mountain exercise; the acoustics were breathtakingly perfect.'

13 *December* 1961

Cleopatra is given a massage on a marble slab. Still photographs are taken but 'Liz won't allow them in print. She has absolute approval on everything.'

18 *December* 1961

Philip departs for London, and Christmas in South Wales. It struck him later that though he'd been introduced to so many of the stars involved with the film, 'I had not met Cleopatra herself, Elizabeth Taylor.'

25 *December* 1961

Taylor says this is 'the best Christmas I've had', and had ordered her poultry from Chasen's, plus two Virginia hams.

26 *December* 1961

The budget is $24 million and Taylor has phlebitis. She had to be carried on to the set like an eighteenth-century invalid in a bath chair.

31 *December* 1961

The Burtons throw a New Year's Eve party at 'Roman Chez Bricktop' in the Via Veneto. Bricktop's was named for Ada 'Bricktop' Smith (1894–1984), the proprietress, a black American jazz singer and dancer, who smoked cigars. She'd run a club in Paris before the war, a club in Mexico during the war, and in 1951 opened the club in Rome, where guests included the Windsors and King Farouk. She was admired by Duke Ellington, Josephine Baker and Cole Porter. Bricktop appears in Woody Allen's *Zelig*, to tell the camera how Porter could never find an adequate rhyme for 'You're the top, you're Leonard Zelig'.

Burton ingratiates himself with Taylor by (an old trick) topping up her glass – Eddie is trying to cut her down, which she resents. 'I was spoiling her fun,' admitted Eddie. Sybil also put on the alert, intercepting glances. 'I suddenly looked at Rich and saw him looking at Elizabeth. It was the way he kept his eyes on her, and I thought, hello!'

One of the guests is Hedda Hopper, who told her readers, 'All the years I've known Liz, I've never seen her this happy, contented and congenial. She looks absolutely radiant.' It's the sort of burble said of a bride on her wedding day.

15 *January* 1962

On top of everything else, Taylor wants to adopt a baby with a deformed pelvis. 'I want her all the more because she's ill.' Petra Heisig, renamed Maria, is from Mering, Germany. 'Her legs were twisted so badly that one was practically facing around the wrong way,' as if marching forwards and retreating simultaneously – useful for a German. Her birth parents were overwhelmed. 'How could we ever have imagined that Elizabeth Taylor, of all people in the world, would come into our lives. We had to let the baby go.' No doubt parents felt that way when Bette Davis, Joan Crawford and Mia Farrow wanted to adopt – screen goddesses appearing from the sky. Louella Parsons, in her gossip column, predicts the Fishers will divorce.

22 January 1962

Taylor and Burton's first scene together – Antony and Cleopatra and the Roman Senators. Taylor arrives on set with Eddie, two secretaries, two maids, make-up people and hairdressers. She is wearing a mink, which she ostentatiously let drop to the floor. Burton was to write later about her 'breasts jutting out from that half-asleep languid lingering body, the remote eyes, the parted lip'. Wanger notes how the actress and the actor were 'intently talking . . . You could almost feel the electricity between Liz and Burton.'

26 January 1962

Mankiewicz to Wanger: 'Liz and Burton are not just playing Antony and Cleopatra.'

27 January 1962

Burton appears in the make-up trailer at Cinecittà and announces in his Old Vic voice, 'Gentlemen, last night I screwed [fucked, nailed – sources differ] Miss Elizabeth Taylor in the back of my Cadillac.' He didn't have a Cadillac. He had a black-and-white Lincoln.

30 January 1962

At a party in the Villa Volpi, a neo-classical palazzo belonging to Contessa Nathalie Volpi di Misurata, the wife of Giuseppe Volpi, founder of the Mostra Internazionale d'Arte Cinematografica di Venezia (the Venice Film Festival), as well as being Mussolini's finance minister, the talk is all of Cleopatra – how Hollywood has brought back the mood of Ancient Rome and the Italy of the Medicis and Borgias.

5 *February* 1962

Burton assures Wanger, 'I will not allow anything to hurt my career or my marriage. And I won't do anything to harm Liz, who is a wonderful person.' Wanger, no fool despite what everyone always thinks, could appreciate the danger and the appeal: 'The excitement Liz requires of life could be supplied by Burton because of his strength, experience, and the dreams he opened up.'

13 *February* 1962

Burton flies to Paris to appear as a RAF pilot in *The Longest Day*. Eddie breaks the Cuckold's Code, which implicitly states the wronged husband must fume in silence, by speaking to Sybil: 'Your husband and my wife appear to be deeply involved. You know they're continuing their affair?' – 'He's had these affairs before, and he always comes home to me.' – 'But they're still having their affair. You don't know Elizabeth. This time, he's not coming back.' Burton is furious with Eddie for the indiscretion – for daring to bring Sybil directly into it. When Taylor asks him, 'Why did you tell Sybil?' Eddie answers forlornly, 'Because I love you and would do anything to keep you.'

14 *February* 1962

Eddie leaves Rome 'on business', in fact to see how the decorators were getting on in tax-efficient Gstaad, where he and Taylor had acquired the sixteen-room Chalet Ariel, a two-storey timber edifice with overhanging eaves. $285,000 was spent on purchasing the property, with another $100,000 going on renovations.

Burton takes Taylor out for the evening to the Via Veneto, Taylor wearing a leopard-skin coat and matching hat. That's a lot of leopards.

15 *February* 1962
According to Jack Brodsky and Nathan Weiss, publicists on the picture, Taylor and Burton are 'the hottest thing ever'. The Fox high-ups fear the public 'will crucify her and picket the theatres if she breaks up another family'. In the event, there was no moral indignation, only an excited curiosity. Attitudes towards celebrity (and adultery) were changing.

16 *February* 1962
Sybil escapes to New York, staying in Roddy McDowall's (vacant) apartment on Central Park West. She agrees to a meeting with Philip, now living locally. It's hard to imagine the distress she felt, if she singled out Philip for comfort – but she needed someone who'd known him for a long time, who felt for him as she did. Philip is devastated to be told by Sybil 'she had left Richard because of his involvement with Elizabeth Taylor', the first he'd known of it.

He sends Burton a stiff reprimand in the post, as well as a cable. There are temperamental phone calls. 'Richard had been infuriated by my letter . . . Richard's anger was met by mine . . . I didn't speak to him again for two years,' though Burton still instructed Aaron Frosch to pay Philip's tax bills.

Philip's tongue started to swell up, a growth appeared in his mouth and he lost his voice – oral cancer? It was cured by a course of antibiotics, and Philip put it down to psychosomatic stress. 'I suppose it must have been the fear of losing Richard, because I felt that if Sybil lost him, I would too.'

Taylor, fearing Burton would be affected by Sybil's dramatic departure, and to regain the initiative, attempts suicide by 'trying to break through a glass door and had to be restrained,' says Wanger.

Burton indeed tries to call it all off: 'It was fun, while it lasted.' To no avail.

17 *February* 1962

Fearful Burton will choose Sybil over her – 'Imagine, a guy turning her down!' said Brodsky to Weiss – Taylor is taken to the Salvator Mundi Hospital to have her stomach pumped, after an overdose of Seconal. 'I needed the rest, I was hysterical, and needed to get away.' Her mood swings do not go unnoticed by the film crew: 'One day Taylor is bubbling, the next remorseful.' With Sybil in New York, mustering support, 'She [Taylor] wants to junk everything.'

18 *February* 1962

Having decided to go to Gstaad, then Milan, with the idea of catching a plane to New York, Eddie found himself in Lisbon. By some means – teletransportation? – he phones the Villa Pappa (or Papa) from Florence. Burton answers. 'What are you doing there? What are you doing in my home?' asks Eddie in a surprised way, unaware Burton had returned from Paris – and Taylor seems to have been speedily sprung from the clinic, too. 'What do you think I'm doing? I'm with my girl.' 'She's not your girl. She's my wife.' 'Well, I'm fucking your wife,' is the reply Eddie receives, almost autistic in its honesty. Both men threaten to murder each other. 'I'm going to come up there and kill you,' says Burton. 'Stay right there, I'm going to kill you,' says Eddie, who later told Roddy McDowall, 'In Italy, the courts are easy on crimes of passion.'

Searching for one of her favourite medical metaphors, Taylor says to Wanger, 'My heart feels as though it is haemorrhaging.'

19 *February* 1962

In an act of calculated stupidity, Burton makes a statement to the press, thus giving the press something to dwell upon:

'For the past several days uncontrolled rumours have been growing about Elizabeth and myself. Statements attributed to me have been distorted out of proportion, and a series of coincidences have leant plausibility to a situation which has become damaging to Elizabeth.

'Mr Fisher, who has business interests of his own, merely went out of town to attend to them for a few days.

'My foster-father, Philip Burton, has been quite ill in New York and my wife, Sybil, flew there to be with him for a time, since my schedule does not permit me to be there. He is very dear to both of us.

'Elizabeth and I have been close friends for over twelve years. I have known her since she was a child star and would certainly never do anything to hurt her personally or professionally.

'In answer to these rumours my normal inclination would be simply to say no comment, but I feel that in this case things should be explained to protect Elizabeth.'

His more succinct (though equally dishonest) precis: 'It's all bloody nonsense.'

20 February 1962

Burton denies he'd authorised the denial. It is too late. Newspaper reporters from every country, photographers with their flashguns – what Fellini had in *La Dolce Vita* named the *paparazzi* (swarming and persistent wasps or mosquitoes whizzing about on mopeds) – invaded Rome, invaded the production. Cameras were hidden in hairdos, cameramen hid in trees and bushes. Journalists pretended to be priests collecting donations. 'His name has become a household word,' said Wanger of Burton.

27 February 1962

On what Taylor was to decide was 'the most miserable day of my life' (thus far), Eddie organises her thirtieth birthday party at the Borgia Room of the Hostaria dell'Orso. He gives her a $250,000 emerald necklace and a Bulgari mirror, in the shape of an asp, also encrusted with emeralds. He later spoilt the munificence somewhat by sending

Taylor the bill. 'I probably paid it,' she said resignedly. Burton, meanwhile, tells people the Oliviers named their son Richard after him, 'and he's their son's godfather.' Richard Kerr Olivier, born the previous December, was named after Sir Laurence's brother.

1 *March* 1962
St David's Day, so Burton crapulous. Patricia Tunder, a chorus girl from *Camelot*, is openly his escort.

3 *March* 1962
Sybil returns. Burton takes Patricia Tunder into his dressing room at seven a.m. and doesn't emerge until ten. When Taylor complained, he said, 'Don't get my Welsh temper up.'

8 *March* 1962
The newspapers all quote Burton's remarks and iterations about how he'd never leave Sybil, so the scene where Antony leaves Cleopatra in Alexandria, goes back to Rome, and marries Octavian's sister: life is imitating art in distorted fashion; and Cleopatra, when she hears about this, stabs the bedclothes, the mattress and Antony's clothes in the wardrobe – Taylor acts it all out with such genuine derangement, she dislocates her thumb. 'We had to send for Dr Pennington.'

9 *March* 1962
Budget now $27 million. Recent disasters and delays – $200,000 because of a sandstorm and $17,000 because a cat had kittens under the floor of the set, which had to be dismantled. Michael Hordern, hired for eight weeks and remaining under contract for nine months, recalls 'the poor little mother was enticed out with pieces of raw liver, but the kittens took a while longer to extricate.'

Louella Parsons tantalises her readers: 'It is difficult to appraise how the world will react to another scandal involving Elizabeth.'

10 *March* 1962

Louella Parsons comes clean with her readers: 'Elizabeth Taylor has fallen madly in love with Richard Burton.'

'The report is ridiculous,' comments Eddie.

13 *March* 1962

Burton and Taylor are now 'so close you'd have to pour hot water on them to get them unstuck,' Brodsky tells Weiss. Taylor tells Eddie she loves Burton. 'We can't bear to be apart, even for a matter of hours.' Burton is all over the place; he is vaporising. 'I'm leaving Sybil and going off with Elizabeth' alternates with 'I can't leave Sybil. I'm not going to see Elizabeth anymore.'

16 *March* 1962

Sybil returns to London.

18 *March* 1962

The Milanese weekly paper *Gente* prints telescopic-lens shots of Taylor and Burton embracing and leaving Bricktop's at three-thirty in the morning. They are also spotted at Tre Scalini in the Piazza Navona, and the Taverna Flavia. Not cheap joints by any means. 'They are very expensive,' says Burton, almost with surprise.

19 *March* 1962

Eddie says, 'Elizabeth, I'm leaving,' and she doesn't see him for two years, if longer. He is in a mental hospital, according to rumours. 'You know, you can ask a woman to do something, and she doesn't always do it,' he says, sounding like a Thurber husband in a cartoon about the battle of the sexes.

Taylor's parting shot to Eddie is like a line from *The Flintstones*, in which thirty-two years later she will play Pearl Slaghoople: 'No one walks out on me, faggot. I'm more famous than the Pope, and the Queen of England, who always walks around like she's got a poker stuck up her ass. I'm even more famous than General Eisenhower.'

The Rolls, parked in Milan Airport, is stolen 'by thieves'.

21 *March* 1962
According to the production log, Taylor left the studios at 12.25 p.m., 'having great difficulty delivering dialogue'.

22 *March* 1962
Rex marries Rachel Roberts in Genoa.

27 *March* 1962
Sybil issues a denial: 'I was furious about it. Richard was furious, so was Elizabeth. You see, Richard and I have known Elizabeth since she was married to Michael Wilding. Naturally, we're all very friendly.'

28 *March* 1962
Rex collects Rachel from the airport, where she shouts at the customs officials and the police are called. Embassy personnel have to sort it all out, as Rex only knows two words of Italian – '*Stupido!*' and '*Idioto!*' – neither of which is helpful.

29 *March* 1962
Eddie issues a statement from his hospital bed in the Gracie Square Hospital: 'One thing is undeniable. I love Liz, and she loves me. The marriage is fine, just fine. The only romance between Burton and Elizabeth is the romance they play as Antony and Cleopatra.' Gracie Square Hospital, opened in 1958, was (is) a psychiatric facility at 430 East Seventy-Sixth Street.

The front page of today's issue of New York's *Daily News*, dominated by the tabloid headline 'Eddie Fisher Breaks Down: In Hospital Here; Liz in Rome', is turned into a screen-print by Andy Warhol.

Flanking the rather cartoonish drawing of the pair of them are photographs of a neighing horse and a child in a wheelchair.

30 *March* 1962
Eddie holds a Press Conference in the Sapphire Room at the Pierre. He says tales of his wife's involvement with Burton are 'preposterous, ridiculous, absolutely false'. Over the transatlantic phone line, however, Taylor refuses to deny the rumours. 'Eddie I can't do that, because there's some truth in the story . . . There's a foundation to the story.' The headlines are Pop Art classics: e.g. 'Liz Turns Down Eddie's Ocean Phone Call Love Plea'.

Eddie goes to see Frank Costello, *consigliere* to the Luciano crime family, who'd once said to him, 'Anything you need, you come to me.' Unfortunately, this is real life, not a novel or a television series, so this potential plot strand peters out. Not even Eddie wanted to be responsible for having a mobster's goons break Burton's legs. 'They'll even cut off his dick if you want that done, too,' Costello offered.

31 *March* 1962
Burton and Taylor go to Bricktop's and the next day photographs of the couple appear on the front pages of the tabloids: 'Liz and Burton Frolic In Rome'.

1 *April* 1962
Emlyn Williams, visiting Rome on a mission of mercy from Sybil, leaves a note for his former protégé, pointing out with forced wit that, 'as it is April Fool's Day could it be Richard Burton's year to play the part?' Williams adds, of Taylor, 'Look here, she's just a third-rate chorus girl.' Burton, speaking to Emlyn in the car, on the way from the airport, states calmly, 'I'm going to marry her' – conveying his earnestness, his uncloudedness, by saying it in Welsh, which made it an incantation: *Dwi am briodi'r eneth 'ma.*

Williams, recalling all this twenty-two years later, in the Service of Thanksgiving Address, and having realised, I think, it had marked the precise moment when Burton was damned, said he never forgot Burton's 'mischievous devilish twinkle', in the back of the car, in Rome.

Williams himself was playing a part (or replaying a part) – in Rattigan's *The Deep Blue Sea* (1955) he was Sir William Collyer, the judge who fails to fathom the depth of emotion Vivien Leigh feels for Kenneth More, and whose good practical (if conventional) advice means nothing, in the face of overwhelming physical passion.

2 April 1962

'It's an insane asylum here,' Weiss tells Brodsky. On the same day, officials at the German orphanage wonder what was meant to be happening with the adoption of Maria. 'She was nine months old, covered with abscesses, suffering from malnutrition, had a crippled hip, and I just loved her,' Taylor suddenly remembers.

The person put in charge of the adoption, by the way, dealing with the complex official foreign language paperwork, was Taylor's money shark, Kurt Frings (1908–1991), a native of Germany and the nephew of Cardinal Josef Frings, one of the few Roman Catholic eminences to stand up to the Nazis. Kurt had been the lightweight boxing champion in the Reich – *Leichtgewichtmeister* – and a ski instructor in the French Alps, where, in 1938, he married Ketti Hartley, who wrote the story turned by Billy Wilder, in 1941, into *Hold Back the Dawn*, starring Olivia de Havilland.

Kurt was refused an American visa, so lived over the border in Tijuana. Eventually allowed into America, he in 1956 founded the Kurt Frings Agency Inc., in Beverly Hills, and his clients, in addition to Taylor, were Audrey Hepburn, Hildegard Knef, and Lucille Ball and Desi. His net income for 1960, after having negotiated Taylor's *Cleopatra* contract, was $190,747.58. Another client was the Viennese Maria Schell (1926–2005), who also assisted with the

Maria adoption and after whom Petra was renamed. I have seen press photographs of Taylor, Eddie and Kurt Frings arriving at Munich-Riem Airport [*Flughafen München-Riemü*], sometime in January 1960, the three of them having been to visit Maria Schell in Wasserburg.

Meanwhile, Taylor and her three (other) children, Michael, Christopher and Liza, are taken by Burton in his Lincoln to Corsetti's Restaurant in Torvaianica, where they eat lobster and ice cream. The adults drink Chartreuse, which is filthy stuff.

3 April 1962

The Fishers announce their intention to divorce, Sybil collapses, and Emlyn tells the press: 'I just cannot imagine that Richard would throw away his life like this. [He and Sybil] are exceedingly happy and he adores his daughters.'

7 April 1962

Burton in Paris for further work on *The Longest Day*. Forty press photographers greet his arrival. He meets Sybil, but tells the press (jokingly), 'I think I may kill myself.' Romance with Taylor pooh-poohed.

8 April 1962

Burton and Sybil dine at Maxim's. 'I am married. I am married,' he insists to the press. Some sources, however, quote him as saying, 'I am still married. I am still married,' which is grammatically slightly different, implying only a precarious present tense, the future altogether something else again.

Taylor and her opulent breasts are left in the care of Mike Nichols, who is visiting Rome, and who had befriended Burton and Sybil during the *Camelot* days on Broadway. 'I can't leave the house,' said Taylor. 'We're surrounded,' by all the maddened press photographers. She puts a scarf over her head as a rudimentary disguise and

Nichols drives her off to spend the day at the Villa d'Este, the fountain-crammed Renaissance gardens at Tivoli – where crowds point and say, 'That's Mike Nichols!'

Nichols reflects, of his future Martha: 'She never had a life of her own. Every movement had always been public,' where she'd rise to the occasion – and every moment, as the director of *Who's Afraid of Virginia Woolf?* would discover, was a half-waking fantasy. Wandering the wet gardens, she had said to him, of her beauty, 'I can't wait for it to go,' which it quickly did when she became a bun-jaws, and which did her no harm as she won a second Oscar for turning herself into the vindictive ruin in Nichols' Albee film.

Taylor asked the hairstylist on *Cleopatra*, Paul Huntley, an employee of Stanley Hall Wig Creations, 'Do you do personal wigs? I have a dear friend who's a comic in New York, and he wears one of the worst wigs I've ever seen.' Nichols, who even had to glue on false eyebrows, was incredibly sensitive about his alopecia, so I wonder how all that went down? George C. Scott, for example, was never forgiven for having said to him, during a run of *Uncle Vanya*, which had almost co-starred Burton (instead of Nicol Williamson), 'Slap on your wig and get your ass down to the theatre!'

12 *April* 1962
The Vatican begins issuing rebukes – the notorious 'erotic vagrancy' open letter in *L'Osservatore della Domenica*, where Taylor and Burton are ticked off for displaying 'the caprices of adult children'; they are blamed for 'this insult to the nobility of the hearth, which millions of married couples judge to be a beautiful and holy thing'. Taylor is described as 'an avaricious vamp who destroys families and devours husbands', which actually isn't an exaggeration. 'Where are we all going to end up?' asks the Pope rhetorically, before answering his own question: 'In an erotic vagrancy without end or without safe port, in which three years

means "for a lifetime" . . .' The 7,000 extras love it. '*Bacci! Bacci!*' they roar – 'Kisses! Kisses!'

21 *April* 1962

Taylor and Burton go to Porto Santo Stefano for the Easter Weekend, pursued by paparazzi with their telephoto lenses. Taylor returns with a bruised face and can't be photographed. Burton says he spent his time reading Aldous Huxley and 'learning *Hamlet* in Italian'.

Accounts of what occurred vary enormously – did Burton and Taylor go in one car, two cars, with chauffeurs or without? Taylor said, 'I bumped my nose on an ashtray,' when asleep on the back seat and the vehicle hit a pot-hole in the road. Skouras was unpersuaded by this explanation, and referred to 'the beating Burton gave her in Santo Stefano. She got two black eyes, her nose was out of shape, and it took twenty-two days for her to recover enough in order to resume filming.' Another version is that Taylor and Burton were in a soft-top Lancia, Taylor took a swipe at Burton (who was at the wheel) – annoyed he expressed guilt about Sybil – and when the car swerved into a ditch she clouted her conk on the dashboard.

Burton gives his side of the story in his diaries – but not until getting on for a decade later, 13 August 1971, by which time it had settled in his mind as an alcoholic anecdote ('We drank to the point of stupefaction and idiocy'), not dissimilar to the rambunctious anecdotes about pissing in his armour at Stratford after a day on the beer, a combination of bravado and chagrin.

As Burton tells it, 'I had driven E from Rome in the small hours in a rented car – a small two-seater Fiat as I remember . . . All the world press were searching for us. We thought we had got clean away.' After breakfasting on Cognac ('perhaps we had two'), they found their villa, 'gambolled like children, scrambling down the rocks to the sea and enjoying ourselves as if it was the last holiday.' Then the photographers ('there were hundreds') discovered them. 'We were well and thoroughly trapped.'

The couple had to hide indoors. 'We tried to read. We failed. We couldn't go out . . . For some reason E said that she was prepared to kill herself for me. Easy to say, I said, but no woman would kill herself for me . . . Who remembers from so long ago with everything shrouded in a miasma of alcohol what was said . . .' What he did remember distinctly was Taylor standing over him with a box of pills in her hand, 'saying that she could do it . . . whereupon . . . she swallowed them with gusto . . . She then, I think, took herself off to bed in an adjoining room.'

It's like Juliet taunting Romeo – a huge self-dramatising gesture, seemingly about love and death but really about possession, or possessiveness, and not dissimilar to Taylor in Munich with Eddie, wanting to get her way. Burton, who has 'vague memories of trying to get her awake', then has to find 'our sometimes chauffeur Mario' – so a chauffeur is present suddenly? – and there follows a 'hair-raising drive' back to Rome, 102 miles away, with Taylor dropped off anonymously at the Salvator Mundi Hospital. Burton returns to his own accommodation and refuses to answer the phone to 'disaster-lovers' like McDowall 'and almost everybody'.

This is high drama, and I assume an authentic sketch, certainly a candid one. But questions arise. First, how could Taylor deal with death so lightly? Did she assume, like Cleopatra, there'd be life after death – that death was there to be survived? Secondly, why is there no sense or indication, in Burton's journal entry, that he was afraid? Nor is there retrospective terror, even if he's grateful that, 'I didn't want any repetition of that awful Easter.' His tone is cool, almost humorous – what he chiefly sees, on looking back, is ridiculousness – the ridiculousness of Taylor's indestructibility. You'd have thought he'd find the incident more troubling – and as an afterthought he writes, 'In that year also Sybil had a go at knocking herself off.'

23 *April* 1962

Having said she'd not return to Rome, Sybil returns to Rome. Paparazzi photographs of Burton and Taylor smooching on the beach in Porto Santo Stefano had been published in the London papers, which even Sybil couldn't pretend not to have seen. 'Richard loves Elizabeth more than me,' she said to Roddy McDowall, earnestly hoping he'd contradict her.

Taylor took *another* handful of pills and was back having her stomach pumped in the Salvator Mundi, a private facility at 67, Viale delle Mura Gianicolensi, which had opened in 1951 but had never been so busy. The staff there must have been standing by the front door with their hoses and nozzles aimed in permanent readiness.

27 *April* 1962

Kate arrives from London. Sybil and Burton go to meet her at the airport, in separate cars.

3 *May* 1962

Taylor's parents arrive. They'd actually liked Eddie, so Taylor cried and couldn't work the next day. Another arrival is Sheilah Graham, who shrewdly notes Burton 'is enjoying all the publicity'. She also predicts with one hundred per cent accuracy, 'Unless he abandons the bottle, I doubt whether he will make it to old age.'

8 *May* 1962

Skouras watches a five-hour rough cut. He falls asleep with his worry beads.

14 *May* 1962

Further Skouras bombast, as he assures Mankiewicz the rushes promise 'public appeal surpassing anything put on the screen'.

19 *May* 1962
Sybil visits Burton, so Taylor couldn't work. 'She stayed up crying all night and her eyes were too swollen to shoot.'

'It's best for Rich to be free to work out his own future,' Sybil is heard to say.

22 *May* 1962
Iris Faircloth Blitch, who'd been elected to Congress, from Georgia, in 1955, informs the Attorney-General that Taylor and Burton must have their visas revoked on 'the grounds of undesirability'. Taylor and Burton, says Iris, show 'no concern for either the Flag or the people and show no respect for cherished institutions or God speaking in the name of American womanhood.' Iris, incidentally, was a signatory of the Southern Manifesto, which demanded racial segregation.

Michael Aloysius Feighan (Democrat, Ohio) also wades in, asking Dean Rusk at the State Department to revoke Burton's visa, as the actor was altogether 'detrimental to the morals of the youth of our nation'.

29 *May* 1962
Completion of Taylor's interior scenes at Cinecittà.

1 *June* 1962
Wanger is 'taken off salary' by the Fox board. He is blamed for all the delays, the bad and disrupted scheduling, the corrupt underlings. The unit manager had blood transfusions ('and finally passed away') and his replacement, Franco Malgi, whose uncle owned the elephants, 'proved to be completely untrustworthy', according to the Fox files. The numbers on the studio payroll are reduced to six hundred and six. There are ninety Americans, three hundred and fifty Italians and sixteen British crew members – so who are the remaining hundred and fifty? Ibo? Zulu? Inuit? Interest payments are $7,000 a day. Sundries

included $100,000 on paper cups. The asp – actually a Sardinian Garden Snake [*Natrix natrix cetti*] – cost $3.40.

9 *June* 1962

Taylor, based at the Regina Isabella Hotel, Ischia, is unable to work because of 'infected teeth'. The studio keeps an ambulance standing by in case she does anything dramatic.

13 *June* 1962

Battle of Actium scenes at Ischia. Cleopatra's two-hundred-foot barge costs $277,000. The purple sails are made of nylon because the silk and cotton ones faded in the sunshine. Marcello Geppetti's stolen pictures appear in *Oggi*, of Taylor and Burton lounging very companionably in bathing costumes.

Geppetti (1933–1998) in fact was the very stills-cameraman who'd inspired the 'Paparazzo' character in *La Dolce Vita*, where he is played by Walter Santesso. He worked for the Meldolesi-Canestrelli-Bozzer Agency and had taken pictures of Anita Ekberg firing arrows at the press, Audrey Hepburn out shopping, Bardot in the buff, and so forth. He was a pest.

Time runs, however. These days Geppetti's work is the subject of monographs and exhibitions. The *fucking nuisance* has become a respected figure. For example, in a degree course on 'famous images' (ARTH 923) offered by the Department of the History of Art at the University of Pennsylvania, 'Taylor and Burton's First Kiss' is considered 'iconic', and is studied alongside other Sixties images by Warhol and Cecil Beaton.

19 *June* 1962

Burton and Taylor visit Gracie Fields' restaurant La Canzone del Mare, Capri, and are shocked to discover newsreel cameras running behind the curtains. When Peter Sellers went there he was even more shocked, as at the end of tea Gracie handed him a bill ('This is for you, love'). He thought he'd been there as Gracie's personal guest, popular artiste-unto-popular artiste.

23 June 1962

Completion of Taylor's exterior scenes – with the arrival of Cleopatra's barge at Tarsus. The pots of pink and blue smoke on deck obscured everything. The exterior location at Ischia costs $500,000.

It is now 272 days since Mankiewicz started production in Italy and 632 days since Mamoulian had tried to begin the film at Pinewood. Of her 228 days of shooting at Cinecittà, Taylor didn't turn up on fifty-seven occasions, worked only 122 days in total, and was late ninety-nine times, at a waste of fifty-three studio man-hours.

As one of the crew observed, 'You know how she got time off for her period? She was having three or four periods a month.'

News Taylor was no longer needed is kept from the press, in case 'it would bring down Sybil' and Taylor would try and top herself again.

26 June 1962

Skouras announces his retirement.

11 July 1962

Taylor and Burton attend the Festival dei Due Mondi (The Festival of Two Worlds) in Spoleto, where there was a performance in the Teatro Caio Melisso of Tennessee Williams' *The Milk Train Doesn't Stop Here Anymore*, starring Hermione Baddeley. In due course this would become *Boom!*, about which the playwright would say, 'a beautiful picture, the best ever made of one of my plays ... Eventually it will be received with acclaim.' As it has been, by me.

Taylor later packs up and leaves for Gstaad – she'd not yet seen Chalet Ariel. There were three lorries for her pets, six lorries for her 'furnishings' and the children's toys, and four Rolls-Royces to convey herself and her staff, including nannies.

28 July 1962

Production wraps, seven months late. The cast had been kept on the payroll, 'for weeks or months before ever appearing', at a cost of $125,000 daily. The location shoot in Egypt was no different to the rest. Taylor couldn't go, as she'd received death threats for making contributions to Jewish charities. None of the equipment turned up, the generators and lorries, wigs and costumes – cargo went to Beirut or maybe Bayreuth by mistake, then Naples. The Egyptian extras rioted.

Burton returns to Céligny, but because he keeps nipping over to Gstaad to see Taylor, and because Jessica receives the autism diagnosis – and Sybil put the blame for her daughter's condition on the frenzy of the affair; the paparazzi's blinding flashbulbs; the reporters infiltrating the house and peering in through the windows – Sybil attempts suicide. 'Reading always relaxed me,' she told Elaine Dundy, Kenneth Tynan's wife. 'Then I was in Céligny and I looked down at the page and couldn't read it. Then I knew I was really in trouble.' She attempts to cut her wrists. ('I saw the scars,' said Dundy.)

6 August 1962

News of Marilyn Monroe's death reaches Taylor, who believes it was an accidental overdose rather than suicide, or murder. 'I was stunned. I thought it would have been me,' she gasps melodramatically, even puzzlingly. It says a lot about Taylor that the death of Marilyn was a tragedy all about *her*. 'I felt so depressed and sad because I myself couldn't reach her and she was a generous and sweet girl.'

(She'd also manage to make the death of Princess Diana all about *her*: 'I know what it's like to be chased in a car by the paparazzi.' If that wasn't a sufficient enough parallel, Taylor also claimed on one occasion in Paris she'd been offered Henri Paul as her driver: 'I recall that he wanted to drive fast and I recall that I said, "No way!"')

12 *August* 1962

All this splashy drama – yet back in Loughborough, England, let's remind ourselves, Philip Larkin was immobile at the sink, 'washing the same old colander, the same old saucepans, the same old cooking knives and forks ... You may say there's nothing very awful about this, but all the same I think there is – I *feel* it as awful, anyway.'

Awful, and funny, and moving: the dull routine, a sense of waste and of time passing, which filled Larkin with nervous dread – his suspicion there must be a better, less inconsequential life going on elsewhere. Yet even Burton, who in most respects was living exactly that magical life, could be suffused with ennui. He drank, he said, 'to burn up the flatness; the stale, empty, dull deadness that one feels when one goes off the stage.' It could have been worse; he could have been doing Monica Jones' washing-up or rinsing Eva Larkin's smalls.

13 *October* 1962

There are 600,000 feet (or 120 country miles) of exposed negative to examine, running ninety-six solid hours. Having spent six weeks in the editing suite, Mankiewicz reduces a twenty-six-hour rough cut to eight hours. Darryl F. Zanuck, Executive Head of the Fox Corporation, sees a version lasting four hours and thirty-six minutes in Paris. Other sources say the version he saw ran for five hours and twenty-minutes. He dislikes the 'awkward, amateurish battle episodes'.

16 *October* 1962

Cuban Missile Crisis. The prospect of global annihilation of lesser importance to the press than what they are calling the scandal of

'Dick and Liz – The Story Behind Those Red-Hot Rumors!'; 'How Liz and Burton Make Love'; 'How Liz Makes Sure He'll Never Want Another Woman'; and much more in the same strain. 'How did I know the woman was so fucking famous,' says Burton disingenuously. 'She knocks Khrushchev off the front page.'

20 November 1962

Cuban Missile Crisis resolved. 'Liz and Burton: Will Marriage Kill Their Love?' ponder the papers.

6 December 1962

To make *The V.I.P.s*, Taylor and Burton arrive at Victoria Station, having taken the train from Geneva. They depart in separate cars, Taylor in a Jaguar MK10, Burton in a shooting brake. The destination is the same, nevertheless: The Dorchester, where they reside in adjoining suites – The Terrace and The Harlequin – along with secretaries, nannies, children, a personal housekeeper, baggage handlers and a chief of staff.

Sybil is abandoned in Hampstead. She (again) attempts suicide with aspirins and a carving knife, or so says Tom Rubython in *And God Created Burton*: 'In a moment of pure desperation, [Sybil] leaned over the bath and drew the blade across her wrists, screaming as she did it ... Ivor and Gwen, alerted by the nanny ... put towels round her wrists and rushed her to the casualty department of the Royal Free Hospital in nearby Pond Street, a few minutes away.' But the Royal Free Hospital didn't open in Pond Street until 1974.

23 December 1962

Talk about a person being in two (or three, or four) places at once, in a letter to Robert Bolt of today's date, David Lean, installed in the Beverly Hills Hotel, lists Joe Mankiewicz as being one of the directors, along with Billy Wilder and Richard Brooks, who 'have all been round here to deliver their feelings [about *Lawrence of Arabia*] in person. They are all so bloody generous.'

Lawrence of Arabia (released on 10 December) and *Cleopatra* (to be released six months hence) were the sprawling epics of their day – 227 minutes and 251 minutes long respectively; ten and nine Oscar nominations respectively. Lean's film received astonished plaudits – in 1991 the Library of Congress deemed it 'culturally, historically [and] aesthetically significant.' Where the Burton-Taylor film mostly got derided, the critics pissing and moaning about budgets, by contrast, according to Kevin Brownlow, his biographer, Lean was told he had made 'quite simply, the most impressive film [anyone] had seen in their lives'. Lean fully believed as much himself, as if he was Michelangelo and here was a cinematic Sistine Chapel.

I find *Lawrence of Arabia* unendurable – all that billowing pink sand and empty desert vistas, like David Lean's souvenir photo album of his long holidays in the Middle East. Despite the furnace heat of Jordan, it is ice cold. The performances are execrable, apart from Claude Rains, who spends his scenes pretending to be somewhere else: 'On the whole, I'd rather be in Tunbridge Wells.' Omar Sharif, Anthony Quinn (in a ridiculous false nose – he's Abanazar in panto), Donald Wolfit, Jack Hawkins, José Ferrer – they are required only to shout and glower, the English chaps furiously shuffling documents at a desk, barking at junior officers, and Johnny Foreigner jabbing daggers into desks or generally maltreating tabletops. Alec Guinness as Faisal floats about in beard glue and Jedi gear. At the centre of the farrago is Peter O'Toole, shrieking, screwing up his face to make his eyes bulge, completely unsympathetic, retentively homosexual. And no women. Not one. And no humour. Not a shred, only risibility. How better the film would be had Lean cast Richard Briers, Jimmy Edwards and Dickie Henderson.

No human drama, either, only camels and politics. I never know one tribe from another, or why everyone hates the Turks, or what the

British interests are or were, or even what years are being covered. It is both thin dramatically and clotted, squashed. Anthony Quayle's Colonel Brighton doesn't seem to know what's going on, either. The only emotion on display is anger, as everyone is in a bad temper, the militaristic expectations of honour and self-sacrifice, the duplicitous operations, bringing out the worst in everybody.

Lawrence of Arabia is a thoroughly dated costume drama – stiff collars, clanking spurs; the soupy easy-listening score from Maurice Jarre. *Cleopatra* had and has much more going for it – for one simple reason: despite everything, it has nothing really to do with Ptolemaic Egypt, Rome's Civil War, classical history lessons. It is a shrine to Taylor. 'Other women cloy the appetites they feed, but she makes hungry where most she satisfies.'

29 *December* 1962

Blizzard conditions in Britain, with snow falling and drifting and remaining on the ground until 6 March 1963. The average temperature is minus 2.1 degrees Centigrade, 30 degrees Fahrenheit.

23 *January* 1963

Taylor is in The London Clinic with a twisted knee. Burton waits in an adjacent pub, the Devonshire Arms.

11 *February* 1963

Death (by carbon monoxide poisoning) of Sylvia Plath, at 23 Fitzroy Road, Primrose Hill.

7 *March* 1963

Zanuck, the new Fox president 'in full control', sacks Mankiewicz, as the budget climbs to $37 million during the editing, dubbing and re-shooting process. 'What has happened to Mr Mankiewicz is disgraceful, degrading, humiliating and appalling,' says Taylor. But Mankiewicz was 'semi-mad at this point', by his own admission, waking up at dawn to swallow Dexedrine, plus receiving three injections a day to keep himself going. The dialogue he'd been writing was gibberish – not even Rex Harrison could say, when Caesar is distributing honours to the centurions and officials, 'For each of our distinguished senators, each medal inscribed with the name of him for whom it is intended.' I think that speech ended on the cutting-room floor.

Along with much else. The fellow entrusted with the shears was Elmo Williams (1913–2015 – which means he only lived to be 102), who was instrumental in the success of Zanuck's *The Longest Day*, where he'd been the second-unit director responsible for combat episodes, the endless booms and bangs. (Elmo would later be involved with *Tora! Tora! Tora!*: more booms, more bangs.) In January or early February 1963, *Cleopatra* was screened in secret for him by Zanuck at the Studio Boulogne and, 'Well, for five hours the projectors ground out what Mankiewicz thought was a masterpiece.'

With a preference for gunfire and bombs, Elmo had no patience with exposition, conversation, disquisition – all the things Mankiewicz was good at, which a glance at *All About Eve* or *Suddenly, Last Summer* confirms. Hand-holding the 70 mm celluloid over a lamp, not even bothering to find a proper editing desk, Elmo chopped away with a kitchen scissors. 'Mainly I removed scenes of Taylor,' Elmo says in his memoirs, *Elmo Williams: A Hollywood Memoir* by Elmo Williams (2006). He then got rid of a further twenty-six minutes, crowing to Zanuck, 'It's vastly improved.'

Promoted by Zanuck to the position of 'head of all foreign-produced feature films', Elmo then ordered new battle scenes, filmed, as were the Aqaba sequences in *Lawrence of Arabia*, in the sand dunes of Almeria: 'Antony on the battlefield leading his Roman Legions to victory', was the brief.

Burton, however, busy with *The V.I.P.s*, or unamenable, wasn't available. A double named John Sullivan was used. To further camouflage the star's absence, the Battle of Pharsalia sequence was set at night, with flickering torches, smoke and shadows. Rex Harrison wasn't the least put out by any of this: 'My boy,' he said to Elmo, 'there will be no one on stage but me – an actor's dream.' No one else at all, except for a few thousand horsemen and extras. There were cavalry charges, chariots, battering rams. Stables had to be built for the horses, which kept getting loose – the mischief of gypsies it was rumoured. The Spanish police were offered bribes to impose some order.

Beginning on 23 February, and at a cost of $224,000, there were eight days of re-shoots at Pinewood – Caesar's death, bits and pieces on a terrace, in a garden, inside Antony's tent, where Burton had to huff and puff whilst describing how, despite a depleted force, he'll meet Octavian's legions, alone if necessary, and wishes to be granted only an honourable way to die. Taylor was wanted for replacement close-ups, as Zanuck and Elmo thought, when reacting to the Battle of Actium, she'd looked 'bloated', not a flattering thing for her to hear. With everyone ready, she kept not turning up – until a Sunday, when she could claim 'golden' overtime. 'There was no apology from her,' said Elmo. 'You can see why I don't have fond memories of Elizabeth Taylor.'

Mankiewicz hated the interpolated epic segments, when he got to see them: 'I don't want to be another DeMille!' One of the Hollywood panjandrums rallying to his defence – Joseph L. Mankiewicz's not Cecil B. DeMille's – was Billy Wilder, who cabled Zanuck his 'disgust' about the 'brutal and callous dismissal of people' (the original obviously in capitals): 'No self-respecting picture maker would ever want to work for your company. The sooner the bulldozers raze your studio the better it will be for the industry.'

31 *March* 1963
Wanger and Joan Bennett are spotted by Noël Coward in the Shaw Park Beach Hotel & Spa, Ocho Rios, Jamaica. 'He had recently

shot her agent in the groin,' says Sheridan Morley in a footnote to
Coward's diaries – but that incident was by now twelve years in
the past.

2 *April* 1963
Sybil arrives in New York and Aaron Frosch announces a 'legal separation'. Burton, however, stresses to Stanley Baker, 'Nothing will
change the way I feel about Sybil. Nothing will break our marriage.'
Sybil never sees or speaks to Burton again – as Kate told Tony
Palmer: 'My mother never spoke to my father again. She felt there
was no point in being friends or trying to maintain a sort of civil
friendliness.'

3 *June* 1963
Pope dies, ostensibly of stomach cancer, but maybe the actual cause
was a surfeit of Taylor and Burton. When John XXIII had said,
'We like to call Rome a Holy City. God forbid it becomes a City of
Perversion,' Burton announced, 'Fuck it, let's go to fucking Alfredo's
and have some fucking fettucine.'

12 *June* 1963
The final cut, screened at the premiere, at the Rivoli Theatre, New
York, runs for four hours and three minutes. Further trims were
later made, reducing *Cleopatra* to three hours and twelve minutes.
A black-and-white dupe print of the first cut, 'exactly as it was
shown to me by Mr Mankiewicz in Paris,' was, says Zanuck, depos-
ited under bond at the Lyon Van & Storage Company, where
possibly it remains.

Fifty-five of Cleopatra's costumes are shipped to America aboard
the SS *Cristoforo Colombo*, where they go on exhibition. (The
cockroach-riddled ship is scrapped in 1982.) Fox had hoped Cleopatra's
royal barge, built to Plutarch's specifications, and last seen somewhere
near Ischia, would end up as a restaurant at the 1964 New York World

Fair, but transportation and restoration costs, estimated at over $2 million, proved prohibitive. What did happen to all the big props, I wonder?

Taylor and Burton don't attend the gala premiere. 'Everyone was insulted,' said Elmo Williams. 'Then to make matters worse [they] sent their secretaries to occupy those two centre seats.' Well, I find that funny anyway.

Everything descended into a muddle of claims and counter-claims and litigation, as people blamed each other for misstatements about integrity and executive ability. Taylor and Burton were sued for $50 million, Fox arguing the picture was hurt by their 'scandalous public conduct'. Taylor was singled out for 'suffering herself to be held up to scorn, ridicule, and unfavourable publicity as a result of her conduct and deportment'. Fox later apologised and gave her a few more million.

Skouras accuses Wanger of having 'demonstrated a reckless and wanton attitude, spending money lavishly, without any thought of economy'. The final cost, including distribution and marketing, was $62 million.

Nevertheless, *Cleopatra* remains in New York cinemas for sixty-three weeks, and went into profit in 1966, when ABC paid $5 million for television rights – and additional (or revised) statistics were to be flung at us: the 26,000 gallons of paint, 6,000 tons of cement, 150,000 arrows, 8,000 pairs of shoes and 26,000 costumes.

12 *July* 1963

Witchfinder-General Feighan, who has got himself appointed Chairman of the House of Representatives Immigration Subcommittee, is still fulminating: 'I want to know, is Richard Burton guilty of adultery?' Cheeky. Burton summarised the entire rising tide of passion and ego by saying, 'I left a perfectly good woman to be with a lunatic.'

15 January 1965

Fox pompously sued Peter Rogers, the producer of *Carry On Cleo*, for infringing their copyright, by duplicating the poster artwork completed by Howard Terpning – Terpning at my time of writing is still with us at ninety-five, and he also painted the posters for *Lawrence of Arabia* and *The Sound of Music*. In Rogers' version, Burton, Taylor and Rex Harrison were replaced with Sid James, Amanda Barrie and Kenneth Williams. Charles Hawtrey peers from under the couch. The court hearing was at 10.30 a.m. Quintin Hogg pointed out to the prosecuting counsel, Sir Andrew Clark QC, that *Carry On Cleo* was a comedy 'consciously spoofing the established drama' of Fox's *Cleopatra*. 'Everyone had made the connection and the poster offended nobody.' Mr Justice Plowman agreed.

When it was over it still wasn't over. Elmo Williams, who'd won the Academy Award for editing *High Noon* (all those ticking clocks), continued trying to abridge the bloody thing, endlessly dickering to make narrative sense of what was left. On top of everything else, differing versions were required for different territories. For the Philippines, eight scenes went as 'too sexy'. The Spanish print cut any close-up containing bosoms. In Malta and Ireland, love scenes were censored and Cleopatra's entrance to Rome truncated. Few countries were permitted to see Taylor's chubby bare back massaged by handmaidens, one of whom was a sixteen-year-old Francesca Annis. Nothing of anything at all was seen in Egypt until 1968, when President Nasser personally overruled a ban on anything to do with Taylor, who'd caused an upset in the Middle East after she'd married Eddie and converted to Judaism in Las Vegas. As Taylor said, 'I was involved with *Cleopatra* for five years on and off, and surely the film must be the most bizarre piece of entertainment ever to be perpetrated.' She was not wrong. The film was a way of life.

In late 1962, and throughout 1963, there were still further re-shoots and extra sequences, insertions required here and there – 'After several months we both had to go to Paris to do some additional scenes on *Cleopatra*,' said Taylor of herself and Burton, who in the meantime had made *The V.I.P.s*. Had they lived until the twenty-first century and beyond, no doubt there'd be more to do – and what remains is a dappled patchwork quilt, which seems to undulate on a spicy breeze. Cinematographer Leon Shamroy being unavailable, as he was shooting *The Agony and the Ecstasy* with Charlton Heston (Burton had been offered and turned down the part of Michelangelo), Claude Renoir, grandson of *the* Renoir, latterly took the cap off the lens. The only thing I know about Claude Renoir, lighting cameraman, is that he went blind. Is this why the re-done Battle of Pharsalia, which begins the film, is an anticlimax? We see no fighting. Caesar has been victorious. In the background, in evening gloom, are bodies, campfires, lots of smoky plumes. Rex Harrison is told Pompey, his opponent, has fled to Egypt, and all we see of Pompey, later on, is his severed prop-head in a garden urn. A narrator was brought in. Sequences freeze and turn into paintings or murals – cracked frescoes as if on a vase or wall.

I don't think anyone knew what they were doing by this stage – Mankiewicz's response to any question, any comment, was that everything was a 'phantasmagoria of frantic lies'. In that much that goes on in *Cleopatra*, especially in the first, Rex, half of the film, concerns political machinations and manoeuvrings – business, duty, administration; affairs of state; a concern for position; rivals and allies; people coming in and out with scrolls, documents, messages – this all reflects, rather well, the jockeying for power in Hollywood, the psychology of commerce and what occurs in any organisation when there are roles, debates, objections to committees (senates) and interference. I've made a lot of Taylor's indispositions, but an argument may be made – and it has been made by Sydney Guilaroff, the nelly in charge of wigs – that the deciding factor in the move from Pinewood to Rome was not after all the star's illnesses but, exactly as they are satirised in the Sellers classic *I'm All Right, Jack*, the truculence and obstinacy of the British trades unions, problems with work permits and visas, labour laws, restrictive practices, clearances and the closed shop. Guilaroff himself had to slink back to Hollywood, after a stoppage had been called when he, the hair man, had adjusted a costume, which was the designated task of a dresser, who belonged to the wardrobe department. 'The British unions had won the battle,' he said, 'but had lost the war, as the production would have provided hundreds of jobs for British craftspeople,' who instead reverted to normal Pinewood fare, such as Norman Wisdom comedies.

Wanger wrote, in his memoir, that studio executives, the businessmen on any continent, were always 'operating ... out of insecurity and fear', and kings and tyrants are people who put a stop to dithering, and offscreen this role was played by Zanuck, with Elmo, his henchman, Antony to his Caesar. Spyros was the ex-Caesar, who if he wasn't exactly stabbed to death on the Ides of March, was at least in retirement. Darryl Francis Zanuck, as Head of Production, had founded the Twentieth Century Fox Film Corporation in 1933. He spent time in London during the Blitz and, awarded the rank of colonel, he shot documentary war footage in Tunisia. In Africa, he was photographed next to safari trophies, like rhinos. He was one of those cigar-chomping moguls famous for his pronouncements: 'Don't say yes until I've finished talking'; 'There was only one boss I believed in, and that was me.' A contemporary of Irving Thalberg and David O. Selznick, he seemed to believe himself to be Ike or Montgomery, or Patton, in a hard hat stomping around movie sets as if they were battlefields; and he was the presiding genius behind *The Longest Day*, which was efficiently made in Paris when *Cleopatra* was inefficiently being made in Rome. I suppose the chief difference between those projects was: in the former, *no fucking Taylor.* But there is Burton, as the RAF pilot, and for him and for everybody (McDowall has two scenes), D-Day was a welcome respite from *Cleopatra,* and so here is the Second World War, with Vincent Korda the art director, with no blood or pain. Hit by a bullet, soldiers silently topple like skittles.

Burton is in taciturn military mode, drinking beer in the mess with a dreadful Donald Huston. 'You mean, he bought it?' It's like a revue sketch with Jonathan Miller and Alan Bennett. Later, we see Burton wounded, leaning against a barn door, being stoical, growling about the folly of war. He brings or is allowed to bring a Shakespearean dimension, an oracular tone – those snarls and barks, which he copied from Olivier; the pent-up whispers, the sneers. Here is a man, Burton, having a few days off in Paris, leaving Taylor behind in Cinecittà, who was supremely successful (famous, rich) in a profession he never believed in (or so he'd always say) – never wanted to be part of, had no sympathy with – and yet his reluctance is what makes him interesting, as here, as the crashed pilot asking for morphine. He'll march no further; no worse has heaven to give. We don't know the fate of his character – in *The Longest Day,* actors are introduced only for events, and Maurice Jarre's propulsive score, to overtake them: John Wayne, Robert Mitchum, Henry Fonda – all the way to Richard Wattis as a paratrooper, alighting in the forecourt of Nazi headquarters: 'Awfully sorry, old man. Simply landed here by accident.' And if Wattis, a peerless English character actor and comedian with a distinctive slightly quacking grand voice – if the telly was on in another room, I'd know immediately who it was – commands his few seconds on screen effortlessly, so Burton, too, has a special quality; the charge of his personality apparent in the stillness of and around his helmetless airman.

If Zanuck was now a pragmatic Caesar, for some years, however, he'd been behaving like Antony, an 'amorous surfeiter', in Shakespeare's description, given to 'lascivious wassails'. In 1956, he peremptorily gave up Fox, abandoned his wife, Virginia, who'd appeared in silent pictures, in Santa Monica, and moved to Paris, to be with a succession of mistresses: Irina Demick, Geneviève Gilles and Juliette Gréco. Again, it's as if *Cleopatra* is an allegory of Hollywood behaviour – the mouldering grandeur and fragmented porticoes; the contrast between Roman ideals of government, practicality, war and masculine might and decisiveness, which Zanuck had briefly had enough of, versus Egypt's oriental heat and decadence, Nile lyricism and mirth and calamity – and yet there came a moment, as for Octavian (in Shakespeare's play – but McDowall implies as much) when 'Our graver business / frowns at this levity', and Zanuck, operating as an independent producer, with Fox as his distributor, frowned at the costs of *Cleopatra*, fearing it would swamp the commercial chances of *The Longest Day*, which amongst other things was to launch Irina Demick, who played Janine, a girl in the Resistance, as a star. That never happened. Irina was to appear in *Those Magnificent Men in their Flying Machines* and *Prudence and the Pill*, but her career tapered off in the Seventies, after *Ragazza Tutta Nuda Assassinata Nel Parco*, an Italian exploitation horror about (I assume) a totally nude young woman assassinated in a park.

Zanuck was more successful in the boardroom. Despite the amorous interlude or indulgence amongst the French, he remained a major Fox shareholder – and to save *The Longest Day* he made the studio cancel Marilyn Monroe's *Something's Got to Give* (a decision precipitating Marilyn Monroe's suicide); 260 acres of the Fox backlot in California was sold off to become a shopping centre; and he quashed any hopes Mankiewicz still harboured of assembling a pair of separate pictures, one with Cleopatra and Caesar (like Shaw), the other with Cleopatra and Antony (like Shakespeare). Zanuck had the perspicacity to realise audiences would only really want to pay to watch Cleopatra and Antony – because not for a second did anyone in the world think of Cleopatra and Antony as anything less than Taylor and Burton, Liz and Dick to the tabloids, hard drinking, extravagant, full of ecstasy and egotism. They were playing the roles in public and in private – common knowledge by now – and to hell with wives, husbands, children, duty. 'How it hurts, how love can stab the heart,' says Cleopatra, as portrayed by Taylor. 'I had to be with Richard. I knew it was wrong. I knew it would hurt people. I knew. I *knew*. But I also knew what I had to do ... I had to be with Richard,' said Taylor, behaving more like Cleopatra than Cleopatra, a creature of sheer will. Whatever misgivings Burton may have had deep down, and reflecting the title of Monroe's lost film, he simply had to give in to it.

* * *

'Excited about going to Rome, Mr Burton?' Burton had been asked by a reporter, before leaving America, in the autumn of 1961. 'Of course. I love the place. The Italians are like the Welsh.' With *Cleopatra* completed, he changed his tune. 'I never want to see the place again as long as I live,' he said firmly. But the fact is, he and Taylor were often in the Eternal City. *The Taming of the Shrew* was made for Zeffirelli at the newly constructed Dino De Laurentiis Cinematografica Studios (Dinocittà) in 1966, and in the August of that same year, Burton and Taylor filmed *Doctor Faustus* at Cinecittà, utilising *Cleopatra* personnel. *Boom!* was made on location in Alghero and Isola Piana, Capo Caccia, in Sardinia, and in the studios in Rome, in 1967. Also in 1967, though the story takes place on a military base in Georgia, Taylor made *Reflections in a Golden Eye*, with Marlon Brando, at Dinocittà. *Candy* was made in Rome in 1968. *The Assassination of Trotsky*, set in Mexico, was produced in Rome, in October 1971. Burton paid $150 a week to have use of 'my old dressing room' at Dinocittà. *Divorce His, Divorce Hers* was made in Munich and Rome in November 1972. *Massacre in Rome* was made right where the Nazi atrocities had occurred, in January 1973. De Sica's *The Voyage*, chiefly shot in Sicily, Milan and Venice, required the RAI [Radio Audizioni Italiane] Dear

Studios, Rome, for its interiors. *Wagner* was filmed at many sites throughout Italy. There may be other Italian projects I've yet to catalogue – for instance, Burton's narration for *Florence: Days of Destruction*, a fifty-one-minute documentary, broadcast by the BBC on 11 December 1966, about the city's floods; as *Per Firenze*, and originally produced by RAI, this was directed by Zeffirelli as a fundraising effort and shown first in Italy on 23 November. The text, impressively delivered by Burton in both English and in the Italian language, was written by Furio Colombo, a professor at the University of Bologna, editor of the newspaper *L'Unità*, and a member of the Italian parliament. Another Italian thing: wearing their costumes for *Reflections in a Golden Eye*, Taylor and Brando appeared in a short sequence for *Gala de l'Unicef*, promoting voluntary blood donation, rolling up their sleeves on behalf of the Associazione Volontari Italiani Sangue (A.V.I.S.). Three armfuls, if Burton, present on the set, sportingly joined in. A private photo album, containing goofy snapshots of Taylor, a bearded Burton and a face-pulling Brando, was apparently given by Taylor to Michael Jackson, who left it in a taxi in Germany, the careless fucker. Published in *Elizabeth Taylor 1932–2011: Queen of the Silver Screen*, the pictures are hesitantly captioned by an Andre Deutsch editor as having been taken 'possibly in Mexico'. Possibly not, as Rome is in the background. People seem to be having a festive time, but Brando's recollections of Burton were unfavourable. Referring, in his memoirs, *Songs My Mother Taught Me*, to 'Elizabeth Taylor, whom I liked, and Richard Burton, whom I didn't,' Brando says Burton was 'already drunk' and bleary-eyed by noon and that alcohol rendered him 'a mean drunk', who was in the habit of making 'racial slurs', particularly about Brando's Tahitian offspring, of which there were many. 'When he kept it up, I turned to him and said, "If you make one more comment of any kind about my children, I'm going to knock you off this boat."' Burton was saved from a dunking in the harbour by Taylor ('Oh Richard, stop that now'), but it is an ugly anecdote – Burton and Brando too alike, perhaps, each the proud possessor of bad tempers, finding the needling of a rival male irresistible.

Italy, anyway, was the place the Burtons travelled to – the weather, the light, giving a sharper outline; the lyricism. A study could be made of the importance of Italy, Rome particularly, in Burton and Taylor's lives; the Sixties; the monuments and fountains; the international cinema community; the overlaying of antiquity and the pagan with the Vatican and its rococo decor. 'My wife and I wouldn't mind spending the rest of our careers in Italy playing Shakespeare,' said Burton wistfully. Muriel Spark was there – Taylor's version of her novella, *The Driver's Seat*, is another unseen pearl. It is a Seventies version of *Pandora's Box*, in which in 1929, Louise Brooks searched for Jack the Ripper, for a glinting knife to be plunged into her flesh. 'Dear Miss Spark,' wrote Taylor, in a letter now housed in the National Library of Scotland. 'Thank you so much for your lovely letter and your enthusiasm at the idea of my playing Lise. I cannot tell you how pleased and flattered I am. I shall do my very best to live up to your faith in my portrayal. Richard and I are, and always have been, great fans of your enormous talent and look forward very much to meeting you . . .' Taylor as Jean Brodie? It's a thought. Burton in *The Ballad of Peckham Rye*? A very good thought. Anthony Burgess was there. In one of his books, he says that, when addressing their sweethearts, on the back of soldiers' envelopes, during the war, a variation of S.W.A.L.K., sealed with a loving kiss, was I.T.A.L.Y., I trust and love you. Another was B.U.R.M.A., be upstairs ready my angel. N.O.R.W.I.C.H., knickers off ready when I come home, doesn't work because of the 'k' needed for knickers, obviously. Burgess' Roman novel was *Beard's Roman Women*, and Joe McGrath worked with Burgess on an adaptation of the Enderby novels, with the intention of offering the screenplay to Burton, who'd have been excellent, perfect, as the fundamentally lonely and crapulous poet, beset by a succession of crazy girlfriends. Enderby's dark ladies, indeed, were not unlike the steamed-up Burgess' terrified description of Taylor, when in the pages of *The Listener* in 1963, and protesting too much, he wailed like a banshee, calling her 'the limit of frothy insubstantiality, a jaw-dropping vision of totally meaningless allure, Yves Saint Laurent icing, delectability of fairy gold, the poor little box of tricks of Zuleika Dobson.'

Sellers was there, making *The Bobo* and, with De Sica, *After the Fox* ... Maybe Gregory Peck and Audrey Hepburn started it all off, with *Roman Holiday* – a princess at large in the post-war capital – and there was a unique stylishness: Vespa and Lambretta scooters, Olivetti typewriters, Lamborghini Miuras and Maserati Ghibli cars, Ferragamo, Gucci, Armani and Valentino fashion goods, shoes, handbags, and Bulgari jewels and accessories. Burton said there was no accommodation lovelier than a suite at the Grand Hotel de la Minerve, Rome. I wonder, looking at the period lamps, cooking pots, radio sets, televisions and Zanussi washing machines – these streamlined, elegant household appliances, with which a modern Cleopatra would cram her palace: how much do these geometric sculptures owe to the lines and planes of Futurism? *Futurismo*, as explained by Marinetti, advocated not only unmusty things like speed and technology, but also militarism, aggression and actual war. An Italian coffee percolator, as I know from experience, is liable to explode. The flashbulbs of omnipresent photographers were artillery fire. Cinecittà, after all, was constructed in the Fascist era, opened by Mussolini in 1937, and became so popular with American filmmakers it was known as Hollywood-on-the-Tiber. *Roman Holiday* is an early instance, as was *Quo Vadis*. On her three-month honeymoon with Nicky Hilton, in the summer of 1950, Taylor visited the set of the latter, as Sydney Guilaroff was constructing hairpieces for Deborah Kerr. As the director was Mervyn LeRoy, who'd directed *Little Women*, Taylor, for fun, played a 'Christian prisoner in [the] arena', an extra or crowd artiste. Taylor, said Sydney, 'poured out her heart to me.' Her marriage was a senseless torment. Looking back, *Little Women*, *Father of the Bride*, *Father's Little Dividend*, and the rest, were cruel, misleading, mendacious, as regards a girl's destiny.

Patriarchal propaganda. 'Real life for her was filled with disappointment and bitterness.'

For whom is it mostly not filled with those things? (Antony and
Cleopatra?) On 2 August 1967, Burton wrote in his diary, 'All the bad
things that have happened to me have almost always happened in
Rome,' a conviction he came out with again, four years later: 'A lot of
things happened to me – and us – in Rome.' It was evidently a spot
notable for a heady psychological climate, where love was irrational,
fidelity a farce. Rome, as Elizabeth Bowen wrote, 'jumps to the senses
immediately, at the same time keeping a puzzling element'. It gave
scandal a piquancy. It's where the egotism of a big love affair could
have a backdrop – where Taylor and Burton were strong, physical,
throbbing, and had the illusion of behaving in an uncontrolled way.
It's where the problems of their personal lives bubbled up like lava.
'What a dreadful and terrible day,' Burton also wrote in 1967, when
working on *Doctor Faustus*. 'All my pettiness and resentment and
idiocy all rolled up into one day. I'll blame it on Rome.' There
were tranquil times, too. On 5 May 1966, filming *The Taming of
the Shrew*, Taylor and Burton found a roadside trattoria, near a
church: 'The voices of the choir drifted on the air like an invisible
mist . . . We stopped eating . . . to listen. It was one of those moments
which are nostalgic before they're over . . . [The moon] shone on us
from the cloudless night.' Time present and time past are both perhaps present in time future, etc. There were never, in fairness, many
moments like that one. Mostly Burton and Taylor were pulling each
other to pieces, and this made them happy. I sometimes wonder,
indeed, whether, after *Cleopatra*, they ever did make a full, thorough,
exit from the world of that film. Figuratively or imaginatively speaking, Taylor and Burton always remained in Rome – all those films
they made about a couple's rage and combativeness; people consuming themselves, like a fire; angry moods, angry glares. That their final
project together, on stage, was *Private Lives*, fits the pattern, fulfils
their destiny.

Cleopatra was there beforehand, also, for Taylor, with her (many) coquettish, wily characters, who goad, who provoke, and for Burton, too, with *Camelot*. On 10 April 1966, he received 'a long telegram from Josh Logan asking me to do *Camelot* for Warners ... don't want to much.' Richard Harris was to be King Arthur on celluloid, and I resent him in the role because he's not Burton (Harris was an irritable, nastier, actor) – though like anyone I prefer Vanessa Redgrave as Guinevere to Julie Andrews. Vanessa is lusty. Julie is no-nonsense. When Julie sings (I have the LP) about 'the simple joys of maidenhood' there's absolutely no randy undercurrent or subtext. Vanessa (later Burton's Cosima Wagner) has a slightly blurred, dazed sexuality. It's terrible hokum – and to think Burton was in a revival of *Camelot*, in 1980, rather than playing Prospero or Lear, parts on offer from Anthony Quayle and John Dexter. But Burton (in the clips surviving from *The Ed Sullivan Show*) makes Arthur come off. The role attains depth. And in that the story is about adultery, the corruption of noble ideals, one can see how it contains *Cleopatra*, except in that film, and in real life, Burton is or was more like Lancelot – and the film of *Camelot* picks up with the appearance of Franco Nero. Lancelot is willing to throw self-control away. He can barely control his impatience with the tedium of chivalry, Arthur's boring ideas about 'might for right', the gentle May Morning hobbies of picnics and pressing wild flowers. The music is jaunty. Irritatingly jaunty. Nevertheless, Arthur, in Burton's characterisation, has a conscience – the wracked conscience of Antony – who in the hunting scenes and snowy forests presides over elaborate codes of conduct, perceives how Camelot (the place) and the Round Table (its symbol of concord) are corrupted by deceit and sinful passion. Arthur's court experiences, deals with, virtue and dishonour. And in that those medieval myths and legends – Malory by way of T.H. White – are an allegory of seduction, and of love and fatedness, maybe *Cleopatra* is the *Camelot* Burton should have been in, or else *Cleopatra* is the *Camelot* Burton had already been in – his once and future enterprise – with Taylor his

Guinevere. The difference being, where Lerner and Loewe concocted a comic romp, an entertainment, *Cleopatra* is a serious saga of betrayal and ruin.

* * *

It is one of the great Sixties films, along with *A Countess from Hong Kong, Casino Royale*, Tati's *Playtime* and Fellini's *Satyricon*. Everyone involved heartily hated it. 'They had cut out the heart, the essence, the motivations, the very core, and tacked on all those battle scenes,' commented Taylor. 'The finished film you saw is a complete distortion,' Mankiewicz told an audience at the Festival du Cinéma Américain de Deauville, on 7 September 1984. 'A parody of what I wanted to do. I disown it. Zanuck hammered it to pieces with that polo mallet he used to carry.' When asked why he didn't attend the premiere in New York, Burton sighed. 'We'd just had it with *Cleopatra* by then. The whole thing. It was years of my life.' As Hume Cronyn summed up, 'There was a certain madness to it all.' But also a spaciousness, the white skies, the dry air. Like the ocean liner in Chaplin's film, the Sixties styles in the Sellers Bond spoof, Tati's city of glass and Fellini's ancient mosaics and monsters, what consumes me, when I personally watch *Cleopatra*, is the beauty of the world on view – it is another world, one full of images of feeding, feasting, cloying, glut, hunger, festivity, sweetmeats, melting, tasting, savouring.

As creatures of mythology, Antony and Cleopatra are longing for another (self-contained) world, and here it is: large gleaming floors, no dust, no mess; echoing vaults and antechambers. Egypt and Rome are identical – people walk out of one throne room and into another, and if the Mediterranean separates Alexandria from Italy we see little of it. *Cleopatra* is a film, chiefly, of interiors. The crowds don't appear or muster very often. For all the notorious chaos surrounding the production, what we see is clean, immaculate, thrillingly empty, filled only by Alex North's score, a perfect period mix of slithering, hypnotic, Oriental jangling and druggy New Age California: Shakespeare's Cleopatra described such music as the 'moody food / of us that trade in love'. Nevertheless, it is muted – never any bustle. Actually, those palaces could be a hospital or a very expensive private clinic – and *Cleopatra*, as we know, was made in the midst of illness. Often, Taylor doesn't look like a voluptuary. She is bloated and poorly, with a greasy sheen. Instead of heralds and fanfares, one expects an ambulance siren, stretchers, a red blanket.

The huge sets, nevertheless, look like sets – onyx and bright yellow burnished gold panels, with cobra, serpentine, imagery embossed on lamps, door-handles, sword blades, bed-frames and woven into hair-braids. Everything snakelike is glittering, gorgeous, and somehow evil, like Satan seducing Eve: 'Oft he bowed his turret crest, and sleek enamelled neck, fawning, and licked the ground whereon she trod.' The chairs are very Sixties – Taylor's eye make-up and fringe are very Sixties; the murals and melting purple light are Sixties psychedelic hues. Lacking only white telephones, the rooms, indeed, like the business convention in *Playtime*, could be a Hilton hotel suite, motor show or department store furniture exhibition, e.g. the objects placed on Cleopatra's dressing-table, the coloured thin-stemmed glass bottles, the bikini-clad dancers sent to amuse her, the way Taylor lolls on a couch in diaphanous sheets and wisps: all is on deliberate display, as if for sale – and in the story, the juggled loyalties of Romans, Egyptians and neighbouring kings, all come with a price tag attached, exactly like the costs of the grain and corn they are keen to purchase and exchange. When Antony escapes to Egypt, after the ignominy of Actium, and he hates himself and is full of worry and fury, the gold of the palace becomes greenish, turquoise, bilious; there is a sourness to the gold – it is as if there is now a taste of copper on the tongue. Again, the settings are a portent of mood and impulse, as Antony finds himself at 'the very heart of loss' – the loss of his pride and rank; the loss of face; the loss of trust. As applied to Burton – the loss of

Sybil and family and esteem of old pals ('To choose Elizabeth rather than Sybil was lunacy,' said Robert Hardy; 'He lost himself when he married Elizabeth Taylor,' said Stanley Baker); and counteracting loss, he found freedom, but it was a horrifying freedom. The reality he'd known existed now no longer. Burton's complexion as Antony is gold and brown, like an Aztec perhaps, with a bone structure and grandeur of form to rival Classical sculpture – bright polished bronze, weathered marble contours, impending animal movement, animal energy, the effect precise and also paradoxically distorted; artificial, yet real, organic.

It's towards all of that – a final act (in the theatrical and operatic sense) exploring the idea of extinction – that *Cleopatra* builds, with the forming and dissolving of alliances, the violence and intrigue. In the abandoned Peter Finch footage, Caesar, mounted on a white stallion, leaps from his ship in Alexandria harbour, clatters up the palace steps, and dramatically entered Cleopatra's presence. Rex Harrison, by contrast, wrapped always in a mantle of West End light comedy, strolls through the marketplace, meets the Egyptian dignitaries on a terrace – including Richard O'Sullivan, from *Man About the House*, as an elaborately accoutred Ptolemy – and says in his Rex Harrison way, 'You all look so impressive, any one of you could be king.' I can never get enough of that voice, the ringing clarity of the enunciation, words and phrases coming out like sips from a honeycomb, literally mellifluous; the continual suggestion of impatience and rebuke and derision. His eyes, whether he's Dr Dolittle, Professor Higgins, or Julius Caesar, are narrowed to slits, like, said Rachel Roberts, 'embrasures in a medieval fortress behind which archers fired arrows and poured boiling oil.' It's this refusal of his to be impressed that characterises the scene where he greets Cleopatra, when Apollodorus (Cesare Danova, his role much cut) unrolls her from the carpet, and Rex is a difficult customer in the department store, scrutinising the stock. Rex is urbane, at ease with the politics, power, diplomacy, receiving and dismissing deputations – coping with the

tax riots, the civil wars and the transportation of treasure and plun-
der. All this is meat and drink to Caesar. Informed by a cross
Cleopatra his troops have managed to burn down the Library of
Alexandria, only Rex could elicit a laugh with the line, 'So I've been
told. I'm extremely sorry.' Quite matching him in this *Blithe Spirit*
manner, when Caesar comes in at light-infantry pace and distracts
Cleopatra, Taylor says, semi-witheringly, 'Oh, it's you.'

Taylor always liked weaker vessels, pets, invalids, horses, dogs,
gerbils, Michael Jackson, so her Cleopatra starts warming to Caesar
when he gets 'the falling sickness', or epilepsy – George Cole, as the
deaf-mute servant, Flavius, is on hand with a stick to wrench apart
his master's jaw, to prevent him swallowing his upper-set. (Fifteen
years later, Taylor met Cole again in Leningrad, when he replaced
James Coco in *The Blue Bird*: 'George, I thought you really were a
deaf-mute when we did *Cleopatra*!' She'd never heard him say a dicky
bird.) Romance of a kind ensues, a child named Caesarion is born,
whom Cleopatra hopes can one day be monarch of both Rome and
its territories and Egypt and north Africa, i.e. of the entire known
world – and Caesar then scoots back to Italy, a journey taking several
years, as he has unspecified things to do in Asia Minor. Cleopatra
follows some years later again – hence the big set-piece, where Taylor
makes her ceremonial appearance on top of a big black sphinx, pulled
by lots of grunting Nubian slaves, like a British sovereign on a gun
carriage tugged to Windsor by sailors. She looks precarious up there,
but it was Rex who kept blowing his lines, much to the enjoyment of
Michael Hordern. For each take, it took a full two hours to marshal
the procession of camels, elephants, panthers, zebras, senators and
soldiers. As Hordern described it, there were fifty trumpeters on
Arab horses, followed by charioteers and 'bowmen shooting arrows
with coloured streamers into the air. Dancers flash by ... A group of
men waving gold fans reveal a moving platform on which are golden
temples, obelisks, pyramids, winged girls ... Everything is gold.' And
so on and so forth. Doves are released, handmaidens strew blooms,

Caesar is carried to his throne on a palanquin – and Rex dried. 'Okay, we'll go again,' said Mankiewicz. They gave up after the third attempt. 'Okay, it's a wrap. We'll go again tomorrow.' If they did, none of the mobile zoo is in any version of *Cleopatra* I have seen – the Bengal tigers, dwarves, donkeys, and slaves, 'who weren't black enough,' said Burton, 'so they were painted blacker.' It has all gone – either abandoned at the time, or edited out later. Little of the extravagance remains on screen – mainly Taylor, in an elaborate headdress, which 'weighed about fifteen pounds and was two-and-a-half feet high', in the actress' own estimation, coming down off her motorised Sphinx to give Rex a silly wink.

Hordern lurched up to Rex in the bar afterwards and crowed, 'When I was watching you today, being carried along, with all those bloody animals, and when you got to the top of the stairs and then made a bloody arse of yourself in front of all those people, do you know, I was bloody delighted!' Rex smacked him in the mouth for his effrontery – though in Hordern's memoir, it is he, Hordern, who smacked Rex in the mouth. 'What with one thing and another, and probably the demon drink, Rex rather foolishly . . . was very rude. I was very rude back and I am afraid I leant across the table and struck him rather hard . . . He was a mercurial character, Rex Harrison.' And it is in Rex's favour, I think, that he didn't mind being unlikeable – as when McDowall wanted to photograph him: 'Well, you see, Roddy, that is, well, I'm sorry, but, well, the fact is, I just don't like you.' Nor do I. His Octavian is epicene and shouting – mewling. They should have kept Keith Baxter, Blodwyn of the Valleys, who was instead now playing Hal for Orson Welles.

Rex was an imperious person, perfect for Caesar. And if, in the film, Antony is Caesar's rival, as actors, too, Harrison and Burton joust and spar – the Shakespearian and the polished light comedian; Burton's churning, effortful manner, and Rex's impenetrable, shining and wholly exterior performance style. Burton is darker, murkier. He didn't want to escape or deny his origins, but romanticise them. Harrison, crisp, detached, cruel, reptilian, was born in Liverpool, but he was his own invention. Both men were conscious of their voice, their vocal beauty; and their authority was attractive to women. Rex was in *Anne of the Thousand Days* on stage, Burton on film – and as Burton said of Henry VIII: 'mad, I think... He is certainly demonic. Great charm and stupendous outbursts of rage.' The actors will continue their relationship in *Staircase* – and also in real life, e.g. at the charity opening of *A Flea in Her Ear* and there was a mix-up with limousines: 'I don't mind Rex telling me to fuck off, but I do wish he'd stop taking my Rolls.' When he, Caesar, is stabbed in the Capitol on the Ides of March, he reacts not as if he is being assassinated but, being Rex, as if he is being compelled to witness frightful bad manners. But at least the way is left clear for Antony to be with Cleopatra – and, says Rex in his autobiography (1974), 'Richard and Elizabeth came to stay with me at the villa in Portofino for several weeks when the film was over... I think we all enjoyed the peace and relaxation, looking up into the olive trees and out to the distant sea.'

When Cleopatra was with Caesar, their embraces were as stiff and formal as perhaps Taylor's were with Michael Wilding. At last, with the arrival of Burton, there is sexual emotion. Their kisses have an intensity. Their dialogue is an affirmation and a premonition: 'Antony, what has happened?' – 'To me? You have happened to me'; 'For so long now you have filled my life, like a great noise I hear in my heart'; 'Everything I shall ever want to have or hold or look upon or be is here now with you'; 'I will never be free of you'; and when Antony has to endure an arranged state marriage with Jean Marsh: 'Have you ever really left her?' – 'No,' which is the answer Suzy Hunt and Sally Hay feared they'd receive if the subject of Taylor came up – and Taylor went around saying, of herself and Burton, to anyone who'd listen, 'In my heart, I will always believe that we would have been married a third and final time ... From those first moments in Rome, we were always madly and powerfully in love.' Cleopatra's political ambition was also Taylor's policy with divorce settlements: 'Take a little, then a little more, until finally you have it all!' Mankiewicz, scribbling the dialogue in bars or his hotel room the night before the cast had to deliver it, or even handing out lines on scrap paper there and then on the set, simply seemed to be transcribing Taylor and Burton's vocal delight in each other – something Eddie never appreciated: 'To have waited so long. To know so suddenly. Without you, this is not a world I want to live in,' and other sentiments from the Barbara Cartland style manual. 'Fisher is jealous of the lines Burton has,' reported Brodsky to Weiss, the Fox publicists.

And now that Taylor has died, in 2011, twenty-seven years after Burton died, *Cleopatra* has assumed added poignancy: Cleopatra is always talking about death – she's having her mausoleum built from early on, visiting it, inspecting it; important scenes take place next to Alexander the Great's tomb (Cleopatra and Caesar talking about their dynastic plans; Cleopatra and Antony talking about the forces of destiny) – 'A kiss, to take my breath away'; 'Nothing changes, except life into death'; 'You and I will prove death so much less than love ...' Do they? Can anyone? When Larkin wrote, as the final line in 'An Arundel Tomb', 'What will survive of us is love,' he's never fully convinced (*blurred, vaguely, faint, hardly, helpless, scrap, almost* make up the poem's reticent vocabulary) – and in *Cleopatra*, love is like death because moribund. There's nowhere for it to go. Octavian and his armies are on their way. Antony has been disgraced, swept up into Cleopatra's world and made a directionless drunk – Burton does a lot of swallowing from huge golden goblets. Though he doesn't speak Shakespeare, his manner is Shakespearean, when Burton, as Antony, is gripped by the grog, stupefied by gaudy nights: 'Fill our bowls once more; let's mock the midnight bell.' The Midnight Bell is the public house in Patrick Hamilton's *Twenty Thousand Streets Under the Sky* (1935), incidentally, which is all about pie-eyed prostitutes, wastrels with cirrhosis, dead-end existences.

What we are left with, in the chilled palace sets (they look refrigerated – vaults for people who are already dead), is the helplessness of the characters' love; all for love; and like Taylor and Burton, a public spectacle is made of it. Their banquet on the golden barge is like a Vegas floor-show, at the Desert Inn or the Tropicana, where Taylor had accompanied Eddie in June 1958. Or else an orgy in Fellini, with bejewelled palm trees and romping satyrs. Taylor's bath scenes, too, are a Sixties commercial for soap or skin cream, and through the windows surely that is not the Nile, but a view of Vegas hotels and casinos – like in Mel Brooks' *History of the World*, where Caesar's palace really is Caesar's Palace. Heroic love, *Cleopatra* demonstrates, can no more be sustained than international or civic peace. Unrest, revolution, war – Antony and Cleopatra's love is like that, truces changing into troubles; love not a reprieve or remission but a continuation of strife, with more scrambling. The characters, like the actors playing them, are campaigners, hit backwards and forwards from victory to defeat, alienation alternating with reconciliation. Historical concerns and erotic concerns – irrational violence and sensual obsession – are inextricable.

Though there is plenty to deride: characters have names impossible to pronounce – Sosigenes, Pothinus, Euphranor, Valvus, Archesilius; battles are perfunctory (Actium is toy boats on a tabletop, for the most part, instead of an epic confrontation at sea); Robert Stephens and Martin Landau don't do much except stomp around in red cloaks barking orders; Finlay Currie, John Alderton, Laurence Naismith and Desmond Llewellyn are in the credit-roll, yet I've never seen them; George Cole brings with him an expectation of Cockney spivery, Flash Harry from *The Belles of St Trinian's* or Arthur Daley in *Minder*; Richard O'Sullivan belongs with Seventies sideburns, Sally Thomsett and a flatlet; and despite all the hullabaloo, nothing much happens for long stretches (Burton puts on or removes his leather armour, taking all day to buckle and unbuckle the straps) – yet to me none of this much matters. What counts are those huge empty halls, which emphasise the characters' aloneness. The story, at least with Shakespeare, is antiphonal: Egypt and Rome, lovers and soldiers, living and dying. In the film what I notice are closeness and distance. Intimacy with Cleopatra is dashed, when Antony returns to Rome and Octavian orders him as an expedient to marry Octavia – Jean Marsh presiding at table like Lady Bellamy in *Upstairs, Downstairs*, the series Jean created. This segment parallels Caesar's legitimate Roman marriage to Gwen Watford's Calpurnia. On both occasions the Senators have an excuse, equally xenophobic and misogynistic, to sneer at Cleopatra as foreign, as a 'whore', who is not one of us (she's a woman, for a start); and as an outcast, a 'gypsy', she rattles around uncrowded rooms, existing in a kind of limbo. What therefore redeems Taylor as an actress – by which I mean: what makes me watch her; what makes me take her seriously – is that though she is blowsy and coarse, her weight varying from scene to scene (often she is outright fat in the scanty costumes); though she can be idiotic (that wink) and grotesque (the fish-wife screech '*Antony!*' when she feels deserted – the actress' way of calling out to a Cinecittà assistant was to say, 'Hey, Shithead!'); nevertheless, Taylor is vivid and swift. There is something severe underneath – her will or wilfulness. You can see with Burton – he's fascinated; his muscles and nerves alerted. His eyes devour her, as if she is something that has ripened on a tree.

Burton's face and frowning expression always suggested a darkness within him – with Taylor in his sights and thoughts we get a sense of a power in the darkness beneath him, the rocks and stones and mines of Wales, the fables and fairy tales, rose gardens, thorns; and these are Taylor's components, too, her attraction to folklore and familiars, the cats and rats, horses and riders, even elephants (in *Elephant Walk*) on view in everything from *National Velvet* and the *Lassie* films, to *The Sandpiper* [*Actitis hypoleucos*] or *The Blue Bird*, the latter made in Russia between 20 January and 11 August 1975 and scarcely released by Fox in 1976. If a rarity, it's because the subtitles are in Cyrillic. Taylor shape-changingly materialises as a peasant mother in a shawl, a warty witch in an orange cloak, and as the Spirit of Spring in a silver crystalline headdress, made of wire and beads by Sydney Guilaroff. Dyed doves fly about. Coloured paper leaves dot the lawn outside Mona Washbourne's cottage. George Cole, blessed with speech, is a dog in a woolly suit. George Cukor was the director. Maurice Maeterlinck's play, aimed at children, about the search for the blue bird of happiness, if we ignore the homily in the finale (happiness is all about you already – you simply have to learn to look), might more credibly be about the search for luxury, particularly where Taylor was concerned – and from the outset Taylor, and Burton, shared an appetite for wonders, waste, frivolity.

And they were similar in another way, too – as spoilt children. Shakespeare's Antony is an 'old ruffian', a version of Falstaff; Burton's is the needy Lost Boy Taylor described to Michael Aspel: 'The first day on the set he was hungover and very vulnerable, and his hands were shaking. He asked me to hold the coffee up to his lips and I was gone. He was so sweet.' It was a moment of recognition. Burton had been as cossetted by sisters and relatives, all those women in Wales, as Taylor had been by the Hollywood studio system, and she'd long been a sexual connoisseur or predator – she received 1,065 invitations to college proms in 1947, prompting L.B. Mayer to observe, 'Our child star has suddenly developed an elegant bosom and become a fully-formed lady.' Nicky Hilton's parting shot was, 'Every man should have the opportunity of sleeping with Elizabeth Taylor.' With Michael Wilding she was Lolita ('I wish you'd stop treating me as if I had a child's mind inside a woman's body. Why don't you invite me out to dinner tonight?'); Todd introduced her to the brutality of sex and its implications ('This girl's been looking for trouble all her life. Now she's found somebody who can give it to her. Me, I'm real meat' – sometimes the quotation is, 'Me, I'm red meat'); Eddie was a sex slave whom Taylor discarded ('I really understood how a woman could destroy the man who loves her,' he reflected) – and all this is usually the male's role or prerogative, or initiative. Taylor's lewdness was

344

unabashed: 'You come right now,' Taylor and Todd used to command one another, particularly when guests were within earshot. 'I want to fuck you this minute.' And within a year of their being together, Burton would be heard saying to the assembled company, e.g. in Puerto Vallarta, when shooting *The Night of the Iguana*, 'My sexual presence is herewith summoned.'

In terms of *Cleopatra*, and Cleopatra, these passions and appetites are 'the habitual craving of a licentious nature' (Coleridge); she is 'voluptuous, ostentatious, conscious, boastful of her charms, haughty, tyrannical, fickle' (Hazlitt); and no doubt more things besides. But in Rome, in the early Sixties, there was also the booze. Eddie tried to cut down Taylor's drinking, Burton encouraged it – vodka, grappa and ouzo mixed, 'Ivan the Terrible' cocktails; brandy disguised in Coca-Cola bottles. The drinks bill at Villa Pappa was between $450 and $700 a week. It's why Taylor grew plump – though the dozen chickens and forty pounds of bacon she charged to the budget daily would have found their way to her hips.

Eddie said, with understandable acrimony, that Taylor mistook Burton's 'alcoholism, bitterness, and the anger that led to violence, for independence and self-confidence', which maybe she did. Yet she also helped transform those deficiencies into his strengths, and he was able to give the appearance of independence and self-confidence (what a romantic buccaneer he seemed), which, when combined with his earnestness and pessimism (his Welshness), brought about, brought forth, the actor he was now going to become, with Taylor as his frequent co-star, the pair of them always seeming to be engaged, as Gavin Lambert said of Elsa Lanchester and Charles Laughton, in 'an angry bondage game', notable for its mutual intimidation and cunning.

'Who can control his fate?' asks Othello. I've always thought of Taylor and Burton as a comical couple. Their ridiculous side is what is mostly on display. But as regards the question of fatality – questions of accident and of chance – when I think more deeply, as I am doing

345

now, today, they are tragic. In the end, obsessed with desire for each other, with possession, they were left utterly alone. As unreachable as ghosts, they were unaware of the rest of us – at best, impatient with the rest of us. We – other people, that's to say – are not to be cared about. 'I don't like Negroes,' said Burton, in the sort of riff found offensive by Marlon Brando. 'I don't like Jews. Nor Russians. Nor Italians. The only people I do like are the Welsh, and of them I only like the miners. The only miners I like are my family . . . and I don't like all of them.' Nor did he. They, the Jenkinses, would come for a holiday in Switzerland, arriving very early (a Welsh trait), staying ages (another Welsh trait), and expect a full programme of entertainment and refreshments to be laid on. 'Will broke my swordstick silly bastard and fell to boot,' Burton jotted in his diary, of a typical visit, in July 1975. 'Putting [him] in hospital tomorrow. He's a mess. Wife Betty fucking stupid. Daughter [Rhian] fat and staggeringly tongue struck.'

Taylor and Burton were feral, fierce, and fantasy became their reality, with an absence of responsibility, no need for commonplace woes, e.g. cooking the tea, making the beds, supervising the homework, hoovering. (Correction: on 29 May 1966, because 'the servants had all gone to Mass', Burton 'boiled myself a couple of eggs'.) There were secretaries to answer letters, or toss letters away. (When Hilda Jenkins expressed surprise at seeing the mail ripped up unopened, she was told, 'They're only rubbish!') They were people who by their behaviour or actions did not wish to be inhibited – and who seemed to question ultimate values (liberty, justice), by mastering their environment, putting their own happiness and pleasure first, other people's misery second, or nowhere. This was all a great threat to life, moral life. And if they thought the advantage of stardom was the freedom it conferred – at last, a life unhindered – Taylor and Burton were to discover it was only another way of being held prisoner. There would be no escaping the shackles of age, illness, expectation, mortality, even one's own personality, the inner landscape of guilt and self-loathing. Some things really can't be avoided. It is the lesson of Faustus, who wants and expects free will, only to find he's still subject to what Larkin called 'the unbeatable slow machine / That brings what you'll get'.

It is equally possible that as I think about Taylor and Burton more deeply still, tomorrow, next week, next year, they will have become comic again, though in a different way.

PART FOUR
THE AGE OF VULGARITY

The Pop Art elements: 'Any art that is successful in projecting positive feelings about life has got to be heavily erotic,' said Claes Oldenburg. The Burtons were gorgeous and monstrous. 'No crime is vulgar,' said Wilde, 'but all vulgarity is crime. Vulgarity is the conduct of others.' Yet no one sets out to be vulgar, just as they don't intentionally make mistakes, and I can find a harmony in vulgarity – form and design in its gaudy pleasurableness, as represented on the Burtons' poster art. The Burtons had a thrusting quality – and a brash glamour and majesty; and also an elegiac quality now that everything they were a part of has vanished: dancing with Vic Damone, singing with Frank Sinatra, having a drink with Farley Granger and Shelley Winters; seeing Kirk Douglas, Victor Mature and Mickey Rooney in Chasen's or the Brown Derby; white gloves, hats, blue velvet slacks, purplish lipstick; hairstyles by Sydney Guilaroff and Alexandre de Paris; dressing up to descend the steps of a silver aeroplane, which sparkles in the sunshine. I never knew this world, but I was always able to picture it and draw sustenance from it.

'FUCK!' bawled the baritonal Richard Burton, in the vestibule of the Hotel Capo Caccia, Sardinia, when on 11 August 1967 he found himself with 'thousands of bags all over the place, nine children, six adults ... I screamed *fuck* out of drunkenness ... To scream *fuck* in the lobby was the only possible way to meet the justice of the day.' Possibly so. There were many similar days to do justice to. At the

Grand Hotel Timeo, for example, in Via Teatro Greco, Taormina, Taylor broke a guitar over Burton's head. Rex Harrison, seeing four-teen pieces of luggage piled up at Reception in the Hotel Lancaster, Paris, plus the cages of cats and dogs and turtles, wondered out loud, 'Why do the Burtons have to be so filthily ostentatious?' John Gielgud, directing *Hamlet* in Toronto and Boston, early in 1964, said that, 'Even when I went out to lunch with [Burton] between rehears-als, there'd be four or five of the entourage sitting at adjoining tables, preventing people coming up and talking to him.' In Toronto, Burton and Elizabeth Taylor took the Presidential Suite at the Sheraton King Edward Hotel. In Boston they put up at the Copley-Plaza. When they arrived at Logan Airport, there were five thousand screeching fans, grabbing at their clothes, snatching at their hair, behaving as if Taylor and Burton were The Beatles. The police lost control. Is any sympathy deserved? Marlene Dietrich, staying at the same hotel as Burton and Taylor, overheard them complaining about the sheer volume of fans besieging the place. 'My dear Richard, my dear Elizabeth,' she said, with her Germanic lisp, 'if you want to escape the crowds, don't stay in the same hotel as me.' There is stardom, superstardom, and mega-stardom.

'That sort of celebrity is so very hard to cope with,' said Gielgud. 'They had to exercise the dogs on the roof. There was a man with a machine gun in the corridor outside their room.' The ructions were similar the following year in Dublin, whilst the filming of *The Spy Who Came in from the Cold* went on at Ardmore Studios. John le Carré couldn't believe it. Taylor was disrupting shooting by turning up in a Rolls-Royce, accompanied by the likes of Yul Brynner and crates of champagne. 'The reputedly seventeen-strong Burton house-hold . . . occupied the whole of one floor of Dublin's grandest hotel,' The Gresham, in O'Connell Street, where the retinue was augmented by 'various children by different marriages,' plus nannies and tutors and, said Le Carré, 'the fellow who clipped the parrot's claws.' There is now The Elizabeth Taylor Suite at The Gresham, one hundred and thirty metres square, containing a four-poster bed seven foot three inches wide.

Franco Zeffirelli also visited The Gresham, for a preliminary talk about *The Taming of the Shrew*. He, too, was struck by the atmosphere of a chaotic Ruritania. Taylor had acquired a bush baby, which had 'rampaged around the rooms, knocking over lights and vases', before clinging, terrified, to a pipe in the bathroom. The chief problem, however, was the human zoo. 'It was difficult to cope with their entourage,' wrote Zeffirelli in his autobiography, usefully entitled *Zeffirelli*. 'They had a court of about twelve people, ranging from lawyers to hairdressers, and this gossiping, opinionated set had to be mollified and won over ... I always knew when this tribe was coming my way; there was the tell-tale chink of gold bracelets and necklaces.' In 1973, this same crowd mustered at the Grand Hotel in Rome, before shifting to the Miramonti Hotel in Cortina d'Ampezzo, for Taylor to star in *Ash Wednesday*. The producer Dominick Dunne witnessed a slightly servile Burton stooping to clean up the dog mess. He also saw the thirty monogrammed steamer-trunks, Raymond Vignale, the major-domo, in a uniform of white mink, and Taylor getting herself attired as if 'for a ball at Buckingham Palace'. Taylor and Burton proceeded to descend the hotel's marble stairway in state, 'like the king and queen [they] were', and formally greeted their guests – not ambassadors or grand dukes but rather bathetically their own hairdressers, photographers, make-up people and the chauffeur. 'They had,' says Dunne, 'the largest entourage I had ever seen, and the people who worked for them worshipped them,' as they knew full well on which side their bread was buttered.

The train, in the Shakespearean sense of the word, which by 1969 was costing Taylor and Burton $800,000 a year, was ever-expanding, like the cosmos. 'We need so many people to help us and they need to be paid,' said Burton, who perhaps thought he was eligible for the Civil List or revenues from the Duchy of Cornwall. In alphabetical order, the lackeys were: Jim Benton, 'useful with mail', secretary and cocktail-maker – he gave Burton the swordstick Will broke and he was later in the Cedars of Lebanon Hospital with hepatitis; Ron Berkeley, the make-up man who with a plasterer's trowel was responsible for concealing Burton's deep pockmarks; André 'Bobo' Besançon, housekeeper and caretaker in Switzerland, where he hanged himself in the garage; Claudye Bozzacchi, hairdresser and manicurist; Gianni Bozzacchi, her husband, house photographer; Valerie Douglas, whom Burton called his 'manager' and Graham Jenkins said was 'Rich's personal secretary' (she'd be in charge of his funeral arrangements); Richard (Dick) Hanley, inherited from Mike Todd, and who packed the crocodile suitcases and died of Aids; Bobby La Salle, bodyguard, who when he knocked someone out cold claimed they'd 'fainted'; John Lee, another suitcase-packer and luggage captain; Caroline O'Connor, Taylor's nurse, who was 'forever pumping doses of drugs' into her patient; Chen Sam, Egyptian-Italian 'business-manager and spokesperson', educated in Rio de Janeiro, who had a working knowledge of pharmacology, obtained prescriptions, and was put in charge of Taylor's charitable endeavours and perfume promotions; Gaston Sanz, chauffeur; Gaston Sanz's wife Anne, another suitcase-packer, who was given the star's cast-offs, including the Dior dress worn at the *BUtterfield 8* Oscar ceremony and Tiziani and Karl Lagerfeld clobber, worn in *Boom!*; Raymond Vignale, above-mentioned, a 'creeps-giving middle-aged pouff' (according to Burton), the butler, who carried Taylor's jewels and pills; Brook Williams, drunken hanger-on; Bob Wilson and wife Sally, dresser and barman ... This circus was always on the move, from film to film, from London to Switzerland to Mexico, to God knows where else, Hungary, Yugoslavia. They'd fly from Paris to Geneva in a turbo-jet twenty-five-seater private plane, 'with thirty-two small bags'. Thence by helicopter to Gstaad. Lawyers and agents joined the peregrinations: Frings, Frosch and (Hugh) French. Kennamer, the medicine man, was often in attendance, e.g. when Taylor's piles burst: 'He came over within ten minutes ... mucked about and put a bandage around her arse.' I've never liked the sound of Rexford Kennamer. Nor did Eddie. When Eddie asked him why he, Kennamer, refused to tell Taylor to stop mixing alcohol and tablets, the doctor said, 'Because I don't want her to lose confidence in me.'

A cult of sycophancy is endemic in dissolute (and tyrannical) circles. Only flatterers are wanted. True friendships fade, and Taylor couldn't see how funny and bizarre she was being when she came out with things like, 'He's one of my friends. He's really my friend. I loved him,' when the President of Egypt, Anwar Sadat, was assassinated in Cairo in 1981. Letters were returned or burnt – admittedly there were up to seven thousand pieces of mail a week, also deliveries of voodoo dolls (there must have been quite a collection eventually) and messages from the Ku Klux Klan. Telephone messages were not passed on. Hugh French rejected scripts without Burton and Taylor's seeing them, e.g. *The Fixer* (Alan Bates and Georgia Brown), *Goodbye Mr Chips* (O'Toole and Petula Clark). Robert Hardy was banished from the presence ('In the end I sent a telegram and that wasn't answered'); grandees like Gielgud and Alec Guinness were ignored (Burton 'didn't seem to know half of what went on'). Douglas Wilmer's experience was typical: 'I tried once or twice to contact him, when he and Taylor were staying at The Dorchester, but he had adopted the Hollywood pattern and surrounded himself with an impenetrable wall of minions. My messages were never returned.'

Money and fame had always isolated Taylor, the MGM princess. 'I have known many child actors,' said Joseph Losey, 'and have seen how their lives, no matter how successful, are later ruined, like, for instance, the most extreme example, Elizabeth Taylor.' Interesting. What did he mean? Having directed Taylor and Burton in *Boom!*, Taylor in *Secret Ceremony*, and Burton in *The Assassination of Trotsky*, Losey placed Taylor amongst the damned, I think, because her every moment was improbable; she had a child's introspection; she was overtrained in the arts of seduction (in seemingly being pleasing) – the art of getting her own way, e.g. getting Michelin laureate Anton Mosimann out of bed at two a.m. to cook her a dinner of roast beef and mashed potatoes. There was a child's – more like a baby's – need for instant gratification of basic needs. Emotional travails were exaggerated. She was very insistent, direct, keen to make an entrance – as if coming down from the nursery to be adored. She was always late, never learned to tell the time, yet expected others to be punctual, on hand when required. Michael Powell, for example, turned up for dinner at The Georges V in Paris. 'We sat and waited for Liz Taylor,' he recalled. 'After Burton and his entourage had made twelve long-distance telephone calls, Liz came down with her hair piled on top of her head. It was midnight, more or less.' Her illnesses guaranteed plenty of pampering, placed her at the centre of concerned bustle. The ramifications of her having been a child actress were, in the main, that past and present selves were blended. 'I have the body of a woman, the emotions of a child,' she said in 1952. 'I stopped being a child the minute I started working in pictures,' she nevertheless said half a century later to Paul Theroux. Which was it? Zero childhood or perpetual childhood? What's clear is that between her childishness and her relation to the adult world there lay something unbridgeable. Like a fish lying low in the pond, Taylor was watchful, suspicious, never quite trustful. If thinking about her makes me uncomfortable, it's because she retained a child's terrible tenacity. 'She frightens me far more than Goneril or Regan,' as T.S. Eliot said of George Eliot's Rosamond Vincy – and like the haughty and manipulative beauty in *Middlemarch*, Taylor expected the world to be 'ordered to her liking,' and she was 'gracefully vicious' when it wasn't.

And the effect of this on Burton? His inflexibility met hers, with this great difference. In an absolute sense, Taylor had made acting and living the same thing. She was always on show, always photographed. She could only be herself as a star, wearing silver shoes. Burton, by contrast, was aware that as a public person he was behaving in a different manner – that there was, as Shakespeare would say (Sonnet 111), his 'public means, which public manner breeds'. A true (or truer) self, or private being, lay elsewhere, and was unreachable, though there are glimpses in his diaries. But the chief immediately obvious thing was he literally stopped venturing outside. He was left alone with himself. There is a strange little moment in the journals, when Burton says an offer has come through from Stan Stennett to play Baron Hardup in panto in Porthcawl. 'Impossible of course'. Of course. Why *of course*? Burton was, in 1971, remote from any conception of the strolling player, the end-of-the-pier tatterdemalion. Burton is not going to do anything unexpected – yet nor is he lacking in a sense of his own importance, which was to annoy Marian Seldes, who appeared with him at the Plymouth Theatre, New York, in *Equus*, in 1976. Burton seemed so regal, when he complained he couldn't afford to work on stage: 'He was getting $10,000 a week for this engagement. It seemed to me that much money could pay for anything. It irritated me because I have had this same conversation with successful and rich actors before. They all need more money.' Greed is part of the pattern, and with Taylor in his life Burton's was an enclosed existence – the star in Swiss chalets, private planes and yachts, opulent hotel suites. He was always in lovely places – Italy, Switzerland, Mexico – but his response was a sort of paralysis or defensiveness, which did nothing for his underlying uncertainty, his loss of identity, which is why he drank.

In 1977, Burton said to Paul Ferris that for the past two decades he'd 'very rarely gone out, except when commanded to, in a sense'. No gardens or open fields or public pavements or parks; only shielded rooms, artificial light, where he existed in a yellowish glow from cigarettes. What struck me, watching Tony Palmer's documentary, *In From the Cold?*, is how caged Burton and Taylor are – the atmosphere of claustrophobia, as they descend an aeroplane's steps to be instantly jostled by cameras and reporters; the crowds engulfing them, pushing them, as they try and move from a darkened limousine to a hotel lobby or tumble into the wood-panelled exclusivity of Chasen's and the Brown Derby; the sheer permanent intrusiveness and attention recorded in grainy newsreel footage. All the crowd scenes and mobs – Burton never looks happy; he can't accept the adulation, not fully. For all the graces and luxury, dinners, first nights, private railway carriages, his expression suggests he wishes he wasn't there. For a Welshman from humble origins, everything has turned into a *performance*, to use the word with a Tony Hancock sigh of exasperation. Taylor, meantime, is unperturbed by the elbowing fans and pressmen, who yell out things like 'Kiss me, Dick!' or 'Liz is a bad girl!' She has the movie star's strength of character, and understood (in ways Burton did not) that publicity was intrinsic to their careers – that a star was a creature of the brash mass media, the television and newspapers, which documented every tantrum, journey, meal and, yes, kiss.

They were always crushed and squashed – and if Taylor was metaphorically speaking malformed as an infant by the studios ('I always swore I wouldn't end up like Judy,' she declared often enough – and she was conscious of that much at least), Burton, likewise, was trapped by his upbringing (all those siblings and relatives), and then he was hemmed in by his fame, and his guilt. Burton and Taylor were walled in, the pair of them, insulated, by their reputation and glory, and, safe in their landscaped, pricey enclosures, of blue pools and palm trees, it was here, if anywhere, where they were free to become wild things, furred and feathered, with clothes and fashions flown from Paris or London; here they lived with insolent abandon – as when Burton popped up from behind a mound of caviar, saying to the dozens of servants, 'The rest of you can go now. I'm going to fuck my wife.'

* * *

Of course, she wasn't his wife for ages, not until 15 March 1964, when the ceremony took place in a hotel, the Ritz-Carlton, in Montreal. If the planets had collided with *Cleopatra*, that gave the public two full years to think about morality, respectability, publicity, celebrity, in a new way. 'You'd think we were out to destroy Western Civilisation or something,' said Burton with a sort of pride. (I have also seen the quotation attributed to Taylor.) Other cultural shifts were occurring: The Beatles' first LP, the end of the *Lady Chatterley* ban, the suicide of Sylvia Plath, a lot of it 'too late' for, say, Philip Larkin (b. 1922), but manifestly not for Burton (b. 1925) or Taylor (b. 1932), who took sexual intercourse in their stride; whose turbulence and radicalism – that's to say: their aptitude for not doing the sensible thing – and whose illicit affair helped liberate the Sixties, precipitated the sexual revolution of the Sixties. There is a sense with Burton and Taylor that they are breaking out, breaking away – girls having boyfriends, enjoying sex, without ties and threats of babies and domestic drudgery. This was brave, tough. It went beyond the practical and the sound – and Taylor and Burton suggested anybody's life could now be like that. As Henry Miller observed, 'They were never afraid to act out their true feelings,' and this element of non-stop performance is the key. Everything was theatre. They never belonged to themselves alone, were always in public – social events, the social jungle.

Hence, the first post-*Cleopatra* venture, *The V.I.P.s*, directed by Anthony 'Puffin' Asquith. Contracts were signed in November 1962 and it was made during the icy Christmas and New Year period and released on 7 August 1963. The screenplay by Terence Rattigan, it is set in an airport and an airport hotel, and is all about arrivals, departures, separations, reunions. Burton's character, billionaire Paul Andros, an oil tycoon or plutocrat, and Taylor's character, mink-clad, Givenchy-attired Frances Andros, move from hot places to frozen places, fly between Bermuda and London and Switzerland, searching, as it were, as dissatisfied rich people often do, for the blue bird of happiness, and despite the subdued eroticism – symbolised somehow in the immaculate table-settings and crystalware in the flashback, briefly glimpsed – there's a very definite sense that on everyone's mind is the knowledge romance cannot last, and will be replaced soon enough by a great hole of emptiness and suffering. Paul prefers to be away on business trips, a sphere where only power, ruthlessness and success need be recognised, not warmth, not conciliation. He gets his butler (Dennis Price) to select and wrap the expensive gifts he brings back, e.g. diamond bracelets. Frances sees through the generosity: she'd prefer 'the odd toy duck from Woolworth's if it was chosen by you,' she laments. Meantime, Frances/Taylor is having an affair with Louis Jourdan, plans to elope with him – she says she appreciates (it is a novelty) his 'helplessness', but Louis Jourdan is soon revealed as rather spineless, nervous of Paul/Burton, who is like Mike Todd reappearing from beyond the grave to reclaim Taylor's affections. Jourdan does a lot of sneaking and hiding behind pillars. But Jourdan has one good line. Paul turns up at the (fog-bound) airport armed, as Eddie did in Rome. 'Killing me won't get your wife back,' Jourdan says, when threatened.

Where have we heard all this before? Gone through all this before? Burton gives a coiled, dejected performance as the disappointed (cuckolded) husband – and the triangular relationships here follow the plot essentials of Rattigan's *The Deep Blue Sea*, with Taylor as Hester, Burton as the equivalent of the about-to-be-walked-out-on High Court judge, fighting to keep his dignity, and Louis Jourdan as the useless, feckless, boulevardier, never convincing as a future husband. It is also a return to *Cleopatra*, and the palaver surrounding *Cleopatra*, and Taylor and Burton are giving performances that belong in *Cleopatra*; and Rattigan will have been entirely aware of this when, in *The V.I.P.s*, Taylor, or Frances, makes threats of suicide, yields to illness and collapse and hysteria, has consultations with lawyers and doctors. Wounded vanity is on display. Also explored is the way an apparent victim (Taylor's character, but Burton's too) retains every advantage. The jealousies and plots, the disgust and outrage – the *scenes* – come straight from Cinecittà, from Villa Pappa and Chalet Ariel. Everything is a re-enactment. Puffin Asquith's cinematographer, incidentally, Jack Hildyard, was Mamoulian's cinematographer, on the aborted Pinewood *Cleopatra* shoot. This only adds to the three- or four-way mirror effect, the kaleidoscopic way

Taylor and Burton's life, their daily living, was as dramatic – indeed as melodramatic – as their art, i.e. these stories, successively modified, in each of their films, about the predicaments of love and desire; about how the hunger for love and sex is not the same as the need for affection and company. They had an instinct for spectacle – for what would steal the show, gripping onlookers, tabloid readers, gawpers generally. And like his forensic barrister in *The Winslow Boy*, who sees through special pleading and surface chat to penetrate how people and things have come to be as they are, Rattigan, taking Taylor and Burton, saw their personal furies, their ruthlessness, and in *The V.I.P.s*, another film with a bad reputation, which no one has watched for decades, the playwright involves them in a plot about choices, consequences.

They don't completely have the screen to themselves, however. Taylor and Burton's romantic dilemma is muffled not only by the bad weather wrapped around Heathrow, but by the other players and their miscellaneous problems, which seem to be mainly financial: Orson Welles' movie mogul needing to flee his tax liabilities; Margaret Rutherford needing cash to save her stately home; Rod Taylor needing funds to bridge a bank loan. The director explained: 'It's my first portmanteau film and it's difficult to do – just as you're getting interested in one story, you're whisked off into another ... I hope the various moods won't clash.' But there's only one mood, which is operetta-ish. We have the fog everywhere, and we have Miklós Rózsa's omnipresent orchestral score – wonderfully full-volume and bittersweet surging cellos and violas, pulsing with Viennese rhythms, turning *The V.I.P.s* into an edifice of whipped cream. Burton and Taylor are further encompassed by Equity's roster of comic character actors: 'There's today's VIP List,' says Richard Wattis to Ronald Fraser. The check-in desk, or what in those days was the Departure Counter, is manned by Lance Percival. Up in the Control Tower, fretting about the grounded planes, is Michael Hordern. His assistant is Frank Williams, the vicar from *Dad's Army*, last seen in

Lincoln Green shooting arrows in *Ivanhoe*. David Frost is the airport pressman. Richard Briers is the weather-forecaster, Reginald Beckwith is the room-service waiter, Terence Alexander a captain, and Peter Sallis is a doctor on call. In a big emotional scene with Burton in the hotel, Taylor smacks her palm against a wall-mirror, shattering the glass, drawing blood. 'At least you now have physical proof of my feelings for you,' she says to Burton, who is prompted towards tenderness. Where are we now? Back in Porto San Stefano?

'It's quite superficial,' says Sallis, dabbing the wound. 'Extraordinary accident. With some of my patients I'd have suspected [slight pause] a little intake.' Sallis was always to be knowing and sardonic – chiefly as Norman Clegg in *Last of the Summer Wine* for thirty-seven years – and Maggie Smith, quick and demure, as Rod Taylor's secretary, Miss Mead, is recognisably Maggie Smith, with her jumpy glances and tearful voice, rising up the scale towards hysteria. There's a splendid (if preposterous) scene, where Maggie, flapping her wrists, simultaneously shy and bold, persuades Burton to write a cheque, to cover Rod Taylor's tractor investment. She's the Personal Assistant with a crush on her boss, and Burton's character is touched by this – it is beautifully handled, beautifully choreographed. As is the whole entertainment. Welles and Margaret Rutherford do a slow dance around each other, like Falstaff and Mistress Quickly. As the Duchess of Brighton, Rutherford is a great clown, rummaging in her tartan suitcase, dropping her gloves, losing her travel documents, pushing her crumpled hat back on her head. She's up in the bar with a brandy, she totters about in red shoes, her hatbox falls off the luggage rack four or five times. When Rutherford is on the screen, the Vienna Woods symphonic score is replaced by a jaunty woodwind madrigal, as if the actress has wafted in from Shakespeare's magical places where oxlips and nodding violets grow, sweet musk-roses and eglantine. Stringer Davis, contractually in every film she was in, as they were a married couple, is the night porter, to whom the Duchess describes her beloved crumbling castle: 'They have a better show of daffodils there than anywhere else in the county, so they say.' There's a depth of feeling here, beyond what the line suggests – not spring profusion but wintery loss. Dame Margaret Rutherford won the Oscar for Best Supporting Actress, beating Diane Cilento, Edith Evans and Joyce Redman, who were all in *Tom Jones*. Her statuette was accepted by Peter Ustinov. At the ceremony, held on 13 April 1964, in the Santa Monica Civic Auditorium, Rex Harrison, nominated for his Julius Caesar, lost to Sidney Poitier, but *Cleopatra* won Academy Awards for Art Direction, Cinematography, Costume Design and Special Effects.

The *V.I.P.s* has majesty. The music, the Panavision format, the splendour of the Sixties architecture – the modernist air terminal, impressively recreated at Elstree, with its wide teak staircases, big picture windows, ceramic murals. The cast is perfectly assimilated to the luxury of the First-Class Lounge, the Blériot Suite. The film is about glamour – the glamour of big stars on the big screen; cigars, cocktails, top hats, champagne in a silver bucket. In the twenty-first century, this has all gone, replaced by a multiplex smallness, no-frills flights, a popcorn stink. Air travel is classy no longer. When Burton and Taylor arrive, as here, by helicopter, they are like gods descending to earth. Burton's Andros wears a well-cut Pierre Cardin suit, a cashmere coat, a red scarf. Burton's voice retained more Welshness at this period – and we believe in his crisis of conscience, his love, his need; especially as Taylor, in this film, is not blowsy but subdued, crushed, almost, when she says: 'I wanted to be treated like a wife, not an expensive mistress . . . I don't belong to anyone . . . I'm a person not a possession.' Soap operetta dialogue, to be sure. In the film, Burton's character threatens to kill himself, so Taylor runs back to him, awkwardly leaving Louis Jourdan in the lurch. It's not a very solid foundation for reconciliation – and will Welles' promise to pay Margaret Rutherford for the use of her stately home as a film location be kept? Will Maggie Smith and Rod Taylor be happy raising tractors? What I do know is after *The V.I.P.s*, Taylor did nothing professionally except bask, lying on the beach or a sofa, very much as Burton's possession, until they made *The Sandpiper*, in the August of 1964. One lingering postscript – when Dennis Price died, in alcoholic obscurity in the Channel Islands, in October 1973, a huge floral tribute arrived at the church, Ste Marie du Castel, Guernsey, upstaging the funeral. It was from Taylor and Burton. 'The wreath was very large and caused concern among the family, who did not know what to do with it,' according to Price's biographer.

* * *

With *The V.I.P.s*, the final scene to be shot is the one opening the film – the silent sequence on the yacht anchored at evening off Villefranche-sur-Mer. Taylor, in an ermine-trimmed white dress ('Givenchy designed it for me'), her hair piled up elaborately, and wearing gigantic emeralds and diamonds worth $340,000, arrived on the set hours late, followed, wrote Francis Wyndham in *Queen Magazine*, 'by a little entourage of secretaries, attendants, friends,' and by Burton, who kept up a running commentary – nonsense about dogs ('that little puppy could be a killer'), Hollywood profligacy ('do you know, they bought me out of *Camelot*') and how wigs are made ('Somewhere there's a bald nun going about'); and as Puffin wanted Taylor to look reflective and sad in a close-up, Burton recited lines from Hopkins' 'The Leaden Echo and the Golden Echo': 'How to keep back beauty, keep it, beauty, beauty, beauty, from vanishing away? ... So be beginning to despair ... despair, despair, despair, despair.' That must have cheered everyone up – and at Taylor's request Hopkins' elegy was recited, by Colin Farrell, at her funeral, on 24 March 2011. When Wyndham asked, 'Have you any plans for another film after this?' Taylor's reply was dismissive, but telling: 'I'm never, never, never going to make any more plans ever for the rest of my life ... At present I just feel one great big *nothing*.' It's how she was, when turmoil was in abeyance. Taylor's dressing room, nevertheless, seemed full of simmering danger – big drinks and ringing telephones, bright magazines with Taylor's face smeared on the cover, a terrier bitch chewing at her necklaces ('she loves to teethe on diamonds'), snapping Sealyhams and hissing Siamese cats. This is a witch's lair, and like supernatural figures who have to get a move on when the glow-worm shows the morning to be near and begins to pale its ineffectual fire, the stars had to scurry promptly back to Switzerland, their ninety-day tax allowance in the United Kingdom being exhausted.

Burton had *Becket* to prepare. 'Can you imagine me as a saint?' he said to his brother Graham. 'The critics will die laughing.' Nowhere was there much laughter. This must have been a wretched period. By Graham's account, Burton was drinking heavily, with Bloody Marys for breakfast, vodka and tonics during the remainder of the day. There were 'terrifying bouts of depression and ill temper when he became a stranger to us all,' especially when *Becket* began shooting at Pinewood, when Burton was always on the booze with O'Toole. To Kenneth Tynan he said, using the conditional tense and making everything seem hypothetical, 'I couldn't be unfaithful to my wife [i.e. Sybil] without feeling a profound sense of guilt' – and Mankiewicz, watching events continue to unfold, commented, 'Richard ... tears himself to pieces, maddened with guilt ... He has given up everything that truly matters to him,' meaning Sybil and their daughters and what they represented of family history. Again, the only testimony about Sybil comes from Tynan's wife, Elaine: 'What defeated her was to be dependent on [Burton's] love, on his being finally there, whatever had gone on in the dark and in the distance, [to be dependent] on the fact that he would finally come back to her, and then he didn't.' The hotel suites, the expensive landscapes, with everything happening in a blaze of sunshine, only made Burton see that his real self – the spectre of Richard Walter Jenkins – was left somewhere in the grey sedge of the valleys; and this was why at moments of triumph he was depressed, brooding – why he couldn't respond. There was interior stagnation. *Becket* is about this bind.

It is stagey – aware of itself as a literary work – but I can see why actors want to play both roles, the archbishop and the king, or alternate the roles, as each is mad and selfish, after their own fashion; each switch from sulks to riot. And what I feel with Burton here is that his performance doesn't lie outside his own life. Thomas Becket's blemishes, his disenchantments, are the actor's, which in the film (and Anouilh's play) are built up as cosmic blemishes and disenchantments. Like Taylor, Burton had been galvanised by elopement, romance, passion; neither was good at ordinary normal life. They needed an atmosphere of explosions and confusion – of (metaphorically) non-stop military coups. So what kind of plane did Burton expect his relationship (and marriage) with Taylor to be on? How would it be made endurable? Because if he lived – if he was sequestered – in all those posh hotels, on jets and aboard yachts, in Riviera villas in the sunshine, in chalets in the snow, and was never anywhere for long, then the meaning, the answer, is to be found in the way his (and Taylor's) energy was deployed – dissipated – in mess and muddle, in the bedlam of fame and money and bad films. Burton and Taylor, I think, wished to be in some realm or sphere where they could be disengaged, where they could ask, or wonder, what their feelings were evidence of. (Are there, indeed, meanings in the world, which can be put into waking thoughts?) Perhaps the most alarming outcome is that, as for Becket and for Faustus, there is no longer a belief in good and evil. Truth and virtue are revealed as only comforting illusions – proof, were it required, morality doesn't exist. Abandoning Sybil and the children – they were exposed as fragile attachments, reduced to feelings of protectiveness and pity merely. And if one sort of history was lost, could a new one not be remade?

Taylor may not have been working on any feature film, but she did her best to play at and seem Welsh, eclipsing Sybil in everybody's mind. She hung around the *Becket* set, telling everyone, 'I really love Richard, even in his Welsh darkness.' The pair of them visited Pontrhydyfen inconspicuously in a Rolls. Taylor realised this journey was a test, and that their love for each other could at this moment have 'disintegrated and turned into anything from disgust to shame'. They went to Aberavon to see Elfed and Cis. There was a tour around picturesque Taibach and Port Talbot. They stayed overnight with Hilda – the lavvy was a tidy step, so Taylor was handed a personal pisspot. They went to see Detective David Jenkins in Gowerton, who said: 'We found her quite charming . . . anxious to be accepted by us all. We still felt for Sybil, but everybody . . . was prepared to move on.' Well, who wouldn't be? This was *Elizabeth Taylor*. It was like a Royal Progress. 'The gasp of wonder could be heard the length of the valley,' said Graham Jenkins. To further win over the locals, Taylor knocked back pints at The Miners' Arms and sportingly permitted the Pontrhydyfen citizenry to slap her flank and examine her teeth, as if she were prize bloodstock. She went to Cardiff for the rugby, where there were bigger crowds outside the Queen's Vaults than inside the Arms Park. Everything seemed to have gone swimmingly, though I don't know whether it was now or later, or how much later, Cis was heard to remark, 'We all rue the day when he met Elizabeth.'

* * *

It is difficult to put spiritual struggle on the screen. Burton attempted to do so more than most – howling at battlements or in empty forests about Satan and burning in hell. He was not like James Dean, George C. Scott, Brando, or any contemporary person, exerting themselves to be real – rather, he had a 'huge, outsize quality, rather like Russian actors,' said Anthony Page, who directed Burton in *Absolution*, where he is a Jesuit schoolmaster, who at one moment recites Hopkins' 'The Leaden Echo and the Golden Echo' to his class. 'There's nothing too small or mean about Richard's acting,' Page continued. 'He has that marvellous, dry, cutting edge.' One of the reasons why his films are bad (though I don't think so), or have received a bad press, is that Burton is often simply too passionate – or too simple and too passionate – for the specific story or genre, action capers or sci-fi pieces, which are slight, negligible. His primary power, his physical being, is out of scale – so there is a lack of connection, though this is not the case when he is with Taylor, where her sexual histrionics match his theatrical gusto. What I have noticed, though, is that in Burton's films with Taylor, and in the films he made on his own, but where Taylor (and her strong personality) was still in the background, he starts to recede – he loses the ebullience, his complete confidence in himself, as displayed in *The Robe* or *Alexander the Great* (typical macho line of dialogue: 'There's not world enough, and not time enough, for these men to escape my vengeance'), even *Look Back in Anger*. What this means is we have, instead, Le Carré's Alec Leamas, the Broadway Hamlet, George in *Who's Afraid of Virginia Woolf?*, a perspiring Petruchio, Graham Greene's Brown, in *The Comedians*, and so on. Burton, the embodiment of proud Shakespearean kings, paradoxically grew up, matured as an actor, when he started playing broken men. None more so than in Tennessee Williams' *The Night of the Iguana*, where he gives us another of his priests who've gone to the devil, first seen chasing his congregation out into the rain, fulminating and having a nervous breakdown. 'My life has cracked up on me,' he says (like Dysart in *Equus*) – and he's next found in reduced circumstances, working as a tour guide, conducting complaining old Baptist ladies around Mexico in a charabanc. John Huston's picture is in black-and-white, yet we feel we see the green leaves and red parrots. We certainly register the tropical heat, the mist, the mould.

As with *Cat on a Hot Tin Roof* and *Suddenly, Last Summer*, the former set on a plantation and the latter in a gothic greenhouse – and where Taylor's sexuality in both instances was unpeeled – Williams' worlds are never natural. They are wildernesses filled with symbolism. Mexico, likewise, an uncomfortable place of dysentery and sweat, in *The Night of the Iguana* has a pulpy, mystical mood – the jungle, the moonlight, the thunder and lightning flashing on the sea.

Like the airless New Orleans Blanche DuBois finds herself in, it is a milieu where characters come to cope with their pain. The iguanas, these great silent scaly lizards, like dragons, which are trapped by the locals and prepared for the pot, have much emblematic work to do. Noble and doomed, they have survived from primeval times to be (literally) easy meat – and Burton's character, the Reverend Shannon, gazing at the streams and rivulets and the jolly natives, at the boys selling writhing iguanas at the roadside, tells his busload of old biddies in their straw hats that what's on show here is 'a fleeting glimpse into the lost world of innocence'. If we have Eden, there has to be the snake – is this Shannon? Are the women characters variations of Eve? The marketing for the film was deliberately erotic: 'One man – three women – one night', stated the trailer and the poster, with the stress on bondage and beach orgies. If Shannon is having a rubbish time with the grotesque Baptists ('Don't make me take steps,' one of them threatens), at least another of them has brought along an impossibly blonde granddaughter, Sue Lyon, Kubrick's Lolita. She flirts with Burton's character, swims next to him, infiltrates his hotel room. Later, she dances with the receptive beach boys. ('I'm sure you know she's underage,' everyone is warned.) The secluded hotel itself – like the house in *Boom!* it is on a terrace high above the sea – is run by Ava Gardner, who plays the role of blowsy widow Maxine as if she's Elizabeth Taylor, i.e. as a slapdash strumpet. Maxine, despite being merrily fucked by the beach boys in the surf every night, has, we learn, been rather ruined and disappointed by love and by life. Somehow, she seems already to know the Rev. Shannon, from a former association. Finally, there's Deborah Kerr, a watercolourist, always smiling sweetly. Was there ever another actress with such manners? She's righteous, but not self-righteous. Having seen her just lately in *Bonjour Tristesse*, *Black Narcissus*, *Separate Tables* and *An Affair to Remember*, and now *The Night of the Iguana* – yes, of course I can see Kerr is ladylike and can convey (embody) chastity in ways that weren't priggish or self-satisfied; but she does also have a warm

369

quality, a sympathetic understanding, which you'd never get or sense in, say, Katharine Hepburn, who was brittle and egotistical or (when called upon to be benevolent) superior; nor was she ever mad, like a lot of movie queens; there was nothing coarse or deranged, or frayed. When, impeccably attired in a bonnet and linen veil, Kerr, as Hannah Jelkes, goes down the hill at the end of *The Night of the Iguana*, you don't feel sorry for her. 'Some people take a drink, others take a pill. I just take a few deep breaths,' is Hannah's parting shot – perhaps Joyce Grenfell is Kerr's closest parallel. Deborah Kerr had great strength – and if Burton's character responds to her character, it's because Kerr's splendour is a demure version of Taylor's, in the same way Ava's is a parody version, and Sue Lyon's Charlotte could be Velvet Brown fondling a fetlock.

When Burton's agonised vicar goes on about ruling his own per-turbed spirit, defending himself against Satan, what he means is he has to curb, rein in, sexual potency. Whilst there is a luridness to the material, there is also comedy – all these women fearing and desiring Burton; all these criss-crossing vibrations and agitations. Burton, beset, plays a man for whom most pleasurable things are forbidden, which adds to the eroticism. He alters from shot to shot: plump, lean, perspiring, bearded, clean-shaven, dishevelled, groomed, like Mil-ton's Devil in *Paradise Lost*, experimenting with appearances. Aware of sin, of sexual frustration and temptation, Shannon is aware, acutely, of the danger of youth, loveliness, wholesomeness – these are unstable conditions, and a person can all too swiftly find themselves 'crossing the border of sanity'. Burton plays his role as a man who knows he's attractive, and is faintly amused by the attention – but he does go mad. Shannon walks barefoot on glass. He drinks ('I'm a bad drunk') and wants to embark on the 'long swim to China', i.e. drown himself. For his own safety, he is trussed up like an iguana, tethered in a hammock. Deborah Kerr, like somebody's cousin Rachel, brews him poppy-seed tea. 'What's this, Mr Shannon?' she asks with brisk concern, like a nurse at the Front. 'Hell and damnation,' he replies, which for Burton were familiar places. Puerto Vallarta, the location, three hundred miles north of Acapulco, was soon another familiar place. Burton and Taylor, and John Huston, invested in property thereabouts. The sets for *The Night of the Iguana*, in Mismaloya, overlooking the brilliantly blue Bahía de Banderas, remain there to this day, inaccessible on an overgrown hillside.

* * *

Taylor is all over the film, though not appearing in it. She was every-where on the set, too, and tried to run Ava Gardner over with the drinks trolley. Luckily, she was mostly distracted by dysentery, insects and poisonous lizards. Taylor's feet were bitten by tropical fleas or sandflies called chigoes, which burrowed under the cutane-ous and subcutaneous dermal layer, fed on her blood and laid their eggs, causing ulcers to form. Taylor's arrival in Mexico, neverthe-less, was no less eye-catching than Cleopatra's into Rome. She brought seventy-four suitcases, filled with hot-weather clothing, including her forty new bikinis, bought in Paris. Calling themselves 'Mr and Mrs Heyman', Burton and Taylor had flown from Montreal by way of Toronto to Mexico City (where there was a crush at the airport), and thence by private plane four hundred miles to Puerto Vallarta, on 22 September 1963. Shooting commenced a week later, wrapping on 30 November. Then, everybody got divorced.

Sybil was granted a divorce in the Supreme Court of Jalisco, at Guadalajara, on 5 December, on grounds of Burton's 'abandonment and cruel and inhumane treatment'. On 14 January 1964, Taylor served an 'abandonment petition' on Eddie, blaming him for walking out on her in 1962. Judge Arcadio Estrada, in Puerto Vallarta, gave him twenty-one days to respond. Eddie didn't do so – 'I am not going to be part of the slanging match,' he said. The judge therefore ruled that as Eddie hadn't contested Taylor's petition, he, Eddie, had 'pre-sumably confessed to Elizabeth Taylor's charge that he had abandoned her', and the divorce was granted on 8 March, though other biographers say 5 March, and others again 6 March. Eddie wanted (and won) $750,000 tax free and $250,000 a year for ten years. 'Eddie's demands are in the realm of the fantastic,' said Burton, 'and quite intolerable.' Which prompted Eddie to say, absolutely justifiably, 'I hardly think Mr Burton is one to lecture on morals, integrity and honesty, to me or anyone else.' Eddie had been cleaned out by Debbie Reynolds, who'd received, in her divorce settlement, in 1959, a house, cars, $40,000 annually in alimony and child support, and a $100,000 insurance policy on Eddie's life. Plus, she kept all her own property, including a home in Palm Springs, where she put some of her money to good use constructing a tunnel and canopy for her pets so they could be protected from the elements when let into the garden to defecate. Taylor, in her turn, worth $10 million in her own right in the early Sixties, kept the Gstaad chalet, the Rolls she'd given Eddie as a present, and all the jewellery. Though she filed for divorce in Puerto Vallarta, the lawyers she retained, Phillips Nizer Benjamin Krim & Ballon LLP, were a shit-hot New York firm, who also had offices in Geneva. They were instructed not to be generous – and Taylor, indignant Eddie received a single penny cent, refused to pay any legal costs. When, years and years later, and Taylor was married to John Warner, she'd throw people out on the street if they so much as whispered Eddie's name: 'Get out! Get out of here! Leave my house this instant! I will not have that name mentioned in my presence. I will not tolerate it!' Burton always called Eddie 'deplorable, absolutely deplorable,' and Taylor would mumble, 'that schmuck, that fucking schmuck.' Litigation lasted until 1967, as Eddie wanted a share of Taylor's Swiss corporation, MCL Films, which owned thirty-five per cent of *Cleopatra* – Taylor had by then made $7 million from *Cleopatra*: her salary plus ten per cent of the gross. Whatever the outcome was, the poor schmuck went bankrupt in 1970, with debts of $916,000. Sybil, meantime, was benefitting from what Burton called 'my Welsh Presbyterian puritanical background', in other words his capacity for exultant guilt, and he bought her a large apartment in The Eldorado, an Art Deco co-operative, at 300 Central Park West and West Ninetieth Street, in Manhattan. He gave her half a million dollars in cash for three years, and there were trust funds for the daughters. The settlement package was worth at least $2.3 million, which in today's figures would be $20,618,071.90.

The joke is, were any of these Mexican divorces valid? Sybil should have been present in person, in the Guadalajara courtroom, yet wasn't. And was the marriage to Mike Todd in Acapulco valid, after the Wilding divorce? 'No one was ever married to anyone really,' Burton quipped – Ponti's Mexican divorce was not recognised in Italy, for example, and his marriage to Sophia Loren resulted in a bigamy charge. Everything had to be done from scratch in France. As for Taylor and Eddie, the President of the Academia Mexicana de Estudios Jurídicos, or Mexican Academy of Legal Studies, asserted that Arcadio Estrada, who was not a judge but only a Notary Public (since 1949) in Acapulco, and who was not Arcadio Estrada but Julio Garcia Estrada, 'usurped jurisdiction', and the Puerto Vallarta divorce was 'null and void', which meant perhaps Taylor for the remainder of her days was still Mrs Nicky Hilton? Nicky, by the way, was by now a certified lunatic, running around brandishing a loaded gun, pursued by male nurses and psychiatrists, who were on permanent call. 'He was gone almost to the point of no return,' said Kennamer, who had had him sectioned in the Menninger Psychiatric Hospital, Houston.

Adding to the farcical circumstances, who should be in Puerto Vallarta but Michael Wilding, now employed in a minor, ceremonial, capacity by Hugh French. It was Wilding's task to sort out his ex-wife and Burton's accommodation, and he found Casa Kimberly for them, on Calle Zaragoza, a mile from the beach. He put up mosquito nets around the windows and beds. He obtained cans of insect spray. He placed bouquets of flowers around the property to greet Taylor and Burton on arrival and had a tray of Dry Martinis at the ready.

'Dear, dear Michael,' said Taylor, 'only you would think to do all this!' Casa Kimberly is another of those dwellings that shrinks or expands depending on the source – ten bedrooms, eleven bathrooms, three kitchens; four storeys and a pool measuring forty-seven foot by seventeen foot; seven bedrooms, a forty-foot-long white-tiled living room and open courtyard; six bedrooms and six bathrooms. There was a tropical garden of coconut palms, banana and papaya trees. The house, which rambled across both sides of the street, connected by a pink stucco arched bridge, appealed to Burton so much he purchased it for $40,000. His description in the diaries is like a touristic Kodak Ektachrome: 'I started to dream of Puerto Vallarta and the bedroom patio and sunbathing . . . and walks through the cobbled town at dusk and boating to deserted beaches . . . church bells . . . steel bands, donkeys braying, cocks crowing . . . Serenaders staggering on marijuana coming to do homage to Elizabeth at four in the morning . . . and perhaps the iguanas have come back to live on the roof. You never know.' Taylor inevitably grabbed the place in their divorce, but couldn't bear to visit after Burton's death. Casa Kimberly was abandoned and sold in 1990, complete with the contents – Taylor's clothes, magazines, paperbacks. It was run as a bed-and-breakfast for ten years, and by the time I found out about it, it was half-demolished, gutted, a crumbling concrete block, mostly scorched rubble and piles of masonry, surrounded by barbed wire. It was almost palpable, the feeling that romantic dreams ended up like this – the gorgeous ceramic tiles chipped away in the stagnant heat, the whitewashed walls 'trailing in bougainvillea' (as a visitor said in 1970) derelict. 'We'll never leave this place. We love it too much,' said Taylor in the Sixties, adding slightly ominously, 'Besides, there's nowhere else to go.' She and Burton filled it with orchids and ran around with no clothes on, a sight definitely worth missing. I looked Casa Kimberly up on the web in 2021, and it is now a 'restored' boutique hotel.

* * *

Burton and Taylor made big claims for each other. 'He is the ocean. He is the sunset. He is such a vast person,' she said of him. 'She's the most astonishingly self-contained, pulchritudinous, remote, removed, inaccessible woman I had ever seen,' he said of her, and sounding like Meredith Jones, too. 'She looks at you with those eyes and your blood churns, I tell you.' No doubt. Soon enough, however, unremitting proximity led to put-downs, sarcasm, blows: 'Fuck you,' 'Go fuck yourself,' and similar imprecations. 'Piss off out of my sight,' etc. Taylor called Burton 'a boozed-up, burned-out Welshman!' When she was particularly annoyed with him this was truncated to, 'Oh, you . . . *Welshman!*' Service was returned in kind, with Burton saying of Taylor, 'She has the shape of a Welsh village girl. Her legs are really quite stumpy.' Chivalrous to the end, Taylor was also 'Miss Tits', 'that fat little tart', a 'French tart', 'that fat Jewish wife of mine', 'Shumdit', 'Snapshot', 'Booby' and 'Buon Appetito', which he misspells 'Bon Apetito.' It's true she enjoyed good grub. John Warner called her 'Chicken Fat' and 'My Little Heifer'. But Burton's criticisms went beyond weight and appearance – he liked to mock Taylor's lack of formal education: 'Oh yes, I forgot. You don't know any Shakespeare, do you? Not one bloody word that doesn't come out of the dictionary of clichés.' Her reply was very cool: 'I don't know anything about the theatre, but then I don't need to. I'm a star.' I think she won that round. In the ways they needled each other, it's as if by some quirks of fate and psychic energy, *Who's Afraid of Virginia Woolf?* was forming itself for them in the future. Burton was to be found in the bars of Puerto Vallarta, reciting Dylan Thomas. 'I have to get out of the clutter of my house,' he explained. Back at Casa Kimberly, the anecdotes and poetry lectures becoming repetitious, the drinking and the rudeness becoming more coarse, Taylor was heard to murmur, 'Does the man ever shut up?' Another Welsh trait: garrulity.

Words, words, words, of course, are Hamlet's province. By 26 February 1964, Burton was on stage in Toronto speaking them. He and Taylor flew first to California to see Taylor's parents – there was what the *Los Angeles Times* called 'an event of nearly riotous character' at the airport, with fifty pressmen and innumerable autograph hunters and a few detractors forming their usual baying crowd. One placard read: 'Drink not the wine of adultery!' – a neat conflation. Some sources have Taylor and Burton staying in the Presidential Suite at the Beverly Wilshire Hotel; others say Bungalow 5, the Beverly Hills Hotel. On 28 January, they proceeded to Canada, whether by train, the Super Chief from Chicago, under the names 'Walter Rule' and 'Rosamond Sutherland', who sound like characters in Scott's *Waverley*, or whether directly by plane from Los Angeles, with the laughable amount of luggage, guarded by Jim Benton, going separately – frankly, we'll never know. Burton was to be paid $10,000 a week to play Hamlet, plus fifteen per cent of the ticket sales. That much I do know. Rehearsals and previews at the O'Keefe Centre were followed, on 22 March, by rehearsals and previews in Boston, before the Lunt-Fontanne Theatre, on Broadway, was reached on 9 April – Shakespeare's quatercentenary. Burton's eighteen-week run, one hundred and thirty-six consecutive performances, was seen by 204,000 people and took $1,718,862 at the box office. 'You're the Frank Sinatra of Shakespeare,' Burton was told. Eddie was once dubbed 'the Jewish Sinatra'. What does that make me? 'The Frank Sinatra of biography'?

Burton had played the role often enough – at the Assembly Hall, Edinburgh, in September 1953, when Kenneth Williams for some undisclosed reason didn't get to be Osric; at The Old Vic in 1954; and then there were ten performances at Kronborg Castle, in Denmark. His Hamlet, in those days, was spry, cocky, princely. He had a forthrightness. There Burton was, an Elizabethan avenger, when everything was in store for him. As a man and as an actor he possessed a gravity, or what in *Measure for Measure* is called 'a more strict restraint'. He was scornful of the absurdities of desire or love or human warmth – he believed this gave him integrity. ('I find it very difficult to allow my whole life to rest on the existence of another creature,' he'd said – the boy who had no mother.) Emotions had no place. Sybil,

for example, had not roused him – his feelings towards her were faintly patronising: 'I felt very protective towards her. She was very giggly and bright and sweet and innocent and selfless,' like Ophelia. Burton had contempt for imperfections and compromise. It was important to him to maintain his separateness. ('I demand absolute loyalty. I demand obedience. I must have my own way.' Crikey.) What he lacked or had eradicated was any danger of entanglement – and then Taylor turned up. She brought disorder into his life. She thought the challenge of physical fights, tantrums, roaring panic, was what love meant, what having a relationship meant. 'When a woman like Elizabeth loves you,' Burton said with what must have been if not bitterness, then an awareness of incapacitation, 'she is not happy until she owns your soul.'

So, the Hamlet he became in 1964 was going to be markedly different from his earlier personification – because by now, aged nearly thirty-nine, he has been matched with a she-devil; he's been swallowed up by life's complexities and contradictions, which are not to be resolved. The play can accommodate all this, of course. *Hamlet,* beyond the courtly pageants and duels, has an ominous, desaturated atmosphere, and its prevailing theme is uncertainty: wars, invasions, espionage, assassination. Nothing is fixed or reliable. Paranoia is underneath. The country's boundaries with Sweden, Norway and Poland are disputed. Elsinore may be attacked, clouds change shape, language slips and slides, turning speech into guessing games and riddles. Solid flesh melts, in the tomb, life reduced to a sticky dew. The play is full of references to mortal illness, 'foul disease', leprosy, pleurisy, poisoning. Time is out of joint. The black sea crashes on bleak rocks. Everyone is mistrustful, everyone is suspected – they place each other under secret observation, paying for spies. Ghosts walk and can be conversed with. Paranormal phenomena need consideration. It is a night world of graveyards, the watchmen on the battlements, gloomy candlelit interiors of greenish slate. There is also the metaphor of theatre – acting, disguise, donning masks, including the mask of madness. What is the difference between public and private behaviour ('I have that within which passes show') – and in the midst of this dissolving society, Hamlet is expected to make decisions, demonstrate practical intelligence. He wishes to see the Ghost for himself, to ascertain Claudius' guilt. That which is true, Shakespeare seems to imply, is that which can be verified. But is there anything that persists? Can anything, indeed, be said to make sense, when you get right down to it? All those famous soliloquies of his: Hamlet allows any actor playing him to flail about in unfathomable mental activity, spouting lines to do with the inner-dimensions of intention, will, desire, memory, fear. In 1954, Burton's Hamlet saw destiny and self-destruction as a clear trajectory. A decade later, he's more weary, stale, flat: 'an unweeded garden that grows to seed', in Shakespeare's image. Gielgud, who'd directed the actor when young and lettuce fresh in *The Lady's Not for Burning* (1949) and *The Boy with a Cart* (1950) now found Burton (as he wrote in a letter to Paul Anstee) 'pretty gross and red' in appearance, and (as he wrote in a letter to Emlyn Williams), 'he does put away the drink, and looks terribly coarse and heavy – gets muddled and fluffy and then loses all his nimbleness and attack.'

Gielgud's production was modern-dress, the gimmick being the audience was watching 'a pre-dress rehearsal run-through'. In July 1964, it was recorded on blurry videotape using a system called Electronovision – primitive monochromatic smudges and a mono-aural soundtrack. The effect is like watching something beamed spasmodically from outer space, or even picked up by science-fictional means from the seventeenth century. There is enough there to grasp, nevertheless, the groggy quality of Burton's prince. He has a pallor. You suspect foul breath. The 'rehearsal' clothes are cheap-looking, but preferable to tights and doublets, the Elizabethan costumes Burton always looked bad and false in. There's no scenery, only a conglomeration of dark corridors, with black curtains, black boxes, black trestle tables, black cushions. According to William

Redfield, who played Guildenstern, Burton was perspiring a lot, as drinkers do. 'I go raving mad on gin,' he was heard to say. 'Uncontrollable. Vodka's the thing. Or whisky. Or tequila, when I'm in Mexico,' where he recently was. Despite the length of the run, Burton never fully mastered his lines, which could throw other members of the cast. Did the audience notice? He allegedly spoke the soliloquies in German one night. 'He muddled along one way or another,' said Redfield, 'and worked his way out of most messes.' Taylor wanted to put him on tablets to cure his nerves. 'What sort of dosage might help Richard to relax before a performance?' she wanted to know. What kind of pill, if any, would help him most, 'without undesirable side-effects?' As Burton, by Taylor's own admission, 'never takes pills, not even aspirin,' her decision to slip him Dexamyl was like something that happens in the play, where characters are drugged or poisoned unwittingly. The result was Burton needed to be prompted from the wings. 'He resembled a gibbering lunatic,' said Redfield, who himself would find fame as one of Jack Nicholson's gang in *One Flew Over the Cuckoo's Nest*. Burton 'all but gave up the ghost', and his performances became so startling, the cast speculated how much Dexamyl Taylor had actually been giving him – also known as Purple Hearts, Dexamyl is a pharmaceutical which elevates mood, suppresses the appetite and induces amphetamine psychosis: hallucinations, persecution mania, aggression, all perfect for *Hamlet*; and Hamlet was starting to reveal Burton totally. As he said to Kenneth Tynan, 'I played it [as] myself – that is, Richard Burton playing Richard Burton playing Hamlet.'

Gielgud, who had himself played Hamlet as lofty and intellectual, was less than convinced by Burton's volatile temperament: 'Have a care as to shouting. You shout brilliantly; both you and Larry Olivier do – two splendid cornets. But these hunting calls you do so well can be tiresome when sounded too often.' Good advice, though in fact Burton cannot sustain Olivier's implacable patrician coldness. And as the Broadway production was preserved on a complete original cast album, a four-disc Long Player boxed-set, distributed by Columbia Masterworks, we can hear for ourselves how Burton's voice was suggestive of a smoky fire burning, of sandstorms and glass-blowers' furnaces. There is a lustrousness to the voice and bearing, a ferocity; and a suggestion, always, of elegy, of the streams and mists of Wales. Burton said he disliked Gielgud's own 'mellifluous-voice business. It's old-fashioned now, I think.' But he himself was hardly averse to a honeyed lilt – and what he brought, in addition, was a sense of dark forces gathering, fireballs, explosions. 'Violence sits hunkered behind his eyes like a watchful Cheyenne,' Redfield thought – and Burton, at rehearsals, was exasperated by Gielgud's indecisive fusspot irritability, which the director disguised behind gabbling good manners. 'He gets bored with what he did yesterday and wants to change it again,' with the result Gertrude spent the entire play with her back to the stalls. Had they seen her face, audiences would have been able to recognise Eileen Herlie, who was Olivier's Gertrude in the film they'd made in 1948. Born in 1918, Eileen was bizarrely eleven years younger than Olivier, who played her son. That's nothing. When Burton was born, Eileen was still only seven. This stretches any Oedipal interpretation of the Hamlet–Gertrude relationship to the limit. Herlie was in any event perhaps not Gielgud's cup of tea. She put him in mind of 'a fat landlady who keeps a discreet brothel on the Côte d'Azur'.

It was as if, as a director, Gielgud was behaving like Polonius – that character, by the way, was taken by Hume Cronyn, a Cinecittà refugee or veteran, who said the entire *Hamlet* undertaking 'was enveloped in the mystique of the Burton-Taylor romance. It was a replay of the hysteria that had existed throughout the world press during the latter half of the filming of *Cleopatra* in Rome. It was inescapable.' Cronyn recalled the 'hullabaloo' in Toronto and Boston, the 'general madness' of the crowds at airports and outside hotels, the 'great roar' that went up when Taylor and Burton appeared at the stage door of the Lunt-Fontanne. 'Mounted police kept a passage open across the sidewalk between the alley and the open door of the limo. But it was still a gauntlet of snatching hands, cheers, jeers, and waving autograph books.' Taylor, waving like royalty, mouthed under her breath, as surely the Queen Mother never did, 'Fuck you, and you, and you, dear!' One gets the feeling she was in charge. If seats were sold out, even in the O'Keefe Center, which had room for 3,200 patrons, it's because audiences wanted to watch Taylor glittering with jewels in the front row. Her most significant action, however, and it would have been part of her campaign to dominate Burton completely, like when she played at being Welsh, was to get in touch with Philip, who had been out in the cold for two years. 'He needs you,' is apparently what Taylor told the foster-father on the telephone. 'Richard needs you. Please come.' The appeal or entreaty was an absolute echo of the summons Philip received from Burton himself, during *Camelot*, when Philip had announced gleefully, 'Richie needed me,' even if Lerner and Loewe weren't so sure. Now, regarding *Hamlet*, 'Richard was in such a state he couldn't go on without a word from me,' is how Philip remembered it.

* * *

There is such cruelty in desire. 'I knew it would cause havoc in my private life, with my wife and children and sisters,' said Burton of his obsession with Taylor. 'We were hurting a lot of people and we knew it,' said Taylor, though this only made her the more resolved: 'I knew what I had to do, God help me.' Angels and ministers of grace, defend us! as Hamlet might say. Like Burton, Taylor was brutal towards Sybil, Kate, Jessica, and Eddie – and she was equally brutal towards Burton, her love (her version of love) adhesive and corrosive. *Hamlet*, it may fairly be said, fine and large in its five acts, explores the clammy bonds, or fetters, of affection – Taylor would have made a splendid Gertrude ('Th'mperial jointress to this warlike state'), whose relationship with Claudius involves lust and gluttony and 'bodes some strange eruption'. The wedding in Canada was a hole-in-the-corner affair – as bad as Gertrude and Claudius' in Denmark, where the baked meats at the elder Hamlet's funeral wake were wheeled out again as cold cuts at the nuptial breakfast. There were no guests, save the entourage. ('That tremendous princeliness does isolate you in a funny way,' said Gielgud, who wasn't invited.) The province of Ontario not recognising Mexican divorces, and the province of Quebec not yet having come to a decision about recognising Mexican divorces, Burton and Taylor had to fly in a privately chartered Lockheed Jet-star from Toronto to Montreal, where a civil ceremony took place in the grounds of the Mexican consulate. This was followed by another civil ceremony, conducted by a Unitarian Church of the Messiah pastor, in Suite 810 at the Ritz-Carlton. 'You both have suffered great travail because of your love,' intoned the Reverend Leonard Mason. Burton was drunk all day – from now onwards he'd always look slightly sick – and Taylor wore Bulgari jewels and a bridal gown adorned with yellow ribbons, designed by Irene Sharaff, the Oscar-winner from *Cleopatra*. Her hair extensions were entwined with hyacinths.

Reaching out to Philip, on the face of it an attempt to broker a reconciliation, also suggests Taylor's power of provocation. Philip had once taken over Burton, and to take over Burton, Taylor took over Philip. It was part of her sense of ownership. Everything for Taylor was conquest and disputation, and to flatter Philip ('I, for one, thank you, Phil, because if it hadn't been for you I probably would never have met Richard') was part of her possessive intensity. For Philip's tutorials and presence in Toronto created only awkwardness – his going behind Gielgud's back with 'notes' the least of it. Indeed, Burton's relationship with Gielgud was already a version of Burton's with Philip – the homosexual wariness and appreciation (Gielgud had recently said: 'He has enormous dash, panache and enthusiasm, and yet a certain brooding thing which is also very beautiful'); Burton's spontaneity and verve as an actor, his magic effects, compared with the way Gielgud was donnishly refined, if watery. And it had all been Taylor's doing, beginning with the telephone call on 2 February – Philip hearing her voice, 'to my great and somewhat unsettling surprise.' Burton did not meet him at the airport. When Philip went to see *Hamlet* in the evening, Burton was in a state, and left the stage. The Interval dragged on – people started a slow handclap and stamped their feet. Burton refused to go on with the show. Hume Cronyn had to fish Philip out of the audience, for him to go round and have a word with the star in his dressing room. 'This was so unlike Richard I have come to believe it couldn't have happened; I must have dreamed it,' said the foster-father. Philip's presence completely threw him – though Philip's belief was that Burton felt outshone by Gielgud, who (unseen) spoke the lines of the Ghost. In the hotel afterwards, 'I gave him detailed comments and suggestions,' said Philip. 'But my main purpose was to restore his confidence,' which ebbed.

The next day, Philip stayed in his room, expecting Burton to be in touch – Burton called reluctantly in the late afternoon, prior to Philip's return to New York. 'It seemed I had failed to reassure him ... I did my best to repair the damage I might unwittingly have caused.' On 3 April, Philip went to see the production again in Boston. 'Richard was electrifying,' and therefore there was no requirement for any 'late [night] note-giving session.' Philip travelled back to New York by train, in the company of Burton and Taylor, who required a police escort to conduct them to the Regency Hotel. Though Burton visited Philip's house, he wasn't interested in being shown around, nor did he 'eat the lunch I had prepared'. With Burton in Manhattan, Sybil left town, not returning until 29 September, when her ex-husband and Taylor began making *The Sandpiper*, a long way off, in Big Sur, California.

Like Jesus, Hamlet's chief role in life is to be a son – the scenes with the Ghost, his father, with Gertrude, his mother, with Claudius, his stepfather – who goes out of his way to say, 'think of us / As of a father'; 'no less nobility of love / Than that which dearest father bears his son / Do I impart toward you.' From every angle the prince is required to examine and obey the demands of filial duty, succumb to family ties and responsibilities, take seriously the nature of kin and of blood relationships. Hamlet's own scenes are interspersed with the Polonius / Laertes / Ophelia sequences, where, again, paternal force is flexed, children coerced. Yet there is no reconciliation for Hamlet with parental figures, as there wasn't for Burton. Silence without hope was what it boiled down to. His biological father, Dick, or Dic Bach, whose full name, like Burton's, was Richard Walter Jenkins, had died in Neath General Hospital at half past four in the morning, when not a mouse would be stirring, on 25 March 1957. His last words were 'Where's Richie?' He was eighty-one and had lived with Hilda, his daughter, at 4 Penhydd Street, Pontrhydyfen, since 1938. He was always awash with booze when the prodigal returned – 'Drink up, boys, Rich is home!' Burton would fill the old man's pockets with pound notes, and sessions at The Miners' Arms were referred to as 'going for his medicine', or poison. Burton did not attend the funeral, remaining in Céligny. 'He was always an enigma to me,' he told Graham. 'But blood is blood and I feel very empty today.' As Claudius says, describing due human process: 'You must know, your father lost a father, / That father lost, lost his . . .' Old man Jenkins had been a nightwatchman in Port Talbot, walking to work – essentially the same job as Barnardo, Francisco and Marcellus, the Elsinore sentinels, charged with the midnight round. As with Hamlet and the elder Hamlet, was there a congruence – a sense of doubling or duplication – between Richard Jr. and Richard Snr., his spring and water-source? 'For many years I made my father the loveable rogue,' admitted Burton. 'But he was a useless drunk.' And how impressive was it really that for the actor to endure the Broadway run, his dresser, Bob Wilson, a black man who was Burton's Best Man in Montreal, was serving Martinis and bourbon-on-the-rocks in the dressing room and from the wings?

Even as a child, it was said of Burton, by Pontrhydyfen neighbours, 'He's the exact copy of Dick,' and his diaries in later life are an alcoholic chronicle: 'I quietly got sloshed' – 'I have been more or less drunk for two days' – 'I was more or less stupefied with drink all day long . . .' He was drinking to forget, to extinguish the fire – there's no enjoyment in it, only self-loathing, with everything (as in *Hamlet*) tending towards fragmentation, slipping and wavering. Seemingly heedless, Dick was a father who didn't face up to fatherly obligations; nevertheless, a father's name meant something. Everything disappears into the void, but a name still means something. Dick Bach, said Graham, 'could never quite reconcile himself to Rich assuming another name,' and when, under Philip's sway, Burton became Burton, he, Burton, was to live between two worlds – a genetic and psychological inheritance, and as a stepson or ward; on top of which was the reality of a career, grabbing at money and pleasure, all this happening a long way from South Wales. As he was to say, 'After what I am and what I've come from, where can I go but to the top?' Taylor, having released Philip back out of the genie's lamp, also invited Cis and Elfed over to New York to see *Hamlet*, paying their first-class airfare and for a suite at the Regency. 'Oh Rich, if only Mam could see you now,' said Cis delightedly, as the limo was rocked by fans and the mounted police failed every night to contain people behind wooden barriers. Taylor, incidentally, to make her royal exit from the theatre, was always in a new outfit – an example of Performance Art in itself, as deeply coloured as dreams, as Oscar Wilde might say, had he been there.

* * *

Hamlet was a son – and Burton was also a brother. Shakespeare was fascinated by fathers and sons, fathers and daughters; but he also examined fraternal liaisons, sundered twins, good and evil siblings – Don John and Don Pedro in *Much Ado About Nothing*, Duke Senior and Duke Frederick in *As You Like It*, come immediately to mind, also Orlando and Oliver, in the latter comedy: 'Wert thou not my brother, I would not take this hand from thy throat.' There is always a lot of deadly rivalry, continuous competitiveness, which can amount (as in *Hamlet* and as in all the History plays) to usurpation and fratricide. It is time to bring Ivor into the narrative. He was nineteen years Burton's senior, and biographers describe a mythical figure, like a warrior encamped outside Troy – he was a boxer; he played rugby for Neath and Aberavon; he swam the ten miles from Mumbles to Port Talbot. Hilda said of Ivor and Richie, 'You wouldn't think they were brothers, more like father and son.' When Edith Maud Jenkins died in 1927 and Richard Walter Jenkins proved himself incapable of coping, 'Ivor, now twenty-one ... came to the rescue,' said David. 'He took command of us,' and was not congenial. Their mother had left debts of £300, which is £20,947.58 in today's money, and Ivor insisted they each of them pitched in to repay this. Pay packets were handed over; Ivor insisted household expenditure was recorded in a ledger, 'which [he] meticulously inspected every evening.' Hilda was not even permitted to set aside a bob a week for a wristwatch. Ivor's 'occasional heavy-handedness made him very unpopular,' said David, the policeman, who was not given to exaggeration. Graham, generally more fly, went along with this view: 'I was never able to get close to him.' I recognise the type. In Wales they'd be known as a man's man, sergeant-major sorts in charge of rugby practice in a secondary modern. Ivor was in the Royal Army Service Corps during the war. He then worked as a bricklayer, notable for the military crease in his trousers and sparkling boots. 'He was strong, tough and bristling with confidence,' said David. Old Dic Bach 'seemed to accept Ivor was in charge, and never quibbled about his dictates'. Burton, nearly a generation younger, saw only a figure to hero-worship: 'Richard looked to Ivor for fathering in the same way he looked to Cis for mothering,' and in the same way he looked to Sybil for mothering. As Burton wrote in his diary, 'Ivor has always been a kind of God to me.' He certainly represented the world's hardness. Unsentimental, masculine, Ivor was contemptuous of frailty or foibles in any form, believing illness, for instance, was the fault of being 'mentally weak or masochistic'. He couldn't stand Philip, need-less to say, neither liking nor trusting him – Philip was left in no doubt there was 'an ambivalence in Ivor's original attitude to me', and Ivor had 'an uneasy embarrassed look on his face' whenever Philip was around, as Christopher Isherwood noted in 1961. Philip, in his turn, thought the elder brother was too much of a drinking partner. Was this why, by the Fifties, Ivor and his wife Gwen were the earliest, founding members of the entourage? Burton bought them a house in Squire's Mount, Hampstead – indeed, he and Sybil had quite a little property empire in the district: 3 Squire's Mount; 10 Squire's Mount; 11 Squire's Mount, including an adjacent cottage they called The Cwtch; 6 Lyndhurst Road NW3, which in 1953 was turned into flats they rented out. When David said Ivor had a 'supportive role' in Burton's coterie, it's hard to pinpoint what he and Gwen did, beyond babysitting for Kate and Jessica. Maybe Ivor collected rents and had minor administrative duties – anything of importance was dealt with by Aaron Frosch of Weissberger & Frosch, East Fifty-Sixth Street, New York. Hilda called Ivor 'King Farouk' and David dubbed him 'the well-known Scrooge of the family', so in the pre-Taylor days, perhaps this pompous arsehole kept a lid on Burton's spending, especially as before the escape to Switzerland, ninety-two per cent went in income tax. Ivor was known to drink in The Wells Tavern in Well Walk.

That's the key – the pre-Taylor days. According to David, Ivor only 'slowly and reluctantly' accepted Taylor. When Taylor made her Royal Visits to Pontrhydyfen, everyone caved in, 'with the exception of Ivor'. During the ructions in Rome, Ivor was 'Sybil's main source of sup-port,' and they waited together in Céligny for Burton to come to his senses and return – something that was practically as well as emotion-ally difficult as, to keep Burton at her side in Gstaad, Taylor burnt all his clothes in the incinerator. Ivor represented the appeals 'for stabil-ity, for loyalty, for the family' – he was instinctively against what

Burton now wanted; he would also have been envious of Burton as a father – he and Gwen were childless: how could he, Burton, throw that good fortune away? Ivor additionally believed Burton to be the main cause of Jessica's autism. 'Ivor's long hostility towards Richard sprang as much from this conviction as from his more general abhorrence of adultery and divorce.' But not from any abhorrence of violence. Eddie was delighted when he heard Ivor had beaten Burton up: 'That was the best day I'd had in several weeks.' There was another fight in The Load of Hay, Praed Street; yet another when Burton went to Cardiff for the rugby, early in 1963, and was called 'a shit who's done the dirty on his wife'. Ivor was present at these affrays. Various accounts say Burton fractured his spine and damaged his eye. Graham was required to play his out-of-action brother's double in reverse-angle shots in *The V.I.P.s*. 'There were six of these little monsters against Ivor and myself,' as Burton put it in his diary, as if Paddington or Wales were the Wild West. Who could tell whence came the flying fists and boots? 'I was caught off balance and felt my feet giving way.' Why mightn't it be Ivor as aggressor? On another occasion, Burton and Ivor attacked the waiter at the Hotel Negresco, in Nice, for his 'lousy service'.

So, the man Isherwood described as 'a stolid bucolic brother' was a drinker, an overbearing bully, but not one too proud to take Burton's shilling as 'personal manager'. Though Ivor refused to speak to Burton for over a year (and 'Ivor's reaction shattered him'), there was evidently a rapprochement, as in 1964, Ian Fawn-Meade, a business associate of Cy Endfield, who directed *Zulu*, remembered seeing Burton 'with an elder brother', whom he calls 'an ugly brute of a man', arriving at a party thrown by Stanley Baker at his Wimbledon home. 'They are both drunk,' says Fawn-Meade, and they babbled 'in fluent Welsh', though that didn't mean they were drunk or sober or anywhere in between. (Taylor was expected but 'does not arrive'.) Ivor and Gwen's chief task, however, was to fly back and forth across the Atlantic, bringing Kate, and Liza and Maria, to stay in Switzerland

and other European resorts. 'Ivor and Gwen as guardians', is a frequent phrase in Burton's diaries, denoting comings and goings. Ivor
and Gwen collected the children from their schools, returned them in
one piece, saving Burton and Taylor the trouble. 'Ivor and Gwen were
delighted with Gstaad,' wrote Burton in 1967. But in addition to chap-
erone duties, Ivor had another essential function: he was the sole link
to Sybil, the one person from whom Burton could find out things
about Sybil, when Kate was gathered up from her mother for holidays –
and indeed Ivor was pleased for Sybil when she remarried, which
Burton wasn't. He begged Stanley Baker to intervene: 'Please don't let
her get married.' Sybil's new husband, Jordan Christopher, a pop
singer, was sixteen years her junior. (He died in 1996, aged fifty-five.)
In 1965, on the day of the wedding, Ivor and Gwen were on hand to
look after Kate in Quogue, Long Island, the home of Aaron Frosch,
the lawyer, who now converted Sybil's alimony into augmented trust
funds for the two daughters, even if to all intents and purposes Jessica
had ceased to exist.

Burton's fireside chats with his brother went round in circles – 'We
sat around endlessly talking of this and that – mostly about Kate and
Sybil.' If Ivor felt conversation was growing too introspective, he
knew how to get the subject changed. He'd bring about 'a cosmic fart
that shattered eardrums'. But something was about to occur that
shattered more than eardrums. On 23 July 1968, André Besançon,
whom Burton had employed since 1957 to be caretaker and lawnmower of the house in Céligny, hanged himself in the garage. Burton
took the jet to Geneva the next day to attend the funeral, accompanied by Ivor, Gwen and Brook Williams. Some sources say Kate
and Liza were also of the party. Taylor had been in hospital, the
Fitzroy Nuffield Nursing Home, since 21 July, howling about 'the
destruction of my womanhood' and having a hysterectomy, so she
definitely wasn't present. ('Thank God it's not cancer,' said Dick
Hanley.) There are, said Detective Chief Inspector David Jenkins,
'confusing versions' of what followed. 'No one knows the whole

truth,' conceded Graham. 'In what appears to have been a freak accident,' in the cautious words of Professor Chris Williams, editor of
Burton's diaries, Ivor was rendered paraplegic. 'Ivor's fall was an accident, or was it?' Burton asked himself, in those diaries. A good
question – and a terrifying one, akin to Macbeth's assertion, 'To
know my deed, 'twere best not know myself.' We have enough evidence, from journal entries, of Burton's bad temper, his loss of
elemental control ('I drank steadily all day long yesterday ... Nothing could drag me out of my tantrum'), and being back in Céligny
was to find himself in a fatal context – it's a place unvisited for years,
more or less on Taylor's orders, and she had always refused to go
there, hysterectomy or no hysterectomy. It was full of memories of
Sybil. Being here brought everything back. Indeed, Taylor didn't
want the funeral-goers even to stay at Le Pays de Galles – she wanted
everyone to drive afterwards to Chalet Ariel. But the menfolk got
pissed in the Céligny restaurant, Café de la Gare. (Where were the
womenfolk, or at least, where was Gwen?) By one account, thirty-
seven demi-litres of white wine were taken. 'We're not driving
anywhere. We'll stay here. It's my home,' said Burton. As dusk fell
(though as this was high summer, sunset wouldn't have been until
after nine o'clock), Ivor apparently went on ahead to switch on the
mains electricity and get the hot water going; or another version:
'The idea was that Ivor could go in and find the sheets so that Gwen
could make up the beds.' Whatever the reason for his toddling away
from the table to go to Le Pays de Galles, and whether he was alone
or accompanied, 'Ivor, uncharacteristically, tripped,' as David has it.
He fell over a metal doormat, or a boot-scraper, or went backwards
and hit his neck on a windowsill, or he stumbled over a paving slab,
or he smacked his chin as he went down – every book on Burton pictures it differently. Paul Ferris says Ivor 'slipped in snow and broke
his neck'. Penny Junor, persisting with the snow theme, says Ivor was
found 'lying with a broken neck in the snow where he had fallen
nearly two hours earlier. Richard had asked for a snow grille to be put

on the front door, which was hidden by the heavy snow. In reaching up to get the front-door key from its hiding place on the lintel, Ivor had caught his toe in the grating and fallen.' Snow? In July?

Was it misadventure, a fluke, horseplay that went wrong – or the conclusion to a serious argument? If Ivor went over in the dark, how come it was dark – what time was it by now? 'Richard was never able to talk to any of us about it,' said David, who as a policeman surely would have wanted a few more hard facts established. Graham says Burton was already in the house (with Gwen – and the girls?) when the lights came on, and went back out to find Ivor. After a spell he returned. 'Ivor's hurt. I'm getting an ambulance.' Ivor was taken to Intensive Care in Geneva, and later to the National Spinal Injuries Centre, Stoke Mandeville, where according to various accounts he was completely paralysed, paralysed from the neck down, or paralysed from the waist down. Taylor, in any case, 'held Rich responsible for what had happened', i.e. had everyone gone to Gstaad instead of remaining in Céligny to get drunk, the accident would not have occurred; Graham also found his brother at fault – he knew what Ivor and Burton were like together, getting more boisterous, pushing and shoving, 'throwing punches, wrestling, running'. Ivor would have slipped as 'part of a silly game'. Yet why does Graham, in his memoir, then quote Wilde ('Each man kills the thing he loves') – because that suggests something altogether more criminal, amounting even to attempted manslaughter. But what if it was attempted murder? As Tom Rubython says in *And God Created Burton*, 'The most viable explanation ... is that Burton and Ivor got into a fight over Sybil when they got back to Céligny ... Something one of them said ... sparked a fist fight between the two intoxicated brothers.' It's Hamlet Senior and Claudius scrapping over Gertrude in the Elsinore orchard. There's a dramatisation of the incident in a deeply resonant television film made in 2011 by S4C – *Burton: Y Gyfrinach* [*The Secret*], with Richard Harrington as Burton and Dafydd Hywel as Ivor. The dialogue is in Welsh, which whilst authentic – the Jenkinses spoke

Welsh amongst themselves – does rather cut down on the number of viewers who can follow any of it. But none can complain about seeing the actual Céligny in the background.

This is my belief, anyhow – a deliberate furious push. Burton had been provoked, riled, and he retaliated. Too much emotion altogether; obsession and claustrophobia – for Ivor was a sort of double: a Jenkins still a Jenkins, untainted by a career in artifice, mummery, multiplicity; a drinker and rugby enthusiast, seemingly completely straightforward. And Ivor represented a division in Burton's being; Ivor was the self he'd left behind, when Burton longed for a new life outside Wales – and Burton always looked back in anger: 'Thank God I never have to live again through those terrible years of puerility, of idiocy,' which is also an indictment of Philip, and the spare room at 6 Connaught Street. If Burton idealised Ivor ('I don't know what I would do if anything happened to Ivor'), it was in a way that could never bode well – for there was something in Ivor that discredited Burton – and that nothing in any of the accounts hangs together, that the narratives are at variance, makes me think the person we need is Miss Marple. We need a street plan, a site plan, bits of string and coloured drawing pins. The timings, the position of the various suspects (what happened to Brook?) in the village, in the house, in the outbuildings and grounds: all this requires clarification. If Gwen said the electricity was off, when did she ascertain and impart this and to whom? If she spent the afternoon 'with a friend', who was that? Did the emergency services compile a report? Weren't rudimentary questions asked by the Corps de Police Cantonale de Genève? Burton, says Graham, 'never did talk about it in any logical way,' as how could he – as what we have here gives way to evil; is pledged to the powers of darkness. Though Burton had said of Ivor, 'He was the nearest of a father to me,' what had father figures meant? Dick's fecklessness, Elfed's nastiness (Elfed stole Burton's 1940 diary and scrawled in it: 'At four o'clock Richard Walter shits his pants'), Philip's clamminess, and Ivor's own kind of threat: it added up to family deadlock. Ivor, in particular, was critical of the things most precious to Burton – he was loyal to Sybil, when what Burton wanted was allegiance to Taylor; and what in any event did fame as an actor mean to Ivor, if anything? He didn't know anything about the arts, as Graham testified. Ivor would have been the one to rub in the idea acting was effeminate: 'I have never quite got over the fact that I thought, and I'm afraid I still do think,' Burton declared to Taylor in 1973, 'that acting for a man – a really proper man – is sissified and faintly ridiculous. My heart, unlike yours, is not in it.' A bit late to say that, ducky.

Burton's idea of the shape of his life was that he was a tragic and solitary figure – and when Ivor went off in the ambulance to Geneva, he 'disappeared' for ten days, on the run until he knew Ivor was not dead, i.e. not killed. Where did he go? Chalet Ariel in Gstaad, presumably. Any witnesses? It's like Agatha Christie's vanishing act, when in 1926 she couldn't be found, was feared to have committed suicide, and was located after eleven days by Dustin Hoffman in Harrogate, if the film with Vanessa Redgrave is to be believed. Burton's own memory of the aftermath turns him into Hamlet, Macbeth, Richard III: a tragic hero beset by ghosts. 'When [Ivor] died,' Burton said in 1977, 'I had vivid dreams. I thought he was there in the room with me, smiling. But it was a fantasy, of course, and it became a nightmare for me to go to sleep because of those dreams.' The alleged attempted murder, never seen, only done – and what's done cannot be undone: Burton 'was utterly devastated by the accident and by Ivor's helpless misery,' concurred David and Graham. Owls scream and crickets cry. Back in Britain, as Graham recalls, the news was kept from the family. 'You're not supposed to know,' Jim Benton told Hilda. Ivor was refusing visits. He survived for four years. He was fitted with a surgical collar, so he could sit up. The best he could do was twitch his toes. He went swimming with assistance. He stood up with assistance. He had a motorised wheelchair. 'Richard found it almost unbearable and his own visits [to Stoke Mandeville – where Jimmy Savile was at large] grew less frequent.' The brothers watched sport on the telly, but if there was nothing on the box, 'Then he would have to talk to Ivor and he just wouldn't know what to say,' as Cassie, the sister who was a nurse, reported. The diaries record the pity: 'Ivor is very near the end. Death is written all over his face . . . He can barely speak. He is already dead. I wish he were' (July 1971); a few months later, he's still alive, though running a temperature and he can't keep food down. Burton somehow arranged for Ivor and Gwen to sojourn in Gstaad – an orthopaedic bed, pulleys, grips and other gadgets were installed. Then Ivor's heart started to fail. He had a stroke. He went into hospital in Geneva with a malfunctioning kidney. Back in Stoke Mandeville, Burton paid £100 a week for Gwen to stay permanently nearby, in the New Bell Inn, Aston Clinton. There was some sort of bother about fresh towels: 'I went mad,' said Burton, and Taylor had to bash him 'round the head with her ringed fingers' to shut him up, which made him worse: 'I had sufficient sense to stop myself . . . If any man had done that I would have killed him.' Burton took ages to simmer down. 'I still boil with fury when I think about it.' Ivor died on 19 March 1972, when Taylor and Burton were in Budapest, and he was making *Bluebeard*, the one about locked rooms and grisly secrets.

* * *

When, on 9 August 1964, *Hamlet* came to an end on Broadway ('Not even John Barrymore could draw crowds like this every night,' said the stage doorman), Taylor and Burton travelled to Paris, for interior shooting on *The Sandpiper*, which is set in California. MGM paid Weissberger & Frosch $30,000 for negotiating the contracts. The stars took six first-class suites in the *Queen Elizabeth*, and the restaurant manager commented, 'They enjoyed their fame enormously,' which implies they enjoyed a conspicuous raucousness enormously. Debbie Reynolds was also aboard. 'Who the hell cares about Eddie Fisher?' she and Taylor agreed – I visualise them cackling. At the Hotel Lancaster, Taylor and Burton occupied twenty-one rooms – space for the governesses, tutors, secretarial assistants, nurses and the chauffeur. The pet dogs accompanied the humans into restaurants, and had to be fed from the menu. I wonder if this solicitude was inspired by *The Sandpiper*, where Taylor's character, an artist, Laura Reynolds, sees all living things as equal – 'The only way you can tame anything,' she says, 'is to let it fly free.' Perhaps that philosophy made more sense in the Sixties (the only way you can recognise freedom is to keep it in a cage – it amounts to the same thing) – but the point about *The Sandpiper* is it is a diagram of Taylor and Burton's relationship, with Taylor a force of nature, tossing her black mane, a romantic survivor, always ready to give or receive a surge of emotion, and Burton the ordained headmaster, the Reverend Dr Edward Hewitt, with his Latin conjugations, who sees himself as a Jesus figure, tempted in the wilderness, convulsed by sin: 'I can't dispel you from my thoughts!' he says to Taylor, as if it is her fault. Completing the triangle is Eva Marie Saint, as Hewitt's wife. With her helmet of very fine silvery hair, and wearing pale yellow outfits, and fawn or olive-green outfits, everything about Claire Hewitt, Eva's character, is bleached, straw-coloured – and points to Sybil. There seems to be no blood in her body; a wisp of a person (yet look what she does to Cary Grant in *North by Northwest*) – and all this contrasts with Taylor's dark ultra-violet ways. Normally, Taylor is rasping, combative, belligerent. She moves awkwardly, a waddle. She's not a graceful actress. She's given to flouncing. She has no poise – and is what Keats would call 'a real woman'; which is not by any means the same thing as a mere woman or only a woman. In this beautiful film – the letter-box format, the Panavision lenses, the Metrocolor processing – where I find I warm to her and she has tenderness, we have what appears to be an exploration of Taylor's temperament: what it is like being trapped by having to be a woman (and treated as a whore, because a single parent); the meaning of various notions of liberty and independence, 'without any sense of guilt'. For *The Sandpiper* is about adultery – which is to say, modern attitudes to marriage bonds; notions of honour and virtue are examined; social laws and rules: 'A woman is a wife, a mother, and a – what else? Unful-filled and in her place.' And if not put in their place, slut-shamed. By her very presence Taylor seems to demand: what right have men got to make women feel ashamed?

The exteriors were shot in the Carmel Highlands, Big Sur, where Taylor's character's beach hut was constructed at a cost of $35,000. The languorous landscapes are important – the surf and sky, set to music by Johnny Mandel's Academy Award-winning song, 'The Shadow of Your Smile'. It is a paradise of waterfalls and woodland streams, and Taylor, as in the *Lassie* films, is at one with the wilderness, 'the sea, the mountains, the birds, all of it'. Laura had a son out of wedlock (a black mark against her), so when Danny (Morgan Mason – actual son of James Mason) shoots a deer, the authorities intervene, threatening to have him sent away to reform school. As he's from a 'broken home', he obviously has to be 'disturbed'. Laura is outraged, saying how proud she is to be a single mother, damn everyone else to hell. 'Are you trying to shock me, Miss Reynolds?' asks the Episcopalian Burton. Taylor is angered by everyone's condescension. There's a gen-uine flash of temper. Burton is pompous – yet crackles with interest suddenly. He has met his match. He goes to visit Taylor's wooden house on the cliff, which is lit by oil lamps. If this is meant to suggest Laura is too poor to be connected to mains electricity, at least Taylor had twenty-two costume changes. The interior, put together on a sound stage in the Studios de Boulogne-Billancourt, with the cush-ions, copies of Chaucer, ethnic blankets, interesting pebbles, an open fire – who'd not find all this bohemian clutter attractive? The contrast is stark, comprehensible by the dimmest audience member. There is Burton, in his starchy school, which expects conformity, stamps out originality, and where Eva Marie Saint dresses elegantly and wears white gloves like a duchess at a fête; or else there's the pagan boldness of Taylor's way. (It's the same division of sensibility as found in *Equus*.) Here is a woman who goes about in purple tops and smocks with purple bobbles, refusing to be ashamed. Anyway, she long ago saw through men and their requirements: 'Men have been staring at me and rubbing up against me since I was twelve years old,' and Laura could be speaking for Taylor herself, the child actress, who'd said in 1949, when making a film called *Conspirator*, 'How can I concentrate on my education when Robert Taylor [her co-star; no relation; he's also Ivanhoe] keeps sticking his tongue down my throat?' The director of *The Sandpiper* was Vincente Minnelli, who'd not only directed Taylor's child-bride films with Spencer Tracy – *Father of the Bride, Father's Little Dividend*: films that fed into and were at such variance with the repulsiveness of the Nicky Hilton marriage – he was also the husband (for six years) of Judy Garland and his daughter (b. 1946) was Liza Minnelli – so here, I may reasonably surmise, was an expert on female exploitation, female hysteria. Not that Taylor's Laura is hysterical. Her awareness that venality only comes from men already gives her the advantage – she doesn't require protectiveness, thank you. When Robert Webber's flirtation becomes outright molestation, she has no qualms about going for him with an axe.

Burton always had, as Fitzgerald said of Gatsby (and Gatsby was another self-invented person), 'an instinct towards his future glory.' It's a glory lit by purgatorial fires. In *The Sandpiper* there are actual bonfires, flickering in the dunes, where the hippies strum guitars and hold parties. One of the hippies, Charles Bronson, is a sculptor – his redwood carving of Taylor with her big breasts is like a prow of a ship-of-the-line in Nelson's navy. Burton's repressed Dr Hewitt doesn't know where to look, though he keeps returning to the beach house for further looks, under the pretext of commissioning Laura to design the stained-glass windows in his new chapel. Laura has awakened Hewitt from his puritan snooze, obliterated his reserve – she knows at once he wants to pry into her sex life, using prurience as a means of gathering evidence against her, when the school becomes by order of the court Danny's legal guardian. She says, well, men have been eliminated from her life, they're such bastards. She's happier, these days, looking after a baby sandpiper with a broken wing.

Burton's character says, well, she needs to find the right kind of man. 'Does your wife know you're here?' Laura asks, and suddenly Burton is impersonating a man tormented by lust. Indeed, he's so deranged, he stops wearing a tie. In two shakes of a lamb's tail, the pair of them are on the beach, covered in salt spray. She's in cream and red. He's in light blue. The sky is orange. 'I must invite your contempt,' Burton says to Eva Marie Saint later on, allowing himself the grammatical luxury of the future conditional. In any event, the future is sealed, everything laid down – professional disgrace, disappearance. The film ends in an unresolved way, with Burton driving off on his own. Betraying his wife for an unmarried amateur artist has proven too much, though Hewitt is careful not to place too much blame on Taylor's free spirit. Laura has simply completed a process: 'It was my betrayal of myself that began years ago . . .' When? Maybe Original Sin is meant or implied?

* * *

In my imagination, when the somewhat morbid Hewitt leaves *The Sandpiper*, he arrives as Alec Leamas in *The Spy Who Came in from the Cold*, made in early 1965. Cold is the right word, too. There's scrupulously nothing here as 'warm as a dove's nest among summer trees' (Keats); nor is there a bracing blue cold, either. It's the coldness of refrigerated moods; chesty coughs and snivels; the cold East Berlin streets and freezing puddles; the leafless trees in the London parks (though Dublin Zoo was the location used); the cigarette ash non-colours and smoky shadows of the rooms and buildings – Oswald Morris, the cinematographer. The skies are like soaked newsprint and there is a clammy coldness to all the personalities: Cyril Cusack as the icicle Control; the various agents and double agents, Michael Hordern, Robert Hardy, Rupert Davies, Warren Mitchell, whose pallid faces register humiliation and hurt and fear. Le Carré's world is deliberately not glamorous – this is not Bond's province of tuxedos, chromium cars and exotic cocktails. The physical experience here is of cheap flats, stuffy pubs, railway station urinals and bad meals. The film, in fact, could almost be about Burton's face – puffy, pustular, slightly bloated, sleep-deprived. He has a stye on his eyelid. Leamas is a man who knows about the mottled looking-glass world he moves in, the moral trapdoors and the double-cross, but not until his final moments, straddling the Berlin Wall, does he know the full extent of the deceptions. There's always another twist, another turn. Serving the national interest (in Control's hostile exhortation), exposing Hans-Dieter Mundt, Head of East German Security – being called upon to be selfless (to the extent of getting himself sent to prison for contriving an assault on Bernard Lee) – is only another facet of betrayal and corruption; the grown-up view or less deceived approach is that all this has to be accepted eventually as an ordinary sense of reality, the reality of what Leamas calls 'seedy little men, henpecked husbands, queers'. Burton's wan face – bright blanched, like the lily on the snow – registers the State's rottenness, blends with the weariness of wet Fleet Street, where Leamas makes use of a cigarette vending machine, whilst wondering whether he is being followed; blurs with the waves and mist coming off the North Sea, when Leamas poses as a defector in windswept Scheveningen, on the Dutch coast, and tells Sam Wanamaker about a covert operation in Holland. Leamas is, in Le Carré's words, a man 'negotiating his own destruction', and within this crepuscular, heavily symbolic landscape, Claire Bloom's Nan stands out as an innocent – and she's played like the virgin amongst unicorns; but she's involved, also, as a Communist Party delegate, keen to visit and support the German Democratic Republic. Her ideals are dangerous, and as always with Le Carré (Smiley and the philandering Lady Ann; Karla and his daughter – mentally troubled and kept hidden, like Burton's Jessica), love is 'the human error', making a person vulnerable. Apart from the books being ace Cold War thrillers, Le Carré's works are equally fairy stories about ogres and maidens, good and evil. Contrary to Chaucer's Prioress' motto, *Amor Vincit Omnia*, it doesn't conquer all, it undermines all, and though Le Carré was an anti-sentimentalist, nevertheless he was the poet of soiled Edens. Looking at the East and at the West, here we had warring systems: the Soviet bloc's suppression and suspicion; their belief in rational necessity. The fixed features of Beatrix Lehmann, as the President of the Tribunal, leave us in no doubt of that. And then our own Western preferences for private judgements, our ironic acknowledgement of the contradictions and nuances of human nature. These different ideas of truth and justice neutralise each other, and as both philosophies involve loss and conflict, what we have in *The Spy Who Came in from the Cold* are people who think they have power who are suddenly rendered powerless: Hordern, Hardy, Wanamaker and Oskar Werner, and so on, are peremptorily treated by the next person in the chain of command, told to get out or to take the car round the back. There's peril and paranoia. No one is safe. Burton gives a great performance – as great as any performance in the history of cinema – and he is absolutely suffused with guilt and shame; with a final powerlessness and dejection; with a sense of the pointlessness of human aspiration and desire. Which makes me wonder, was Burton always out in the cold? (Tony Palmer's documentary [1988] was called *Richard Burton: In from the Cold?*). Where or what was home, warmth, safety? Where could he be in order not to be outside?

* * *

It must have been awkward having Claire Bloom on hand again. Burton 'wasn't very nice to her. Understandably, I suppose, with Elizabeth there,' said Martin Ritt, the director. Elizabeth was indeed there, making a fuss, making a silly nuisance of herself, disrupting the night shoots by arriving in a chauffeured limo with Franco Zeffirelli. 'Oh Christ, Elizabeth, you fool!' Burton shouted, as embarrassed by the invasion as Ritt was by the ostentation. On 3 March, Taylor's Rolls, driven by Gaston Sanz, managed to run over and kill seventy-eight-year-old Mrs Alice Maud Bryan on Stillorgan Road. The inquest, which Taylor attended, was two years later. Sanz, a judo black belt, whom David Wood describes as this 'squat Basque in dark glasses who had apparently seen service in the Free French Commandos during the war,' was unsteady behind the wheel because his sixteen-year-old son had recently been fatally wounded in a shooting accident. Mrs Bryan was buried in the graveyard at Killiskey Parish Church, County Wicklow, where the lettering on the tombstone has already worn away. The inscription might well have lasted longer if written on water.

Bloom rather enjoyed the discomfiture: '[Taylor] settled for feeling extremely uncomfortable having me around' – and as Le Carré himself pointed out, 'Elizabeth can scarcely have enjoyed the spectacle of the two of them [Burton and Bloom] flirting on set,' so Taylor was like a shadow watching them, as she was when Geneviève Bujold looked like being a threat during *Anne of the Thousand Days*. What's interesting, as Bloom says in her memoirs, is Burton, who had casting approval, 'could certainly have vetoed my appearance had he wished; I was surprised when he chose not to.' Yes, Bloom is exceptional as Nan Perry ('Liz Gold' in the novel – which sold 200,000 copies in hardback), the crushed idealist. She's good at portraying diffidence and simplicity – and though subdued, she's proud and haughty, too. But what was Burton's concealed purpose, especially as Bloom, and others involved with the production, found him taciturn, chilled through? He refused to do extra takes, for example. 'It's good enough for me,' he'd say firmly. When Ritt said, 'It's not good enough for me, Richard,' Burton snarled, 'Don't fuck around with me.' When drunk, which he always was after lunch, a boorish streak emerged – as it had in the way he spoke to Puffin Asquith when making *The V.I.P.s*: 'What kind of fucking shot is this? This is ridiculous.' Leamas is a portrait of solitude, and it could be argued Burton was getting fully into character as washed-up, broken-down, burnt-out. I don't think it's that, however. I think with Bloom there, and his insisting Bloom was to be there, rather like in *Brief Encounter*, which one day he'd remake with Sophia Loren, Burton was being given a glimpse of another fate, a different life. As Bloom says, 'Richard believed he had won a paragon among women,' and she, Bloom, didn't appreciate having all this flaunted: 'Where I had failed, another woman [Taylor] had succeeded,' i.e. in vanquishing Sybil.

But what was this paragon exactly? Taylor was impetuous. She liked people to be eager to serve her, pay homage. The centre of her own life, she expected to be the centre of everyone else's life. She was hard and relentless, always appearing at Ardmore Studios and bellowing 'Richard!' across the set – Bloom thought Burton frightened of her, which partially explains his distracted, disconnected manner, made worse by his drinking wine and spirits from breakfast onwards. He couldn't remember his lines, cue-cards had to be used. The scene where Leamas emerges from a cellar and climbs an iron ladder took days – the contents of the Johnnie Walker bottle in Burton's coat pocket quickly gone. In the midst of this, Bloom, married since 1959 to Rod Steiger, had to come to terms with the strung-out residue of her genuine love and affection – and what she now saw was commonplace: disunion, resignation. In trying to see Burton as he really was, in trying to find fault with a man she'd worshipped, here was the conquering male ego who'd rejected her because he'd wanted someone altogether larger, who had lofty goals – and Burton had duly found all these in Taylor, who was gross, bossy, melodramatic; who was someone or something repulsive to the likes of Bloom, who couldn't have been more different – opposites, like Disraeli and Gladstone. As Sheilah Graham perceived, Bloom, as a person, was 'self-contained and gives an impression of coldness', where Taylor, by contrast, simmered and boiled over, bringing with her a sense of giant moths, chameleons, queer light, tambourines and the stench of phosphorus.

For his part, on the set of *The Spy Who Came in from the Cold*, Burton was aware of mismatch, trapped by dreams coming true: 'I can't go to a pub anymore. Elizabeth is more famous than the Queen.

I wish none of it had ever happened,' he told Le Carré, a big admission, and not entirely an honest one. Research by me has disclosed Burton fortified himself in Kavanagh's Bar, New Street, The White Horse Inn, George's Quay ('Ladies Not Served', so Taylor wasn't allowed on the premises), public houses in the Blackpitts area and Malpas Street, The Comet, Swords Road, Santry, and Cusack's, North Strand, where Taylor took a piss in the gents – the locals still talk about the incident. Le Carré was bidden to Dublin ('Richard needs you') in the hope he'd be a buffer between the actor and Ritt, the actor and Taylor, and the actor and Taylor's retinue. The chief problem, however, lay between Burton and Bloom – he was irritated (as Philip Roth would be) by the way she'd seem full of sorrow, making him remember, simply through her presence, when they were younger, gentler, and it was now as if those times had never existed. 'Our paths never crossed again,' said Bloom, and in 1965 she was relieved. Like Le Carré, she'd had a vexing evening in Burton and Taylor's suite at The Gresham, where the stars were installed for ten weeks, having arrived at Dún Laoghaire on the mailboat on 9 February. Taylor remained a disembodied voice on the intercom. 'Richard?' – 'Yes, darling?' – 'Who's all there?' She refused to be gracious, a shouting match began, and as guests hurriedly left, it looked as if a boxing bout might soon commence, complete with bells and a sponge in a bucket.

Taylor, whilst hanging around, was 'constantly drinking from a champagne bottle,' said Ritt disapprovingly, and Le Carré reportedly saw Taylor slapping Burton around. Ernest Lehman, who adapted *Who's Afraid of Virginia Woolf?* for the screen from Albee's play, also witnessed violence: 'Elizabeth loves to fight. She was constantly hitting and punching Burton.' Why did he endure it? She also thwacked Mike Nichols when he laughed at one of her mistakes. She wouldn't be mocked or patronised. I think what's going on is Taylor and Burton wanted the opposite of anything that could be described as restraint, deprivation. The pair of them – their minds and feelings – were in conspiracy to push themselves forward. As stars, they were there purely to be looked at – they had a loudness, a thrusting quality. They were able to get away with anything. They were glorious rebels who'd altered the social and historical landscape, brought in a novel kind of moral life, yet their devotion could never be brought into harmony, except momentarily, as Tolstoy said of his own married state. Was their talent reduced by the chaos? Strangely, I think not. It was organically necessary. But the thing is, after the extravagance and the passion, there has to be a sense of limitation – a sense of the utter banality of existence: this is the horror glimpsed by people who witnessed their scenes and squabbles, which represented, or was a response to, triviality and aimlessness. It's what Lawrence called an awareness of 'the nervous horror of the world', which is what Burton was realising in 1965, even though he was paid a quarter of a million sterling to be in Le Carré's film, plus twenty-nine per cent of the gross.

Not quite twenty years later, Oona Chaplin, who knew Bloom from *Limelight*, ran into Burton in Switzerland, and he said to her, 'Please give her [Bloom] my undying love.' Bloom thought this a strange message to receive – *undying*? There'd been no attempt at contact since *The Spy Who Came in from the Cold*. They shared no scenes in *Ellis Island*. When Burton died soon afterwards, however, heartache returned, which Roth was put out by – and it was to Bloom, on 22 August 1984, Gielgud sent condolences: 'I am very sad about Richard Burton . . . and I can't help feeling very sorry for Elizabeth, of whom . . . I became very fond when we saw a good deal of her over the American *Hamlet*.' Gielgud says he'd last worked with Burton in Vienna, when making *Wagner*. 'He was looking terribly ravaged . . . his back and arms were giving him trouble.' He mentions to Bloom that, 'We have the Memorial Service . . . at St Martin's, where I have to read some Shakespeare, with Emlyn to speak the address and Paul Scofield also taking part. I dread the crowds and reporters as you can imagine.'

Burton's remark to Oona; how he'd behaved back in Dublin; now his death at what Bloom says was 'the wastefully early age of fifty-nine': what Bloom had was an awareness of Burton's loneliness. He was a man who'd cast off human warmth. I mean what the *absolute fuck* can it have been like, at the end, fobbing off Anthony Quayle (who wanted to direct him as Prospero) and John Dexter (who wanted to direct him as King Lear) and instead instructing Brook Williams to book the hotels for *Exorcist II*, *The Wild Geese* and *The Wild Geese II*? Burton's sudden death meant the latter reservation in Berlin had to be cancelled, the hotel losing out on expenses charges of $150,000. At least Burton, of all people, may have noticed the wistful Shakespearean allusion: 'Winter's not gone yet,' says the Fool to Kent and Lear, 'if the wild geese fly that way' (Act 2, Scene 4). And he was fifty-eight, Claire, not fifty-nine, when the curtain fell.

* * *

The boredom and dissatisfaction they took with them to Smith College, Massachusetts, when *Who's Afraid of Virginia Woolf?* commenced production, on 6 July 1965. Seventy security guards mustered by the Deputy Sheriffs' Association kept back onlookers. The film remains banned in Nova Scotia for its 'obscenity and blasphemy': thirteen 'goddams', twelve apiece of 'Jesus' and 'Christ', seven 'buggers', four 'screws', four 'sons-of-bitches', and two references to 'must have made it in the sack'. The censor also found persistent references to scrotums and balls – I suppose because *Who's Afraid of Virginia Woolf?* is a castration drama, with Taylor's Martha, as noisy as Jerry Lewis, one of cinema's tireless witches, her every utterance to Burton's George an order: 'I said fix me a drink'; 'I said get over there and answer that door'; 'I said come on in.' It's a horror movie – it even begins with a shot of a full moon and scudding clouds – and Taylor and Burton deliver their lines as demonic cackles. They chew on their food like werewolves. Sandy Dennis (twenty-six) and George Segal (twenty-eight) are lambs to the slaughter. Everything takes place at night, in a house from which none can escape, where moths cluster around the lamps and trees sway and creak, as if we are in the middle of a forest, instead of an academic community. Except, of course, an academic community, far from being a centre of enlightened learning, enquiry and debate, is always a nest of envy, failure and smugness, where, as Mike Nichols said, the stakes are so low. The cluttered and detailed set, with the insanitary kitchen ('What a dump!' says Taylor, mimicking Bette Davis in *Beyond the Forest*), the unwashed plates and discarded Kleenex, could be Richard and Mary Ellmann's unwelcoming place in St Giles, Oxford, or John Bayley and Iris Murdoch's quarters in Steeple Aston and, later, Charlbury Road. Seemingly civilised, people with strings of degrees and qualifications can quickly become feral, taunting each other with their sense of inadequacy. (Losey's *Accident* treads a similar path.) The characters in *Who's Afraid of Virginia Woolf?* have no humour, no irony, only forces, challenges. They try to make each other angry. Though trying to remain polite, there is hatred in the exchanges, under the veneer of congeniality – and Taylor and Burton, amidst the cigarette smoke and tiredness, the atmosphere of staleness, completely blossom. It is their entire marriage, crammed into a single picture. The interpersonal games, where everything is loaded and risky; the extent of Martha and George's provocation; the taunts – 'You make me puke!', 'You burn me up!', 'You make me sick!', 'George makes everyone sick!': rage and joy are the same, playfulness and fury are the same.

People who drink, when they stop, are still never fully sober, they are poisoned, and as Nichols said of Burton, 'He had either drunk too much, or needed to drink more.' *Who's Afraid of Virginia Woolf?*, therefore, is about reaching saturation point, physically and mentally. Let's consider this for a moment, consider where we are. Burton is stage-trained; he knew about elocution. He had made financial investments with Sybil (chiefly property – he was not profligate). He could fold his clothes, having been a draper's assistant at the Taibach Co-op on thirty shillings a week. Then (boom!) Taylor is there. Her chief contribution was vulgarity, sloppiness. For her, it was high time to be sloppy – after dozens of films being dutiful: all those daughters, wives, mothers, where she'd have composure, decorativeness, in those period frocks (*Ivanhoe, Beau Brummel*). Here Taylor was, in the Sixties, unbuttoned. What's fascinating about her is her instability; her unique compound of muddle and egotism – or rather, the ruthless way she used a suggestion of being unstable to exert or demonstrate her power and her will. All this, Burton found stimulating and compulsive, though it worried outsiders. 'She was wearing him down,' said Nichols of Taylor's effect on Burton, and it's true he never loosened up, at least not as an actor. Cary Grant is loose-limbed, under the cashmere. Rex Harrison is permanently ironic – wittily freely-floating and controlled (the comedy of superciliousness); David Niven had a dapper flexibility; but Burton, in the Sixties, is somehow ferocious, pained, weary. He is both present and distant, like a public monument, the king on the balcony. And what always interests me about Burton as an actor is he is operating on two levels, in two different worlds: the one of observed and coherent rules, the other involving his more precarious, provisional view of himself, which he tried to keep secret – his sensibility, which had something shadowy, rueful, tough about it. I am always aware of this – of his temperament, which was tarnished, unsuave and, to use the word Burton chose when talking to Tynan, which he believed was an encapsulation: *febrile*. Despite the large Welsh family, Taylor and the retinues, I think he preferred being on his own, figuratively if not actually. 'I have to have a lot of space on the stage [and elsewhere], a lot of space that I can move about in, without being bothered by too many people.' His separateness, which represented stability, in performance, could come over as plaintiveness, and his voice had an acid edge: the cigarettes; sulphur; hell.

All of which is on cacophonous display in *Who's Afraid of Virginia Woolf?*. Watching it again (and again), Burton's performance is something to wonder at. 'I am George,' he said to Ernest Lehman, in the same way he'd assure Nevill Coghill he was the reincarnation of

Faustus. 'George is me.' Taylor also laid claim to Martha ('I'm loud, and I'm vulgar'), and Nichols, who'd insisted on three weeks of rehearsal, deliberately drew on the possibility the roles would infect them, that Taylor and Burton would get caught up in it, allow it, in some fashion, to disarrange them, take them over, and sound, as it were, deeper notes. Taylor, remembered Nichols, was 'very physical', needing to know about her clothes, movements, business with props. Burton preferred to dwell on the lines, the poetry. During the rehearsals and the months of the shoot, everyone sought the rhythms in the script, the speeds, the press and release – the emotional and literal staging, characters going from chair to chair, crossing the room, leaving the room. There's a lot of overlapping dialogue, sudden silence, punctured by ice clinking into a glass. Nichols was impressed by Taylor's movie acting. She seemed to be doing as little as possible – you'd only notice the nuance when the rushes were printed. Actually, directors always said that. Though Taylor was late for appointments, though messy and disorganised, she had, within her storminess, and despite her impatience and fluctuations (which were actually the source of her acting style), the ability to brew magic. Mankiewicz said, after *Suddenly, Last Summer*, 'She has done it mostly by instinct.' Puffin Asquith commented, after *The V.I.P.s*, that Taylor possessed 'a natural, instinctive acting talent.' It was all done wholly unselfconsciously, which is why, with Taylor when she was with Burton at any rate, though not (in her final phase) when Taylor was with Michael Jackson, I'll resist calling her camp. Camp is the art of deflection; it is about something other than it seems to be about. For all the flapping and extravagant mannerisms, the characteristic of camp is caution. It is studied. With Taylor, in everything she made with Burton, and in what she made without Burton though he was very much still around (*Reflections in a Golden Eye, Secret Ceremony, The Only Game in Town, X, Y & Zee*), there is no element of masquerade. 'Come on, love, what is it you do?' Burton once asked her. 'She just smiled. She doesn't really know. That's the truth. She doesn't know what it is she does.'

Bette Davis very much wanted the role of Martha – she'd have made it camp, as Rachel Roberts did when she played it in Bath (opposite her husband at the time, Alan Dobie) – but with Taylor, her essential nature informed what she did with the part, 'feeling what's there, simplifying and ripening' the material, as Nichols said. And with Burton, there are extended shots of him listening. He's often the one to whom the moment is happening: 'Boy, you're really having a field day, huh? Well, I'm going to finish you,' threatens Martha; 'I wear the pants in this house because somebody's got to, but I'm not a monster, I'm not,' she rails, a line mimicked by Gene Wilder in *Young Frankenstein*. 'You aren't man enough . . . You haven't got the guts,' is another sneer. 'Before I'm through with you,' is a further phrase accompanied with a lot of glaring. In a sequence where Martha is telling Nick and Honey about the time her father, the president of the college, 'Got the idea all the men should learn how to box . . . Daddy put on the gloves himself, Daddy's a strong man . . . and he asked George to box with him and George didn't want to . . .' – the dialogue is left behind as the camera follows George, who leaves the room and finds a gun in the garage. The hand-held camera in pursuit, he returns, comes at Martha with the weapon, which shoots out a toy umbrella. Nevertheless, the murderousness on his face is real.

We are inside with Burton's George, absorbing these terrible taunts – yet in terms of biography, the scenes recreate what we know of Taylor and Mike Todd. 'You're not going to fucking step all over me like you stepped on everybody else in your whole life,' Todd had warned her once. When Taylor arrived at Todd's house, Todd punched her in the face. 'She tolerated being hit,' said Eddie, who witnessed this. 'Maybe she even needed it to respect a man.' The scenes in *Who's Afraid of Virginia Woolf?* recreate what we know of Taylor and Michael Wilding, too: 'You're nothing but a coward,' she'd said to him. 'To think that the man I once loved turns out to be nothing but a coward.' This because Wilding had turned down taking over as Professor Higgins from Rex Harrison in *My Fair Lady*, because of epilepsy symptoms.

It's exactly the sort of thing the restless and cruelly critical Martha would say to George. Wilding and Taylor separated on 19 July 1956. Wilding returned to Marlene Dietrich. They fucked so energetically, 'they broke the double bed in the guest room,' according to Maria Riva, Dietrich's daughter. Dietrich came on the set of *Who's Afraid of Virginia Woolf?* and 'ignored Elizabeth Taylor totally,' said Nichols. Incidentally, in *Touch of Evil*, it is one of Taylor's old wigs that Dietrich is wearing, hence adding to the gypsy blowsiness. 'He was some kind of a man,' her character, Tanya, a character that suggests Taylor, says of Welles' Quinlan. 'What does it matter what you say about people?' I've always thought that a neat critique of biography.

Like a Francis Bacon painting of figures turning themselves inside out, *Who's Afraid of Virginia Woolf?* is difficult to look at. The purple entrails, the splatter of bodily fluids, and the equivocation of sex and death, on Bacon's canvas, becomes, in Taylor and Burton's performances, what Freud, when describing the id, called a 'cauldron of seething excitations', a display of basic urges and drives: biting, punching, grasping, weeping, laughing. In fact, Taylor and Burton in *Who's Afraid of Virginia Woolf?* are insane. The *OED* defines the id as the 'instinctive impulses of the individual', and that's Taylor and Burton here, as they expect instant and continuous gratification of expanding appetite. It used to be a dangerous game to watch *Withnail and I*, matching Richard E. Grant tincture for tincture – it would be a suicidal or murderous game to try it on with *Who's Afraid of Virginia Woolf?*. The tale doesn't begin until half-past two in the morning, when George and Martha pile out of one party and stagger drunkenly home. 'Well, I don't suppose a nightcap would kill either one of us,' they agree, upon reaching their lounge. 'Will you give me my drink, please?' They get through bottle after bottle. It is an alcoholic epic. 'Hey, put some more ice in my drink, will you? You never put any ice in my drink'; 'There aren't many more sickening sights than you with a couple of drinks in you and your skirt up over your head, you know . . .' When George Segal and Sandy Dennis arrive, as witnesses to these ritual demonstrations and heightened actions with or through which their elders keep themselves aroused, they are plied with booze: 'Make the kids a drink, George. What do you want, kids? What do you want to drink, huh?' Nick asks for Bourbon on the rocks, 'if you don't mind,' which inspires a sarcastic riff: '*Mind?* No, I don't *mind*,' says George, with the pissiness of a philosophy professor. 'I don't think I *mind*.' The sickly, simpering Honey overdoes it on the brandy and is sick. Despite the pints of liquor consumed, everyone jams into a car for more beverages at a roadhouse.

After the drinking, the driving. You can't quite believe this nocturnal session, the extent of the drinking and fantasies playing out. Sandy Dennis gets pie-eyed and shrewish. George Segal is butch, tries to be combative. 'I know when I'm being threatened,' says Burton, levelly and menacingly, the beast in the jungle. Taylor changes into tight trousers and a loose blouse, to dance along seductively to a jukebox. The word games, the aggression, the changing moods: what appears at first to be a lot of random befuddlement, to be blamed on those tumblers of jungle juices, does coalesce – around notions of virility, fertility. Everyone bullies everyone else. Honey has had a phantom pregnancy, or possibly an abortion, and Nick feels he was trapped into marrying her. Though he goes upstairs with Martha, he's too puddled to do anything, to his chagrin – all the men Martha knows seem to be flops, a noun reiterated throughout the drama. Career flops, erotic flops: 'You're all flops . . . I pass my life in crummy, totally pointless infidelities . . . A bunch of boozed-up impotent lunk-heads . . .' Most sex, the film seems to say, is bad sex – and as Ernest Lehman's previous screen adaptation was *The Sound of Music*, I do wonder if the very chaste and proper relationship between Captain von Trapp and the nun Maria in the pristine Salzkammergut is what we have here in reverse, in a parodic distorted circus-mirror sort of fashion, with George and Martha braying instead of singing; everything discordant; the squalid faculty digs instead of a lakeside villa; the sparkling colour of Austria instead of a putrescent corpse-like black and white; lots of obedient von Trapp children, instead of George and Martha, and Nick and Honey, with no children at all. Throughout *Who's Afraid of Virginia Woolf?* there are references, hints, concerning Martha and George's absent son. Is he away somewhere, or dead, or is he entirely imaginary, a figment of the couple's elaborate role-playing? 'Our son ... He's our comfort.' We don't need any of this Act 5 mystery, frankly, with Taylor and Burton. They transcend it, knock it aside. They don't behave like people who have or who have had children. On the contrary, they are each other's lives – there's nobody else. The imaginary child business is something only they know about, is part of their weird intimacy. And as the film grinds towards its final reel, George and Martha, who'd seemed such enemies, are actually close, 'wanting the loved-one to be one's best self,' as Nichols has it. Who else can they love? There's nowhere else to go. It is the young couple who are not close, whose confidence in each other has fractured, whose love is betrayed or exposed as mawkishness. 'Do we mean love, when we say love?' asked Samuel Beckett. Love is merely a madness.

* * *

Who's Afraid of Virginia Woolf? is the life Taylor and Burton were living, and Nichols knew exactly how they lived. He'd known Burton personally for ages – *An Evening With Mike Nichols and Elaine May* was running at the John Golden Theatre, on West Forty-Fifth Street, when, from December 1960, *Camelot* was running at The Majestic, on West Forty-Fourth Street. Nichols had been in Rome, so could see something of the Fox decadence seeping in now at Warner Brothers: Taylor's dressing room was filled with bushels of white roses and lily of the valley; printed instructions were given out to everybody, 'Don't greet the Burtons unless they greet you first.' The stars refused to work before ten in the morning or after six at night, and in any event never arrived on set until twelve-thirty. 'We almost never got a shot

before lunch,' said the director. The alcohol; dizzy spells; disorienta-
tion; suppressed (and actual) violence – Taylor really did have her
head smacked on the car roof. True to form, during pre-production,
when Lehman met her at the Beverly Hills Hotel, Taylor was having a
tooth capped – and of course was allergic to the anaesthetic, a side-
effect of the thyroid pills she was taking to control her weight. During
the shooting, Taylor sent telegrams to Dr Carl Heinz Goldmann in
London, one of the *Cleopatra* physicians, demanding an urgent
consignment of 'pink pills' – Diconal, or dipipanone hydrochloride,
an opioid analgesic tablet equal in strength to morphine. Her make-
up took hours, followed by long big meal breaks. There'd be a few
hours of filming, but Nichols, to tap Taylor and Burton's unconscious,
or to encourage them to do so, preferred night shoots in the cold. This
gave *Who's Afraid of Virginia Woolf?* something solid, realistic – the
emotional wreckage, the extreme states, the sense of breakdown,
which Nichols had suspected in his stars' natures, in their existence,
as long ago as *Cleopatra*, when he'd helped distract the paparazzi. He
wanted his own film to have that silvery Giuseppe Rotunno appearance, inspired by Fellini.

The last day of shooting was 13 December 1965. *Who's Afraid of
Virginia Woolf?* was released on 29 June 1966 to massive applause, and
Taylor's percentage netted her four million dollars in the first year
alone. This on top of her $1.1 million fee. Burton was on a flat fee of
$750,000 with no share of the gross. There were Academy Awards
for all, or nearly all: Art Direction, Cinematography, Costumes,
Sandy Dennis, Taylor, but not Burton, who was robbed of the accol-
ade, as he was his whole life, this time by Paul Scofield, who, said
Burton in his diaries, 'walks like a pimp, he's got a patently false
voice.' I agree. It's the honk of a pregnant camel, whether as Sir
Thomas More or anything else. (I saw Scofield on stage as Don Quixote
and Oberon.) But Burton's comments may have been a reflex of
pure envy – Scofield lived modestly in Sussex, nothing he did was
ostentatious, he followed the classical theatre path, was respected

and admired and never in the gossip columns. He was (as David Hare reminds me) everything Burton was guilty about not being. 'Scofield is Burton's counterlife. Hence the bad-faith bitchiness,' argued Sir Hare, in a letter to me the other day.

For the record, those carrying off the Best Actor statuette down the years instead of Burton were Anthony Quinn (1952), William Holden (1953), Rex Harrison (1964), Lee Marvin (1965), John Wayne (1969) and Richard Dreyfus (1977). *Richard Dreyfus?* Otherwise here is a mid-twentieth-century gallery of masculinity – something dependable about those fellows, who have a martial bearing, good to go on patrol with. And compared with all of them, Burton is the wariest actor who ever became a star. He flinches, retires, eludes; he steps back from people. Look at his interaction with other male stars – James Mason (*The Desert Rats*), O'Toole (*Becket*), Clint Eastwood (*Where Eagles Dare*), Lee Marvin (*The Klansman*) – there is no camaraderie. Though I never doubt Burton's powers of sympathy or perception, he resists any rapport with audiences, too. There's a caustic tone, a cynicism – frighteningly exploited as the Nazi in *Massacre in Rome* ('Hitler Ordered It. The Vatican Wouldn't Stop It. The World Would Never Forgive It') or O'Brien in *Nineteen Eighty-Four*, though present also in *The Spy Who Came in from the Cold* and *Who's Afraid of Virginia Woolf?*. It's why Burton was not a natural comedian – he couldn't risk being laughed at. Nevertheless, if George and Martha were ever members of the Smith College, Massachusetts, Amateur Dramatic Society, and they'd been cast as Petruchio and Katherina in an end-of-term production of *The Taming of the Shrew*, Burton and Taylor's production of *The Taming of the Shrew* is what students and teachers would have had to queue up and buy tickets for. It is full of grabbing and pummelling, the characters knocking each other off stools and ladders. The script is non-stop insult: 'You peasant swain! You whoreson malt-horse drudge! You whoreson beetle-headed flat-ear'd knave!... Here's snip and nip and cut and slish and slash...' As ever, it makes me wonder: is there a core of bonkersness in being an actor, being a star? *The Taming of the Shrew* was made in the spring of 1966 in Rome – and Mike Nichols, on holiday, hung around the set with his girlfriend, Mia Farrow, a Shakespearean waif in those days, before she became eldritch in later life, and who Burton said was 'so goody as to invite suspicion of affectation,' though he misspelt that in his diary (11 April 1966) as 'affection'. Farrow is sexy as the devil-child, alongside Taylor in *Secret Ceremony*.

Shakespeare's Italy was Warwickshire – I've always relished the local references to chestnuts in a farmer's stove, hazel twigs, crab apples, pippins, oyster jars, rush-candles, hunting dogs, morning roses, and parsley in the garden to stuff a rabbit. Taylor and Burton's Italy was Italy, exacerbated by Zeffirelli, who gives *The Taming of the Shrew* the look of grandiose Renaissance paintings, which is the look he always gave his operas – alchemical libraries, globes, hour-glasses, cathedral lanterns, cobwebs, with plenty of peeling gilt. Zeffirelli adored crowds, movement, market places, marching bands, soldiers, campfires, citizens waving from upstairs windows. The colours are russet reds, dusty pinks, quince yellows. Burton as Petruchio would seem to be in his element here: speaking the language of Shakespeare – 'a mad-cap ruffian', 'a mad-brain rudesby' – or what remains of it. Paul Dehn's screenplay, the final draft carrying a date-stamp 15 March 1966, prefers action to words; but as Dehn was the one who did the script for *The Spy Who Came in from the Cold*, and *Goldfinger*, if it comes to that, and as he, during the war, had trained Allied agents in the knacks of silent killing, going on covert missions into Occupied France and Norway (Le Carré very impressed by all this), his knowledge of battle is what's required, as we watch *The Taming of the Shrew* for the unbridled clashing of Burton and Taylor: 'You can throw your wife about,' Burton said with uncertain logic. 'With Elizabeth I was permitted to do extreme physical things.' They knock over and throw furniture at each other, race around barns and lofts, burst into orange and lemon stores and appear on rooftops. They collide with wine barrels, roll terracotta flagons across stone floors, fling fruit, fall through trapdoors and land on fleeces. They get tangled in hoists and pulleys. It is all less than athletic – and actor and actress waddle through the sequence, utterly out of puff. Stunt doubles take over to swing on ropes.

In fact, one feels sorry for Kate, with this brute being pesky. Burton's Petruchio swaggers, flashes glistening porcelain veneers, shakes his shoulders to indicate merriment. Is he drunk – or stupid? There is a great deal of meaningless hearty laughter – of a Brian Blessed sort – in place of actual Shakespearean text. Despite the over-scaled panto acting, nevertheless I can see in the boorishness of Petruchio the bullying aspects of Sir Toby Belch, who Burton played in The Old Vic 1953 / 1954 season (when Michael Hordern was Malvolio), and the tyrannical aspects of Henry VIII, in *Anne of the Thousand Days* (where Michael Hordern will be Anne Boleyn's father) – these are all characters who hurl goblets and cutlery everywhere to indicate irascible high spirits. Petruchio, the roistering libertine, when he grows older and fatter, evolves in the canon into Falstaff – what a Falstaff Burton would have made. What a Falstaff perhaps he already was, drink coming first, extensive continental lunches and snacks coming first. 'A bottle of Dom Pérignon for Mr Spinetti!', who was playing Hortensio. 'Some smoked salmon sandwiches and two glasses,' was Burton's cry – though in private he was dismissive of Spinetti ('He is fairly worthless') as Falstaff is of his hangers-on, Bardolph and Pistol. Zeffirelli thought the regular parties in the dressing rooms were very detrimental. 'The whole feast would stretch until four p.m., when they'd saunter back for a couple of shots, inevitably the worst of the day.' Burton particularly liked Tuscan tripe and a soup of vegetables and beans, made by Zeffirelli's aunt, the dish ferried from her kitchen to the studio in a big limousine. Taylor also ordered hamburgers and hot dogs from Nathan's in New York, no foreign muck for her. 'A surprise dinner or party was always cropping up.' Apart from Hordern, who is funny as Baptista, Katherina's father, doddery and harrumphing, however, the finished film gives little sense of the supporting players, who vanish in a hurricane of bows and ribbons, feathers and fluff: Spinetti, Alan Webb, Alfred Lynch, Cyril Cusack – though there's always an element of watchful malice with Cyril Cusack; and an academic paper could be written on Michael Hordern's transformation from sombre character actor into comic genius. Here, Shakespeare's verse is entirely exchanged for his non-stop multi-layered groans, guffaws, wheezing, mumbling and snickering. Incidentally, what a lot of lonely well-off men with troublesome grown-up daughters or wards, whom they are keen to marry off, Shakespeare put in his plays: Lear, Prospero, Shylock, Brabantio in *Othello*, Leonato in *Much Ado About Nothing*, Egeus in *A Midsummer Night's Dream* – every one of them capable of being reduced to Hordern's virtuosic sighing.

Michael York and Natasha Pyne have little to do, save dally in a blonde fashion – they ought to be a junior Petruchio and Kate, as Nick and Honey are a junior George and Martha. Everything between everybody is tremendously *knockabout* – elbowing, bruising, clout-ing. Incidentally, Zeffirelli came first to Burton and Taylor's notice in Paris, when they were shooting *The Sandpiper*. They attended his rehearsals for a stage version of *Who's Afraid of Virginia Woolf?*, which opened on 1 December 1964 at the Théâtre de la Renaissance. Zeffirelli's production had originated in October 1963 at the Teatro La Fenice (Venice), and had also been seen at the Teatro d'Oggi (Milan) and Teatro Valle (Rome). Quite what Taylor and Burton made of what was called *Chi ha Paura di Virginia Woolf?* and of an Italian cast speaking Italian – well, no doubt they got the gist. Maybe it made more sense in a foreign language you couldn't follow – pure noise, like passages of music, theme and countertheme, hurtling along; love as a kind of army clashing by night.

* * *

When there are no money worries, no practical, domestic or business concerns; when there are other little people to take care of these things – then Taylor and Burton were left solely with each other, with their emotions. And how quickly love turns into ennui, or plain irritation. Setting each other tests, bringing things up: 'That's one of the differences between us. Elizabeth has a very limited vocabulary. I have an immense vocabulary'; 'I love four-letter words,' Taylor countered. 'They are so terribly descriptive. They just give me a good feeling'; and of Burton's literariness, she grew jaded with his 'intoxication of words. It's a Welsh disease, I'm sure.' The drink exaggerated everything, coarsened everything. With actors such as these, I don't see life and art as separate – it's a single flow, public and private images overlap, blend; reality and fantasy, history and fiction: realms merge. And anyway what is meant by 'great acting'? Taylor and Burton carried on playing themselves. If in *Who's Afraid of Virginia Woolf?* they were playing themselves, in *The Taming of the Shrew* they were playing themselves, because it's a continuation – people screaming and fighting, hurling things at each other, quarrelling, love having made them into maniacs; love not as a bond, but as destruction.

Zeffirelli's main disadvantage, when shooting began, was he wasn't Nichols. 'I'm not sure I like Zeffirelli,' Burton wrote in his diary on 21 April 1966. 'I think he's a coward and devious with it. He cannot look you in the eye either physically or mentally. As a mind and personality, he's not a patch on M. Nichols. But he has flair shall we say.' Decoded, this suggests homophobia. (Though would Burton have been rude about Visconti?) Franco was swishy, and enjoyed the company of those Bronzino boys cast as extras. There'd been a silly contretemps over costumes – Burton and Taylor wanted the clothes to be designed and made by Irene Sharaff, who'd created the banana-yellow chiffon wedding dress for Montreal, which when put up for auction at Christie's after Taylor's death carried a pre-sale estimate of $40,000–$60,000. Zeffirelli wanted historically accurate jerkins, smocks, bodices and hats, sewn by Danilo Donati. In the event, Sharaff did the outfits for the two stars, Donati did the togs for everyone else, the hundreds of swirling cloaks, plumed caps and coloured laced corsets – and if Nichols had wanted *Who's Afraid of Virginia Woolf?* to be Felliniesque, it's nevertheless Zeffirelli who made use of Fellini's costume designer (Donati is responsible for *Roma*, *Satyricon*, others) and Fellini's composer, Nino Rota, who fused jigs and circus bands with ecclesiastical choirs and tolling bells.

The whole giddy edifice is opulent and turbulent, but in terms of sexual politics very horrible. The basic idea is a man's good Christian duty is to dominate and break a wayward strong-willed woman (as one would a brood mare) with force – physical force. That is the natural order of things. Men must be 'masters to their females', as it is said in *The Comedy of Errors*, and a girl is but a possession, a *thing*: 'She is my goods, my chattels; she is my house ... my field, my barn': Petruchio's list is all-encompassing. 'My horse, my ox ...' I'm rather reminded of Taylor, during her divorces, when spoils were divided, who always fought over *things*, the jewels, the oil paintings. When she divorced Burton the second time, on 1 August 1976, she kept the diamonds, fine art, Casa Kimberly and the yacht, the *Kalizma*, which she hadn't managed to grab when she divorced Burton the first time, on 26 April 1974. Nothing new here. Back in the Fifties, Taylor's settlement took a year longer to work out than her actual marriage with Nicky Hilton had lasted. In February 1952, she refused to sign the papers until granted Hilton stock, Cadillacs, trinkets worth $50,000 and all the wedding presents: Wedgwood china, sterling silver canteens of cutlery, Italian hand-embroidered tablecloths and napkins, five hundred pieces of Swedish crystalware and six entire coffee services. I suppose anyone in the hotel business like Conrad Nicholson Hilton Jr. would find all this surplus to requirements, but still – it's an indication of Taylor's greed. It is also an indication of her strength, which underpins her Katherina, who has a sceptical sort of air throughout *The Taming of the Shrew*, narrowing her eyes – we often see her eyes in close-up, peeping through shutters – or lifting her eyebrows. Her most affecting line (which is repeated, to make sure it has sunk in) is: 'Of all things living, a man's the worst,' which is perhaps Paul Dehn's re-write of the original Shakespearean notion, 'There's small choice in rotten apples.'

Nonetheless, were audiences, in the Sixties, unthinkingly on the side of a lusty male, who subjects a woman, who makes her feel the back of his hand? The scene in the rain, where Burton and Cusack leave Taylor in the mud and wet – not funny, just as all the cuffing and pinching is not funny. When Katherina tidies up Petruchio's castle – she gets to be domesticated, wants to make it nice ('I'm going to do the housework and the cooking,' Taylor had said when newly engaged to Nicky Hilton): it's improbable. What is probable is that, as in *Who's Afraid of Virginia Woolf?*, the heavy-going banter between the characters is spoken ironically, becomes a private game, with sticky resonances. Petruchio is initially interested in Kate (as Roderigo is in Desdemona) because she's rich – and people did wonder to what extent Burton had been drawn to Taylor for her fame. Eddie had never been in any doubt on that score. 'Why don't you leave her alone, Richard? She's my wife. I love her.' – 'You don't need her anymore,' Burton had replied. 'You're a star already. I'm not, not yet. But she's going to make me one. I'm going to use her.' Mankiewicz heard Burton say similar things, though possibly (and does this make Burton less or more culpable morally?) what Burton made use of was being in love. Truman Capote, who saw Taylor when *Hamlet* was running on Broadway, was convinced: 'She loved him, but he didn't love her. He married her because he wanted to be a movie star. That was the career he wanted – money, money, money.' There again, Ava Gardner thought the absolute opposite. 'He gave her love, he gave her sex, he gave her the diamonds, he gave her the greatest care when she was sick and in pain. I never figured out what she gave him.' The mistake being made is to assume Taylor and Burton were separate categories, when like Katherina and Petruchio they were in a sense conjoined, compounded, 'To bandy word for word and frown for frown.' Or maybe it's more accurate to say they were like Solange and Claire, the maids in Genet, 'each of whom is the other's bad smell'.

* * *

It is now Burton's great fascination with the character of Faustus – a man who sells his soul for fame and riches – made itself manifest. He'd first seen Marlowe's play at the Shakespeare Memorial Theatre, in Stratford, where a production had opened on 12 July 1946. He was with Philip, who said they stayed 'in a large private house with rooms for summer visitors'. Hugh Griffith was Mephistopheles. The actor playing Faustus later moved to New York and became the Marlboro Man. Also amongst the cast, depicting sins and temptations, were Donald Sinden, Elizabeth Sellars and Margaret Courtenay. On the lawn outside their summer let, Philip encouraged Burton, aged twenty, to recite Faustus' final soliloquy ('Earth, gape ... Ugly hell, gape not', etc.), which was to become one of his favourite party pieces. What's clear even from this early date is Burton was fascinated by the idea of damnation, by the sense of trespass and retribution – by a general sense of doom, and a belief in the Devil. Orson Welles was similarly entranced. He played Faustus on stage in 1937, aged twenty-two, and adapted the story several times, as *Bright Lucifer*, *Lucifer Rising* and *Time Runs*, where Eartha Kitt was Helen of Troy. So what *is* the story, as it might appeal to these heroic actors with their booming, beautiful voices? Clearly, Faustus is utilised as a self-portrait, bent to the actors' will: the man of learning and discrimination, who masters the world, fate, history – and who wants more. (Barry Humphries' memoirs were entitled *More Please*: despite his being lavished with life's luxuries, the Australian music hall artiste was always left with 'a vague feeling of unfulfilment: where was the rest?') And plenty more indeed comes Faustus' way – at the cost of guaranteed destruction, guilt flowing into dreams, existence shadowed by evil. He becomes somebody else, a darker version of himself. The light fails, conflict replaces harmony, and Burton (and Welles – I don't know about Barry Humphries) was fully aware of the bargain he'd made, which required all those successive transformations and relinquishments: changing his name, changing his wives, changing his language – Welsh supplanted by English literature and culture, English manners and courtliness, English tradition. Burton lost his mother, moved in with his sister, had to learn English to attend school. Then he moved in with Philip, taking on Philip's diction and airs and ambitions for him. All these major alterations; all this loss, as he got rid of what was there before. Parents, family, education; a classical actor and then a movie star: what was Burton's sense of himself, as he let his life go by? Going to Exeter College and not being a Jenkins: 'If I had remained Richard Jenkins, I would have done everything different,' Gianni Bozzacchi, Taylor's personal stills photographer, heard him assert – though doing *everything differently* is what the non-Italian Burton would surely have said. 'Basically, I don't like Richard Burton very much,' he is quoted as saying in one of the many biographies.

He was always adjusting to new realities. To what extent did he eliminate the past? Remember the past? In 1975, Burton opened a bazaar in Hackney, at the behest of Sheran Hornby, and didn't much rejoice in the experience: 'Very depressing. I have forgotten the class from which I come,' and in the November of the same year Burton was in South Wales, and he's now too grand for it. He walked out of Neath's Castle Hotel, and was then upset by the modesty of the 'executive' Beach Hotel in Aberavon: 'Overall feeling of grime.' Burton remained Welsh as far as valour and faith went, and he liked wearing a patriotic red, but it is like a lost identity. Who is this stranger? Paradoxically, despite the attachment disorders, as a child he was surrounded by love and affection; as he was as an adult by wealth and women. Professionally he was acclaimed, at least at first – Richard had riches everywhere; and so, like Tolstoy, with his money and accomplishments, Burton was 'confronted with a great blank', which was filled with alcohol and bad sex.

'I remember screwing everybody in a large company over a year or so to get one woman,' he reminisced in 1968. 'I got her. I wish I hadn't now because she was an evil virtuous bitch and filthy minded . . . But I got her.' (Who was this, I wonder? Not Claire Bloom? In their autobiographies, Julie Andrews and Joan Collins ruled themselves out as conquests.) There was a nastiness and misogyny behind the glamour, what Woody Allen dubs anhedonia, a belief happiness is a brief distraction from endemic suffering. 'Why, this is hell, nor am I out of it,' says Mephistopheles of his life on Earth.

Burton was more or less murdered by fame, and in a way, like Faustus, he didn't seem to age, or he aged slowly – until suddenly, in his fifties, he looked like a man in his seventies. His voice had the same measured deepness – it was a voice appropriate for funerals – and he was always capable of a lingering, rasping echo and an oozing, sounding brass. Burton was always ripe or ripening; slowly sinking. It was Nichols who frequently spelt out, in Tony Palmer's documentary and elsewhere, that 'Richard was in the grip of a fantasy of having sold his soul to the Devil,' and before arriving in Rome, on 15 March 1966, to make *The Taming of the Shrew*, Burton and Taylor, honouring a promise made to Nevill Coghill, the Exeter fellow now installed in the Merton chair, that they'd do something to benefit the University Theatre Appeal Fund, had been busy on stage at the Oxford Playhouse, appearing in a few live performances of *The Tragical History of Doctor Faustus*. The undergraduates had been rehearsing for two months. Burton and Taylor slotted themselves into the show for ten days. 'It was unspeakably better than anything I had foreseen,' said Coghill diplomatically. Professor Coghill, in addition, could see the point of Burton's identification with Faustus, when he said, 'Who else can speak poetry like that and make it part of the living story he is enacting?' Despite the carousing and womanising, Burton had always been a bookish, private, serious man, obsessed with literature and language, and if everyone else had been ready to go on stage, aware of their moves and lines, since well prior to the start of Hilary Term, on 3 January, he and Taylor arrived punctually, on 31 January.

* * *

Burton was forty, Taylor thirty-three, and in the words of David Wood, a student at Worcester College, they were 'risking their reputations on sharing the stage with us' – but they mucked in manfully, were 'happy and relaxed', thoroughly enjoying the parties, where the youngsters (in Taylor's phrase) 'puked up in the john'. Taylor gave away Burton's spare clothes, if she thought people looked shabby: 'You can't go around like that!' They kept in touch, too – Wood was invited by Taylor to Burton's birthday party at The Dorchester, in 1975. Egalitarianism only went so far, though. There were plenty of signs world-class celebrities had descended on Oxford. Burton and Taylor materialised in a green Rolls-Royce driven by the bodyguard and reckless driver Gaston Sanz. Sanz even accompanied Burton to the Gents, so the star never risked being vulnerable and alone. Rehearsals were held in the gymnasium of the Oxford police station, in St Aldate's, as the premises could be sealed from press intrusion. Every so often, without looking or asking, Burton threw his arm backwards over his shoulder – Sanz would instantly be there, to place a lighted cigarette between his master's nicotine-stained fingers. The Burtons, married for two years, a couple for four years, were, Wood remarks, by now 'something of a double act', like Laurel and Hardy or Martin and Lewis. They retained suites for daytime use at The Randolph. The ballroom was taken over as an office for agents, managers, hair and make-up personnel, valets and dressers. Overnight was spent at The Bear in Woodstock, where dinner was on offer to the young cast – many of whom, in later life, went on to be High Court judges or Establishment grandees with knighthoods. When it was Wood's birthday during the run, Taylor gave him a smacker on the lips: 'I still glow at the memory of this spontaneous gesture of affection.' I bet he does.

Burton, who'd grown a beard for the part, made no secret of the fact personal parallels were all too apparent – that he'd sold his soul for earthly delights. As Wood and his colleagues could see, comparisons were to be made every day 'between the character and the actor' – Burton the penniless actor from South Wales, who'd played kings and princes at Stratford and The Old Vic, who'd thrown away a traditional and respectable career doing the classics, to become a big Hollywood star, married to a bigger, splashier, Hollywood star. Private jets, jewels, fur coats, an entourage, unimaginable wealth ... 'Everyone is offered a choice,' Burton explained to the company. 'One easy, one difficult.' The difficult choice is more rewarding, at least materially. Burton was now so lordly, or regal, he never carried money. Sanz paid for everything. The boot of the Rolls was filled with fan mail, which Burton and Taylor never bothered to open. The stars were getting too apart from real life – and no wonder Burton identified with Faustus, telling the company the final speech in the play, where Faustus begs for his soul, was 'the greatest in English drama'. Indeed, against a soundtrack of clock chimes and knocking heartbeats, speaking these majestic lines – 'Stand still, you ever-moving spheres of heaven, / That time may cease and midnight never come' – Burton's 'melodic tones were excitingly apparent', and Wood witnessed what seemed to be like the opening up of 'a magic circle of space around him to portray his power'. This is what Burton had always been able to conjure up – the sensual (or sexual) nature of acting; the erotica of any great art, the pleasurable tingling. Remembering being in the Fry play *The Boy with a Cart*, back in 1950, Burton said, 'I could feel the absolute stillness of the audience. The atavistic hairs on the back of my neck rose and I thought: what an extraordinary feeling. That was the first time I felt a sense of the power of acting ... That's when I thought: I'll go on with it.' The creative urge or stimulus, what Burton called the 'throbbing fervours', provoked 'the strangest sensation in my penis'. Picasso said he painted with his penis. It's the same idea.

Opening night was 14 February, Valentine's Day. Tickets, normally six shillings and sixpence (thirty-two-and-a-half pence) were now changing hands for a fiver, or a hundred quid in today's figures. It was all 'the most publicised three weeks in Oxford's seven-hundred-year history', everyone was saying, which might be hyperbole, except this was *Elizabeth Taylor* and *Richard Burton*. As Helen of Troy, on Taylor's head was twenty pounds in weight of wig. She'd had her costume specially designed by Irene Sharaff, who did another variation on the lavish gold dresses from *Cleopatra*. With The Randolph as their dressing room, Taylor and Burton scurried through the kitchens, went across the covered hotel car park and down an alleyway, to reach the Stage Door of The Playhouse. 'All I do is kiss Richard and move around,' said Taylor, which was true. But as Wood adds, as the apparition of Helen of Troy, throwing Faustus lascivious glances, 'she became a fantasy, a phantom bathed in dry ice.' Maria Aitken, who played an angel, has confirmed, 'When they kissed, it was the single most electrifying moment I have ever seen in well over half-a-century of theatre-going.'

A valet was in the wings, to hand Burton a sustaining tot of whisky and a burning cigarette every five minutes. Taylor was also escorted by her minions to her entrance upstage left. The minions then raced behind the scenery to greet her on her exit downstage right. There was a glass of gin in readiness on a cushion. At the finale, the audience, amongst whom were Harry Secombe and Stanley Baker, gave the stars fifteen curtain calls. There were nine minutes of solid applause. There'd been huge press interest, of course, so it is not edifying, reading how mocking, sneering, contemptuous and cynical the national reviewers all were, opinions formed in advance. It's as if Burton and Taylor were fair game for being rich and famous. 'What do you expect from a pig but a grunt?' said Coghill of the average newspaperman. Burton, said the critics, 'has scaled himself down'; 'an eagle among a covey of well-meaning sparrows'. An LP recording with the student cast was made by EMI one Sunday in

Putney. Taylor was present, and credited on the sleeve, despite her non-speaking role. 'I'm here to make the sandwiches.'

* * *

With Zeffirelli's filming completed – Burton's Faustus beard was his Petruchio beard – forty-eight undergraduates arrived in Italy for the *Doctor Faustus* filming to begin. It looks to me as if props from *The Taming of the Shrew* were recycled, especially as John DeCuir was again the production designer – black candles, skulls, a stuffed alligator, astrological instruments. Welles, in his theatrical version, wanted complete darkness (the stage hung about with black velvet), out of which bestial shapes appeared, tigers and lions, in flashes of fire and shafts of light. The Seven Deadly Sins were giant puppets. Infernal spirits were heralded by shrieks and yells. The play was an exorcism rite, Faustus standing inside a cabalistic pentangle, and the whole thing derived from Welles' production of *Macbeth*. Burton's *Doctor Faustus* derived from *Hamlet*. There are lots of skeletons, maggoty corpses, puffs of green smoke; we are in the catacombs, which could be the rotten Danish court or the Prince's quarters in Wittenberg. Burton is the mad and lonely scholar, his study a purple cave, and what makes him sign the deed of gift – 'Faustus has bequeathed his soul to Lucifer' – is a vision of Taylor, 'the pride of nature's works', who makes nine appearances throughout the film, shimmering about, her face sparkling with glitter or painted gold and silver. These statues she is made into have precise physical form. Her Helen of Troy (she of the thousand ships, sunk) goes in for long mermaid hair and costume jewellery. There are also lots of lovely girls, the 'undergraduettes', one must suppose, a blonde mob, who as Faustus approaches turn into grinning hags, which will have been frustrating. 'I am wanton and lascivious and cannot live without a wife,' Faustus has to remind Mephistopheles, a stone-bald student who never washed and grew

427

up to be an Associate Professor of Philosophy at Brandeis, named Andreas Teuber, who died in 2021.

Burton starts out under a lot of crêpe old age make-up, which disappears as he signs away his soul, and his hair becomes a ruddy chestnut, or as Peter Kay would say, prematurely maroon. Gábor Pogány's camera picks out windowpanes, telescope lenses, magnifying glasses – scientific instruments belonging to the scholar, with which he is meant to see clearly; but with Faustus, all now is distorted, his (moral) vision blurred. He wears primitive spectacle frames, as Michael York does in his schoolmaster disguise in *The Taming of the Shrew*. Whenever it looks like he may repent, Taylor returns, with metal coils springing through an orange head dress, and without offering much resistance, Faustus is saying, 'Lips, suck forth my soul.' Which Taylor's lips seem successfully to do. Taylor is like the Bride of Dracula, writhing around, snarling and laughing humourlessly. The expression on Burton's face suggests he is fully aware sexual curiosity and horror share the same territory. He once said of Taylor (as previously mentioned), 'She is not happy until she owns your soul,' and Taylor, here, is the person who drags Burton's Faustus down under the floorboards, into the flames of 'eternal damnation', and the film ends with a lot of jangling music, whispering voices and insistent chiming bells.

As the character who destroyed the metaphysical order, there's Marlowe's Faustus and Goethe's Faust; Berlioz's opera *La Damnation de Faust* and another Faust opera by Gounod. Liszt composed *A Faust Symphony*, a musical portrait. In Mann's novel *Doctor Faustus*, the maestro, Adrian Leverkühn's diabolical pledge – he's mad before he goes mad – is to infect his central nervous system with the spirochete, in the belief syphilis, a manifestation of the Devil, will guarantee the composer twenty-four years of crazy creativity. I like *Bedazzled*, directed by Taylor's one-time squeeze Stanley Donen, released in 1967, in which Peter Cook's Devil tries to corrupt Dudley Moore's Stanley Moon. It's interesting that at the same time Burton and Taylor were working on the Faust legend, Cook and Moore were drawn to the same theme (of inner-demons) – *Bedazzled*, originally entitled *The Sale*, a parody of the Faustian pledge, is an allegory of the comedians' strange show business marriage, the entrapments of a double act: 'Course there's no call for angels now, is there' – 'No, you don't see much of them these days, do you? Mrs Wisby saw one actually the other day in the garden. She saw this angel. It turned out to be a burglar.' Cook, who'd read Modern Languages at Cambridge, knew his Goethe: 'Let but the Spirit of All Lies with works of bedazzling magic blind you; then, absolutely mine, I'll have and bind you.' As Dudley summarised everything to Cook, to show he understood it, 'a short-order chef, useless with women, crippled with a lack of self-confidence, who sells his soul to you, a cruel but debonair Satan . . .' The Pete and Dud relationship is an exact parallel of Mephistopheles and Faustus, and Pete and Dud are also possibly Taylor and Burton in satirical guise – and Burton and Taylor's *Doctor Faustus* is as much a personal fantasia as any of these antecedents.

* * *

When Faustus says ''Tis magic, magic that hath ravished me!' and as Burton gasps and declaims, rocking his body from side to side, tilting backwards, what he means is the black magic of celebrity. There's a mass of material benefits, glory and riches. Gold coins are heaped throughout the film, like piratical booty. In terms of Burton's own career, though he said three-quarters of it went before he saw it, on wages for guards and aides, after *Cleopatra* thirty-six million dollars came his way, in straight fees alone. Contracts stipulated first-class travel for up to eight persons. A limo was to be on twenty-four-hour call. Burton's name came first on posters, in lettering bigger than the title. He had approval for script changes and casting decisions. Taylor had similar privileges. It was all money and anarchy – Burton and Taylor arriving in a helicopter in Wales, with hairdressers and secretaries; Burton dishing out jewels ('It made me feel good. A feeling of power. Real power'); Taylor's eager acceptance. Burton interpreted Faustus as an explanation (possibly an exculpation) of his own shamelessness – the crowds of girls – and his neediness and ambition and paranoia, which were chips off the old block. 'I am neurotic,' he once said. 'My father, slashing away at the coal face, smashing out [his] anger and passions and fury . . . was shaking with neurosis,' amongst other stimulants. Or as Faustus put it, 'My heart's so hardened I cannot repent,' though his heart, Burton's, may still be filled with pride and despair – and if he was subject to damnation, the process ('then will I headlong run') began immediately: his treatment of Sybil; the fate of Jessica; the fate of Ivor; the Academy Award he never won; the alcoholism and physical decrepitude (cervical laminectomy, 26 March 1981; perforated ulcer, 7 October 1981); the mockery of the press (*Doctor Faustus* was 'an oddity that may have some archive appeal', *Variety*; Taylor appears in 'waves of candle smoke, dry-ice vapour and vulgarity that swirl through the sets', *Time*); the loneliness and the knowledge bliss was not everlasting. 'And then return to Helen for a kiss,' says Faustus – but it is the vampire's kiss. Troy was destroyed for her. The 'eternal beauty' is a she-devil, who in Burton and Taylor's film is first seen inside a geodesic dome – a Sixties architectural favourite, invented by Buckminster Fuller. The (unrealised) Oxford arts centre was to be a geodesic dome. Helen's final metamorphosis, when Faustus attempts to embrace her, is to turn into a pillar of disease – which is quite true to Marlowe's play, which is crammed with references to pestilence. As Christopher Ricks said in a lecture I attended, when I was a Junior Research Fellow, '*Doctor Faustus* and Hell on Earth', and which is printed in *Essays in Criticism* (April, 1985), bubonic plague was rife during the years surrounding the play's composition, in the sixteenth-century. Londoners were infected with running sores. Theatres were places of contagion. The language of the play – 'a plague on her', 'a plague take you', 'And hell shall after plague their treachery' – contemplates disease and contemplates the soul:

'But mine must live still to be plagued in hell.' Mann's Leverkühn is likewise 'pinched and plagued with hot pincers' – this the price of Faustus' gratification, his experience of what Hazlitt called 'all the fictions of a lawless imagination'. And it was Taylor who was Burton's 'shortcut to riches, love, knowledge and power of all kinds', to use the words of Keith Thomas, in *Religion and the Decline of Magic*, when describing sixteenth- and seventeenth-century spirit-raising.

Faustus' communing with Helen of Troy – what we see or sense is Taylor's ownership of her husband; and by now with her Burton had become a different person, like Macbeth after the murder: 'To know my deed, 'twere best not to know myself.' Taylor had become a fantasy figure ('Bewitched', jotted Burton in his diary. 'Bewitched by her cunt and her cunning'), almost impersonal, static, rather than a person, completely realised. Burton's diaries are full of the fear he's going to lose this magical sense of her – as of course he did. When they were attending to each other's wishes and dreams they were close; when it became manageable and factual – food and fucking – something essential was extinguished. The blushing and the flushing; physical or bodily sensations – the frenzy or purple riot: they could recreate this, prolong it, return to it methodically in movie roles (all these films which parade their passion and are love stories with unhappy endings), but not in ordinary life, which required stimulants and depressants, drugs and booze, and which couldn't evolve, couldn't progress. Taylor and Burton couldn't have babies together, for example; they became ossified, rooted to the spot, as creatures of romance and legend – self-centred and mutually oppressive. They were aware of the impression they were making, too; they were aware of everything they were doing, on screen, and in their very public private lives, at airports, on the decks of yachts, when they threw tantrums, quarrelled, the round of kissing and reconciling. Their tiresome misbehaviour had a childish intensity. Her to him: 'For Chrissakes, shut your fucking mouth. I'm not finished talking yet.' Him to her (at the Round House's Cinema

City Exhibition on 10 October 1970): 'Shut your mouth, woman.' They'd found their own private corner of hell.

* * *

As Montgomery Clift had died of 'occlusive coronary artery disease' (drink and drugs) on 23 July 1966 – the very day they were shooting the hilarious sequence where Katherina falls off her donkey into the muddy pool – his role as Major Penderton in *Reflections in a Golden Eye* was going to have to be recast. Lee Marvin turned it down. Apparently, Burton turned it down, perhaps because, despite *The Night of the Iguana*, he had in the meantime gone off John Huston, writing in his diary, 'Huston is a simpleton. But believes himself to be a genius. And a self-aggrandising liar. Cunning at it.' Burton had a puritanical – and pedantic – tendency to sniff out pretension, though as a witch-finder general in this regards sometimes he was simply bitchy: 'She seems pathetic to me' (of Maria Callas); 'those tiny button eyes in that great arse of a face' (of Anthony Quayle); 'a monster of staggering charmlessness and monumental lack of humour' (of Lucille Ball); 'a mass of affectations . . . He really is a shallow little man with a very mediocre intelligence' (of Laurence Olivier). First, Burton, who had a reflective, ruminative temperament, is seeing himself as superior to these people – but these are critical remarks about private personae, not denigrations of artistry. Indeed, the purpose of the artistry is to cover up, shift away from, how one can come over in real life. 'Half the fun of playing other parts,' Burton had said in the Fifties, when making *The Robe*, the one about the Roman who executed Christ and converted to Christianity, 'is getting away from your own disgusting self.' Secondly, perhaps that was the importance of Taylor. In the priggish climate of the Fifties and early Sixties, her spoilt ego and selfishness were such, she challenged the notion and convention of disreputableness and social aberration. The disgusting self may be admitted, indulged, in the quest for pleasure – as she said in old age, looking back: 'When I think about the Sixties, I'm glad I knew the wildness, glamour and excitement, when I was in my prime. The parties, the yachts, and the private jets and the jewellery. It was a great time to be young, alive and attractive and to have all those goodies. I enjoyed it.' Where Burton saw morality, a need to preserve notions of a high ideal, Taylor saw appetite. And this is why he saw through John Huston – the affected Anglo-American-Irish drawl and the riding to hounds at St Clerans, County Galway; his proficiency with his fists; the big game braggadocio; the courtliness a mask for cruelty. Burton didn't want to respond to the charm. Nor do the Welsh like swank. Additionally, Huston's being a literary man, cultured, making films based on Melville, Toulouse-Lautrec, Kipling, Arthur Miller, and so forth: Burton's contempt, I think, is tinged with envy. *Reflections in a Golden Eye* was another literary project, from a novella by Carson McCullers. Burton was fully aware of it, having discussed the work with Peter Glenville, in May 1965. Taylor read the book in Puerto Vallarta in 1963. If Burton is not in the film, it'll be because he'd have been required to play the same role yet again – more cinematic squabbling, more spousal fisticuffs. His place is taken by Marlon Brando.

We are in the Deep South, except we aren't. Georgia is the De Laurentiis Studios, where in the autumn of 1966, Burton was involved in post-production work with not only *The Taming of the Shrew* but also *Doctor Faustus* ('There's a lot to be done with it and we may have a most interesting piece by the time we've chopped, changed and diffused the weaker spots.') *Reflections in a Golden Eye* is like *Who's Afraid of Virginia Woolf?*, in that we are on campus, this time an army campus. Taylor is the sex-starved wife of Major Penderton, who lectures on Clausewitz and is completely prissy – Philip in his ATC uniform with MBE medal – with a curious strangulated voice. At one point we see him in the bathroom, smearing his face with Nivea cream. He talks to the men about the necessities of leadership, about how leadership qualities are acquired; he is moved by the idea of men living only amongst men – a life that's clean, without ornamentation or feminine clutter. It's a deeply misogynistic philosophy, not unlike that of Colonel Kurtz in his heart of darkness, or Sherlock Holmes, who in *The Sign of Four* tells Watson, who has got engaged to Mary Morstan, 'But love is an emotional thing, and whatever is emotional is opposed to that true cold reason which I place above all things. I should never marry myself, lest I bias my judgement.' Less a speech in favour of a detective's deductive methods, I've always thought, than Holmes rationalising homosexuality, and *Reflections in a Golden Eye* is a thoroughly homosexual film, and homophobic. One of Penderton's officers is denied promotion because he drinks tea, listens to classical music and reads Proust. In the closed society of the military base everyone watches each other, for signs and signals that might give them away – there are shots of staring eyes, snatched glimpses, veiled looks. Taylor's Leonora, meanwhile, the daughter of the chief-of-staff (as Martha was daughter of the college dean), flirts forlornly with the soldiers, taunts her husband in public, and goes off riding on her own. Also off riding on his own is Robert Forster's Private Williams, the object of Penderton's suppressed lust – Brando picks up and treasures a sweet-wrapper the soldier discards, as if it's a love token. Williams, says McCullers in her book (published in 1941), 'moved with the silence and agility of a wild creature or a thief'. One of Williams' oddities is to ride naked in the forest. Exactly as in *Equus*, equestrian paraphernalia is rendered erotic – the riding boots, whips, saddles, horseflesh. Leonora's mount (to quote from McCullers – and this exactly rendered in the film) is 'a chestnut stallion ... His coat was curried smooth as satin and his mane was thick and glossy in the sun ... a light froth of foam showed on his muzzle.' Taylor, who in her jodhpurs looks like Dawn French, at one point slashes Brando across the face with her riding crop. As usual, when her scenes involve animals – going back to *National Velvet* and *The Courage of Lassie* – what Taylor is responding to is the animal in man, and if Penderton is unable to respond to her needs and drives,

434

Williams proves decidedly creepy, stealing into Leonora's room at night to sniff her discarded clothes and perfume bottles. Penderton mistakes the nature of the nocturnal visit – he thinks he's the object of the tryst. When he realises his error, he gets a gun. Williams is shot (executed) not because he's Penderton's wife's putative lover, but because he, Penderton, is a rejected suitor.

Critical and biographical commentary on *Reflections in a Golden Eye* is generally irrelevant and offensive, e.g. Brenda Maddox calling Brando 'the fairy guardsman' or Roger Ebert describing (without outrage) the jeering audiences in Chicago. We are told about falling grosses. Actually, Huston and his cast and crew made an adult film and they should all have been proud of it. *Reflections in a Golden Eye*, Taylor's first film without Burton since *BUtterfield 8*, deals with how wretched people tend to be in their real (as opposed to professional) lives and relationships, how mismatched. Brando shows us the agony of the secret life, the desires and longings beyond conscious control. As an actor, he has no fear of embarrassment – indeed, he elicits it, and gives a thoroughly masochistic performance. I don't believe Montgomery Clift, had he lived, could have had this sheer presence on the screen, this great weight. (He'd have been more suited to playing the Williams character.) With Brando there's this sense of a mountainous person collapsing, as 'the thought of the soldier tantalised him continually,' as McCullers described it. Could Burton have been so free? Brando's freedom is that he remains remote, a quality Burton saw in Taylor likewise. 'They are remote,' he said of Brando and his wife, seeing them together on screen. 'You can't quite catch them.' They swim, as it were, far away from land. Burton's Penderton, I feel sure, had he played the part, would have been Antony, Andros, Hewitt, George or Petruchio. We'd be fully aware of every saucy doubt and fear. Nevertheless, Brando and Burton always did things grandly. Both of them, in the end, contrived to hate acting, its childishness and lack of manliness. They were indolent and self-destructive: eating (Brando), drinking (Burton). Julie Harris, who is in *Reflections in a*

Golden Eye, is good here – and though she means Brando she could equally be speaking of Burton: 'He didn't love acting, he didn't love the theatre and he didn't respect his own talent, but his gift was so great he couldn't defile it.' Their physical presence may not be gainsaid. Burton had a naturalness and authority; Brando strove for a naturalness (the 'Method', etc.) yet it's always artifice, magniloquence, his performances reek of, which are as mannered in their way as Congreve or Vanbrugh. He had the nobility of brute strength (Kurtz carrying on up the jungle; Don Corleone in his darkened library), as Burton did in *Alexander the Great*, or when he threatens to erupt in *Look Back in Anger*. As actors, they had access to similar amounts of pride and gloom. When I was watching *Last Tango in Paris*, I kept thinking how inconceivable it would have been for Burton to be as open as this, completely unselfconscious, mumbling the dialogue, giving a performance that is incoherent, smudged. And indeed, Burton hated it, was 'absolutely revolted. I didn't know where to look . . . it did not turn me on, it turned me off.' It is not though, Bertolucci's film, a work intended for arousal – in fairness, Burton saw the picture at the Ponti villa, with Sophia Loren adjacent. But it is a work intended to show sex as obliterating, annihilating; sex as death and sex as infertility: anal sex, fingers up the arse, pillow talk about pigs fucking and vomiting in your face. There is scrupulously no tenderness, only simple brutal fornication, and yet . . . and yet . . . Maria Schneider, as the rich girl (we are taken to the family's country estate), doing what she wants, lashing out, abasing herself, kittenish: is this Taylor, too? She said often enough, whether of Burton or Mike Todd, 'We had a ball fighting,' and here in the empty orange apartment as anonymous as any hotel suite, is a couple doing exactly that, slapping each other, flinging themselves against walls, wanting to be subservient, and resisting it.

Burton's version of this, a pale imitation, scarcely heard of, is *Obsession*, with Tatum O'Neal. She's fifteen-going-on-sixteen, he's whatever he was in 1980, fifty-five, a depressed painter called Ashley St Clair (Christ), who hasn't picked up a brush in a decade. 'When an artist stops working,' he says, 'he finds sick ways of destroying himself.' He dozes in a porno cinema ('Did I snore?'). He quotes William Blake. Vivaldi tinkles in the background. His studio is a big barn that must be a bugger to heat. Tatum says, 'I know that certain people shouldn't get all tangled up together, but they can't help it. They do because they . . .' – 'Have an affinity,' says Burton's character, cutting across her, completing the sentence. Ashley then says he's sixty, which is not an age Burton reached. Tatum tries to tell him, 'You're great and strong and young,' but Burton's dry and stricken artist isn't going to be deluded. The rich bronze of his face in the dull yellow light retains an implacable Red Indian blankness. 'Are you attracted to me, I mean physically?' the girl presses. 'Yes,' says Burton, swallowing audibly. As the painter's new model, and I wish she hadn't been asked to do this, she strips off to display hairy forearms, big brown monkey nipples (to use a phrase from *Who's Afraid of Virginia Woolf?*) and puppy fat, exactly like the Taylor in Burton's romantic diary descriptions ('I think her arms should not be overexposed . . . She should never wear low-heeled shoes'), and it's Tatum, readers will recall, who took the Taylor role in the remake of *National Velvet*, which was called *International Velvet*. In spite of the topless scene, however, where Tatum's Sarah Norton tried to become Ashley St Clair's new muse, *Obsession*, which also went by the title *Circle of Two*, and which was the last feature film of Burton's to be released when he was alive, doesn't quite become another *Lolita*, even though Burton says of Tatum in the buff: 'You are the most perplexing, intriguing girl.' The film lacks what it should be about: illicit sexual heat ('I have the strongest kind of feeling for him,' the girl bleats to her parents – the idea is that it's the youngster who does the seducing); and instead (perplexingly, intriguingly) the mood is of impotence. With Burton there, wearing brown or brownish woollen pullovers, which aren't saggy but immaculate; with his hair given a brownish, reddish rinse (I kept trying to work out where the parting was, whether an expert had stopped him seeming bald) – all this helps make the elderly artist and his youthful model theme (a favourite of Picasso's; it's the relationship in heaps of Woody Allen films) decidedly deathly. I can't think of another Burton picture so filled with death, the fear of death, the fear and morbid certainties of old age, though in 1974, and *The Voyage*, Vittorio De Sica was already making predictions: 'Richard was a man ready to die. A man killing himself . . . It broke my heart to see him.' A sombreness settles over the actor, in *Obsession*, when he talks about dust and smoke as 'things that settle'. Burton is heavy, fatalistic, not quite fully present. 'Hey, where are you?' Tatum says to him, aware his mind is elsewhere. It's a fragment, I'd venture to say, of what his Lear might have been like, the characters here in the end more like the king and Cordelia than Humbert Humbert and Dolores Haze, especially when Burton is given the line, 'The most beautiful sounds in the English language are the names of flowers.'

Brando is regal, too, but it's a king of the jungle nobility, e.g. the scene in *Last Tango in Paris* where they make gorilla noises, thinking it's the only honest kind of speech. The primitiveness Burton overcame, as a youngster, Brando exults in – and Burton would have had too much taste (or 'taste') to be like Brando, when he dangles a dead rat. Actually, Brando, as he is in *Last Tango in Paris*, made at the same time as Burton was in Budapest making *Bluebeard* (directed by the Dmytryk who'd directed Brando in *The Young Lions*), would view Burton's idea of art and taste as fake, like the cosmetics on his character's wife's laid-out corpse. Good taste is something to jeer at, be repulsed and made angry by. Paul, Brando's character, has a hatred of refinement – when ordering champagne at the dance hall he puts on a silly-ass English old-boy accent. In his turn, Burton was repelled by Brando's clownishness, the tangled appearance, rudeness, fatuousness – yet during *Hamlet* rehearsals, in 1964, Burton had been overheard saying of Brando, 'He surprises me, he's the only one who does.' So, whilst I can see Brando gave performances Burton could never have given, Brando's performances, particularly as exemplified by the one in *Last Tango in Paris*, and by the mettle or essence Brando implied generally (do find *The Nightcomers*, where he's Henry James' Peter Quint) – all possess qualities shared by many of the roles Burton did attempt – the nasty eroticism, the feelings of debasement, the exhibitions of power and torment.

There's a carelessness about Brando that Burton with his obsessive puritan guilt would disallow, unless he could let drink overtake him ('Had a good row with [Taylor] and accused her ... of lousy taste,' 2 June 1965); he was constrained by the precepts of Philip, a man who if he was cultivated, was cultivated, as Tolstoy would say, 'like a cucumber in a greenhouse.' And it's the pent-up psychology of Philip that Brando manages to portray in *Reflections in a Golden Eye* – the actor perfectly indicating the 'constant state of repressed agitation', the 'diseased obsession,' as described by Carson McCullers ; and in *Last Tango in Paris*, there's truth to the way grief makes the character deranged, as Taylor was when Todd was killed, and when she heard Burton had died. She was 'completely hysterical,' said Victor Luna. 'I could never have that special place in her heart she keeps for Burton.' At the finish, nothing much matters. Everything is reduced to nothingness and vulgarity; to bodily fluids and damnation. It occurs to me now, Burton went through his career with a look of disgust on his face; the dry bumps and craters gave his skin the quality of a seashell; his eyes had red flecks, the red the colour of a hospital blanket. The reddish glow and sickliness, the burnished copper tones – a gift to great lighting cameramen, like Vittorio Storaro, who photographed *Wagner*, and Taylor in *The Driver's Seat*, and who was also responsible for the Francis Bacon colouration, ghastly peacock greens, prepuce pinks and glans greys, for Bertolucci, in *Last Tango in Paris*.

* * *

By 9 January 1967, Taylor and Burton were in Cotonou, Dahomey, making *The Comedians*, and having dinner with Peter Glenville and

Alec Guinness. I'll leave them there in the gross West African heat, eating 'cold ham, spring onions, radishes, cheese, bread (lovely long loaf)' – Burton makes a Ploughman's sound like a brand-new discovery – in order to look at a broader cultural context. For though specific films, specific events, about which a big fuss was made at the time, have disappeared from public consciousness (Royal premieres, Royal receptions, Royal charity galas, with Taylor and Burton in evening attire to the fore in any receiving line), Taylor, certainly, remains present, constant, as one of Andy Warhol's chief images, along with Elvis, Mao, Marilyn, Jackie O, electric chairs, knives and guns, in his stream of screen-prints – the Pop Art fabrication of a tab-loid front page with a headline and picture: 'Eddie Fisher Breaks Down; In Hospital Here; Liz in Rome' (black polymer paint on canvas), now in the Museum für Moderne Kunst, Frankfurt; 'The Men in Her Life' (six-foot-ten-inches by six-foot-ten-inches), belong-ing to the Morton G. Neumann Family Collection, Chicago – Taylor at the races with Mike Todd and Eddie, a stuttering, faint image repeated thirty times (silk-screen ink on synthetic, fast-drying, water-based polymer paint on canvas); a version was sold for $63.4 million in 2010 by Phillips de Pury and Company, New York. 'National Velvet' (eleven-foot-four-and-three-eighths-of-an-inch by six-foot-eleven-and-a-half-inches) – forty or so images of Taylor on a horse; 'Double Liz' (six-foot-seven-and-three-quarters-of-an-inch by six-foot-eleven), where she's disappearing into the blackness of the rolled ink; ''65 Liz', two panels, one empty, Collection Irving Blum, New York; 'Ten Lizes' (six-foot-seven-and-one-eighth inches by eighteen-foot-six-inches), in the Musée National d'Art Moderne, Centre Georges Pompidou, Paris, where they call it 'Dix Liz': char-coal images, none is flattering – as if trodden underfoot, or a peeling hoarding, putting me in mind of Larkin's Prestatyn poster, where in the once-cheerful picture the girl's breasts and thighs are defaced: 'Huge tits and a fissured crotch / Were scored well in . . . Very soon, a great transverse tear / Left only a hand and some blue.' 'Blue Liz as

Cleopatra' makes use of a publicity still, particularly the Egyptian earrings. There's a darkish blue background and Taylor's image gets blacker and blacker, disappearing into the night. 'Early Colored Liz' has an olive-green background. Taylor has pinkish skin, and there's an embalmed effect to the lips and eyes. A Wall Street hedge fund manager, Steve Cohen, sold one in November 2013 for $20.3 million. In November 2014, at a Contemporary Art Auction at Sotheby's, an 'Early Colored Liz' sold for $31,525,000.

There was an exhibition of some of these daubs at the Ferus Gallery, Los Angeles, between 30 September and 30 October 1963. Warhol was typically banal in his statements. He liked depicting Taylor because she was beautiful, 'and if something's beautiful, it's pretty colours, that's all.' Nevertheless, if beauty, according to Keats, was always meant to be interchangeable with truth, the truth for Warhol, with his fondness for tragedies (plane crashes, car accidents, suicides: people and things crushed, pulverised, exploding, falling), is that Taylor always looked as if she'd be joining what he'd called (when Marilyn Monroe died) his 'death series'. Warhol had started clipping Taylor's photographs out of the *Daily News* and *LIFE Magazine* (the issue dated 13 April 1962) 'when she was so sick and everybody said she was going to die.' The process was mechanical. 'You pick a photograph, blow it up, transfer it in glue onto silk, and then roll ink across it so that the ink goes through the silk but not through the glue.' (Got that?) The artist duplicated the same image, but it was coming out slightly differently each time. 'It was all so simple – quick and chancy. I was thrilled with it.' (No doubt.) Warhol, having prepared his screens coated with light-sensitive chemicals, squashed and squeezed oil-based enamel and vinyl inks through the mesh, onto unstretched rough canvas or linen, laid out on the studio floor. Pencil tracings taken from the acetate photographic blow-ups established a rough guide for the position of lips, eyelids, hair. The artist was fond of sleazy ripe colours, raspberry jam scarlets, bruise-blues, poison apple greens, reminiscent less of undimmed life than putrefaction, and which anticipate Brando's wife's corpse in *Last Tango in Paris*. The off-register lines, the masking tape and stencilled blocks make everything lurid, sloppy, glossy. The result is Warhol made Taylor less than one-dimensional. Like a Coke bottle from Atlanta or a soup can label, we know what's there without having to look at it closely.

This is a big compliment. Like Heinz tomato ketchup, Kellogg's cornflakes, Brillo pads, Del Monte pineapple chunks, Typhoo tea or Kraft cheese spread – commodities essential to Western civilisation, Taylor is also by now a commodity; it takes less than a split-second glance to recognise the brand. We flip past her pictures, as we would a magazine advertisement for shower curtains or high-buttoned boots or electric typewriters. We don't much notice it, nor do we judge it. She has a throwaway quality – and I suppose what Warhol did was raise questions about intrinsic value; the banality of great stars; the difference between ordinariness and celebrity; uniqueness and uniformity – all those mass-produced flattened images. It soothed Warhol – it's a sort of commingling – to know 'Liz Taylor drinks Coke and, just think, you can drink Coke too . . . All the Cokes are the same . . . Liz Taylor knows it, you know it.' Taylor, her life a spectacle, manipulated by the popular press, reliant on commercial photography, public relations, promotional personnel, was a person-as-a-luxury-good, but nevertheless one that was machine-made – in the literal sense, the celluloid clacking and whirring through the sprockets, the technical splices, the scratches and jaggedness, everything illuminated by the harsh lamp in the projection booth. Taylor, as it were, in her films, magazine profiles, paparazzi shots, newsreel glimpses, and now in Warhol's studio, was coming off the assembly line. 'One of my assistants, or anyone else for that matter,' said Warhol, 'can reproduce the design as well as I could.' And indeed, one of his employees did do exactly that – in 1963, Gerard Malanga was hired on a salary of $1.25 an hour to print Elizabeth Taylor portraits. He remained busy in Warhol's studio, known as The Factory, for seven years.

Warhol was himself a commercial artist, his work owing much to the European tradition of Alphonse Mucha, who illustrated calendars, soap wrappers, paper labels for bottles of toilet water, cosmetics and colognes; he drew advertisements for elegant Prague department stores and effulgent menu cards for the restaurants – shopping and eating as theatre. (The Warholas were from that locale – Slovakia.) Domestic objects, the utilitarian, perfume, hair oil, pomades, have, or are given, elements of frictionless fantasy. Ice creams, sweets, balloons, boxes, stationery and bill-heads were covered with intertwining flowers and leaves, tendrils, pistils. Warhol's Fifth Avenue window art was similarly joyous and playful – shoes with gold-leaf laces – so why do I feel it was deathly? Because it is not built to last long. The world of fashion (and of money): it will pass. And the more Warhol's images of Taylor (and Elvis and Marilyn and Jackie O) are reproduced, the colours leaking, the lines breaking in on each other, the soot-black contours, though not blurred exactly, losing definition, the emptier his subjects seem. The repeated images are variously faded or gummy. If we look at these faces and take them at face value, 'even beauty,' said Warhol, 'can be unattractive. If you catch a beauty in the wrong light at the right time, forget it! I believe in low lights and trick mirrors. I believe in plastic surgery.' Taylor's artificiality was bright and shiny, when the fan magazines are looked at, or Warhol's portraits are looked at. She looks extraterrestrial, unlikely to be hindered by earthly concerns. To Warhol, Taylor was in the same class as Picasso or the Queen of England, 'nothing and nobody can ever intimidate them.' In his diaries, she's chiefly notable for not turning up at functions, which adds to the mystique. Warhol is always hoping Taylor would attend his gallery's private views, for example – she never does. 'It would have been great if Liz Taylor had come to the opening. That would have made it something, wouldn't it?' he wrote on 11 January 1977. Later that same year, after a Liza Minnelli concert, Taylor, at last viewed by Warhol in the flesh, 'was glaring at me for some reason, giving me that look like she'd scratch my eyes out.'

At an Aids Benefit at the Javits Center on 29 April 1986, 'Liz Taylor was late because she was getting a dress from Calvin [Klein] . . . Then Liz came in and everybody went crazy and mobbed her . . . What do you have to do to be that famous?' The following month, there's a Taylor tribute at the Lincoln Center – clips, speeches, etc. – and she was an hour and a half late. 'Her mother was looking beautiful. She was the one person Liz thanked,' said Warhol. And thanked in a peculiar, gynaecological, or uterine, way, too: 'There's just one person I'd like to thank, first for giving me birth, and for being there for me all of my life – my mother.' When Taylor's mother used to phone up ('Can I speak to my baby angel girl?') it was the factotum Raymond Vignale's job to fob her off. Come December, at another charity gala, to raise money for the Creo Society, the fund for children with Aids, Leonard Bernstein, Marilyn Horne and Linda Ronstadt are present, but speeches are scrapped 'because Liz Taylor didn't show up'.

Her tardiness and absenteeism are part of the glamour – and as Warhol said, 'It would be very glamorous to be reincarnated as a big ring on Elizabeth Taylor's finger.' His shivers of delight, as he observed her thoughtless rudeness ('Liz Taylor yelled at me for leaving Diana [Vreeland] alone,' 29 October 1977); her weight gain ('Liz looked like a belly button. Like a fat Kewpie Doll,' 6 March 1978; 'Liz looked very fat, but very beautiful,' 28 October 1978); and her weight loss ('Liz's one beauty problem now is that when she lost the weight her nose never did get smaller. The liquor's still in it,' 5 May 1986) – the effects she has on him are almost ecstatic: '*Ohhhh*, Elizabeth Taylor, *ohhhh*. She's so glamorous.' Warhol is the devotee of a cult, and Taylor's function is not to be accessible. Her worshippers must put up with degradation, defilement. The worst occasion for Warhol must have been when he appeared with her as (according to the script) 'a rich creep of undisclosed nationality and occupation', in a rare film called *The Driver's Seat*, the one based on Muriel Spark's novel and made in Rome, between August and October 1973. Warhol took the trouble to organise a luncheon in her honour. Taylor ate none of the food, greeted none of the guests, and departed early in a temper, having first locked herself in the lavatory and called for a doctor. Warhol thought his tape recorder had scared her off – probably she'd finally had enough of Warhol's calling her by the detestable (to her) diminutive 'Liz', plus, at that stage, she'd yet to be presented with one of these precious pictures of herself, with which the artist had made his fortune. Also, her marriage to Burton was collapsing. Nothing was settled or normal.

There again, when had it ever been? Taylor was not frightened of anything, and could tame cheetahs, stallions and baboons – in Botswana, 'About five to fifteen baboons surrounded our suite,' said Burton. 'It was a phenomenon never seen before. It would of course occur when Elizabeth was here … Quite scary.' She never allowed herself to be rebuked by Hollywood moguls ('I won't take that kind of nonsense'), and if Mankiewicz, during *Cleopatra*, was forced to concede, 'a late Taylor was still better than no Taylor at all,' then Brian Hutton, the director of *X, Y & Zee*, unthrilled by the way the actress wouldn't get to the set until eleven, before she left it again to take luncheon until three, concluded: 'All her life, this is what she did. She's Elizabeth Taylor. She comes down to the set when she wants to come down.' She was never less than robust, definite. 'She had the simplest egotism,' as Virginia Woolf says of somebody in *Mrs Dalloway*, 'the most open desire to be thought first always.'

* * *

Warhol was her court painter, as Nicholas Hilliard, who created those miniatures frothing with pearls, ruffs and lace, was for Queen Elizabeth I. Taylor eventually manoeuvred the Pop Artist into giving her a portrait – not an actual screen-print, as it turned out, but an offset lithograph on wove paper, from an edition of three hundred published by the Leo Castelli Gallery, New York, in 1964. Inscribed 'To Elizabeth with much love Andy Warhol', it was included in her sale at Christie's on 14 December 2011. Her own copy of what Feldman & Schellmann, in the *Catalogue Raisonné,* simply entitle 'Liz', was given an estimated pre-sale value of $30,000–$50,000. It went for $662,500. Surrounded by flamingo pink, there are large green shapes accentuating Taylor's eyes – she looks like Batman's arch-enemy The Joker. You can see what Warhol meant when he said he'd taken 'a cheap photo of Liz [which had] turned the painted face of a human being into something blank, blunt, bleak, stark,' with the subtlety of a giant advertising billboard. The same reductive stunt is played by the artist on dollar bills and the Mona Lisa, icons that are likewise multiplied to infinity. The technique may be discerned in *The Driver's Seat*, which is a strange film, almost experimental. The only DVD I managed to find had been badly transposed from video, yet the blurriness and jump cuts added to the mood of it, which was accentuated, also, by the out-of-tune piano soundtrack and the distorted, taut voices.

Though we are in Rome, the city is not actually specified – and if it is not Ancient Rome on view (statues, ruins, fountains), Seventies Rome is antiquated enough, the modern hotel atriums, the department stores with escalators seemingly moving between heaven and hell. I wonder how a big star like Taylor was persuaded to be in a small-scale – cheap – operation, but it is interesting, seeing her having to be awkward and wary, unsupported by any entourage. Taylor is the only person in the world, other than Garbo or Marlene Dietrich, who could play this improbable role; a person who is stared at and surrounded, and also lonely, isolated. Her character, Lise, is nervous, anxious, convinced she is being watched, scrutinised, laughed at behind her back, jeered at – or worshipped. Lise is cross with everybody, and has a right to be. She is in a state of nervous breakdown, brittle and angry. A thing like a smudge on a water-glass can tip her over the edge. With Taylor, whatever she is doing, the film gets to be about Taylor – an investigation of her mysteriousness, revolving around the conundrum: is what is true the same as what she imagines to be true? (Warhol again: 'Who wants the truth? That's what show business is for – to prove that it's not what you are that counts, it's what you think you are.') Here, Taylor's Lise spends an eternity choosing and buying a dress, which makes her look like a harlequin. 'People in the north know nothing of colours', so the character is covered in lurid lemon-yellow tops and cotton skirts with orange, mauve and blue zigzag patterns. There is a long scene, where she's in bra and panties and we watch her do her face, in a way Warhol had long admired: 'the Liz Taylor-in-*Cleopatra* look, long, straight, dark shiny hair with bangs [fringe] and Egyptian-looking eye make-up.' She gazes at herself in mirrors, as in *BUtterfield 8*. Lise is very intent – on what? The men she meets (Warhol amongst them) are arrested and interrogated. Lise can't be found, nor her behaviour pinned down. There seems to be a complex (or messy) structure – are we seeing flashbacks or flashforwards? Has a crime been committed? By whom? Against whom? There is something of *Don't Look Now* about the police inquiries, the mannered cutting, the air of menace – all in this Italian bright light, though we could equally be in North Africa – which reminds me of another of Warhol's explanations as to why he connected Taylor and morbidity, his sense of something about her decaying and ill: 'I have lots of southern themes in my paintings. Flowers and Liz Taylor and bananas, which all the monkeys down there eat.' The explanation for everything is that Lise is searching for death, for deliverance. It's the Louise Brooks *Lulu* idea, that a girl's greatest dream is to be fatally stabbed by a sexual maniac: 'I think he's around the corner somewhere, now, anytime.' The man who'll save her is the man who'll obliterate her.

Being about sex and madness and death, or what Muriel Spark calls 'a potential for catastrophe', *The Driver's Seat* is a fairy tale: Ian Bannen with his wolf teeth and bags of rice; Mona Washbourne the sweet old granny, with a soft gurgling posh voice ('How very kind you are!'); the city as a forest, with random screams and gunfire ('terrorists popping up everywhere!'); Warhol as a white-clad angel

447

of death. Lise finally meets death in the woodland glade of the Borghese Gardens – she's Cleopatra organising her suicide: 'First tie my hands. Tie them with my scarf... Kill me! Kill me!' The Satie piano score is angry, jabbing. Vittorio Storaro, the cinematographer, washes out the colours – it is almost wholly white, which highlights the print's scratches. *The Driver's Seat* is Taylor's death film – a story about how to get rid of yourself, discarding keys, passports, documentation; the sheer relief at being able to do all this, and at the finish we get a sense of how things click and fall into place. Formally, in *The Driver's Seat*, the present and the future are flung at each other, to convey the psychic premonitions. The work is sophisticated (and Eliotic, structurally: 'Time present and time past / Are both perhaps present in time future, / And time future contained in time past'); it is also deliberately a creation of bad art, which is to say Pop Art, a film that is like a book badly transcribed from tapes and then mistyped. As Warhol himself said, 'I wanted to do a "bad book", just the way I'd done "bad movies" and "bad art", because when you do something exactly wrong, you always turn up something.' I have a feeling this is why I am drawn to and admire and see things in the Taylor and Burton films everyone else has predictably wanted to sneer at. 'The same old Hollywood stuff' (*The Sandpiper*); 'It is of an awfulness that bends the mind' (*Doctor Faustus*); 'A fuzzy unconsummated work' (*Boom!*); 'Decorous titillation' (*Bluebeard*) – these all reviews from *The Times*.

Biographers tot up the disparagements, unaware Taylor and Burton's is a Pop Art story. Their abundance and violent greed belong with comic books and bubble-gum machines – with Roy Lichtenstein's enlarged comic strips of lovers kissing. The vulgarity of Cleopatra's triumphal parades; the car Taylor drives in *A Place in the Sun* (the shark fins and chrome); the wealth on show in *Father of the Bride* and *Little Women* (nice homes with lace curtains and patchwork quilts); the mansion in *Giant* and the transatlantic travel of *The V.I.P.s*; the pungent and sweet gardens in *The Sandpiper* and, earlier, in *National Velvet* or the *Lassie* films (where England was created by shoving daffodils and hydrangeas into the Californian soil; the wardrobe department had to find bagpipes and bowler hats); or Taylor's book about Nibbles: here is America as a sacred great good place, the consumerism of the American Dream, represented by kitchens with juicers and toasters, food in the fridge, neon lights. As Warhol said, Taylor is 'too conscious of being the cat's meow, the star of stars. She has the makings of an empress, but there's also something tawdry and a bit cheap about her,' which is to be cherished – it's how we have Martha or Katherina; it's why people were afraid of her (they are afraid of Lise, in *The Driver's Seat*). She'd instantly protest against any delay or frustration of her will.

It is a fantasy existence, too, which Taylor, and Burton, demanded, an image of desire, like a magazine spread – and Taylor and Burton flooded magazines, newspapers, television bulletins, hoardings, luminous posters. The pair of them became products, registered by the public and discarded quickly (before more of them was demanded: 'Photos of Elizabeth and Richard, whether alone or together,' testified Gianni Bozzacchi, 'sold for rafts of money'), along with cardboard boxes, plastic, cotton buds or lipstick tubes. In this glittering chaos, where their photographic images were turned into mass-produced grainy silk-screens, where urban junk and fast-food counters prevailed (hamburger with fries, hot dogs with mustard); in this world where suddenly everything is the same and everything is jettisoned and vanishing: Burton and Taylor's work – the kitsch Italy of Franco Zeffirelli, the white marble clifftop villa built by MGM in *Boom!*, the tropics in *The Comedians* (Taylor 'blooms in hot climates,' said Burton) – is part of art history and the jet set; Condé Nast poses, swimsuits, blue pools. Consider the importance of lingerie, a subject in itself, in Taylor's films, in *Cat on a Hot Tin Roof* or *BUtterfield 8* or *Secret Ceremony* or her Rosie Probert in *Under Milk Wood*. Taylor is forever showing off the tops of her stockings, adjusting her garter belt and panty girdle – actually, in an old-fashioned Forties or Fifties way, which Pop Art loved. The more modern Sixties girl, who'd wear no tights or knickers, just a hastily buttoned man's long shirt, or a short skirt and a cropped haircut, is post-Pop Art, thinner-looking, hermaphroditic, in psychedelic prints. As Taylor regretted, 'There's no tits anymore. If there are, they're fake balloons ... It's all become slightly androgynous. That's not very sexy.' It's sexy enough in *Secret Ceremony* or *X, Y and Zee*, where Taylor frolics with Susannah York. That film is a hymn to vinyl, suede, feathers, bright-coloured mesh or textured tights and dresses of linked plastic discs and squares.

Halston designed yellow outfits to go with Taylor's yellow diamonds, aquamarine ones to go with her sapphires. She'd always emptied the shops: 'I never wore hats before, but Mike [Todd] said he likes them, so I went out and bought fifty.' When Burton was making *The Spy Who Came in from the Cold* in Dublin, Taylor bought him thirty-seven bespoke suits. Possibly she was still replacing the wardrobe that went in the Gstaad furnace. They had a pair of matching $120,000 Kojah mink coats, each requiring forty-two pelts. Then there were the jewels, which are hard, multi-faceted, but with no centre. They exist to catch the light, and are formed deep under the earth, in lava pools, the spawn of fire and ice. What does it say about a person, that they are obsessed with huge diamond brooches and bracelets, emerald gee-gaws? Asked, 'What is Pop Art trying to say?' Warhol was gnomic as usual. 'I don't know,' he responded, like Peter Sellers in *Being There*. I think when we look at the burgeoning Pop Art market in the Sixties and after, and when we look at the fees Taylor and Burton commanded – here are activities quite consciously commercial, lives run as a business. 'The truth is,' said Burton disingenuously, 'we live out for the benefit of the mob the sort of idiocies they've come to expect.' What Pop Art is about, is money.

* * *

The Coronation of His Majesty Bokassa the First, Apostle of Peace and Servant of Jesus Christ, Emperor and Marshal of Central Africa, in Bangui, in the Central African Republic, in December 1977, is what Burton and Taylor's conduct puts me in mind of – Bokassa I, in a ceremony inspired by Napoleon, wanted horse-drawn carriages, a gilded bronze eagle-shaped throne, a mantle covered with pearls, and troops of mounted soldiers trotting up and down in brocade. Crates of Moët and Lafite Rothschild were shipped from France – all these luxuries flown to the African bush. The effect was the opposite of dignified, and as with Burton and Taylor, and Cleopatra's entry into Rome, what scores is vanity and self-importance – and covetousness, avarice.

Between 1962 and 1966, when their percentages of the gross, profit participation bonuses and the sale of television rights were added, Burton and Taylor's films had made $200,000,000, and they couldn't get through the stuff quick enough. On 23 October 1968, for example, Burton recorded in his diary, 'I had only recently given [Taylor] a £127,000 diamond ring simply because it was a Tuesday. I enjoy being outrageous.' Sometimes I don't appreciate hearing how he enjoyed being outrageous. On 21 May 1967, for instance, they bought a luxury yacht, the *Kalizma*, which had seven double-berth state rooms, three bathrooms, and an armoury containing sub-machine guns. The vessel, an Edwardian motor launch, weighing 290 tonnes and capable of ten knots, was built by Ramage & Ferguson, Leith, in 1906, and had previously been known as the *Minona*, *Cortynia* and *Odysseia*. Scottish shipbuilders Ramage & Ferguson, by the way, also provided craft for the kings of Siam, Portugal and Sarawak. One hundred and sixty-five foot from stem-to-stern, a fantasia of walnut and chrome, with a steel hull and timber decks, the *Kalizma* was refitted for its new owners in Genoa, at a cost of $240,000. Burton spent a further $100,000 on radar equipment. The rest went on Chippendale furniture and mirrors, a dozen Regency dining chairs, and rosewood sofas upholstered in yellow silk. The Wilton carpets were notoriously ruined by the *fucking pets* and replaced every six months. 'It's a splendid toy and a lovely luxurious home,' Burton said in his diary. The toy's upkeep was $150,000 a year. When, in February 1968, the *Kalizma* was in dry dock, and Burton was in London making *Where Eagles Dare*, the 200-tonne *Beatriz of Bolivia* was rented from the Patino tin family at £1,000 a week (or $2,400) and moored near Tower Bridge. The boat was purely for the dogs, Cuthbert, Georgia, Oh Fie and E'en So, which were kept onboard, circumventing United Kingdom quarantine restrictions. In May 1969, and *Anne of the Thousand Days*, it was the turn of the *Kalizma*, anchored off Princess Steps, to serve as a kennel.

An en-suite Owners' State Room, plus four other cabins, were frequently redecorated – a hand-carved mahogany bed was installed. 'No bunks for us.' There was a saloon, a reading-room. It is still afloat. Sold by Taylor in 1995, the yacht is to be found in the Far East, steaming in South-East Asian waters around Borneo and Malaya and the Maldives. It is available for charter at $70,000 a week – let's go! Taylor and Burton's chief entertainment in mid-ocean was watching not projections of their own films but cine films of the Carry Ons – *Carry On Cleo* was a favourite, with its recognisable sets and costumes, recycled gold laurel wreaths, Nubians left over from Pinewood and Talbot Rothwell dialogue ('My end is in sight' – 'You'd better do yourself up quick. You can't meet her looking like that') out-classing any speech provided by Joe Mankiewicz for *Cleopatra*. Then there was *Carry On Henry*, for which a champagne launch was held at The Dorchester on 7 October 1970, when Burton was in town making *Villain*. Sid James was again wearing Burton's clothes, discarded after *Anne of the Thousand Days*. James, of course, was the comical version of Burton – the lasciviousness and rascality; the automatic assumption of leadership; the tough leathery face and wiry hair. James, originally a South African hairdresser, was a self-creation, as straight, randy Cockney Everyman. 'Your hand on it,' says Terry Scott's Cardinal Wolsey, in Anthony Quayle's scarlet robes. 'I didn't even put my finger on it,' replies Sid's Henry VIII, with his mix of filth and nonchalance.

I don't know the fate of their aeroplane. On 30 September 1967, 'so we could fly to Nice for lunch,' Taylor and Burton bought a Hawker-Siddeley de Havilland 125 twin-engine executive jet, which as Burton admitted was a purchase 'beyond outrage'. Taylor wanted Losey's production designer Richard Macdonald (a Royal College of Art graduate) to decorate the cabin in an ornate Regency style, with plasterwork panels, lace pelmets and Christ knows what. 'Where am I going to put the fireplace?' Macdonald asked, which Taylor thought was a serious question. They used it to land in RAF Abingdon, for example, when *Doctor Faustus* received its premiere in Oxford, a fortnight later, on 15 October 1967. They did indeed fly in it to Nice to spend the weekend on their boat, boarding the *Kalizma*, the walls now adorned with Monets, Van Goghs, a Picasso and, on a plinth, an Epstein bust of Churchill, at Saint-Jean-Cap-Ferrat. 'Might buy this plane or one like it,' Burton had announced airily. He used it to go to Geneva with his daughter Kate, Taylor's daughter Liza, Emlyn Williams' son Brook, and Ivor and Gwen, to attend André Besançon's funeral – when Ivor met with his paralysing 'accident'. When Burton completed the purchase, for $960,000, 'She [Taylor] was not displeased.' And keeping Taylor pleased was a priority. The studios had given her a Cadillac with solid gold keys when she was sixteen, and she expected gifts thereafter. All her husbands heaped her with jewels and trinkets. Nicky Hilton, in addition to a £10,000 platinum ring, a £5,350 engagement ring and a £3,700 wedding ring, gave Taylor Hilton hotel stock, which she sold in the Nineties for a profit of $21.7 million. Michael Wilding, despite being the father of her two sons, was cast aside for being (his words) 'a boring old appendage', and one not so flush. Todd, in between wrestling with Taylor on the floor, kissing and making up, gave her a $25,000 tiara, which she wore to the Oscar ceremony in March 1957, when she presented the statuette to the Best Costume Designer. Her wedding present had been a $80,000 (or $90,000, or even $250,000 – sources differ) diamond bracelet. Todd also gave Taylor a 29.7-carat ring, explaining 'thirty carats would be vulgar and in bad taste.' Taylor wore it at the numerous *Around the*

World in Eighty Days galas. Eddie Fisher paid for ten dresses from Dior, ten from Yves Saint Laurent, a Jaguar car, fur-lined coats and the $325,000 chalet in Gstaad.

So, Burton knew what was expected, if he was to maintain what by now had become 'a beautiful doughnut covered in diamonds and paint'. For Taylor's thirty-fifth birthday there was a £160,000 diamond and emerald bracelet. 'I introduced Elizabeth to beer. She introduced me to Bulgari,' Burton tried to joke – during *Cleopatra* he gave her a Bulgari 18.61-carat diamond and emerald necklace and pendant set. On 16 May 1968, the thirty-three-carat Krupp Diamond – named for a wicked industrialist who'd used forced labour during the war – was purchased for £127,000 (or $305,000). The Picasso in the *Kalizma* was acquired at Sotheby's on 4 July 1968 for £9,000, and the Monet for £50,000 – entitled 'Le Val de Falaise', it would today be valued at approximately ten million. The Peregrina Pearl, allegedly once presented by Philip of Spain to Mary Tudor in 1554, and which adorns Spanish queens in Velazquez portraits, was bought for $37,000 and given to Taylor as a Valentine's Day gift in 1969. Most famously, there was the whopping stone, the 69.42-carat diamond, also acquired in 1969, for which on 23 October Burton paid $1.1 million. Cartier designed a necklace for it, and insurers insisted it was always accompanied by bodyguards. Taylor rather enjoyed arranging for what became known as the Burton-Taylor Diamond to be placed on a bed of lettuce and paraded around the Lanai Restaurant in the Beverly Hills Hotel. 'It won't seem out of place in the yacht parked in the Bahamas or the Mediterranean ... It sort of hums with its own beautiful life,' said Burton. A spokesman for Sotheby's, New York, commented, 'Miss Taylor was very anxious to have the diamond and Mr Burton was very anxious that she should have it ... Mr Burton gives presents because he likes giving them.' Taylor said, 'I have a lust for diamonds, almost like a disease.' And we know how much she relished diseases – her all-consuming fevers, her turmoil, her operatic restlessness and languidness, her tendency to rush around like a

Donizetti heroine. Hence, all those Paris nightgowns trimmed with lace she wanted from Mike Todd, and which Todd's secretary, Peggy Rutledge, obtained from Bergdorf's, or from Andrew Sinclair, when he directed her in *Under Milk Wood*. For her short scene, says Sinclair, Taylor wanted 'three Parisian nightdresses', costing £600 apiece, which was 'half our total costume budget'. She also insisted upon a 'luxury trailer' at Pinewood, didn't appear until noon, and didn't want to appear at all in the afternoon. Burton, and O'Toole, had to take her out for a boozy luncheon, after which they finally got the shot of Rosie Probert laughing at Captain Cat's tattoos.

It has been estimated that Taylor cost Burton $1,000 an hour, between 22 January 1962, and their first scene in *Cleopatra* – 'the future in an instant,' to quote *Macbeth* – and their second divorce, in Haiti, on 1 August 1976. Not that it ended there. Three years afterwards, lawyers were still squabbling over who was due what percentage of the Vicky Tiel boutique in France and an apartment in Tenerife, worth $202,000. 'Richard pays all the bills,' Taylor said nonchalantly – and because he wanted to be 'rich, rich, rich, or at least as rich as my wife,' he invested, on behalf of both of them, in a company leasing jets to tycoons, in 158,400 shares in Harlech Television, which generated dividends of £100,000 a year, in the Paris dress shop and a 685-acre plantation in the Canaries, a farm in County Wicklow, the art (Modigliani, Van Gogh) and precious stones ... Not a penny was paid in income tax – and to avoid customs and excise duty (blabbed Eddie), jewels were hidden in Taylor's medical bags. The lawyer Aaron Frosch spent years of his life creating holding companies in Bermuda, founding corporations in Nassau, opening numbered accounts in Geneva: Interplanetary Productions Ltd; Atlantic Programmes Ltd.; Safety Programs; Oxford Productions; Taybur; Bushell Productions Inc. Though registered as company assets, the paintings and the jewels all went Taylor's way during the marital break-ups, all the goods and chattels, full ownership of the companies, the H T V stock – not exactly equitable, but Burton, when he wasn't rapacious and demonic, was austere, ascetic. What's interesting about him is the hedonism coexists with his puritanism, and his irresponsibilies and improprieties were also penitential – Burton was always working through his guilt, taking pleasure in his holy fears. Taylor nabbed the Neiman Marcus minks, of course – garments, as Burton said in his diary, that perpetuated 'the legend of immense wealth and distant unattainability which is the very stuff of glamour.'

Their accommodation had a castle-in-the-air quality. Burton and Taylor even wanted to buy the Sardinian clifftop villa built for *Boom!* – until it needed to be explained to them as to a child that there was no roof, no electricity or plumbing, and that it was in fact only a film set and merging fantasy and reality can only go so far. Luxury, nevertheless, came at a price well within their means. When Burton and Taylor attended the Taormina Film Festival, and stayed in the Il Principe Hotel, Catania, the staff were informed, 'Don't you understand that Elizabeth Taylor is coming to this hotel and that she must have nothing but the very best?' Into the eight-room suite the stars brought one hundred and fifty-six suitcases. The luggage contained outfits the world would be allowed to glimpse only the once. Taylor ordered a hundred new ensembles a year from Halston, for example, who confirmed, 'She refused to be seen in public more than once in the same design.' Her habits in the Sixties continued in the Seventies. Between April and October 1976, for instance, she bought twenty-one dresses, four capes, six pairs of shoes and a turban from Halston, and expected a forty per cent discount. Had you been standing outside the Hotel Santa Caterina, in Amalfi, during one of Taylor and Burton's arguments, you would have seen a lot of the clothes being thrown out of the window. Evan 'Buddy' Richards, a Texas-born designer and trained opera singer, whose label, founded in 1963, was 'Tiziana Roma', corroborated the extravagance and squandering: 'Elizabeth wears a dress only once – just once . . . This pink dress is to be thrown away. Five or six hundred dollars' worth of ermine are on this cape.' When 'Buddy' died in 1994, aged seventy, a box containing about three hundred sketches was discovered in his archives, of outfits devised for Taylor by a 'Tiziana' employee who'd left 'Buddy' in 1969 to be his own man – Karl Lagerfeld. Wispy long white dresses plastered with milky yellow daisies, embroidered ivory silk frocks, feathered capes like miraculous wings ... Some of these drawings, with fabric swatches attached, were sold by Palm Beach Modern Auctions on 6 January 2014. These were clothes perfect for a day of heat haze, in Italy's southern glare. 'Tiziana of Rome' is credited for 'Miss Taylor's gowns' in *The Comedians* and for 'Gowns' in *Boom!* Did any of this lot come flying through the casement?

* * *

Burton and Taylor retained suites in hotels in cities they never visited. If they did visit, in their wake was the pillage of an invading army – dog shit and dinner trays at the Plaza, New York, the usual mess of dog shit and empty bottles at the Grand Hotel, Rome. The 'clean-up from the animal excrement' from the carpets, curtains, mirrors and furniture at the Four Seasons Hotel, New York, took days. Asked to recommend a hotel in Yugoslavia, however, Taylor had to admit, 'I don't know. Whenever I was in Yugoslavia, I stayed with Tito,' which I think a wonderfully unselfconsciously comical remark. This would have been mainly in 1973, during the pre-production and production of *The Battle of Sutjeska*, also known as *The Fifth Offensive*, and a film which is as Burton predicted when reading the script, in June 1971, 'a series of loud bangs'. It's all about Tito and the partisans in the Balkans during the war when, between May and June 1943, they were circled by the Germans. The partisans are stern men with big moustaches, who cry when picking flowers for their beloveds, and then fall in battle.

I've seen few films in Serbo-Croat, and as Burton is dubbed – by one Petar Banicevic, a member of the ensemble at the National

Theatre in Belgrade, who had an uncredited role in Mel Brooks' *The Twelve Chairs* – we lose his prize asset, his voice. Burton had written to Wolf Mankowitz, imploring him to look at the script and 'save me at least from the wreck by making my speeches sufficiently believable and speakable so that I wouldn't end up as a permanent glottal stop,' but if any of Mankowitz's contributions remain, they are in the hit-and-miss subtitles. Referred to by his troops as 'Comrade-Commander-in-Chief', Burton's Tito is perhaps Burton's Owen Glendower, in the Yugoslavian mountains instead of Welsh hills. He certainly gives one of his stern, imperturbable militaristic performances, informing us 'a very big offensive is in operation', to rid the land of Anton Diffring and Hardy Krüger, Nazis who plan to exterminate 'everything that breathes', including peasant women and children – 'poison the water, kill the wounded'. Burton is mostly on a ridge or sitting under a burning tree, listening to reports and bulletins, issuing orders. There are lots of explosions. Lots. As it grinds on, and the bodies pile up (actual historical casualties were 7,543) grey and green and drab, like rocks in the river, it becomes like an epic tableau, the weariness, the sacrifice, with the occasional artfully placed patriotic flag. Irene Pappas, as is usual with her, washes and rolls bandages and does her eternal suffering mother-dolorosa thing – identical to her Catherine of Aragon in *Anne of the Thousand Days*. The film is brutal – dogs machine-gunned, horses blown up or tipping sideways into raging torrents. It is all somewhat shuffled together, with shaky continuity – I saw a deleted scene once where Burton wanders silently amongst his soldiers at night, like Henry V before Agincourt. It was an artistic error not to have included that.

The Battle of Sutjeska is not dissimilar to Taylor's *The Blue Bird*, the one made in Leningrad: an obscure Communist enterprise, ropey production values, primitive cinematic equipment and facilities, and what's left of any of it available on a degraded print. Nevertheless, such was Burton's fascinated fondness for leaders and kings – not only for impersonating them ('I am the son of a Welsh miner and one would expect me to be at my happiest playing peasants, people of the earth; but in actual fact I'm much happier playing princes'), but also for seeking out their company ('We were invited to have lunch with the King and Queen of Greece' – diary, 19 October 1971), he and Taylor were more than willing to spend a summer with Marshal and Mrs Josip Broz, at the Presidential Summer Residence, on the Brijuni Islands, in the Adriatic. They stayed at the Presidential Villa, travelled on the Presidential Yacht and Presidential Plane. Burton found the leader-for-life of the Socialist Federal Republic of Yugoslavia 'surprisingly small and delicate. Little short arms and legs and a small head with little features,' which suggests Wee Georgie Wood. Nevertheless, Tito carried with him an 'atmosphere of dread' and the way he never raised his voice or grew demonstrative was, says Burton, 'deadlier than any Hitlerian rant.' Wherever they went, with Tito and his wife, Burton and his wife were greeted by applauding crowds. Servants were always nervous. There were military escorts snapping to attention. Tito explained that the caves and tunnels beneath Vanga Island were filled with gunboats and submarines – as if the beauty and tranquillity of the place was a facade. Pula airport, for example, and the Istrian coast, thronged with 'helicopters, tanks, jeeps and armed soldiers everywhere,' said Gianni Bozzacchi, who was of the Burtons' party. When with his henchmen, the Marshal was markedly 'less friendly' and his speeches ('the heroism of the mighty dead', etc.) platitudinous. Rapport between hosts and guests was stilted because everything about politics and reminiscences of the war had to be filtered through interpreters – 'interminable translated conversation'. With Tito at the wheel of a Lincoln Continental ('a present from the people of Zagreb' – though Bozzacchi says the donor was President Nixon), Burton and Taylor were taken to visit the private Presidential Zoo. Bozzacchi, their personal photographer, took a snap of Taylor and Mrs Broz offering a bun to an elephant, though at first glance it's not easy to tell which one is the elephant. As if they were international statespersons exchanging official gifts,

459

Taylor and Burton gave the Titos a pedigree Alsatian puppy. Taylor was presented with Tito's Fabergé-esque cigar holder. Burton got a bunch of roses.

During the making of *The Battle of Sutjeska*, though offered accommodation on land, at Kupari, near Dubrovnik, the stars preferred to remain aboard the *Kalizma*. Each day Burton was taken to the set by helicopter – frightening rides in all weathers through ravines, with many a near-miss. Though the film won the Best Anti-Fascist Prize at the Moscow International Film Festival in July 1973, where George Stevens was on the jury, though in fairness he was outnumbered by East Germans and Bulgarians, *The Battle of Sutjeska* is not the first thing you think of when Burton's name comes up. Bozzacchi says, 'I never saw the finished movie, and wasn't sure it ever got out of Yugoslavia.' Chief Inspector Jenkins was also confounded: 'One of the strangest choices [Richard] ever made,' he writes in *Richard Burton: A Brother Remembered*, 'was to appear as Marshal Tito ... But a film produced by his own government could not be expected to be a study in candour, nor present a shrewd character analysis. Richard was, quite frankly, mad to agree to do it ... I have never seen the film and know no one who has.' Brother Graham, who'd followed the caravan and gone to Belgrade, hoping to sample 'Yugoslavian largesse', was nevertheless sent on his way. Taylor and Burton were within Tito's compound, and (said Graham) 'the palace was denied to me. Security forbade me or anyone else not of the elect to step beyond the stout iron gates which separated ordinary mortals from the President.' I think that's the significant point: *ordinary* mortals, the *elect*.

* * *

It's interesting that as these stars became megastars, the only people they wanted to mix with were dictators, minor tyrants, seedy royalty, i.e. tricksters and frauds – shooting was held up one day during *Who's Afraid of Virginia Woolf?* because the Duke and Duchess of Windsor

460

wanted to drop by at the studio and say hello to Taylor and Burton. With Sally, who was to be his widow, Burton even associated with the Duvaliers, and he bought a house in Haiti, a place renowned for its voodoo cults and a murderous secret police, the Tonton Macoute. The Chief Inspector accompanied his brother and Sally to the island for Christmas 1983, and whilst David Jenkins noticed the 'malnutrition, disease and illiteracy', Burton (in his diary) saw only 'highly coloured buses jammed with people ... No servant problem ... No tax.' He believed the country easier to reach from Europe than Puerto Vallarta, and he'd first got to know it, in August 1976, as a good place for a quick divorce. The dissolution of Burton and Taylor's brief second marriage (ten months) took place in Port-au-Prince – all a defendant needed to do was go to the Office of Divorce for Foreigners at the Ministry of Justice, fill in the form ('Statement of Grievances'), attest there'd been 'incompatibility of character', and within twenty-four hours everything would be rubber-stamped by the Dean of the First Instance, all at a cost of fifty American dollars. Burton was back in February 1983, to divorce Suzy Hunt. 'Strongly tempted to buy a place here,' he jotted in his diary (28 February), 'Longing to buy a place here' (3 March), 'Longing to have our own home in the sun for Sally' (4 March). Baby Doc loaned Burton his helicopter, for the scouting about. By the year's end, Burton had purchased L'Habitation Courvoisier, Etang du Jong, Pétion-Ville. The Chief Inspector helped escort thirty-nine trunks of belongings from Los Angeles, which included lots of books. There were also twelve suitcases.

On the face of it, Haiti was 'free of all other associations', i.e. Burton had not been there with Taylor. The climate was nice – but the real appeal was the way Burton was feted by Baby Doc, Jean-Claude Duvalier, who was 'obviously a powerful force'. And what a lot of peculiar amnesia is in evidence. Graham Greene, having gathered material for *The Comedians*, had said, 'I have never felt such pervasive fear in a country as in Haiti.' At the end of the film adaptation, Taylor's character murmurs 'Poor Haiti!' as she and Ustinov escape to Miami, and she looks from the plane window at the Caribbean island ravaged by deforestation, over-population, terror, doubt and confusion. Burton, in person, saw none of that – or forgot he'd been told about any of that. He was met at the airport by dignitaries, whisked to an audience with the President, which lasted one-and-a-half hours. He was photographed beaming with the Duvalier clan – and Baby Doc, in his turn, had forgotten how Papa Doc had once furiously instructed his ambassadors to make protest against anyone who had any connection with Greene's novel and the cinema version, from the MGM board downwards, which (so the State Department in Washington was told), 'constitutes an inflammatory libel against Haiti. From the first to last the film presents an utterly distorted picture of Haiti, its people and its government.' Mexico concurred, banning the film, as did the Dominican Republic, as did Franco's Spain, as did France (Haiti having been a French colony) until March 1970. Papa Doc, decreed his embassies, in letters despatched with wax seals, 'believes that President Johnson will join Queen Elizabeth in an agreement to suppress the producers and actors and deny their right to work.' Yet here we are, not all that many years later, and Burton was invited to a white-tie banquet at the Presidential Palace to see in the New Year, and was never deterred by 'tonight's intimations of continued corruption in high places'. Haiti, to Graham Greene, 'really was the bad dream of the newspaper headlines' – arrest, torture, summary execution – whereas the horror of the island for Burton, as his brother described it, was the way his suicidal drinking 'coincided eerily with the nightly beating of drums in the surrounding hills'. David Jenkins and Sally, and the ubiquitous Brook, sat fearfully downstairs, whilst from upstairs came the noise of glasses being broken and empty bottles rolling across the floor. 'There was something utterly pathetic,' commented the Chief Inspector, 'in his being in such isolation, thwarted even in his attempts to get another drink.'

When Burton did appear, he was bullying and impossible, frighteningly restless – as his character was, coincidentally enough, fifteen years earlier, in *The Comedians*, which though set in Haiti was filmed, of course, in Dahomey. Burton's character, Brown, is, said Greene, 'a person who would like to be better than he is but cannot.' Emerging from the tropical steam, living amongst frangipani trees, flame trees and oleanders, Burton was like a ghost in the noonday sun. And in Dahomey, also, he and Taylor had been bidden to meet President Christophe Soglo at the Palace in Cotonou, a building full of mosaics and big reception halls, erected in 1964, three years before they arrived. The President was proud of the concealed wall lights and his wife's racks of shoes. Dahomey had received independence from France in 1960, and was to endure nothing but military coups and Marxist-Leninist takeovers. Soglo was himself overthrown later in 1967. Burton said he was 'very black' and 'married to a white wife and has seven children.' He tended to paw Taylor who, as later with Tito, played at being 'charming and very feminine'. Addressed by staff as 'Mon General', though his rank had been that of colonel, the President had a habit of turning up on the set, expecting to be entertained. 'I searched for [Elizabeth] because he quite clearly wanted to see her and not anybody else.' Would they have put up with this sort of infringement or invasion from any other sort of person? There was an affinity, I think, because these despots they spent time with – Taylor, in the years after her final divorce from Burton, befriended the Iranian ambassador, Ardeshir Zahedi, and in May 1976 flew on the inaugural flight from New York to Tehran to suck up to the Shah – were, like the film stars, all similarly lonely, unable to trust anyone, no longer capable of natural social intercourse. Taylor spent the Shah's money on caviar luncheons and couture clothes. The Empress, Farah Diba, gave her a kaftan woven with gold and silver thread – Taylor was photographed wearing it, along with a lot of Persian costume jewellery, on the balcony of her Dorchester suite. She looks like one of those ululating fortune tellers Irene Pappas was known

463

for, in an epic containing much sand. And though the Shah was deposed in February 1979, and the Pahlavi family sent into exile, Taylor managed to carry on being imperial. Her security force included sixteen people, who'd clear the way before she entered a room ('It's part of the glamour and attraction of Elizabeth Taylor'); she wouldn't get in a lift unless her guards 'checked it out first'. When she was poorly, she whizzed about in a gold-plated wheelchair with emeralds inlaid in the armrests.

As Burton had said, though by April 1970 financial overheads – insurance premiums for the jewels, the yacht, the various properties, including Puerto Vallarta; lawyers and agents' fees – came to about $600,000 a year, their wherewithal and business activity was that of 'one of the smaller African nations', with all that that unfortunately implies of corruption, nepotism and ostentation. For the Royal Command Film Performance of *The Taming of the Shrew*, on 27 February 1967, at the Odeon, Leicester Square, attended by Princess Margaret ('infinitely boringly uncomfortable to be around,' in Burton's view), the Jenkins goblins were ferried from Pontrhydyfen in a fleet of Rolls-Royces. Fourteen suites, filled with floral bouquets, were booked for them at The Dorchester. Christopher Plummer played the piano at the party, which ended at dawn the next day with hymn singing. 'Hey, Jenk,' said a Welshman to Burton, overcome by the marble grandeur of the lavatories. 'Doesn't it make your cock look shabby in here?' Or then, on 6 October 1970, there was the wedding at Caxton Hall of Michael Wilding Jr., eighteen, to Beth Cutter, nineteen. The incredibly young couple were given an all-expenses-paid honeymoon, commencing at The Dorchester, a Jaguar car, $100,000 in cash (some sources convert this to £35,000) and a house in Hampstead, which cost £43,700. A flower-child free-spirit, Michael's wish was to start a commune in Wales, so he and his bride were duly waved off to Ffynnon Wen, Goginan, Ponterwyd, with $40,000-worth of drums, guitars and amplifiers, a trajectory Burton simply couldn't understand: 'I made it up and Michael is trying to make it down ... I still get goddamned mad, when

I think what it took to climb out.' Here is Burton the man divided against himself; the prince and the pauper – a person Michael, nevertheless, could understand very well indeed: 'Mama has only Richard Burton on her mind,' he once said with some bitterness, 'and he likes to live like a Roman emperor.' Lucille Ball was more sarcastic than satirical when Burton and Taylor appeared in *I Love Lucy* and she dropped a curtsy, calling them 'Your Highness' and 'Your Majesty'.

* * *

They were at their most monarchical, when residing at the Duna-International Hotel, in Communist Budapest, where Taylor's fortieth birthday party was held in February 1972. Two hundred three-page telegrams were despatched, including this example preserved by Kenneth Williams:

> We would love you to come to Budapest as our guest for the weekend of 26th and 27th February to help me celebrate my big 40th birthday STOP The hotel is very Hilton but there are some fun places to go STOP Dress slacks for Saturday night in some dark cellar and something gay and pretty for Sunday night STOP Dark glasses for hangovers in between STOP Lots of love Elizabeth and Richard STOP P.S. Could you RSVP as soon as possible to Intercontinental Hotel Budapest so I know how many rooms to book STOP.

Williams didn't go, though on 18 February he conveyed 'my unspeakable thanks to you both for asking me. I was dancing about the room, I was so thrilled . . . It certainly seems light years away from those halcyon days in Swansea and that production of *The Seagull*.' It was more important for him to be at Pinewood playing the role of Sir Bernard Cutting in *Carry On Matron*. Nor did Arthur Koestler attend. He felt the 'climate' of Eastern Europe 'unhealthy for me'. (He later killed

465

himself in a railway carriage.) Nevertheless, eighty people did make their way to Hungary for what Burton called 'the endless weekend', many of them travelling from Heathrow in a specially chartered British Airways Trident jet. Susannah York, Michael Caine and Margaret Leighton had been Taylor's co-stars in her recent film, *X, Y & Zee*, her most psychedelic work. (The New York premiere had been held on 26 January, exactly a month earlier.) Margaret Leighton's presence meant her husband was invited – only Michael Wilding. Michael Wilding Jr., however, refused to leave his trust-funded Welsh enclave: 'I just don't dig all those diamonds and things.' Billy Williams, the *X, Y and Zee* cinematographer, turned up, as did Joseph Losey, Victor Spinetti, Yul Brynner's ex-wife, Doris, Kurt Frings, the German-speaking agent, John Springer, the publicist, and Marjorie Lee, the woman in charge of The Dorchester's VIPs. Ron Berkeley, the make-up chap, was on hand, as were Alexandre de Paris and Gianni Bozzacchi. Francis Warner came from Oxford and promised Burton a Hon D.Litt and a knighthood, none of which came off. Nevill Coghill and Stephen Spender represented the intelligentsia, though Stephen Spender had no idea who Taylor and Burton were. The only crowned head, if you can call her that, who turned up, was Grace Kelly – without Rainier, but with a lady-in-waiting, who grew excitable when the dancing started. Taylor arranged with Budapest antiques shops to borrow antiques for Grace's suite, to make it less, well, like a Hilton. Everybody's accommodation was filled with trays of champagne, whisky, wine and Russian vodka, in addition to arrays of out-of-season blooms. Other guests were allegedly David Niven and Marlon Brando, though no photographic evidence exists to prove their presence. It all reminds me again of Jean-Bédel Bokassa's naff Coronation with all the no-shows. He was snubbed by Hirohito of Japan, the Shah of Iran and Omar Bongo of Gabon. There were few delegations of senior diplomats. General Franco sent an antique suit of armour, which turned out not only to be not antique, but not appreciably old. The most prominent guest in the end was the Prime Minister of Mauritius, Sir

Seewoosagur Ramgoolam. At Taylor's party, I do know Frankie Howerd was there. Frankie and his partner Dennis Heymer got stuck in a lift with Raquel Welch, so she was perfectly safe.

There were plenty of relatives and to spare – Taylor's brother Howard, his wife and children, for example; Christopher Wilding and Aileen Getty – but the do does seem to have been dominated by a full complement of the Welsh lot, who managed to turn the occasion into a provincial jamboree. It was over half a century ago, but I still cringe to hear about the way my countrymen, who with what Burton called 'their still-retained sense of wonder', were bowled over by everything, e.g. the trip on a plane, the view of the Danube, indoor bathrooms and flush lavatories. Burton's brothers were predictably clueless about 'dinner' not being at noon, black-tie, dress-shirts and caviar ('It's like lava bread' – which when Snowdon erupts is collected by locals in buckets). Anticipating the Jenkinses would feel out of place, Burton had asked them to bring along cine films of rugby matches, which they were able to watch in one of the suites, when they were not boozing and singing ethnic ditties about saucepans ('sospans'). 'Graham got sloshed very quickly,' recorded an embarrassed Burton in his diary, and Hilda cornered Ringo Starr. 'My husband and I did have an awful shock when Ringo and Maureen split up. We sat with them at the Duna in Budapest,' Hilda reminisced later. Hilda also mistook Michael Caine for James Mason. Poor Princess Grace had to endure a fortis-simo chorus of 'We'll Keep a Welcome in the Hillside', then the hymns started.

There were three chief events, where the Jenkinses got ample chance to show everyone how enchanting they were. First, a cocktail party in the Presidential Suite; then the party on the Saturday night, with a buffet of Hungarian eats, held in the Tokaj Cellar, which was decorated by the *Bluebeard* art department with candles and cobwebs, which Cis wanted to hoover up; then the actual birthday gala in the Belle Vue Supper Club on the twelfth floor, which was filled with

467

three thousand red and gold balloons brought from Paris. White lilacs and red tulips decorated the tables and guests ate Chicken Kiev and chocolate cake. There was a thirty-piece orchestra, which soon enough abandoned 'I Left My Heart in San Francisco' to vamp along with ethnic ditties about saucepans. Norman Parkinson took official photographs of Burton and Taylor, wrapped in furs, the tips of their noses glistening, surrounded by soft-focus lights and frozen mist. 'I've always wanted to be older,' Taylor the eternal child star announced, as 'Happy Birthday to You!' was sung to her – and sung to her again *in Welsh*; Taylor, the public baby, who'd never known humility, who since her MGM days had demanded applause. 'Madam's done quite well, hasn't she?' said Frankie Howerd, who will have been in closer proximity to busty substances this weekend than at any other moment in his entire life. Rampant, on either side of his and Dennis' fireplace in Somerset, by the way, were swords given to them by Burton, which had featured in *Cleopatra*. A significant absentee in the Tokaj Cellar and the Belle Vue Supper Club was Philip – surely he'd have received a telegram? He makes no mention of the party in his memoirs, saying only that Taylor wrote from Budapest to thank him for a kaftan he'd not, in fact, sent.

Burton and Taylor in Budapest 'created more stir than the Revolution of 1956,' said Graham – not that Taylor had heard of the Revolution of 1956. When Brook's brother Alan asked her about it, she looked blank. As the Chief Inspector said, 'We were so enveloped in comfort, the poverty around us seemed almost unimaginable,' so no one bothered to imagine it. Certainly not Burton, who presented Taylor with the canary-yellow diamond cut in 1621 by a court jeweller of the Mughal Emperor, which in 1627 had been given by Shah Jahan to the Empress Nur Jahan Mumtaz Mahal. Crafted in the shape of a heart, set amongst a latticework of rubies and jade, and suspended as a pendant on a silken cord, which Taylor wanted replaced by a golden necklace, it cost Burton $900,000, or £350,000. At the auction held on 13 December 2011, *The Collection of Elizabeth Taylor: The Legendary*

Jewels, it went for $8,818,500. There is a slightly fuzzy Pathé newsreel of Burton in Budapest, showing the trinket off to the press, somewhat idiotically draping it on his forehead. There were Cartier and Bulgari personnel invited to the party, maybe even Monsieur Cartier and Signor Bulgari. By the way, at that Christie's auction, organised not that many months after Taylor had died, La Peregrina sold for $11,842,500 and the Krupp Diamond sold for (another) $8,818,500 The grand total for all chips, stones and rocks was $115,932,000. The Burton-Taylor Diamond had been sold off years before, in 1979, to the jewellers and watchmakers, Mouawad of Geneva and Dubai. Taylor used the $4 million proceeds to fund John Warner's political ambitions. John Warner died in May 2021. His most notable achievement as senator was to ban pay-cubicles in airport lavatories.

* * *

Their lives, shut and locked: the Venice Film Festival, and being entertained by Onassis on his yacht, where the bar stools were upholstered in whale foreskin; parties thrown by people with names like Countess Marina Cicogna or Florinda Bolkan; the Roman nobility visiting the studios to watch the *Cleopatra* shoot, as Parisians once spent an hour's diversion at the morgue; a reception at Kensington Palace on 23 June 1971, where Princess Margaret said of the Krupp Diamond, 'How very vulgar,' and Taylor replied, 'Yeah, ain't it great. Want to try it on?' Ma'am Darling did so. 'Not so vulgar now, is it?' the actress said, before leaving the gathering for Geneva, thence the Caribbean, not on the face of it a direct route. Burton and Taylor paraded in the paddock before the Grand Prix d'Arc de Triomphe, drawing more interest from the punters than the horses. 'I'm always pleased and surprised by that sort of thing,' said Burton, puffed up. There was the Gala de la Croix Rouge Monegasque, held in the Salle des Etoiles of the Monte Carlo Sporting Club, on 7 August 1971, Grace and Rainier's Red Cross Ball, at which Taylor and Burton were guests of honour. 'It's phenomenal, the continued attention we get. Literally there must be millions of words written about us and hundreds of thousands of photographs.' Princess Grace had another party, The Scorpio Ball, to celebrate her fortieth birthday, at the Hôtel Hermitage, in Monte Carlo, where Taylor spent all night flashing the Taylor-Burton Diamond, upstaging the hostess, former star of *To Catch a Thief*.

Burton and Taylor were frivolous and shallow, out to shock rather than impress. The drinking, the filming, the spending: this was their real life, and they did not experience self-doubt. Indeed, Burton was the first to get in with a bit of rude snootiness. 'Aren't you thrilled to be meeting me, love?' he was overheard asking a fellow guest at an ambassadorial reception. 'You're a cunt. I hate all this fucking privilege,' he said to his host at a black-tie dinner. 'You bore me,' he'd often tell a companion at table. 'You remind me quite distinctly of a hungry vulture,' he said to the wife of a Swiss diplomat. Taylor was no help calming him down. 'Richard, take a drink. You are so goddamned dull when you are not drinking.' Sometimes a letter of apology would arrive a day or so later: 'Why do we hurt those we love the most, and I do mean you?' – to which someone once had the presence of mind to reply, 'Because, Richard, you've had so much experience at it, and I do mean you.'

Their prosperity was not a burden – and as Lytton Strachey said of Queen Elizabeth I, what happiness to be able to 'pulverise the material and remould it in the shape of one's own particular absurdity'. Burton and Taylor's private times, the squabbles, the sleaze, the colossal film sets, the performances, the sex fantasies ('I was unquestionably seduced and I teased her about it for the rest of the day . . . After all these years the girl can still blush,' though the next minute she'll have locked him out and he's kicking the door down): it was all as much a part of life – of their total meaning – as what they ate or dreamt or sought. When, in one of the many biographies, I find Burton quoted as saying, 'I know you, Elizabeth, because I am you . . . I have always been my own greatest concern, and I have never been able to abandon that notion, and neither can you' – what I have to ask is, how do we know he said such strangely pertinent things, spoke such words? It is soap opera dialogue, or Iris Murdoch dialogue. Elliott Kastner wanted to cast Burton and Taylor in *A Severed Head*, which was made eventually with Ian Holm and Lee Remick. Maybe some pages of the script floated off into the world.

Their main problem, as I'd see it, is the company they had to keep – Taylor and Burton completely avoided people who didn't have power and fame, in case such sorts might want some of it ('It seemed strange that [Richard] didn't seem to have real pals,' said Stanley Baker); so they gravitated to their own kind, and Burton's diaries are dotted with references to Ari and Maria or the Rothschilds – Burton and Taylor were often staying at Ferrières, Baron Guy's chateau. On 16 November 1968, for example, it was Baroness Marie-Hélène's birthday, but she was too vain to wear specs and never recognised anybody. 'It is I, Hamlet the Dane,' said Burton, hoping to supply the old ratbag with a prompt. At Ferrières, in December 1971, was the famous Proust Ball, which Burton and Taylor attended, along with the Duchess of Windsor, Grace of Monaco, Audrey Hepburn – and Andy Warhol, who said, 'It was just unbelievable.' Burton shook the Pop Artist's hand and 'was so sweet'. In his diary, Burton, less saccharine, said Warhol 'looked like a cadaver when still and a failure of plastic surgery when he moved ... [a] horror-film gentleman.' Yet high society was now filled with affectless ghouls, who seemed to have dispensed with solidity, who had become detached, deathly – like Maria Callas, a phantasmal presence, living out her last days at 36 Avenue Georges Mandel, Paris, where Burton went to admire her 'black-eyed animation', though not her 'massive legs'. In her turn, Callas 'told me how beautiful my eyes were and that they demonstrated a good soul.' It's more likely what she meant was a kindred soul. In the mentions of her in his diaries, Burton treats Callas as a sad nuisance. There's no sympathy – she'd been abandoned by Onassis, who'd married Jackie Kennedy. Her voice had gone. Burton had no real appreciation or grasp of Callas' gigantic and vivid artistry. Yet her tragic dimension or capacities in performance resembled his own – her full-throated acting style; and Callas was instinctively correct to picture or imagine herself as playing Lady Macbeth to Burton's Macbeth, in a version to resemble Pasolini's non-singing *Medea*. Macbeth is the one big part Burton really should have played – that excess of brooding; the weight and density of that guilt. (If Callas was Lady M., who was Taylor to have been, sneered Burton? Well, why not Donalbain? Why not Lady Macduff, killed with her babies?) Like Callas, Burton in his tones of voice conveyed an anguish always. And there are other obvious similarities: from Greek obscurity to international fame; a private love life that fascinated the press and gossip columnists; Mediterranean yachts and the international jet set; contracts and high fees. Burton and Callas put notoriety first, and in their final projects (Callas' tours, masterclasses and recitals; Burton's *Wagner*) their faces are haunted – they look diseased. And as regards the penetrating vocal genius ('I have this pyrotechnic ability with my voice,' said Burton), the shades, the colouration: I'm not sure Callas' voice was beautiful; it isn't creamy – but it could hold ecstasy and terror. With Callas, there's always a harshness (as if she's shaking her fist), and also, as with Burton, total command – Gielgud was forever telling Burton, when he was Hamlet, 'don't be so sure of your speeches and movements' – he couldn't do it. Gielgud wanted a '*confused* wildness' (his italics) – Burton couldn't do it. Whether playing exquisite girlishness or maddened harridans, Callas redefined beauty, in fact, like Modern Art's severe angles and abstraction. And if there are any points of comparison with Taylor, it's I feel she and Callas never expressed emotions they do not naturally have, made gestures they don't trust. Even when they are (as it were) happily singing of love or contentment, the audience knows the mood is doomed; the heartbreaking frailty of everything; the romantic notion everything is perishable; the inevitable prospect of humiliation, renunciation. Angela Vickers (*A Place in the Sun*), Rebecca (*Ivanhoe*), Leslie

Lynton Benedict (*Giant*), Sussanna [sic] Drake (*Raintree County*), Maggie Pollitt (*Cat on a Hot Tin Roof*), on and on, Flora 'Sissy' Goforth (*Boom!*) are Taylor's equivalents of Norma, Lucia di Lammermoor, Manon Lescaut, Gilda. I'd have been keen to see the proposed adaptation of *Oliver!* with O'Toole as Fagin, Burton as Bill Sikes and Taylor as Nancy. It would have been something more than a musical, if less than grand opera.

* * *

Maria Callas, in the way Burton describes her, resembles Wallis Simpson – a wizened and bristling creature pathetically clinging to vestiges of lost looks and erotic power. If the diary is any guide, Burton and Taylor saw the Windsors about once a month, particularly in 1968, when they were back and forth to Paris, making *The Only Game in Town* and *Staircase*. 'They have always enjoyed the company of show business people,' said the Duke's Private Secretary, by way of an explanation, 'and then what with Mr Burton being Welsh and the Duke's old connections – Prince of Wales and all that – there was lots of common interest.' Wallis and Taylor enjoyed discussing medical matters, Taylor not slow to describe 'when I choked on my phlegm, when my eye was almost gouged out, when they nearly amputated my leg.' They'd dine on the Île Saint-Louis and then have drinks at the Plaza Athénée, Burton and the Duke singing the Welsh National Anthem 'in atrocious harmony'. On another evening, at the Comte de Rives' place, Burton 'became very sloshed and sang and recited poetry'. Like Soglo of Dahomey and Tito of Yugoslavia, the Windsors came to the studios, oblivious they were disrupting shooting, getting underfoot. At a further dinner, this time with the Von Bismarcks, Burton picked up Wallis and swung her around, like one of the rag dolls in Taylor's *Raintree County*. Gradually, over the years, Burton found the Windsors increasingly 'chipped around the edges'; the Duke had pouchy, sagging blind

473

eyes and walked lumberingly with a stick. 'His memory has gone completely and then comes back vividly in flashes.' Wallis was openly gaga, repeating at interminable length her theory Tito is the natural son of a Hungarian count.

I find the association of Burton and Taylor and Wallis and David wholly fascinating. It's like Gielgud's description of the Elsinore court, when he told the cast of *Hamlet*, on 26 February 1964, a Wednesday, as it happens, that they needed to suggest 'a certain malice and wickedness. They're bad, shallow people, the people in this play. They all have a zestful superficiality, which should create a feeling of corruption.' In Burton's diary we go from 'We all got on famously' in 1967, to 'Rarely have I been so stupendously bored' in 1971. There's something gothic and lingeringly deathly about this friendship, if it might be called that. The Windsors were people who'd had their chips. Who did Burton and Taylor believe themselves to be, hanging out with faded aristocrats in a foul atmosphere of misery and bitterness, cloudy with whisky breath, smoke, faded silks, and a sense of disintegrating exaltedness? Dominick Dunne sensed a connection – here were people who had nothing to do save supervise the flower arrangements and the seating arrangements and ensure 'the steamer trunks [were] packed for their endless peregrinations in pursuit of pleasure', or as I'd see it, flight from boredom. Edward and Mrs Simpson and the Burtons: it is like a period drama written by Julian Fellowes about class tensions and hierarchies. Even Rainier and Grace, said Burton, 'don't feel too happy outside their realm as they can never be sure how they are going to be treated.' What would happen if their Ruritanian trappings were derided? What if no one respectfully bowed as they passed? Beneath the augustness, the Windsors, and the Monaco mob, are as nothing, void and null, without everyone agreeing on the importance of protocol. There was no greater beauty than rank nor, with the Windsors, no greater need for every illusion of it. Burton once made the mistake of calling the Duke 'David', an overstepping-the-mark moment, which 'wasn't well received'. He expected any moment to be rebuked for calling the Queen Mother 'Her Dumpy Majesty', but the Windsors did appreciate that one.

The Windsors had little to do but accept hospitality, were dying for a bit of fun – they were, in reality, defeated, held back, the scandal which defined them, the Abdication Crisis, vanishing into the past – as matrimonial scandal and front page 'vulgar sensationalism' (Burton's phrase for it) defined the Burtons, too. There might be seen to be a fatal similarity here – growing insignificance and listlessness, the striving for a regal bearing getting to be ravaged, ancient grandeur now grotesque. Plus the way Taylor and the Duke liked tasteless clothes, such as orange tweed. At dinner one night, Burton had the temerity to say to Wallis, 'You are, without any question, the most vulgar woman I've ever met,' meaning, I think, that he saw through her as a woman, empty and menacing, who could cut up rough – and I have to ask: what is all this bandying about of the word or term vulgarity? Mike Todd had said when warned about his splashing out on jewellery, 'It's vulgar to count money,' and Todd was the biggest vulgarian who ever lived, a man who'd gone bankrupt twice, and who'd left, after his debts were paid off, only $13,000. Taylor wanted a two-ton replica of an Oscar to go on his grave, an idea Todd's son, Mike Jr., considered 'vulgar', which it surely was – as vulgar as one of Taylor's birthday parties at Studio 54, when the cake was a model of her boobs in icing with cherries for nipples. An expensive alarm clock Frank Sinatra gave Taylor and Burton was, said Burton, 'vulgar', and when first taking Taylor to South Wales he'd warned her it was 'a squat and ugly place full of rain' – which was a repeat of what he'd told a reporter in July 1953 (other sources say 1956), when he turned up in a Jaguar Mark VIII and stated, 'My valley is vulgar but honest.' On that flying visit he'd stayed with Cis and Elfed at 73 Caradoc Street, and who'd have blamed them if they'd slammed the door in his face. 'I couldn't settle down here,' Burton told the press. 'The life's too starved. But I was born here and I like to come back.' Occasionally.

In June 2011, a wrinkled handwritten letter, composed by Burton and sent to Gianni Bozzacchi, was offered for sale by an auction house in New Hampshire. Dated 27 April 1973, it ranted on about *Ash Wednesday*, which Burton deemed 'essentially vulgar at its base and vicious in its implications.' Possibly – it's about Taylor as a middle-aged woman undergoing extensive plastic surgery, so as to retain the interest of her husband, Henry Fonda. It's true there's something nasty and shallow about the idea of cosmetic interventions, as the removal of subcutaneous tissue, the nips and tucks, fool nobody. But because, in the film, Taylor's character succeeds in attracting the interest of Helmut Berger's character, Burton thought, or feared, Taylor was carrying on with Helmut Berger. 'Day after day,' he says in the letter, 'I sit here vulgarised,' by the film itself, which is 'violently against my taste' and by what he thought 'my wife is doing,' professionally and personally. Why wasn't Burton cast in the Henry Fonda role?

Evidently, he was bored and frustrated, felt redundant, at having nothing to do, save attend to Taylor on location, at Cortina d'Ampezzo. To Burton vulgarity was pejorative; his duty was to denounce it. Even of Laurence Olivier he says, 'that vulgar streak in him is shaming.' We might be back in a valleys chapel, where Burton's father's way of voicing moral disapproval was to say of someone or something, 'a bit *fancy*.' (In my own Wales, for your house to have a bay window was getting above yourself.) Burton seems to use the word *vulgar* as a synonym for unsophisticated – or in regard to Sinatra's alarm clock, or Wallis Windsor, over-sophisticated. Anyway – not quite in balance; something or someone drawing attention to themselves in an embarrassing way, like Robert Hardy's fastidious good manners, which lost direction and were slightly *off*. Holding doors open or standing up when a lady enters, tipping your hat, and so forth and so forth, composing bread-and-butter letters, offering your seat, 'has to be done with an indefinably unobtrusive grace . . . Hardy, whose manners are meticulous nevertheless manages to make himself faintly obtrusive.' It's a good point, making us see that what is vulgar is that which is sham, that which is all gesture and pretence. Vulgarity, at a basic level, is crude showing off, and lacks style – a clumsy flamboyance, linked with self-advertisement, and this is why Waugh had to chastise his daughter, Margaret: 'I am told you drive recklessly. Don't do that, it's vulgar.' But not everyone can settle for being demure, much to the irritation of Cecil Beaton, who on 19 February 1968 was invited by Universal to take a picture of a person he called 'the loathsome Elizabeth Taylor'. To get out of the assignment he said his fee would be a prohibitive $5,000, which was duly declined. 'She's everything I dislike,' said Beaton, who was additionally alarmed when Universal mentioned Taylor was intending to bring eighteen people to the shoot. Instead, and for a hundredth of his going rate, Beaton photographed 'the eccentric Australian', Barry Humphries – who in Dame Edna mode was a parody of Dame Taylor. Indeed, Edna is on record as saying her double chins were Taylor's recycled love handles, found in a dumpster outside the offices of a Beverly Hills plastic surgeon.

In December 1971, Beaton was photographer for the evening at the Proust Ball. I shall quote at length: 'I have always loathed the Burtons for their vulgarity, commonness and crass bad taste, she combining the worst of American and English taste, he is butch and coarse as only a Welshman can be.' Butch, coarse, me? Beaton, himself insecure socially (and artistically: how *hard* is it to be a photographer?), thought that amidst the Parisian café society, Taylor and Burton were 'extremely embarrassed and self-conscious', like provincial interlopers. He goes on: 'She wanted compliments. She got none. I asked her to hide a shoulder, lean forward, and went forward to this great thick revolving mass of femininity in its rawest.' Beaton felt nothing but 'disgust and loathing at this monster. Her breasts, hanging and huge, were like those of a peasant woman suckling her young in Peru. They were seen in their full shape, blotched and mauve [and] plum. Round her neck was a velvet ribbon with the biggest diamond in the world pinned on it. On her fat, coarse hands more of the

biggest diamonds and emeralds, her head a ridiculous mass of diamond necklaces sewn together, a snood of blue and black pompoms
and black osprey aigrettes. Sausage curls ...' It's true Taylor was carrying gems worth $3 million. Alexandre de Paris did what was left of
her hair. Baron Guy surrounded his chateau with five hundred
guards. But Beaton's is more than scorn. His complete hatred and
revulsion are quite something. We hear all the time about homophobia. This is heterophobia, the loathing by the queer who can find no
boyishness, no androgyny (as Beaton celebrated in Garbo or Katharine
Hepburn), only total womanliness. He's frightened, frankly, by the
child-bearing attributes – frightened, perhaps, that as in a nightmare
Taylor will come after him, eat him up. I've met chaps like this, wearing stained flannels and minor public-school ties, seeking refuge in
their men-only London clubs, who hold the crazy belief women are
out to snare them, are full of tactics, like Red Riding Hood's disguised granny. Actually, this is one of the witch's incarnations in *The
Blue Bird*; and Taylor is a folkloristic *vagina dentata* keeping company with wolves in *BUtterfield 8*, *Who's Afraid of Virginia Woolf?*,
Reflections in a Golden Eye, *Secret Ceremony*, *Night Watch* ... Maybe
Beaton, his house in Dorset later inhabited by Madonna, would have
preferred Taylor later on, when she looked less a female, more of a
female impersonator?

The people Beaton did admire were the thoroughbreds. He was a
snob, so any old earl or countess would do. The well-born, the well-
connected. But Beaton was right, though, to have spotted something
inside that was hard and unyielding, as Taylor was quite keen on the
disagreeable impressions she made. Burton himself was alarmed by
the ways 'the eyes blaze with genuine hatred and contempt' during
their arguments. 'Her lovely face becomes ugly with loathing.' Taylor
could be a complete bitch, and Burton wasn't exactly tranquil.
'Richard loses his temper with true enjoyment,' Taylor said, 'He's like
a small atom bomb going off. Sparks fly, walls shake, floors vibrate.'
We sense something of that in the way he was cast as Richard Wagner,

when Tony Palmer dwells on images of water, mist, fire, smoke –
elemental destruction giving birth to a new planet or to a hero:
'Richard, Richard! It has begun!' says Cosima, going into labour.
Wagner is the artist who wants to be everything, fusing music and
drama: 'I have seen a theatre of flames!' There's a fabulous shot of
Burton, in a silk top hat and an astrakhan coat, reclining in a gondola,
going under a bridge – floating into the dark, and coming back into the
light. He's wearing a pale blue cravat, and his eyes are the colour of the
milky green water. His handsome lustrous watchfulness is undimmed –
and the masterful nine-hour film is a homage to – is hypnotised
by – Burton's face, Burton's skull, which, suffused by golden filters, is
pale, ill, old, the russet hair going white. You never doubt the sensuality
of the music, wild and bold, emanates from such a man, and Palmer
made what turns into a great elegy. I've never seen Burton lose himself
as thoroughly in a role; there's none of his impatience with getting a job
done – the melting edges of the character, and of Burton himself, who
said to his brother Graham, 'I am close to Wagner. I could be Wagner.'
He listens to a *Ring* rehearsal, or maybe *Tristan*, and murmurs, 'It is all
that I would have it be, wonderful, wonderful, wonderful.'

* * *

Another line I recall from *Wagner*: 'To be revolutionary is often the
sign of an artist,' and where Burton and Taylor were revolutionaries
is in the way their sense of power, their energy and neediness, made
them live their lives flat out, and their alleged tastelessness and
shamelessness are what personally I prize and find increasingly
expressive. Back in October 1969, the *New York Times* had admonished them, in ways the Vatican had admonished them: 'In this Age
of Vulgarity, marked by such minor matters as war and poverty, it
gets harder every day to scale the heights of true vulgarity,' the sarcastic implication being the jewel sprees were a pretty good attempt
at finding an antidote to the residual paranoia of McCarthyism,

racial unrest, nuclear winters, Arctic drilling, Pentagon briefings and other irks under God – prompting Taylor to say unrepentantly, 'I know I'm vulgar, but would you have me any other way?' Would we? There can be a vulgarity of the emotions and the intellect, as well as too much importance given to display. Aldous Huxley defined vulgarity as 'too conspicuous a show of vigour', and that is what we have in *Boom!*, let alone *Who's Afraid of Virginia Woolf?* and *The Taming of the Shrew*; and though there will be people always disgusted by Burton and Taylor's materialism – and the stars do stand in marked contrast to our twenty-first century's chilling and arrogant neo-puritanical and practically fascist politically correct modes of thought (if you can call it thought), where everyone is crushed and 'cancelled' if they can't be controlled and signal virtue – I absolutely refuse to disapprove of them. Burton and Taylor uplift me; they never make me feel sad or sorry for them or superior to them. It's why *Private Lives*, the angry banter and the affection, was perfect for them, bringing the couple, though twice divorced, together again, at the Lunt-Fontanne Theatre, New York, in May 1983, at $70,000 a week each. 'All the futile moralists who try to make life unbearable,' says Amanda to Elyot, or maybe it is Elyot to Amanda, 'Laugh at them . . . Laugh at everything, all their sacred shibboleths. Flippancy brings out the acid in their damned sweetness and light.'

Liking to believe everything, at root, is comical, Burton had expressed a similar sentiment when he put in his diary, in June 1970, 'Elizabeth and my wildest quarrels are fundamentally ridiculously funny.' Were they? 'I used to belt him and he hated it,' Taylor bragged. 'Finally he belted me back and my eardrum did not function.' Hilarious, like Punch and Judy. Nor was there comicality in Ivor's death, Jessica's existence, Sybil's treatment. But it's true life can be reduced to nonsense, and when Taylor and Burton were at large, they were joyously vulgar in that they were a ludicrous intensification of themselves. 'If you have a world-famous figure,' said Tennessee Williams of Taylor, 'why be selfish with it?' Taylor wore her diamonds to the wedding of

Simon Hornby and Sheran Cazalet, making fellow guests the Queen Mother and Princess Margaret look like they'd been dressed by Oxfam (15 June 1968); Burton was seen around town in a mink jacket worth £3,000 (9 February 1969); Taylor wore a yellow kaftan and the Krupp Diamond to the Eton-Harrow cricket match at Lords (11 July 1969). The Paris premiere of *The Taming of the Shrew*, for instance, at the Opéra Garnier, was a particularly marzipan night. Taylor, flanked by eight armed guards, wore a Van Cleef and Arpels tiara, valued at £400,000 (though Burton said £1,200,000), containing gold and diamonds shaped like roses, which was perched upon an Alexandre de Paris hairpiece. Dinner companions were the inevitable Windsors and Rothschilds. French cabinet ministers milled about. In the Pathé newsreel, dated 29 September 1967, we could be in Zenda.

Other descriptions of Taylor and Burton's surroundings – we could be in outer space. The *Private Lives* dressing rooms, for example, were a maelstrom of chintz and lavender, silk flowers, Alvin, Taylor's parrot, and an aquarium containing crabs. I wish I'd seen *Private Lives*, which closed in November 1983. The critics carped, but Taylor and Burton played themselves, rather than Coward's Amanda and Elyot – except Coward's Amanda and Elyot did anticipate the Burtons, as well as bringing up to date Beatrice and Benedick's 'incessant trivial flippancy'. It was Alvin, incidentally, who was responsible for Taylor and Burton's final communication. During the run of *Private Lives*, Taylor called Burton in the middle of the night in great distress, convinced she'd gone blind. Burton heard loud crashes and yells ('Shit! Hell!'), finally an explanation: 'Alvin knocked my Jack Daniel's over.' Anyway, a false eyelash had got stuck.

Fashions change, as they must. Today we are given an excess of personal information – people are too openly revealed. There is something about Burton and Taylor in the gossip columns that foretells the ubiquity and dirty delight of social media, Twitter, TikTok, Instagram, jingles, ringtones, and the rest of the *total shite*, but in themselves, to my mind, and in their films, which generally await re-evaluation, they are like posters of palaces and golden domes in a travel agency window, advertisements for a land of smiles, a place which will stay just out of reach. One of the chief attributes making Taylor, in particular, unfashionable now, or at any rate uncontemporary, is the thoroughness of her womanliness, which so nauseated Cecil Beaton, and as a woman she never felt oppressed. There was no spot or streak of the kind of masculinity (paradoxical virility) found in modern girls – Angelina, Charlize, Scarlett or Emily Blunt – who like to jump about, wielding guns and kicking ass as super-heroines, as physically adroit at the martial arts as any bloke. There's no feminism in Taylor's femininity – though keen on raising money to support charities involved with massacres, holocausts, annihilations and Aids, Taylor was mercifully free of today's cooked up 'issues' about gender politics, people not wishing to be either male or female, but free to undergo hormonal therapy and genital reconstruction surgery, to become something else again, floating about on the spectrum, the human spirit in total anxious confusion. Taylor was a wife, a mother: a domestic goddess, openly adoring men. She retained ideals of courtship; her Fifties idea of being a bride. On the other hand, there is her defining role in *National Velvet*, where her hair is cut off so she can pass for a male jockey –though (unlike Garbo or Dietrich or Hepburn or other Cecil Beaton favourites) Taylor (and it's why she remained erotic) when mature retained a woman's curves, breasts, hips, belly. She was massy, swollen, substantial, in flux. Even as Martha, in *Who's Afraid of Virginia Woolf?*, Taylor never stops being a woman – indeed, Martha is desperate to be, to remain, a woman, and is in agony she can't bear a child, and can only invent one. As Taylor plays her, her yearning is womanly – and the sexual tingles the more intense because implied, veiled, never shown directly, e.g. all the dropped lingerie, unmade beds, dressing-table scenes, which can be found in many of Taylor's films, in fact. Taylor's spell was never broken, and Burton was there to maintain the magic, and focus desire. And I'll say this of him, in addition – and it's something he said or implied himself, when, surveying the supporting cast of *Anne of the Thousand Days*, he'd commented that, barring a select few, actors are, on the whole, 'derivative and repetitive and tedious and run-of-the-mill'. Unlike with Burton, there's a lack of authority in modern actors – no *force*. Their voices are thin and reedy; their personalities are thin and reedy. This is because they mainly know only television. There's no calibre; no grain to anything – everything badly made, like fitted wardrobes with a door hanging off. They can't carry a scene, or use the voice, the body, as an instrument. Charisma is a physical thing: commanding the space; in the twenty-first century all that seems to matter is the image, which is transparent, and feels dead.

What's impressive with Burton and Taylor is they refused to behave as if love and sex should be sentimentally tame and lily-white. What they brought out was what Camille Paglia calls 'the magic irrationalism of sex... its Dionysian energies and ungovernable intensities', and by these means, with Burton and Taylor, vulgarity was artistry. They were romantic animals, in pursuit of liberty, with the erotic underlying thought and behaviour, where it was sublimated, inexplicit: through food ('I rather like being given ... the best seat in the restaurant, the best food in that particular restaurant,' admitted Burton. 'I think eating is one of the greatest pleasures in life,' admitted Taylor), particularly rhapsodies about ice cream; through the jewels reflected in the swimming pool at Villa La Fiorentina, St-Jean-Cap-Ferrat ('I had a huge rock on my finger. It was all mad and marvellous'); through the sea twinkling outside the *Kalizma* portholes ('Living with Elizabeth on the *Kalizma* ... and never living on land again ... Moving all the time ... Seek the sun as much as possible'); through images of the rain droplets Taylor gazes through in a photograph by Bozzacchi ('Elizabeth's mythical beauty reflects everywhere' – the caption is probably better in Italian); through the plentiful drinks ('Ah! How I'd love the panacea of a drink now'); through the places ('Puerto Vallarta ... and ice-cold home-made lemon juice ... the memory of being salt-cleaned and clear-skinned') – all of that which makes for

483

moisture, wetness, dissolves into a flow – the fluidity, the subliminal flux and flow of sexual desires, which are like dreams, and therefore not solid, not substantial. Like perfume. It was inevitable Taylor would evolve into an aroma, be boiled down to pheromones – as hadn't Cleopatra decreed: 'I am fire and air; my other elements / I give to baser life?'

The House of Taylor, launched by Parfums International, a division of Chesebrough-Ponds, in January 1987, brought in an annual gross of $70 million, of which the star received $12 million. The marketing campaign, costing $10 million, was organised by Ogilvy & Mather, and Taylor, who went on a tour of selected boutiques and department stores, had polished lines to deliver: 'I have a passion for love, food, children and animals. I have a passion for life in everything I do.' Protected in a purple box, the fragrance was called *Passion*. Other products, down the years, earning $1 billion over two decades, were named *Passion for Men, White Diamonds* ('It's as white hot as the depths of a diamond with an endless brilliance'), *Diamonds and Emeralds, Diamonds and Rubies, Diamonds and Sapphires, Sparkling White Diamonds, Brilliant White Diamonds* ('It's diamonds in a bottle') ... Contemplating all this, I rather sympathise with Marlene Dietrich, who said, 'Why don't you swallow your fucking diamonds and shut up?' Ingredients chucked in the cauldron included lilies, tuberose, narcissi, jasmine, patchouli and sandalwood. 'Perfume is more than just an accessory for a woman. It's part of her aura. I wear it even when I'm alone,' Taylor told prospective purchasers. She seems to have been aware, as was Marcel Proust, that though invisible and ephemeral, and hard to describe and define, perfumes, lingering on clothes, pillows, car seats, or caught on the breeze, trigger potent associations – are associated with events, even events that never took place, except in fantasy. Smell is part of intimate erotic attraction – and all this was the sales pitch.

I almost wish I'd experienced her most obscure picture, *Scent of Mystery*, the brainchild of Mike Todd's son, Mike Todd Jr. At various points in the film, a kidnap romp set in Spain, involving Denholm Elliott, Peter Lorre, Leo McKern and Diana Dors, odours were sprayed into the cinema auditorium – tobacco, oranges, shoe polish, bread, coffee, lavender, peppermint. I'm not sure my olfactory faculties are up to coping with bouquets of Denholm or for that matter Diana, who surely suggests tins of tuna. Taylor in a gardenia cloud played the abducted heiress. Though Smell-O-Vision did not catch on in 1960 – and I wonder how many cinema patrons choked to death before it was scrapped – who's to say it's not ripe for rediscovery, e.g. applied to the remastered cowboy bean-eating scene in *Blazing Saddles*, or in terms of Taylor and Burton, the rancid reek of chicken drumstick leftovers in *Who's Afraid of Virginia Woolf?*, Italian kitchen aromas and donkey sweat in *The Taming of the Shrew*, sulphur in *Doctor Faustus*, the medicine-chest fetor in *Boom!*, the greasy fast-food diner in *Hammersmith is Out*, and so on and so forth. Taylor's granddaughter, Naomi Wilding, has said, 'I still associate my grandmother so strongly with gardenia. Even now, a chance whiff will bring it all back,' exactly like memory in Proust. And there we have it: what will survive of us is our pong, and exactly as Warhol predicted, in death Taylor became a brand, something to be packaged and sold in quantity, with a range of facsimile jewellery, as well as posthumously brewed perfumes in royal blue vessels – *Forever Elizabeth*, *Violet Eyes* and one called simply *Gardenia*: 'Inspired by her life. Designed for yours.' Why does that sound such a threat? Possibly because, if Taylor and Burton teach us anything, it's passion is actually paradoxically solitary, disorientating. Who wants all this volatility? Passion – or *Passion* – might accurately stink of rot and disease, black waters, green earth.

With some of her proceeds, Taylor bought herself the Duchess of Windsor's Prince of Wales feathers brooch, for $623,000. She's wearing it on her lapel when interviewed by Michael Aspel. She tells him, 'It's the only piece of important jewellery I've ever bought [for] myself,' and remembered how, when she and Burton had visited Wallis in Paris, 'this was our favourite piece of jewellery.' It therefore represents a conjunction or confluence: the love of diamonds, the love of Burton and things Cymric, grand pals, plenty of money. Asked by Aspel what was the most extravagant thing she and Burton ever did, Taylor says, 'We'd be in mid-air, flying from one country to another country, and all of a sudden we'd decide to fly to Venice for lunch.' Sometimes she and Burton had said it was Nice. Is this an example of vulgarity? Not to me. Taylor made light of herself. She wasn't vulgar, because she had nothing to prove. She didn't need to show off, because she'd always been a success, ever since childhood, when her mother removed the hobby horses, saddles and bridles cluttering her bedroom to instead install a walnut settee and framed watercolours of roses. She'd always lived in marble dwelling-places, and this had long-lasting effects. Taylor was 'kept in a cocoon by her mother, by her studio, by the fact she was the adored child who had everything she wanted since she was eight years old,' summed up George Stevens, with exasperation and complete amazement. 'From early childhood, she had lived in a world of fantasy. She doesn't know any other world,' concluded Walter Wanger, of his Cleopatra. Was Wilde right when he said, 'There is something vulgar in all success' – and of course he preferred the idea of the noble failure, the fallen giant, this being how he thought of himself; or was Cocteau nearer the mark when he argued, 'Sometimes wealth seems to me as amazing as genius'? The latter sentiment would be endorsed by Warhol. I prefer to combine the twin notions, see vulgarity as having the potential for genius – it's an antidote to drabness and uniformity; the triumph of the bizarre over the ordinary. There's something magnificent about Burton and Taylor disappearing aboard their yacht – agreeing to meet people, who'd turn up on the quay to watch the *Kalizma* steam over the horizon. And with Taylor in his life, Burton, too, as a star, or deity, simply needed to pose, or loll, or bask, on yachts, on hotel balconies, getting (like Taylor) fat (or thin), boozy, blowsy. Stars don't have to do anything – with Taylor and Burton there's nothing discrepant behind the facade, no hidden truth to be got at. They had a disturbing frankness. They didn't give in to things – though it's the case Burton never loosened up, he was physically stiff, as if his body, anyway, rebelled at the liberties it took.

If, historically, they have become famous not for their art but for their affairs, scandals and bad behaviour, then, in the end, it's those very things which are part of their art, indivisible ultimately from achievement. In the past, as has always happened, I'd fall quite out of love with my subjects, having spent years in their company. I never want to see them again – Sellers, Olivier, particularly Burgess; though not Hawtrey. One gets too entangled. With Burton and Taylor – the opposite. I grew to hold them in huge affection. They are almost innocents, in the equivocal way Miles and Flora, Henry James' haunted children, are innocents. I admire Burton's bookishness, and naturally his South Welshness. He's proof you don't have to live in South Wales to remain an old devil, to be there still temperamentally. And there is Burton and Taylor's glamour and majesty, which possess an elegiac quality, now everything they were a part of has vanished: dancing with Vic Damone, singing with Frank Sinatra, having a drink with Farley Granger and Shelley Winters; going on a date to Chasen's or the Coconut Grove with Herman Wouk or Kirk Douglas or Victor Mature or Mickey Rooney; girls wearing white gloves, hats and coloured slacks, dressing up to descend the steps of a large silver aeroplane, which sparkles in the sunshine. I never knew this world – I am from Bedwas, Machen, Bassaleg, Newport: Monmouthshire, which somebody suddenly decided to start calling Gwent. But I was always able to imagine it, draw sustenance from it. I was reminded of these specific Californian details by Monica Lewis (no relation), the widow of Jennings Lang – Jennings Lang being the man shot in the bollocks by Walter Wanger. Passion, says Dorian Gray, makes one think in a circle.

PART FIVE
SEPARATIONS

How does a marriage turn out? Taylor and Burton, like Antony and
Cleopatra, were already living on past glory. After all the wild scandal
and drama about coming together, the films they then made were
about couples at war and splitting up. Equality and fairness were
never feasible. It's obvious what will happen. 'It was like waiting for a
hand grenade to go off,' said one of their directors, 'because they were
privately in a very bad way and publicly pretending everything was
all right.' Though things never went this far, Alberto Moravia, upon
whose novel Il Disprezzo *(1954)* Godard's Le Mépris *(1963) –*
Contempt *– is based, said of his distressing quarrels with his wife:*
'There were days when I wanted to kill her. Not to split up, which
would have been the reasonable solution, but to kill her, because our
relationship was so intimate and so complex, and in the end so vital,
that murder seemed easier than separation.'

They belonged to an era of bad marriages: Peter and Britt ('I told her
that I needed at least a year to educate her and teach her how to act
and give her a knowledge of great world drama,' Sellers told Richard
Burton of his twenty-two-year-old Swedish spouse – a tall order); the
Snowdons ('a snob-ridden load of shits' – Burton's diary, 20 October
1969); Rex and Rachel ('Rex is fantastically tolerant of her drunken
idiocies. She wouldn't last forty-eight hours with me and he's had it for
seven years'); Ted and Sylvia. Elizabeth Taylor was particularly on
Plath's super-sensitive radar. In her private journals Plath says, 'Liz

Taylor is getting Eddie Fisher away from Debbie Reynolds, who appears cherubic, round-faced, wronged, in pin-curls and house-robe – Mike Todd barely cold. How odd these events affect one so. Why? Analogies?' (2 September 1958, when the poetical couple, whose own wedding was two years earlier, were in Boston). The themes in Plath's poetry – death and rebirth; love and vengeance; disease and terror – certainly have parallels galore in Taylor's life and career. (*Secret Ceremony* could be a Plath poem), and Burton appeared to women as Hughes did to Plath, 'a large hulking Adam ... with a voice like the thunder of God – a singer, a storyteller, lion and world-wanderer, a vagabond who will never stop' (17 April 1956). There's plenty more in this style: 'He has a health and hugeness' (19 April 1956); 'I see the power and voice in him that will shake the world alive' (3 May 1956); 'That big, dark, hunky boy, the only one there huge enough for me ... My black marauder; oh, hungry, hungry. I am so hungry for a big smashing creative burgeoning burdened love.' One rather feels Hughes existed mainly as subject-matter for Plath's letters home or her journal jottings – an erotic fantasy-figure, the focus of domination and submission games. These sketches of Hughes are, as the late biographer and essayist Janet Malcolm said, examples of those 'layers of heated self-absorption', placed by Plath between herself and the chill of the void. Taylor used her men in similar, compulsive, ways – as if they were never exactly real or outside of her own mind. Her hectic personality, shrill, dissonant, bent on destruction, seemingly needed to be won over and tamed – 'Some women need to dominate,' Taylor said once, 'others need to be dominated, and I'm one of them' – but for how long? It was always necessary to reassert the upper-hand, or whip-hand, as with poor Larry Fortensky, who was put off by grandeur. 'He wanted to go to McDonald's wherever we were,' said Taylor, who initially enjoyed the novelty. 'I'm not like your other husbands. You're not going to push me around,' he'd promised. They'd met at the Betty Ford, were married in 1991. Larry was Taylor's construction worker pet, her Action Man toy, or adopted baby, who she dressed in inappropriate Valentino, Versace and Armani clothes. The end was inevitable. 'Don't contradict me in public, it's embarrassing,' Taylor told him embarrassingly in public.

She was not an ordinary woman, who'd never been encouraged to bother about education. 'I bet all those girls going to UCLA wish they were Elizabeth Taylor,' said Taylor's mother, at around the same time Plath, only eight months Taylor's junior, and also born in 1932, was a prize pupil, studying hard for Smith and, later, for the Fulbright to Newnham. But if they were similar in being more resourceful and aggressive than they pretended, Taylor and Plath also liked dreaming up the kind of sexual male figure put by Emily Brontë into *Wuthering Heights*. I wonder if they saw the 'Du Pont Show of the Month', broadcast on 9 May 1958, by NBC – an adaptation of *Wuthering Heights*, in which Burton plays Heathcliff? It was a live show, which everyone believed had come and gone. In 2019, a blotchy kinescope recording was discovered in the Library of Congress. The first thing to note is Cathy isn't Yvonne Furneaux, as advertised at the time, but Rosemary Harris, a last-minute replacement. Yvonne, as Elisabeth Yvonne Scatcherd, was a graduate of St Hilda's College, Oxford, and had appeared in *The Mummy* before being cast by Fellini as Mastroianni's ex-wife in *La Dolce Vita*. Rosemary Harris had been Burton's Desdemona, and in *Wuthering Heights* there's a lot of dying upon a kiss. 'Catherine Earnshaw,' howls Burton's Heathcliff, 'may you not rest as long as I am living. Haunt me! Be with me always!' We then switch to a commercial break for detergent and frozen food.

Harris is bony and wan. In the blurry, almost blueish television tape, she as good as glows, like ectoplasm. The paper snow falls softly. The small sets (the studio was in Brooklyn) reverberate. Burton, as swarthy as a pirate, bangs through doors, cracks a whip in the direction of the fireplace, upends pewter tankards and scatters the dogs. 'Take any form,' he says to Cathy. 'Drive me mad, only don't leave me in this abyss, where I cannot find you! Alone! Oh God, not alone!' There is a lot of Old Vic declaiming and projecting, which must have been intolerable coming out of those myopic boxy Fifties tellies. Unless, of course, audiences in those days were more than willing to be convinced this was what great acting was meant to look like, i.e. a chap in costume being showy and loud. Nevertheless, Heathcliff (a murderer) is an iconic Burton role, an angel of darkness, wild-eyed, cursed, drawing lightning. His kisses are like bites – Harris must have been black and blue. Her main recollection of the programme is she hadn't had time to learn her lines, so the script was hidden under pillows, behind cushions, pinned to window frames. Denholm Elliott was Edgar Linton and Cathleen Nesbitt, Burton's mother in *Staircase* and *Villain*, was Ellen Dean.

* * *

I'm sure Brontë fashion, so to call it, is how Burton would've behaved with Taylor, nevertheless, when he sent her urgent and frank messages, like 'Will you, incidentally, permit me to fuck you this afternoon?' That's indubitably Heathcliff to Cathy, as is a note dated 10 May 1969, when Burton said he loved Taylor more than 'buckets of brine poured over a boiling body ... [more] than sanity smoothed over madness.' Their love was perilous, needing images of storms and clashes by night, and the grotesque physical details in *The Comedians*, for example, were ideal – the hot red dust, the pagan gods and zombies, brought into sympathetic or symbolic play, like tormented spirits wafting about the Yorkshire Moors in Emily Brontë or the minatory fossils, diamonds, cinders, glass and bones found in the works of Sylvia Plath, whose body rests in Heptonstall churchyard, ten miles south of the Howarth parsonage. Duvalierville, in the film, is a place of secret police murders, electrical blackouts, cripples living under piles of leaves, cock fights and voodoo ceremonies, where a witch doctor bites the head off a hen, quite graphically, too. We are miles away from the genteel – yet Burton's Brown and Taylor's Martha Pineda play an adulterous game by the rules of bourgeois

Europe or America: 'Can't you take me somewhere where we'll really be alone?' implores Taylor, like Emma Bovary in Rouen.

This film could be Flaubert; or it could be *Peyton Place*; or the Crossroads Motel – as Brown has arrived in Haiti to dispose of a hotel he has inherited, a pretty colonial-era building of filigree wooden lattices. The staff has scarpered. There's a dead body in the empty pool. But still. Taylor is married to Peter Ustinov, an ambassador. 'He never asks questions,' she says, which is handy, because her affair with Burton's Brown has lasted 'three months, three years, three decades', i.e. Mrs Pineda has lost all track of time, especially when she's upside down on the back seat of Brown's car, and Burton kisses her throat and bites (in Heathcliff mode) her lips, eroticism on the cusp of cannibalism. Peter Bogdanovich, incidentally, first watched *The Comedians* with a paying audience, and said the snogging scenes elicited unease and tittering. People 'were embarrassed, suddenly reminded that Taylor and Burton were married, that they must do things like that in private ... It jarred them, took them out of the film.' If, like me, you can be inside and outside the film (any film) simultaneously, then the disquiet here is exactly what is required – exacerbated by the sinister beat of the drums we always hear, the arrests and disappearances, the disrupted funeral services. Illicit love, sexual jealousy, awkward glances, saying one thing and meaning another – as Ustinov's character says, 'It's a horrifying world. I sometimes think Haiti is no different from life anywhere.' This is certainly Graham Greene's message, the novelist roaming the planet to persuade himself horror is always real, nothing else is. And if snatched sessions with Taylor's Martha Pineda, foiled assignations and uncomfortable fucks, are one part of the story, Burton's relationship with Señor Pineda is another, more interesting part. By which I mean, Burton's scenes with Ustinov, their mutual silent resignation and concern, the way they remain polite and courteous, with an undercurrent of dislike and competitiveness. 'Life is fairly lonely here at times,' says the ambassador, meaning more than in 'our sheltered diplomatic existence'. Ustinov, who is usually slightly overblown as an actor, who (as with Poirot) liked to seem he was pull-ing the piss, is subdued, serious. 'People are staying indoors. Who can blame them.' He conveys the gnawing melancholy and defeat of the cuckold. 'I can always lie to you,' says Taylor, and is this how she was with Michael Wilding? 'You always forgive, don't you?' She isn't com-plimenting him on nobility of character, either, but rubbing in his distasteful sense of failure and redundancy. Burton, who was always serious, in his scenes is unnerved. 'I have no pride,' he tells Martha Pineda. 'I steal a kind man's wife . . . When you're not with me . . .' he tails off, romantically agonised, his face creased up. Burton smokes cigarettes in an angry way. 'You can't be jealous of the past,' Taylor tells him. 'Yes you can. One day I'll be the past,' he replies. Wouldn't it be marvellous if we all managed to speak like that in real life?

The title Greene chose is a complicated one. The people in the film don't seem to realise how comical they are, in their very earnestness ('Can't you please try and see how a family feels? Can't you?' – 'No'); they are also comedians in the French sense, as actors, *les comédiens*, trying out different roles, aware of being miscast ('We can't always play the parts you have written for us'), those who think they exist independently suddenly thrust into a plot masterminded by others, as happens to Brown, when he gets involved with the rebel militia. There's also comedy in the usual broad sense. Duvalierville, a des-erted construction site, is like Tativille, in *Playtime*. Topsy-turvy things occur. The secret police confiscate a coffin at a funeral. Alec Guinness, the bogus Major Jones, a con man and pickpocket, dresses in drag, undulating up the embassy steps with a bundle on his head, pretending to be a native cook. Paul Ford (Bilko's Colonel Hall) and Lillian Gish give a music-hall turn as a pair of proselytising vegetari-ans. 'One day we may build a theatre-in-the-round for vegetarian dramas,' they announce, and what they have on offer may well have proved beneficial to the steamy Taylor and Burton. 'Eliminate acid-ity from the human body,' says Paul Ford's Smith (Smith, Jones, Brown: Greene was having a laugh), 'and eliminate passion.' Later,

Burton about to be shot by the police, he is saved by Lillian Gish, who always had an angelic, fairy godmother demeanour. 'Plain and simple, nourishing, with no ugly sense of repletion,' she says of the vegetarian products, which like magical talismans save the day. But few people are plain and simple. 'Jones is as crooked as hell', pretending to supply arms to Papa Doc, yet the closest he came to guns was managing a cinema in Assam and introducing officers to girls. Burton's Brown and Taylor's Mrs Pineda weren't playing gin rummy. Ustinov is aware his successful family man image is a facade. Everyone is acting. Haiti is a theatre of cruelty.

If *The Comedians* has an oppressive atmosphere, it's because the theme is the strength or pressure of forbidden emotion, what Greene would think of as sin. Burton and Taylor are often placed by Peter Glenville against blue backgrounds – blue tiles, blue glass, blue bed sheets – and though Miró may have said blue was the colour of his dreams and Derek Jarman was in raptures over the 'fathomless blue of bliss', in *The Comedians*, and elsewhere, cobalt blues and electric blues mean blue funks, the lamentation of the blues in jazz. Haiti is a place of unrest (in every sense – and Burton bought a thirty-five-acre estate there in June 1976) and so is Sardinia in *Boom!*, where the beautiful blue skies and sea – ultramarine, indigo, cerulean – are used by Joseph Losey to counterpoint a story of sickliness and morbidity, or maybe it is more the case that where Burton and Taylor were concerned, nature was simply compelled to go about adjusting itself, atoms and molecules recalibrating, physics and chemistry finding a new luminescence.

* * *

As mentioned at the outset, this book began when I had needles in my arm, an arterial line in my neck, a catheter up my cock, and a gastro-nasal tube and other pipes and garden hoses attached to transparent plastic bags, which filled soon enough with green algae. A nil-by-mouth patient in National Health pyjamas, I made more than a passing resemblance to Kim Jong Il, who as luck would have it had died that week in Pyongyang. There was a morphine drip or pump, allowing for weird, inflamed thoughts. Sweat poured through my matted hair, drenching the pillows. Though there was no view through the hospital window, because there weren't any windows, this didn't matter because my vision vanished, or anyway an ability to focus – some diabetic symptom, I learned later. There were bright lights, white flashes, and as the exterior world was a sequence of abstract shapes, I felt more in the world of *Boom!* than the Poldark (honestly) Ward of the Royal Cornwall Hospital, Truro. In *Boom!* there is an ape on the white marble terrace, which drinks from a golden bowl. There are talking birds in cages. Who can resist a film where there's a hunchbacked Nazi dwarf? There are golden domes, coloured feathers, lush gardens. Like a Balinese shadow puppet, Burton's shadow is projected on the wall. According to the Tennessee Williams short story upon which the drama is based, 'Man Bring This Up Road', his character, Chris Flanders, is an uninvited guest with a sinister extra dimension as, no less, 'the Angel of Death'. Chris (Jimmy in the original, Burton for our purposes) uses as his calling card a slim book of verse, privately printed. It earned him a small reputation, long in the past. 'He was a good bit older than he appeared to be,' says Mrs Flora 'Sissy' Goforth, the art patron, whose secluded Mediterranean villa the man has invaded, in the hope of free hospitality. Burton is first seen emerging from the surf and shingle – from the depths, from the shallows, at the edge of the sea. He has scaled the cliff and, dusty and perspiring, 'stood blinking anxiously in the fierce noonday sun,' as Williams describes it. 'I climbed the mountain and I'm tired, very tired,' is Burton's first line. Sissy denies him refreshment, and he slinks away to sleep for hours and hours in a room with 'painted cupids on the celestial blue ceiling'. There is no breakfast when he wakes, only the emptiness of 'the painfully brilliant white table'. Sissy, it seems, is starving herself, because 'they once found a trace of sugar in my urine'. The visitor, however, is her nemesis. Whenever he turns up to live off rich elderly women, black-mailing them possibly, or providing sexual favours, like William Holden in *Sunset Boulevard*, they die soon afterwards. Flanders might as well be wearing a cowl and carrying a scythe. Or else he is the shrouded ferryman with his oar, collecting his fare in an outspread skeletal palm. Instead, Burton is put in black samurai robes and he wields a sword. 'People are always amazed at how little I change,' he says with an ominous glint, for who should have arrived but the devil.

All this ritualistic behaviour (done on stage as *The Milk Train Doesn't Stop Here Anymore* and a vehicle down the years for Hermione Baddeley, Tallulah Bankhead and Olympia Dukakis) was described by Losey as Williams' trying to convey 'a feeling about life and about death'. *Boom!* is 'a film about emotion, a film about music – the music of the sea, the music of words, and the music of images'. None of which is tremendously helpful, especially not so in 1968, when what I would have preferred to go and see in Bedwas Workmen's Hall, had an adult accompanied me, was *Carry On Up the Khyber*. It probably never came to Bedwas in any event. *Boom!* cost $4,592,762 and by 1974 was still $3,795,452 in the red. The marble for the villa set, transported from the same quarry as used by the Romans for the Colosseum, cost (or wasted) a million. Nevertheless, Burton always maintained to Losey that, 'We'll all be proud of it one day. It contains what I consider to be . . . a magical combination of words and vision.' I'm still unper-suaded by the words – 'Shit on your mother!' Sissy says to the servants; 'Yoo-hoo! Coo-ee!' trills Noël Coward – but what's on show is defin-itely visionary. Sissy's great clifftop retreat, with bas-reliefs in plaster, modernistic carvings, chinking Calder mobiles, and swaying, billowing curtains, is less a home than a fortress, or as we discover, a mauso-leum. There's an X-ray machine in the stark bedroom. Diamonds and furs vie with pill bottles. Taylor's Sissy coughs and chokes, cries out for morphine injections, lurches from one frantic distraction to another ('You seem very wrought-up, dear,' says Coward – described in the cast list as The Witch of Capri). She has blackouts, total eclipses of memory, gags on tablets, splutters on brandy. Is this hypochondria or a genuine cancer? As regards the actual film, it's both. At the end, the Burton character reverently lays out her corpse – she's as posed as Cleopatra – removes her jewels, drops a diamond ring into a chalice and tosses it into the sea in propitiation. Williams had had Sissy say, 'I am colder-hearted than the gods of Old Egypt,' and Taylor grasped there was something in *Boom!*, something stagnant and humid, and something to do with power struggles and surrenders, with which she could connect. For where, with Burton, I have had to seek the documentary evidence, sift through the sources, listen to the testimony of eyewitnesses, piece together scraps from his diaries, to get a sense of his past – with Taylor, there it all is on the screen. She grew up on celluloid. In *Boom!* asphyxia is part of her exhibitionism, and what I personally find admirable is her refusal to be nice. Taylor's Sissy, 'a dying monster', is snappy, snarling, and won't be contradicted. She slaps the servants, flings crockery on the rocks, hurls food through windows, orders dinner and luncheon trays to be removed – particularly when other characters are famished. Noël Coward, arriving in a funicular or aerial gondola, comes for a meal, sits in a huge golden throne at a table set with golden cutlery, and is served nothing edible, only a glistening, bristling mutant fish. Attired in a dinner jacket cut by tailor Douglas Hayward, he, Coward, always managed to look sleek and common simultaneously, don't you think? Meanwhile, Sissy dances before him in a spiky helmet made from glass rods and beads. 'Everything you do or say,' she is told, 'is like you're playing a game.' There is sitar music, Sixties noises, composed variously by Johnny Dankworth, Michel Legrand and John Barry.

It is meant to be a sexual set-up ('I need myself a lover,' says Sissy – Sissy, by the way, or Sisi, was the name of the errant Empress Elisabeth of Austria, assassinated in Geneva in 1898), but the film is too macabre for that, with the whooping birds and ferocious guard dogs, the noise of the surf lashing the shingle, the harshness of the light, the cactus landscape. It is a frightening atmosphere, intimidating. Taylor's Sissy, in motion in white hats and scarves edged with lavender, her white muslin kaftans resembling floating shrouds, whilst a bundle of temper and irritation, at least goes quiet when given an injection in the stomach. Dictating her memoirs over an intercom, Taylor delivers a long monologue about her sexual experiences when young – which taught her a sexual experience was always going to be like an assault, even when mixed with desire. Having been lying on her bed, twisting and turning, she moves, in her negligee, to the terrace, convinced, 'Sooner or later a person is obliged to face the meaning of life.' Fortunately, she comes face to face with Burton, who picking up on the mood, listening to the waves, says, 'Boom! The shock of each and every moment of still being alive ... Death is one moment, and life is so many of them.' Well, I'm not going to bother denying that. 'Are you frightened of me, or attracted to me, or both?' asks Burton, gazing at Taylor in fascination – gazing at her in a way he never did with other actresses. It isn't lust particularly, or polite male interest – it's like he's drinking her up, drinking her in, as African violet bunches do water. And she is dark and gorgeous in the white clothes and hoods trimmed with lilac. What we are seeing is an opera (without an orchestra) or fairy tale about their relationship: sex and death, beauty and death. 'I do anything I have an urge to do,' says Sissy, a line that could be Taylor's own. 'I've never in my life met anyone like you,' says Burton's character, echoing Burton in his own diaries, when on 20 October 1968, after she'd made *Secret Ceremony* and he'd made *Where Eagles Dare*, he wrote: 'After nearly eight years of marriage [actually four] I look at her when she's asleep at the first light of grey dawn and wonder at her.' In *Boom!* the sun leaves the terrace, leaving behind the intimations of madness and disease. The ambience gets to be ghostly and gothic – the more so, paradoxically, given the blue and white cool. Taylor is suddenly bloated and vampiric. She looks like she's grown fangs, as in *Doctor Faustus*. (In his *Notebooks*, Williams, in an entry dated 29 August 1953, says Sissy was 'a composite of various vampires I have known,' e.g.

Peggy Guggenheim.) We move to the deathbed sequence ('I have lots of art treasures in my bedroom, including myself'), and the film finishes with all that histrionic scurrying, Taylor's Sissy's euphoria and depressive rage, Burton's speechifying about the 'absolute naturalness of nature' – and I can quite see why *Boom!* wasn't commercially successful, and money went down the drain. It is arty and experimental. It's wrong in so many obvious ways. There's no story worth following. Nothing happens. Characters spout daft dialogue. Taylor and Burton are too old – or is it they are too young – for the roles. *Boom!* would perhaps have been better served by an actress good at grimacing, Bette Davis, say, and as Chris Flanders, oh, some young boy, like the Scandiwegian in *Death in Venice*; or if made today, Cate Blanchett and someone erotically evil and cajoling like Jonathan Rhys Meyers.

But none of this matters or is of consequence – because it was Taylor and Burton who were in *Boom!* It's about them – a fact not even Losey appeared to grasp. 'I think it is very beautiful, but I would be hard put to say what it's about, you know,' the director told Michel Ciment. Yet at an instinctive level, Taylor and Burton had fully surrendered to the gravitational pull of the material – Sissy's greed is Taylor's ('I give nothing away. I buy and I sell,' says Williams' heroine); the way Sissy sees traitors everywhere and has fits of panic ('I've been plagued by imposters'): this is the paranoia of the rich star; the wealthy woman in her villa at high altitudes, surrounded by thorns, is Taylor, with Burton, isolated in hotel suites, in Switzerland, in Puerto Vallarta – and finally there's the dying Taylor in 700 Nimes Road. In 2015, the photographer Catherine Opie published a book, called *700 Nimes Road*, which catalogues the star's empty rooms and piles of possessions – Taylor's medals and awards, her sofas and shoes ('a portrait of Elizabeth Taylor through her home and belongings') – and what's spooky is that when Opie began taking her snaps, in January 2010, the actress was still upstairs, bedridden, so, 'Unfortunately I never had the honour of meeting her.' Instead, in Opie's opulent volume, there's the strange feeling of how a star can still be present whilst being absent – the blue rivers of the carpets, the coloured glass ornaments, the Cartier jewels in scuffed red leather boxes. It brings to mind how what I'm struck by when reading Burton's diaries is the sunshine, the Mediterranean or Californian or Alpine or Mexican locales: we are a far cry from soggy, monochromatic Britain, its foggy fields and hills. And then there is the entourage. Sissy's Duchess of Windsor-sized retinue of guards, a masseuse, manicurist, hairdresser, nurse and doctor is probably smaller than the court Taylor and Burton employed, which, as Melvyn Bragg stated, was 'based on the over-protective and self-inflated model of the eighteenth-century German princelings'. All those hirelings – to make them feel isolated. (Opie had to negotiate her way past heaps of them – who still thronged Nimes Road when Taylor was officially demised.) The Goforth emblem is a golden Welsh dragon.

* * *

Capo Caccia, Sardinia, may be hot, but the villa on its crag is an ice palace. The clear blue water and infinite cloudless sky suggest not abundance, but meaninglessness. The opulence signifies waste. I am prompted to count the ways Taylor and Burton described each other, when they wanted to seem surrounded by poetry. 'She is like the tide, she comes and she goes,' Burton wrote on the verso of a photographic portrait of Taylor taken by Gianni Bozzacchi. 'In my poor and tormented youth, I had always dreamed of this woman.' Taylor's picture of Burton also sought aquatic imagery. He was oceanic. He was a downpour. 'I had wanted to be free,' she said, 'running in the rain on the grass, and nothing to tether me ... And Richard and I went that route together.' This all suggests a sort of weightlessness, like the emotional and topographical vertigo of *Boom!* and Taylor was so responsive to the film, she gave Losey an oval-shaped Cartier watch ('To Joe with love – Elizabeth' the inscription) along with an entreaty: 'Dearest Joseph, Till the next one – please make it *soon*.

All my love. P.S. Don't forget all about me.' The director responded with alacrity. *Secret Ceremony* was underway in February 1968, four months after *Boom!* had wrapped. It is another work with the quality of a vision, and is about the deep eccentricity of its two stars, Taylor and Mia Farrow – three if we include Robert Mitchum. Five if we add Peggy Ashcroft and Pamela Brown. Six – don't forget the house. I know this house, 8 Addison Road, Kensington. It was used in *The Life and Death of Peter Sellers* as the home or lair of the soothsayer, Maurice Woodruff, played by Stephen Fry. The actual Maurice was somewhat seedy, living in Swiss Cottage with cats and cobwebs. He died of a sudden heart attack in 1973, at the age of fifty-six – did he see that coming? In the HBO biopic he became sleek and booming, conducting his seances in a vast echo-chamber clad with gleaming turquoise ceramic tiles, which as I said at the time put me in mind of Orson Welles' personal pissoir.

Debenham House, to give the location its official title, Grade 1 Listed since 1969, was built in 1905 for Ernest Debenham, of (defunct) department store fame. The exterior is smothered in the sort of Doulton ware normally used for flower vases – the idea was that the glazing would resist London pollution. Under a large dome, the interior is filled with shiny green and blue panels, mosaics, marble fireplaces, stained glass, and mahogany inlaid with mother-of-pearl. The fixtures and fittings were manufactured by the Birmingham Guild of Handicraft. A first-floor gallery, connecting upstairs rooms, gives the effect of a balcony overlooking a public square in somebody's fantasy idea of Morocco or Persia. More than lavish, it is oppressive, heavy-going, the colours too strong, the sort of place a sultan would lock his harem up in. Here, with the tinkling of astrological bells, Maurice summoned the shade of Sellers' late mother, who from the far-beyond encouraged the credulous Goon to keep playing Inspector Clouseau, and not to think of himself as the great and serious actor who'd emerge (too late) in *Being There*. In *Secret Ceremony*, Debenham House is a similar house of the dead. The sole inhabitant is Mia Farrow's Cenci, a mad girl with lots of hair, long, skeleton fingers, and a dangerous beauty. She's like an overly-knowing child in Henry James – disturbingly erotic, creepily flirtatious, Maisie Farange, say, and in many respects fully aware of her effect on others. 'Crazy people never look their age,' says Peggy Ashcroft, Cenci's aunt, who pilfers bric-a-brac from the occasional tables. 'She's twenty-two, if she's a day.' In 1968, Mia was twenty-three and going through her divorce from Sinatra – as Ava Gardner had unkindly cracked at the start of that brief marriage, 'I always knew Frank would end up with a boy.'

She is or was certainly androgynous, a slender, evil Alice in Wonderland sort, enticing the voluptuous Taylor down into her rabbit hole – Taylor pulpy, matronly, Mia so thin, so vaporous, mirrors can hardly throw back any reflection. Taylor is Leonora, a name from opera (*La Forza del Destino*; *Fidelio*), and she's marvellously operatic here, posed next to all those peacock-coloured, deep purple glazed tiles, the greens almost black – a spectacular moment, which during her college days much moved Camille Paglia, who has written: 'Elizabeth Taylor in a violet velvet suit and turban suddenly walks across the screen in front of a wall of sea-green tiles. It is an overcast London day; the steel-grey light makes the violet and green irides-cent. This is Elizabeth Taylor at her most vibrant, mysterious and alluring, at the peak of her mature fleshy glamour.' Professor Paglia goes further: 'This vivid, silent tableau is for me one of the classic scenes in the history of cinema,' in which case she and I are the only ones (not on drugs) to have suspected such a thing – and we first find Taylor's Leonora in her own flat, trying on an orange wig. She washes and lathers her face and sets off to place blooms on the grave of her drowned child, at Kensal Green Cemetery. It is a sight scarcely to be believed, Taylor on a Number 27 red London bus. The spidery Mia finds her in St Mary Magdalene, a Catholic church in Rowington Close, Paddington. Everything looks bleak, like a cleared bomb crater after a holocaust. If people come together, it's because there's

no one else. 'I'm not who you think I am,' Taylor tells Mia. 'What the
hell do you want from me?' Mia wants a mother, and Taylor's Leonora,
it is established, wants a daughter – and *Secret Ceremony* watches the
pair of them acting out how to handle adult life, capering about the
mansion, examining music boxes, chiming clocks and porcelain dolls.
There are wardrobes filled with pink cloaks – the clothes belonged to
Cenci's real (dead) mother. There's a big sunken bath, suitable for
Cleopatra, a dressing table with ivory-backed silver brushes. We
watch a prolonged scene, where Mia brushes Taylor's hair and calls
her 'Mummy'. She makes her mother-surrogate a hearty hot breakfast, delivering it upstairs on a silver platter in a dumb waiter. Taylor
tucks in and burps – and by falling in with the role-playing Leonora
shows herself to be equally as deranged, especially when Robert
Mitchum, Cenci's stepfather, appears and disrupts the intensifying
sensual relationship between the women. There's been the hair
brushing sequence ('Do you want to touch my hair?'); they take a
bath together. If they are mother and child, this is now an incest
game – and Mitchum's Albert is thoroughly predatory. 'Incest is a
boring symptom of the private property system,' he maintains, as his
stepdaughter trims his moustachless beard. Apparently, he is a professor of some sort: 'All the little sophomores think I'm just baffled,
benign . . . Until we get to the parking lot. Then I grab them.' He grabs
and rapes Cenci in the kitchen, so she swallows a fatal overdose. Laid
out in her coffin, in the Art Deco dining room, she looks translucent
and quite exquisite, in her shroud. It suits her. When Mitchum comes
in, Taylor stabs him.

It's a film about how grief and loneliness make people insane, driving out love. It's about dreams and lunatic behaviour. The house, for
all its luxury, is tomb-like. When the characters give themselves over
to the role-playing, to supposed re-enactments, it's as if they are in a
half-life, dead already. Cenci, when sleeping, with her hair carefully
spread across the pillows, is in a funeral parlour pose. The flower
arrangements in the mansion are funeral wreaths. I am spellbound by

the film, which is no longer solely a film, to my mind, and more of a purple dream. To watch these works – all of the things Taylor and Burton did – which border on hallucinations, again and again, is like seeing a sculpture or painting, which has been created, destroyed and re-created, as if out of nothing. When my back is turned, adjustments seem to have been made, effected, here and there, as I spot new things, like in M.R. James' *The Mezzotint*. Alterations, variations, always emerge; elements have changed – how so? All is part, perhaps, of my inflamed liver, erratic T-cell count, palpitations, elevated temperature. There again, everything is only appearance: how actors and actresses move across a room, their interplay, morning and night, in summertime and wintertime. But I don't only mean the external likeness or the sequence of facts, which biography traditionally is fond of – for what about the emotions, sensations, desires, which physical appearance provokes? Taylor and Burton's way of being – that is the thing. I feel intense joy, mingled with fear, in the presence of art, artistry, artists. And in *Secret Ceremony* I see what Keats in *Endymion* calls characters or beings who 'pass into nothingness', and the whole blazing enterprise is a lesson in mortality.

* * *

My only disappointment is Burton doesn't play Mitchum's part – and not only because of the eulogy to Taylor's tits ('You look more like a cow than my wife'), which sounds like an authentic Burton sentiment, or because of the male swagger, but because of the incestuous or quasi-incestuous longings. In his diaries, the references to Liza Todd are, if candid, aberrant: 'I have developed a love for that child that is in danger of becoming obsessive'; 'I cannot take my eyes off Liza. Her eyes are the most beautiful I've ever seen and I love her to the point of pain' (June 1969, when she was twelve). As when Humbert Humbert is thrilled and appalled by Lolita's slovenliness, Burton is affected by the way Liza leaves undergarments scattered about the bathroom. Her dress, shoes and socks are erotic litter. When she's fourteen he has a conversation with her about masturbation, 'a perfectly normal part of growing up'. At Christmas 1971, 'Liza is a bundle of energy and I spoil her with shamelessness though I have to mentally belt her now and again.' At Taylor's fortieth birthday party in Budapest, the following February, Liza 'gave me thunderous goodnight kisses, several to each side of the face'. When Ivor dies, Burton writes, on 23 March 1972, 'Sweet Liza is here which makes up for a great deal of the pain.' What are we being asked to accept? In 1979, he bought her a car and an apartment, Kate Andersen Brower informs us in her Taylor biography. 'If Richard wants to be the Big Daddy to Liza (and it seems to me he already has by presenting these items) it's OK by me,' Taylor told Aaron Frosch – and the lawyer had evidently thought it a subject worth raising. 'Very generous,' said Taylor, 'but rather confusing.' Quite so. A lot is happening here, psychologically: sin, lust and guilt (the major Burton themes); feelings touching on disharmony, disequilibrium, defilement – semi-explored with Tatum O'Neal in *Circle of Two* or *Obsession*; the seen and the unseen. There's also an allure between Burton's Father Lamont and Linda Blair in *The Heretic*: 'Evil is gaining,' he says to her. 'Good and evil are struggling within you' – though I find it hard to know when the podgy, porcine Linda Blair is the girl Regan and when she's the green-faced growling effigy with the swivelling head. She looks the same.

The Burton story is always one of decadence and sexual hunger, volcanic passions, the exhilaration of danger. Ivor and his death (or murder – as I view it to have been) was Burton at his most demonic. 'The very notion of Richard Burton not killing a man who stands in his way strains credulity,' said William Redfield, explaining in *Letters from an Actor* why he thought the star a rubbish Hamlet, not credible at quibbling. Burton had a need to command. He had a vehemence. People were frightened of him. 'Rich stood up. He was shaking, though [whether] from anger or alcohol, I could not tell. "You little bastard," he shouted. "How dare you tell me how to behave. Who do you think you are?" There was a lot more of this,' is the remembrance of his brother Graham, who was sneered at for having risen no higher in life than manager of the Afan Lido Sports Centre, Port Talbot. 'It was fatal to oppose him,' said his other brother, David, who saw Burton be beastly to Sally. 'Richard baited her again and again and again . . . There was nothing we could do to stop him.' He was beyond good and evil. No one was to stand in his way, not even a minor character actor like George Rose (the gravedigger in the Broadway *Hamlet*) – 'Nobody is going to protect me from George Rose; nobody is going to protect George Rose from me' – not Laurence Olivier, Burton telling him to his face he was a 'grotesque exaggeration'; not any director: despite what had been decided upon in rehearsals, 'Once I'm on stage there's nothing anyone can do.' Kenneth Tynan praised Burton in print ('his voice cuts urgent and keen'), had placed him squarely in the Great Tradition, which descended from Garrick and Irving – so Burton (who would not be beholden) when he met him was belittling, shit-stirring. It amused Burton to introduce Tynan to Humphrey Bogart by saying, 'Bogie, this is a Mr Ken Tynan who wrote about you recently . . . and described your face as "a triumph of plastic surgery" . . .' Burton enjoyed the discomfiture. Tynan was 'devastated . . . never recovered his aplomb and remained for the rest of the evening a stammering and stuttering skeletonic death's head.' It's not humour showing – it's hostility. He was similarly as sadistic in Rome, at a reception where much drink had been taken. Tynan was to record the interview with Burton for the BBC, which is transcribed in *Acting in the Sixties*. Taylor was shooting *Reflections in a Golden Eye*. 'How would you like to go to bed with her?' Burton asked the critic, with unpleasant jollity. 'To be quite candid, Richard, I doubt whether I'd be capable of making it with Elizabeth' – 'You mean you couldn't get it up?' – 'Something like that.' Burton then bellowed to Taylor, who was across the room: 'Elizabeth! Do you know what our friend Ken just said about you? . . . He said he didn't think he'd be able to get it up for you in bed.' Taylor turned and glared at Tynan: '*That* is the

most *insulting thing* that has ever been said to me. *Leave my house!'*
Flowers and the form letter of apology arrived the next day. But still.

The reason Burton was not in *Secret Ceremony* is because in January
1968 he was in *Where Eagles Dare*, the popular and callous war film,
where Germans are machine-gunned, stabbed and blown up without qualm. There's not much dialogue, save the repeated call signal,
'This is Broadsword calling Danny Boy.' Michael Hordern and
Burton recite it like a solemn verse from Shakespeare. The film,
though, is comic strip heroics, with Burton and Clint Eastwood scurrying about in the snow, tussling on top of cable cars and planting
dynamite in a castle dining room. Mary Ure, last seen with Burton in
Jimmy Porter's attic, is a blonde, resourceful killer. Or is she? I'm not
sure I've ever fully followed the plot's double-cross mechanics, or
even if I know if it comes to that whether I'm watching *Where Eagles
Dare* or *The Guns of Navarone*, another one about daring raids on a
Nazi lair. All is intermixed in my mind, which one has Mary Ure, or
is it Irene Pappas; where exactly David Niven, Anthony Quayle and
Patrick Wymark are to be found and whose side they are on. Patrick
Wymark's daughter Jane was in college with Victoria Wood, I know
that much. Stanley Baker is on a Greek fishing boat with explosives.
Kirk Douglas skis down a Norwegian fjord. Everyone is playing at
being a commando. I think Michael Caine may be involved, kidnap-
ping Winston Churchill. A soldier goes over a water wheel. Burton,
with never any gross air of parody or self-parody, always reliable at
being the guilt-ridden, mournful soak, in *Where Eagles Dare* is
required to be the action hero. He snaps into focus, becomes severe
(the reverse of weakness); he plays the role of (the anonymous-
sounding) Major John Smith with a continuous snarl. Here is the
military man doing his duty, making the best of it – the impossible
mission. He's the same when in uniform in *The Desert Rats, Bitter
Victory, The Longest Day, Raid on Rommel, The Battle of Sutjeska, The
Wild Geese* and *Breakthrough*. Burton was concerned with masculinity; there was an anxiety about maleness, pride, vainglory. What I

particularly note is Burton's boldness – yet there's also a dimension, which though invisible, nonetheless is there: a sense Burton is amused (in an ironic, bitterly victorious manner) by his taste for rhetorical flourishes, for splendour, even if what he's doing under the soundtrack's march of drums is pretending to drive a bus through a hail of back-projected bullets. *Where Eagles Dare* made him 'in excess of £8 million', according to brother Graham.

* * *

Burton was intellectually amazingly curious and high spirited, like Faustus; he was also deeply bored, sated (the explanation for why he needled Tynan). As Sybil, dishonoured and abandoned, had said, 'At first he is bored with someone. Then he becomes boring. Finally he bores himself.' He dominated and discarded women, e.g. his treatment of Susan Strasberg (who went on to have a similar relationship with Christopher Jones; she sought to be abused, her virtue mangled) and Claire Bloom (Rod Steiger and Philip Roth next in the queue). Burton had a detachment that seems barbarous. Taylor, at least, with her long black hair, her huge appetite for food and sex, was a permanent distraction – but even regarding her he was heard to announce, on the set of *Ellis Island*, in July 1984, a month before he died, 'I didn't think I would ever feel this or say this, but I don't want to see her ever again.' On the other hand, he was also going around telling everyone, as during *Wagner*, 'I can't live without her.' Excruciatingly, in his last days at Céligny, he called Sally 'Elizabeth'. This was only to bring about a prophecy from 1973: 'When I am on my last bed and nearing the eternal shore . . . the words Elizabeth, Elizabeth, Elizabeth . . . will be on my lips.' Who said love is always to do with happiness? It's a paradox that Burton and Taylor's greatest works are about marriages breaking up. Jealousy, betrayal, cruelty, are the subjects; love and pride; a sense of complicity – an awareness of repulsiveness, in the ways they were occupied with each other.

Francis Bacon had a point when he said, 'Being in love in that extreme way – being utterly obsessed by someone – it's like having a dreadful disease.' I never find Taylor and Burton's eroticism lively and joyous. There is much disenchantment, grossness, moments of revulsion, pure aggression, like that description in *The Golden Bowl*: 'What was Maggie's own sense but that of having been thrown over on her back, with her neck, from the first, half-broken and her help-less face staring up?' They chose to make the films they made, moreover, chiefly because the subjects excited them sexually, or else intensified their private predicaments and dramas. Adulterous, star-crossed, filled with romantic troubles and regrets – through their characters Taylor and Burton could realise, as it were, the feel of each other. The impulses behind (or within) performances are their tan-trums and frustrations, a manifestation of the sexual itch. As Burton wrote in his diary, Taylor 'is a wildly exciting love-mistress. She can tolerate my impossibilities and my drunkenness ... I'll love her till I die.' Maybe this wasn't something she was totally aware of, if what he called her in public was, 'You fucking sagging-tit no-talent Hollywood cunt.'

Whilst this is all faintly disturbing, the erotic charge is more mys-terious for being dispersed, diffused, amongst variously perfunctory or sophisticated objects like cigarettes, jewels, furs, dinners, drinks. For example, the furniture in *Who's Afraid of Virginia Woolf?*, the smudged glasses and kitchen mess (the set-decorator won an Academy Award); the fog in *The V.I.P.s*; the concoctions of witch doctors and voodoo in *The Comedians*; the dry Tuscan summer (and thunder shower) in *The Taming of the Shrew*; the marble terraces, the crystal-ware, the glistening sea and Sardinia in *Boom!* To this day there are colonies of monkeys and flocks of parrots in Sardinia – descendants of escapees from *Boom!* Taylor and Burton were seduced by climate – the snow in *Where Eagles Dare* or the desert in *Bitter Victory* and other war films; the damp of *The Spy Who Came in from the Cold* and *Under Milk Wood*; the Great Outdoors in the *Lassie* films and the shadowy lake in

A Place in the Sun; all the way to the rainy windows in *Divorce His, Divorce Hers*. Something seems to seep out of them, gets to be over-heated. There is a lurid air, with actions and endeavours sliding and collapsing, as in their penultimate screen outing, *Hammersmith is Out*, made in Cuernavaca, Mexico, in May 1971, and which won Silver Bears in Berlin in 1972. 'Very wild and formless but just the kind of thing that I would like to do at the moment,' said Burton. It's certainly a weird film, the more so because the DVD I finally found was a third-generation dupe copied from an ex-rental VHS, which gave it a faint, fuzzy quality. It is not, either, as all the biographies state, a version of the Faust legend, but, rather, Satan's tempting of Jesus in the wilder-ness. Burton is Satan, an escaped lunatic. ('One of my earliest memories,' he says, 'is of a woman and a snake.') But it's as if they have all gone mad: Peter Ustinov, the urbane and polyglot producer of Mozart operas, the author of plays and novels, a cosmopolitan gent, here directs a picture about nose picking, farting, coarseness. He makes an appearance as a German psychiatrist, chuckling over a text-book he's reading, *Studies in Anal Retention*. It is a Peter Sellers role, like Sellers' student-of-the-mind in *What's New Pussycat?*. Actually, now I think of it, and remember Ustinov's oriental accent in *One of Our Dinosaurs Is Missing* or *Charlie Chan and the Curse of the Dragon Queen*, in which Rachel Roberts is seventh-billed (below Roddy McDowall and above Michelle Pfeiffer), plus his flowery Poirot – perhaps he tended to be a cartoonish actor, despite an urbane reputation, which is why his seriousness in *The Comedians* stands out. But none is serious here, only zany. Taylor enjoys herself as Jimmie-Jean Jackson, the bawdy waitress in a diner called 'You Wanna Eat'. She's Martha again from *Who's Afraid of Virginia Woolf?*, sporting a succession of grotesque clothes and capes. She dances by a pool, wearing a zebra-print cloak, and her fat legs and bulging thighs are hideous – and a premonition of how Taylor will per-manently be or look in the years to come, in the likes of *A Little Night Music* or *The Mirror Crack'd* or, my Christ, *Sweet Bird of Youth*, where the combined talents of Tennessee Williams, Nicolas Roeg and Gavin

Lambert turned her into a hag. Yet she's defiant, also, deliberately pro-vocative, concentrated. Burton's Hammersmith, unblinking in a white shirt, speaks in an accent so English, so modulated, he could be George Sanders (b. St Petersburg), and the psychopath escaped from his cell is definitely a precursor of the Hannibal Lecter played by Anthony Hopkins (b. Port Talbot.)

* * *

As with Sellers' *The Magic Christian*, released in 1969, the disjointed scenes in *Hammersmith Is Out* see wealthy movie stars satirise money and power. We go from the asylum to an open-air cinema to a topless nightclub, where the band is called The Tits: women with swinging udders, under the rule of George Raft. There's a pharmaceutical fac-tory, an oil business, a castle in Spain, though the location is no doubt still somewhere in Mexico. The Jesus figure is an uncouth hospital orderly, Billy Breedlove, played by Beau Bridges, and to me there were as many Bridges at large, Lloyd, Jeff, Beau, as Brontës or Cusacks. When he, Beau, gets exasperated with Jimmie-Jean and wants to kill her, though I'm not aware Our Lord felt that way about Mary Magdalene, is that how Burton felt on occasion – or how Taylor felt? 'We are fighting and have been fighting for a year now over everything and anything,' wrote Burton in his diary in 1969. The daily tally of vodka and Scotch bottles didn't help. 'I wish to Christ he'd just get out of my life,' Taylor confided to Norma Heyman a year later. 'It's been growing on me for a long time.' Norma also overheard Taylor say to Burton, in Puerto Vallarta, 'I dislike you and I hate you.' Divorce, when it came, was quite as satisfyingly muddled and uncertain as the complications of devotion and living together: 'Our natures do not inspire domestic tranquillity,' Burton had said, with some pride. Not for them games on the lawn, picnics. Everything was too ardent, too much on public display – like the way Burton chewed Taylor's ear and kissed her in *The Comedians*. Their sexuality was out in the open – this was not Celia Johnson and Trevor Howard in the buffet at Milford Junction. Taylor and Burton were not inhibited and sub-urban. They were the most exciting thing to have happened to each other, and as Taylor said, on 20 July 1973, when they first officially separated, 'Maybe we loved each other too much. I never believed such a thing was possible.' Her line echoes what she came out with about her parents, whom she blamed for overprotecting her ('Maybe they loved me too much. They had no life of their own, especially my mother'); and if the sentiment originated with Othello ('then must you speak / Of one that lov'd not wisely, but too well'), Taylor, like the noble Moor, was never one for understatement. Indeed, in her press release about the bust-up (which she said was 'a good and con-structive idea' – 'Pray for us,' she added) she sounds exultant, as if giving a close-up to a movie camera, like Gloria Swanson in *Sunset Boulevard*.

And trying to work out and follow who was where, why and for how long, is like determining the random peregrinations of (and I think this is a Julian Barnes phrase) sprites pissed on margaritas. On 4 July, a fortnight before her speaking to reporters in her Othello style, Taylor was visiting her mother in Los Angeles and staying at 1600 Coldwater Canyon with Edith Head, who'd designed the cos-tumes most recently for *Hammersmith Is Out* and *Divorce His, Divorce Hers*. Gossip has it that Taylor had a fling with Peter Lawford and Peter Lawford's son, Christopher, who was eighteen and with whom she visited Mae West. 'Christopher, let's get the hell out of here,' she said, realising Mae was the Ghost of Christmas Yet To Come. We next find Burton and Taylor together at Aaron Frosch's house at Quogue, Long Island, but they fell out and Taylor went on her own (plus entourage) to the Regency Hotel in Manhattan. 'Elizabeth is like a spoilt child. She enjoys undermining me. One gets tired of it,' said Burton. The scene then switches to Rome, where Taylor makes *The Driver's Seat* with Andy Warhol. 'Gee,' said the Pop Artist, 'she has everything: magic, money, beauty, intelligence.

Why can't she be happy?' Because when you have everything, you have everything to lose.

Burton had been in Italy since 12 July, staying with Sophia Loren, whom he'd not previously met, at the Villa Ponti in Marino – in August they were to star together in *The Voyage*, to be made in Palermo. In August 1974 they'd again appear together in a remake of *Brief Encounter*, to be made in Winchester. Sophia found her guest nervy, awkward, maudlin, except when 'words and quotations tumbled from him as from a literary cornucopia'. Notwithstanding, she still beat him at Scrabble. 'In our talks, Richard always took full blame for his trouble with Elizabeth.' If he sounds lonely and forlorn, at least there was always the solace of his entourage. Like King Lear, he arrived at Sophia and Carlo's place with a doctor, a nurse, a secretary and two body-guards, if not a hundred knights. He was trying to dry out, 'to get into shape' for Taylor's arrival on 23 July. Burton waited in a green Rolls-Royce for her to land in a Mystère jet at Fiumicino Airport. She appeared with two Shih Tzu dogs and a black cat called Cassius. They started arguing immediately. At Villa Ponti, Sophia said Taylor was 'tentative and ambivalent about Richard,' whose 'personality under-went a disheartening change; he became much more aggressive, and sometimes rather violent in his reactions.' He'd fallen off the water-wagon. 'I am desolate,' said Taylor. 'If two people are sick of each other, or the sight of one another bores them, then they should get divorced . . . as soon as possible,' said Burton. Hence, John Springer, the publicist, on 31 July announced that Aaron Frosch was drawing up papers to 'legally conclude' the marriage.

Taylor, after nine days, moved into Rome's Grand Hotel, where, systematically pulling leaves off a potted plant, like Honey compul-sively picking at a paper label in *Who's Afraid of Virginia Woolf?*, she jabbered to Warhol about how 'I don't want to be that much in love ever again . . . I didn't reserve anything . . .' Taylor did what she always did to claim attention. She fell ill, entering the Scripps Clinic in La Jolla, California, complaining of stomach cramps. Burton was in Sicily, shooting *The Voyage*, when on 28 November (some bio-graphical sources say 10 December) he was informed by Taylor ('their first communication since his arrival,' noted Sophia) that she was about to undergo a three-hour operation to remove an ovarian cyst. She expected him to fly to her side. This was on a Friday. Shoot-ing had to continue on the Monday. On 7 December, according to contemporary newspaper bulletins, Burton sailed on the *Kalizma* to Naples and flew to London on (another – or maybe the same) char-tered Mystère executive jet, before transferring to a Pan Am flight to Los Angeles. 'I understand my wife is pretty sick,' he told reporters. 'I shall be going to see her in hospital as soon as I get off this plane.' He went to California and back over the Pole in twenty-four hours, 'an emotionally disturbing trip,' according to Sophia. 'Thank God it wasn't cancer,' Burton said to her, and he paid Ponti, who was pro-ducing *The Voyage*, $45,000 in compensation for each of the days he was absent. That Christmas in Puerto Vallarta, Burton gave Taylor a thirty-eight-carat diamond he'd found in Naples, presumably on the short trip between the harbour and the airport. 'You've never seen anyone heal so fast,' said Taylor.

By the New Year, however, Burton was drinking with both hands again. In March 1974, shooting *The Klansman* on location in Oroville, he was consuming Martinis with Lee Marvin, falling into camellia bushes, chasing teenage waitresses and chatting up hotel reception-ists. 'I didn't know what the hell I was doing,' he claimed later. Taylor visited the set. 'I could hear them fighting at night in their room,' said a crew member. 'There were screams and then a door slammed. I looked outside and Elizabeth was on the ground where he'd flung her.' Burton made his way to St John's Hospital in Santa Monica, where for six weeks he was fed intravenously and given blood trans-fusions for chronic alcoholism. His liver was so shot, it couldn't metabolise the Antabuse medication – the Disulfiram tablets, which provoked an allergic reaction to ethanol: flushing, throbbing, puking, sweating and vertigo. Founded in 1942 by the Sisters of Charity of

Leavenworth, the Providence St John's Health Center was where Nat King Cole, Dom DeLuise and Blake Edwards died. Burton could sleep no longer than in forty-five-minute batches, as he had nightmares about the killing of Ivor – love and death were at last finally in alignment. 'After all,' as Quentin Crisp once wrote, 'as a test of whether you still mean something to somebody, being loved can never be a patch on being murdered. That's when somebody really has risked his life for you.' Meanwhile, Taylor was coming out with her Chamberlain-at-Munich statements for the press. 'With deep regret,' she intoned, 'the reconciliation had failed and the marriage had died of irreconcilable differences.' We cut now to Switzerland, where Frosch is organising the divorce in Berne. On 26 June the judge in the courtroom at Saanen asked Taylor (Burton not being present, pleading illness), 'Is it true that to live with your husband was intolerable?' – 'Yes, life with Richard became intolerable.' Twenty minutes later, she phoned him up: 'Richard, do you think we did the right thing?'

They didn't think they had, though there were prolonged peccadilloes. Taylor sailed around the Mediterranean on the *Kalizma* with Henry Wynberg, with whom she was to go into the lucrative perfume business. *The Driver's Seat* received its premiere in Monaco, in aid of Grace and Rainier's Red Cross charity. Burton's squeeze was Princess Elizabeth of Yugoslavia, the daughter of Prince Paul of Yugoslavia and Princess Olga of Greece and Denmark. 'I'm going to marry her,' said Burton. 'I want her to be my wife. I want to be with her for ever and ever and ever. I love her, I truly do. I love her so much, so deeply, it hurts' – except what he did was hide away from her in Squire's Mount. Perhaps word reached him she was already married, to Neil Balfour, a barrister, merchant banker and Conservative MEP. When, in October 1974, Taylor heard about Princess Elizabeth of Yugoslavia, she had her back put in traction and had trouble with her teeth. Six months later, in May 1975, she went to the Soviet Union to make *The Blue Bird*, with 2,800 pounds of excess luggage. Burton moved back to Céligny with a Playboy Bunny, Jean Bell, whom he'd first seen with staples in her midriff. ('You look nice. Why don't you join me?' was his practised courtship line.) Jean's son, Troy, was enrolled at the local school. Taylor returned from Leningrad with a temperature of 104 and amoebic dysentery, contracted, she claimed, from hotel ice cubes. She met Burton on 11 August at the Hotel Beau Rivage, Lausanne. The encounter had been arranged eight days earlier, and Burton was trepidatious: 'What will it be like seeing her again? I'm a little scared . . . keep my fingers crossed,' he told his diary. 'Someday, somewhere, you son of a bitch, something will make you realise you can't live without me,' said Taylor, once more sounding like she's spouting movie dialogue. Their remarriage was announced. On 20 August off they went to Israel and in September by Lear jet to South Africa. In Johannesburg, Taylor decided she had lung cancer, which was cured by a Valium pill. 'I had about twelve hours to contemplate death,' she later said of the experience. For the record, Taylor was to live another thirty-six years.

It was a ruse, to get Burton to the altar – in actuality, an outdoor ceremony on safari in Botswana, conducted in the Chobe Game Reserve, Kasane, on 10 October, by the District Commissioner, Ambrose Masalila, an elder of the Bantu-speaking Tswana tribe. The witnesses were employees from the Chobe Game Lodge. As of 2005, Masalila was a government minister, urging the Botswanan Parliament to pass the Customary Courts (Amendment) Bill, which sought to broaden the age limit for which corporal punishment may be imposed, in order to reduce congestion in prisons. 'Whipping by the cane', instead of a gaol term, was to be the fate of rapists, pimps, burglars, robbers and anyone 'endangering the safety of a person travelling by rail'. Back on the banks of the Chobe River, the bride and groom exchanged ivory wedding rings, purchased in a mud hut shop for forty dollars. 'Married Elizabeth Zulu fashion,' Burton noted in his diary. Both of them were drinking ('got shamefully sloshed') and getting ill in the heat, blacking out, having the shakes – no wonder, with double brandies first thing in the morning. Gavin de

Becker, their bodyguard or 'security specialist' in Johannesburg and Botswana, and author of *The Gift of Fear: Survival Signals That Protect Us from Violence* (2001), distinctly remembered that, though Burton was meant to be detoxifying (this no secret), Taylor poured him murderously big gins: 'Giving alcohol to a guy who can die from drinking was somewhere between passive-aggressive and aggressive-aggressive.' As Burton said when he returned from Africa, looking back as at a hallucination, 'It was like a huge dream. It was very curious. An extraordinary adventure. Doomed from the start, of course.' Surveying the elephants, rhinos, hippos and buffalo, and at the crocodiles in the swirling currents, Taylor had been the one to say she wanted to be married again, 'in the bush, amongst our kind.' Their *kind?*

* * *

A brief digression about Sophia Loren, who had the same-size booby-doos as Taylor and (if Peter Sellers is to be believed) Princess Margaret. Burton was much taken with her 'vulpine, almost Satanic face', so he must have known some funny looking foxes is all I'm saying. Loren, 38–24–38, was surely more rounded than sharp-snouted and craggy or bushy-tailed. It's also Taylor who was proverbial for her cunning; who'd paw at her food, sniff out jewels, snap at husbands. Loren had (has – she is about the only one who still liveth at my time of writing) more openness, more peacefulness. 'Everything you see,' Loren once said, 'I owe to spaghetti!' This can be believed. Whether she was playing a countess from Hong Kong, or a Viennese princess, a Greek peasant, an Arabian temptress, or any number of gypsies and courtesans, Loren remained very *Italian*, with an unmistakeable dark dignity. She glows onscreen and evoked what Auden, in his great poem about the *Mezzogiorno* (the idiomatic term for the southern part of the peninsula), catalogued as strong sunlight, vineyards, dagger-edged shadows, the noise of Vespas, and the works of Pirandello, Bernini, Bellini – and no doubt Vittorio De Sica. *The Voyage*, from a novel by Pirandello, was directed by De Sica. During the shoot of the film, Burton remarked on how he'd 'spent all night in bed with Elizabeth for real and all day in bed with Sophia for unreal. Not bad when you come from the bowels of the earth.' He'd have meant Wales and his poor background, needless to say. He always had to speak romantically, mythically, about the miners and his own origins – coal as black gold; colliers as Kings of the Underworld, princes out of folklore; the pits, the rivers, the iron bridges; everything primeval, intensely masculine – strength, hulking, thunderous, singing; a general hugeness. Burton had a deep virility – a ruggedness that was also refined. When off the drink (e.g. when interviewed by Dick Cavett) he was subdued, almost shy or bashful, too, like Wagner's Siegfried listening to the languages of birds. It's why I find Tony Palmer's epic *Wagner* a culmination. The Welsh origins are there – the growling, groaning orchestrations; industrialisation, trains, steam, molten lava in the ironworks; the artist who wants to be everything, rising up, thirsting for power, throwing off constraint ('I must live on, and suffer', etc.): this all bubbles up from Burton himself ('I must have beauty, splendour, light around me,' says his Wagner); the Burton who was wild and bold (there always seems to be more of him) and who as an adult existed, figuratively if not always literally (but often literally) in scarlet and gold rooms, decorated with mirrors and lacquered wood, and which, when I look at it all, at Burton and his world, seems blurred at the edges, like a daguerreotype, a photogravure, found in a drawer.

But as rough and tough as life was in the valleys of the Principality – 'Above all else, he never forgot his roots, the rock he was hewn from,' said Brook Williams, confounding the organic and the inorganic, at Burton's Memorial Service at Bethel Chapel, Pontrhydyfen, on 8 August 1984 – it wasn't exactly Italy under Mussolini and the Nazi occupation. I mean, look at Loren's world. She was born, in 1934, in a charity ward for unmarried mothers, in the Clinica Regina

Margherita, Rome. Her feckless father, Riccardo Scicolone Murillo, did a bunk, and Loren was raised by relatives in Pozzuoli, near Naples, her formative years filled with the 'fear of having nothing to eat, fear of other children taunting me at school, because I was illegitimate', plus the fear of the narrowing dictates of the fascist regime, the fear of Allied bombing, the fear of Nazi reprisals, which Burton will have known about, after playing Colonel Kappler, Chief of the Security Service, in *Massacre in Rome*, made in January 1973, based on a true story, and produced by Carlo Ponti. On 23 March 1944, a partisan device killed thirty-two SS troops. Ten Italians have to be shot for each German lost, orders Hitler, shouting down the phone from Berlin and backed up by Leo McKern and Peter Vaughan. It is Burton's Kappler's job, sitting at a desk with a fountain pen, drawing up the list, to select the 320 victims, which after he'd with alacrity condemned all local Jews and Communists unfortunately left one or two to find if the quota was to be filled. Prisoners were escorted to the Ardeatine Caves, near the Appian Way, and murdered in batches of five – a bullet at point-blank range. 'We are soldiers, doing our duty,' says Burton, believing he is sounding reasonable, to Marcello Mastroianni, who plays Dom Antonelli, a flustered priest, whose church is a hiding place for enemy agents. As with Burton's O'Brien in *Nineteen Eighty-Four*, it is another of Burton's beyond-good-and-evil performances, his Herbert Kappler a hollow man with nothing left except devotion to duty ('I'm going to do my duty,' he tells Mastroianni, getting him to kneel down ready for execution), sticking to rules and regulations and supporting a cause he no longer believes in, a political system he knows has failed, except, 'I'm afraid of disorder' – and though the Nazi is stripped of all illusion, Burton's genius is to show how his character takes a wry, ironic comfort in this: the world truly has been reduced at last to extinction and pain, 'a circle of misery and fear and death,' as Sherlock Holmes concludes in *The Adventure of the Cardboard Box*, the one about a pair of severed human ears packed in a parcel of coarse salt and posted to an adulteress in Croydon.

We spend much of *Massacre in Rome* nevertheless almost liking Kappler – he has a knowledge of Old Masters, knows his Homer by heart. He becomes friendly with Mastroianni, who is similarly intellectual. He is clearly good at his job – but his job is monstrous: the bureaucracy of evil, where a person surrenders their human individuality, accepts human helplessness, and freedom is a concept to be resented. Instead, here is a man who has become an efficient machine, dedicated to the logistics of human slaughter: finding the execution and burial sites, 'a large natural death chamber'; examining the maps and statistics concerning the limestone grotto. The film touches on, too, the evil of the Pope, who won't intervene and prevent the Ardeatine Caves atrocity, because he perceives the similarities between Church dogma and Nazi dogma – and the Nazis are a useful and worthy bulwark against atheists. Burton is almost tender, the way he holds a prisoner's head before shooting them in the nape of the neck. He could be a farmer or butcher or barber, calmly going about his daily tasks. And this is the greatness of Burton's performance – the dignity of the man, his diligence and resignation; his dead calm – and then we see what he is actually doing, what he has been asked to do, which the expostulating Leo McKern calls 'a symbolic necessity'. Burton does look good in the uniforms.

Personified on the screen by the ubiquitous and generally pretty gormless Brook Williams, Erich Priebke, the real-life Kappler's deputy, who took enthusiastic part in the massacre, reading out the roll-call of hostages, and who with Vatican assistance escaped to South America, died on 11 October 2013, aged a hundred. And all of this sort of thing was real life for Loren, likewise. Each night her family had to crowd into railway tunnels for shelter. Loren remembered the 'hot, stinking atmosphere'; the unwashed bodies (water mains had been blown up; electricity long cut off); the lice and scabies, the rotten food and the rats. 'My young eyes saw one appalling, gruesome spectacle after another,' such as children shot in the street, German snipers picking off shoppers at random. The film for which she won the Best Actress Oscar in 1961, *Two Women*, 'corresponded with this childhood period of my life,' which was marked by her mother screaming along with the sirens, people begging for bread, angry voices, protests. Italian females were at risk of rape from both the retreating Nazis and the liberating forces. It's almost crass to mention that Taylor, at the same moment, was making *Lassie* films and weeping about fucking Nibbles. Loren had more cause to be crazy, to start laughing like the mental home patients in *Suddenly, Last Summer,* than anybody.

Loren's only escape, in the immediate post-war period, was to visit the cinema, the rigged-up opera house, the Teatro Sacchini (later demolished and the site now a police station), where she lapped up the performances of all those iconic huge American men who within a decade would be her actual co-stars – Anthony Quinn, John Wayne and Clark Gable. Furthermore, having always been sickly, ostracised, and mocked as a *stuzzicadenti* (toothpick), suddenly, aged fourteen, Loren found her breasts bursting forth and she was wolf-whistled in the open street. She fast turned into what Frank Sinatra approvingly dubbed 'the mostest,' and Romilda, her mother, a powerful force, who, as Carlo Ponti said, 'transferred to Sophia everything she had wanted for herself,' noticing her daughter's newly curvaceous figure, entered her for beauty pageants, something Loren surprisingly enjoyed, didn't see as exploitation: 'My nervousness seemed to fly off me.' Instead of becoming a strutting, preening performer, however, playing up to everyone's attention – and the camera's unremitting attention – Loren conveyed (or embodied) a naturalness, despite the constraints of incipient stardom, with its requirement to be artificial. Accoutred, as she would be throughout her career, in corsets, garters, exaggerated bras, low-cut bodices and big hats, Loren retained a decorum. As a child, after all that 'pain, rejection and humiliation', she was serious, pensive, and on the screen, though she swaggers, she is always guarded, never fully carefree – and was good (because Southern Italian) at being motherly, matronly. There's something dependable about her: look at the way she cradles co-stars, like O'Toole, when he's Don Quixote, in *Man of La Mancha*, Peck, when he's the abducted hieroglyphics professor in *Arabesque*, or Brando, when he's an ambassador and she's a stowaway in *A Countess from Hong Kong*. Most recently we had *The Life Ahead*, directed by her son, Edoardo Ponti. There's no vanity in this performance, of an elderly Auschwitz victim in the shabby port of Bari, earning a crust looking after prostitutes' abandoned children. Loren is scrubbed of make-up; her hair is a tangle. She wears huge false teeth and never smiles – yet conveys warmth, goodness, and anguish. Grey and decrepit, Loren is still impeccable. Style, as Quentin Crisp said, survives beauty.

After triumphing in those Miss Italia beauty contests, where the prize was a train ticket to Rome, Loren was cast as a handmaiden to Deborah Kerr in *Quo Vadis*, which was shooting at Cinecittà. Carlo Ponti, a producer, who was thirty-eight and married with two children, told her, 'You have an interesting face. I was watching you.' Dirty bugger. Also smitten was Vittorio De Sica, who'd direct Loren in fourteen films, starting in 1954 with *L'Oro di Napoli*. 'You have juices running in you,' he said, meaning I assume a vibrancy, something not manufactured by drama schools. 'Act with your entire body,' he recommended – an almost silent-movie mandate, later appreciated by Chaplin when, in January 1966, Loren was cast in the undervalued *A Countess from Hong Kong*. She was statuesque, a model, whom Chaplin could mould and make expressive – and what the cast had to do was copy him. 'Chaplin's method,' said Tippi Hedren, who appears briefly as Brando's wife, 'was to act out all our different roles ... He'd get out there on set and say, "OK, do this," and show us how. He'd become Sophia Loren. He'd become me and Marlon.' Wearing Brando's outsize pyjamas, taking pratfalls, kooky and with lots of charm, Loren is the Chaplin tramp figure – and this is acting as pantomime or a children's game.

In the early Fifties, Loren was in a host of Italian language B-movies, where she often wore bathing suits. It was Ponti who negotiated a

$200,000 fee for her to appear on location in Spain and in the studio in Hollywood, in *The Pride and the Passion*, when Ava Gardner withdrew. Loren's leading men were Sinatra and Cary Grant. Of the latter, 'We were constantly in each other's company,' said Loren, 'and such wonderful company Cary was!' Ponti, however, operating like Professor Higgins set on captivating Eliza Doolittle, steered the actress his way. She'd met him when she was fifteen, 'got seriously involved with him' at nineteen – and they were together until Ponti's death aged ninety-four in 2007. It was a relationship requiring strength and survival instincts as, when Ponti attempted to divorce his first wife, Giuliana Fiastri, in Mexico, he and Sophia were condemned by the Vatican as 'public sinners' – another version of Taylor and Burton having been branded erotic vagrants. When, again in Mexico, attorneys exchanged marriage vows on Ponti and Loren's behalf, Ponti was prosecuted by the Italian state for bigamy, his divorce not recognised, and Loren, like a medieval saint about to be burnt to death, was accused of 'concubinage'. The pair of them were hounded for, this time, 'public adultery'. In the end they moved to Paris, became French citizens, and went through the processes all over again – a fully legal civil wedding took place in 1966. Not that their life was tranquil. It is hard to keep track of the kidnap attempts, miscarriage calamities, jewel robberies, art collection and real estate confiscations and tax problems. Loren even spent a month in prison in 1982 for some obscure fiscal reason. But should anyone wish to revive screwball comedy, and if equivalents of Carole Lombard, Jean Harlow and William Powell can be found, there is a plot worthy of Preston Sturges ready to be filmed – with Burton, Taylor, Sybil, Nicky Hilton, Eddie Fisher, Mike Todd, Michael Wilding, and everyone else, scrabbling around in Mexico in a spiralling panic, trying to find out to whom they might still remain married. There's a classic title in readiness: *It Happened One Night*.

Meanwhile, Loren made energetic films with Marcello Mastroianni, e.g. *Yesterday, Today and Tomorrow*; Hollywood epics, e.g. *El Cid* and *The Fall of the Roman Empire*; the spy romp with Gregory Peck (she's still remembered in South Wales for scrambling across Crumlin Viaduct) called *Arabesque*; and *The Millionairess* with Peter Sellers. Sellers, mistaking the plot of the picture with off-screen actuality, fully believed Loren wished to come and live with him in Frognal Lane. He left his wife and children and set himself up in a swanky London flat – the first sign of his madness. It's the case, nevertheless, that by now Loren was an overwhelmingly glamorous star, redolent of white furs, glittering receptions in hotel lobbies, flashbulbs, flower-laden suites, jewels and multi-million-dollar contracts. She'd arrived in Taylor's world. And like Taylor, it's true Loren's sexual characteristics, the hips, the bust, are never less than those of a total woman. In *The Voyage*, for example, she's required to run in from a green garden wearing a lot of translucent chiffon. She is seen in boudoirs wearing corsets and snow-white bodices. Loren's character, Adriana de Mauro, is described as 'a girl of powerful temperament', and would be a perfect match for Burton's Cesare Braggi, but instead she marries the brother, Ian Bannen's Antonio Braggi. These people are Sicilian royalty, or something, and are obliged to pair off by decree, obey the commands of patriarchal wills and inheritance laws. Ancestry gives these people obligations. In a charged scene, it is Burton's Cesare who has to turn up at Loren's house to inform her she has to get betrothed to Ian Bannen, like it or lump it.

It is very much a historical, stuck in the past, film – Burton, in a succession of turn-of-the-century silk suits, walks through golden salons in country villas, grand hotels and Palermo palaces; there is a lot of damask and gilding. It's a theatrical film, too, with the carefully positioned antique furniture – almost a toy theatre, in fact – and yet under the artifice, emotions are rippling. Burton's face betrays the romantic agony of having to watch somebody you love being married to someone else; Loren in her turn is able to imply what it feels like, having to go through a wedding with the wrong man. One almost feels sorry for Ian Bannen, for coming between these stars – he's additionally handicapped by being dubbed. Why? Too Scottish? When he speaks in *The Voyage* he sounds like silly ass Jonathan Cecil. Fortunately, perhaps, he's not around for long. As when rabbits or puppies are handed over to children in thrillers and we know at once the pets are doomed, when Antonio shows off his flashy new motor car, we know at once it'll crash. It does so. Ian Bannen goes over a cliff (as, in 1999, the real Ian Bannen was to be killed in a car crash, near Loch Ness) – so won't this leave the way clear for Adriana and Cesare to get together? Regrettably, as in *Hamlet*, it's against the rules to marry a widowed sister-in-law, and in any case, Cesare has a reputation – 'God knows what Cesare does on those so-called business trips of his,' insinuates Adriana's mother. But Adriana is undaunted. 'I'm happy, happy, so terribly happy,' she coos. In the next scene she is given a terminal diagnosis – she's been somewhat breathless: not with passion, as the audience may have assumed, but cardiological 'issues' as they'd be called today. Thus, the journey or voyage of the title, as Burton takes Loren from Sicily to Naples to Milan by trains and boats for consultations with bald, bearded doctors. Each specialist wears pince-nez spectacles. The news imparted is uniformly grim: 'Any emotional shock could have serious consequences,' so Burton finally glues his mouth to Loren's in the back of a hackney carriage. They head for Venice – it's going to be death in Venice – and Loren, in chalky make-up, croaks on the carpet. To the last she's still happy, so terribly happy. The film doesn't so much fade out or dissolve as ring down a curtain.

* * *

It's not only owing to the costumes that the characters move stiffly. The whole thing is old-fashioned, the locations and decor of *The Voyage*, or *Il Viaggio*, as it is sometimes called, reminding me of *The Leopard*, which is set in 1860. (Would Burton have been as good as Burt Lancaster in that? I think so. I really think so. Don Fabrizio,

Prince of Salina, last of an ancient aristocratic line, is another of his lost Lears.) *The Voyage* is full of lemon groves, fountains, huge yellow and blue chambers, vestibules with blood-red velvet walls, polished tables laden with baskets of fruit. It is baroque, and very formal. As a tale of thwarted love, it could be Eddie (Bannen), Taylor (Loren) and Burton (Burton), if they'd behaved themselves. The theme of illness – illness as moral judgement – is also normally a Taylor attribute. But Loren is altogether saner than Taylor. And if Taylor, with her midnight colouration, was good at conveying neuroses, Loren's chief attribute is her almost biblical eloquence and radiance. I can see how this affected Burton. He's more at ease, less defensive, than when playing opposite Taylor, who made him tense up as an actor, drove him towards self-consciousness. Perhaps Loren reminded him of his sister, Cis. 'From the time I moved in with Cis,' Burton remembered of his childhood, 'I never cried again for my mother. She was more mother to me than any mother could ever have been. She was innocent and guileless and naive to the point of saintliness.' But shrewd and intelligent, too. I'm reminded of Proust's observation about the loss of a mother or a mother-figure: even if one doesn't get over one's greatest sorrows, one always survives them. The stoicism of the sentiment, the paradoxical triumph, is what plays – plays out – on Burton's face in *The Voyage*, and it is as if Loren has implicitly insisted on this sense of containment, of circumspection.

She does so again in *Brief Encounter*, which would seem to have been an odd film for Hallmark Cards Inc. to try and replicate, the David Lean original having classic status as an enshrinement of Englishness. Burton as Trevor Howard? Howard did become a roaring boozer; by 1980 he was Sir Henry of Rawlinson End to the life ('If I had all the money I'd spent on drink, I'd spend it on drink'), but in 1945, as Dr Alec Harvey, there was a gentler, more reflective quality. Burton captures that, and adds a lassitude. He seems adrift. Burton, in addition, was not only replacing Trevor Howard, he was replacing Robert Shaw, who'd elected to be Quint in *Jaws* instead of playing the provincial physician. In certain ways, Shaw did resemble Burton. There were the seasons at Stratford and The Old Vic. They were alcoholics, in their graves not as old men – Shaw was only fifty-one when he died in 1978. They both played Henry VIII, and had Mary Ure in common. Like Burton, Shaw had an irritable temper and sense of command, e.g. General Custer or the Squadron Leader in *Battle of Britain*. (Why wasn't Burton in that one? Everyone else is. I particularly like Olivier throwing out orders to Michael Redgrave, Trevor Howard, Patrick Wymark and Harry Andrews: all these actors who have to defer to him.) Shaw was an intelligent, prickly man. He published novels. Pinter admired him – he's in *The Birthday Party*. His voice is in the slightly quavering tenor register (like Michael Redgrave's), suggesting a radio signal picked up over enemy territory at risk of breaking up – a certain crackle, interspersed with a sudden bark, sounds tuning in and out, until the wavelength is found, as internal dials and valves are adjusted. Shaw seemed temperamentally brittle, with a touch of impatience always – he was not an actor (or man) who relaxed, whereas at least Burton was capable of a salamander stillness. Shaw's laughter was mocking, villainous. He was ideal as the Sheriff of Nottingham in the elegiac *Robin and Marian*, as the mobster in *The Sting* and Mr Blue in *The Taking of Pelham One Two Three*. He could never be smooth, except when being deceptive – I can't quite see him in *Brief Encounter*. I'd fear Loren was about to receive a karate chop across the back of the neck.

As for Loren's Anna replacing Celia Johnson's Laura – here we have Italian emotion rather than English twittering reserve and repressed hysteria. Nevertheless, a famous film about English reticence has been made into a strange comedy about famous film stars, where the joke (which I for one accept) is that audiences are expected to believe Burton and Loren every day take public transport. 'I live in Basingstoke,' says Burton, who could more credibly announce his address as being on the moon. In the buffet at Winchester railway station, there's a black lady instead of Joyce Carey. Stanley Holloway is played by

Christopher Benjamin. Lean's original made the trains demonic, dragonish, screaming in the night. Here we are in summery rural Hampshire and Dorset – it could be Titfield. Though ostensibly the modern day – it was shot in colour in August 1974 – the film is already as antiquated as the world of *The Voyage*. Businessmen wear bowler hats. The stationmaster greets passengers by name. Jack Hedley, as Loren's dull husband, Graham, is preoccupied with his lawnmower and Airfix models – the English adult male still a schoolboy at heart. Hedley, who died on 11 December 2021, aged ninety-two (spookily as I was writing this page), represents all those husbands in traditional plays, films and novels who at best only half-listen to their wives – this is how it is meant to be with ordinary domesticity. Graham Jesson is a solicitor, fretty about rights of way – symbolic, eh? Loren's Anna at least can get out of the house, as she has a job, voluntary work probably, at the Citizen's Advice Bureau, where she listens to accounts of marital woes. At a park bench on her lunch break she meets Burton. 'You seem exotic and foreign to me,' he says, because her sandwiches contain something never before seen in Winchester or Titfield: *prosciutto*. He's as taken aback as Cary Grant in *To Catch a Thief*, when Grace Kelly munches on a delicacy called *Quiche Lorraine*.

Burton is the seducer, or perhaps it's more he's lonely. He turns up at Loren's office to take her for a cheese salad. They go to see a Mystery Play, where the prophecy of Isaiah is enacted by amateurs in a quadrangle. ('He is despised and rejected of men; a man of sorrows, and acquainted with grief', etc.) Loren is running a risk, especially as her friend Dolly spots her in the crowd. Burton is more concerned to talk about his interest in dust and diseases of the lung – the Welsh miners' malady of silicosis, caused by the inhalation of coal or steel particles. It's the one moment in the story (as it was for Trevor Howard) when the doctor can be openly ardent – I wonder if Noël Coward was remembering Astrov, the doctor in *Uncle Vanya*, describing his forestry maps to Yelena, the young wife of the crabby Professor Serebryakov? Loren's Anna, like Chekhov's character, isn't much

531

keen on the subject or hobby-horse, to which she pays scant attention – but she does appreciate her new admirer's animation. The next thing we know, Loren starts wearing bright yellow frocks and nicer make-up. She's making an effort, so it's Burton's Alec who grows cautious, who can see only dejection in their incipient affair. 'We are in love with each other,' he says categorically – and in a tone he must use when telling patients their polyps are malignant. Loren admits she has guilty feelings about her children, about the mendacity adultery involves, the deceptions. In its off-key way, therefore, we are again back with Taylor and Burton in Rome, in 1962. It's exactly the same dilemma. 'I know it's going to cause pain to others,' Burton's Alec here admits. Decency, self-respect – all is crumbling. The reality is degrading – as is shown in the scenes in John Le Mesurier's flat. The would-be lovers almost get as far as taking their coats off when John Le Mesurier, playing a hospital colleague, Dr Stephen Lynn, comes back early. 'I do think you should have warned me,' he says angrily to Burton, convinced he has interrupted something illicit. 'One of the nurses, was it?' he mutters, coming across what seem like props in a farce – Anna's wicker bag, scarf, and so forth. Comic actors are always best at seriousness. Without laughter as their goal, their intensity is surprising. (For example, Norman Wisdom and Fulton Mackay in *Going Gently*, which is about a cancer ward; or Leonard Rossiter in anything.) Here, Le Mesurier, doing the scene slightly drunkenly – his character is tired and snappish – is instantly able to imply the sordidness of what he has come across, or thinks he has come across. He is mocking and is reproving and full of malice. He demands his key back: 'I can't promise to be away for a while.' He has that Sergeant Wilson way of rubbing at his eyebrow, but Le Mesurier's brief cameo, as Dr Stephen Lynn, has more sudden complexity than all the years he spent in *Dad's Army*. 'I've been offered a job in Australia,' Burton tells everybody, and it's as if he is faced like a convict with being permanently transported.

Brief Encounter was always about a lot of abstractions: decency

and compliance, cowardice and heroism, selfishness and sacrifice –
all these wartime themes. Did that work in the Seventies? All that
agonising about 'sleeping together'? Not so brief, either: all those
Wednesday afternoons add up. Brevity is for the home life with Jack
Hedley – the kids off to bed as their mother comes through the door;
the mostly silent and always dour husband slinking away to glue his
toy trains or stare at the Monopoly board. Loren, her face a mask of
suffering, resembles the effigies of penitents her Anna and Burton's
Alec look at in Winchester Cathedral. She also says she pines for
Naples, where the most you'd expect from Celia Johnson is she'd
hanker for the wool shop in Carnforth. Trevor Howard did have an
eagerness, with a faint undercurrent of dissatisfaction: Alec as he
portrayed him needs more from his career. Burton's grave dignity is
far more imposing – his grand poetic manner, as a country doctor,
has the authority, and the courtly manners, of Arthur in *Camelot*, or
his King Mark of Cornwall, in *Tristan and Isolde*, which was made in
Ireland in the summer of 1979 and remains an obscurity. (Instead of
Wagner on the soundtrack it's The Chieftains.)

Actually, Tristan (the strapping Nicholas Clay – those thighs,
those curls; and now he is dead at only fifty-three) and Isolde (Kate
Mulgrew), are another pair, like Antony and Cleopatra, who are up
to Taylor and Burton tricks: love that is morbid because it can't survive in the intractable real world; love that cannot be domestic and
ordinary, but instead is star-crossed and selfish, sustained by magic
potions and spells. The film is very Celtic. King Mark resides in
barrel-vaulted smoky halls, with ox-skins and pelts strewing the
floors, torches and brands providing the illumination. He drinks
from horn goblets and says things like, 'Is all well with you?' to Cyril
Cusack. Nevertheless, the subject is trust and the breaking of trust
('To trust oneself unto another'), and it's interesting that here Burton
finds himself in the Walter Wanger or Spyros Skouras, or Joseph
Mankiewicz, position, a senior citizen outmanoeuvred by a virile
person, a person in his prime. Burton is poised here, unruffled,

looking at Clay's Tristan with a sort of reproach – for how dare Clay be younger, lovelier, and modest with it. Tristan is sent to Eire as an emissary to ask Isolde if she'll marry King Mark – 'But he's *old!*' she says, and definitely doesn't want to fuck him. 'The lady is not pleased with Cornwall,' Burton says with heavy irony, as if it's a line from a Shakespeare History play, or perhaps he means his bride isn't impressed with the tourist attractions in Redruth or Lostwithiel. But it's too late. Adultery has been accelerated by the love drug (when belatedly released in 1981, the film was retitled *Lovespell*); King Mark is a cuckold; Isolde has not been able to resist Tristan's body, when she tended his wounds in the palace sauna. Witnessing their clinch, Burton glares and snarls. Tristan and Isolde escape from the castle and Burton, wearing a crimson jerkin, gives chase with a pack of hounds. The lovers expire amongst the rocks – Burton looks on, powerless before such a bond. And what's to be noted is how he has aged with incredible refinement – and is able to suggest, as in his work with Loren, as in his work from the beginning, in fact, what Oscar Wilde meant when he told Robert Ross, after he'd visited Constance's grave in Genoa: 'I brought some flowers. I was deeply affected – with a sense, also, of the uselessness of all regrets. Nothing could have been otherwise, and life is a very terrible thing.'

* * *

In all of his films with Taylor, Burton is surrounded by representa-tions and penalties of wrongdoing. All the characters he played lose their job and position – sacked and disgraced teachers, priests, doc-tors, army officers. They are left with nothing. They discover they are in hell. What a strange, dreamlike atmosphere there is, too, in those films. There was an inevitability about Burton and Taylor's self-destruction, on screen and off; their fates and fortunes. With Loren, by contrast – she and Burton don't possess each other, not to any com-parative degree. As a romantic team it's as if they are wearing Sunday clothes. *The Voyage* and *Brief Encounter* are significantly about not yielding fully to temptation; are about being responsible. What, I am therefore wondering, would Burton's life and career have been like had he not become infatuated with Taylor? In partial answer, here is a list of all the things he was first offered and rejected – an alternative Burton, as it were: T.E. Lawrence of Arabia (O'Toole); Bond (Connery); Mark Antony in MGM's *Julius Caesar* (Brando); Douglas Bader in *Reach for the Sky* (Kenneth More) . . . I press the pause button here briefly, freeze the frame, to describe Kenneth More, in the Fifties one of the biggest British box office stars. He indeed played Group Captain Sir Douglas Bader (who'd lost both legs in a flying accident) after Burton had rejected the role. *Reach for the Sky* (1956) is a film about British grit and determination, mixed in with our jocular demeanour. More had bounce, a playfulness – also a valiant goodness. Full of charm, he was never shallow, and he avoided being or seeming a shit. He shouted his lines a good deal, was always gaily chattering, jollying everyone along. He was dependable; a good chap in a crisis – as Richard Hannay in the re-make of *The Thirty-Nine Steps*, as Second Officer Lightoller in *A Night to Remember*, about the *Titanic* sinking, and as Captain Scott aboard the Raj-era steam train in *North West Frontier*, keeping up the spirits of Lauren Bacall by singing 'The Eton Boating Song'. More had an Englishness in the way Burton had a Welshness – almost as if they are deliberate (and definitive) exemplars. More was clubbable (a tie-wearing Garrick stalwart), enthusiastic, puppyish (if on the old side), breezy; Burton was saturnine, solitary, glowering, determined to be accepted at his own valuation, a demon of owls' cries and yellow gorse. More was always in movement, chucking a gnawed chicken leg into the kitchenette in *The Deep Blue Sea*, clambering over the *Queen Elizabeth* during a transatlantic crossing in *Next to No Time*, or as Ambrose Claverhouse, in *Genevieve*, leaping on and off his 1905 Spyker 12/16 HP Double Phaeton. Burton, by contrast, preferred to stay still. I can only imagine the boiling fury he'd have brought out in Bader – none of the determinedly jovial waddling about on tin legs More went in for, as easily parodied in *Beyond the Fringe* ('We need a futile gesture at this stage to raise the whole tone of the war'). What connects the two actors (who share a brief scene in *Now Barabbas Was a Robber*; they are also in *The Longest Day*): an underlying seriousness of purpose; they had expressive eyes – More's eyes often betray an anxiousness; and perhaps when looking in Taylor's ardent eyes, Burton saw a reflection of Burton. In which case Burton and Taylor's 'mutual terrorism' (Iris Murdoch's phrase) was going to be inevitable. Finally, like a golden glow beneath the glaze or the lustre of a bowl or plate, there were More and Burton's voices, those lovely soothing male voices that held the note of lamentation.

To revert to my list, Burton wasn't the consul in *Under the Volcano* (Finney); the Pilot in *The Little Prince* (Richard Kiley – though in March 1974 Burton narrated the LP, which won the Grammy Award for Best Children's Recording); Christ in *King of Kings* (Jeffrey Hunter); *The Sea Wolves* (Gregory Peck); *Robbery* (Stanley Baker); Napoleon in *Waterloo* (Rod Steiger); *Camelot* (Richard Harris); *I, Claudius*, to be directed by Tony Richardson (unmade); Shakespeare's Antony to the Cleopatra of Vanessa Redgrave (unrealised); a film of *Coriolanus* set in South America (a pipedream of Philip's); alternating the roles of Richard III and Buckingham with John Hurt (maybe the drink talking); the Stevenson / Dylan Thomas / Christopher Isherwood *The Beach of Falesá*; *Long Day's Journey into Night*; a biopic of Orde Wingate; *The Corn is Green*; Sartre's *Le Diable et le Bon Dieu*, with Gielgud ('in French . . . I shall ask Barrault to direct it,' stated Burton in his diary); the Earl of Warwick in Otto Preminger's *Saint Joan* (Gielgud); Fry's *Curtmantle*, another Henry II / Becket confrontation (mounted at the Aldwych by the RSC with Alan Dobie); a biopic of Simón Bolívar (unrealised); *Goodbye Mr Chips*, from a Rattigan script and with Leslie Bricusse songs (O'Toole); Churchill in *The Soldiers*, which Tynan discussed with him ('Over my dead body!' warned Taylor); Caliban and Prospero in films of *The Tempest*; *Don Quixote*, with a script written by Ronnie Lubin and

Waldo Salt, with either Ustinov, Guinness or Zero Mostel as Sancho
Panza (O'Toole with James Coco – and Loren as the Dulcinea: *Man
of La Mancha*); *Oedipus*, adapted by Lawrence Durrell (done eventu-
ally with Christopher Plummer); *McKenna's Gold* by Carl Foreman
('Christ what a lot of rubbish one reads'); *A Guide for the Married
Man*, directed by Gene Kelly (Walter Matthau); *The Man from
Nowhere*, a Joe Losey project; *The Antagonists* by Ernest K. Gann,
about Jewish resistance to the Roman Empire in AD 72; Coward's
Hay Fever; *The Savage is Loose* (George C. Scott – made in Puerto
Vallarta); Huston's *The Unforgiven* (Burt Lancaster); *The Last Days of
Mussolini*, produced by Josef Shaftel (Rod Steiger); Nelson in *Bequest
to the Nation*, more Rattigan (Peter Finch or was it Glenda Jackson);
The Canterbury Tales, set in the Channel Islands; *Abakarov*, to be
made in Israel ('Have a feeling this film won't surface either') . . .
Plus, the many mentions of *King Lear*, all abortive. I have found a
letter Olivier wrote from 4 Royal Crescent, Brighton, on 14 August
1975, to Mia Farrow, of The Haven, Dawes Green, Dorking, Surrey,
saying he'd like to cast her in a Granada play, *The Fighting Cock*, by
Jean Anouilh. 'I'm suggesting Richard Burton to play the General,' a
role Rex Harrison had performed on stage, directed by Peter Brook,
between December 1959 and February 1960. Burton would have
been good as the peppery military man, less sure-of-foot on the
home front in peacetime than upon a conventional battlefield. The
General heartily detests the modern world and its developments,
'eye-catching rubbish, supersonic junk, push-button gadgets.' All he
can see are 'ideas without thinking, money without sweat, taste without the trouble of acquiring it – there are glossy magazines that take
care of all that for you.' The General, poignantly rather than contemptuously presented, is a washed-up creature, sensing 'the yawning
chasm of despair, with me in front of it like a great baboon'. He's
afraid he'll be exposed before wife, children, friends, as 'really a bum-
bling old fool . . . I felt lonely suddenly and chilly, as if I were quite
wet with rain.'

It's fascinating Olivier thought of Burton, when looking at this script. There's a tendency towards angry self-pity in the General – he is a reactionary old shag – and though that is apparent in Dysart's monologues about failure and emptiness in *Equus*, which by February 1976 Burton was playing at the Plymouth Theatre, New York, wheedling isn't what we want from this actor. Burton was a star. He'd achieved Taylor's status, could equal her in self-admiration. Stars no longer need to act; they don't have to exert themselves in performance. This is what became clearer to me as I thought about Burton's work with Loren, where he is free of Taylor's crude egotism. He can sit there opposite her in the Winchester refreshment room – actually the Brockenhurst and Shawford stations on the Southampton to Bournemouth line were the locations used; he can sit alongside Loren in the atrium in a Sicilian *castello* – and he doesn't need to do a thing. There is the beauty of a still life – Paul Newman managed this, and Steve McQueen. There they are on the screen. We have no right to ask for more. They have achieved what Roland Barthes in *Camera Lucida* calls 'the impossible science of the unique being'. Burton had thrown off genealogy, when he ceased being a Jenkins. His life originated with him. He escaped from his inheritance, if not from the inhibitions of the past – the rhetorical language and the singing and the pulpit of the Grade II Listed Gibeon Welsh Independent Congregationalist Chapel, Alma Terrace, and Noddfa [Sanctuary], the rival chapel on Commercial Road, Taibach ('our other world,' said Graham), which gave him a formative, never to be undone sense of heaven and hell and damnation: 'All the actors [in Wales] went into the pulpit, the greatest stage in the world,' Burton told Tynan in that interview he gave in Italy. 'It dominated a village in a chapel. You stood hovering like a great bird of prey over the people in the village; you said, "I will tell you what is wrong with you, and let me examine your soul." The greatest pulpit in the world . . .' A preacher as actor as Mephophelean moralist – and Burton created an identity of his own, out of naturally acquired impressions and sensations; and the paradox with Burton is that he couldn't be other than he was. He was not transformative, like Sellers or Olivier. He was a declamatory actor – or so it seems. Actually, I have concluded, he was a reticent actor. The quality of his reticence is what I have come to admire most. He never specifies what is on his mind – his desires and fears. I mean, what were his personal feelings? What lies beyond, or beneath, conventional scrutiny? The diaries aren't fully helpful, beyond being a record of obvious states like anger, grossness, or physical details of lust. What actually are the levels of consciousness and behaviour reached? Domestic routine (packing, unpacking, travel); private silly baby talk (Taylor's front bottom is a 'divine little money box'); blotto admissions ('sloshed all day long'). The decorated surface, appearance – and then psychological needs and drives, and the whole question of memory and looking back (things lost; things that turn up again), of which we are ignorant.

Which is all part of how I think Burton is set apart from what he does, from his own dramatic effects. 'I told him what was required and he did it,' said John Boorman of *The Heretic*. 'If I asked him to adjust his reading, he simply changed it without comment.' In her book *The Making of Exorcist II: The Heretic*, Barbara Pallenberg's mentions of Burton are few and fleeting. He keeps disappearing. 'I'm leaving,' he suddenly announced at a press conference, pushing back his chair. 'Are you going, then?' asked Boorman, slightly incredulous, when Burton 'gets up to leave [a rehearsal] without explanation'. Nevertheless, Boorman was able to tell he was in the presence of genius: 'It was a source of pride in him to make any line, any situation, believable. What he offered was this extraordinarily modulated range of harmonies that we could call upon for whatever the scene required . . . I saw that he was intensely shy and private, embarrassed to talk about things directly . . . He kept a sense of detachment from the film as a whole, which in many ways suited my methods as well . . . He's extremely vulnerable to the camera. He allows it, or maybe he can't help letting it look into his very soul, and this nakedness is something he himself can't bear to confront. I think that is also why he doesn't like to rehearse. He clearly wants to preserve what he feels to be the privacy of that moment when the camera turns and he is alone with the lens.' Detachment is not non-involvement. As a good actor, Burton picked up 'on the tones of the picture' and got 'an instinctive feeling of what you're trying to do in those non-verbal areas that defy description'. For Taylor, Burton always defied description, especially his appeal: 'It's not the way he combs his hair, not the things he wears; and he doesn't think about having muscles. It's what he says and thinks.'

As Father Lamont, in the Boorman film, he's required to be possessed by demons (conjured up by Linda Blair) – and the notion of evil and the devil was never far away with Burton; and when Burton is strangely not there as an actor, when he gives a performance and delivers his lines and yet seems elsewhere, he can be quite frightening. We cannot imagine his thoughts. It's almost as if Burton is watching the characters he plays from afar: he seems familiar, but he is alien – nevertheless, despite the detachment, even the contempt, he's (as critics have said of Shakespeare) continuously present to us as a personality: he conveys impatience with artifice, he is unflinching, like a model soldier under fire; but he is not oblivious. Despite becoming a star, reliably on parade as kings, princes, archbishops, commanders-in-chief, there remained something unconfident, unconvincing in the self-display: the survival of the uncertain Welsh boy with his vulnerabilities is what gave everything he did its depth, its mystery.

Would it have made any difference, had Burton taken on any of those rejected or scrapped projects? My favourite is the scheme, mooted in January 1971, that he should play Baron Frankenstein and Taylor the Bride of Frankenstein, in *Frankenstein: The True Story*, written by Isherwood and Don Bachardy, which was duly made for television in 1973 – with Leonard Whiting and Jane Seymour. Ralph Richardson is the Blind Hermit, John Gielgud the Chief of Police

and Michael Wilding – Michael Wilding! – is a laird of some description. Which prompts me to mention, there is a sequence of rather
scary snaps taken in 1997 by *Life* photographer Harry Benson, of
Taylor and her (benign – the only chunk of her which was) brain
tumour. Benson had heard she was to have an operation and called
her publicists: 'Just ask Elizabeth, she marches to her own drum.'
Taylor granted permission for Benson and his camera to be present
'before, during and after the operation. I photographed an X-ray
of her brain as well.' There she is – with a shaven head and
Frankenstein-sized cranial sutures and staples. Benson correctly
divined Taylor would see all this as a good means of keeping in the
public eye. It's evidence of her strange mixture of medical candour
and showmanship – it's almost an instance of Performance Art.

Burton was never as brazen, and in any case, early on in his career,
choices weren't his to make. In 1953, Peter Brook wanted him for
MacHeath, the rapscallion in *The Beggar's Opera*. 'There was a young
actor named Richard Burton who seemed perfect for the role, but the
time was not ripe, his name not sufficiently known to make the inves-
tors and distributors feel secure.' The role went instead to Olivier,
who in the Restoration hats and wigs, and pinching snuff, was something epicene out of Sheridan or Congreve – where what Brook had
originally wanted for his John Gay adaptation was 'the stinking air
of Hogarth'. Instead of the flouncy, colourful, almost *Carry On* romp
he ended up with, full of bedpans and bed sheets – and Kenneth
Williams appears as a potboy – Brook 'saw in my mind a rough energetic film in black-and-white, with a coarse and virile highwayman in
the lead.' Brook had thought Burton, at the time appearing in a
season at The Old Vic and about to make *The Desert Rats* and *The
Robe*, suitably 'violent and harsh', by which he must have meant capable of violence, capable of harshness. Yet note how all these things
Burton didn't do are on the whole rather literary notions – Anouilh,
Rattigan, Sophocles, Cervantes. Sometimes a man simply wants to
pretend to climb up cliffs or ride on the roof of a cable car, as in *Where*

Eagles Dare. I was watching Anthony Hopkins in *When Eight Bells Toll* (1971), another Alistair MacLean yarn, and wondered whether it was mounted with Burton in mind, especially as the producer Elliott Kastner was the Elliott Kastner who produced *Where Eagles Dare, Villain, X, Y & Zee* and *Equus.* It has plenty of action, casual killings, secret agents imprisoned in castles. There's a yacht that resembles the *Kalizma.* Robert Morley is a Whitehall mandarin, pouting and preening. Charles Gray dubs poor Jack Hawkins' post-laryngectomy voice. Nathalie Delon from *Bluebeard* is the seductress. The difference between Hopkins and Burton? The former scurries up crags on ropes, goes deep-sea diving after pirates and gold bullion – he takes the caper seriously, if slightly stupidly, blankly. He handles himself in fights. Burton was always too world-weary, never quite wholehearted, in such scenes – the doubles and stuntmen do it, like valets living the lives of their masters. Burton is detached – his growling grandeur. And he was like that right at the start, in *Alexander the Great*, made in Franco's Spain, between February and July 1955, where he makes an almost piss-taking first entrance carrying a dead leopard. Were that Hopkins, we'd have had to see him killing the leopard. Hopkins takes it all rather earnestly – nor is he a sexual being. Fame didn't quite come for him until later – Hannibal Lecter and so on – when he was a notable character actor. I've never thought of him as a star, in the sense of romantic star. (Though of course he can dominate, as when he filled the Olivier stage as Lambert Le Roux in *Pravda* – 'the biggest fat fucking star I ever saw,' said David Hare. I agree. But it was a pantomime bigness.)

I'd like to have seen Burton as James Tyrone in *Long Day's Journey into Night*, a role Olivier excelled in – and he'd have understood the good and evil separation within the alcoholic son, when drink makes Hyde emerge from Jekyll and he says to his brother: 'I'd like to see you become the greatest success in the world. But you'd better be on your guard. Because I'll do my damnedest to make you fail. Can't help it. I hate myself. Got to take revenge. On everyone else. Especially you.' I can't picture him as T.E. Lawrence or James Bond. I can picture him in Losey's *The Man from Nowhere*, an unmade film talked about in 1967, which had originated with Hardy Krüger, who died on 19 January 2022, aged ninety-three. (Krüger is a fellow mercenary with Burton in *The Wild Geese*.) Burton would have been a gangster washed up on the beach of a desert island after a storm. The locals think it's Jesus Christ returned to Earth. *The Man from Nowhere* might have been Burton's stab at themes from *The Tempest*. Then there's Nabokov's *Laughter in the Dark*. Does footage survive? I've heard a rumour something was shown at the Bradford Film Festival in 2002. Adapted by Edward Bond for Tony Richardson, the story was moved from Berlin in the Twenties to London in the Sixties. They shot for two weeks in June and July 1968, with Faringdon House, Oxfordshire, and Sotheby's as the locations. Taylor turned up unannounced on the set 'in a dazzling white outfit with a high white torque,' recalled Richardson. She wanted £10,000 to appear as an extra – a somewhat conspicuous extra. 'It was worth it for the publicity,' she reasoned. Richardson had to explain the budgetary constraints to her, so she said she'd settle for a fancy outfit from Paris instead, plus the cost of the fittings. Burton, meanwhile, was misbehaving – though perhaps only behaving in the same way as when in Italy. 'He was hours late, unpleasant to the crew and other actors, sneering about the script. He'd take hours off for lunch.' There was an important sequence in Bond Street, with rehearsals called for seven-thirty a.m. Burton arrived at noon. 'Faced with my anger,' said Richardson, 'he turned round and walked off the set . . . He was in breach of contract. I fired him.' Oh fuck. It was as if Jimmy Porter from *Look Back in Anger* had returned, still unwilling to accept discipline. That's a film I often go back to, by the way, as it captures Burton in the raw, displays a lot of his anxieties and hatreds, his sexual domination ('I've no public school scruples about not hitting girls. You slap my face and I'll lay you out' – 'You would,' says Claire Bloom, 'you're the type.') He is the devil, and Richardson, more in harmony with Burton in those days, immersed Jimmy in smoke and steam, from kettles, laundry tubs, passing trains.

Burton can at least be relied upon to have read Nabokov's novel. Perhaps what threw him was a sentence about his character (Albert Albinus – changed by Bond to Sir Edward More) found in the opening paragraph: 'He loved; was not loved; and his life ended in disaster.' What a frightening, prophetic encapsulation. Burton was replaced by Nicol Williamson, with his peculiar up-and-down-the-stave gurgling voice and over-intense demeanour. 'I'm thoroughly convinced I'm better than him,' Williamson said ungraciously – and untruthfully. Williamson's moody nervous energy was always out of all proportion, and he was physically repellent, a sort of human hyena, crouched as if ready to spring, gnashing his teeth, crushing bones, capable, I felt certain, of spraying rivals with his secretions. Words gushed uneasily amidst his chattering laughs and howls. Siân Phillips remained in place as Lady More. Anna Karina, the Danish beauty, played the teenage girl, a cinema usherette, with whom Sir Edward becomes obsessed, and who plays sado-masochistic games upon him when he is blinded in an accident. It's a story about exploitation and humiliation – how a mature gent can be undermined. There's a trace of *King Lear* in the material: Gloucester's loss of vision, Lear's loss of metaphysical vision ('I stumbled when I saw'); the horribleness of little girls, the Goneril or Regan daughter-figures. *Laughter in the Dark*, released finally in September 1969, was a flop. Joely Richardson said, 'Sacking Burton had finished [my] father's career as a film director.' As Tony Richardson made by my reckoning twelve further flicks, the Welsh curse wasn't that potent – though in April 1970 Richardson was complaining loudly to Isherwood and anyone who'd listen he'd lost all his money when backing was withdrawn 'after he'd gotten rid of Richard Burton'. Yet let's look at this from Burton's perspective. He was given the ignominious heave-ho on 8 July 1968, accused by lawyers acting for Woodall Films of being 'unpunctual and unprofessional'. He'd have

been enraged, belittled. On 23 July, André Besançon committed suicide in the Céligny garage. The gardener had been going around
Switzerland pretending to be Burton's 'business manager,' carrying
an important-looking attaché case containing only his lunch. Burton
was informed the next day, Wednesday 24 July. He flew with his party
to Geneva for the funeral on Friday 26 July – but as he had lunch that
day with Hugh French at The Dorchester and visited Taylor in hospital, it is likely the funeral wasn't until Saturday 27 July, after which Ivor
suffered his 'accident'. So where did everyone stay on the Friday night?
More questions, more puzzles. But at least we have a sense in this
period of Burton's festering feelings, spitting, lashing out.

Another one that went down the drain is *Jackpot*, which was never
completed. Burton was Reid Lawrence, a 'crippled' actor involved in
an insurance swindle, who attributes his recovery to divine interven-
tion. The director was Terence Young, who'd made the first three
Bond films, as well as *The Klansman*, where Burton was drunk and
incapable. 'Burton drunk is better than most actors sober,' Young
told the press, whilst shooting *Jackpot*. Hardly a helpful or an encour-
aging observation. Robert Mitchum and Audrey Hepburn had
turned the film down. Burton, when making *Brief Encounter*, tried to
interest Loren, mentioning the project to her when they stayed on
location at The Bush Inn, Alresford, Hampshire. In the end his co-
star was Charlotte Rampling, and I have seen photographs of a scene
in Nice Airport, where Burton is in a wheelchair and Charlotte
Rampling is doing the pushing. Standing to one side is Jean Bell. James
Coburn was also in the cast, which suggests what a very bland and
breezy Seventies international production this must have been, as
cool as a four-pocket safari jacket. *Jackpot* was underway, postponed,
underway again, and finally cancelled, between February and July
1975. Taylor appeared as 'Herself' in a mocked-up Oscar ceremony,
filmed at the Los Angeles Music Center. It was following all this that
she and Burton found themselves getting remarried in Botswana –
an episode which would have made another typical Seventies screen

romp, with Robert Wagner and Stephanie Powers. On 20 August, Taylor's temporary partner, Henry Wynberg, was seen leaving London for Los Angeles with eight suitcases. 'I have nothing to say to anyone,' he snapped to reporters. *Jackpot* fizzled when the backers, the Irwin Trust Company Ltd. simply ran out of money. All it had to show for itself was litigation, as the cast sued for payment. Terence Young was never to have much luck in this regard. The straight-to-video *The Jigsaw Man*, with Michael Caine and Laurence Olivier, was patched together, and *Inchon*, paid for by the Moonies, in which Olivier impersonated General MacArthur, had a troubled history, was heavily re-edited and never distributed.

If Burton wasn't in Huston's *Under the Volcano*, the role of the dipsomaniacal, hallucinating consul played in the event by Albert Finney, it's because he'd died, which is also why he's not to be found in *The Quiet American*, made finally by Phillip Noyce in 2002. Michael Caine is Thomas Fowler, the Graham Greene character going (as Graham Greene characters must) to seed during the Indochina War. Caine doesn't have Burton's rotting grandeur, but Brendan Fraser, as Pyle, who is not as innocent as he at first seems – he has the brutality of the person who has a 'cause' and who believes in 'the bigger picture' – possesses Burton's male beauty (since lost). Burton was offered Pyle in the first version of *The Quiet American*, made in 1958, directed by Joseph L. Mankiewicz. Audie Murphy played it. Michael Redgrave was Fowler. But Burton and Mankiewicz would know each other soon enough.

* * *

He loved; was not loved; and his life ended in disaster. Taylor, by contrast, had complete resilience, her recuperative skills seemingly supernatural. She was certainly accustomed to being worshipped. Compare her with Marilyn Monroe for a moment. They were both sharply shaded violet, green and sunflower-yellow Andy Warhol icons, rendered as startlingly hyped-up mass-produced cheap art, with inflated values; they were notorious for their maladies and public pain; they were famous for their celebrity men (DiMaggio and Arthur Miller in Monroe's case) and for the way acting was being – 'It's amazing, the way she can just switch on,' said Puffin Asquith of Taylor. 'You sit there and wait,' said Billy Wilder of Monroe. 'You can't start without her . . . It demoralises the whole company. On the other hand, I have an Aunt Ida in Vienna who is always on time. I wouldn't put her in a movie.' Yet where Monroe was genuinely self-destructive, Taylor only courted self-destruction. Her ego remained stable. She had animal faculties (hence her enjoyment of the Chobe nuptials; she was photographed snuggling up to a cheetah named Taga at the Kruger National Park game reserve, South Africa, in 1985; in 2005 Bruce Weber did a series of pictures of Taylor and a bear named Bonkers) – it was in her nature to need a scrap, and she was 'bestial, intent, real' (Larkin), expecting other people to do exactly what she wanted all the time. As Eddie said, with a mixture of admiration and horror, 'Elizabeth lived by her own rule: she wants what she wants when she wants it.' Her advice to him was, 'When you want something, just scream and yell.' From her earliest films, as a child star, opposite Nigel Bruce or Donald Crisp, and wearing a hat, gloves and ankle socks in matching colours, she flirted and was pertinacious with grown-up males, either simpering or shrieking to get her way: the untamed shrew.

It's why I tend to withhold sympathy as the hospitalisations mounted up: Cedars of Lebanon, Los Angeles, 9-16 January 1951, when she was put on a diet of baby food; or insisting she be taken to the UCLA General Hospital because a twisted colon, sciatica and a throat infection had been brought on by the death of James Dean. After falling over on Beaverbrook's yacht at Nassau in November 1956, she was flown to the Columbia-Presbyterian Medical Center, where her crushed spinal discs were looked at by Dr Dana Winslow Atchley (1892–1982), a diabetes specialist who had an affair with

Anne Morrow, the wife of aviator Charles Lindbergh, and Dr John Kingsley Lattimer (1914–2007), chairman of the urology department, and later the physician who investigated the injuries to assassinated President Kennedy. Taylor was discharged on 20 January 1957 and flew to Acapulco to divorce Michael Wilding. On 16 November 1957, complaining of a 'slight case' of appendicitis in Hong Kong, Taylor recovered after a few hours. Nonetheless, she entered the Cedars of Lebanon on 17 December for its removal – Rex Kennamer was in attendance and though he charged the patient $25,000 he did little except lay out and fold Taylor's clothes. Between 26 November and 13 December 1959, Taylor was in the Harkness Pavilion of the Columbia-Presbyterian, saying she had pneumonia – a prelude to *Cleopatra*, which was an epic of non-stop ailments and high temperatures: 'My subconscious let me become so seriously ill, I just let the disease take me,' Taylor famously announced, like Callas in a flowing white gown beginning an aria on a cardboard battlement.

Burton was always having to fret as she 'moans and groans in agony'. In February 1969 he told his diary, 'Suddenly she's an old lady.' Back Taylor would go to the Cedars of Lebanon (since 1961, the Cedars-Sinai Medical Center) 'for tests and rest', or else she'd be in the UCLA (University of California) Medical Center wanting 'abdominal pains' investigated, when all she needed was a good crap. After the Botswana comedy, in November 1975, Taylor went into the Wellington Hospital, St John's Wood, with back and neck discomfort ... By 1986, with Burton two years dead, she was going about plastic surgery and liposuction procedures. She had an entirely new set of teeth installed – her lower jaw thrust forward in a permanent stubborn grimace, like a baboon. In 1989, she was told she had Temporomandibular Disorder (TMD), caused by grinding her choppers. The answer was stronger painkillers. During the years 1980 to 1985, Taylor was already taking twenty-eight different kinds of sleeping pill and tranquilliser. Then, in the Nineties, came hip replacements, arrythmia, candidiasis, treated at the St John's Health Center, Santa Monica, and the Aaron Diamond Institute, part of the New York University School of Medicine. If some of her doctors, Skinner, Gottlieb and Roth, were reported to the Medical Board of California for falsifying Taylor's records, how could anyone of even average intelligence collate and keep abreast of those records? The physicians were reprimanded but not criminally charged. The Deputy Attorney General said, 'It was a classic case of abuse involving multiple prescriptions, multiple controlled substances [obtained from] different pharmacies at the same time.' Eddie had long ago spoken about the way Taylor bullied doctor after doctor into prescribing what she wanted: 'That's the wrong one, you cocksucker, don't try to give me that fucking shit, give me the right one.' Then she discovered the joy of morphine injections, which Eddie had to administer. When it was politely suggested she might see a psychiatrist about her pills and addictions, Taylor threw a tantrum, stripped off her clothes and got into her Cadillac, 'this hysterical naked woman trying to drive . . .'

It's very strange. Where Diana Dors, say, who had a swollen pulpy paleness or sheen, and of course Monroe, were honestly beaten up by life, Taylor never did seem to suffer or become diminished, not in the same manner. She'd never show (or embody) emotional disintegration – what in *Night Watch* are called 'latent neurotic patterns'. *Night Watch*, for example, made in June 1972, when Burton had his five minutes as a St Peter's College don, seems to be about Taylor's character cracking up, pushed around by Laurence Harvey, who as a natty business executive resembles Ronald Allen in *Crossroads*. 'There's a doctor here,' Taylor says fearfully, 'and they are planning on sending me away,' as in *Suddenly, Last Summer*. The big twist is that Taylor's been the one manipulating the murder plot from the outset, like *Gaslight* in reverse. Bangs, crashes, creaks, footsteps, the works. I mentioned Diana Dors, who was similarly buxom, similarly brassy. How did Taylor avoid Dors' fate? Or to put it the other way around – why did Dors never rival Taylor? How did Taylor become famous in ways Dors (who worked with Joseph Losey in *Steaming*) never managed to pull off? For Dors ended up as a ghoul in horror films, e.g. *Nothing But the Night*, where she is obliged to crawl through hedges and streams and is chucked on a bonfire at the finish; or else she's a madam in wilting sex films, such as *The Amorous Milkman* and *Keep It Up Downstairs*. She's the slatternly concierge in *There's a Girl in My Soup*, a randy widow after Harry H. Corbett in *Steptoe and Son Ride Again*, the corpse of her husband still in the bed. Dors became a fat scold, having been a curvaceous pin-up. She and Taylor are very similar (the one an over-bleached bottle blonde, the other raven-haired); neither can be accused of timidity or of going out of their way to be ladylike (as Angela Carter said, 'Diana Dors scarcely seems to come from the same country as Deborah Kerr') – yet tragedy clung to Diana Dors, not only because of the early cancer diagnosis. She was never allowed to soar – perhaps she never transcended Swindon? And there's Taylor, who remained unaffected at root by what came her way. She'd be alongside grief and pain, but it never quite touched her. All those illnesses or acquaintance with illnesses – they didn't reach her. She was outside of them – her fame and her stardom made her a separate thing; again, like Callas, who could undergo the torments of an opera plot, yet keeps on singing. The stylisation, the artifice, takes over, and Taylor got through life by being outside of it – literally, too, in Switzerland or on the yacht, where epidemics, floods, famines, civil wars, nuclear bombs, are never things she'd know or face.

As Michael Wilding noted, she never cooked, sewed, cleaned or grew vegetables. 'Elizabeth wanted the pets around her all the time' – four dogs, four cats, seven rabbits and a duck – 'but she didn't want to do anything with them.' When it came to being a parent, she was never 'closely involved,' said Raymond Vignale, her waspish chamberlain, who wore a white mink jacket with jewelled buttons. Even so, her non-maternal feelings or habits were to prove influential, inspirational, to feminists – in *The Lost Daughter* (2021), for example, Jessie Buckley's

Leda Caruso, at the end of her tether, finds she hates her own children. The (admittedly tiresome) toddlers hold her back, are in her way, so she (literally) shuts the door on them, storms off. Leda goes to the cinema, conveniently a revival house, and is struck by a line in *The Last Time I Saw Paris*, where Taylor coos to the newborn in its cot: 'The last nine months I've devoted to you, sweetheart. Now I'm going to have fun!' This is all the confirmation Jessie's character needs – a disturbing pretext or validation for abandoning family ties, breaking taboos. She later turns into Olivia Colman, an academic with plenty of time on her hands, mooning about on full pay in Spetses. Dakota Johnson, who actually looks like Taylor, stabs her in the belly with a hatpin – a sort of divine (Greek) retribution for her selfishness.

Taylor never signed autographs, was more likely to scribble 'Fuck off!' on proffered pieces of paper. Interviews were rarely granted. She destroyed the negatives and contact sheets of photographs she disliked. If she was habitually late, it's because her time was more important than the other fellow's. Everything was a gesture. There was never any indication there was ever a fragile girl somewhere inside. If she wanted to be beaten into submission, it's so she can kick and bite right back. What she wanted from husbands was pretty basic. 'He hasn't fucked me for weeks,' Taylor complained to Norma Heyman about Burton, as early as 1970. Their second marriage drooped because, 'The trouble is, he can't get it up anymore,' Taylor told a journalist, Charles Laurence, in Burton's hearing, over lunch at Scott's fish restaurant in Mount Street. During her Washington phase, which ended in 1982, she told Warhol her main problem was 'John Warner wasn't fucking her', even though she'd spent $1.2 million on the campaign trail, getting him into the Senate. Taylor hated being a politician's wife: 'You are a robot. They even tell you what you can wear.' In the midst of this – seeing Warner adopted as a Republican Party candidate; attending his swearing-in; appearing alongside Ronald and Nancy Reagan at a Presidential Convention in Detroit – she in May 1980 made *The Mirror Crack'd*: 'It's not every day we have a real live film star actress and her film director husband living here in St Mary Mead,' says Margaret Courtenay, a villager, of Taylor's Marina Rudd and Rock Hudson's Jason Rudd, though no less out of the ordinary surely than Burton and Loren waiting for the stopping train to Brockenhurst, Hampshire.

We are now not in the Texas of *Giant* but in Agatha Christie's teacup territory of guilty vicarages and polite psychopathology. Angela Lansbury, last seen opposite Taylor in *National Velvet*, sports bleached eyebrows and is Miss Marple – a prelude to her Jessica Fletcher in two hundred and sixty-four episodes of *Murder, She Wrote*. The idea is that Hollywood has invaded rural England – idyllic cottages, garden fêtes, peach jam, and where Charles Gray is the butler – to make a picture about Mary, Queen of Scots. An uncredited Pierce Brosnan is an actor on the set, clutched to Taylor's bosom. It's a wonder after that that James Bond didn't have a strabismus. Kim Novak, a 'peroxide floozy', is Lola Brewster, Marina's rival. Lola is married to the producer, Martin Fenn, played by Tony Curtis in a hilarious wig. There's plenty of fatuous bitchery. Taylor's Marina, who if mingling with strangers wears a floral hat, the blooms seemingly growing straight out of her head, is the pill-popping has-been movie queen (Claire Bloom lacking compass in the Joan Hickson version; Lindsay Duncan too discerning in the Julia Mackenzie version), who makes life impossibly difficult for Rock, who is trying to direct the historical romp. 'My love, you're so good for me,' Taylor tells him. 'You always have been.' He keeps his composure when she trots late on set and knocks over a rack of pikes or are they halberds. If he noticed the hairy Taylor has the traces of a moustache in close-ups, Rock fails to mention it. There are tantrums and breakdowns, let alone death threats. 'Can you think of anyone who might want to kill you?' Taylor is asked – and where to begin? 'Somebody's trying to kill me, aren't they?' she replies, quick as a flash, missing little. 'I'm an actress. I act,' she then says, as if that is an answer to everything. Like a lot of these final phase films – *A Little Night Music, Malice in*

Wonderland, Poker Alice – it's as if Taylor is plunged into a cartoonish, parodic reconstruction of her MGM and Fox heyday. 'I want her to be happy,' says Rock to Curtis. 'God knows, she's been through enough.'

It's true Taylor had gained the weight Rock lost, and to her credit, his death from Aids inspired Taylor's extensive charity work. 'Without homosexuals, there'd be no Hollywood, no show business,' she said, dedicating herself to the American Foundation for Aids Research and Aids Project Los Angeles. Taylor was the first celebrity to acknowledge and support the crisis – and *The Mirror Crack'd* is about illness. Marina had 'a child that was born an imbecile', and went round the twist when told by doctors of the hopeless prognosis. 'She never recovered from the shock,' as Burton, in his turn, had had to absorb the shock of Jessica's destiny, at a time when people had a horror of disabilities – and he never absorbed the shock, he never got over the horror. Agatha Christie apparently based her book (published in 1962 as *The Mirror Crack'd from Side to Side* – an extra mark for those who spot the Tennyson allusion) on news reports about the pregnant Gene Tierney, star of Mankiewicz's *Dragonwyck* and *The Ghost and Mrs Muir*, who contracted German measles from a fan – this was thought to have caused Tierney's daughter's mental retardation. Daria Antoinette Cassini was born in 1943, deaf, blind and mentally handicapped. (She survived until 2010.) Meanwhile Tierney (who died in 1991) had her own long-standing psychiatric troubles, was a patient at Taylor's second home, the Harkness Pavilion, and underwent electroconvulsive therapy. In the film, therefore, it is Taylor's Marina who is the mad killer. She was once kissed by a girl with rubella, so, coming across her years later, poisons her. Taylor's final scene is to lie dead on a couch, clutching a yellow rose – her Cleopatra pose. Suicide? Or a mercy killing by Rock? It's left to Miss Marple and her nephew, a senior policeman played superciliously by Edward Fox, to put two and two together and make it all seem not too implausible. 'What,' asked bonny Margaret Courtenay, whom at first I thought was Dawn French, 'would a Chief Inspector from

Scotland Yard be doing in St Mary Mead if it wasn't for the murder of Heather Babcock?' Now, there's a question.

* * *

There's a line in *The Mirror Crack'd from Side to Side*, where Christie is describing Marina – who is Gene Tierney, but the words also apply to Taylor: 'She had a great power of love and hate but no stability.' Taylor became the queen of ostentation. This was inevitable. The alternative would have been to go mad, deprived and bled by Hollywood of essential ordinary life – like the lassitude and macabre grandeur of Norma Desmond in *Sunset Boulevard*; or the schizophrenia of Vivien Leigh, whom Taylor replaced in March 1953 as Ruth Wiley in *Elephant Walk*, which was filmed in Ceylon and is tropical and lush and sinister. Some of Leigh's footage survives in the finished product, and Leigh and Taylor mix and merge and meld in the reverse-angle dialogue shots and long shots, as if they are indissoluble like chemicals in the developing tray. Taylor's Ruth Wiley is demure and works in a London bookshop. She wears Leigh's clothes. When she marries Peter Finch and goes to live in his tea plantation – the bungalow foolishly built astride an ancient elephant trail – she does a lot of running along vast corridors and on and off verandas. She's in and out of stores, larders, cellars, indignant at the 'shocking waste' of food – there's still rationing in England. There are monsoons, natives dancing and rhythmic drumming, as in *The Comedians*. Taylor, in lavender chiffon, is the only woman in the Far East – yet Finch prefers the company of the drunken Garrick clubmen sorts, who drink and play billiards. Dana Andrews strums Chopin. Leigh would have focussed on Ruth's sexual frustration, in the face of her husband's preference for the company of his vile scrounger mates. She'd be a version of Blanche DuBois, lonely and febrile. With Taylor, I always expect her, as Ruth, to take command, not to be shy and deferential, never to break – for the elephant stampede to be something Taylor can surmount, has perhaps psychically organised. The chairs in the bungalow are like thrones, and Taylor's Ruth sits there like Cleopatra – she's altogether pinker, softer than Leigh, who could be quite hard, porcelain, though Leigh played Cleopatra, too. There are elephant carvings in the brickwork, elephant symbols and ciphers woven on Finch's suits, tusks everywhere, like the motif of golden serpents in the Egypt of *Cleopatra*. Finch (briefly Julius Caesar seven years later) glowers when he sees an actual bull elephant – some sort of man-mastering-the-animal-kingdom idea is intended. So what does that make Leigh and Taylor? Females of the species to be broken in?

Taylor, in the pale yellow and mushroom-coloured beige dresses (by Edith Head) is rather indifferent to Peter Finch. It's as if she realises full well the only possible purpose of the empty sleek bungalow set, made of white marble and black ebony, is that trumpeting herds of wild elephants can rampage through it. Not for her Leigh's humid passions and crack-up, brought on by the heat. If this is a version of *Rebecca* – Finch the stubborn, taciturn Max de Winter (Olivier – Mr Vivien Leigh – in Hitchcock's film); the Ceylon tea plantation a colonial Cornwall, the house another Manderley (each dwelling destroyed at the finish) – nevertheless, Taylor isn't Joan Fontaine, either. She had an earthiness, which always protected her from being fragile – or of course camp. She's almost not intelligent enough in a human way to be camp. Animals are incapable of camp. Taylor could never, as it were, step outside of herself, detach or separate herself from herself, to be camp, as Mae West or Tallulah Bankhead did, or as Faye Dunaway does. She's instinctive, not deliberative. It's interesting that the stage play chosen for her by Zev Buffman – rehearsals began in January 1981 – was *The Little Foxes*, which had been a success for Tallulah Bankhead on stage in 1939. In the William Wyler film two years later, Bette Davis took the role of Regina Giddens – and it was another opportunity for Bette, an angry Pekinese in more or less human shape, to sneer and snarl as she goes up and down a wide staircase.

The title of Lillian Hellman's drama is an obscure biblical allusion – Chapter Two, Verse Fifteen, of the *Song of Solomon*: 'Take us the foxes, the little foxes, that spoil the vines; for our vines have tender grapes.' The idea is that wild things destroy nice things – the greed and graspingness of it all. Economic progress means destruction, is Hellman's message. The setting could be the Ambersons' mansion (the cinematographer is Welles' Greg Toland) – and Regina's big scene is the one where she doesn't budge, declining to race for the medicine bottle, and allows her husband to expire on the stairs of angina. We are in high (as in ripe) gothic territory – Regina avid for her inheritance, dealing with her horrible cheating brothers, negotiating with the bankers and God knows what over stolen bonds, loans, collateral, papers kept in a strong-box. We are in the Deep South. Black people exist to be exploited. Everyone is exploited. In this fight for survival, Regina is thoroughly calculating – and Taylor refused to play the role in any obvious, domineering way. 'There is a certain vulnerability to Regina,' she said perceptively. 'She's a woman who's been pushed into a corner. She's a killer, but she's saying, "Sorry, fellas, you put me in this position." ' Which they had. *The Little Foxes* opened at The Parker Playhouse in Fort Lauderdale on 27 February, settled at the Martin Beck on Broadway between 7 May and 5 September for one hundred and twenty-three sold-out performances, before touring to Washington, New Orleans and Los Angeles. The production came to the Victoria Palace, London, for sixteen weeks, from 11 March 1982. In the audience on opening night was Princess Diana.

Taylor in the play and elsewhere doesn't play with masks or strike false attitudes – she wouldn't know what any of this means. She's capable – as capable as anybody – of exaggeration, but not of frivolity: earthy, she is earthbound. She can't take flight, which is why as the Queen of Light, the Mother, Witch and Spirit of Maternal Love in *The Blue Bird*, where bands play and characters skate on a frozen lake, Taylor is as natural and homely as the luxuriously-appointed

stripped pine kitchen, or the patchwork quilts, with which George
Cukor, the director, surrounded her, during the nine months they
spent in five (non-airconditioned) sound stages at the 'Lenfilm' and
'Sovinfilm' Studios in Leningrad, which were run by the All-Union
Corporation for Joint Productions, a body overseen by the Soviet
State Cinematic Committee, which didn't like anything in the script
(by Colin Higgins and Hugh Whitemore) that could be subversively
symbolical – hence the deletion of any mention of Christmas, though
it is a Christmas fable. Richard Pearson, in a brown duffel coat, plays
a bread loaf. Harry Andrews is a tree. Robert Morley is Father Time
('You'll have to take it or leave it / You have to believe it / You're all in
the hands of Fate'). Jane Fonda, dwelling in a castle made from
anthracite, is a black fairy – 'I am in charge of all Nature's secrets,' so
she'll have her work cut out. Ava Gardner is a sort of Red Queen, who
seems to live in a circus. You watch it agog. Who's on next?

Patsy Kensit is Taylor's daughter, Mytyl. At a glance old Patsy
lived a fast-motion burlesque of Taylor's life, had everything for
Taylor gone completely wrong: the child star, whose ambition was 'to
be more famous than anything or anyone', who grew up to have a
huge number of husbands; who believed her father to be an antiques
dealer – in fact he was involved with the Krays. Patsy ended up on
Loose Women and *Celebrity Big Brother*, though perhaps remains best
known for having been Mrs Jim Kerr and Mrs Liam Gallagher. Mona
Washbourne turns up as the Grandmother – when Mona turns up,
e.g. in *The Driver's Seat*, I know I am in the presence of an extraordinary person: her bubbling layers of understanding and sympathy.
Edith Evans, with whom Burton played one of his best scenes, in
Look Back in Anger, and with whom he was luminous in *The Last Days
of Dolwyn*, and Sybil Thorndike, who appeared alongside Burton on
Sunday 28 February and Sunday 17 March 1954, when The Old Vic
Club and the Vic-Wells Association gave a staged reading of *Under
Milk Wood*, must have had these qualities, though these ladies were
more obviously capable of veering off to display asperity or grandeur.

Mona had a rich, lulling Dundee cake voice . . . Anyway, in *The Blue Bird*, time is suspended (as it is in *Elephant Walk*, where everyone, the servants included, is in thrall to Peter Finch's late father, 'the old master', whose ivory-bedecked chambers are retained as a shrine); there are plenty of allusions to Lewis Carroll's Wonderland archetypes, or to Oz and Narnia: temptations to be resisted, perilous journeys to be undergone, the characters mad as hatters. But most of all, even though Jonas Gricius, transliterated also as Ionas Gritzus, the Soviet director of photography – who was in addition President of the Lithuanian Cinematography Union – had never worked with colour stock before, so Taylor looked bright red and Cicely Tyson vanished and all that could be seen in the murk were her teeth; even though James Coco's gall bladder got inflamed, Freddie Young caught pneumonia and the ballet master and choreographer Leonid Yakobson died; even though the American and Soviet units worked from different scripts and never coordinated their work schedules; even though plugs were pulled at five-thirty prompt as overtime was against Communist principles ('Soviet officials don't believe time is money,' wept American co-producer Paul B. Radin); even though the equipment was antiquated, the cameras, light meters and editing desks, and Soviet babushka women worked the studio lights and pulleys; even though the budget soon climbed from $2.4 million to $8 million; even though the birds dyed blue died of toxic shock – nevertheless Taylor at the height of the Cold War, in March 1975, got the KGB to intervene and bring cases of Jack Daniel's, cans of chilli and boxes of frozen American steaks personally to her hotel. And over all *The Blue Bird* – about the joys of home; don't leave, don't go anywhere: that is the only source of happiness (which rather negates ambition, exploration) – is a film for Taylor to demonstrate (like Garbo) her affecting qualities, as a Madonna ('all mothers are rich when they love their children'), and the more so to demonstrate her disruptive qualities, as the Russian folkloristic Baba Yaga, crossing forests and green oceans to lure men to their deaths.

Even when silly, she's solemn. Taylor's rage and impatience won't abate on command, as it wouldn't for Bette Davis. She's not capable of an atmosphere of irony, which is why when she's immersed in the blowsy late films, or *Secret Ceremony* or *Reflections in a Golden Eye*, instead of being camp they become, with Taylor, about the facts of life, principally grief and loneliness and bitter jealousy. Her vulgarity and brashness, which would lead most performers off in the direction of pantomime, with Taylor are natural characteristics – I'd never imagine her in an Oscar Wilde play, for example, though she could do so: 'That guy is amazing. I would love a part with him,' she said of Stephen Fry, and spoke of doing Lady Bracknell. Taylor would not have been a model for Beardsley or somebody in a Firbank novel. But Picasso may have been transfixed by her substantial curves and bouncing bosoms, when he went through his neo-classical period, painting ample women cavorting on beaches – he ought to have had another look after *Ivanhoe*. And Warhol's screen-prints are absolute. According to Warhol, *Boom!* was 'the movie Judy Garland had wanted to star in so badly'. Would she have made it better, or worse? Definitely very different. Taylor and Garland, launched by Louis B. Mayer, knew what audiences expected of them, knew what's effective. They were both needy women, shedding and gaining fat, fond of high drama, living in worlds of their own – as Flora 'Sissy' Goforth lives in a world of her own. But where Garland was vulnerable, febrile, ravaged, as it were, by fire, the world slipping away, what distinguished Taylor, lurid and sensational in appearance as she was, is that the world was there for her to dominate and control. She was never a victim.

* * *

Her non-victim status is apparent in another Tennessee Williams gothic extravaganza, and like *The Blue Bird*, a fairy story, *Sweet Bird of Youth*, which Taylor made for NBC-TV in July 1989. 'Blue is the colour of distance and it is also the colour of memory,' Williams explained lyrically. 'A symbol of longing for the "sweet bird" [of] all the ideals that have crumbled along with the family fortunes and mansions.' These are plays, therefore, about the unattainable, the irretrievable. Maurice Maeterlinck and Tennessee Williams seem to have visited the same aviary or zoo, moreover, when searching for their tokens and types. In *The Blue Bird*, which is seasonally snowy, bread, sugar, fire and water, let alone elms and oaks, and foxes and bears, behave like human beings. In *Sweet Bird of Youth*, which takes place at Easter in the fictional southern resort of St Cloud, particularly with Taylor, a human being becomes inhuman: Alexandra Del Lago is as hard as any diamond, ruby, sapphire or emerald. This was Taylor's fourth Tennessee Williams film, after *Cat on a Hot Tin Roof*, *Suddenly, Last Summer* and *Boom!*; or her fifth if her hanging about in Mismaloya during *Night of the Iguana* is added. She measured out her life in Tennessee Williams works; and what I now see is how, with commendable physical forcefulness, she played dead against the playwright's themes and ideas. He believed he'd created roles showing the destruction of the non-conformist, the grinding into particles of deluded misfits, wistful martyrs, lost souls, sad romantics who inhabit dilapidated houses and cling to a faded elegance. Taylor is too severe for this – her subject is survival.

Hence, her Alexandra del Lago, who also goes by the name the Princess Kosmonopolis, an actress in the Gloria Swanson tradition, is a cyclone of magenta hair and purple stoles and feathers. When, at the start, we see her race from a cinema premiere, convinced her new movie is a disaster ('After failure comes flight' – more bird imagery), Taylor isn't making an exit, she's making an entrance. She swoops into The Royal Palms Hotel, an edifice of Art Deco, bringing with her a beach masseuse or gigolo, named Chance, played by Mark Harmon, voted by *People Magazine* the 'Sexiest Man Alive' in 1986. Three years on, the title may still be retained. Nicolas Roeg's camera lingers on his hairless torso as he comes damp out of the shower, a white towel loose

560

around his waist. Chance, the 'travelling companion', or male whore, has got nothing except his looks and erotic vitality – and Taylor wants plenty of what the script calls 'the distraction of lovemaking'. When Harmon tries to blackmail her over her drug dependency, Taylor simply challenges him right back, wanting to be fucked more regularly than ever: 'I need the distraction *now*. When I say *now* I mean *now*, not later.' It's as if Tennessee Williams, or Gavin Lambert, who wrote the 'teleplay', had been listening through the walls, a glass tumbler pressed to their ear, when Taylor was with Eddie. Harmon's Chance is easily put in his place, too: 'By the time I was your age [thirty-one],' she says, munching a croissant, 'I was already a legend.' By the time Taylor was thirty-one it was 1963 and the world was first seeing *Cleopatra* and *The V.I.P.s*. You can't keep autobiography out.

Tennessee Williams hoped to be writing about the cruel passage of time: 'Nobody's young anymore,' is one of the lines. 'Time. Who can beat it?' Harmon, whose Chance is Dorian Gray, is told, 'Youth is the only thing you've had, and you're past it.' Now he is merely 'the ghost of a golden boy'. These platitudes and insults pour forth from an Alexandra del Lago, the Princess Kosmonopolis, who is of course envious, as Sissy Goforth is envious (and fearful) of her male escort – Harmon's Chance, like Burton's Chris, is a memento mori: a reminder of death, and as such as allegorical as anything in Maeterlinck. As in *Boom!* mortality is represented by Illness. Alexandra moans and mutters in bed ('Princess has bad dreams!') and conveniently brings in her luggage her own portable oxygen tank and mask, plus accessories. 'Help! Oxygen!' she says – again, were Williams and Lambert in the corridors of The Dorchester on those fateful winter nights in 1960 and 1961? 'My nerves! My heart!' pleads Alexandra del Lago, the Princess Kosmonopolis, whimpering beneath the bedsheets.

Were the role played by Vivien Leigh or Judy Garland (and Geraldine Page was in the 1962 film, opposite Paul Newman), there'd be sympathy, concern, over these palpitations and asthma attacks. Not with Taylor. Maladies for her brought rhapsodic moments – when her

Alexandra learns her new film was a hit after all, she rises like a phoenix, and drops Chance instantly: 'Legends don't die easily. They hang
on long, awfully long!' With any other star this would be a delusional
climax, followed by kind strangers enticing them into the asylum's
wagon, a lobotomy procedure scheduled for later on. And one of the
ways Taylor twists or adapts the material to suit her own temperament, rather than serving the self-pitying, inflamed temperament of
the author, is by sending it up. Alexandra del Lago, the Princess
Kosmonopolis, is full of vanity, but Taylor is not vain. In her coloured
plumage of kaftans and white mink, she's a great cube or sphere – like
a creature from The Muppets, swaying about the hotel suite on Miss
Piggy trotters. It is a strange and monstrous transformation – 'When
monster meets monster,' she says to Chance, realising they are as connected, the pair of them, as beauty is to the beast. Taylor is rounder,
more squashed, than ever before, her nose more of a snout; she's unable
to walk in a straight line, and I realise what Quentin Crisp meant
when, in September 1989, he was asked to give a name to the person he
most admired: 'Elizabeth Taylor, because she is so beautiful, so rich
and so courageous in fighting her many illnesses and because she is
wonderfully funny, something for which she never gets any credit.'
Well, I'm giving her credit now. She took Tennessee Williams' tragedies
and made them comedies. Similarly, she took Maeterlinck's whimsy
and gave it ominous depth – for the universe of The Blue Bird is as cannibalistic as anything in, say, Suddenly, Last Summer, with the
anthropomorphic loaves of bread and barley-sugar sticks gleefully
scoffed by Mytyl and Tyltyl. 'Oh, how good they are!' says Mytyl,
sucking on barley sugar formed by one of Sugar's fingers. 'Does that
hurt you much, when you break them off?' – 'Not at all,' says Sugar.
'They grow again at once.' Useful.

Because of the Leningrad cuisine, the poisoned James Coco's
scenes were laboriously re-shot with George Cole, but one piece of
casting in 1975 never occurred, which I for one regret: Crisp wanted
Taylor to play him in The Naked Civil Servant. When the budget was

announced, 'Secretly I would have thought that Elizabeth Taylor could have been persuaded to act the part of me for a fee as large as that ... Instead, Danny La Rue was discussed, but the part went to John Hurt.' Hurt at least was to be Winston Smith opposite Burton's O'Brien in *Nineteen Eighty-Four*. Was there ever a more ill looking actor? Emaciated and pouchy, Hurt always looked like an unshaven patient only recently discharged as a hopeless case from the cancer ward. (Pancreatic cancer got him in 2017.) But in May 1984, when the film was made at RAF Hullavington, Swindon, at Alexandra Palace, Beckton Gasworks and in Battersea Power Station, Burton was the one who was the burnt-out case, with three months remaining. 'No one escapes,' says O'Brien, in defiance of Maeterlinck or Tennessee Williams, where characters fly from anguish and pain, elope, particularly into fantasy. 'There are no martyrs here.' Yet isn't Big Brother the same as the big brooms in fairy stories, sweeping people out of the way?

* * *

Taylor and Burton's time together – from 1962 until their deathbeds: 'You know, Elizabeth and I never really split up, and never will,' Burton told Graham, on the last occasion the brothers saw each other, in July 1984; Taylor's house was adorned with framed pictures of Burton: 'He's where I can keep an eye on him, and he'd better believe it' – was a midsummer night's sex comedy. The *opera buffa* of their existence came to mean more (certainly to the public) than their art: their feuds, rejections, distresses; their bravado and ruthlessness. It was a veritable battle of the sexes, a perverse dance routine, with lots of coiling and writhing; the powerful man who wins the powerful woman, and vice versa, who then subjects her to his will, as she subjected him to her will – each only (at best) seemingly domesticated, seemingly dependent, because in actuality held securely in bondage: 'I woo'd thee with my sword,' Theseus reminds Hippolyta, 'and won thy love doing thee injuries.' Bereft of Burton, Taylor had said, 'If I'm away from Richard I feel like half a pair of scissors' – but there's nevertheless still blade enough for her to jab, for her to lash out with and cut. (It'll be Burton's most obscure project, the narrative voice he provided in 1961 for a Czechoslovakian puppet version of *A Midsummer Night's Dream*, made by Jiří Trnka. Not even I have seen it, except in the original Czechoslovakian – enough to appreciate the carved wooden stop-motion models, with their unchanging expressions; the dissolves and overlays; the colourful jittering and skittering.) Burton, who'd said when cast in *Cleopatra*, 'I've got to don my breastplate once more to play opposite Miss Tits' – his breastplate remaining handy from *The Robe* and *Alexander the Great* – was initially appealing to Taylor because he was masterful, because he was fearless. 'Richard has given me a sense of reality,' she cried in their first days. 'I am now a woman, and that's infinitely more satisfying than being an actress. I'm a woman who needs to be dominated.' I think what this means, when decoded, is she liked to be fucked with vigour, mewing when orgasm was achieved. (Presumably Burton *barked*.) 'I think sex is absolutely gorgeous,' Taylor informed the press in 1964, in case there was any doubt. 'My interest always increases with satisfaction,' as she would say in *Sweet Bird of Youth*. In *X, Y & Zee*, Taylor is also minxy: 'A girl has to be quite grown up to be expelled for kissing a nun,' she says to Susannah York provocatively. As Henry Wynberg, who accompanied Taylor to Leningrad, vouchsafed, 'Let's just say, she put her heart into it,' and put her back out doing it.

But the masochistic yearning to be misused was part of a game, maybe one Taylor was not wholly aware she was playing, which is another of the contradictions within herself that makes her interesting – her vagaries and her distractions; her way of working by instinct. What went wrong with Burton is the same as what went wrong with her other relationships: real and dream images collided. Whoever she was with, from blue-veined thin boy Nicky Hilton onwards, they were made instantly into a famous couple, photographed for magazines, and they wanted to be granted total permissiveness – though in fairness to Michael Wilding, he didn't. He was embarrassed by the crowds outside Claridge's on their wedding night, in February 1952, but Taylor fancied playing to them: 'We are not circus performers!' he said. Oh dear. The circus ring or carnival booth was exactly where Mike Todd belonged. Twenty-seven years Taylor's senior, when he said, 'Elizabeth, I love you and I'm going to marry you,' his assertiveness held an allure. 'Soon as I finish my dinner, I'm gonna fuck you.' His plane crashed, and the marriage would have done so – Todd and Taylor were too combustible. There were lots of 'Fuck you!', 'No, fuck you!' arguments at airports. With Eddie, the entire marriage was a maelstrom, begun in the Donizetti grief at Todd's death and concluded in the Offenbach lust of Burton's bewitchments. As Eddie concluded about Taylor, paying her a backhanded compliment, 'I've never known anyone who was more honest about her feelings,' but they were uncontrolled feelings.

The paradox with intimacy is that it can create or expose distance – separation. Who knows what free-roaming fantasies are unspooling inside the head of one's partner or partners, during a sexual embrace, or at any time? To suspect this causes misery, which is where it began unravelling with Taylor and Burton. 'We only really enjoy working together,' Burton had said, at a reception to launch Harlech Television (HTV). 'It's total comfort for both of us ... We can tell just by looking at each other's eyes if we are at all off-key. We don't have to say a word.' This is similar to the supposed rapport Hardy described in *The Return of the Native* between Eustacia Vye and Clym Yeobright, the diamond merchant, back from Paris: 'They were like those double stars which revolve round and round each other, and from a distance appear to be one,' i.e. they are only appearing to be one – an optical (and emotional) illusion. Before long Burton was also saying, 'We totally misunderstand each other ... We operate on alien wavelengths. [She is] as distant as Venus – planet, I mean.' If there's an absence of any real interconnection or fusion, well, only Our Lord knowest the secrets, the devices and desires, of our hearts. The complexities of living with another person, and the risks involved, whether or not it is Taylor, Burton, or anyone else: every relationship can become unmanageable, intractable; couples lie next to each other, holding each other's hand, yet are separate, at best moored like lobster boats, gently rocking. With Taylor and Burton, finally, or possibly quite quickly, it's their intensity that kept them apart; their love was a matter of the kind of life they were living: tumultuous, public, fervent, blind – and Taylor was blind to most things outside of herself. Burton was always impressed at the way she could shield herself from ordinary or average people, as if she'd gone into a trance, a state of suspended animation: 'Her public persona was aloof and enormously difficult to break.' She didn't want to be side-tracked from herself, to be reduced. The men she married were ideas to her – almost abstractions – rather than actual individuals, so she was soon left unsatisfied, unrealised, by them, the perfect unions in disarray, volatility the essence.

'Nothing comes off until the ring goes on,' she'd said to Nicky Hilton, when she was seventeen and they got engaged. Her tantalising manner soon enraged him ('I'm so goddamned sick and tired of looking at your face'), and the marriage was over before the end of the honeymoon. Taylor called MGM to say, 'Send someone to bring me home. I can't take any more of this.' Wilding's English graciousness, his ability to live life according to a pattern, grated, as did his prudence: 'We were living in a kind of cloud-cuckoo land,' is how he summed up his marriage to Taylor. Her reaction to Todd's death was to play the role of screaming widow. 'Mike is dead and I'm alive!' she told the press on 11 September 1958. In *Cat on a Hot Tin Roof*, which was released nine days later, one of her lines, spoken under duress to Paul Newman, is, 'Skipper's dead and I'm alive!' Taylor's marriage to Eddie was an odd way of resurrecting Todd, as she later saw: 'All Eddie and I had in common was Mike, and that was sick. Boy, did I realise how sick it was,' like necrophilia. 'I tried to copy him,' Eddie admitted of his predecessor, 'from the tips of his shoes to the way he combed his hair.' Eddie even ordered the same dishes as Todd at Chasen's. Burton's temper and male pride put Taylor in mind of Todd. 'I adore this man,' she'd murmured, when Burton poured her the sixth or seventh glass of wine, at their first social meeting in Rome. When he called her a 'cunt', she was excited. Their official legal separation and first divorce brought about another alignment. The director of *The Driver's Seat* remembers Taylor saying, 'I have had one sad day in my life and that was when Mike Todd was killed. I never thought I would have another. I was wrong. Today is the second sad day in my life. I am desolate.' Nevertheless, Burton had long since ceased being a rare man to her, a powerful stimulant. He was someone to whom she could say, 'Now, you shit-faced bastard, give me a drink.'

* * *

What lies beneath, in a relationship? How fragile is our hold. How rapidly deterioration sets in. Division coming out of unity; proximity turning into absence; confusion and silence: all this is there for us to watch in *Divorce His, Divorce Hers*, Taylor and Burton's final appearance together on the screen, filmed between September and November 1972 in Rome and Munich. Belittled by critics when shown the following February ('Miss Taylor looks good and Mr Burton sounds good. Leave it at that,' *New York Times*), it's actually an important analysis of how a marriage need not, as in *Who's Afraid of Virginia Woolf?*, be a fight to the death, but, rather, a fatal journey towards indifference, airlessness. People can gratify each other, then they can't. When, inwardly jaded, partners stop idealising each other, physical pleasure, which was once rounded, as it were, melting, becomes, instead, a mass of drives, an affair of sharp teeth and claws, bone and gristle. Men and women, certainly Burton and Taylor, show a great capacity for cruelty, and for suffering, becoming as animalistic as monkeys, squatting in the dirt, lapping from stagnant water.

Maybe we'd have had more of this had John Osborne continued to be involved, which he was from at least the end of August 1970, when Burton told his diary: 'John Heyman [has] commissioned John Osborne to write two plays – a sort of *Rashomon* for E. and I to do on T V for Harlech, which should get that lot off my back.' Burton sent Osborne a 'short delighted note. I hope it's some good.' He also jotted, 'Osborne starts work on Monday.' By my calculation, that would have been Monday 31 August 1970. As for Harlech Television, this was named not after the Welsh town and castle but for David Ormsby-Gore, the fifth Baron Harlech, who'd led the consortium hoping to run the new regional channel, which began broadcasting in May 1968, following a franchise review the previous year. Colour came in on 6 April 1970, a big event in my own home in Bedwas, Monmouthshire, except we had to instal extra aerials to pick up English-speaking programmes from the Mendip mast in Somerset, as otherwise all that was on locally from the Wenvoe mast in Glamorganshire was *Pobol y Cwm*. The Welsh signals managed to reach as far as Victoria Wood, then a drama student in Birmingham, who called it *Pobol y Quim*. As Kingsley Amis has an indignant character say in *The Old Devils*, 'Do you know they have wrestling in Welsh now on that new channel? Same as in English oddly enough except the bugger counts *un-dau-tri* etcetera. Then the idiots can go round saying the viewing figures for Welsh language programmes have gone up. To four thousand and eleven.'

Burton attended a shareholder reception at The Dorchester in March 1969, where the host was Ormsby-Gore. 'I will doubtless see a great many other people. I shall loathe it all,' said the star. The main director-shareholders were Burton and Taylor, Stanley Baker, Sir Geraint Evans (I saw him sing Verdi's *Falstaff* in Cardiff), Harry Secombe (the tiresome Goon) and Wynford Vaughan-Thomas, who'd been taught English Literature in Swansea by Dylan Thomas' father. In other words, no greater group of professional Welshmen or stage Welshmen could throughout history have been gathered in one place – Wynford, along with another media Welshman of the period, John Morgan, were always smirking with blackened teeth and smoking in the background if newsreel cameras captured Burton arriving by train in Fishguard or if he was showing off a diamond. Another one was Emrys Walters from *Wales Today*, who in December 1962 forgot to ask Burton about Taylor, preferring to use up his interview slot solemnly wondering what Burton thought about the rugby match between the London Welsh and Aberavon, held at the Old Deer Park, Richmond, the previous Saturday. Burton boastfully said he'd played for both sides in his time, and had been 'fairly fast, fairly nippy'. This was preferable I suppose to John Morgan, who disrespectfully said Taylor was 'boring' until she'd had a few drinks, when 'she becomes very lively and flirtatious'. Perhaps it was more she found the company of all these distinguished citizens of the Principality something of a trial – and in any event, flirtatious or boring, she and Burton were the principal shareholders in HTV 'by a considerable amount'. In August 1969, Burton was telling his diary, 'We'd better do something, much as I'd rather sell and get out … They are quite hopeless.' Not that he and Taylor had bothered to attend directors' board meetings or make any contribution to policy.

More than a year after first learning of Osborne's involvement – and Burton's being pleased on that score – some sort of screenplay was in existence. On 21 October 1971, when he was in Rome shooting *The Assassination of Trotsky*, Burton writes in his diary: 'Have just started [reading] another piece – the long-promised play for TV of John Osborne's called *Separation*. Actually it's two parts, one called 'His' and the other 'Hers'. I gather it's about a marriage break-up, one play of an hour from her point of view and the other from his. We must do something for Harlech especially as it's made us some money, though that's incidental, and see if we can help keep the franchise or consortium or whatever they call it.'

569

Patriotism was coming into it, and cupidity. Taylor and Burton had bought £100,000 worth of shares when they were priced at two shillings and sixpence (twelve and a half new pence) each. They opened on the stock market at a pound. 'Fairy tale stuff,' said Burton of his windfall. Taylor said their HTV shares would benefit the National Society for Mentally Handicapped Children, Mencap as it became later, but nothing was received by them, which was true to form. She promised to endow a $1 million research foundation for cardiovascular disorders, in memory of Montgomery Clift. The American Heart Association heard nothing further. After the 'Carry On Up the Jungle' episode of their second marriage, Taylor promised she and Burton would pay for a hospital in Kasane, Botswana. The Ministry of Health in Gaborone confirmed in 1977, two years after the wedding ceremony, that financial assistance had 'not yet been forthcoming ... Miss Taylor had changed her mind'. If there's no point in an anonymous donation – and one of Taylor's (unnamed) friends told Kitty Kelley, 'I'm afraid there's not much anonymous giving on Elizabeth's part ... She definitely wants credit for her generosity. It helps soften her public image' – how much better to allow the press to learn of a splashy bit of munificence, and then quietly cancel it. After Todd's demise and as a tax dodge, Taylor presented the Los Angeles County Art Museum with her Renoirs, Pissarros and Van Goghs, and a year later, 'she took them all back', the gallery's records, seen by Brenda Maddox, indicated. She'd been concealing assets from probate assessments. Around about this time, December 1959, as Christopher Isherwood indicated in his diary, a furrier visited Taylor at her and Eddie's bungalow at the Beverly Hills Hotel, 'coming in with a coat of Russian sable [worth] $11,000'. Taylor wanted to defer payment for two years, shocking the furrier rather. Then she had a better idea. 'She may rent it to the studio for her new picture, BUtterfield 8, and get it that way' – another fiscal dodge, where she'd get what she wanted for nothing, plus claim for the deduction of an allowable business expense. She was good at this.

Decades after the release of *Under Milk Wood,* Andrew Sinclair found out from the brother-in-law of his producer, Jules Buck, why the film had never made any money: 'It wasn't distributed properly because Burton and Taylor and O'Toole each had a million dollars written off their taxes for making it. The film had to make a maximum loss.' In on the plot were Buck, Hugh French, John Terry and David Higham (all now deceased, as is Sinclair) – fraudulent contracts, forged signatures. 'The most extraordinary deals for under-the-table money had been done.'

Burton was not averse to stringing people along. As part of his Oxford fantasy, he promised to build the university an arts centre, informing Nevill Coghill how he would be able additionally to rope in 'the Gettys and Onassises of this world', who'd 'write us a splendid little cheque'. Coghill was thrilled: 'It is a dream of a lifetime made real.' But it remained a dream and was never real. Coghill was fobbed off into having to contact Aaron Frosch – and further appeals to Burton personally (Coghill's smile was starting to get rather frozen) were ignored ('Do you think Aaron could be authorised by you to let us have the payments?'). The existing Oxford Playhouse was not replaced, though I think a rehearsal room bore Burton's name, or maybe a stationery cupboard. Burton didn't get his Honorary Doctorate, either. 'This is a great blow which I know you will feel as sharply as I do,' Coghill said to Frosch, who no doubt couldn't give a fuck. People who might have given a fuck on a sort of related topic would have been the goblins, who were told by Valerie Douglas, Burton's business manager, and a Frosch associate, the night before Burton's funeral: 'Don't forget, I want to talk to you guys tomorrow. I have some news for you.' The news was that though, over the years, Burton had generously bought houses for Cissie and Elfed, for Hilda and for Ivor and Gwen, and Tom was given a bungalow – and everyone received cars – Burton had not transferred actual title. Everyone had a lifetime interest, of course they did, but ultimate ownership remained with Bushel Productions Limited, Burton's offshore company, or one of them, based in Bermuda. Awkwardness over this is why Douglas did not want any of the Jenkinses travelling to Céligny for the burial – she didn't want to face them. She also vetoed the idea of Burton's being buried in Pontrhydyfen. 'I have already told you,' she said with unnecessary sternness to Graham, 'the funeral has to be in Switzerland. For tax reasons.'

Anyway, 'We do own so much of Harlech Television that we thought we should really do some work for them,' Burton told reporters at the end of 1971 – though in his diary entry for 7 December he was apprehensive: 'The TV films of Osborne's seem to be very confused. Nobody seems to know what is going on.' At least the project allowed him to evade having to do something for Lew Grade, which would have involved donating his fee to Princess Margaret's charity, the St John Ambulance Brigade. As he told Ma'am Darling in a phone call, 'we had two far better ones [scripts] by John Osborne (I hope we have) . . . We had already contracted to do the two Osborne plays for Harlech TV . . .' Harlech is twenty-five miles from Snowdon, as a matter of interest. But it is unsavoury, unedifying, seeing Burton wriggle, pretending to commit himself, withdrawing, advancing, being vague, mentioning big sums only for them to vanish. And Osborne vanished, too. The screen credit for *Divorce His, Divorce Hers* goes to John Hopkins, who was drowned in his swimming pool in July 1998, aged sixty-seven, and was best known for writing fifty-two episodes of *Z Cars*. He was also to be responsible for *Smiley's People*, with Alec Guinness as the enigmatic spy. Hopkins contributed to things like Play for Today, Armchair Theatre, The Wednesday Play, and so forth. *Talking to a Stranger* (1966) was Hopkins' – four plays looking at four different interpretations of what happened over one weekend – and structurally that's similar to Burton and Taylor's film.

Yet in my view, Osborne's fingerprints remain all over it – and in his papers kept in the Harry Ransom Center, part of the University of Texas at Austin, the draft, contained in three notebooks, was entitled *Separations*, plural, not *Separation*, singular. Osborne certainly had experience in this area, having undergone many flurried marriages: Pamela Lane, Mary Ure, Penelope Gilliatt, Jill Bennett, Helen Dawson. You'd not want to have been in the vicinity of any of them – evidently Osborne didn't much enjoy being with anyone at close quarters for long, except Anthony Creighton when they were on a houseboat. It is my contention Mary Ure was on his mind in *Separations* – born in 1933, so a year younger than Taylor; 'a tough little girl from Glasgow', in Tony Richardson's estimation. She spent three years at the ironing board as Alison Porter on stage in *Look Back in Anger*, before co-starring with Burton in the film and having to say to the camera how Jimmy Porter's was 'the old story of the knight in shining armour, except that his armour didn't really shine very much.' Ure had been in the West End with Paul Scofield in *Time Remembered*, the Anouilh play Burton did at the Morosco with Susan Strasberg. She was Paul Robeson's Desdemona, Charles Laughton's Bottom's Titania . . . So, an *actress*.

Osborne married her at the Chelsea Registry Office in 1957 (Tony Richardson the Best Man), and they lived in a house in Woodfall Street, Chelsea, bought by her father, which burned down during one of their arguments. The fire brigade rescued them from the roof. Osborne treated her cruelly – 'squalid . . . I was ignoble,' he admits in his notebooks. 'He flayed her, just like Jimmy Porter,' said Doris Lessing, who saw them in a restaurant. When Osborne and Ure dined at Emlyn Williams' house in Pelham Crescent, did they try and behave themselves? Ructions aren't recorded, though the other guests were Burton and Sybil, and everyone was amused that the pretentious and stuffy Emlyn had hired a butler for the night. Osborne immediately had an open affair with Jocelyn Rickards. Ure went in for heavy drinking, mood swings, blackouts, which her doctor coyly attributed to 'salt deficiency'. A lot of Spode crockery was flung about. She tried to drown herself in Tony Richardson's Californian pool and was rescued by Joan Plowright. 'She luxuriates in scenes,' wrote

Christopher Isherwood, who'd observed some of the hysterical sob-
bing. Isherwood also thought Ure's relationship with Osborne
'undoubtedly masochistic . . . He doesn't take the trouble to be nice
to her, but I suppose she likes it.'

Did she? Would anyone? Ah, men and women – and it's true Ure
went through it all again with Robert Shaw, with whom she had been
having a concurrent liaison since 1959, and by whom she became
pregnant – Colin was born in August 1961. Peter Brook, who'd
directed Ure as Ophelia, in the Scofield *Hamlet,* said she was perfect
in the role because perfectly mad: 'She was beautiful, pure and rud-
derless. The seeds were already there in her performance' – the seeds
of her destruction. Ure and Osborne were divorced on 15 March 1963,
and she married Shaw, who formally adopted Colin. Ure died in 1975
from 'the effect of alcohol and barbiturates resulting in vomiting and
asphyxiation'.

* * *

It all sounds like a condensed version of Taylor and Burton in many
respects, and it was all going on at the same moment *Cleopatra* was
going on. Adultery, betrayal, suicide attempts, drinking, hospitals;
people thinking bad behaviour made them more interesting; the
curtain never coming down . . . On the day the house caught fire in
Woodfall Street, Rouben Mamoulian was sacked, Eddie injected
Taylor with Demerol, and Mankiewicz was paid $3 million by Fox
for the production company he co-owned with NBC. But as big
as Osborne and Ure – and Osborne and his other wives, e.g. Jill
Bennett – were on the British cultural map, Burton and Taylor were
bigger, much bigger. They stood alone. They still do. In *Divorce His,
Divorce Hers,* made not in the HTV Studios in Bristol as intended,
but in Germany and Italy, because Taylor's quota of tax-free days in
the United Kingdom had run out – 'We've got to be out of this country the minute I've finished this film [*Night Watch*], otherwise we're

into tax for two million pounds,' the actress decreed from her dressing room in Elstree; in this, their final collaboration, Burton is the beast in the jungle, a leonine businessman named Martin Reynolds, who has something to do with a mine in Africa. I can watch it often entirely for Burton and Taylor being themselves: the arguments and making up, the love which is hate, the passion, which meant once disagreements and opposition arrived, as in real life they do, the stars were instantly open to – and at risk of – fear, hostility, disappointment and, especially, resentment. They felt wounded, affronted. There was a loss of confidence: 'We had something special,' says Taylor's character, Jane Reynolds. 'We had something more than most.' Did they? Taylor and Burton in themselves, I mean. It seems to me, in these last days of winter, as I set down my impressions and reach towards the end of making my notes, that what they, or she, liked best were shiny objects, the 'intense transparency' (Proust) of precious stones, stimulating food and drink – the main problem with the Soviet Union, during *The Blue Bird*, was you couldn't 'order a Jack Daniel's . . . You couldn't even afford the vodka.'

Initially, Taylor enjoyed Burton's drunken self-lacerating moods; but he was always going to be guilty of cruelty and egotism. His love, her love, could never be fresh and pure. Like the people in Tolstoy's *The Kreutzer Sonata*, they had nothing in common after 1962 except the way they used each other to obtain 'the maximum amount of pleasure' – hence the frequent and increasing expressions of hostility, the round of quarrels on flimsy pretexts ('I tell her, "You're not Jewish at all." She turns white with rage') and the patching up. Plenty of directors and cast members witnessed the volatility. Joseph Losey said that on Sardinia they were 'unimaginably awful', arriving on the set of *Boom!* 'screaming, drunk and abusive'. They'd say they wanted each other dead, allege physical assaults – this mixture of violence and the sexual charge: 'Terrible fights we have,' said Taylor. 'Once we're cuddled up in bed it will all be forgotten.' Such a picture is unconvincing, and Burton's version positively unnerving: 'It is quite impossible to take an argument seriously with Elizabeth naked, flailing around in front of you. She throws her figure around so vigorously she positively bruises herself.' There's an image to set back a boy's puberty by several years, reminding me of Marlene Dietrich's condemnation: 'She's just a tart with breasts and very little talent,' an assessment which is only half right, if that. I think the best or most perceptive observation, effacing the falseness, was made by Keith Baxter, during *Ash Wednesday*, which was made immediately after *Divorce His, Divorce Hers*: 'Taylor was determinedly cheerful ... but it was obvious to everyone she was fighting like a tigress to save her marriage. When Richard's unhappiness made him cruel, sometimes very cruel, she ignored it ... She loved him unreservedly, and any future without him appeared to her an abyss.' Meanwhile, when a man like Burton 'is possessed of a fierce masculine pride while his wife is being courted and pampered, that temper is liable to explode, and Richard's fuse was short.'

The hysteria and unhappiness are apparent – more than apparent – in *Divorce His, Divorce Hers*. Osborne said he was thrown off the project because Taylor and Burton wanted the story to unfold in places where they could reside aboard the *Kalizma*. 'The most important aspect of the script,' he told Paul Ferris, 'seemed to be that most of the locations should be in either Mexico, Acapulco or the South of France, where the Burtons' yacht was conveniently moored. I ignored this instruction and followed the presumable premise of the two titles. When I presented the script of the Richard version, a kind of resentful hysteria seemed to break out, which seemed to imply that I had not followed my brief.' I can't see how John Hopkins made any material alterations – Munich is 348 miles from the sea, and Rome is not the Bahía de Santa Lucia nor the Côte d'Azur. Osborne's original conception holds – we could almost still be in Bristol – and what has happened, given the actor and the actress involved, is that modern Rome, or the Rome of the early Seventies, is superimposed upon Ancient Rome, which is to say the

Cinecittà Rome of the early Sixties. For Burton and Taylor: no more haunted a place.

Antony and Cleopatra are coming apart. They look smart, however, swanky. I like the look of Rome in the Seventies, the hotel foyers of goldish glass and fuchsia upholstery, the clothes – nicely cut jackets and gowns, Taylor in strange lilac creations, emphasising her dumpy shape. ('Get me Edith Head in California,' Taylor told Waris Hussein, the director. 'She's so good with shoes.') She wears a primrose minidress, gigantic ivory earrings, coats that are far too short, and hats with veils. Breathless and throaty, like Vivien Leigh's, her accent seems to hark back to the Forties – had someone told her to take elocution lessons? In 'the Richard version', the idea is he's the tycoon, never parted from his crocodile-skin briefcase. Domesticity is something he hasn't much time for – Martin Reynolds is a man of deals, contracts, business meetings, important phone calls. Barry Foster, his previous film Hitchcock's *Frenzy*, where he's the serial killer, is Burton's secretarial assistant, looking after the luggage, laughing at the boss' pleasantries, opening doors. This is all Burton's character requires by way of human company – and Taylor's Jane Reynolds feels very left out. Martin is particularly bored by his children. When he is obliged to take them out for an afternoon, he wants the nanny to tag along. 'Will I see you tomorrow?' asks his daughter. 'Of course, as long as I'm here.' He's not going to be there, or anywhere in the vicinity. He intends being far away in Africa for at least several years – 'I must do it,' says Burton in his devil's voice. It's as if he needs this excuse to keep away from family life, from the muddle of domestic demands – he's always looking at his watch when the children are around, scarcely able to control irritation: 'How long [will you be away]?' – 'Well, I don't know.' Christmas is hell ('There was so much anger,' reports the nanny) and it's then that he strikes his wife – which she thinks means at least she's been noticed. Taylor cowers, is subservient. It's poignantly done, the characters trying to reach out to one another, but somehow stopping short, flaring up – and is this how Burton was with Sybil, when she came to be replaced; when money and fame mattered more than affection; when power and the importance of masculine power held sway? Burton used to talk a lot about his Faustian-sized decisions. And how many of us are forced to choose in those decisive ways? How many of us have really engaged with choice? We dress suitably and convention-ally, behave ourselves, smile politely and appropriately. We put others first – we go about life never making a fuss. In Burton's terms, this all adds up to passivity. It's what he rejected. In *Divorce His, Divorce Hers*, it is pitiful, the way Taylor's character tries to interest and keep him, and he is indifferent. 'What do you want to, err, do?' she asks finally, terrified of the answer – which will broach the reality of sepa-ration. Burton is the lone male with nothing to give his family, except alimony: 'We have a right to expect more from you,' Taylor says finally.

In what we might call the 'Elizabeth version', the sadomasochism is intensified – if love and desire are pretences, the punches and beating are authentic, as is the loneliness: 'Have you seen Daddy?' – 'No.' The Taylor character pleads for 'a few bruises, some broken bones', as if perverted outbursts are preferable to apathy. Taylor is more vampish, now the story is seen from her point of view. She chooses an orange colour scheme and strides more confidently amongst her 1972 furnishings – furry swivel chairs, a large lamp on a curved stand, cer-amic parrots. (The interiors were shot at the Bavaria Filmstadt, Geiselgasteig, south of Munich.) This time Jane Reynolds has even taken a paramour, to provoke her husband. 'You shouldn't have left me alone in Rome,' she tells her husband. 'Who is it?' he wants to know. 'Someone I know?' – 'Of course. Do you think I'd go off with a stranger?' The wife in *Divorce His* would never have spoken up like that in *Divorce Hers*. Unfortunately, or comically, Burton's rival is played by Ronald Rudd, dead at forty-seven, though he looked eighty-seven, who resembled rubicund Sir Billy Butlin, and who never rose much above doing an episode of *Softly, Softly* and *The Saint*. He's also dubbed with an imperfectly synchronised growly voice. Burton's character, nevertheless, still finds business meetings his preferred sphere – the negotiator fluent with a balance sheet, out of his element when confronted with emotion. Only in nocturnal telephone calls is there intimacy – Burton and Taylor, or the people they are playing, get on better than when they are actually together, and Taylor can get away with a line like: 'I am permanently adrift. I see no end.' That's no worse than what Chekhov's characters utter, when the temperature falls in the samovar. It's not a sentimental, happy (or resolved) ending, either, by any means, when Burton says, 'We should be together,' and Taylor says, 'I always thought we would be. Then one day we weren't.' What the telly plays have shown, with sympathy in my opinion, is the essential insecurity of this great vaunted love of theirs, as if they were waiting for it to be over, searching, probing, for cracks: 'Once I let you out of my sight, you might never come back.'

* * *

Burton and Taylor had wanted Brian Hutton to direct 'the Osborne plays' as Burton always called *Divorce His, Divorce Hers* in his diary. Hutton had been in charge of *Where Eagles Dare* and *X, Y & Zee*, also *Night Watch*, so perhaps had had quite enough, thank you very much. He's on record as saying Burton 'was pissed three-quarters of the time' throughout the making of the former, and as for the latter pair of pictures, here's what he babbled: 'When I finished the second Elizabeth Taylor picture I thought, well, what am I wasting my life doing this for? I mean, a gorilla could have made those movies. All I had to do was yell "Action" and "Cut. Print", because everybody was doing what they had to do anyway.' If you say so, Brian. He started a new career as an estate agent and died in 2014. His name is seldom mentioned in the same breath as Pier Paolo Pasolini. Also, gorillas are perfectly capable of sign language, can clamber up the Empire State Building and seduce Fay Wray – everything Taylor looked for in a man. Anyway, Waris Hussein was given the assignment – he'd recently made *Henry VIII and His Six Wives* with Keith Michell, and went on to direct *Edward and Mrs Simpson*, with Edward Fox as David, Duke of Windsor, a performance Burton admired. Hussein's metier, therefore, could be seen to have been problematic, slippery relationships, men and women and the madness of sex. His own relationship with Burton and Taylor was definitely slippery and problematic. 'They had a dysfunctional relationship and I was in the middle of it,' he said in 2013, and Waris had begun his career working with rubber monsters in *Doctor Who*.

It wasn't only the way the stars had reacquainted themselves with the sybaritic habits surrounding *The Taming of the Shrew* (long luncheons served by white-gloved waiters – Victor Spinetti even visited, for a session of 'hysterical nonsense') or the pathological unpunctuality (Taylor was two hours late for her only exterior scene in Rome: 'She flicked her scarf on Take Two. Which is all we got. She flicked her scarf, walked up to the camera, kissed the lens, got into her car and left') that upset Hussein, which turned *Divorce His, Divorce Hers* into 'the worst experience' of his professional life; nor even the unprofessionalism – exactly as during *The Spy Who Came in from the Cold*, Taylor came unannounced to watch Burton at work and was a thorough disruption, like the circus was in town: 'Suddenly there was uproar in the distance, hooting horns, a glare of lights.' Taylor emerged in her mink from a black limousine. 'Don't worry about me, Waris. I'll just stand in the corner and watch' – as if Taylor could ever achieve, or wanted to achieve, a state of camouflage. An alarmed and embarrassed Burton disappeared into a bar and got dead drunk, emerging 'with a magnificent display of temper' (according to Carrie Nye) to deliver a line worthy of a Shakespearean king – or perhaps Donald Wolfit playing a Shakespearean king in *The Dresser*: 'I am old and grey and incredibly gifted.' Actually, somewhere in his brain, Burton was misremembering Yeats' 'When you are old and grey and full of sleep / . . . Murmur, a little sadly, how Love fled / . . . And hid his face amid a crowd of stars' – and, it has to be said, when the camera closes in on Burton's wonderful face, the exotic, dark Welsh look does have a sort of Red Indian stillness, suggesting unfathomable distance, disquieting strength.

So – Hussein put up with all of this. He put up with Burton's saying, 'Fuck off! I am Lear! I could play Lear!' and 'I could have been King Lear! I could've played Lear!' Perhaps by now in his mind that's exactly who Burton thought he was, the deposed monarch, making his way through storms. But what was beyond his, anyone's, ability to resolve was the fact, as Hussein said, 'a lot of what happened was due to [Burton and Taylor's] own personal unhappiness. It was a bad time for all concerned . . . The scripts echoed their lives, the chaos of their lives.' Like *The Mousetrap* running forever and cast with different actors, *Divorce His, Divorce Hers* could tour the provinces with Peter and Britt, the Snowdons, Rex and Rachel, Ted and Sylvia, Osborne and Ure. In a lot of their films, Burton and Taylor are arguing, as if poking each other with tridents. In *Divorce His, Divorce Hers*, Burton keeps walking out, Taylor can't decide whether or not to pursue him – Cleopatra criss-crossing the Aegean, Katherina on her donkey falling in puddles. Or in other films, on other days, Burton is the hunter, Taylor the one being elusive, for whom capitulation (including caring for children or accepting responsibilities) meant weakness. They could both be very cold, using charm to simulate warmth. You wonder if what they are both avoiding is faithfulness, finding themselves tied down. 'Long may we live to love and torture each other until death do us part . . . and even then,' Burton said in his toast to Taylor at her Fiftieth Birthday Party, held at Legends disco, Old Burlington Street, when she was in town to rehearse the transfer from Broadway to the Victoria Palace of *The Little Foxes*, which opened on 11 March 1982. They'd not had anything to do with each other for five years, apart from daily phone calls. 'I bred her in my bones,' Burton said – but his bones were not well. He had all the alcohol-related illnesses, gout, epilepsy, arthritis, bursitis – bursitis being a stiffness and inflammation in the spine and neck, the booze causing crystals to form in the joints. Burton often said it was sciatica or pinched nerves, but it was the booze and the tobacco: overstimulation generally. There were rumours, surrounding that Legends do, on 27 February, that Burton came to the house Taylor was renting, 22 Cheyne Walk, and committed intimacy – rumours Taylor laughed off: 'He was too drunk to find his way down the street, let alone into my bedroom.' Nevertheless, they agreed to appear in *Private Lives* the following year, when Taylor gave up on Coward and threw food into the audience. Burton, by then, had given up on everything. 'Elizabeth can't look after me. I need Sally. She takes care of an old man.' Lynne Frederick served the same function for Peter Sellers, lining up pill bottles. When Burton died, Taylor 'was completely out of control,' said Victor Luna, who'd only recently given her a Cartier ring worth $300,000. 'I realised then how deeply she was tied to this man, how vital a role he had played in her life.' Sally's reaction was to bar Taylor from the funeral. 'Can't you get it straight,' she flung at Brother Graham. 'I don't want Elizabeth here.' – 'You have no right to make demands of the family or of Elizabeth,' Brother Graham flung right back. Sally had spent a grand total of twenty-six months with Burton, which adds up to less than Anne Boleyn's thousand days.

At the Memorial Service at St Martin-in-the-Fields, Taylor sat next to Cis. The customary widow's seat in the front pew was occupied by Brook, who wanted to protect Sally from buffetings in the aisle. Sybil was not there, or anywhere. 'It was all too long ago,' agreed the Jenkins family. Twenty years. I've been writing this book for more than half that time. And the conclusion reached, about art, about life; the public and private lives; the acting and the reality – is that there is a kind of unity within the circle of Burton's existence, and Taylor's. It was all a continuous enterprise. There have been biographies and chronologies – and the more thorough they are, the less satisfactory, in my estimation. What I've attempted here, instead, is what Roland Barthes, in his book on Michelet, author of the nineteen-volume *Histoire de France*, called that operation to discover, if possible, 'an organised network of obsessions,' a campaign to find 'the tissues, the humours,' in the medieval meaning of that word. And if I have myself been obsessed – the feverishness of my own illness, when I was in hospital in immense distress, and the room seemed to lose its shape, tilting and sloping, inspiring me to investigate the at once hot and cold nature of Burton and Taylor's life and work, then what's happened is I have finally reached the extreme point where sickness and health, life and death, the real and the imagined (or the dreamt), the past and the future, high and low, goodness and badness, as André Breton has it in the *Surrealist Manifesto*, 'cease to be perceived as contradictions'.

Epilogue

There were always wild crowds in South Wales – 'busloads coming in to see them,' according to Hilda Jenkins, who'd be out on the door-step in Pontrhydyfen, ready to greet Richard Burton and Elizabeth Taylor with their personal Him and Hers piss-pots, there being no upstairs sandbox in Penhydd Street. What Kenneth Williams chiefly recalled about Swansea, when he understudied Burton in Chekhov, were the outside water-closets, which were 'cold and draughty for passing motions'.

Michael Sheen, who grew up in Port Talbot, remembers there were framed photographs of Burton and Taylor 'in every pub in the area'. Sheen must have started drinking early, as these 'iconic images' were 'imprinted onto my psyche from the moment I became conscious'. Did I myself ever glimpse or pass the stars on a rainy evening in the street, over half a century ago? On one of their visits, in between the fancy-dress balls, parties, racing through airports and auctioning dia-monds, Taylor and Burton would have been welcome – more than welcome – to come and see my puppet theatre, in the attic above the butcher's shop and the slaughterhouse, in Bedwas, Monmouth-shire. As I painted my backdrops of a fairy-tale forest, I seemed to know, even as a child – particularly as a child – that the point of enter-tainment, and certainly of cinema, was that it was about what real life was *not* like, a fantasy 'we think is out there but can't see,' as Warhol put it.

Taylor's origins were in the magazines and movies of the Forties, the era of Bing and Bob, Big Bands, such as Glenn Miller, Bogie, Rita

Hayworth, Mickey Rooney, Warner Bros cartoons, Bugs Bunny, Tom and Jerry, Disney. There was something old-fashioned about her glamour – ice-blue lipstick and shoes matching the headboard and the curtains: she belonged more with Doris Day and John Wayne, rather than Peter Fonda or Mick Jagger and Sixties drug madness. Even when Taylor became a Sixties icon, thanks to Warhol, the screen-prints were based on a vintage MGM publicity still, to which the painter added turquoise eye-shadow, a blood-red mouth, like the Batman Joker's, and yellow, green and mauve backgrounds. Everything is so flat, the image is not in two dimensions, it is barely one dimension: Taylor has been skimmed, reduced to a camera's shutter-speed; all she requires from us is a flash of recognition. And she was always recognised. Warhol owned a house in Montauk, Long Island, which 'I rent ... to friends every summer and wait to be invited.' Taylor went for a weekend with her hairdresser and Firooz Zahedi, cousin of the Iranian ambassador and staff photographer for Warhol's *Interview Magazine*. Though a private, unannounced visit, 'All the cooks, waiters and maids from the Montauk Yacht Club were waiting on the dock to have their pictures taken with Elizabeth.' Similarly, when making *The Blue Bird*, Robert Morley said to her, 'No one will know you in Leningrad,' and persuaded her to put a scarf over her head and stroll the streets. Within minutes, the Russians were climbing over their chairs to get a better view. 'Miss Taylor,' said Morley, 'was rather paranoid at this point.'

With Burton, if his hair had a light red shimmer, it's because he was always the devil – *Ma' lwc y diafol arnat ti*: touched by the Devil's luck – and so much was signified by his rich and smoky voice; the smoke streaming from both his nostrils; the way he snatched a single cigarette from the pack – long Marlboro Lights ('Looks like these lethal goddamn things will be with me to the end of my days,' he told Dick Cavett); the click or rasp and a speck of flame appeared, shaded by his hand. Was Burton aware the smoke made him harder to see, his ice-green eyes harder to see, and that everything about him, hot and glaring, swirling in the light, indicated damnation, corrosion? Maybe being an actor in the first place is a kind of primal sin: Burton was going to permit himself to be transformed into other, more interesting people – colourful roles, acclaim, position. Any exertion, any deal made or bargain struck, is going to be an example of ambition, pride, which got Burton away from Wales and its blackened moss, which made Burton Burton, with Philip as his Mephistopheles. As he said to Barbara Pallenberg, when making *The Heretic*, which was about demonic possession: 'I certainly wouldn't begin to try to describe what acting is, what I do . . . I've done it all my life.'

He did return to Wales professionally the once, for *Under Milk Wood*, in January 1971. Lower Fishguard, the location, does look idyllic, the green promontory and eighteenth-century houses (one of them inhabited by Wynford Vaughan-Thomas), the groves, birdsong, copper-coloured streams and rounded hills. What a sexy story it is, too – Dylan Thomas' fascination with breasts and bottoms, silk stockings, feather-beds; the constant references to rosy-red glistenings, milkiness, butteriness, drifting, slobbering, lapping, lolling, and 'being up to no good in the wash-house'. It's a kitsch Wales, no doubt, but preferable to valleys' gloom, chapel dourness. What Burton could respond to was the eroticism of the sea and the foam and the waves; the bobbing boats, cockle women, cows and dogs and herring gulls. Susan Penhaligon is in the gorse with her goats, drawing on her tits with lipstick. Angharad Rees is Gossamer Beynon, Ann Beach is Polly Garter. Though Burton speaks the narration, he doesn't speak on camera. He rolls around in a shed with Pat Kavanagh, whilst Ryan Davies holds their coats. He wanders through the Pembrokeshire woodland, fumblingly making the sign of the cross, fag in hand. He looks intensely sad, like a ghost, and in fact Burton often had this quality of solitude, detachment: 'You don't want to get too involved with people,' he'd told Emlyn Williams.

When had he worked out that this was a policy he'd be best suited to? When his mother died? When he left Cis and Elfed's house and had to live with Philip? When he left Pontrhydyfen for Port Talbot and Port Talbot for the wider world? (And from the wider world into tax exile? It was one of his delusions Céligny was exactly like South Wales – and his family went along with this: 'My impression of Céligny when I first came here,' said his sister Catherine, or Cassie, 'was that it was the next place to Wales. Delightful. I thought it was so similar.') But Switzerland! Mexico! Haiti! Burton never had another proper home – life with Taylor was itinerant – and even Philip's rooms were rented. This stranded, homeless quality is there in his performances, in his demeanour. By which I mean, the conflicts in Burton's upbringing, his sense of angry inferiority, his uneasiness, are what, all his adult life, he dramatised in his work. Burton was the loneliest of actors – the king in his court, or Dysart in his consulting room; the officer with his men ('The truth is, it's a suicide mission' – the plot of *Raid on Rommel* in a nutshell); the soldier charging into an Austrian castle, machine gun blazing; the bandaged Morlar in his hospital bed in *The Medusa Touch* ('The thing is, we are nearer The Dark Ages than we care to admit'): Burton was not a mixer. His detachment was literal: 'I really cannot bear to be touched and I very rarely allow myself to touch other people – physically touch them, I mean.' For such an avowed libertine, he was never romantic. Burton was not good at giving (or receiving) a screen kiss. He can make the tone of his voice seductive – but not his body, which was stiff and unyielding. He cannot melt. (What he was good at was grappling, fucking.) Anyway, it was up to the camera to find him.

You never sense complete outward calm with Burton – fears and resentments are bubbling to the surface, as if he has emerged bristling from the animal kingdom. This is not how I think of Olivier, for example, whose upper-middle-class credentials are obvious; the bishops, colonial governors, prelates in the background – the ecclesiastical, establishment furniture. Or Gielgud's world of the Terrys and the Trees. Or for all his chimerical antics, for all that he was determinedly anonymous and featureless, even Peter Sellers had roots in music hall and Muswell Hill synagogues. But Burton – what can we do save make vague attributions of Welshness, describe him as a unique compound of hot coal and cinders, left over from a primeval Welsh forest? (The only comparable great figure is Ralph Richardson, whose ancestry was surely in another world entirely, with Merlin's mists and magic.) Burton also never tried to be anything other than an actor – he didn't return to Oxford; he was never trained in any other field. He held no professional qualifications. James Mason was an architect. Leonard Rossiter was a clerk in the claims and accident department of the Commercial Union Insurance Company. Roy Barraclough was a draughtsman and worked in an engineering factory for eight years. Avis Bunnage was a telephonist, as was Kathleen Ferrier. Ian Lavender 'thought about' being a policeman, Deryck Guyler trained for the Anglican priesthood (before playing Macduff on radio), and Hattie Jacques and Sid James were hairdressers. Arthur Lowe was a clerk in a bicycle spare-parts and accessories warehouse in Manchester. He later became a time-and-motion inspector at an aviation factory, which was constructing planes for the Fleet Air Arm, one of whose pilots was Laurence Olivier. Victoria Wood was a barmaid in Birmingham. Peter Cook expected to enter the Foreign Office. Wendy Richard 'harboured dreams' of a career as an archaeologist. And Burton? There was only the spell as a draper in Taibach. He may have loathed the job, but when Rigsby is trying to impress a prospective new tenant in *Rising Damp*, he says, 'It's a very, very fashionable area here, you know. We had the manager of the Co-op drapery staying here last year. He never complained.'

Was there an element of self-indulgence to Burton's solitude, i.e. he didn't mind it, didn't object to it? It's why he was a natural as military commanders or priests. Kenneth Williams, his understudy in *The Seagull*, met Burton again at Pinewood in May 1978. Williams was making *Carry On Emmannuelle*, Burton, whose 'enormous Rolls [was] outside', was filming *Absolution*, in which he's a Father Goddard. 'You're looking very fit,' Burton told the hypochondriac comedian.

'Keeping yourself very spare.' Burton went on to tell Williams how he'd been driven to drink by Hollywood, by the charity do's 'organised by stalwart matrons covered in rhinestones'. Williams thought Burton had 'a grave and urbane air now, like a man who is doing penance', which he was. When Burton died, six years later, Williams was aggrieved to recall all the hope and all the promise: in front of Burton, eternity's sunrise – and how sad it was now to remember Burton's swaggering assurance, when he'd told everyone, 'I shall go to Hollywood, but it won't corrupt *me*. Sybil and I come from these valleys, and that's where our values are.' And then came Taylor, to shock and excite him, whirl around in his head: Taylor, mad for pleasure, maddened by the banal, who to play Rosie Probert in *Under Milk Wood* had insisted on elaborate eye make-up. 'That won't do,' said Andrew Sinclair, understanding nothing. 'You're a Welsh sailor's whore . . . You can't look like that' – 'I *always* look like Cleopatra,' the star replied, dismissing him. Taylor had certainly created a Sixties look, a Pop Art look, echoed by Mary Quant and Paco Rabanne, which was feline, sphinx-like, static, black and blue, and set off by a geometrical haircut, like something found on a frieze, Ancient and Space Age simultaneously. 'I think Egyptian dress and make-up are very becoming to a woman,' Taylor said firmly, and did Burton fall into pitch darkness when she came along? In Italy for *Cleopatra*, he did what no one can ever do: fantasy and the fulfilment of one's wishes actually converged – and it could easily be argued the great disaster of Burton's life was his involvement with Taylor, which brought about the Faustian pact, the gaining of earthly riches and celebrity. Taylor was like one of those witches or water-spirits in a fairy tale, coming to enchant Burton: beauty, and its costs. There he was, or there he'd been, the ingrained theatrical actor, keeping himself still, immobile, controlled – and he was plunged into Taylor's world, another world than this one, which was quite opposed to The Old Vic formality, let alone standing in stark contrast to Edwardian Wales and its inhabitants. He never expected Sybil to reject him as she did, never to see or speak to him again – the pain of that; the pain of Jessica being as she was, a living symbol or embodiment of pandemonium. 'The father of my children will never be Elizabeth Taylor's fifth husband,' Sybil said, wide of the mark. 'I love Sybil, but in a different way,' Burton said, hurtfully and transgressively. 'My love for Elizabeth is more complete, more necessary.'

So – total turmoil; a mismatch of style and manners; this clashing, punch-drunk love of Taylor and Burton's; all the entangled workings of sex and power. So – furthermore – who would Burton have been if nothing had happened? If Taylor's bejewelled bosoms hadn't come wobbling towards him, what then? Had Burton behaved himself, not been a boozer, a carouser, a womaniser, an over-reacher; had he dedicated himself to the routines of the classical stage – he'd have been John Neville. Actually, Neville took his own dedication to crazy self-less extremes and disappeared, first, to the Nottingham Playhouse, then, for the remainder of his days, to Canada. 'I want to serve a community,' Neville had said in October 1963, when Burton was shooting *The Night of the Iguana*. 'In London I feel I'm just serving a business.' Neville founded and ran repertory theatres in Edmonton and Halifax, which was like going to the Dominions and doing altruistic community work on a ranch. He succeeded, where Burton at Oxford had failed, in building arts centres, where plays ran alongside orchestral concerts, jazz, poetry readings. He was to make few films, though *The Adventures of Baron Munchausen* is a rococo thrill, thanks to Terry Gilliam. Shunning anything commercial, it's as if Neville set himself in deliberate opposition to Burton, though at one time their careers ran in close parallel: Neville was Fortinbras to Burton's Hamlet, at the Assembly Hall in Edinburgh, in 1953; they were together in *King John*, *Coriolanus* (where Neville's character said of Burton's: 'I tell you, he does sit in gold, his eye red as t'would burn Rome') and *The Tempest*, for The Old Vic Company, between 1955 and 1956. Neville was Orsino when Burton was Toby Belch, the Chorus when Burton was Henry V. On 21 February 1956, they began their celebrated run, alternating Othello and Iago – an interesting experiment: 'I fetch my life and being from men of royal siege,' says the Moor, yet though each actor was good at appearing to be aristocratic – and a glance at Neville's characters is a long list of dukes, generals, knighted professors, judges and high commissioners – their beginnings were humble enough. Neville, Burton's senior by six months, was born in Willesden (in 1925) and raised in Neasden, his father something menial on the Council. And unlike Wales, you can't romanticise Willesden and Neasden. Both men were, nevertheless, children of the Twenties, with its post-war mass unemployment and hunger marches. Neville sang in the church choir at Stonebridge Park and, like Burton, was taken on trips to see plays at Stratford. He saw action off Normandy and Japan as a signalman in the Royal Navy, when Burton was in the Royal Air Force. Neville attended the Royal Academy of Dramatic Art, where one of the students in his year was Robert Shaw. He was taught to speak – and to value – Shakespearean verse by Robert Atkins, at the Regent's Park Open Air Theatre; this was Neville's equivalent of Burton's apprenticeship with Philip and Emlyn Williams – an apprenticeship with its roots in the Beerbohm-Tree and Henry Irving tradition, where acting is a product of mellifluousness.

When they appeared in the theatre together, newspaper headlines seemed to promise a boxing bout: 'The Willesden Wizard v. The Welsh Wonder' and 'Battling Burton v. Nipper Neville'. Though there were similarities – they'd been in Christopher Fry verse plays and the refined efforts of Jean Anouilh; Claire Bloom was Burton's Ophelia and Neville's Juliet; they worked with all the same people (Donald Pleasence, Alan Badel, Michael Hordern) – it's the differences which stand out. Neville had a courteous, lovely elegance, a fineness, which was never feminine. (He had the sweetness of Robert Donat.) He was an unobtrusive actor, with considerable poise, spryness. Though he didn't overdo the vocal music, Neville was nevertheless musical in his delivery, which held a note of elegy. Neville always struck me as a sort of stricken deer – his Bosie (opposite Robert Morley's Wilde) was nearly sympathetic; he was a non-eccentric Sherlock Holmes. He had a critical intelligence, and searching standards – with none of Burton's snarling wariness, Burton's intensity. Neville had a hawk face, Burton was crow-black, sloe-black. Burton did a lot of glaring. Neville was fair to Burton's foul – he could never match Burton's sensationalism, his independent mood, or cadence, of cosmic desolation; nor Burton's nerve.

Asked to reflect, in later life, about what he thought had occurred with his erstwhile stablemate, Neville's words were diplomatic: 'Burton followed the path into films and it's a very difficult path to kick once you've chosen it.' As Burton himself admitted in his diaries, 'Money is very important,' and Tony Richardson's comment on the subject was undiplomatically blunt, as well as sharp: 'Richard and Liz Burton,' he told Christopher Isherwood in August 1964, 'are completely corrupt; they think only of money.' This will be why Richardson, seeing himself as an avenging angel, exacted punishment during *Laughter in the Dark*, when Burton was sacked. For they'd made a success of *Look Back in Anger*, in the pre-Taylor era. John Osborne's figure of Jimmy Porter, though socially new, in Burton's incarnation was a character in Dickens, the chatterbox in his attic rooms – the laundry, the kitchen utensils, the gas fires. Jimmy is profane and infantile, and puritanical – obsessed with sexual purity and gentility and respectability. Similarly, George Jacob Holyoake, in *A Subject of Scandal and Concern*, the television play Richardson directed, was somewhat righteous, landing himself in prison for having announced in a public lecture in 1842: 'I am of no religion at all. I do not believe in such a thing as God. The people of this country are too poor to have any religion.' I wonder how this chimes with *Henry V*, when the king says of the enemy, before Agincourt, 'We are in God's hands, brother, not theirs.' Isherwood saw a performance at The Old Vic in February 1956 and commented, 'Burton spoke this exactly right, curtly, almost impatiently, without the slightest pathos ... I am amazed to find him so good.' Henry, Jimmy, Holyoake: they are fatalistic, providential, ironic. These were the precise qualities Sophia Loren found in Burton twenty years later, when she said he was 'like a grand Shakespearean king, broken upon the wheel of preordained tragedy.'

The discovery made by Burton and Burton's characters is that nothing much can be done about upheaval. Nature is stronger than the will – which I'd take to be the beautiful theme of *Under Milk Wood*. People squabble, gossip, get through the day; they dream about murder, ghosts, weddings, rebellion and delinquency. But mostly what happens is they sit doing nothing in the sun, no different from the cat on its sill. What matters is the appetite: eating and drinking, hence Thomas' references to food, meat, sweets, lollipops, fish; and tumbling into bed: 'You can tell it's Spring.' By the way, Burton was taken with Pat Kavanagh, who before she became an over-revered literary agent wanted to be an actress. Burton invited her to Puerto Vallarta, but no doubt she had a more important date to keep with little Jeanette Winterson. In his own diaries, however, Burton seldom smells April and May. Somewhat portentously, only a sulphurous pit beckons. The Day of Judgement, he wrote in August 1980, when he'd been reading Kafka, and also watching *The New Avengers*, though it's Kafka which tipped him off, 'is a summary court in perpetual session', a statement he took to mean that the supreme and severest judge searching and scrutinising the soul is oneself: 'I am the prosecutor and defender, Satan and Saint ... I am totally responsible for all my sins and goodnesses. And I am alone.' Alone with the horror and emptiness of life? Except Burton took some delight in the infernal, did he not? In his bearing and manner, he was a man who lies in ruins, like an ancient civilisation lies in ruins. So – once again – what of Taylor, who at the end of *Under Milk Wood* is laid out as a corpse, with coins on her eyes? (The nearest she got to Fishguard was her 'luxury trailer' at Pinewood.) I can see the two of them were erotic gluttons. I can see theirs was a satiated love. I can see Taylor was reduced to being a sexual being ('I was unquestionably seduced,' Burton once said, after seeing her in a negligee. 'After all these years the girl can still blush'); but why should this be any kind of reduction?

I know Burton's own stabs at prose-poetry were third-rate Dylan Thomas ('Your breasts jutting out from that half-asleep languid lingering body', etc. – so her breasts were wide-awake?); and other people's estimates were meaninglessly hyperbolic (Taylor was 'the world's greatest movie star' according to Warhol) or meaningfully spiteful. Here's Orson Welles, in a story told by Henry Jaglom. In 1983, Welles was scoffing away at Ma Maison, the restaurant located at 8368 Melrose Avenue, in West Hollywood, when Burton made his approach: 'Orson, how good to see you. It's been too long. You're looking fine. Elizabeth is with me. She so much wants to meet you. Can I bring her over to your table?' The polite overture does not go down too well. 'No,' snapped Welles. 'As you can see, I'm in the middle of my lunch. I'll stop by on my way out.' Jaglom attempted to be conciliatory: 'Orson, that was so rude. He actually backed away, like a whipped puppy.' Explaining himself, Welles said, 'Don't kick me under the table ... Richard Burton had great talent. He's ruined his great gifts. He's become a joke with a celebrity wife. Now he just works for money, does the worst shit. And I wasn't rude. To quote Carl Laemmle, I gave him an evasive answer. I told him, "Go fuck yourself."'

That Welles deserved an ice bucket tipped over his big head is not to be denied – and anyway how much of this is apocryphal? Taylor didn't need to 'meet' the great man, as if this was going to be the first time and an introduction was required. She'd actually known Welles since *Jane Eyre*, made in the spring of 1943, when he'd said of her, 'she had a neck like a swan'. Taylor and Welles had jointly narrated *Genocide*, a documentary about the Holocaust, produced by the Simon Wiesenthal Center, which won an Oscar in 1981. Welles also co-starred with Taylor and Burton in *The V.I.P.s*, and he provided the voice of Winston Churchill for *The Battle of Sutjeska*. Burton and Welles: they were well-read, eloquent men, with golden speaking voices.

What, in any case, was Burton doing in Los Angeles in 1983? During the final full year of his life, he was in Haiti getting divorced (from Susan) or in Las Vegas getting married (to Sally). Taylor took up residence in the Betty Ford. It was also, nevertheless, the period of *Private Lives*, and having opened on Broadway in May, where it ran for sixty-three performances (some even without understudies), it toured to the Forrest Theatre, Philadelphia (July), the John F. Kennedy Center for the Performing Arts, Washington (August and September), the Shubert Theatre, Chicago (October), then to the Wilshire Theatre in Los Angeles, where the show closed on 6 November. It's theoretically possible, therefore, that Welles, who played Noël Coward's Elyot opposite Gertrude Lawrence's Amanda on CBS Radio in 1939, may have encountered Burton and Taylor in California that autumn – but I harbour doubts. The marriage to Sally Hay had been on 3 July, so it is unlikely the groom and his new bride would have been apart in order for Taylor to seem, in Jaglom's report, very much with Burton as a couple; nor was Taylor ever only an appendage ('a celebrity wife'); and they hadn't been married to each other for seven years; nor would Burton have allowed himself to be intimidated, belittled, by Welles, by anybody. Burton did not pay court. Yet the fate Welles describes, and criticises, was, surely, his own? The Welles of *Citizen Kane* who ended up doing dog food and frozen peas commercials, who threw away his genius and never settled to finish anything and was hopelessly unprofessional ... My suspicion is that Jaglom was using Burton as an allegory of what had happened to Welles himself, describing Welles by default. Welles' women, Rita Hayworth, Dolores del Rio and Eartha Kitt amongst them – do they add up to a bestiary, to rival Taylor?

But Welles' contempt, regardless of its authenticity, or true target, was echoed by another poisonous little egomaniac. Here's Dirk Bogarde, who in his letters to Joseph Losey referred to Burton as 'a Welsh bastard' (that's nothing; Noël Coward called him 'that silly little Welsh cunt' – but this was meant affectionately) and who, after having had a think about *Boom!* and *The Assassination of Trotsky*, said: 'I resented Burton for his betrayal of his own talent and craft. I don't give a shit about Burton personally. You can't be jealous of anyone who's better than you are, and he was better than me – but not as a screen actor. He couldn't act on the screen and I hated the way [Losey] was selling himself so cheap . . .' All this schoolmarmish disapproval. Bogarde never got over losing Losey to Burton and Taylor – Losey going after money and fame. (He was still whining about it in the Nineties.) There's a lot of distinct rancour here, negativity, coming from an actor who had appeal in the *Doctor* comedies and conveyed a fine donnish superciliousness in *Accident*, and unadulterated superciliousness in everything else, before descending into Continental or intellectual pretension, with outings for Visconti, Cavani, Resnais and Rainer Werner Fassbinder. Considering Bogarde's appearances on stage were few – the last one before his death in 1999 being in an Anouilh play at the Oxford Playhouse in 1958, his praise ('he was better than me') is faint: Bogarde was only ever a screen actor, with a rich repertoire of twitches and sneers, arched eyebrows, nostril flares. You are fully aware of the cogs and wheels, pendulums and clicking counterweights. There's something sour about him always, too, which is easy to mistake for fastidiousness, choosiness. Look at the way Bogarde fiddles with a starched napkin or polished soup spoon as Gustav Von Aschenbach. He's a prissy person, bitchy. He's frightening in *The Servant*. Actually, Bogarde would have been fascinating as Burton's co-star in *Staircase* – the angry queen. Bogarde's malice, I suspect, like Welles', derived from a realisation that, when it came to Burton, they are looking at themselves in a distorting mirror: Burton the monarchical leading man, who impersonated Henry VIII, Churchill, Tito, Wagner and Trotsky, as imperial a person as ever Welles was; the Welles who was Cesare Borgia, Benjamin Franklin, King Saul, Cardinal Wolsey, the Emperor Justinian, and so forth; and then there is Burton the lusty heterosexual ('I intend to roam the globe searching for ravishing creatures') and Bogarde the painfully repressed homosexual. They could be the identical twins – except Bogarde was four years older – in Christopher Fry's version of Anouilh's *Ring Round the Moon*.

Anyway, I refuse to see waste or failure. Who'd not want to be Taylor for a day or Burton for an afternoon? You don't need to watch *Anne of the Thousand Days* to be reminded how Burton had become a regal person – in the ways he held himself – expecting deference and complete attention. Because when, in fact, had he not been a pampered sun king? He was a royal baby in his family, always adored by Cis, and by Philip. *Anne of the Thousand Days, Doctor Faustus, Where Eagles Dare, Villain, Bluebeard, Equus, Wagner* only express or expose how what he'd become in adulthood is what he always was: self-centred or stubborn, cranky, deadpan, aspiring to be magical and elusive. Whether he was playing good or evil characters – characters going to hell and in varying and various states of hopelessness – there was a directness about Burton, nothing furtive or underhand. I suspect he hated secrets. A rhetorical question such as William Redfield's – 'Will Burton confine himself to film and deteriorate as all actors who so confine themselves inevitably must?' – I find pissy in the extreme. (Redfield the Guildenstern in the 1964 *Hamlet*.) I disagree with the notion that to be a great actor, only the stage is the thing; moreover, that if money is made you are a wastrel. When Redfield asked, in 1967, 'What will Richard Burton's future be? Is there ... disillusion or even disaster ahead?' he clearly couldn't wait to sit by and watch ruination – Redfield's tone is crowing, hostile. He is willing Burton to fail. You can tell what he and many another wanted was to see Burton overtaken by dread and emptiness, instead of fulfilment; wretchedness, isolation, stagnation – whereas what Burton did, even as his work demonstrated hope abandoned, was to make any ugliness beautiful.

Biographies, obituaries, newspaper articles – even now – tend to denigrate Burton and Taylor, with allowances made for *Who's Afraid of Virginia Woolf?*. We are told to dislike their work, from the mid-Sixties onwards. But they – those films, and Taylor and Burton in themselves – capture an era, which can be seen, all these decades later, to have had its own strange beauty. It is all like a period hotel interior: just as it is about to be gutted and lost, you see the point of it. Though considered vulgar in their day – and remembering Wilde's statement, 'No crime is vulgar, but all vulgarity is crime. Vulgarity is the conduct of others' – I can find harmony in Burton and Taylor's displays; form and design in their convictions about life, in their enjoyment of wealth and stardom. When Patricia Losey said the couple were 'stuck in their sealed world and determined not to receive new ideas or change themselves in any way,' to me this is part of the appeal – and good for them – not the rationale for condemnation. There was something about their jet-set court that reminds me of Titania and Oberon's bower in a Peter Brook production of *A Midsummer Night's Dream* – everyone loafing about picking at room-service dinners; in the background the sound of plucked sitar strings, the occasional gong or bell; a Western idea of Indian palace life; crimson feather fans and eiderdowns; white sheepskin rugs; chromium furniture; fluorescent yellow light. Very druggy and lazy, salaried 'friends' and hangers-on everywhere – Taylor dressed in Vicky Tiel jumpsuits, mini-dresses and satin wraps, none of which suited her.

Burton and Taylor: we can only watch such figures at a distance. We can't emulate their behaviour. They are dream images, light and matter in conjunction. John Gielgud appreciated as much – in 1971 he waxed nostalgic to Emlyn Williams about 'Richard Burton coming into our lives, and now it's all like a dream'. The point about the stars is we can take pleasure in their beauty, in their misrule, revel in it. Their concern was their own publicity, which was part of their artistry. Zev Buffman, who produced *Private Lives*, learned never to announce in advance where he may be turning up with his illustrious cast, as two hundred photographers would be there first, pushing and shoving. As when Burton was in *Hamlet*, nearly two decades previously, and Taylor came to watch, if crowds pulled their hair and ripped their clothes, it was a routine they must have welcomed, even egged on, if they put up with flashbulb torment night after night after night. As Sheilah Graham sardonically noted, though the Regency Hotel on Park Avenue and Sixty-First Street had a perfectly good back door and a hidden parking lot, Taylor and Burton 'preferred to feel their fame by plunging into the crowds waiting for them in front of the main entrance'. The spotlights, the photographic blow-ups – they fucking *asked for it.*

In Boston for the *Private Lives* previews, in addition to conceding 'Noël must be spinning in his grave', Burton agreed, when thinking about his ex-wife, 'Elizabeth and I know each other so well by now . . . we are beyond caring what people think of our motives.' Though I applaud this disinterestedness, actually Burton and Taylor worked best when there was a sense of incomprehension between them, a distance. I prefer it when they are working hard to keep their image of each other intact – wanting each other to be different, to retain their enchantment, and never to be wearisome. (They were the Fred and Ginger of recrimination.) Continuously emotional, often to be found in her films going through cupboards and wardrobes, throwing clothes on the bed, Taylor was both 'a woman of quick spirit' and a 'sluttish spoil of opportunity', as Shakespeare says of Helen of Troy. She was like a pony, charging about on a field. As for Burton, I would argue that everything the odd and solitary Philip had taught him, about the importance of artistry, the high intellect and refined taste, he had to discard. He had to become simple and straightforward – almost desolate. This he achieved. And yet, 'the greatest men fail, or seem to have failed,' said Wilde, who could be describing the manner in which Burton took on Henry VIII, Churchill, Tito, Trotsky, Wagner: he finds in them facets of his own proud grand Welsh doom; he gives them the treasure of his voice. True failure will only be so if we have to be reminded our heroes (and it is always a mistake to meet them in the flesh) are after all ordinary, with feet that in ancient times walked upon England's pastures green. Welsh pastures, too. 'Jesus Christ was unquestionably a Welshman,' Burton used to boast, with questionable theological authority. But who wants the pedestrian, the pedantic? I personally want everything concerning Burton and Taylor to be louder, more clamorous, more garish, like unicorn herds carved in crystal. How much better, than mine or yours, a life like Taylor's, who was able to both proliferate and to vanish, becoming a perfume or series of psychedelic prints.

To the brazen, all is brass. The history of the making of *Cleopatra*, for example, may have been about illness, and moral and physical corruption, but it was chiefly about money – pornographic amounts of money – and I don't know whether to laugh or cry when I realise *Carry On Cleo*, its counterpart, with Amanda Barrie in Taylor's discarded costumes as 'that bird who rules Egypt', and Sid James making lip-smacking references to 'cementing our alliance', ran up a grand total for Peter Rogers and Gerald Thomas of £165,802. The latest estimate for the grand total of the Fox *Cleopatra* is $60,000,000, or $546,670,588.24 in today's figures, and I still find Charles Hawtrey funnier than Hume Cronyn. And Taylor was never to change her ways. Everything was like *Cleopatra*, whether her fortieth birthday party in Budapest or, at a cost of $1.5 million, her sixtieth birthday party at Disneyland when, four months after the Fortensky nuptials, the castle was lit up in bright purple: 'It's going to be the best party of my life,' Taylor said, extending an invitation to her thousand closest friends. Amongst whom, on 27 February 1992, was Barry Humphries, who told me: 'Attendance was huge, because everyone wanted to go on the rides for free and without queuing. Gifts had to be passed on arrival to beefy security officers. Small presents were segregated from more substantial and promising donations. I think things were discreetly weighed. Once inside, and after security checks, we were herded onto a popular ride called It's A Small World. Only then did guests begin to realise they were all barred from the grown-up rides because insuring these celebrities was too expensive, even for the birthday girl, wherever she was? All these famous and unrecognisable people in their finery were huddled in foetal positions on that little train, while the speakers bleated out the inane song, "It's a Small W-o-r-r-l-d!" Pirates of the Caribbean was the next treat and there was a Disney hireling in piratical déshabillé at the prow of our boat, doing an habitual spiel, but no one was listening. Mickey Mouse then announced Miss Taylor's propinquity. We observed a caged walkway, guarded by an armed security detail, and soon the little form of our hostess appeared, waving abstractedly in all directions, amidst cheers and hosannas from the obedient crowd. Kiddie food circulated. It was over. A few desperate sorts took to the rides again. We left early, disdaining another sojourn in that very small world of which we had been vouchsafed but an enticing glimpse. Limo drivers stamped out their cigarettes. We got the economy gift bag, containing a bottle of White Diamonds perfume and a sweatshirt emblazoned with the Warhol portrait.'

Taylor said she went to Disneyland 'for the child in me'. She'd first gone there in 1962, when she'd enjoyed Frontierland with Eddie, Michael and Christopher, who wore cowboy attire. For her party, thirty years later, armed guards with torches and Alsatians patrolled the perimeter, stationed at fifty-yard intervals. A no-fly zone was declared by the Federal Aviation Administration. It all had the air of a concentration camp or the Potemkin village, with Main Street, Fantasyland, Tomorrowland and Videopolis thronged by the likes of Carrie Fisher, Esther Williams, Bowie, Elton, Barry Manilow, and of course Barry Humphries, who was out of his Dame Edna disguise, as otherwise Taylor would have been upstaged. What a lot of presents and knick-knacks would have been accumulated that night – and what chiefly survived of Taylor was the bric-a-brac, collected by the house clearance men: those people in long brown coats who give the inheritors a fistful of notes for the wardrobes and picture frames, the candlesticks and chipped His and Hers chamber pots. Her being Elizabeth Taylor, the leftovers were in a different league, but the principle was the same: what was to be done about the sheer amount of *stuff*?

Amassed from Bel Air and Gstaad, Taylor's clothes and jewels were auctioned at Christie's Rockefeller Center headquarters, between 13 and 16 December 2011. There were two hundred handbags, thirty pairs of cowboy boots, hot-pants embroidered with daisies. Taylor's copy of *National Velvet*, estimated at $2,000 went for $170,500. There was an abundance of Mucha lithographs, Galle vases, lots of Lalique. Her taste distinctly veered towards Art Nouveau – tendrils, pistils, bindweed, the sensation of being trapped and frozen or petrified underwater. There were 1,778 lots, including one of Cleopatra's wigs (estimate in pounds – £7,000), which raised £103 million in sterling. Everything Taylor had touched had extra, occult value. In April 1986, the William Doyle Gallery sold the contents of Rock Hudson's New York apartment, 'just comfortable nelly junk,' said Warhol. 'There was only one sort of nice thing, a wooden box that was so ugly, Elizabeth Taylor had written on it.' Actually, a footstool, which Taylor has inscribed in purple ink: 'E.T. stood here, she had to because she couldn't reach the sink. R.H. is a love, and I thank him always – even tho' he is one foot taller. Your always friend, Elizabeth'. Estimated at $200, it went for $1,400. A good investment, like the painting by Rufino Tamayo (1899 – 1991), entitled *Mujer en un Interior*, sand mixed with oil on canvas, which Taylor and Burton gave to Peter Ustinov, as a parting gift after they'd all made *Hammersmith is Out* in Mexico. Elongated, striated fields of lilac and lemon, columns of colour, stripes with a few dots, which somehow depict a woman indoors, it was sold by Ustinov's heirs at Sotheby's, New York, on 17 May 2023, for $609,000. Then there's Taylor's den or lair or cave. Her 7,000-square-foot ranch-style house at 700 Nimes Road, previously occupied by Nancy Sinatra, was put on the market in May 2011, with an asking price of $8.6 million. It was sold for $11 million and 'redeveloped'. Taylor spent her final days chatting on the phone to Colin Farrell (you can see why she'd have been attracted – a Celtic gypsy prettiness) and at her funeral on 24 March 2011 he recited Hopkins' 'The Leaden Echo and the Golden Echo', which had been a

Burton favourite. At the time of my writing this leaf, MY [Motor yacht] *Kalizma* was moored at Port City Colombo Marina, Sri Lanka.

Burton's leavings were less lavish. In December 2015, his widow, Sally, donated his copy of *Harrap's New Shorter French and English Dictionary* to his school, the Dyffryn, in Port Talbot. I don't know what became of it, as Dyffryn Comprehensive closed in 2018 and was demolished. According to the ownership signature, Burton had purchased the book in January 1977. Four words were underlined: *maussade* (gloomy), *torticollis* (stiff neck), *le retraite* (retirement) and *s'engouer* (engulf; to become infatuated). Perhaps Burton's entire existence can be distilled into that vocabulary. It is a recapitulation. He'd long since said, 'You think women have been my passion. The real passion in my life is books.' Nearly. Not quite. Look at this description in his diary (19 August 1980) of a Vodka Dry Martini: 'double, ice cold, the glass fogged with condensation, straight up and then straight down and the warm flood [of] the painkiller hitting the stomach and then the brain and an hour of sweetly melancholy euphoria.' Why, *that* is passion. Burton drank for its effects, as if this was romantic; as if it was expected of him, intrinsic to his dark vocal power, to empty bottle after bottle, drinking, smoking, coughing. Sitting with Richard Harris in Tshipise, in the Limpopo province of South Africa, making *The Wild Geese*, Burton and his co-star agreed, 'We drank because we loved it!'

If he never returned in triumph to the classical stage, he went one better: Burton turned into a classical stage. The Richard Burton Theatre, part of the Royal Welsh College of Music and Drama, or Coleg Brenhinol Cerdd a Drama Cymru, opened in June 2011. It seats a hundred and eighty. Coronavirus restrictions notwithstanding, in November 2020, he was to have been an exhibition, 'Becoming Richard Burton', at the National Museum of Wales, Cardiff, or Amgueddfa Genedlaethol Caerdydd – costumes, posters, ephemera, material selected from the Swansea Archive, displayed in glass cabinets. Of his large family, none is left. Brother Graham perished of

Alzheimer's Disease in December 2015, aged eighty-eight. He'd lived in Cwmavon, two miles from Port Talbot, and the funeral was at Margam Crematorium. One far-off memory had never faded. Graham remembered Richie 'at thirteen, walking across the schoolyard with a cigarette in his mouth. I'd watch in awe. He started drinking at fifteen. He was five-foot-nine and could get into pubs . . . He was notorious.' His eyes glowing like coals, the old devil, born to do battle, stood already in the sun, ravenous, ready to pounce.

ACKNOWLEDGEMENTS AND SOURCES

Persons

If Richard Burton was touched by the Devil's luck, so was I when it came to the innumerable courtesies I received, during the thirteen-year period researching and writing this book. For advice, stimulation and general moral support, grateful thanks are due to the following, even if many are now demised: Robert Bathurst; Andrew Biswell (Director, The International Anthony Burgess Foundation); Judi Bowker; Gyles Brandreth; Sarah Broughton; Andrew Brown; Craig and Frances (Welch) Brown; Andy Budgell (Dame Elizabeth Taylor website); Eric Colleary (Cline Curator of Theatre and the Performing Arts, Harry Ransom Center, University of Texas at Austin); the late Barry Cryer; the late Dame Olivia de Havilland; Susie Dowdall; Adam Endacott; Duncan Fallowell; Stephen Frears; Stephen Fry; Leslie Gardner; Michael Gove; Bunty Gunn; Rik Hall; Sir David Hare; David Harries; the late John Heald; Michael Herbert; Bevis Hillier; David Howard; the late Barry Humphries; Richard and Sara Ingrams; Steve Jacobi; Angela John; Rebecca John; Catherine Jones; Philip Kemp; the late Herbert Kretzmer; Sam Leith; Quentin Letts; the late Jeremy Lewis; Richard Littlejohn; John McEntee; Joe McGrath; the late Hugh Massingberd; the late Steve Masty; Jonathan Meades; Daphne Merkin; Robbie Millen; the late Jan Morris; Harry Mount; the late Mavis Nicholson; Garry O'Connor; Gary Osborne; Richard Osborne; Jasmine Palmer; Tony Palmer; Molly Parkin; Sandra

Parsons; Becky Percival (United Agents, on behalf of Sir Michael Holroyd); Nick and Chris Prescott; Dominic Regan; Griff and Jo Rhys Jones; Sir Tim Rice; Bernard Richards; Jon Riley; (Lord) Andrew Roberts; the late Michael Rush; Peter Stead; Laura Thompson; Jim Tucker; the late Patrick Tull; Barry Turner; David Weston; Francis Wheen; Michael and Hilary Whitehall; the late Dame Barbara Windsor; Clair Woodward; Toby Young.

Publications

Agee, James. *Agee on Film* (New York, 1969).

Agee, James. *Film Writing and Selected Journalism*, edited by Michael Sragow (New York, 2005).

Albee, Edward. *Who's Afraid of Virginia Woolf?* (New York, 1962).

Allan, John B. *Elizabeth Taylor* (New York, 1961 and 2011).

Alpert, Hollis. *Burton* (New York, 1986).

Amburn, Ellis. *The Most Beautiful Woman in the World: The Obsessions, Passions, and Courage of Elizabeth Taylor* (New York, 2000).

Anger, Kenneth, *Hollywood Babylon* (San Francisco, 1975).

Anger, Kenneth. *Hollywood Babylon II* (London, 1986).

Anon. 'Body of film producer snatched from cemetery', *The Berkshire Eagle* (Pittsfield, Massachusetts), 27 June 1977.

Anon. 'Philip Burton, 90; Taught and Adopted Richard Burton', *The New York Times*, 30 January 1995.

Anon. 'Elizabeth Taylor Obituary', *The Times*, 24 March 2011.

Anon. 'Meet Security Guru Gavin de Becker, Protector of Hollywood Stars', *Gulf News*, 8 February 2019.

Anon. 'John Warner, Republican Senator who served as Secretary of the US Navy and married Elizabeth Taylor – obituary', *The Daily Telegraph*, 26 May 2021.

Anon. 'John Warner Obituary', *The Times*, 27 May 2021.

Anouilh, Jean. *The Fighting Cock* (London, 1967).

Aspel, Michael. *In Good Company* (London, 1989).

Barrow, Andrew. *Gossip: A History of High Society, 1920–1970* (London, 1978).

Barrow, Andrew. *International Gossip: A History of High Society, 1970–1980* (London, 1983).

Baxter, Keith. *My Sentiments Exactly* (London, 1998).

Bean, Kendra and Uzarowski, Anthony. *Ava: A Life in Movies* (Philadelphia, 2017).

Beaton, Cecil. *Portraits & Profiles*, edited by Hugo Vickers (London, 2014).

Becker, Gavin de. *The Gift of Fear: Survival Signals That Protect Us from Violence* (New York, 2001).

Ben-Ami, Yoram. *Guiding Royalty: My Adventure with Elizabeth Taylor and Richard Burton* (Albany, Georgia, 2018).

Berlins, Marcel. 'Hanging in the Balance', *The Guardian*, 7 December 2004.

Biskind, Peter (ed.). *My Lunches With Orson: Conversations Between Harry Jaglom and Orson Welles* (New York, 2013).

Bloom, Claire. *Leaving a Doll's House: A Memoir* (Boston, 1996).

Boorman, John. *Adventures of a Suburban Boy* (London, 2003).

Bozzacchi, Gianni. *Elizabeth Taylor: The Queen and I* (Madison, Wisconsin, 2002).

Bozzacchi, Gianni. *My Life in Focus: A Photographer's Journey with Elizabeth Taylor and the Hollywood Jet Set* (Lexington, Kentucky, 2017).

Bragg, Melvyn. *Rich: The Life of Richard Burton* (London, 1988).

Brando, Marlon. *Songs My Mother Taught Me* (London, 1994).

Branin, Larissa. *Liz: The Pictorial Biography of Elizabeth Taylor* (New York, 2000).

Brenner, Marie. 'The Liz and Dick Show', *New York Magazine*, 9 May 1983.

Bret, David. *Elizabeth Taylor: The Lady, The Lover, The Legend: 1932–2011* (Edinburgh, 2012).

Brodsky, Jack and Weiss, Nathan. *The Cleopatra Papers: A Private Correspondence* (New York, 1963).

Brook, Peter. *Threads of Time: Recollections* (Washington, 1998).

Brower, Kate Andersen. *Elizabeth Taylor: The Grit and Glamour of an Icon* (London, 2022).

Burchill, Julie. *Girls On Film* (London, 1986).

Burton, Hal (ed.). *Acting in the Sixties* (London, 1970).

Burton, Philip. *Early Doors: My Life and the Theatre* (New York, 1969).

Burton, Philip. *The Sole Voice: Character Portraits from Shakespeare* (New York, 1970).

Burton, Philip. *You, My Brother: A Novel Based on the Lives of Edmund & William Shakespeare* (London, 1973).

Burton, Philip. *Richard & Philip: The Burtons* (London, 1992).

Burton, Richard. *A Christmas Story* (New York, 1964; new edition with an Introduction by Sally Burton, London, 1989).

Burton, Richard. *Meeting Mrs Jenkins* (New York, 1966).

Burton, Sally. 'Return to Happy Valley', *Mail on Sunday*, 29 July 2002.

Byrne, Gabriel. *Walking With Ghosts: A Memoir* (London, 2020).

Capote, Truman. *A Capote Reader* (New York, 1987).

Carter, Graydon (ed.). *Vanity Fair's Tales of Hollywood* (New York, 2008).

Cashin, Fergus. *Richard Burton* (London, 1982).

Cashmore, Ellis. *Elizabeth Taylor: A Private Life for Public Consumption* (London, 2016).

Caute, David. *Joseph Losey: A Revenge on Life* (London, 1996).

Cavett, Dick. *Talk Show* (New York, 2010).

Cavett, Dick. 'Who's Afraid of Richard Burton?', *The New York Times*, 17 July 2009.

Chrissochoidis, Ilias (ed.). *The Cleopatra Files: Selected Documents from the Spyros P. Skouras Archive* (Stanford, 2013).

Christopher, James. *Elizabeth Taylor: The Illustrated Biography* (London, 1999).

Christopher, James. *Elizabeth Taylor: A Biography* (Maine, 2000).

Ciment, Michel. *Conversations With Losey* (New York, 1985).

Ciment, Michel. *John Boorman* (London, 1986).

Clement, Dick and La Frenais, Ian. *More Than Likely: A Memoir* (London, 2019).

Coldstream, John. *Dirk Bogarde: The Authorised Biography* (London, 2004).

Coldstream, John (ed.). *Ever, Dirk: The Bogarde Letters* (London, 2008).

Cole, George. *The World Was My Lobster: My Autobiography* (London, 2013).

Coleridge, Nicholas and Quinn, Stephen (eds). *The Sixties in Queen* (London, 1987).

Cook, Lin (ed.). *Something Like Fire: Peter Cook Remembered* (London, 1996).

Cottrell, John and Cashin, Fergus. *Richard Burton: Very Close Up* (New Jersey, 1971).

Coveney, Michael. 'Sybil Christopher, Obituary', *The Guardian*, 11 March 2013.

Crisp, Quentin. *How to Become a Virgin* (London, 1981).

Crisp, Quentin. *How to Go to the Movies* (London, 1988).

Crisp, Quentin. *Resident Alien: The New York Diaries* (London, 1996).

Cronyn, Hume. *A Terrible Liar: A Memoir* (New York, 1991).

Daniell, John. *Ava Gardner* (Chatham, 1982).

David, Lester and Robbins, Jhan. *Richard and Elizabeth* (New York, 1977).

Davies, Russell (ed.). *The Kenneth Williams Diaries* (London, 1993).

Davies, Russell (ed.). *The Kenneth Williams Letters* (London, 1994).

Davis, Mark and Earnshaw, Tony. *Under Milk Wood Revisited: The Wales of Dylan Thomas* – Foreword by Sally Burton (Stroud, 2014).

Day, Barry (ed.). *The Letters of Noël Coward* (London, 2007).

Diederich, Bernard. *Seeds of Fiction: Graham Greene's Adventures in Haiti and Central America 1954–1983* (London, 2012).

Dougary, Ginny. 'Elizabeth the First', *The Times Magazine*, 10 October 1999.

Dougary, Ginny. 'Sex, drugs, plastic surgery . . . and the sheer joy of the elasticated waistband', *The Times*, 26 March 2011.

Duncan, Paul (ed.). *Taschen Movie Icons: Elizabeth Taylor* (Cologne, 2008).

Dunn, Anthony J. *The Worlds of Wolf Mankowitz* (Edgware, 2013).

Dunne, Dominick. *The Way We Lived Then: Recollections of a Well-Known Name Dropper* (New York, 1999).

Dyer, Geoff. *Broadsword Calling Danny Boy: On Where Eagles Dare* (London, 2018).

Ebert, Roger. 'Interview with Elizabeth Taylor & Richard Burton', *Chicago Sun-Times*, 17 August 1969.

Eco, Umberto. *Travels of Hyperreality: Essays* (London, 1987).

Endacott, Adam. *The Kenneth Williams Companion* (Coventry, 2018).

Endacott, Adam. *The Kenneth Williams Scrapbook* (Coventry, 2021).

Etherington-Smith, Meredith. 'Queen of Diamonds: Elizabeth Taylor's Life in Jewels', *Telegraph Magazine*, 19 November 2011.

Falk, Quentin. *Travels in Greeneland: The Cinema of Graham Greene* (London, 1984).

Ferris, Paul. *Richard Burton* (London, 1981).

Ferris, Paul. *A Portrait of Richard Burton* (London, 1984).

Findlater, Richard. *Emlyn Williams* (London, 1956).

Fisher, Eddie. *Been There, Done That* (London, 1999).

Fountain, Tim. *Quentin Crisp* (London, 2002).

Fry, Christopher. *The Boy With A Cart: Cuthman, Saint of Sussex* (Frome, 1945).

Gale, John. 'Society Wedding', *Observer*, 16 June 1968.

Gold, Tanya. 'Who's afraid of Burton and Taylor?' *The Sunday Times*, 28 July 2013.

Gopnik, Blake. *Warhol: A Life as Art* (London, 2020).

Graham, Sheilah. *Scratch an Actor: Confessions of a Hollywood Columnist* (London, 1969).

Graham, Sheilah. *My Hollywood: A Celebration and a Lament* (London, 1984).

Grice, Elizabeth. ' "Dad and Liz couldn't be together" – Kate Burton talks about her father's alcoholism and his fiery relationship with stepmother Elizabeth Taylor', *Daily Telegraph*, 14 March 2003.

Guilaroff, Sydney. *Crowning Glory: Reflections of Hollywood's Favorite Confidant* (Santa Monica, 1996).

Gussow, Mel. *Edward Albee: A Singular Journey* (New York, 2001).

Hall, Sheldon. *Zulu: With Some Guts Behind It – The Making of the Epic Movie* (Sheffield, 2005 and 2014).

Harris, Mark. *Mike Nichols: A Life* (New York, 2021).

Harrison, Rex. *Rex: An Autobiography* (London, 1974).

Hayes, Helen. *My Life in Three Acts* (New York, 1990).

Heilpern, John. *John Osborne: A Patriot For Us* (London, 2006).

Henderson, Barney. 'Yours for £18m: the third love of Taylor's life, her jewellery,' *The Daily Telegraph*, 8 September 2011.

Hershman, Gabriel. *Black Sheep: The Authorised Biography of Nicol Williamson* (Stroud, 2018).

Heyman, C. David. *Liz: An Intimate Biography of Elizabeth Taylor* (London, 1985).

Hirsch, Foster. *Elizabeth Taylor* (New York, 1973).

Honnef, Klaus. *Pop Art* (Cologne, 2004).

Hordern, Michael. *A World Elsewhere: An Autobiography* (London, 1993).

Hotchner, A. E. *Sophia: Living and Loving – Her Own Story* (London, 1979).

Hoz, Cindy De La. *Elizabeth Taylor: A Loving Tribute* (Philadelphia, 2011).

Hoz, Cindy De La. *Elizabeth Taylor: A Shining Legacy on Film* (Philadelphia, 2012).

Hutchinson, Tom. *The Screen Greats: Elizabeth Taylor* (London, 1982).

Isherwood, Christopher. *Diaries Volume One 1939–1960; The Sixties: Diaries Volume Two 1960–1969; Liberation: Diaries Volume Three 1970–1983*, edited by Katherine Bucknell (London, 1996–2012).

Jackson, Joe. *Richard Harris: Raising Hell and Reaching for Heaven* (County Kildare, Ireland, 2022).

Jacobi, Derek and O'Connor, Garry. *As Luck Would Have It* (London, 2013).

Jenkins, David. *Richard Burton: A Brother Remembered – The Biography Richard Wanted* (London, 1993).

Jenkins, Graham and Turner, Barry. *Richard Burton: My Brother* (London, 1988).

Jenkins, Graham. 'Obituary: Philip Burton', *The Independent*, 11 February 1995.

Jewell, Derek. 'John Neville turns his back on London', *The Sunday Times*, 6 October 1963.

Junor, Penny. *Burton: The Man Behind the Myth* (London, 1985).

Kane, Vincent. *Kane's Classics: Burton* – BBC Wales Library Services (9 April 1998).

Kashner, Sam and Schoenberger, Nancy. *Furious Love: Elizabeth Taylor, Richard Burton and the Marriage of the Century* (London, 2010).

Kelley, Kitty. *Elizabeth Taylor: The Last Star* (London, 1981).

Kelly, Susan. *Elizabeth Taylor: Her Life In Style* (London, 2011).

Kingsland, Rosemary. *Hold Back the Night: Memoirs of a lost childhood, a warring family and a secret affair with Richard Burton* (London, 2003).

Kukil, Karen V. (ed.). *The Journals of Sylvia Plath* (London, 2000).

Lahr, John (ed.). *The Diaries of Kenneth Tynan* (London, 2001).

Lancaster, David. *Montgomery Clift* (Bath, 2005).

Larkin, Philip. *Letters to Monica*, edited by Anthony Thwaite (London, 2010).

Le Carré, John. 'The Spy Who Liked Me', *The New Yorker*, 15 April 2013.

Le Carré, John. *The Pigeon Tunnel: Stories from My Life* (London, 2016).

Leavitt, Richard F. *The World of Tennessee Williams* (New York, 1978).

Levy, Alan. *Forever Sophia: An Intimate Portrait* (London, 1979).

Levy, Emanuel. *George Cukor: Master of Elegance* (New York, 1994).

Lloyd, Ian. *Elizabeth Taylor 1932–2011: Queen of the Silver Screen* (London, 2011).

Loengard, John (Introduction). *The Great LIFE Photographers* (New York, 2004 and 2010).

Lord, M. G. *The Accidental Feminist: How Elizabeth Taylor Raised Our Consciousness* (New York, 2012).

Loren, Sophia. *In the Kitchen with Love* (Milan, 1971).

Loren, Sophia. *Recipes & Memories* (New York, 1998).

McBride, Joseph. *Billy Wilder: Dancing on the Edge* (New York, 2021).

McCullers, Carson. *Reflections in a Golden Eye* (New York, 1941).

McDowall, Roddy. *Double Exposure* (New York, 1966; new edition 1990).

McGilligan, Patrick. *George Cukor: A Double Life* (New York, 1991).

McGrath, Ellie and Sanders, Richard (eds). *People Tribute Commemorative Edition: Elizabeth Taylor 1932–2011* (New York, 2011).

McLean, Pauline. 'Wife-beater "slur" upsets the family', *Western Mail*, 15 September 1994.

Maddox, Brenda. *Who's Afraid of Elizabeth Taylor?* (New York, 1977).

Maeterlinck, Maurice. *The Blue Bird* (London, 1909).

Malcolm, Janet. *The Silent Woman: Sylvia Plath and Ted Hughes* (London, 1994).

Malone, Aubrey. *Welsh Drinkers* (Talybont, 2009).

Malvern, Jack. 'Taylor's Oscar dress discovered', *The Times*, 24 November 2022.

Mangan, Richard (ed.). *Sir John Gielgud: A Life in Letters* (London, 2004).

Mann, William J. *How to be a Movie Star: Elizabeth Taylor in Hollywood* (New York, 2009).

Marlowe, Christopher. *Doctor Faustus and Other Plays*, edited by David Bevington and Eric Rasmussen (Oxford, 1995).

Medved, Harry and Dreyfuss, Randy. *The Fifty Worst Movies of All Time* (London, 1978).

Medved, Harry and Michael. *The Hollywood Hall of Shame: The Most Expensive Flops in Movie History* (London, 1984).

Merkin, Daphne. *Dreaming of Hitler: Passions & Provocations* (New York, 1997).

Merkin, Daphne. *The Fame Lunches* (New York, 2014).

Miller, John. *Peter Ustinov: The Gift of Laughter* (London, 2004).

Morley, Robert. *Morley Matters* (London, 1980).

Morley, Robert. *Around the World in Eighty-One Years* (London, 1990)

Morley, Sheridan. *Elizabeth Taylor: A Celebration* (London, 1988).

Munn, Michael. *Richard Burton: Prince of Players* (London, 2007).

Newman, Paul. *The Extraordinary Life of an Ordinary Man: A Memoir* (London, 2022).

Nickens, Christopher. *Elizabeth Taylor: A Biography in Photographs* (London, 1984).

Norman, Barry. 'Prince of Players', *Radio Times*, 14–20 August 2010.

O'Brien, Edna. *Zee & Co.* (London, 1971).

O'Brien, Edna. *Country Girl: A Memoir* (London, 2012).

O'Brien, Edna. *The Love Object: Selected Stories* (new edition with an Introduction by John Banville, London, 2013).

O'Hara, John. *BUtterfield 8* (New York, 1935).

Opie, Catherine. 700 *Nimes Road* (Munich, 2015).

Orizio, Riccardo. 'Dear Tyrant' [on Bokassa], *Granta*, September 2002.

Osborne, John. *Damn You, England: Collected Prose* (London, 1994).

Osborne, John. *Looking Back: Never Explain, Never Apologise* (London, 1999).

Paglia, Camille. *Sex, Art, and American Culture: Essays* (New York, 1992).

Paglia, Camille. *Vamps and Tramps: New Essays* (New York, 1994).

Paglia, Camille. 'Paglia on Taylor: "A luscious, opulent, ripe fruit!" ', *Salon*, 24 March 2011.

Pallenberg, Barbara. *The Making of Exorcist II: The Heretic: From the original idea to the finished film!* (New York, 1977).

Papa, Joseph. *Elizabeth Taylor: A Passion for Life – The Wit and Wisdom of a Legend* (New York, 2011).

Parish, James Robert. *Fiasco: A History of Hollywood's Iconic Flops* (New Jersey, 2006).

Parker, Elaine and Owen, Gareth. *The Price of Fame: The Biography of Dennis Price* (Stroud, 2018).

Parkin, Molly (Contributor). *Barry Humphries: Bepraisements on his Birthday*, compiled by Ken Thomson (London, 1994).

Parkinson, Michael. *Parkinson: Selected Interviews from the Television Series* (London, 1975).

Payn, Graham and Morley, Sheridan. *The Noël Coward Diaries* (London, 1982).

Pearce, Garth. 'At home with her husband Michael Ritchie and son Morgan [,] Richard Burton's daughter Kate Burton speaks of her relationship with her father and his wives', *Hello!* 3 August 1996.

Perelman, S. J. *The Last Laugh* (London, 1981).

Porter, Darwin and Prince, Danforth. *Elizabeth Taylor: There is Nothing Like a Dame* (Staten Island, 2012).

Powell, Michael. *Million-Dollar Movie* (London, 1992).

Reed, Rex. *Valentines & Vitriol* (New York, 1977).

Rham, Edith de. *Joseph Losey* (London, 1991).

Richards, Bernard. 'Lenny 'n' Liz', *Oxford Magazine*, Number 408, Trinity Term, 2019.

Richardson, Tony. *Long Distance Runner: A Memoir* (London, 1993).

Ricks, Christopher. '*Doctor Faustus* and Hell on Earth', *Essays in Criticism*, Vol. XXXV, Number 2, April 1985.

Risko, Robert (Foreword). *Forever Elizabeth: Iconic Photographers on a Legendary Star* (Woodbridge, Suffolk, 2021).

Rivers, Melissa and Currie, Scott. *Joan Rivers Confidential* (New York, 2017).

Robin-Tani, Marianne. *The New Elizabeth: Better and More Beautiful Than Ever* (New York, 1998).

Rubython, Tom. *And God Created Burton* (London, 2011).

Ryan, Paul. *Marlon Brando: A Portrait* (London, 1991).

Schulman, Michael. 'Found! A Lost TV Version of *Wuthering Heights*', *The New Yorker*, 'Culture Desk', 16 August 2021.

Seldes, Marian. *The Bright Lights: A Theatre Life* (New York, 1984).

Sellers, Robert. *Peter O'Toole: The Definitive Biography* (London, 2015).

Shaffer, Peter. *Equus* (London, 1973).

Shail, Robert. *Stanley Baker: A Life In Film* (Cardiff, 2008).

Shakespeare, William. *Antony and Cleopatra*, edited by Barbara Everett (New York, 1963 and 1988).

Sheppard, Dick. *Elizabeth: The Life and Career of Elizabeth Taylor* (New York, 1975).

Shore, Robert. *Andy Warhol* (London, 2020).

Sinclair, Andrew. *Down Under Milk Wood: Of Richard Burton, O'Toole and Others, Dylan and Me* (London, 2014).

Sisman, Adam. *John Le Carré: The Biography* (London, 2015).

Smith, Susan. *Elizabeth Taylor – British Film Institute* (London, 2012).

Spark, Muriel. *The Driver's Seat* (London, 1970).

Spinetti, Victor. *Up Front: His Strictly Confidential Autobiography* (London, 2006).

Spoto, Donald. *Elizabeth Taylor* (New York, 1995).

Sprinkel, Katy. *Elizabeth Taylor: The Life of a Hollywood Legend* (Chicago, 2011).

Stead, Peter. *Richard Burton: So Much, So Little* (Bridgend, 1991).

Stead, Peter. *Acting Wales: Stars of Stage and Screen* (Cardiff, 2002).

Sterne, Richard L. *John Gielgud Directs Richard Burton in Hamlet* (New York, 1967).

Steverson, Tyrone. *Richard Burton: A Bio-Bibliography* (Westport, Connecticut, 1992).

Storey, Anthony. *Stanley Baker: Portrait of an Actor* (London, 1977).

Strachan, Alan. 'Brook Williams: Actor son of Emlyn and friend of the Burtons', Obituary, *Independent*, 11 June 2005.

Strasberg, Susan. *Bittersweet* (New York, 1980).

Sullivan, Robert (ed.). *LIFE: Remembering Liz 1932 – 2011* (New York, 2011).

Tanitch, Robert. *Brando* (London, 1994).

Taraborrelli, J. Randy. *Elizabeth* (London, 2006).

Taylor, Clarke. 'Liz Taylor Honored in N.Y. by Film Society', *Los Angeles Times*, 7 May 1986.

Taylor, Elizabeth. *Nibbles and Me* (New York, 1946).

Taylor, Elizabeth. *Elizabeth Taylor: An Informal Memoir* (New York, 1964).

Taylor, Elizabeth. *Elizabeth Takes Off* (London, 1987).

Taylor, Elizabeth. *My Love Affair with Jewelry* (New York, 2002).

Taylor, John Russell. *John Osborne: Look Back in Anger: A Selection of Critical Essays – Casebook Series* (Basingstoke, 1968).

Theroux, Paul. *Figures in a Landscape: People and Places – Essays: 2001–2016* (New York, 2018).

Thiltges, Alexander, Dherbier, Yann-Brice and Burkhalter, Kate (eds). *Elizabeth Taylor: A Life in Pictures* (London 2008).

Thompson, Harry. *Peter Cook: A Biography* (London, 1997).

Thomson, David. *Marlon Brando* (New York, 2003).

Thorne, Jack. *The Motive and the Cue* (London, 2023).

Tiel, Vicky. 'Life with Elizabeth', *Vanity Fair*, April 2011.

Tomalin, Nicholas. 'Burton and Liz set Communist Budapest abuzz', *The Sunday Times*, 27 February 1972.

Trewin, J. C. *John Neville: An illustrated study of his work with a list of his appearances on stage & screen* (London, 1961).

Tynan, Kathleen (ed.). *Kenneth Tynan Letters* (London, 1994).

Tynan, Kenneth. 'Richard Burton Interview', *Playboy*, September 1963.

Tynan, Kenneth. *A View of the English Stage* (St Albans, 1976).

Vermilye, Jerry and Ricci, Mark. *The Films of Elizabeth Taylor* (Secaucus, New Jersey, 1976).

Vitello, Paul. 'Sybil Christopher, Nightclub Founder, Dies at 83', *The New York Times*, 11 March 2013.

Walker, Alexander (ed.). *No Bells on Sunday: The Rachel Roberts Journals* (New York, 1984).

Walker, Alexander. *Elizabeth* (London, 1990).

Wanger, Walter and Hyams, Joe. *My Life With Cleopatra: The Making of a Hollywood Classic* (New York, 1963).

Warhol, Andy. *The Andy Warhol Diaries*, edited by Pat Hackett (New York, 1989).

Warhol, Andy. *Warhol 10 Fois Liz* – Musée National d'Art Moderne du Centre Georges Pompidou (Paris, 1990).

Warhol, Andy. *Warhol Liz* – Gagosian Gallery (New York, 2011).

Waterbury, Ruth and Arceri, Gene. *Elizabeth Taylor: Her Life, Her Loves, Her Future* (New York, 1964 and 1982).

Waterbury, Ruth. *Richard Burton: His Intimate Story* (London, 1965).

Weber, Bruce (ed.). *Andy Warhol's Interview Magazine: Big Elizabeth Taylor Special* (New York, February 2007).

Whitebrook, Peter. *John Osborne: Anger Is Not About . . .* (London, 2015).

Wilding, Michael. *The Wilding Way* (New York, 1982).

Williams, Chris (ed.). *The Richard Burton Diaries* (Yale, New Haven, 2012).

Williams, Tennessee. *Cat on a Hot Tin Roof and Other Plays* (London, 1976).

Williams, Tennessee. *The Collected Stories* (London, 1986).

Williams, Tennessee. *Notebooks*, edited by Margaret Bradham Thornton (New Haven, Connecticut, 2006).

Wilmer, Douglas. *Stage Whispers: The Memoirs* (Tenbury Wells, 2009).

Wood, David. *Elizabeth Taylor's Kiss and Other Brushes With Hollywood* (Market Harborough, 2022).

Young, Caroline. *Roman Holiday: The Secret Life of Hollywood in Rome* (Stroud, 2018).

Young, Freddie. *Seventy Light Years* (London, 1999).

Zahedi, Firooz. 'Elizabeth Taylor: A Little Light Chatter', *Andy Warhol's Interview Magazine* (New York, November 1976).

Zec, Donald. *Marvin: The Story of Lee Marvin* (London, 1979).

Zec, Donald. *Put the Knife in Gently!* (London, 2003).

Zeffirelli, Franco. *Zeffirelli: The Autobiography of Franco Zeffirelli* (London, 1986).

Zeffirelli, Franco. *Complete Works*, edited by Caterina Napoleone (London, 2010).

INDEX